HANDBOOK OF POLITICAL
AND SOCIAL MOVEMENTS

Handbook of Political Citizenship and Social Movements

Edited by

Hein-Anton van der Heijden

University of Amsterdam, The Netherlands

Edward Elgar
Cheltenham, UK • Northampton, MA, USA

© Hein-Anton van der Heijden 2014

All rights reserved. No part of this publication may be reproduced, stored in a retrieval system or transmitted in any form or by any means, electronic, mechanical or photocopying, recording, or otherwise without the prior permission of the publisher.

Published by
Edward Elgar Publishing Limited
The Lypiatts
15 Lansdown Road
Cheltenham
Glos GL50 2JA
UK

Edward Elgar Publishing, Inc.
William Pratt House
9 Dewey Court
Northampton
Massachusetts 01060
USA

A catalogue record for this book
is available from the British Library

Library of Congress Control Number: 2014938766

This book is available electronically in the ElgarOnline.com
Social and Political Science Subject Collection, E-ISBN 978 1 78195 470 6

ISBN 978 1 78195 469 0 (cased)

Typeset by Servis Filmsetting Ltd, Stockport, Cheshire
Printed and bound in Great Britain by T.J. International Ltd, Padstow

Contents

List of figures	viii
List of tables	ix
List of contributors	x

1 Introduction: linking political citizenship and social movements 1
  Hein-Anton van der Heijden

PART I   POLITICAL CITIZENSHIP: APPROACHES AND FORMS

2 Political citizenship: mapping the terrain 25
  Russell J. Dalton

3 Republican citizenship 45
  James Bohman

4 Citizenship, gender and sexuality 60
  Surya Monro and Diane Richardson

5 Multicultural citizenship 86
  Narzanin Massoumi and Nasar Meer

6 Ecological citizenship 107
  Sherilyn MacGregor

7 Urban citizenship 133
  Patricia Burke Wood

8 European citizenship 154
  Espen D.H. Olsen

9 Global and cosmopolitan citizenship 177
  Sebastiaan Tijsterman

PART II   SOCIAL MOVEMENTS: CURRENT APPROACHES AND RECENT DEVELOPMENTS

10 Resource mobilization and social and political movements 205
   Bob Edwards and Melinda Kane

11	The new social movement approach *Christian Scholl*	233
12	Citizenship, political opportunities and social movements *David S. Meyer and Erin Evans*	259
13	Post-structuralism, social movements and citizen politics *Steven Griggs and David Howarth*	279
14	Social movements and emotions *Helena Flam*	308
15	The transnationalization of social movements *Movindri Reddy*	334
16	Social movements and the ICT revolution *Jennifer Earl, Jayson Hunt and R. Kelly Garrett*	359

PART III CONTEMPORARY SOCIAL MOVEMENTS

17	The environmental movement *Hein-Anton van der Heijden*	387
18	The women's movement *Jo Reger*	418
19	The international human rights movement *Ann Marie Clark and Paul Danyi*	440
20	Urban social movements *Pierre Hamel*	464
21	The Tea Party movement *Edward Ashbee*	493
22	The animal rights movement *Lyle Munro*	518

PART IV SOCIAL MOVEMENTS AND POLITICAL CITIZENSHIP IN THE GLOBAL SOUTH

23	Social movements and political citizenship in China *Lei Xie*	547
24	Social movements in India *Dip Kapoor*	572

25	Social movements and political citizenship in Africa *Patrick Bond*	604
26	Political citizenship and social movements in the Arab world *Roel Meijer*	628

Index   661

Figures

2.1	Citizenship norms in established and new democracies	31
2.2	National patterns of citizen duty and engaged citizenship	35
22.1	Modes of animal protection	525
26.1	The modern state at the height of its power, 1960s–1970s	640
26.2	Rising resistance to the authoritarian state	645

Tables

2.1	Categories of citizenship norms and public opinion questions	30
10.1	Means of social movement and SMO resource access and resource types	221
22.1	Correspondence between various perspectives on social movements	533
25.1	Africa's relative labour militancy, 2013, sample of 49 countries (ten most pliable working classes, along with 39 African countries, ranked least to most militant)	611
26.1	Rights in the Middle East, 1500–2013	637
26.2	Comparison between rights in the struggle for independence with the rise of citizenship rights over the last 20 years	644

Contributors

Edward Ashbee is Associate Professor in the Department of Business and Politics at Copenhagen Business School, Denmark.

James Bohman holds the Danforth Chair in the Humanities and is Professor of Philosophy and of International Studies at Saint Louis University, USA.

Patrick Bond is Senior Professor at the University of KwaZulu-Natal (UKZN) School of Built Environment and Development Studies, South Africa, and director of the UKZN Centre for Civil Society.

Ann Marie Clark is Associate Professor of Political Science at Purdue University, USA.

Russell J. Dalton is Professor of Political Science at the University of California, Irvine, USA.

Paul Danyi is a PhD candidate in the Department of Political Science at Purdue University, USA.

Jennifer Earl is Professor of Sociology at the University of Arizona, USA.

Bob Edwards is Professor of Sociology at East Carolina University, USA.

Erin Evans is a PhD candidate at the Department of Sociology, University of California, Irvine, USA.

Helena Flam is Professor of Sociology at the University of Leipzig, Germany.

R. Kelly Garrett is Assistant Professor of Communication at Ohio State University, USA.

Steven Griggs is a Reader in Local Governance at De Montfort University, Leicester, UK.

Pierre Hamel is Professor of Sociology at the University of Montreal, Canada.

David Howarth is a Reader in Social and Political Theory in the Department of Government, University of Essex, UK

Jayson Hunt is a PhD candidate at the Department of Sociology, University of California, Irvine, USA.

Melinda Kane is Associate Professor of Sociology at East Carolina University, USA.

Dip Kapoor is Professor of Educational Policy Studies at the University of Alberta, Canada.

Sherilyn MacGregor is Senior Lecturer in Environmental Politics at Keele University, UK.

Narzanin Massoumi is Associate Lecturer at the London School of Social Sciences, History and Philosophy, UK.

Nasar Meer is a Reader and Chancellor's Fellow in the Faculty of Humanities and Social Sciences, University of Strathclyde, UK.

Roel Meijer is a Lecturer in the History of the Middle East at Radboud University, Nijmegen, The Netherlands, and visiting professor of Ghent University, Belgium.

David S. Meyer is Professor of Sociology at the University of California, Irvine, USA.

Surya Monro is a Reader in Sociology and Social Policy at the University of Huddersfield, UK.

Lyle Munro is Adjunct Research Fellow at Monash University, Melbourne, Australia.

Espen D.H. Olsen is a Senior Researcher at ARENA, Centre for European Studies, Oslo, Norway.

Movindri Reddy is Associate Professor in Diplomacy and World Affairs at Occidental College, Los Angeles, USA.

Jo Reger is Professor of Sociology at Oakland University, Michigan, USA.

Diane Richardson is Professor of Sociology at the University of Newcastle, UK.

Christian Scholl is a Postdoctoral Research Fellow at the University of Louvain, Belgium.

Sebastiaan Tijsterman is a PhD candidate at the Department of Political Science, University of Amsterdam, The Netherlands.

Hein-Anton van der Heijden is Associate Professor in Political Science at the University of Amsterdam, The Netherlands.

Patricia Burke Wood is Associate Professor at the Department of Geography, York University, Toronto, Canada.

Lei Xie is a Lecturer in Politics at the University of Exeter, UK.

1. Introduction: linking political citizenship and social movements
*Hein-Anton van der Heijden**

POLITICAL CITIZENSHIP, SOCIAL MOVEMENTS, AND THE LEGACY OF THE 1960s

From the early days of modern social science onwards, political citizenship and social movements have been core concepts in analyzing major social changes. The anti-slavery movement in the USA, the nineteenth- and early twentieth-century labor movements in Western Europe, and the first feminist wave on both sides of the Atlantic, for instance, have not only functioned as pivotal to analyzing the striving for all different kinds of human (citizenship) rights, but also as paradigmatic examples for defining and explaining major transformations in the social and political world.

Almost five decades ago, Western society (and numerous parts of global society as well) found itself on the eve of one of the most turbulent episodes in modern history. Apart from sociologists like James Scott and Charles Tilly with strong roots in the practice of social history,[1] most contemporary social movement scholars have taken the late 1960s as the starting point for their research endeavors (e.g., Tarrow, 1994; McAdam et al., 1996; Della Porta and Diani, 2006). Actually, it was also around that time that 'social movement studies' established itself as a kind of subdiscipline in contrast to previous studies of collective action, which, rather, took concepts like 'alienation', 'mass behavior' or 'relative deprivation' as their starting point. In the 1960s, black students staged sit-in demonstrations throughout the American South, sit-ins that in their turn would revitalize not only a moribund civil rights movement but also the tradition of leftist activism dormant in America since the 1930s. During the ensuing decade the United States was rent by urban riots, student strikes and massive anti- (Vietnam) war demonstrations (McAdam et al., 1996, p. 1). With respect to Europe, opposition against American imperialism, the May 1968 revolt in France, the worker–student coalitions of the 1969 'Hot Autumn' in Italy, and the pro-democracy mobilizations in locations as diverse as Francoist Madrid and communist Prague are cases in point (Della Porta and Diani, 2006, p. 1). Further, all over the Western

1

world women's groups campaigned for equal citizenship rights for women and men. Environmental groups started to question the 'hidden side' of the prevailing limitless economic growth: pollution of air, water and soil; destruction of nature; exhaustion of natural resources. Finally, in cities as diverse as Berkeley, Paris, Berlin and Amsterdam, but also in countries like Japan, Mexico and Pakistan, students campaigned for university reforms in order not only to improve the quality of their education, but also to turn research and development towards more socially relevant directions.

The civil rights, women's, environmental and students' movements were center-stage among the movements that one decade later would be called 'new social movements', and that would decisively change Western society into a 'social movement society' (Meyer and Tarrow, 1997). These movements, in their turn, would play a pivotal role in the further development of the concept of political citizenship (Dalton, 2008).

For a long time, the concept of citizenship has been the way to define the social and political role of individual citizens vis-à-vis civil society and the state. As early as 1950, Marshall's influential book on citizenship and social class was published. During the late 1960s and early 1970s, in most Western societies a social-democratic, Keynesian welfare state discourse was the hegemonic way of doing and defining politics and citizenship, even in countries where right-wing governments were in charge. Modern citizenship rights drawing from the nation-state typically include civil rights (free speech and movement, the rule of law); political rights (voting, seeking electoral office); and social citizenship rights (welfare, unemployment insurance and health care) (Marshall, 1950; Isin and Turner, 2003, p. 3). Among these three kinds of rights, it was in terms of social citizenship rights that citizenship was considered in those days, and social-democratic parties and labor movements singularly and jointly struggled to improve these rights.

At present, half a century later, the political and social landscape has radically changed. From the late 1970s onwards, neoliberalism, going along with what has been called 'possessive individualism' (Macpherson, 1964), has become the hegemonic social and political discourse. Most of the former 'new social movements' have become institutionalized (e.g., the environmental movement), but at the same time 'new new social movements' like the global justice movement have emerged, not only opposing neoliberalism but also proposing the necessity of global citizenship (rights). Apart from this, during the past 50 years in numerous non-Western countries social movements have decisively contributed to regime change. The former communist block, South Africa, and several countries in the Middle East and Latin America are telling cases in point. Moreover, globalization and the ICT revolution have also impinged on social movements, resulting not only in the emergence of a number of transnational or even global social movement organizations (e.g., Amnesty International, Greenpeace), but also of numerous transnational social movement networks. In sum, the concept of a movement society seems to apply not only to Western, but also, or even more, to non-Western and global civil society.

As touched on above, citizenship has traditionally referred to a particular set of political practices involving specific public rights and duties for a specific political community (Bellamy, 2010, p. xii). In this respect, the past half-century has witnessed the successes of the civil rights movement in the USA, the anti-apartheid movement in South Africa, and numerous other movements striving for legal, political and social rights in all parts of the world. Influenced by theories about post-modernism, post-modernity and post-modernization (Harvey, 1989; Jameson, 1991), these five decades have also experienced the emergence of women's, immigrant, aboriginal, gay, lesbian and other groups, all striving for the recognition of their specific rights and identities. Apart from the new forms of citizenship resulting from this (e.g., sexual, diasporic, multicultural and aboriginal citizenship), from the 1980s onward globalization has brought about new forms of transnational (e.g., European) citizenship, and a reinvigoration of cosmopolitan citizenship.

In the social sciences large bodies of literature have developed on citizenship on the one hand, and on social movements on the other. These two topics of academic interest, however, are often pursued separately and distinctly, as the first traditionally refers to the individual dimension of social and political acting, and the second to the collective one. Besides, as Gaventa observes, those who examine how citizens engage with the state often do so with a focus on participation in the political processes of elections, parties, deliberative spaces or occasionally protest, but not on social movements, many of which emerge outside the formal political arena, and use extra-institutional channels to express their demands. On the other hand, those who focus on social movements have concentrated largely on how and why they engage, and on the dynamics within them, but not necessarily on their contribution to realizing substantive citizenship rights or to building and deepening responsive, more democratic forms of governance (Gaventa, 2010, pp. xi–xii). However, despite these distinct trajectories of development, social movement and citizenship studies have much ground in common. One of the underlying goals of this handbook is to bridge or, at least, to narrow the gap between them in order to lay the foundations for a social science research program that would do more justice to social and political reality.

SOCIAL MOVEMENTS, POLITICAL CITIZENSHIP, AND THE SOCIAL SCIENCES

Seen from a political science point of view, the dominant concept of liberal citizenship refers to the subfields of political theory and political behavior that are related to the individual level of political activity and identity, whereas the concept of social movements addresses the collective dimension of them. Citizenship as conceived of in this handbook and social movements are inextricably connected, but, as said above, in the social sciences the two have gone through quite different trajectories of development and institutionalization.

Until the 1960s social movements were widely seen as forms of irrational or unorganized political behavior, and were studied under labels like 'mass society', 'collective behavior' and 'relative deprivation'. However, vis-à-vis the new wave of movement activity in the USA, the newly emerging resource mobilization approach (RMA) convincingly argued that social movement action could be very rational and effective indeed (McCarthy and Zald, 1977). Conventional as well as unconventional political activities by groups of citizens could result in all kinds of favorable outcomes and successes for them. The resource mobilization approach in its turn proved to be very successful as an academic endeavor. In the 1970s, over half of all social movement and collective action articles in journals like the *American Sociological Review*, the *American Journal of Sociology*, *Social Forces*, and the *American Political Science Review* were based on this new approach, whereas by the early 1980s it was almost three-quarters (McClurg Mueller, 1992, p. 3).

Whereas the US-based resource mobilization approach was mainly interested in the impacts of the different kinds of resources (manpower, money, organizational structures, expertise, networks, and so on) for social movement organizations (SMOs), the Western European 'new social movement' (NSM) approach largely focused on the distinctive features of the recently originated new social movements (postmaterial values, unconventional action repertoire, new middle class constituency, and so on). More recently, this new social movement approach has also addressed issues like the relationship between global modernity and social movements and, from a Foucaultian perspective, the interrelationship between regimes of governance and practices of resistance.

From the 1980s onwards, on the heels of Charles Tilly, political scientists with an interest in social movements became aware that the specific features of an individual political system decisively impinged on the action repertoires, forms of organization, as well as on the successes of these movements (Kriesi et al., 1995). Whereas, for instance, unconventional or even radical action could be effective in one political context, it could be counterproductive in another one. This political opportunity structure (POS) or political process approach has developed into a full, third approach to the study of social movements.

A fourth approach finally (Van der Heijden, 2010, pp. 18–28), addresses the way social movements frame their issues of contention, the social and political discourses in which these frames are embedded, and the individual and collective identities that are formed in different kinds of social movement actions and interactions (social-constructivist or post-structuralist approach). According to this approach, the key feature of a social movement is not its material success but its 'cognitive praxis'. A social movement is primarily seen as a producer of knowledge; by framing an issue in a 'counter-hegemonic' way, by developing points of view that challenge dominant ways of looking at the social and political reality, it points to alternative ways of modeling society (Eyerman and Jamison, 1991).

From the mid-1970s onwards, academic research into social movements has started its process of institutionalization in specialized university departments; in research committees of international professional associations (e.g., the International Sociological Association Research Committees on 'Social Classes and Social Movements' and 'Social Movements, Collective Action and Social Change'); in the publication of thousands of books and journal articles; in several handbooks, for example, the *Blackwell Companion to Social Movements* (Snow et al., 2003), and the *Handbook of Social Movements Across Disciplines* (Klandermans and Roggeband, 2010); in the 1977-founded (and still existing) book series *Research in Social Movements, Conflicts and Change*; in authoritative monographs or collective endeavors covering the field (e.g., Tarrow, 1994; McAdam et al., 1996, 2001; Della Porta and Diani, 1999; Van Stekelenburg et al., 2013, to name just a few of them); and, finally, in a number of specialized academic journals (e.g., *Forschungsjournal Neue Soziale Bewegungen* [founded 1988], *Mobilization* [1996], *Mouvements* [in French, 1998], *Social Movement Studies* [2002], and *Interface: A Journal for and about Social Movements* [2009]).

To be sure, the study of social movements is definitely not restricted to the academic disciplines of sociology and political science. Social movements not only include the anti-nuclear, the civil rights, and similar political social movements, but also innumerable youth, cultural, and religious movements like, for instance, Hare Krishna and the International Naturist Federation. These primary 'a-political' social movements are widely studied by anthropologists, social psychologists, and other social scientists (Klandermans and Roggeband, 2010), but do not really cover the central topic of concern of this handbook.

Within social movement studies, the concept of citizenship has received only sparse attention. This is surprising because, as Bosniak observes, however it may be defined, 'Citizenship is commonly portrayed as the most desired of conditions, as the highest fulfillment of democratic and equalitarian aspirations' (Bosniak, 2006, p. 1). Up to the present day, discussions about citizenship are largely based on two classic models: a 'republican' model based on political participation, and a liberal, rights-based model, emphasizing citizenship as a legal status that can be separated from any involvement in decision-making (Bellamy, 2010, p. xxiii; Leydet, 2011). However, over the past couple of decades citizenship has gradually developed into an 'essentially contested concept' with numerous competing (and overlapping) categorizations and conceptualizations, including citizenship framed in moral terms, as a legal status, in terms of active participation, and in terms of identifying with the political community (whether this be local, national or global) (Kiwan, 2010, p. 100). One way to bring order in this conceptual chaos has been developed by Delanty. According to him, citizenship can be seen in terms of four models, all emphasizing different dimensions of what membership of a political community might entail: rights, duties, participation, and identity (the rights, conservative, participatory, and communitarian model of citizenship; Delanty, 1997, p. 288).

Another relevant contribution in this respect comes from Kiwan. Citizenship, historically, has been by definition an *exclusionary* concept, with the rights and responsibilities of citizenship conferred to only a well-defined subset of people within a society. However, according to Kiwan, with the relatively recent expansion of citizenship to include all members of society – including gender, social class, disability, ethnicity, and religion – there is an increasing interest in *inclusive* theorizations of multicultural citizenship (Kiwan, 2010, p. 102).

Citizenship studies as a field of political and social science research started to develop only in the 1990s, significantly later than social movement studies, and also, in terms of the number of scholars and students, it has remained smaller. Nevertheless, citizenship studies have become firmly institutionalized. Marshall's classic text on *Citizenship and Social Class* (1950) has been cited more than 6000 times in Google Scholar, whereas Kymlicka's *Multicultural Citizenship* (1996) received over 5000 citations. In 2003 the authoritative *Handbook of Citizenship Studies* was published (Isin and Turner, 2003), and at present there are at least two academic journals exclusively addressing this topic of academic interest: *Citizenship Studies* (founded 1997), and *Education, Citizenship and Social Justice* (2006).

In order to articulate the relationship between social movement research and citizenship studies, in this handbook the concept of *political* citizenship will be further explored. Rather than emphasizing traditional conceptualizations of citizenship like the right to vote and the right to be eligible or to stand for office, the focus will be on topics that are also addressed by social movements, for instance, the ecological, gender, and urban dimensions of citizenship.

As for the distinction between the two classic models of liberal and republican citizenship mentioned above, scholars like Benjamin Crick have presented republican citizenship as an alternative to the dominant liberal tradition, a corrective to what Crick sees as the overly individualistic, litigious and inactive nature of contemporary political life (Crick and Lockyer, 2010). A similar interpretation of this concept of republican political citizenship has been suggested by Benjamin Barber in his highly praised *Strong Democracy* (1984). Strong democracy, Barber argues, aims at understanding individuals not as abstract persons but as citizens, so that commonality and equality rather than separateness are the defining traits of human society (ibid., p. 119).

The concept of political (or engaged) citizenship as explored in this handbook is strongly influenced by the ideas as developed by authors like Crick, Barber, and Russell Dalton, ideas that are shared by numerous other scholars as well (e.g., Bellamy, 2010, p. xi). Political citizenship is, as will be elaborated below, the very concept to decrease the cleavage between citizenship and social movement activities, as well as between citizenship and social movement studies.

According to Dalton, institutionally focused, 'rights- and duty-based' citizenship has a restrictive definition of participation – it dissuades people from participating in direct, challenging activities. However, as Dalton observes (2008, p. 88), as over the past decades people have become more educated and politically skilled, they seek different means of influencing policy:

> In contrast [to duty-based citizenship] engaged citizenship taps participatory norms that are broader than electoral politics. The engaged citizen is more likely to participate in boycotts, buying products for political and ethical reasons, demonstrations and other forms of contentious action. These effects are even more striking for internet activism, which is unrelated to citizen duty but strongly related to norms of engaged citizenship. In other words, the norms of citizen duty lead to participation in electoral politics, but do not encourage a broader repertoire of political action.

In order to adequately assess this broader political action repertoire, citizenship and social movements could no longer be addressed separately. This applies in particular to the present era of neoliberalism. The forms of political citizenship and the social movements analyzed in this book have mainly developed during the past three decades, the global neoliberal era. Neoliberalism has structured and shaped the life of every individual and every collectivity to a certain extent, including individual citizens and social movements. The way the neoliberal discourse encourages individuals and collective actors to perceive competition, egoism, and ruthlessness as self-evident; the way individuals are socialized to behave as 'calculating citizens'; the way the 'logic of the market' permeates all spheres of human life and human society – the hegemony of neoliberalism is overwhelming. On top of this, in many cases neoliberal policies have also included a frontal attack on citizenship rights and social movements themselves, for example, the attack on the labor movement under Thatcher. At the same time, however, it is engaged citizens and social movements (or, at least, parts of them) that do not stop to challenge the global hegemony of the neoliberal discourse, and try to develop alternative bodies of knowledge, alternative social practices and other forms of resistance (Klein, 2000; Herz, 2001; Smith, 2002; Hardt and Negri, 2004; Cox and Flesher Fominaya, 2009; Flesher Fominaya and Cox, 2013). It is this background that interconnects the different parts and chapters of this handbook.

ABOUT THIS HANDBOOK

This book aims to be more than a mere description of all different kinds of citizenship and social movement studies; it is intended to function as an academic handbook. In order to fulfill the requirements of such a handbook, the authors of the individual chapters have been advised to include as much as possible the following four topics of attention:

- an overview of the most important research endeavors within the research area of their specific chapter (for instance, multicultural citizenship, the new social movement approach, or the international human rights movement);
- an overview of the most important (theoretical and/or empirical) research results;
- an assessment of the most important middle-range theories and concepts within the specific area of research;
- a short sketch of relevant future developments and future research topics within that area.

As noted before, citizenship and social movements have developed as basically distinct fields of academic research, but the linkages between the two are numerous. As Isin and Turner observe, one of the very reasons for the emergence of citizenship studies has been the emergence of new social movements and their struggles for recognition and redistribution. Major social issues such as the status of immigrants, refugees, and environmental injustices have increasingly been expressed through the language of rights and obligations, and hence of citizenship (Isin and Turner, 2003, p. 1). Citizenship studies, however, as Isin and Turner contend, is ultimately not (only) about books and articles. It is about 'addressing injustices suffered by many peoples around the world, making these injustices appear in the public sphere, enabling these groups to articulate these injustices as claims for recognition and enacting them in national as well as transnational laws and practices, and thus bringing about fundamental changes' (ibid., pp. 2–3).

Apart from this introduction, the *Handbook of Political Citizenship and Social Movements* consists of four different parts: one on the different forms of, and approaches to political citizenship; one on the current approaches to social movements and on recent developments within social movement studies; one on a number of contemporary social movements; and, finally, a part specifically devoted to social movements and political citizenship in non-Western countries. To be sure, this perforce division in four parts reflects the current academic practice rather than the interconnection between citizenship and social movement studies as advocated in this introduction. Hopefully, however, this handbook may contribute to a future research practice in which citizenship and social movement studies are a joint rather than a separate research endeavor.

In the first part of the book, the different approaches to, and forms of political citizenship are addressed. In Chapter 2, Russell J. Dalton gives a sketch of the history and the present status of the concept of political citizenship. Most scholars agree that the concept of citizenship is composed of three main elements: citizenship as legal status, citizenship as political agency, and citizenship as membership of a political community, which furnishes a distinct source of identity (Leydet, 2011). However, as has been elaborated above, during the past couple of decades citizenship has developed into a contested concept with a large number of different conceptualizations and categorizations. The core goal of Dalton's chapter is to provide a succinct overview of these conceptualizations and categorizations, to assess them, and, most of all, to further elaborate and refine the concept of political citizenship. On top of this, Dalton provides us with a fine set of data about the distribution of 'traditional' and 'political' forms of citizenship in a large number of countries all over the Western world.

As has been observed above, whereas liberal individualism has a conception of citizenship as status, civic republicanism has a conception of citizenship as 'practice', thus coming closer to the definition of political citizenship as developed by authors like Dalton. Consequently, whereas at present liberal citizenship is the hegemonic definition of citizenship, in Chapter 3 of this handbook James Bohman elaborates – at a theoretical level – republican citizenship in terms of an alternative to this dominant liberal tradition in the present context of globalization. Topics addressed by Bohman include the concepts of epistemic injustice, communicative freedom, and civic friendship, and the question of to what extent the European Union provides an institutional basis for the further development of republican self-rule.

Chapters 4–6 address three forms of citizenship that have developed as major 'thematic' approaches in citizenship studies over the last couple of decades: gendered, multicultural, and ecological citizenship. Since the 1970s, feminist theorists have criticized the republican and liberal models' shared assumption of a rigid separation between the private and the public spheres (Leydet, 2011). This critique has provided the impetus to the development of a large body of literature on the relationship between citizenship, gender and sexuality. In Chapter 4, Surya Monro and Diane Richardson not only assess this literature, but, importantly, they also expand the object of analysis by introducing the concepts of sexual and transgender citizenship, and by including LGBT (lesbian, gay, bisexual, transgender) groups as social movements in their research agenda on citizenship, gender, and sexuality.

Whereas liberal and republican citizenship define citizenship primarily as a legal status for all members of a polity, during the past decades both models have been challenged by groups that stressed three specific types of demands: special representation rights (for disadvantaged groups); multicultural rights (for immigrant and religious groups); and self-government rights (for national minorities) (Kymlicka, 1996; Leydet, 2011). The research area of (some of) these kinds of differentiated citizenship is addressed by Narzanin Massoumi and Nasar Meer in Chapter 5. Interestingly, in this chapter the authors not only assess the literature on multicultural citizenship, but they also consider how multicultural citizenship and (new) social movement literature, with its strong emphasis on the construction of new individual and collective identities, can be synthesized in the theorization of contemporary citizenship.

A third thematic approach, also challenging the universalist liberal and republican models, refers to the relationship between citizens and the environment. In political science and political philosophy, an extensive debate has developed about environmental or ecological citizenship as a way to achieving sustainability, encouraging individuals to act according to the 'public environmental good'. Perhaps more than any other social

Introduction 11

movement, Sherilyn MacGregor argues in Chapter 6, environmentalism has succeeded in changing the way citizenship is theorized. These theorizations include the greening of liberal citizenship; the importance of individual green virtues in republican ecological citizenship; and, finally, the global responsibilities of post-cosmopolitan ecological citizenship.

Up to the present day, citizenship has mostly been defined as the status of being a citizen of a specific *national* political community. Transnationalization and globalization, however, are increasingly eroding the national state as the exclusive locus of citizenship. At the same time, however, the partial erosion of the nation-state due to globalization has also led to a reinforcement of the role of the 'local state', the urban or metropolitan political community. The impact of these national de-territorialization processes on citizenship will be addressed in three chapters: one on urban citizenship (Chapter 7), one on the impact of the European Union on the reshaping of the concept of citizenship (European citizenship; Chapter 8); and one on the possibilities of global or cosmopolitan citizenship (Chapter 9).

In Chapter 7 on urban citizenship, Patricia Burke Wood analyzes urban citizenship both as a tool of governmentality in the Foucaultian sense of the word, and as an empowering or liberating device. After defining the specifically urban elements of urban citizenship, Burke Wood analyzes three empirical examples of urban citizenship: the urban uprisings that together constituted the Arab Spring; the mass protests in 61 Spanish cities in 2011 under the joint banner of 'Real Democracy NOW'; and, finally, the Occupy movement. She connects these occupations of urban public spaces to Lefebvre's concept of 'right to the city', and also introduces the concept of 'the grid'. Encampment in urban public space, she argues, is a successful disturbance of the order of 'the grid' and *all* that it represents.

In many parts of the world, the European Union is seen as a shining example of what a twenty-first-century polity could look like. Australian political scientist Robyn Eckersley, for instance, has called the European Union the very first cosmopolitan, post-national democracy in the world, 'the closest empirical approximation of a greenish Kantian culture, with intimations of a post-Westphalian culture' (Eckersley, 2004, p. 47). In *The European Dream* the American economist Jeremy Rifkin contrasts the American emphasis on economic growth, personal wealth and individual self-interests with the European emphasis on sustainable development, quality of life and community. Rifkin concludes that the EU is developing a new social and political model better suited to the needs of the globalizing world of the new century and, consequently, that 'Europe's vision of the future is quietly eclipsing the American dream' (Rifkin, 2004, p. iii). In Chapter 8 on European citizenship, Espen D.H. Olsen investigates

12 *Handbook of political citizenship and social movements*

to what extent Rifkin's optimism about the EU can be recognized in the different approaches to European citizenship. Olsen contrasts essentialist with constructivist ideas on the viability of European citizenship; he discusses the normative literature on the desirability, problems and possibilities of European citizenship; and, finally, he assesses the historical and institutionalist research on the emergence of citizenship as a policy field in European integration.

The final chapter of this first part of the handbook, Chapter 9, deals with global and cosmopolitan citizenship, concepts with both strong supporters and opponents. In order to unravel the different arguments, Sebastiaan Tijsterman makes a strict distinction between empirical, normative, and prospective perspectives on cosmopolitan citizenship. Themes being addressed in his chapter include the influence of globalization upon territorial citizenship, the normative question of whether we should foster global citizenship and, finally, the discussion between voluntarists and skeptics about the possibilities of realizing cosmopolitan citizenship in some meaningful way.

In the second and third parts of this handbook, focus shifts from political citizenship to social movements. The second part (Chapters 10–16) addresses the different approaches and recent developments in the study of social movements. A quick glance at the field of recent social movement studies reveals that the four approaches as identified in the introduction of this chapter are still the ones that largely dominate the field, although it is increasingly recognized that the four approaches are complementary rather than contradictory to one another, and that there is also a considerable number of scholars who work outside any of these approaches, or selectively re-work some aspects of them. Nevertheless, Chapters 10–13 not only present the core concepts and most important research results from the resource mobilization approach, the new social movement approach, the political opportunity structure approach, and the post-structuralist approach, but also the middle-range theories and research findings emerging from these, their consequences for future research, and the interconnections between the four approaches. Apart from these four chapters on different approaches to social movements, the three subsequent chapters will address some recent developments: the importance of emotions as analytical category in social movement research (Chapter 14); the transnationalization of social movements due to globalization (Chapter 15), and, closely related to this, the impact of recent developments in information and communication technology on the action repertoires, the organizational structures and the impacts of social movements (Chapter 16).

For numerous contemporary social movement scholars, McCarthy and Zald's (1977) 'partial theory' of resource mobilization and social movements has played a key role in their socialization in social movement research, for instance, in order to define the differences between social movements and social movement organizations (SMOs). The article received almost 4000 citations, and has been seminal in the development of the resource mobilization approach. In Chapter 10, Bob Edwards and Melinda Kane analyze the current state of affairs of this approach, both from a theoretical and an empirical point of view. On the theoretical level the authors develop typologies of different resource types (material, human, social-organizational, cultural, and moral resources), and mechanisms of resource access. In their analysis of the empirical literature they assess a large number of studies, dealing with all kinds of resources. The authors conclude that current social movement research tends to under-utilize resource mobilization theory relative to other theoretical explanation, partly caused by a lack of accessible and reliable indicators with which to measure all types of resources and organizational characteristics.

Social movements themselves rather than social movement organizations are the core topic of attention of the new social movement (NSM) approach. The NSM approach has tried to explain the emergence of the environmental, women's, peace, students', civil rights and other social movements in the 1960s and 1970s. These movements basically differed from 'old' movements like the labor movement, and because of that were called 'new social movements'. In contrast to the 'micro-sociological', US-based resource mobilization approach, the European 'macro-sociological' NSM approach tries to explain the emergence of new social movements by referring to the large structural transformations Western societies had gone through since the end of World War II. In Chapter 11 on this approach, Christian Scholl first of all analyzes the specific contributions of some of the most important NSM theorists: Alain Touraine, Alberto Melucci, Jürgen Habermas and Manuel Castells. Thereafter he discusses three main criticisms and debates. What is *really* new about new social movements? What is the difference between the NSM approach and instrumentalist-structuralist approaches (the 'strategy versus identity' debate)? And, finally, are new social movements not as much about lifestyle as about politics? In the final sections of his chapter, Christian Scholl delves into the relevance of the NSM approach to explain the 'newest social movements' like, for instance, the climate justice movement, the counter-globalization movement, and Occupy.

The distinctive contribution of political scientists to the study of social movements has been the concept of 'political opportunity structure' (POS). POS scholars argue that POS could explain to a large extent the widely different impacts, action repertoire, levels of mobilization, and organizational structures of social movements in individual political systems, for example, nation-states. In Chapter 12, 'Citizenship, political opportunities and social movements', David S. Meyer and Erin Evans start from the observation that social movements are almost all about citizenship. For instance, citizenship bargains structure the form, claims, and influence of social movements, and social movements connect individuals through both formal organizations and less formal networks. Subsequently, Meyer and Evans sketch and discuss the different ways in which the concept of POS has been operationalized in the political process approach, and they reflect on the most promising methodology for finding transformative changes that social movements have induced.

The fourth and final contemporary approach to the study of social movements is the social-constructivist approach. One of the forerunners of this approach is the 'cognitive approach' to social movements as developed by Eyerman and Jamison (1991). According to these authors, the key feature of a social movement is not its material success but its 'cognitive praxis'. A social movement is primarily seen as a producer of knowledge; by framing an issue in a 'counter-hegemonic' way, by developing points of view that challenge the dominant discourse, it points to alternative ways of modeling society. The social-constructivist approach has been elaborated in two different ways: frame theory and discourse analysis. Frame theory (Snow et al., 1986; Snow and Benford, 1988; Gamson, 1992; Benford and Snow, 2000) starts from the idea that social movements try to express their vision on (a part of) social and political reality by means of collective action frames. Collective action frames are action-oriented sets of beliefs and meanings that inspire and legitimate the activities and campaigns of a social movement organization (Benford and Snow, 2000, p. 614). In this respect Benford and Snow distinguish between three 'core framing tasks' for SMOs: diagnostic, prognostic, and motivational framing (Snow and Benford, 1988). Diagnostic framing deals with the way a problem is defined by a social movement organization, prognostic framing addresses the resulting solution strategies, whereas motivational framing provides a 'call to arms' or rationale for engaging in collective action (Benford and Snow, 2000). The analytical framework as developed by Benford, Snow, and their colleagues has been proved very successful and has been applied in several hundreds of social movement studies. Their 1986 article has received almost 4000 citations, their 1988 one over 2500, and their 2000 overview and assessment was cited more than 3250 times.

A slightly different conceptualization of framing has been suggested by William Gamson. According to Gamson, collective action frames in social movements have three important characteristics in common: a feeling of injustice, agency, and, finally, identity. Whereas the injustice aspect refers to 'moral indignation about harm and suffering', the agency side points to the idea that it is possible to alter social conditions or policies through collective action. The identity component, finally, refers to the process of defining a 'we', typically in opposition to a 'they' who have different interests or values (Gamson, 1992, p. 7).

The second way the social-constructivist approach to social movements has been operationalized is discourse analysis. Whereas one could argue that framing theory is based on a positivist rather than on a social-constructivist epistemology, discourse analysis explicitly starts from a post-structuralist point of view. In Chapter 13, 'Post-structuralism, social movements and citizen politics', Steven Griggs and David Howarth examine the ways in which post-structuralism offers a particular style of theorizing and ethos, which is appropriate to doing research into social movements. In contrast to most mainstream theories, the post-structuralist approach starts from the recognition that both interests and identities are contingent and political constructs, with precise discursive conditions of existence. Consequently, the approach draws attention to the ways in which shared interests and identities in moments of citizen mobilization are constructed politically and discursively, as well to the dependence of the group identity that is forged on an opposition to other groups.

After this assessment of the four contemporary approaches to social movements, the next three chapters of this part of the handbook address three recent developments in social movement research. In Chapter 14 on social movements and emotions, Helena Flam criticizes the rational actor model underlying most social movement studies until the 1980s. In their 1977 article on the resource mobilization approach, for instance, McCarthy and Zald posited an analogy between social movements and industry, casting movement leaders as 'movement entrepreneurs' and mobilizing individuals as rational actors seeking to realize their preferences by choosing between different movement organizations. Soon after the publication of McCarthy and Zald's article, the 'emotional turn' in social movement studies took off with a number of studies of self-help groups within the women's movement. A vast array of emotions, these studies showed, makes women, subject to various forms of victimization or stigmatization, form or join self-help groups, and thus enables the development of new collective identities. Subsequent topics addressed by social movement scholars with a focus on emotions include, for instance, the role of friendship and solidarity, but also of grievances, anxiety, and fear in social movements. Case studies discussed by Helena Flam in this chapter address, among many others, the student protest at the Tiananmen Square in Beijing in 1989; the Madres de Playa de Mayo in Buenos Aires; and the enduring action campaign of the Israeli Women in Black.

16   *Handbook of political citizenship and social movements*

In Chapter 15 on the transnationalization of social movements – another emerging trend in social movement studies – Movindri Reddy contends that existing theories fall short in explaining this transnationalization, as they are primarily suited to analyzing social movements in the Global North. Consequently, numerous scholars are inclined to give transnational social movements a coherence and rationality that does not actually exist. What is distinctive about the Global South in our current period of globalization, Reddy argues, is that in many countries the globalization of the economy and the transition to formal, liberal democracy have occurred at the same time. Social movement theories, however, have neglected to analyze and contextualize the marginalization of these countries and social movements emerging from these circumstances.

In Chapter 16, 'Social movements and the ICT revolution', Jennifer Earl, Jayson Hunt and R. Kelly Garrett discuss the impact of new information and communication technologies both on social movements and on social movement research. They sketch the development of this kind of research from humble early examinations of activists' Usenet bulletin boards and the Zapatistas, to the examination of different forms of 'internet activism' across the globe. The authors outline the different positions within the grand debate over the general theoretical impact of ICTs on protest: does ICT usage have no effect on fundamentals underlying social movement theory; does it accelerate knowing processes or otherwise enlarge them; or are social movement theories fundamentally altered through ICT use? Finally, the authors assess empirical research results on the influence of ICT on phenomena like micro-mobilization and participation; organizing and organizations; online collective identity and community.

In the third part of this handbook, research on six contemporary social movements will be assessed: the environmental, the women's, and the international human rights movement, as well as urban social movements, the Tea Party movement in the United States, and the animal rights movement. These movements are not only among the most important social movements of the present era, but they also show the inextricable relationship with specific forms of political citizenship (e.g., ecological or urban citizenship).

The environmental movement and the women's movement are generally considered to be the most important and most influential social movements of the past half-century, and thus should be included anyway. One could, however, argue that the same applies to the labor movement. Obviously, the labor movement has been the most important social movement of the first half of the twentieth century. From the 1970s onwards, however, this movement has lost most of its movement characteristics, at least in Western countries, whereas in several countries in the Global South it remains an important social movement indeed. Consequently, it has been decided not to reserve a separate chapter for the Western labor movement, but to pay ample attention to it in the individual, non-Western regional chapters in the fourth part of the handbook.

Of all social movements discussed in this handbook, the environmental movement is probably the most diversified one. It encompasses both the environmental justice movement in the USA and the 'environmentalism of the poor' movements in the Global South; both the European GMO-Free Regions Network, and the Russian branch of Greenpeace, fighting against the drilling in the Arctic shelf by the Russian Gazprom company. Large parts of the environmental movement have become highly institutionalized and solidly operate within the master frame of ecological modernization. However, in Chapter 17 by Hein-Anton van der Heijden on the environmental movement it is argued that over the decades there have always been groups within the environmental movement that have framed environmental problems as one of the 'routine consequences' of modernity and its four interconnected institutional features: capitalism, industrialism, surveillance, and military power. It is argued that the uniqueness of these 'counter-hegemonic' parts of the environmental movement lies in the fact that they deliberately challenge the very institutional features of modernity, and thus show us a glimpse of what a greener society could look like, both in the Northern and the Southern Hemisphere.

The history of the women's movement, in particular the North American one, is sketched by Jo Reger in Chapter 18. Reger argues that while scholarship of social movements has deeply influenced the ways in which women's movements have been studied, women's movements in their turn have also provided important theoretical concepts and frameworks that are relevant for all social movement research. Examples discussed by Reger include, for instance, the concepts of abeyance; the critique of the concept of 'waves' of protest; feminist work on the intersectionality of social identities; and, finally, the expansion of notions of mobilization and movement outcomes.

In Chapter 19 on the international human rights movement, Ann Marie Clark and Paul Danyi analyze how this movement has made itself a lasting political and moral force to be reckoned with. They describe the growth of this movement since the 1970s; the differences and similarities between the two most important SMOs in the field, Amnesty International and Human Rights Watch; and the three categories within the movement's repertoires of contention: bringing human rights violations to light; incorporating human rights concerns into international law and institutions; and, finally, holding states accountable. Apart from this, Clark and Danyi also discuss a number of debates about the human rights movement, among which the question of what impact the movement has had internationally.

Urban social movements have received an individual chapter not only because of their constituent role in the formation of social movements in the recent past, but, more importantly, because life in the twenty-first-century world will increasingly be lived in urban and metropolitan areas. With more than 60 percent of the world population living in these areas, urban citizenship and urban social movements are expected to become an increasingly important area of twenty-first-century social science research. Urban struggles include, for instance, squatting/rent struggles, struggles around the use of public space, traffic and mobility. In Chapter 20 on urban movements Pierre Hamel reconstructs the debate on these movements, from Manuel Castells's 1972 influential volume on the urban question to recent work of authors like David Harvey, Saskia Sassen and, again, Manuel Castells. In the 'suggestions for further research' section of his chapter, Pierre Hamel stresses, among others, the ongoing tension between structure and agency-based approaches to the study of urban social movements, the emergence of mega-cities in the Global South and the resulting conflicts and movement mobilizations in countries like China, India, and Brazil.

Social movements as conceived of in this volume not only include 'left-leaning' or 'progressive' ones. In the United States, the conservative Tea Party movement has developed into the most influential social movement of the past decades, with many millions of members or sympathizers. Consequently, Chapter 21, written by Edward Ashbee, will try to unravel not only the discourse, but also the organizational structures, the action repertoire, and the impact of this Tea Party movement. Besides, Ashbee tries to systematically answer the question of why there has long been a theoretical and methodological cleavage between surveys of conservative and radical rights movements in the USA on the one hand, and studies of (other) social movements on the other.

The last movement addressed in this part of the handbook is the animal rights movement. In his book on radical environmentalism, Rik Scarce has observed that few of us give a second thought to using animals for food, clothing, and other purposes. However, Scarce contends, vast industries have built up around exploiting tens of millions of dogs, cats, monkeys, and horses for medical research. Apart from this, in the USA alone every year six billion animals are killed for human consumption (Scarce, 1990, pp. 116–18).

In his chapter on the animal rights movement, Lyle Munro in Chapter 22 first of all assesses the literature on the abuse of animals from different disciplinary perspectives: political science, sociology, social psychology, and so on. Thereafter he analyzes the animal rights movement as a stratified movement consisting of three categories: animal welfarists, animal liberationists, and animal rightists. From each branch he discusses the most important SMOs, not only with respect to their intellectual underpinnings, but also their organizational structures and action repertoires.

In the fourth, final part of this handbook, focus shifts from a thematic to a geographic approach, and from a separated to an integrated assessment of political citizenship and social movements. As Stammers (2009) has pointed out, historically the attainment of rights in the North was the outcome of sustained social movement activity. In contrast, many social movements in the Global South have arisen as a consequence of opportunities presented by rights entrenched in relatively recently founded constitutional democracies. In such contexts, social mobilization is, in many respects, aimed at achieving substantive citizenship that yields material gains (Thompson and Tapscott, 2010, p. 2). Consequently, whereas in many Western countries the academic distinction between social movement activism and political citizenship has become somewhat artificial, in most countries in the Global South the distinction has lost most of its relevance: social movement activism and political citizenship struggles are virtually indivisible (cf. Thompson and Tapscott, 2010). Accordingly, the authors of the chapters in this part of the handbook have been asked to take into account, as much as possible, both the social movement angle as well as the political citizenship point of view when analyzing political activism.

The selection of countries and regions for this part of the handbook not only reflects the political relevance and the state of social movement activism and political citizenship in the respective different parts of the world, but also the level of development of social movement and political citizenship research. In Chapter 23 on political citizenship and social movements in China, Lei Xie analyzes in what ways China's restrictive political system limits the options open to people for forming movements or to systematically organize large-scale collective actions. She describes the research about the present state of affairs with respect to five contemporary social movements: peasant, labor, urban, environmental, and women's movements. Subsequently she analyzes the rights consciousness and the conceptualization of citizenship in contemporary China, and the way the concept of political citizenship has been applied in and by social movements.

Contrary to China, India has a rich history of organized and spontaneous social activism from across the political-ideological spectrum. Contrary to China, India also has a rich history of social movement research, including research from the structural-functionalist, the dialectical Marxist, the new social movement, and from a large number of 'in between' approaches. In the first part of Chapter 24, Dip Kapoor meticulously analyzes the numerous research endeavors within these different approaches. In the second part he describes the state of the art with respect to research in four encompassing movements in present-day India: peasant and new farmers' movements; informal economy and industrial working class movements; women's movements; and, finally, human (citizenship) rights movements.

In comparison to India, social movement research in Africa is still in its infancy. Consequently, rather than describing the state of affairs of this kind of research in Africa, in Chapter 25 Patrick Bond describes a large number of social movement activities all over the continent, in which the climate justice movement appears to play a leading role. Much attention is also paid to the macro political-economic context. Is Africa 'rising' as a great new economic power, or is the continent better seen as witnessing early – and potentially widespread – uprisings, in a context of worsening economic conditions, as climate catastrophe also bears down on a billion Africans? It is this question that determines the structure of the chapter on political citizenship and social movements in Africa.

In the final chapter, Roel Meijer first of all analyzes how politics in the Arab world in past and present has impinged on the civil, political, social, and cultural rights of the citizen. The trajectory of citizenship in the Middle East appears to have had different historical phases with different combinations of rights (e.g., civil, political, social, and cultural rights). Thereafter Meijer compares the status of these rights during the period of the struggle for independence with the rise of citizenship rights over the past 20 years. As social movement theory gives agency to the citizen, Meijer subsequently tries to answer the question of how contestation has influenced the position of the citizen. His overall conclusion is that both citizenship and social movement studies can correct the tendency to portray the Arab as passive or indolent, or the exact opposite, fanatic and religious, so reminiscent of the orientalist tradition.

Although some parts of the world (e.g., Russia, South East Asia, and, most importantly, Latin America[2]) have remained unrepresented, this final part of the handbook convincingly shows that political citizenship and social movements, and academic interpretations of them, have developed into an increasingly global phenomenon. Time will tell in which forms and to what extent they will continue to bring about core social transformations, and so again will basically change the world.

NOTES

* The author would like to thank Christian Scholl and Sebastiaan Tijsterman for their helpful comments on an earlier draft of this chapter.
1. Apart from Scott and Tilly, social historians like Hobsbawm and E.P. Thompson should also be mentioned in this respect.
2. There is no lack of studies into political citizenship and social movements in Latin America, but most of them are in Spanish or in Portuguese.

REFERENCES

Barber, B. (1984), *Strong Democracy*, Berkeley, CA: University of California Press.
Bellamy, R. (2010), 'Introduction', in R. Bellamy and A. Palumbo (2010), *Citizenship*, Farnham, UK: Ashgate.
Benford, R. and D. Snow (2000), 'Framing processes and social movements: an overview and assessment', *Annual Review of Sociology*, 26(1), 611–39.
Bosniak, L. (2006), *The Citizen and the Alien: Dilemmas of Contemporary Membership*, Princeton, NJ: Princeton University Press.
Cox, L. and C. Flesher Fominaya (2009), 'Movement knowledge: what do we know, how do we create knowledge and what do we do with it', *Interface: A Journal for and about Social Movements*, 1(1), 1–20.
Crick, B. and A. Lockyer (eds) (2010), *Active Citizenship*, Edinburgh: Edinburgh University Press.
Dalton, R. (2008), 'Citizenship norms and the expansion of political participation', *Political Studies*, 56(1), 76–98.
Delanty, G. (1997), 'Models of citizenship. Defining European identity and citizenship', *Citizenship Studies*, 1(3), 285–303.
Della Porta, D. and M. Diani (1999), *Social Movements. An Introduction*, Oxford: Blackwell.
Eckersley, R. (2004), *The Green State. Rethinking Democracy and Sovereignty*, Cambridge, MA: MIT Press.
Eyerman, R. and A. Jamison (1991), *Social Movements: A Cognitive Approach*, Cambridge, UK: Polity.
Flesher Fominaya, C. and L. Cox (eds) (2013), *Understanding European Movements. New Social Movements, Global Justice Struggles, Anti-Austerity Protest*, London: Routledge.
Gamson, W. (1992), *Talking Politics*, Cambridge, UK: Cambridge University Press.
Gaventa, J. (2010), 'Foreword', in L. Thompson and C. Tapscott (eds), *Citizenship and Social Movements. Perspectives from the Global South*, London: Zed Books.
Hardt, M. and A. Negri (2004), *Multitude: War and Democracy in the Age of Empire*, New York: Penguin.
Harvey, D. (1989), *The Condition of Postmodernity*, Oxford: Blackwell.
Herz, N. (2001), *The Silent Takeover. Global Capitalism and the Death of Democracy*, New York: HarperCollins.
Isin, E. and B. Turner (eds) (2003), *Handbook of Citizenship Studies*, London: Sage.
Jameson, F. (1991), *Postmodernism, or, the Cultural Logic of Late Capitalism*, London: Verso.
Kiwan, D. (2010), 'Active citizenship: multiculturalism and mutual understanding', in B. Crick and A. Lockyer (eds) (2010), *Active Citizenship*, Edinburgh: Edinburgh University Press, pp. 100–111.
Klandermans, B. and C. Roggeband (eds) (2010), *Handbook of Social Movements Across Disciplines*, Wiesbaden: Springer.
Klein, N. (2000), *No Logo. Taking Aim at the Brand Bullies*, New York: Picador.
Kriesi, H., R. Koopmans, J.W. Duyvendak and M. Giugni (1995), *New Social Movements*

in *Western Europe. A Comparative Analysis*, Minneapolis, MN: University of Minnesota Press.
Kymlicka, W. (1996), *Multicultural Citizenship*, Oxford: Oxford University Press.
Leydet, D. (2011), 'Citizenship', in *Stanford Encyclopedia of Philosophy* [online], accessed 1 May 2014 at http://plato.stanford.edu/entries/citizenship.
Macpherson, C.B. (1964), *The Political Theory of Possessive Individualism: From Hobbes to Locke*, Oxford: Oxford University Press.
Marshall, T. (1950), *Citizenship and Social Class and Other Essays*, Cambridge, UK: Cambridge University Press.
McAdam, D., J. McCarthy and M. Zald (1996), *Comparative Perspectives on Social Movements*, Cambridge, UK: Cambridge University Press.
McAdam, D., S. Tarrow and C. Tilly (2001), *Dynamics of Contention*, Cambridge, UK: Cambridge University Press.
McCarthy, J. and M. Zald (1977), 'Resource mobilization and social movements: a partial theory', *American Journal of Sociology*, **82**(6), 1212–41.
McClurg Mueller, C. (1992), 'Building social movement theory', in D. Morris and C. McClurg Mueller (eds), *Frontiers in Social Movement Theory*, New Haven, CT/London: Yale University Press, pp. 3–25.
Meyer, D. and S. Tarrow (eds) (1997), *The Social Movement Society. Contentious Politics for a New Century*, Lanham, MD: Rowman & Littlefield.
Rifkin, J. (2004), *The European Dream*, New York: Jeremy Tarcher/Penguin.
Scarce, R. (1990), *Eco-warriors. Understanding the Radical Environmental Movement*, Chicago, IL: The Noble Press.
Smith, J. (2002), 'Globalizing resistance: the battle of Seattle and the future of social movements', in J. Smith and H. Johnston (eds), *Globalization and Resistance. Transnational Dimensions of Social Movements*, Lanham, MD: Rowman & Littlefield, pp. 207–27.
Snow, D. and R. Benford (1988), 'Ideology, frame resonance, and participant mobilization', *International Social Movement Research*, **1**(1), 197–217.
Snow, D., B. Rochford, S. Wordem and R. Benford (1986), 'Frame alignment processes, micromobilization and movement participation', *American Sociological Review*, **51**(4), 464–81.
Snow, D., S. Soule and H. Kriesi (eds) (2003), *The Blackwell Companion to Social Movements*, Oxford: Blackwell.
Stammers, N. (2009), *Human Rights and Social Movements*, London: Pluto Press.
Tarrow, S. (1994), *Power in Movement. Social Movements, Collective Action and Politics*, Cambridge, UK: Cambridge University Press.
Thompson, L. and C. Tapscott (eds) (2010), *Citizenship and Social Movements. Perspectives from the Global South*, London: Zed Books.
Van der Heijden, H.A. (2010), *Social Movements, Public Spheres and the European Politics of the Environment Green Power Europe?*, Houndmills, UK: Palgrave Macmillan.
Van Stekelenburg, J., C. Roggeband and B. Klandermans (eds) (2013), *The Future of Social Movement Research: Dynamics, Mechanisms, and Processes*, Minneapolis, MN: University of Minnesota Press.

PART I

POLITICAL CITIZENSHIP: APPROACHES AND FORMS

2. Political citizenship: mapping the terrain
Russell J. Dalton

Citizenship has emerged as a central concept in the discourse about the politics of contemporary democracies for several reasons. In theoretical terms, there is a long and rich debate on what makes for a good citizen, with as many possible answers (or more) as the number of authors who have addressed this topic. The concept of citizenship dates from the first democratic polity and before, and theorists – republicans, liberals, neoliberals, communitarians, social-democrats, and others – differ substantially in their definitions of the concept. The exact meaning of citizenship is open to multiple interpretations as displayed in this book.

The concept has such special relevance today because it is intertwined with debates on the vitality of democracy – and this chapter focuses on the content of democratic citizenship. As contemporary publics have become more critical of their governments and politicians, and the policy-making process has become more conflictual in some nations, experts have turned to concepts of citizenship to diagnose the current situation and offer potential remedies. On the one hand, some analysts claim that an erosion of 'good citizenship' has produced the current challenges to democracy, and hark back to an era when these norms were apparently in greater supply (Etzioni, 1995; Putnam, 2000; Stoker, 2006). A typical example is an observation on the decline of civility in public discourse, attributed at least in part to changing norms of citizenship (Elgar, 2012). On the other hand, another group of experts argues that the nature of citizenship is changing, and people are still 'good citizens' just in a different manner than in the past (Inglehart, 1990; Dalton, 2009). In other words, changing norms of citizenship can transform the democratic process without offering a challenge to the vitality of democracy.

This chapter begins by summarizing some of the previous approaches to defining democratic citizenship. I will not discuss the full philosophical history of the concept, because this would fill a volume and many such studies are available (Shklar, 1991; Kymlicka and Norman, 1995; Schudson, 1998; Heater, 1999, 2004). Instead, I try to identify the key elements of citizenship discussed in the contemporary research literature. Then, I summarize current findings on the distribution of citizenship norms in contemporary democracies, and how they are changing. And finally, the chapter discusses other debates on the nature of citizenship in democracies today.

THE NORMS OF DEMOCRATIC CITIZENSHIP

I begin with an open definition of democratic citizenship: the term refers to what people feel is expected of them as 'good' democratic citizens. Reflecting Almond and Verba's (1963) description of a political culture as a shared set of social norms, I define citizenship as 'a shared set of expectations about the citizen's role in politics'. A political culture contains a mix of attitudes and orientations, and images of the citizen's role are central parts of a nation's political culture. They tell people what is expected of them, and what they expect of themselves. These norms also shape other elements of the political process. Indeed, these norms of citizenship are the values that Tocqueville stressed as defining a political culture.

The existence of norms does not mean that individuals approve of these norms, or that their personal values are consistent with these norms. The interaction between norms and behavior is, in fact, an important topic to consider. For instance, someone might say that tolerance is an important norm of democratic citizenship – but then not tolerate others who disagree with their political beliefs. Thus, I define citizenship as a set of norms of what people think they should do as a good citizen.

It is also important to identify what we are *not studying*. Sometimes citizenship is used to describe a legal status as a citizen of a nation. This chapter is not concerned with this specific legal definition of citizenship: who is a citizen, how one becomes a citizen, the legal rights of citizenship. Similarly, a legal approach to citizenship can involve the formal legal relationship between individuals and the state: the rights of citizenship or the legal protections of citizenship. These legal elements are related to the topics examined here, but they involve the norms of citizenship only to the extent that the public defines legal rights or responsibilities as part of their expectations of citizenship. This aspect of citizenship has become especially prominent in European discussions of how to respond to increasing cultural diversity and immigration in these societies (see Chapter 8 by Olsen in this book; also, Balibar, 2004).

How, then, might citizenship be defined? An initial framework comes from Aristotle's observation that citizenship balances two contending roles: citizens are 'all who share in the civic life *of ruling* and *being ruled* in turn' (Aristotle, 1946, Book 3, Chapter 13, Section 1283b; italics added). This simple, insightful statement underlies much of the theoretical literature about citizenship to the present. For instance, the contrast between liberal and republican perceptions of citizenship can largely be traced to whether one emphasizes the rights of citizens in democracy or the responsibilities of citizenship (see Chapter 3 by Bohman in this volume). In reviewing the contemporary literature on citizenship, there are three different aspects of political citizenship that seem central to democracies.

First, public participation in politics is broadly considered a defining element of democratic citizenship (Pateman, 1970; Thompson, 1970; Dahl, 1998).[1] Democracies are based on citizen involvement in political decision-making, even if this participation was initially limited in early democracies or the newly emerging democracies of today. The principle of citizen participation remains a defining element of American democracy, for example, and Tocqueville argued that it was a distinctive element of the American political culture. Similarly, the empirical work of Almond and Verba (1963) argued that participatory norms were central to a democratic civic culture, and more recent research has echoed these themes (Verba et al., 1995).

Because of this emphasis on participation, the current scholarly debate examines the question of whether political involvement is decreasing. One group of experts argues that eroding citizenship norms are decreasing participation in elections and other forms of political activity, which weakens the foundations of the democratic process (Putnam, 2000; Papadopoulos, 2013). Other analysts maintain that the social transformation of advanced industrial societies has increased the ability of the average person to be politically engaged (Inglehart, 1990; Welzel, 2013). This counter-position maintains that changes in norms are leading people to use forms of political engagement beyond traditional electoral politics, and this expands and empowers the political influence of the citizenry (Cain et al., 2003; Zukin et al., 2006; Dalton, 2009). Thus, a central issue for democratic citizenship involves the question of how much people believe they should participate and how they should participate. There is little consensus on how much participation, and in what forms, is beneficial for democracy. There is even less agreement on how much participation actually occurs today.

Second, often overlooked in discussions of citizenship is the other part of the Aristotelian equation: the acceptance of the authority of the state (Tyler, 1990). Autocratic states emphasize the role of the loyal subject as the prime criteria of citizenship, and democracies also stress the importance of state sovereignty. Indeed, acceptance of the legitimacy of the state and the rule of law is often the implied first principle of citizenship, since without the rule of law meaningful political discourse and participation cannot exist. The emphasis on duties and responsibilities of citizenship is prominent in both republican and communitarian definitions of citizenship.

Political philosophy is replete with those who stress the acceptance of state sovereignty – from Bodin to Hobbes to Hamilton – even before the participatory elements of democracy. For example, this logic appears in how the US government presents itself to its new citizens. A pamphlet prepared by the Immigration and Nationalization Service for prospective citizens described the Constitution's importance as first 'everyone is protected by the law' and then 'everyone must obey the law' (Immigration and Naturalization Service, 1987, p.3). Only after this does the pamphlet discuss the rights provided in the Constitution's Bill of Rights, which is paired with a discussion of the duties and responsibilities of citizenship: voting, serving in the army, and paying taxes.[2] The centrality of accepting state authority is quite clear in what most nations tell their citizens. This dichotomy between ruling and being ruled is central to the definition of citizenship. Both are necessary in the modern democratic state, and the proper balance between these principles has been a central element of the philosophical literature on citizenship.

A third element of citizenship involves our relationship to others in the polity. T.H. Marshall ([1950] 1992) described this as social citizenship. The expansion of civil and political rights created a new category of social rights, such as social services, providing for those in need, and taking heed of the general welfare of others.[3] Citizenship thus includes an ethical and moral responsibility to others in the polity, and beyond. The framework of distributive justice provides a theoretical base for equality as a basis of citizenship. Similarly, one of Dahl's (1990) requisites for democracy is that individuals must have sufficient resources to meet their basic social needs; otherwise, democratic principles of political equality and participation are meaningless. Although initially identified with the European welfare state and social-democratic critiques of capitalism, this idea of citizenship has been embraced by liberal interests in Europe and North America (Walzer, 1983; Shklar, 1991; Harris, 1997).

Social citizenship also potentially reaches beyond the nation-state. Contemporary discussions of equality and distributive justice are often embedded in a framework of global human rights and responsibilities. Thus, a socially concerned citizen cares about those less fortunate at home, as well as issues of global inequality and the conditions of the global community. Many scholars now treat citizenship as part of a global community, with global interests and responsibilities (see Chapter 9 by Tijsterman; Held, 1995; Walzer, 1995).

These elements of citizenship – participation, acceptance of state authority, and social rights – are central in defining the possible content of citizenship. Democratic citizenship requires a mix of all these elements, and one can easily point to examples of the detrimental effects when one element – state authority, say – is given too much emphasis over the others. Yet, some analysts assert that all three elements of citizenship are declining in contemporary societies (Münkler, 1997; Putnam, 2000; Stoker, 2006). If the norms of citizenship are what bind people to their polity and each other, then a broad decline would have fundamental implications for contemporary democracies.

EMPIRICAL RESEARCH ON CITIZENSHIP NORMS

The philosophical debate about contemporary citizenship is much richer and more extensive than I have briefly outlined here. Each theoretical tradition posits that a different mix of traits defines contemporary norms of citizenship, or a different mix of these norms is desirable. However, the debate among theorists has lacked one component: what do the citizens themselves think of citizenship? How do people weigh the various elements of citizenship? I will present some empirical evidence on the distribution of citizenship norms based on a battery of questions included in the 2004 International Social Survey Programme (ISSP) study.

Public opinion surveys have only recently begun to study the public's adherence to different citizenship norms. The 1984 General Social Survey in the United States and the 1987 Swedish Citizenship Survey included some initial questions on the duties of citizenship (Petersson et al., 1989; Bennett and Bennett, 1990). These early studies asked only a few questions, but provided a baseline for measuring citizenship norms.

To my knowledge, the first systematic attempt to theorize the components of democratic citizenship and then measure these traits in a public opinion survey was the 1998 Swedish Democracy Audit (Petersson et al., 1998). Petersson and his colleagues reviewed the philosophical literature that we summarized above, and on this basis identified several conceptual categories for assessing citizenship norms. Their national opinion survey then asked Swedes to express the importance of each of the possible norms in their survey.[4] The Swedish researchers defined four categories of citizenship they derived from previous theories of citizenship, and then used these categories in selecting their survey questions, which we list along with the survey items in the 2004 ISSP survey (Table 2.1).

Reflecting its centrality to the theoretical literature on democracy discussed above, Petersson and his colleagues considered the norm of participation in politics as a prime criterion for defining democratic citizenship. The right side of the first row displays the three questions included in the ISSP: the importance of always voting in elections, being active in social or political organizations (participating in civil society), and choosing

Table 2.1 Categories of citizenship norms and public opinion questions

Categories	International Social Survey Questions Regarding the Importance of . . .
Participation	Always voting in elections
	Being active in social or political associations
	Choosing products for political, ethical, or environmental reasons
Autonomy	Trying to understand reasoning of people with other opinions
	Keeping watch on actions of the government
Social order	Never trying to evade taxes
	Always obeying the laws and regulations
	Being willing to serve in the military in a time of need
Solidarity	Supporting people in your country who are worse off than yourself
	Helping people in the rest of the world who are worse off than yourself

Source: 2004 International Social Survey Programme.

products for political, ethical, or environmental reasons. This list was designed to cover a range of participation opportunities, even if it does not include all the possible forms of political action. Moreover, the survey did not ask if the respondent participated in these activities – the questions asked whether they recognize such norms as defining an important part of citizenship.

Petersson et al. (1998) expanded the concept of participation to include what they called the autonomy of the citizen. Autonomy implies that good citizens should be sufficiently informed about government to exercise a participatory role. The good citizen should participate in democratic deliberation and critically evaluate the government. Other researchers have described such items as representing critical and deliberative aspects of citizenship (Denters et al., 2006). The ISSP measures these orientations with a question on keeping watch on the government and whether one understands the reasoning of people with other opinions.

Social order represents the acceptance of state authority as part of citizenship. The ISSP asked two items on obeying the law: never trying to avoid taxes, always obeying laws and regulations. In addition, a willingness to serve in the military is considered to be another measure of allegiance.

Finally, solidarity is a fourth category of citizenship norms that taps the idea of social citizenship. This idea represents the belief from Marshall

Political citizenship: mapping the terrain 31

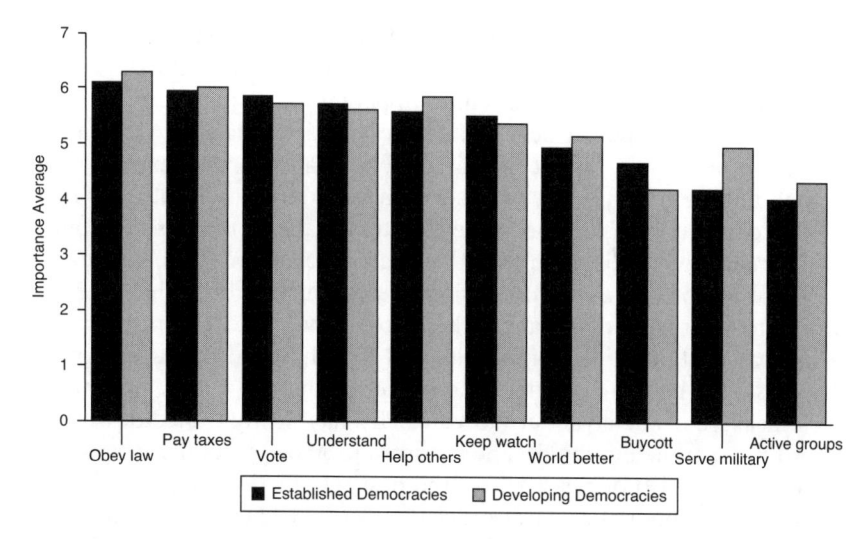

Note: There are 19 established democracies and 19 developing democracies. Buycott means buying products for political reasons.

Source: 2004 International Social Survey Programme.

Figure 2.1 Citizenship norms in established and new democracies

that good citizenship includes a concern for others, which is also reflected on communitarian norms of public spiritedness. The ISSP thus asks about the importance of helping others in one's nation who are worse off, and helping people in the rest of the world who are worse off.

The Distribution of Citizenship Norms

The 2004 ISSP survey asked about the importance of each of the norms in Table 2.1 for more than three dozen contemporary democracies.[5] Figure 2.1 presents the average importance score given to each of the ten citizenship norms for the 19 established democracies in the ISSP as well as for 19 new or developing democracies. On the seven-point scale used in the survey, all ten items score above the mid-point of the scale, and several are heavily skewed with means above 6.0 (also see Denters et al., 2006). Thus, it is not that contemporary publics accept one set of norms and reject others – rather, all these norms are recognized as important, with some variance in salience across individuals.

The social-order items – obeying the law and paying taxes – tend to evoke the most support in both established and developing democracies.

Indeed, support is actually higher in developing democracies, perhaps because of the traditional, authority-oriented political cultures in these nations. This old/new contrast is most apparent for military service, which is significantly higher in new and developing democracies. At the same time, the next most salient norms involve a mix of participation items (vote), autonomy (understand others) and solidarity (help others). Both of the solidarity items display more attention to these norms in developing democracies, which likely reflects the greater social needs in these nations.

These responses come from a single recent survey, but other evidence points to an erosion of certain of these norms over time. For instance, the American National Election Studies and British Social Attitudes surveys have asked whether it matters if one votes, which is widely interpreted as a measure of the civic duty to vote. This has slowly trailed downward over time, paralleling the decline in turnout.[6] More generally, respect for authority has also decreased over the past several decades, which probably erodes support for social-order norms of citizenship (Nevitte, 1996, 2013). In contrast, the shift to post-material and self-expressive values in advanced industrial democracies has probably increased attachments to autonomy norms and social engagement. Thus, norm shift is occurring within the public, a fact that has fundamental implications for how people define their role as citizens and relate to their government.

In summary, citizenship is a multidimensional concept that includes many different potential aspects of the citizen's role in the polity. The evidence from recent surveys suggests that these different norms are endorsed by most people, even if their relative salience varies across time and individuals.

The Framework of Citizenship Norms

There is a distinct logic to these four separate categories of citizenship norms, and so empirical research has attempted to verify that these clusters actually describe people's thinking about citizenship. Petersson et al. (1989, Chapter 8) initially identified two dimensions of citizenship norms: obeying the rules, which was largely the social-order items, and creating the rules, which was primarily participation and autonomy norms. The 1998 Swedish Democracy Audit had a more extensive battery of items and found four citizenship dimensions: participation, deliberation, solidarity and law-abidingness (Petersson et al., 1998). Denters and his colleagues (2006) examined a smaller set of items from the 2002 European CID survey, finding three dimensions that they label: law-abidingness, critical/deliberative principles and solidarity.

There is a great deal of commonality to these results, even if the authors use different labels. And the results partially depend on the number and type of norms asked in the survey. The 2004 ISSP survey includes the longest battery in a major cross-national survey (ten items), and my own research suggests that people perceive citizenship norms in terms of two broad dimensions (Dalton, 2009, Chapter 2, p.8).[7] One citizenship dimension is what I describe as the norms of citizen duty. The three items on social order are the core of this dimension, along with the duty to vote. The fusion of these different items suggests that some forms of participation – such as voting – are motivated by the same sense of duty that encourages individuals to be law-abiding citizens. Citizen duty reflects traditional notions of citizenship as the responsibilities of a citizen-subject that might be most closely identified with a republican philosophy of citizenship. The good citizen pays taxes, follows the legitimate laws of government, and contributes to the national need such as service in the military. Allegiance to the state and voting have been linked together in discussions of citizenship beginning with Tocqueville. Similarly, research on voting turnout stresses the importance of citizen duty as a predictor of voting (e.g., Blais, 2000, p.92). Thus, the clustering of voting participation and order norms into a single pattern of duty-based citizenship has a strong foundation in prior empirical research and democratic theory, such as Almond and Verba's (1963) description of the citizen-subject.

The second dimension, engaged citizenship, includes other elements of citizenship. It involves participation in non-electoral activities such as buying products for political reasons (buycotting – see Figure 2.1) and being active in civil society groups. This dimension also incorporates the autonomy norm – that one should try to understand the opinions of others. Engaged citizens also possess a moral or empathetic element of citizenship, as reflected in the solidarity or public-spirited items of helping others (at home and abroad). This is significant, because some theorists maintain that concern about the community is an element of traditional citizenship values; these surveys suggest just the opposite – that it falls most heavily in the engaged citizen cluster. This suggests a pattern of the socially engaged citizen: one who is aware of others, is willing to act on his or her principles and even to challenge political elites.

These two dimensions of citizenship are not contradictory; they reflect different emphases in the role of a democratic citizen. Both clusters involve a norm of participation, although in different styles of political action. Both define citizenship as a mixture of responsibilities and rights, but different responsibilities and different rights. Although both dimensions are linked to democratic theory, neither completely matches the mix of norms posited in previous philosophical models.

If citizen duty captures the traditional model of republican citizenship, then it leads to a set of predictions about the causes and consequences of these norms. For instance, one expects that duty-based citizenship should promote distinct forms of political participation, policy preferences, images of government, and other attitudes and behavior (Dalton, 2009). In comparison, engaged citizenship partially overlaps with the liberal models of citizenship. These norms stress the rights and social responsibilities of citizenship. Instead of seeing political participation primarily as a duty to vote, engaged citizenship prompts individuals to be involved in a wider repertoire of activities that give them direct voice in the decisions affecting their lives. This evokes the values implicit in Barber's (1984) idea of 'strong democracy'. Even more directly, engaged citizenship overlaps with the patterns of post-material or self-expressive values that Inglehart (1990) has described as a growing feature of advanced industrial societies (also Welzel, 2013). Post-materialists emphasize participatory norms, elite-challenging behavior, and more interested in non-economic social issues. Engaged citizenship includes a responsibility to others in society. Such feelings of social responsibility have a long tradition in European social-democratic and Christian social traditions.

We can also use these two dimensions of citizenship to describe the distinct national patterns in citizenship norms among established democracies (Figure 2.2).[8] The horizontal dimension in the figure represents a nation's score on the citizen duty scale; the vertical dimension is the nation's score on the engaged citizenship scale.

American citizenship norms are not unique, but they are distinctive. Americans are highest in citizen duty. More than most other publics, Americans believe a good citizen pays taxes, serves in the army, obeys the laws, and votes. Several other nations that are high in citizen duty also share a British heritage – Ireland and Britain – plus Australia and Canada in other analyses (Dalton, 2009, Chapter 8). This suggests that cultural elements of citizen duty derive from this legacy, perhaps from a tradition of popular sovereignty and the expectation of citizen allegiance in response. Most Scandinavian nations are located near the mid-point on citizen duty, and the lowest nations include several that have a Germanic background: East and West Germany, Austria, and Switzerland.

Americans also score above most nations in engaged citizenship as shown on the vertical axis, along with several European nations (Portugal, Spain, Ireland, Austria, and Switzerland). Given the tradition of social citizenship in Europe, the relatively high placement of the United States is surprising, since the public in several welfare states (such as Britain, Germany, Sweden, and Norway) score at or below

Political citizenship: mapping the terrain 35

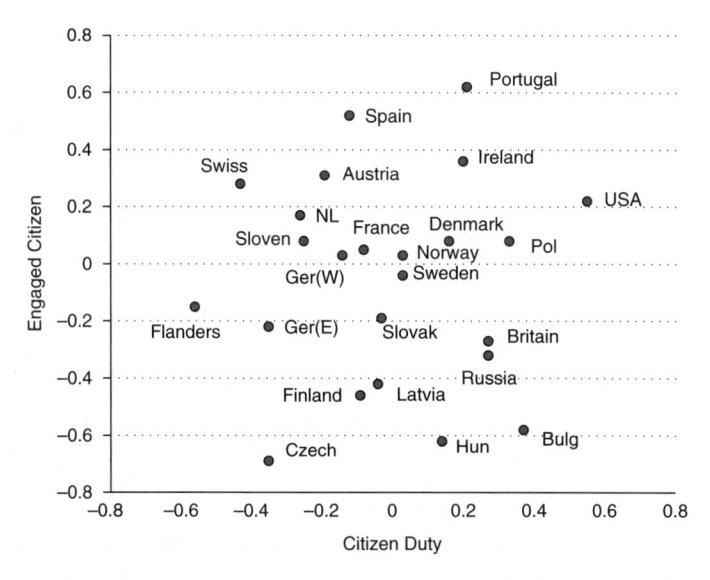

Note: Figure entries are national positions based on mean scores on the citizen duty and engaged citizenship scores.

Source: 2004 International Social Survey Programme.

Figure 2.2   National patterns of citizen duty and engaged citizenship

the overall average. Americans' positive scores on engaged citizenship reflect participatory norms beyond voting and feelings of political autonomy. However, Americans are not dramatically different from Western Europeans on the two norms of social citizenship.[9] Most of the post-communist nations of Eastern Europe tend toward the other end of this dimension, with fewer citizens endorsing engaged citizenship. This appears to be a lingering effect of the authoritarian experience on engaged citizenship in these nations, although the pattern of post-communist nations on this dimension is quite varied, with Poland and Slovenia scoring above the average.

To the extent that these citizenship norms are converted into political behaviors, we should expect that the mapping in Figure 2.2 translates into differences in how different citizens relate to their governments through participation patterns and policy priorities. Both within and between nations, the distribution of citizenship norms should have significant consequences.

THE SOCIAL DISTRIBUTION OF CITIZENSHIP NORMS

Understanding the social distribution of citizenship norms can illuminate the sources of these norms as well as their political implications. Several studies have examined the social correlates of citizenship norms, but here we focus on three factors: generation, education, and gender (Petersson et al., 1998; Rossteutscher, 2005; Denters et al., 2006; Dalton, 2009).

Generational Patterns

Central to our theorizing on citizenship norms is the presumption that the tremendous changes in the socioeconomic conditions of democratic nations have reshaped these norms over the past several decades. To the extent that citizenship norms become relatively fixed during early political socialization, then generational patterns suggest how norms have changed over time – just as a field archeologist tracks changes in societies over time by comparing social artifacts across layers of accumulated deposits.

The predominant assertion is that the norms of good citizenship are waning among younger generations. This ranges from Tom Brokaw's (1997) praise of 'the greatest generation' who came of age during World War II (and implicit criticism of younger generations) to Robert Putnam's (2000) worries about the generational decline of citizenship in the United States. Older generations supposedly embody a sense of duty, participation, and community-mindedness that is lacking among the young.

While criticizing the politics of the young has a long tradition, it has taken on a new intensity in the current discourse on citizenship, and some empirical research supports these claims. Feelings of citizen duty are more common among older Americans (Bennett and Bennett, 1990, pp.126–30), for example, and the belief that voting is a civic duty is greater among older generations (Pattie et al., 2004; Wattenberg, 2002). The erosion of these voting norms is linked to the generational decline in turnout in most established democracies. Similarly, the experts lament the supposed erosion of social-order norms among young generations as well as the decline in collective interests.

While such trends are real, they describe only half of the changing reality of citizenship norms. The norms of being a 'good citizen' have not declined among the young, but the definition of what makes for a good citizenship has changed. The young in most advanced industrial democracies are less likely to think of citizenship in the same duty-based terms as their elders. The decline in citizen duty is at least partially counterbalanced by new norms of engaged citizenship. Research shows a positive correlation between age and citizen duty norms – social order and the duty to vote – while there is a negative correlation with engaged citizenship – autonomy norms, solidarity norms, and participation outside of elections (Rossteutscher, 2005; Dalton, 2009). Such a shift in orientations is consistent with evidence that the young are more likely to support self-expressive and self-actualizing values over security-oriented values (Inglehart, 1990; Welzel, 2013). And norms of engaged citizenship may have benefits for democracy that are missed by narrowly focusing on the decline in duty-based norms, as in the patterns of assertive citizenship described in other chapters in this collection.

In summary, claims about the decline in democratic citizenship among the young are incorrect. Rather, there is a generational shift in the types of citizenship norms that contemporary publics stress. Generations socialized before and immediately after World War II are more likely to define citizenship in terms of a republican framework of citizenship based on duties and obligations. Indeed, one might argue that these are the norms of a good subject (though not necessarily a good democratic participant) in the terms of Almond and Verba's (1963) concept of the civic culture. In contrast, the young reflect a new political reality, and stress alternative norms that should encourage a more rights conscious public, a socially engaged public, and a more deliberative image of citizenship. To the extent that these patterns endure, it suggests a continuing generationally based shift in the citizenship norms of Western publics to emphasize engaged citizenship over citizen duty.

Educational Patterns

Many studies point to the power of education and other social status variables in shaping images of citizenship (Almond and Verba, 1963; Milner, 2002). Nie et al. (1996, Chapter 2), for example, show that education is a key variable in explaining democratic participation and democratic enlightenment, although in different ways. Empirical research consistently shows that the better-educated vote more, are more active in their community, more knowledgeable about politics, and more politically tolerant.

Better-educated, higher-income, and higher-status individuals are thus more likely to subscribe to duty-based norms of citizenship that encourage voting and allegiance to the political system (obeying laws, paying taxes). The formal and informal civics training in most nations presumably stresses these norms, and upper-status individuals are typically more supportive of the norms and principles of the existing political order. At the same time, however, the skills and values produced by education are also important in stimulating participation in the more assertive forms of participation described in this volume as well as broader feelings of social solidarity. Several empirical studies show that the cognitive skills identified with education appear even more directly related to norms of engaged citizenship (Nie et al., Chapter 4; Dalton, 2009). Furthermore, it is commonly asserted that the political ethos in higher education has generally shifted toward the norms of engaged citizenship with increased stress on direct action, the critical role of the citizen, and social responsibility – partly as an alternative to traditional duty-based conceptions of citizenship (Bennett and Bennett, 1990, pp.119–20). Thus, higher-status groups tend to favor social order and feelings of citizen duty, but also the autonomous norms of citizenship and non-institutionalized forms of participation. Good citizenship is important to higher-status individuals in all of its forms.

Gendered Citizenship

One of the most active areas of debate and discussion in this area is the relationship between gender and citizenship (see Monro and Richardson, Chapter 4 in this volume). Feminist scholars have argued that traditional concepts of citizenship were based on the male experience, and have critiqued the traditional model or tried to integrate the interests of women into the traditional concepts (Lister, 2003; Lister et al., 2008). Often, Marshall's discussion of social citizenship provides an entry point because of the social role and interests of women. Other scholars maintain that national policy towards women is guided by liberal, republican or social definitions of citizenship (Siim, 2000).

Recent empirical work has put this theorizing to the empirical test, and asks whether the changing societal role of women impacts on their norms of citizenship. For instance, social norms traditionally discouraged political participation by women, and researchers ask if these patterns still endure (Burns et al., 2001). Similarly, there are theoretical expectations that women will attach greater importance to solidarity and social-order elements of good citizenship. Bolzendahl and Coffé (2009) analyze the same cross-national ISSP survey presented in Figures 2.1 and 2.2. They find no significant difference in participation norms between men and women overall, but their hypotheses about the gender differences in solidarity and social-order norms are confirmed. In a predictable way, the social position of women leads them to bridge the contrast between duty-based and engaged citizenship.

In summary, the collective findings of empirical research on advanced industrial democracies suggests that social modernization – reflected in generational change and rising educational levels – during the latter half of the twentieth century contributed to changes in the importance of different norms of citizenship. The cognitive skills and political resources represented by education provide a basis for a more engaged form of citizenship that goes beyond the deferential, almost subject role of duty-based citizenship. Similarly, these same forces have lessened support for definitions of citizenship based on the duties and responsibilities of citizens. Thus, it is not that citizenship is lacking in contemporary publics – but that the priorities of citizenship are changing.

TRANSNATIONAL CITIZENSHIP

Discussions of citizenship were traditionally synonymous with orientations toward the nation-state. People thought of the political community in terms of Britain as a whole, for example, or their images of the government in London. But in recent decades an international dimension of citizenship has also become more apparent, which appears to involve two distinct forms.

The first aspect of transnational citizenship involves a broader view of citizen rights and responsibilities that extends beyond the nation-state. Often described as cosmopolitan citizenship, this involves a claim of basic human rights and moral values that is explicitly transnational. This framework has a long philosophical tradition, but it has taken on added importance with the influence of globalization and an expanding international system breaking down national boundaries (Archibugi et al., 1998; Held, 2006, 2010). Perhaps the best example of this tension occurs in the European Union, where citizens can adopt both a national and a transnational identity, which only partially overlap (Olsen, Chapter 8 in this book; Dell'olio, 2005). With dual identities it is possible that the norms of citizenship in both domains can also develop separately.

In a broader sense, this cosmopolitan framework involves a sense of common citizenship without limitations to a specific geographical community, often leading to calls for supranational or global political institutions (see Tijsterman, Chapter 9 in this book). But the content of this notion of citizenship is seldom rigorously studied; instead there are theoretical claims of moral and ethical standards that are partially philosophical constructs of the authors. As with national definitions of citizenship, it is likely that the norms of transnational citizenship can also be quite varied across different political communities.

The second international aspect of citizenship involves the interaction between native and immigrant populations. The growth in transnational migration because of globalization has increased the salience of this topic.

On the one hand, migration creates basic issues of who is a citizen, and citizenship thus raises questions of inclusion or exclusion in the political community. Growing immigrant populations in established democracies has prompted reforms in citizenship laws in several nations, sometimes making them more inclusive and sometimes more exclusive.

On the other hand, increasing immigration also generates introspection on the meaning of citizenship, such as the debates of civic education and the content of citizenship in several European nations. The mixing of different populations also produces 'culture clashes' in matters strongly related to the principles of citizenship. For instance, tensions between native Europeans and immigrant Muslims stimulate debates on the rights of women and children in Muslim communities, the appropriate respect for different religious traditions, and sometimes strikingly different definitions of good citizenship that contrast with the categories defined above. In other words, does multiculturalism mean uncritical respect for the differences of others, or accepting diversity within a framework of basic human rights and citizenship norms? Paul Sniderman's work on political tolerance in Europe starkly illustrates these tensions and their implications for definitions of citizenship (Sniderman et al., 2002; Sniderman and Hagendoorn, 2009).

Given the rising interest and importance of this transnational dimension of citizenship, it is an area greatly deserving of more systematic research. We are already theoretically well endowed with claims and counter-claims about the impact of these forces on citizenship. Thus, it is a fertile ground for more systematic empirical study to test these rival theories.

THE IMPORTANCE OF CITIZENSHIP

As the chapters in this book demonstrate, citizenship norms are complex and multifaceted. Contemporary publics believe many different norms are important to good citizenship, and this diversity probably benefits the democratic process. Some aspects of politics depend on an allegiant public, but democracy also progresses because other citizens are more assertive in demanding reforms.

In contrast to philosophical theories of citizenship, empirical research suggests that contemporary publics broadly define the important aspects of good citizenship in two distinctly different ways. Duty-based citizenship reflects a republican tradition that stresses the duties and responsibilities of citizenship, with a limited participatory role. This is a constrained model of citizenship, which generally reinforces the existing political order and existing authority patterns. In contrast, engaged citizenship has a more expansive view of citizen norms. The engaged citizen views participation as important, but this includes direct action and elite-challenging activities. Participation is not just an expression of allegiance and duty, but an attempt to express policy preferences. Significantly, engaged citizenship also includes a concern for others. Thus, engaged citizenship contains elements that are part of liberal and social traditions of citizenship.

Recognition of these different citizenship norms is important because these norms shape the attitudes and behaviors of contemporary publics. The orientations of engaged citizenship are especially important in understanding the political interests of the new social movements discussed in this book, and the assertive style of these new movements. While duty-based citizens may feel they should vote, they are less likely to participate in contentious political activities, such as an environmental protest or a demonstration by a human rights group. In contrast, the broader worldview of engaged citizens and their different framework for political participation makes contentious actions a more normal part of the political repertoire. Changing norms of citizenship, especially solidarity norms, can reshape the policy expectations of the citizenry. And even more profoundly, citizenship norms set the standards for what the public expects of the democratic process.

In short, the norms of democratic citizenship are not weakening as much as they are changing the definition of what it means to be a 'good citizen'. These changes in the norms of citizenship will have both positive and negative impacts on the nature of the democratic process, and contemporary political systems need to adapt to their citizens. Some of the forces and processes of change are discussed in the following chapters of this book.

NOTES

1. Even with the near universal acceptance of the mass franchise, many analysts still prescribe a narrow role for the citizen. The elitist critique of democracy typically argues that too many citizens lack the knowledge or interests to make informed decisions, and thus limited participation is desirable (Delli Carpini and Keeter, 1996; Caplan, 2007). In contrast, see Oppenheimer and Edwards (2012).
2. To point out a small irony, the Prussian government of the nineteenth century also stressed three norms for a 'good citizen': pay your taxes, serve in the army, and keep your mouth shut. This example suggests that citizenship norms in authoritarian and democratic governments share state sovereignty as a core principle.
3. Although this chapter emphasizes the modern roots of social citizenship, these concepts were part of the discussion of citizenship beginning with Aristotle. See Heater (2004, pp.270–84).
4. This basic model has been adopted by several subsequent cross-national projects. The 'Citizens, Involvement and Democracy' (CID) project at the University of Mannheim

included several of these items in a survey of European nations in the late 1990s (Rossteutscher, 2005). The European Social Survey (ESS) asked a short set of questions for 22 European nations in 2002 (Denters et al., 2006), and this survey was replicated in the United States by the Center for Democracy and Civil Society in 2005 (https://www.icpsr.umich.edu/icpsrweb/ICPSR/studies/4607).
5. Information on the ISSP survey and the questionnaires and data are available through the project website (www.issp.org).
6. In addition, Swedish surveys find that the importance of voting has decreased from a mean of 8.7 in 1988 to 8.4 in 2002, based on a ten-point scale. The importance of group activity also declined, as well as another item on solidarity.
7. These dimensions were empirically determined using factor analysis. Factor analysis is a statistical method designed to identify the similarity between different items. I explored several options before deciding on the results presented here. One can identify additional dimensions, but they tend to be weakly identified or overlap with the two basic dimensions presented here. For additional explanation see Dalton (2009, Chapter 2).
8. We used the two-dimensional factor structure described in note 7 for the 19 established democracies in the ISSP survey. We then computed factor scores for the two dimensions, and the average scores for each nation to locate nations in Figure 2.2 (see Dalton, 2009, Chapter 8).
9. I suspect this may partially reflect Europeans' belief that social welfare is a responsibility of the state, while Americans are more likely to also view this as a responsibility of individual citizens.

REFERENCES

Almond, G. and S. Verba (1963), *The Civic Culture: Political Attitudes and Democracy in Five Nations*, Princeton, NJ: Princeton University Press.
Archibugi, D., D. Held and M. Köhler (1998), *Re-Imagining Political Community: Studies in Cosmopolitan Democracy*, Stanford, CA: Stanford University Press.
Aristotle (1946), *Politics*, trans. E. Barker, Oxford: Clarendon Press.
Balibar, E. (2004), *We, the People of Europe? Reflections on Transnational Citizenship*, Princeton, NJ: Princeton University Press.
Barber, B. (1984), *Strong Democracy: Participatory Politics for a New Age*, Berkeley, CA: University of California Press.
Bennett, L. and S. Bennett (1990), *Living with Leviathan: Americans Coming to Terms with Big Government*, Lawrence, KS: University Press of Kansas.
Blais, A. (2000), *To Vote or Not to Vote: The Merits and Limits of Rational Choice Theory*, Pittsburgh, PA: University of Pittsburgh Press.
Bolzendahl, C. and H. Coffé (2009), 'Citizenship beyond politics: the importance of political, civil and social rights and responsibilities among women and men', *British Journal of Sociology*, **60**(4), 763–91.
Brokaw, T. (1997), *The Greatest Generation*, New York: Random House.
Burns, N., K. Schlozman and S. Verba (2001), *The Private Roots of Public Action: Gender, Equality, and Political Participation*, Cambridge, MA: Harvard University Press.
Cain, B., R. Dalton and S. Scarrow (eds) (2003), *Democracy Transformed? Expanding Political Access in Advanced Industrial Democracies*, Oxford: Oxford University Press.
Caplan, B. (2007), *The Myth of the Rational Voter: Why Democracies Choose Bad Policies*, Princeton, NJ: Princeton University Press.
Dahl, R. (1998), *On Democracy*, New Haven, CT: Yale University Press.
Dalton, R. (2009), *The Good Citizen: How the Young are Reshaping American Politics*, revised edition, Washington, DC: Congressional Quarterly Press.
Delli Carpini, M. and S. Keeter (1996), *What Americans Know about Politics and Why It Matters*, New Haven, CT: Yale University Press.

Dell'olio, F. (2005), *The Europeanization of Citizenship: Between the Ideology of Nationality, Immigration and European Identity*, Burlington, VT: Ashgate.
Denters, B., O. Gabriel and M. Torcal (2006), 'Norms of good citizenship', in J. van Deth, J. Ramón Montero and A. Westholm (eds), *Citizenship and Involvement in Europe*, London: Routledge.
Elgar, R. (ed.) (2012), *Civility and Democracy in America*, Pullman, WA: Washington State University Press.
Etzioni, A. (1995), *The Spirit of Community: Rights, Responsibilities and the Communitarian Agenda*, London: Fontana Press.
Harris, D. (1987), *Justifying State Welfare*, Oxford: Blackwell.
Heater, D. (1999), *What is Citizenship?*, Cambridge, UK: Polity Press.
Heater, D. (2004), *Citizenship: The Civic Ideal in World History, Politics and Education*, 3rd edition, Manchester: Manchester University Press.
Held, D. (1995), *Democracy and the Global Order: From the Modern State to Cosmopolitan Governance*, Cambridge, UK: Polity Press.
Held, D. (2006), *Models of Democracy*, 3rd edition, Stanford, CA: Stanford University Press.
Held, D. (2010), *Cosmopolitanism: Ideals and Realities*, Oxford: Polity Press.
Immigration and Naturalization Service (1987), *Citizenship Education and Naturalization Information*, Washington DC: US Government Printing Office.
Inglehart, R. (1990), *Culture Shift in Advanced Industrial Society*, Princeton, NJ: Princeton University Press.
Kymlicka, W. and W. Norman (1995), 'Return of the citizen: a survey of recent work on citizenship theory', in R. Beiner (ed.), *Theorizing Citizenship*, Albany, NY: State University of New York Press.
Lister, R. (2003), *Citizenship: Feminist Perspectives*, 2nd edition, New York: New York University Press.
Lister, R., F. Williams and A. Anttonen (2008), *Gendering Citizenship in Western Europe: New Challenges for Citizenship Research in a Cross-national Context*, Bristol: Policy Press.
Marshall, T.H. ([1950] 1992), in T. Bottomore (ed.), *Citizenship and Social Class*, London: Pluto Press.
Milner, H. (2002), *Civic Literacy: How Informed Citizens Make Democracy Work*, Hanover, NH: Tufts University Press.
Münkler, H. (2007), 'Der kompetente Bürger' (Competent citizens) in A. Klein and R. Schmalz-Brun (eds), *Politische Beteiligung und Bürgerengagement in Deutschland* (Political Participation and Citizenship in Germany), Baden-Baden: Nomos.
Nevitte, N. (1996), *The Decline of Deference*, Peterborough, ON: Broadview.
Nevitte, N. (2013), 'The decline of deference revisited', in R. Dalton and C. Welzel (eds), *The Civic Culture Transformed: From Allegiant to Assertive Citizens*, Cambridge, UK: Cambridge University Press.
Nie, N., J. Junn and K. Stehlik-Barry (1996), *Education and Democratic Citizenship in America*, Chicago, IL: University of Chicago Press.
Oppenheimer, D. and M. Edwards (2012), *Democracy Despite Itself: Why a System that Shouldn't Work at All Works so Well*, Cambridge, MA: MIT Press.
Papadopoulos, Y. (2013), *Democracy in Crisis? Politics, Governance and Policy*, London: Palgrave Macmillan.
Pateman, C. (1970), *Participation and Democratic Theory*, Cambridge, UK: Cambridge University Press.
Pattie, C., P. Seyd and P. Whiteley (2004), *Citizenship in Britain: Values, Participation, and Democracy*, New York: Cambridge University Press.
Petersson, O., A. Westholm and G. Blomberg (1989), *Medborgarnas makt* [Citizen Power], Stockholm: Carlssons.
Petersson, O. et al. (1998), *Demokrati och Medborgarskap. Demokratirådets Rapport 1998* [Democracy and Citizenship: Democracy Council Report 1998], Stockholm: SNS Förlag.

Putnam, R. (2000), *Bowling Alone: The Collapse and Revival of American Community*, New York: Simon and Schuster.
Rossteutscher, S. (2005), 'Die Rückkehr der Tugend?' [The return of virtue?], in Jan van Deth (ed.), *Deutschland in Europa* [Germany in Europe], Wiesbaden: VS-Verlag.
Schudson, M. (1998), *The Good Citizen: A History of American Civic Life*, New York: Free Press.
Shklar, J. (1991), *American Citizenship*, Cambridge, MA: Harvard University Press.
Siim, B. (2000), *Gender and Citizenship: Politics and Agency in France, Britain and Denmark*, Cambridge, UK: Cambridge University Press.
Sniderman, P. and L. Hagendoorn (2009), *When Ways of Life Collide: Multiculturalism and its Discontents in the Netherlands*, Princeton, NJ: Princeton University Press.
Sniderman, P., P. Peri, R.J.P. de Figueiredo and T. Piazza (2002), *The Outsider: Prejudice and Politics in Italy*, Princeton, NJ: Princeton University Press.
Stoker, G. (2006), 'Politics in mass democracies: destined to disappoint?', *Representation*, **42**(1), 181–94.
Thompson, D. (1970), *The Democratic Citizen: Social Science and Democratic Theory in the Twentieth Century*, Cambridge, UK: Cambridge University Press.
Tyler, T. (1990), *Why People Obey the Law*, New Haven, CT: Yale University Press.
Van Deth, J. (2007), 'Norms of citizenship', in R. Dalton and H.-D. Klingemann (eds), *Handbook of Political Behavior*, Oxford: Oxford University Press.
Verba, S., K. Schlozman and H. Brady (1995), *Voice and Equality: Civic Voluntarism in American Politics*, Cambridge, MA: Harvard University Press.
Walzer, M. (1983), *Spheres of Justice: A Defense of Pluralism and Equality*, Oxford: Blackwell.
Walzer, M. (ed.) (1995), *Toward a Global Civil Society*, Providence, RI: Berghahn Books.
Wattenberg, M. (2002), *Where Have All the Voters Gone?*, Cambridge, MA: Harvard University Press.
Welzel, C. (2013), *Freedom Rising: Human Empowerment and the Quest for Emancipation*, Cambridge, UK: Cambridge University Press.
Zukin, C., S. Keeter, M. Andolina, K. Jenkins and M.X. Delli Carpini (2006), *A New Engagement? Political Participation, Civic Life, and the Changing American Citizen*, New York: Oxford University Press.

3. Republican citizenship
James Bohman

While republican citizenship has never really gone away, it has recently undergone a deep and highly original revival of sorts. According to Pettit and others, republicanism offers a distinctive theory of citizenship based on an ideal of non-domination, a conception of freedom that is central to contemporary republicanism. On this account, to be free is to be free from arbitrary power, where such freedom provides the basis for a normative ideal of citizenship. At the same time, republican conceptions of citizenship also include protection from domination at a wider scale on the basis of a variety of institutional mechanisms, including new forms of political democracy. Here we might think of the emergence of participatory forms of deliberative democracy, which often require direct participation and new forms of majority rule. In this respect, such political forms allow for a more capacious form of republicanism, with a wider scale and broader scope for protection of all citizens from the harms of domination. Thus, these newer forms of republican non-domination develop an appealing conception of the benefits of political community. Most of all, this ideal of citizenship provides for various statuses and powers. These intersubjective statuses have broad implications for the ideal of citizenship, including ways in which geographical, racial and gender exclusions can be addressed. Thus, republicanism asks us to imagine a rich political world in which freedom consists of the absence of mastery by others.

As Richard Dagger argues, the revival of republicanism 'occurred simultaneously with a renewed interest in citizenship' (Dagger, 2002, p. 145). It is no accident then that such conceptions of citizenship have re-emerged. But Dagger is wrong to think of it as a revival of citizenship as such. Rather, it is the case that citizenship undergoes a fundamental transformation. Traditional republicanism sees a republic as inherently tied to self-legislation, where citizens are the authors and subjects of the laws, particularly with respect to publicity and self-government. Such republicans, however, often have a fairly narrow conception of citizenship, where only people of a certain type are entitled to be citizens, such as propertied males. Contemporary republicans have over time developed a broader conception of citizenship, even if such citizenship settles on a narrow subset of citizens who qualify for self-rule. Politics, Dagger argues, is the people's business, and republican citizens who qualify as 'the people' will take part in its conduct. In so doing, they purportedly cultivate virtues, making themselves more virtuous by pursuing the common good and deepening their commitment to their community, as Rousseau claims. Even so, Mill argues that people develop their faculties through engaging in public life as active citizens seeking the common good, producing cumulative effects in each person who participates in public life. Indeed, republican citizenship is possible only if there is already a free and equal self-governing political community. For this reason, many republicans take belonging to 'the core of citizens who have a direct share in building a community' (ibid., p. 155). Thus, to be a citizen of a republic is to share with others in a common enterprise and a common fate, where virtuous citizens are likely to put the shared and common interests of all ahead of their own specific interests. However, this older conception of virtuous citizens has recently been challenged, leading to multiple and sometimes juxtaposed interpretations of republicanism, the most important of which is whether republican citizenship is tied to a broader or narrower form of freedom and self-determination.

For the modern critics of classical, early modern republicanism, however, many of these claims seem overly insular and thus no longer appropriate in diverse modern political communities. Indeed, the general tendency to praise one's community may well become part of the problem, rather than the solution, especially given a diverse set of shared commitments and a common ethos that is defended by republicans such as Dagger and Miller. In order to show the whole range of republican commitments, Dagger distinguishes different conceptions of citizenship that are ruled out if the republican community is to be preserved. While the putative claim is that only the common good allows for the emergence of a shared standpoint, for many modern republicans the civic republican claim of belonging may itself be a reason that a shared common good does not create a common ground when the republic faces challenges of diversity within community as such. Such a standard of commonality would make it impossible to seek, and perhaps even create, a common good in most modern communities. It seems unlikely that modern republican communities can survive without such renewals and the periodic reinterpretation of the scope of the common good. Like every other form of human community, republican communities require mechanisms of change, even with respect to non-domination, which would make it possible for citizens to incorporate novel possibilities and new moral claims. Without such change, self-identification would provide only a narrow range of interpretations of the common good as the basis of a shared political community.

Indeed, the second argument that common good republicans such as Dagger offer is the idea that because republican communities develop internally, a republican cannot be a 'wholehearted cosmopolitan' (ibid.). But this ahistorical non sequitur does not follow from commitment to a particular community, since the requirement to share a common enterprise is something that communities can do by creating new norms and developing new forms of life and new ways of sharing and participating in different conceptions of the good with others. For this reason, we should not reify republican communities, which historically have not been immune to internal contestation and exogenous change. On this measure of a shared common good, the idea of the political community remains purely notional, since there are no such communities that Dagger and Miller retrospectively claim to be somehow the more genuine form of republicanism. There cannot be such an inward-looking form of republicanism under current conditions, nor could there ever have been such an effective perfectionist and hence limited community. Once we accept the possibilities of cosmopolitan forms of republicanism, previous accounts become parochial at best and often elitist at worst, both of which show how the common good can be turned into such bad faith.

REPUBLICANISM: A HOUSE DIVIDED

One of the main debates about republicanism turns on the extent and scope of the bonds of the political community. As Miller argues, 'civitas must be a political community held together not just by law and a constitution, but also by relations of friendship and solidarity among citizens' (Miller, 2008, p. 141). These issues of size and complexity are not new among republicans, but had already begun in the eighteenth century, if not before. The results of these debates led republicans to embrace dispersed, federal republics as a third way that could avoid internal corruption, as it also increases the role for popular sovereignty, even as it was balanced with other institutions. From the lens of the present, such claims are parochial at best and dependent on the extent to which the republican community is also guided by internationally shared values and norms. To the extent that republicanism still depends on civic friendship and solidarity, it now becomes much more complex in a diverse world, even as some republicans remain narrow and insular.

At the same time, Miller is certainly correct when he argues that 'successful republics need not be homogeneous' (ibid., p. 142) and thus must reconcile competing claims. While Miller claims to embrace separate traditions within the republic, loyalty towards each other seems best restricted to cases when people act together as participants in a political enterprise. At times, Miller seems to extend this idea to include even the national scale, so long as the ideal of shared peoplehood exists; people will then be tied to others only insofar as they identify with others who are 'your people' to use Miller's term (ibid.).

AGAINST MILLER: WHO ARE 'THE PEOPLE'?

This kind of conception of a 'people' seems to offer a common good only if all have similar, and at times even identical aspirations and goals qua members. In fact, it would seem that the similarity of shared claims fits well when many different claims allow various groups to share common circumstances, even if they are geographically diverse. Even if a common national identity remains important to some of the people, there is no simple way to hold the community together by specific commonalities without at the same time accepting a variety of multiple, interacting identities across those who participate in shared lives together. If these commonalities are shared as the basis of identity, then these arguments leave very little room for wide-ranging dissent (previously a hallmark of republican politics), even within the space of public decision-making. Moreover, economic interdependence and large scle migration are now deeply entrenched features of many polities, republican or not. To use Cerny's phrase, we now live in a world of *raison d'état*, also more apt to endorse the reasons of international law (Cerny, 2010, p. 64). The republican state today hardly registers many of the consequences of modern freedom, including much less homogeneity across groups of citizens. While Miller thus vacillates between two positions, Pettit offers a broader range of arguments for a commitment to an ideal of freedom as non-domination, and, as it is the currency of justice, non-domination is certainly more apt under our current cosmopolitan circumstances.

Even stronger than the supposed commonalities that Miller proposes as the basis of identity, the ideal of freedom as non-domination clearly advances the internal politics of republics by creating the conditions for freedom from domination. At the same time, and despite the fruitfulness of this new republican vocabulary, some contemporary republicans see their view as inimical to cosmopolitanism, following the traditional republican adage that 'to be free is to be a citizen of a free state'. But this in no way follows. While republicans as diverse as Dagger, Miller, and Pettit all must fully accept the necessity of the state under current conditions of politics, such a convergence on non-domination makes the condition of shared liberty possible. In this case, statehood is neither necessary nor sufficient for robust non-domination. Moreover, it is not sufficient precisely because some mechanisms are also necessary to check the tendencies of many republics to establish their own form of imperium over technologically less-developed communities. In modernity, such forms of domination have only increased, with powerful states and private actors often going unchecked and out of the reach of the international system. If informed by this republican legacy of non-domination, republicans could revive the unversalist character of their anti-colonial and cosmopolitan legacy. This difference may have much to do with current strands of republicanism, although it is clear that the rejection of European colonialism marked a divide among republicans. Above all, this Enlightenment tradition does not extol the virtues of bounded political communities despite the existence of a dense, transnational political community. A first step for republicans is thus to endorse the benefits of federal institutions, where federal institutions are based on the dispersal rather than the monopoly of powers. But this conception faces the fact that there is not some single form of the Enlightenment or one specific understanding of republican claims about non-domination.

ENTER THE ENLIGHTENMENT

The Enlightenment republican critique of states and their dominating tendencies, including the expansion of centralized and executive powers among other sources of domination, leads to the gradual decline of the distinctive powers of citizenship. This criticism is consequential for the design of the modern republic, which demands deeper, more protective assumptions about the proper role of citizenship and the powers citizens now must also exercise to avoid domination. That is, supranational institutions must exist if democratic and peaceful citizens are to become more democratic; with this expansion of democracy across borders, it is possible to expand the space for common liberty across borders. Here a more capacious form of republicanism will also include the new circumstances of politics in which transnational political communities live. By the circumstances of politics, I do not simply mean the distribution of social goods, but also the scope and variety of political possibilities, including greater freedom from domination. Historically, both the Federalists and Kant have shared this interpretation of political space, arriving at important conceptions of the idea that a proper transnational order must be cross-cutting and transnational in scope, much like the European Union is today. Indeed, cosmopolitan republicans have long rejected the priority of those goods over the universal values shared by all of humanity. Shared humanity provides the basis of shared identity and interests necessary for overcoming injustice and domination. Thus, under current circumstances of politics, we ought to give priority to overcoming the pervasive harms and injustices of domination. But recognizing such wrongs requires broadening the scope of republicanism beyond states to include all of humanity.

Accepting this basic priority of humanity over 'my people' permits us to broaden the scope of our concerns across borders in our historical period, where moral and political demands become more numerous, including the burdens of practices of injustice, particularly the normality and pervasiveness of everyday injustice, of the rich over the poor, the politically dominant over the voiceless. Following Pettit, domination occurs when there is arbitrary interference, among which are the many possible forms of arbitrary interference that are socially motivated. Among other things, we may include 'financial clout, social connections, communal standing, informational access, ideological positions, cultural legitimation, and the like' (Pettit, 1997, p. 69). On republican grounds even this capacious list needs to be expanded, where the broader and more universal ideal of citizenship provides the basis for the inter-subjectively validated status of non-domination, understood as a form of freedom that is absent in a variety of struggles across borders that put the lie to the idea that republicanism is inherently and properly statist. Of course, one's avowed interests are not always validated by a putatively univocal acceptance of some shared conception of the common good.

These republican arguments can be strengthened, however, if we expand the forms of injustice that can be shown empirically to uncover nearly universal forms of injustice. What I have in mind here are, for example, forms of epistemic injustice, that is, of injustice due to domination with respect to one's capacity as a knower. The analysis of epistemic injustice has been developed recently by Miranda Fricker, who has examined what she considers the two main forms of such injustice, and these can best be understood in a republican manner as a kind of domination. The first, testimonial injustice, concerns domination in which someone is wronged in his or her capacity as a knower; and the second, hermeneutical injustice, occurs when someone is wronged in her or his capacity as a subject of social understanding (Fricker, 2007, p. 7). One such form of injustice occurs when a person's credibility is deflated, and thus is not taken to be a reliable knower. In this case, the hearer is wronged by the speaker in her capacity as a knower. Furthermore, one can be wronged in one's capacity as a knower when a person is wronged in his capacity as a giver of testimony. This may be due merely because of the color of one's skin. Finally, when people are trying to make sense of their social experience, gaps in self-understanding may be caused by the lack of collective resources that are structurally prejudiced, which Fricker calls situated hermeneutical inequality. One remedy is to correct for the ways in which epistemic, testimonial, and other hermeneutical injustices are overcome by corrective and ameliorative virtue. On Fricker's understanding, republicanism can take this corrective further by ending such wrongs through its commitment to non-domination. Here, the point is that there are no persistent injustices without the presence of overt domination, including those that harm someone's communicative status. In this sense, Pettit's more capacious conception is correct in arguing that non-domination requires that not only institutions exercise non-domination, but also work to permit the emergence of a form of counter-power. Thus, Pettit is correct in arguing that non-domination 'represents a form of control that a person enjoys in relation to his own destiny' (1997, p. 51), where the agent qua individual has the power to prevent certain bads from happening to him or her. In this sense, non-domination certainly relies on forms of counter-power.

There is much to be said in favor of Pettit's treatment of domination as a fundamental harm. Nonetheless, missing in this new argument is Pettit's earlier conception of anti-power, which he argued was 'the capacity to command noninterference as a power' (1997, p. 68). While this conception no longer figures in Pettit's current understanding of non-domination, it has advantages over his current arbitrary interference model. Anti-power cannot simply be the control over others, nor is it simply the capacity to have control over one's statuses and powers to resist domination. According to Pettit, it is this power that is a necessary and structural feature of non-domination. Thus, it is better, on his own account, to see non-domination as a positive and creative power to interpret, shape, and reformulate powers collectively by the contents of common obligations and commitments. Or, to use Habermas's terms (1999), communicative freedom requires communicative status, and communicative power is based not on power over others, but rather power over one's own decisional status.

However, as Richardson (2006) and others have pointed out, Pettit's definition of arbitrary interference makes sense only against already existing rights, duties, and roles, (such as citizenship) which carry specific rights and duties that are mutually taken for granted. If domination and non-domination are instead inherently normative notions in this sense, then the normative exercise of a purported power – the power to modify rights and duties – is essential to the idea of domination. Domination on this view is the use of normative powers by the dominator to purport to impose duties and change the statuses of others. Thus, dominators stand in a normative relation to the dominated in a web of authority and roles. The advantage of this conception is that it more clearly distinguishes between cases of systemic and normative powers of non-domination from those that are dyadic and thus non-systemic forms (such cases in which x is dominating y). For this reason, the non-dominating features of citizenship work to generate countervailing and thus communicative forms of power, since it is only qua citizens that people are able to exercise their effective normative powers and communicative freedom.

This account has further advantages with respect to communicative freedom. Democracy is built upon the joint exercise of these powers and capacities that are not under the control of any specific person or group. Even if there is an extant constitutional order, these protections may not be sufficient for citizens to achieve non-domination without such shared powers. But, for citizens, Pettit rightly argues that non-domination is needed for 'ensuring that your social freedom will require eliminating those material and related disadvantages that expose you to the control of others' (Pettit, 1997, p. 86). Given that egalitarian structures characterize the current global order, many of its disadvantages stem from inadequate institutionalization. In the case of destitution within a putative republic, citizens are dominated by these institutions and thus live with the functional equivalent to tyranny and the absence of rights. Destitution is one of the great major causes of domination globally, but it is worsened when republics act in ways that make it even more difficult for citizens to achieve non-domination as protective statuses and powers.

THE EMERGENCE OF MODERN REPUBLICANISMS

The upshot of this argument is that republican citizenship requires, first of all, that everyone has access to basic statuses and powers; and second, that all persons must also have the resources and powers not to be dominated. Only then do all citizens have the right to such statuses and powers. Thus, non-domination is not just the absence of interference; it also establishes a kind of effective and actual equality among citizens to have the right to exercise communicative freedom and powers. One aspect of this kind of everyday reciprocity within a republic is a conception of civic friendship, as has been argued by Spragens (Spragens, 1999, pp. 186–7). On Spragens's understanding of such friendship, civic friendship is already constituted by common interest, common attachment, common purposes, and common values, all of which are parts of the state. Certainly, it is the case that in modern republics common interests and powers are widely distributived, while they now seem to be much more varied, even within a republic. However, even if Aristotle's parsing of such friendship in terms of 'the interests and concerns of life' still holds, these interests and concerns of life are not shared by all and are often subject to a great deal of indeterminacy (Aristotle, in Pettit, 2012).

As we have seen, Dagger and Miller make the same arguments for republics, whose ways of life are shared by all those who belong to the state. Even if some argue in favor of such a way of life, there does not seem to be anything very specific about civic friendship as opposed to constitutional patriotism. Rather, Pettit has offered a republican revival of sorts, one that he thinks can be developed into a new vision of 'what public life might be' (Pettit, 1997, p. 129). Here Pettit seems to side with Habermas when he articulates these ideas of common bonds based on shared historical experience, as can be seen by the fact that there are no grand differences between Germany and Sweden, for example. Moreover, there is indeed a core set of beliefs and practices across Europe, such that all have access to basic human rights, including political capacities. Here the EU has moved in the direction of a larger and internally diverse form of political community, increasing the requirements on democratic openness and constitutionalism. We might think of the EU as a kind of political system, the purpose of which is to constrain power so as to make equality among persons possible, even as it also makes it possible to affirm equality before the law that protects the rights and obligations of citizens. Pettit's arguments embed these conditions within what he calls the dispersal of power condition that aims at protecting all persons, citizens or non-citizens. Such systems create a kind of minimal constitution building that makes it possible to solve problems despite reasonable disagreement, without violating equal respect and consideration, while weighing various arguments and with possibilities, all in such a way as to permit the ongoing review of the condition of dispersal of judicial power (Bellamy, 2008, p. 178).

Central to Dagger and Miller's neo-pragmatist arguments is the importance of civic friendship and shared bonds within the existing boundaries of the state. In fact, they see no alternative if there is to be shared national identity and common language necessary for republican citizenship to work. In a way, that is hard to reconcile with other claims about commonality. Miller argues that any project of transnational identity-building that is consistent with liberal republican principles should not aim to replace national or subnational entities with larger ones (Miller, 2008). Instead, it will have to generate modern identities alongside existing ones. Miller's point here is not to accept the fact that states are unable to overcome the limits of national state building. Rather, he comes to the surprising conclusion that 'the argument for nationality as the basis for citizenship remains robust' (ibid., p. 147). On this basis he argues that 'the political community needs the cement that common national identity provides' (ibid.). Miller goes on to criticize Habermas's arguments of 'constitutional patriotism', the point of which is precisely to have a capacious conception of transnational identity and shared political understandings in Europe. Moreover, in an important passage, Habermas argues that the crucial and global test of constitutional patriotism is whether or not it can turn citizens 'into members who can feel responsible for one another' (Habermas, 1999, p. 113). By rejecting Habermas's attempt at a more universal polity, Miller is able to argue for a conception of citizenship based solely on shared values and norms, while rejecting the test of free and open incorporation that is based on the simple test of mutual, shared responsibility. This means that many states cannot on their own self-conception promote responsibility for all others in the polity, even among those that live within their state. This deplorable condition is often due to non-functioning states and pervasive illegality. The current global system is structured in this way between states and failed states, where borders are the fundamental difference between the two. In the absence of Miller's putative 'cement', republicanism seems on his account to have lost its moral dimension, leaving it entirely unclear if identity building does or does not lead people 'to feel responsible for others' (Miller, 2008, p. 151). Now the 'fact of porous boundaries' entails a broader and more cosmopolitan self-understanding of what is now a global responsibility.

Because of the vast inequalities in life and prospects for people who are situated in various parts of the globe, many discussions of social justice have been concerned with primary social goods. Given the fact of global interdependence, it is no longer possible to think of these issues in terms of distant peoples, since those people have begun to migrate in ever-greater numbers across the globe in search of better life opportunities. Some nationalist republicans have given priority to their fellow citizens. Many cosmopolitan republicans have rejected this view. What is needed is a much more capacious universalism. My main argument against Miller and Dagger is that their republicanism does not turn on identity or particular common good of some of the people. Rather, republicanism must now change its conception in light of the new circumstances of justice under pervasive forms of domination. Today, falling under the control of another is now, more often than not, a matter of deep asymmetries in status and power in the global order. In this global order, many people are excluded so long as they lack legal and civil status. As Hegel already remarked, in *Philosophy of Right* ([1820] 2005), 'to have a status is now a distinction', and this means that there is a difference in life chances between those who live freely in the global system and those who live without its protections that reach down into everyday interactions. Hegel argues that having a status is to be somebody (*etwas*), and to lack one is then to be *a nobody*, for whom the rule of law does not afford any juridical protection. As Kant remarks in *Toward Perpetual*

Peace ([1795] 1970), about those who lack any statuses and powers, they lack 'the original freedom', so that all of us who have such a freedom must carry the burden of realizing the original freedom the scope of which must include all persons and all citizens who have a part in the end of shared freedom. Respecting the rights to freedom for non-citizens requires changes in how we regard non-citizens and their rights and duties. For new forms of republicanism that give a broader role for international law at home, cosmopolitanism is practiced at home, producing what Harrington called 'the empire of law and not of men' (Harrington, 1977, p. 401).

A HOUSE STILL DIVIDED?

It may well be in this case that it is better to unlink such social statuses from any particular political community, since these statuses and basic freedoms can be applied anywhere. Kant ([1795] 1970) argues that any just political order is based on a universal and thus an original and universal right, 'an innate right to freedom'. As Rawls points out about this passage in Kant, the claim to freedom is not dependent upon some antecedent status such as citizenship or any other membership. Rather, such a status makes one 'self-originating sources of valid claims' (Rawls, 1980, p. 543). Slavery remains a violation of all such valid claims, so that the demand for freedom is its own justification. For Kant and Rawls, this original right can be understood as requiring that no one can be bound by others 'except inasmuch as they can be bound by us' (Kant [1795] 1970). Those who live as non-citizens in our midst suffer under this moral harm that one ceases to be a person. The difference here is between those who lack freedom as non-domination from those that do not. Moreover, the emergence of international criminal courts offers many new and fruitful ways in which various forums are present in the international system to adjudicate claims to the loss of freedom.

This sort of adjudication creates the possibility that being a source of self-originating and self-authenticating sources of claims further justifies, in Habermas's terms, the exercise of both communicative freedom and communicative power. Such freedom requires cognitive gains, and in this respect Mill's arguments in *On Representative Government* (1861) for a life of engagement in public life serves to direct citizens to go beyond 'private partialities' and aim at the general interest and the common good in the broadest sense. This emphasis on participation could possibly be transformative, but it seems more likely to be the means to the end, where participation in public life is itself an end. Mill's arguments are certainly republican with his emphasis on the public good, but do not address many of the current basic concerns of republicanism, which are not merely the same engagement beyond the life of the single political community. Rather, all those with deeper aspirations share concerns with freedom, peace, and security, goods that require that all possess them globally.

As Kant has already realized, in solving the problem of peace, any such solution must be transnational. The space of possibilities that the generation of Kant and Madison explored was rather unique. This is not the ideal of governance without government, but rather the ideal of government without a state as the supreme authority as a requirement of peace. In asking these questions, Kant and Madison did not confine themselves to the models of ancient republics. They confronted different and starker realities, including the horrors of colonialism and the increased capacity for violence and destruction that is an inescapable part of modern warfare.

At the same time, Enlightenment republicans were also concerned with rethinking the political idea of distributive sovereignty, that is, a sovereignty that could be distributed across different units and a variety of scales. This distributive solution has in fact become the basis for a form of popular sovereignty, which I will call plural popular sovereignty. There are, of course, limitations on any such multi-level systems, in particular the potential conflict between juridically enforced liberal rights on the one hand and more republican and democratic institutions in which citizens exercise self-rule on the other. Nonetheless, what they all share is the desire to get beyond the domination inherent in the nation-state, where cosmopolitan republics sought to develop a form of political order based on a different sort of public order; that is, a form of political order based on a multi-level political system without any claim to occupy a unique form of the supremacy of one part over the whole. This kind of self-rule has much in common with many features of the European Union, but also one that is able to create the conditions of self-determination, a property that is lacking, but can be universalizable across various republican forms, perhaps in some cases as a form of European citizenship.

Because of their differing views on citizenship, republicans such as Miller and Dagger have quite different views from Rawls, Young or even Pettit (who share aspects of the Kantian tradition). Certainly, many republicans see the need for a conception of the good that was not restrictive. An obvious step is to develop order at the transnational level, where obligations to humanity have a priority over the bounded political communities as such. Indeed, even if fellow citizens within a free state could be said to enjoy non-domination with respect to each other, this status cannot be fully attributed to them, since this state cannot be said to enjoy non-domination as long as they employ dominating relations to other communities. As the eighteenth-century republicans understood their obligation, people do not enjoy non-domination so long as they stand in relations of domination with respect to other political communities. Citizens of imperially expansive republics, however, do not enjoy security in their own capacity to avoid non-domination. This makes non-domination a term of membership or a status that is distinctive social and normative power that operates against the background of normative expectations of the common good.

CONCLUSION

The most basic normative power of citizenship is the positive and creative power to interpret, shape, and change one's most basic powers and those very normative powers possessed by agents who seek to impose obligations and duties on others without being addressed by them. Non-domination is thus best understood normatively, as tied to the exercise of communicative freedom, giving new content to social norms and institutions. In this view, democracy is also a means by which people exercise their normative powers and agency. Normative powers, I argue, are central achievements of democratic institutions in securing non-domination, of members who are self-originating sources of claims. Humanity emerges within constituted democracies in struggles over status and membership, both internally and externally. The function of humanity is thus to function as an addressee to claims of justice that should be answered by the larger democratic community. The point of republicanism now demands the embracing of democratic processes. For this reason, republicanism makes it possible for all citizens to address the political communities of various sorts and to make the case that some practices have retained elements of domination.

On this neo-republican view, democracy is the means by which citizens have what Arendt called 'the right to have rights', as a way to realize non-domination along with others (Arendt, 1968, p. 177). While republican in origin and principle, this right to membership is part of being a member of the human community as such, and in so doing provides the most fundamental normative status: that of being recognized as worthy of being treated as nothing less than a full human being. Republicans now ought to cultivate these statuses and powers so as to achieve what is now a universal accomplishment of the right to freedom of all human beings.

Republican citizenship has been around for centuries. It is also constantly evolving over time, as it faces new challenges such as epistemic and other forms of injustice. Given the emergence of globalization, global institutions are necessary to address issues of the causes of human suffering and of the pervasive lack of freedom from domination. At the same time, it also seems clear that republicanism is beginning to transform itself and to address the issues of global governance. For this to be possible, republicanism must address various types of harms and wrongs. While many forms of injustice are closely related to domination, injustice is also a broader category that encompasses the need for a critical theory of the global order. The role of a transnational institutional order is now central, given how diverse various forms of injustice can be. Given a renewed focus on priority of injustice in cosmopolitanism, such institutions provide the basis for a more capacious understanding of the stakes in dealing with the consequences of domination. Given this priority of justice as a guide to a more capacious republicanism than a single polity, the transnational polity could take on the difficult task of addressing all the complex forms of social and economic inequalities and injustice that heighten rather than minimize domination. This is the task of contemporary republican and cosmopolitan citizenship.

REFERENCES

Arendt, H. (1968), *The Origins of Totalitarianism*, New York: Harcourt, Brace Jovanovich.
Bellamy, R. (2008), 'Republicanism, democracy, and constitutionalism', in C. Laborde and J. Maynor (eds), *Republicanism and Political Theory*, Malden, MA: Blackwell Publishing, pp. 159–89.
Cerny, P.G. (2010), *Rethinking World Politics: A Theory of Transnational Neopluralism*, Oxford: Oxford University Press.
Dagger, R. (2002), 'Republican citizenship', in E.F. Isin and B.S. Turner (eds), *Handbook of Citizenship Studies*, London: Sage, pp. 145–58.
Fricker, M. (2007), *Epistemic Injustice: Power & the Ethics of Knowing*, Oxford: Oxford University Press.
Habermas, J. (1999), *The Inclusion of the Other: Studies in Political Theory*, Cambridge, MA: MIT Press.
Harrington, J. (1977), 'The prerogative of popular government', in J.G.A. Pocock (ed.), *The Political Works of James Harrington: Part One*, Cambridge, UK: Cambridge University Press, pp. 389–566.
Hegel, G.W.F. ([1820] 2005), *Philosophy of Right*, S.W. Dyde, trans., Mineola, NY: Dover Publications.
Kant, I. ([1795] 1970), 'Toward perpetual peace', in H. Reiss (ed.), *Kant's Political Writings*, Cambridge, UK: Cambridge University Press, pp. 114 and 115.
Mill, J.S. (1861), *On Representative Government*, Chapter 3 [online], accessed 7 May 2014 at http://www.constitution.org/jsm/rep_gov.htm.
Miller, D. (2008), 'Republican citizenship, nationality and Europe', in C. Laborde and J. Maynor (eds), *Republicanism and Political Theory*, Malden, MA: Wiley/Blackwell, pp. 133–58.
Pettit, P. (1997), *Republicanism: A Theory of Freedom and Government*, Oxford: Oxford University Press.

Pettit, P. (2012), *On the People's Terms: A Republican Theory and Model of Democracy*, Cambridge, UK: Cambridge University Press.
Rawls, J. (1980), 'Kantian constructivism in moral theory', *The Journal of Philosophy*, **77**(9), 515–72.
Richardson, H.S. (2006), 'Republicanism and democratic injustice', *Politics, Philosophy and Economics*, **5**(2), 175–200.
Spragens, Jr., T.A. (1999), *Civic Liberalism: Reflections on Our Democratic Ideals*, Lanham, MD: Rowman & Littlefield.

4. Citizenship, gender and sexuality
Surya Monro and Diane Richardson

INTRODUCTION

The term citizenship has traditionally been understood in relation to the rights and responsibilities of citizens within a given nation-state (Richardson and Monro, 2012). This classic model of citizenship is associated with the work of T.H. Marshall (1950), a British sociologist who defined citizenship in terms of three stages of sets of rights: civil or legal rights, political rights and social rights. The other traditional model of citizenship has been characterized as the 'town hall' model, which emphasizes the participation of citizens in civil society, and is linked to communitarianism (which emphasizes the responsibility of the individual to the community) and republicanism (where, in a 'republic', the head of state is not a monarch). In contrast to the traditional liberal conception of citizens as autonomous individuals who make choices, advocates of civic republicanism see citizenship as communal, where citizens are people whose lives are interlinked through shared traditions and understandings that form the basis for the pursuit of the 'common good' (Delanty, 2000). Since the 1990s debates over the inadequacies of these two traditional models have led to the development of new ideas about citizenship. It is in the context of such developments that notions of gender and sexual citizenships have emerged, much of it fuelled by (respectively) feminist and lesbian, gay and bisexual, or queer, scholarship. For Ruth Lister: 'feminist theory and research have significantly transformed the theorization of citizenship. And, in challenging the false universalism of the "malestream", it has contributed to a more differentiated analysis better able to frame research into gender and citizenship in a multicultural context' (2011, p. 27).

Historically, citizenship has been constructed in the 'male image' (Pateman, 1988; Lister, 2003), and one of the major contributions that the large literature on gender and citizenship has made to the broader field of citizenship studies concerns a critique of the masculinist nature of traditional approaches (see also, for example, Walby, 1994). Sexual citizenship theories have provided a number of contributions to the field of citizenship studies, including a questioning of the heterosexist assumptions that underpin traditional models of citizenship. This chapter addresses citizenship in relation to gender and sexuality, taking the critiques that these pose to traditional notions of citizenship as a starting point. Both fields have re-theorized citizenship, moving the concept beyond Marshallian models. For example, Sasha Roseneil (2013) discusses a multi-levelled, multi-dimensional citizenship, which addresses economic resources, equality, self-determination and recognition in embodied, intimate and sexual life. This chapter provides an overview and discussion of, first, gender and citizenship, and, second, sexual citizenship, before concluding with a discussion of some of the common themes (specifically, the universalism–particularism debate) and some future directions for research. The chapter does not include the women's movements as 'new social movements', as this textbook contains a chapter of this theme (Chapter 18), but it does include a brief overview of the lesbian, gay, bisexual and transgender movement because this is not included elsewhere in the handbook. The discussion about transgender citizenship is mostly located within the section on sexual citizenship because the transgender movements are more strongly allied with the lesbian, gay and bisexual movements than with feminisms.

A Note about Terminology

While gender and sexuality may be separated analytically, their meanings are intertwined (Bondi, 1998, cited in Hearn et al., 2011; see also Richardson, 2007) and in some cases discussions of citizenship deal with both gender and citizenship (for example, Carver and Mottier, 1998). Wide cross-cultural and trans-historical variance on both gender and sexual identity formations is in evidence (Ramet, 1997); rigid gendered, sexual and other social categories (including racial and classed categories) were developed in the West during the nineteenth century as part of the imperialist drive to develop and embed social hierarchies (Angelides, 2001). Western gender categories, while troubled to an extent by the emergence of transgender as a valid social category in some contexts, remain mostly binaried ('male' and 'female') and the categories of 'heterosexual, lesbian, gay and bisexual' are largely predicated on these binaries (see Sedgewick, 1991; Monro, 2005). In a post-colonial context, the worldwide use of the terms lesbian, gay, bisexual and transgender (LGBT) is problematic, with a concern that international human rights organizations use the terms lesbian and gay, and bisexual and transgender in ways that suggest these are universal terms rather than social categories that have particular local as well as global meanings. Dennis Altman (2001), for example, discusses this in terms of a tension between the 'global gay citizen' and local (homo) sexualities, arguing that global definitions are inadequate to represent local sexual practices, activisms and identities. Jasbir Puar (2002, 2007) has also addressed such issues in her work, arguing that in producing a new global lesbian/gay citizen, whose rights claims go beyond single nation-states, there is a need to be attentive to what circulates as global definitions of lesbian and gay identities and politics.

GENDER AND CITIZENSHIP

Scoping the Field

There has been considerable growth in the literature concerning gender and citizenship at a range of different levels including conceptually oriented bodies of work (Lister, 1997, 2003, 2011; Halsaa et al., 2012) and more empirically based scholarship. Studies pertaining mostly to the individual and issues traditionally placed within the private realm include approaches that discuss care, emotionality and dependency (Hobson, 2000; Lynch et al., 2009, cited in Hearn et al., 2011). Studies addressing gender and citizenship at regional or national levels are plentiful (for example, Fuller et al., 2008; Gökalp, 2010; Saeidi, 2010; Predelli, 2011; Atluri, 2012) and there is a substantial body of work concerning supranational citizenship issues, for example analysis of EU policies (Vasiljevic, 2009; Lombardo and Meier, 2011). Studies of transnational migration and citizenship also broaden the field, including, for example, Rutvica Andrijasevic's (2010) analysis of trafficked sex workers and gendered citizenship issues and Umut Erel's (2011) discussion of migrant mothers as citizens.

Conceptual Contributions

Scholarship concerning gender and citizenship begins with the observation that:

> [c]itizenship has historically been framed by the nation-state and its supposedly gender-neutral, in practice often male, citizens. The concept includes not only formal political representation but also social and cultural rights, and access to state machinery... The nation-state itself has often been characteristically gendered, at least in the sense that its 'making' has usually been a project led historically by men, and at least initially for men or certain classes of men. (Hearn et al., 2011, p. 2)

Much of the gender and citizenship literature focuses on rebalancing the masculinist bias in the traditional citizenship literature, but as part of this, some literature deals directly with diverse masculinities (see, for example,

Oleksy's 2009 collection). There are, of course, wide variations in the ways that citizenship is gendered across, and within, different nation-states, but the extent of female marginalization has provoked examination of the core structures of gender inequality (Hearn et al., 2011). The extension of mainstream notions of citizenship to include women includes a reformulation of the public (paid work, formal politics) and private (domestic and personal life) divide, with a need for greater focus on the informal involvement of women in public life (Monro, 2005) as well as a re-privileging of unpaid caring, as opposed to paid work (Lister, 1997). Traditional models of citizenship rely on a separation between the public and private spheres, but public–private inequalities profoundly affect women's citizenship, for example difficulties accessing childcare may impede women's abilities to participate in work and politics (Daly and Cowen, 2000). It is important to note at this point that the public–private distinction does not play out in the same way (or even necessarily exist) across countries internationally; moreover, the private sphere has provided an important buffer against oppression for some women (see Lister, 2011). Overall, a discussion of the public–private divide sets the scene for an examination of the ways in which gendered citizenship is mediated across a range of rights and responsibilities (social, economic and political); key questions concern the factors that could enable people of different genders to have the status of 'full membership' of a national (or indeed international) political community (Hearn et al., 2011).

Other key conceptual issues for the field of gender and citizenship include the tension between academic analysis of gendered citizenship and the application of notions of citizenship in the policy and practice areas. As Ruth Lister (2011) asserts, the notion of citizenship has been used as an analytical lens *and* a mobilizing tool; however, the inclusion of women following citizenship claims is patchy (Lister, 1997, 2003). Another conceptual issue concerns the limitations of taking a purely gendered citizenship focus in a way that mirrors, but is distinct from intersectionality approaches (McCall, 2005; Richardson and Monro, 2012) that might also address, for example, faith or ethnicity. A further, related theoretical issue is that of the difficulties of speaking about a universal female experience given post-structuralist critiques of the category of 'woman' (see Richardson, 2000) and the challenges that gender diversity raises for a feminism that is predicated on gender binaries (Monro, 2005). Gender diversity, including transgender and intersex, 'does' a number of things theoretically; it destabilizes the notion that women and men are discrete categories and the only categories available to people, and it provokes an acknowledgement of greater diversity in terms of citizenship claims, rights and obligations, including not only those of cisgender (non-transgender) women and men, but also transgender, intersex, androgynous and other gender-diverse people (see the discussion in the section on sexual and transgender citizenship below). There are other broader trends that are reshaping gendered citizenship, including the shift towards a digitally based society (see Crow and Longford, 2000) and increasing globalization; these will increasingly require conceptual attention.

Gender and Citizenship in Relation to Traditional Models of Citizenship

Feminists and other scholars have examined the utility of different mainstream models for women seeking greater political equality. Stephen Leonard and Joan Tronto (2007) provide an historical examination of the way in which republicanism has become equated with masculinity (see also Lister, 2011), discussing ways in which egalitarianism for both women and men can be realized within the republican tradition. Arguably, although republicanism is useful for feminists because of its emphasis on participation and public debate, it can be seen to be masculinist due to the fact that some women are excluded from the public sphere (Bussemaker and Voet, 1998). Surya Monro (2005) notes that liberalism has a number of advantages for women, given the emphasis on equality and the language of freedom and autonomy, but that the emphasis on individualism is frequently masculinist because it is assumed that women take care of the private sphere (freeing up men to engage with public life) and that: 'Neoliberalism is problematic for women because of the focus on the market and avoiding state intervention, which does not support women's equality and is a threat to the welfare state on which many women [in Western liberal democracies] rely' (ibid., p. 151). Kate Nash examines the interfaces between liberalism and feminism in more depth, discussing the dilemmas that liberalism poses for women and contending that:

> [w]hile the feminist critique of liberalism is important to analysing the logic by which women have been positioned outside full citizenship rights, in practice feminists have made some gains by reconfiguring the terms of liberalism around this undecidability [concerning the way in which public–private divide positions women outside of full citizenship]. (Nash, 2010, p. 255)

Another key strand of thinking that informs some models of gendered citizenship is provided by communitarianism; this has advantages for women in that it includes values such as compassion, care and an emphasis on interrelatedness (Monro, 2005). However, there is a tendency for differences to be subsumed under universalist rhetoric, and, in addition, some forms of communitarianism are traditionalist in the areas of morality and gender roles. In practice, communitarian notions of community are often locality based, failing to address communities of interest such as women and sexual minorities (Bussemaker and Voet, 1998). In addition, an examination of particular areas of welfare provision demonstrates a shift towards notions of citizenship that emphasize gendered obligations and caring roles as opposed to rights; see, for example, research concerning single mothers and welfare in British Columbia (Fuller et al., 2008). The deployment of notions of citizenship by agents of the state as a means of fostering active citizenship and therefore placing responsibility for welfare onto members of the population, away from the state, is apparent in the literature more widely and across liberal, as well as communitarian, citizenship regimes. For example, Susan Franchescet and Laura Macdonald discuss the ways in which:

> a serious problem for women in both Chile and Mexico is the fact that governments themselves are deploying the concept of citizenship as a way to legitimate their social and economic policies. While women's movements seek to broaden the meaning of citizenship to include social rights, neoliberal governments employ the rhetoric of citizen activism to encourage society to provide its own solutions to economic hardship and poverty. (Franchescet and Macdonald, 2004, p. 3)

Political Science and Gendered Citizenship

While gender and citizenship scholarship addresses the Marshallian spheres of social, political and legal or civil rights, as well as other forms (for example, intimate citizenship, which overlaps with sexual citizenship approaches; see Lister, 2011 and the discussion below), it is worth flagging up the substantial gender and politics literature that is located within political science (for example, Childs, 2008). This body of literature overlaps with the literature concerning gender and political citizenship, which addresses gender and citizenship within the bounds of traditional notions of political citizenship, and addressing concerns such as feminist movements (Ong, 1999; Franchescet and Macdonald, 2004), and female suffrage and the levels of political representation of women within legislatures and state machinery (Sulkunen et al., 2009). Irma Sulkunen et al.'s (2009) edited collection traces the historical development of woman's suffrage, addressing national specificities (see, for example, Beaumont et al.'s 2009 analysis of woman's suffrage and citizenship in Ireland). The collection also addresses contemporary issues concerning political citizenship and gender, including, for example, women parliamentarians in Iran (Mousavi, 2009) and the influence of Catholicism on women's role in politics in Poland (Gozdecka, 2009). As Lister (2011) notes, women are still vastly under-represented in executives and legislatures, and a concern with this is arguably central to the political citizenship literature. Another key issue is the question of whether women's suffrage, or indeed representation within political parties and the legislature, necessarily entails female emancipation (see Maloutas, 2006). Other developments concern a shift from the focus on analysis from the so-called centre to the periphery (including, for example, emerging democracies) and a move towards post-colonial approaches in Pacific (and other Southern) contexts (see Sulkunen and Markkola, 2009). An examination of women's participation internationally yields insights concerning the nature of political citizenship. For example, Cheryl McEwan, in an analysis of gendered participation in South Africa:

> explores some of the emergent spaces of radical citizenship that marginalized groups and black women, in particular, are shaping in response [to the lack of full implementation of gender equality rhetoric]...while there are possibilities for creating alternative, more radical citizenship spaces, these can also be problematic and exclusionary. (McEwan, 2005, p. 969)

Thus far this chapter has demonstrated that important contributions to the citizenship literature have developed both beyond (or as a critique of) traditional approaches to political citizenship, and within it. A further area of development concerns gender and citizenship in an increasingly globalized world.

Gender and Citizenship in an International Context

Hearn et al. (2011) argue that the concept of citizenship requires evaluation, given the shift towards globalization and transnationalization that is taking place: 'For example, the current economic and financial crisis is important in constructing gendered citizenship, and its limits...as seen clearly in the gendered effects of neo-liberalism as both the precursor of the crisis and a widespread response to it' (ibid., p. 4). As Roseneil contends, the role of individual states globally in mediating citizenship claims and establishing the structures that support citizenship is problematized because 'the largely unfettered operations of capital produce ever greater inequalities within and between nation-states' (2013, p. 3). This, together with the intensification of migration and the emergence of new ethic and national conflicts, problematizes the role of states in addressing injustice for women, gender minorities and others.

Overall, notions of citizenship that originated in the West have been variously interpreted by Southern scholars and others, and the contributions emerging from Southern contexts contribute to the reworking on notions of citizenship in the West (see Lister, 2011). One of the trends emerging from non-Western gendered citizenship scholarship concerns the importance of women's agency in reshaping state institutions beyond either the legal or representative political realms. For example, Shirin Saeidi's (2010) article examines the role of Iranian women in asserting citizenship status, both in collaborating with, and contesting national power structures. Another trend is the move, also reflected in the discussion about sexual citizenship below, beyond a Western-centric and post-colonial form of citizenship that revolves around certain types of rights claims. For instance, Tara Atluri (2012) in a discussion of Hijras' (India's gender-variant persons) citizenship is critical of the relationship between citizenship discourse and those associated with development and international aid, suggesting that 'It is also important to be mindful of how bourgeois Western secular feminist narratives that construct marginal subjects as vulnerable bodies whom we should empathize with might obscure feminist interventions that assert imperial power' (Atluri, 2012, p. 721; see also Herzog, 2008). This argument supports a conceptualization of citizenship that is critical of the dominant Western gendered citizenship analysis. Such a conceptualization may address (amongst many other things) war, poverty, disease, violence, the impact of climate change, and displacement as factors shaping gendered citizenship. For instance, Deniz Gökalp (2010) provides an analysis of Kurdish women in the context of armed conflict in Turkey, analysing the interfaces between violence and nationalism and the ways in which women exercise agency in relation to citizenship.

This section of the chapter has provided an overview of a range of different approaches to gender and citizenship, outlining the main theoretical contributions that gender and citizenship scholarship provides, as well as providing examples of the wealth of empirical studies in this field. The section has addressed the relationship between gender and citizenship literature and mainstream approaches to citizenship, showing how gender and citizenship approaches can work to enrich traditional, masculinist approaches, as well as complementing them by casting scholarly gaze on dimensions of citizenship such as welfare provision and affectivity. While gender and citizenship studies located within political science must not be overlooked, particularly given the limitations to female and transgender franchise and basic democratic rights internationally, it can be seen that there is a need to also address other dimensions of citizenship. The increasingly international nature of citizenship, given changes associated with economics, migration and climate change (see Richardson and Monro, 2012) calls for a sophisticated and strategic form of citizenship analysis, which draws on the insights provided by Southern scholars.

SEXUAL AND TRANSGENDER CITIZENSHIP

Sexual citizenship refers to the gendered, embodied, spatialized claims to sexual entitlements (including free expression, bodily autonomy, institutional inclusion) and sexual responsibilities (non-exploitation and non-oppression of others) (Brown, 1997, p. 5, cited in Hearn et al., 2011). The concept of sexual citizenship crosses the public and the private, and directs attention to cultural, political and legal aspects of sexual activities and expression (Hearn et al., 2011, p. 7). For Hearn (1992), analysis of sexual citizenship includes attention to the socio-spatial aspects of sexuality; while most sexual activities may take place in private spaces, sexual partners may be found in a range of spaces (for example, via the internet, at domestic parties) and sexual citizenship concerns in part movement between different realms (public–private, geographic spaces) and there are issues concerning equitable access to such spaces as well as personal safety. This chapter acknowledges the ubiquitous nature of sexuality and the breadth of sexual citizenship studies. Sexual citizenship issues pertain across the entire population, in terms of issues such as consent to sexual activities, the rights of minors to be free of sexual abuse, sexual and gender-based violence, the rights of sex workers and so on; however, discussions of LGBT sexual citizenships provide a way into many key themes such as the universalism–particularism debate. The section begins with an outline of the lesbian, gay, bisexual and transgender social movements and then addresses different aspects of sexual citizenship, looking first at sexual citizenship and political approaches and then at post-Marshallian approaches, including notions of intimate citizenship.

LGBT Groups as Social Movements

It is difficult to understand concepts of sexual citizenship without reference to the emergence of sexuality-specific social movements because these movements have formed the platform for sexuality-related citizenship claims. This section of the chapter outlines the development of Western LGBT movements, following a historical trajectory (from the 1950s to the present). It does not address Southern LGBT and related movements, which vary widely (see, for example, Steyn and Van Zyl, 2009); it is recognized that this would be outside of the scope of the chapter.

Over the last half-century or more, LGBT people have formed groups and organizations that have been the basis for political action and engagement. Those growing up in the West in the 1950s, for instance, lived through a time when homosexuality was defined as abnormal, unnatural and inferior to heterosexuality (Terry, 1999; Minton, 2002) and some people responded by organizing to advocate for tolerance and homosexual rights. For example, in the USA and in parts of Europe a number of 'homophile' organizations – a term less contentious at the time than homosexual – were formed, often originating in large urban centres such as, for instance, Los Angeles, San Francisco and London (Katz, 1992; Epstein, 1999). These organizations were, on the whole, conservative in their demands, seeking tolerance and civil rights for homosexuals (Richardson and Seidman, 2002). By the late 1960s and early 1970s a very different kind of sexual politics was in evidence. High on the political agenda of the gay liberation movement (which, in the early stages, included bisexual people and gender-diverse people) was to rid society of negative ideas about homosexuality, in particular that it was abnormal and unnatural (Weeks, 2008). This early movement fragmented to a degree soon after it was formed, so that by the early 1970s a shift towards autonomous lesbian organizing took place (D'Emilio and Freedman, 1988). As well as the gay/lesbian split, both trans and bi people were increasingly excluded by lesbian feminist and gay movements, with consequences for political organizing (Ault, 1994; Monro, 2005). The bisexual and trans movements took different (although sometimes overlapping) trajectories, however, with the bi community developing as a grassroots-based community with an emphasis on lifestyle politics and political visibility (Angelides, 2001; Hemmings, 2002). The trans movement grew from its roots in the Stonewall riots in New York in 1969 and the early gay liberation front (GLF) in response to rejection by some gay men and lesbians associated with the GLF and lesbian organizations (Kirk and Heath, 1984), and manifested in organizations such as the Street Transvestite Action Revolutionaries in the USA (Wilchins, 1997).

The lesbian and gay movements that developed in the West in the 1970s and subsequently appeared on the surface to have similar goals to earlier 'homophile' organizations. There were those who still advocated assimilationist approaches to change, but the dominant political rhetoric was one of lesbian and gay liberation – a movement whose aims were not to assimilate into, or seek to reform society, but to challenge and transform it. It was about establishing an egalitarian society and overthrowing capitalism and patriarchy (Weeks, 2008). These new social movements contested many core institutions and cultural values in fundamental ways. Critiques of traditional gender roles and 'the family', including marriage as a social institution, were at the fore (Altman, 1993; Jackson, 2008; Weeks, 2008). In the 1980s, the impact of HIV/AIDs worked to both 'revitalize' and professionalize the gay (less so lesbian) movement, especially in the USA (Brown, 1997; Epstein, 1999; Richardson, 2005). In its inclusion of bisexual men, the practical work that was done in response to the HIV/AIDS crisis opened the door to greater inclusivity of people of diverse sexualities. AIDS also helped to re-establish ties between gay and lesbian communities and, in the early stages at least, led to greater collaboration in political organizing (Epstein, 1999). The 1990s saw the emergence of a new queer perspective on sexuality and sexual politics. Queer was initially put forward by activists 'as a replacement for labels such as "gay" and "lesbian"' and the 'modes of community and self-expression associated with them' (Epstein, 1999, p. 61); it concerned 'a politics of difference' that sought to be more inclusive of sexual and gender diversity, including bisexual and transgendered people, than mainstream lesbian and gay culture was perceived to be. In this sense, in putting forward a new, unifying term that included all sexual and gender minorities – even queer straights (Thomas et al., 2000) – queer saw itself advancing an anti-identity politics that displaced the categories lesbian and gay, *and* heterosexual (Richardson, 1996).

Since the 1990s, a different form of sexual politics has emerged alongside queer that has been highly influential in redefining the goals and strategies associated with LGBT activism. This is a politics whose aims are more reformist than transformist, seeking incorporation into the mainstream rather than critiquing social institutions and practices as did gay and lesbian/feminist activists in the 1960s and 1970s, and the queer and trans activists of the 1990s. This has taken place at the same time as the globalization of lesbian, gay, bisexual and transgender organizing and advocacy (see Adam et al., 1998), with the establishment of transnational networks as well as international organizations (Kollman and Waites, 2009). State institutions and practices supporting LGBT rights have now formed in some parts of the world, for example Europe, have formed including the establishment of the European Union (EU) Charter of Fundamental Rights (2000). This is further supported by the findings of the first comprehensive study of discrimination on the grounds of sexual orientation and gender identity covering all 47 member states in the Council of Europe, which reported that while there is progress on the human rights situation of lesbian, gay, bisexual and trans people in some countries, in others discrimination and human rights violations against LGBT people are continuing (see the Council of Europe report, 2011).

It is within the reformist trajectory of the LGBT movements that citizenship claims arguably fall; the LGBT movement has shifted towards a drive to gain the legal, social, political and other rights that are accorded to heterosexuals, rather than to question the structures that support particular forms of relationships and identities per se. This is not to say that these rights are not crucial, particularly in countries where human rights abuses against LGBT people and non-heterosexual people more widely are commonplace. Rather, it is to question the parameters of rights claims and to ask whether, in attempting to gain the same rights as heterosexual people, some LGBT people are inadvertently supporting traditional norms and institutions such as those relating to marriage. The following section of the chapter provides an overview of LGBT citizenship (which is generally known as 'sexual citizenship') and the literature concerning intimate citizenship.

Sexual and Transgender Citizenship

Scholarly contributions concerning LGBT citizenship that falls within the remit of traditional approaches to citizenship, particularly political citizenship, are somewhat limited. There has been some US- and UK-based scholarship regarding LGBT people and political citizenship. For example, Riggle and Tadlock (1999) have demonstrated that although LGBT people are a part of the electorate, their ability to influence political space has in the past been delimited and the collection edited by Tremblay et al. (2011) covers a number of legislatures. Being 'out' as lesbian or gay has historically been seen as a disadvantage or even a disqualifier for political office in many countries (see Rayside, 1998). This is an under-researched area, however a recent research report on barriers to participation in public life for LGBT people in the UK found that a key issue was the complex feelings, attitudes and experiences associated with being 'visible', including fears for safety (Ryrie et al., 2010) (see also the Equality and Human Rights Commission report *Pathways to Politics* by Durose et al., 2011). In addition, as previous studies have found (Cooper, 2004; Monro, 2006), political parties have typically distanced themselves from advocacy for LGBT equality. This is also manifest in political leadership as Lewis (2005), for example, demonstrates in his analysis of the issue of same sex marriage in the context of the 2004 presidential election in the USA (see Richardson and Monro, 2012, for a fuller discussion of LGBT people and political engagement). Internationally, the picture varies widely. For instance, in India, Hijras have succeeded in gaining political representation and influence, albeit partially because they relinquish aspects of their Hijra identities and gained a political platform via transgender-related rights claims (Atluri, 2012).

There have been much more substantial developments concerning sexual and intimate citizenships outside of the remit of traditional approaches to citizenship, with a new body of literature, emerging in the West in the 1990s, linking 'citizenship discourse and "sexualities" discourse' (Wilson, 2009, p. 74) and subsequently internationally (see, for example, Vasu Reddy's 2009 discussion of sexual citizenship in South

Africa). The relationship between sexuality and citizenship, and the construction of concepts of sexual and intimate citizenship, has subsequently become an important theme across a number of disciplines (see, for example, Evans, 1993; Berlant, 1997; Carver and Mottier, 1998; Weeks, 1998; Bell and Binnie, 2000; Phelan, 2001; Plummer, 2003; Cooper, 2006; Cossman, 2007; Oleksy, 2009). Within this body of work it is possible to identify a number of strands that draw on different epistemological concerns. Some, for instance, have focused on the question of what is meant by sexual rights and responsibilities, including research on the welfare of lesbian and gay citizens (Richardson, 2000b) while others address issues such as breastfeeding, pornography and kinship (see Oleksy, 2009). One of the main strands running through this literature, however, is how claims to citizenship are constituted through specific sexual norms and practices. Specifically, it has been argued by a number of writers that hegemonic forms of heterosexuality underpin the construction of the 'normal citizen' and that, related to this, heterosexuality is a necessary if not sufficient basis for full citizenship (Richardson, 1998; Bell and Binnie, 2000; Cossman, 2007). Moreover, it is important to recognize that this is a dynamic process: such constructions of citizenship both reflect *and* reproduce the privileging of heterosexuality (Richardson, 2000a). In response some writers have contested this link between heterosexuality and citizenship. Bryan Turner, for example, has emphasized parenthood rather than heterosexuality as the defining characteristic of the 'normal citizen' and as the basis for social entitlement, raising the question of whether it is more useful to think about *reproductive* citizenship than sexual or intimate citizenship (Turner, 1999).

The second main strand that runs through the literature on sexuality and citizenship is the articulation of a notion of 'sexual citizenship' or, as some prefer, 'intimate citizenship'. The public/private distinction has been central to how both sexuality and citizenship have been defined as belonging to the private and the public spheres respectively. There might therefore appear to be a certain conceptual tension in bringing together sexuality and citizenship. However, the division between what is understood as the public and the private spheres has been the focus of a great deal of debate, much of it pointing to how it is a socially produced binary and, in many ways, a false distinction. Our 'private' and 'intimate' lives may often be talked about as if they were outwith the public, the social and the political, but in fact they are deeply connected to and regulated by public discourses and social institutions. Nor can we speak about citizenship only by reference to public spheres. It is claimed that a shift is taking place in the locus of citizenship, as increasingly people's everyday 'private' practices are becoming the bases for discussing citizenship (Richardson,

2000a). This is one aspect of what some have referred to as the 'privatization' of citizenship (Phelan, 2001). This can be seen, for example, in debates over 'healthier citizenship', where in addition to smoking and patterns of eating and drinking, 'private' and intimate (safer) sexual practices are also part of how healthy citizenship is constituted. In recognizing that the 'personal and the public cannot be so readily split up' (Plummer, 2003, p. 69), it is possible to open up conceptual space to think about sexual and intimate citizenship. This can include the concept of sexual citizenship understood as involving 'partial, private and primarily leisure and lifestyle membership' (Evans, 1993, p. 64). The sexual citizen here is the consumer citizen, where sexual citizenship rights are expressed primarily through 'participation in commercial "private" territories' (ibid.). This has prompted debate over who such sexual citizenship includes and, importantly, does not include (Bell and Binnie, 2000), especially in the context of socioeconomic inequalities that structure people's access to consumption. It can also include Ken Plummer's idea of 'intimate citizenship'. This he defines loosely as a cluster of emerging concerns over the rights to choose what we do with our bodies, our feelings, our identities, our relationships, our genders, our eroticisms and our representations (Plummer, 1995, p. 17) and it can be understood in terms of both political and social status, constituted through everyday practices (see, for example, Oleksy, 2009, documenting ways of 'practising' intimate citizenship).

As this brief review has indicated, the field of sexual citizenship has developed fairly recently, with some work taking place within the remits of traditional citizenship studies and/or political science, and a new field emerging around a critique of the heterosexuality implicit in traditional approaches to citizenship; this new field stems primarily from scholars taking inspiration from the LGBT and related social movements. Scholars in the sexual citizenship field take varied approaches, including that of intimate citizenship, which overlaps with the gendered citizenship field discussed above (see, for example, Lister, 2011). The chapter will now move on to a discussion of key questions concerning gender, sexuality and citizenship, before outlining some future directions for research.

DISCUSSION AND FUTURE DIRECTIONS

There are a number of overarching themes emerging from the gender and sexual citizenship literature. Some of these, notably a focus on sexual and gender citizenship rights within a political context, will continue to be crucial for future research, given the lack of human rights and equality that many females, transgender people, and non-heterosexual people experience globally. Others are relevant at a conceptual level, and will continue to inform discussions. Of these more conceptual themes, two are examined here: the question of whether the concept of citizenship is useful for scholars concerned with gender, and what is broadly known as the 'universalism–particularism' debate. Questions for future research stem from these themes, as well as other more empirical processes, such as the trend towards globalization and the challenge of climate change.

The Utility of the Concept of Citizenship for Gender and Sexuality Scholars

For a number of feminist authors, the utility of the concept of citizenship continues to be under question. This is apparent in some of the discussions above, for instance Franchescet and Macdonald's (2004) explication of the ways in which neoliberal ideas of citizenship, specifically the 'active citizen' are utilized by the state as a means of structuring access to economic and social resources. The ambivalent relationship that many feminists have to ideas of citizenship is taken up by Roseneil, who argues that: 'Citizenship is a troubling proposition for feminism. Intensely luring in its expansive, inclusionary promise, yet inherently rejecting in its restrictive, exclusionary reality, it is an ambivalent object for those of us committed to radical projects of social transformation' (2013, p. 1). Roseneil acknowledges the many social, political, legal and other gains made for women and other groups that have been attained under the banner of citizenship claims, but also points to the flaws of citizenship, tied as it is to individualistic neoliberalism. In a recent large research project carried out across 13 EU countries, one finding was that the notion of citizenship was of limited use to women's movements and that where it was being used, its scope was limited by the frameworks associated with government funding (Roseneil, 2013; see also Halsaa et al., 2012). Roseneil discusses the 'spectre of incorporation' (2013, p. 4) that haunts feminist engagements with citizenship, in particular in relation to the ways in which citizenship has become framed as a solution to issues such as the 'democratic deficit' within the EU (and elsewhere), pressures associated with the drive to integration, and austerity. She also addresses the ways in which, to a degree, some women, and feminists, have attained inclusion within the citizenship project, presumably raising questions about those women and gender minorities that are still excluded from citizenship. For instance, there has, in the West, been a dominance within feminist theorizing of transphobic thinking (see Monro, 2005) which has contributed to the exclusion of gender-diverse people and to their stigmatization; it can be argued that feminists concerned with citizenship need to address this kind of blind spot in feminist thinking and

Citizenship, gender and sexuality 75

take ownership of their own roles in perpetuating certain types of inequality. Overall, questions will persist concerning the extent to which citizenship can be developed in such a way as to support gender equality, without the interests of subordinated groups becoming subsumed and dispersed by the institutions and processes associated with state machinery.

For scholars working to develop sexual citizenship studies, some common themes are shared with those in the gender citizenship field (such as a concern with the possibility of becoming assimilated into state discourses and institutions, and a questioning of the assumed agency associated with citizenship as discussed below), but other themes are also apparent. One aspect of critiques over the conceptual meaning and use of the term sexual citizenship is a contestation of the locus of sexual citizenship. For some, as was discussed above, this has led to a broadening out of the concept through notions of 'the intimate' rather than only 'the sexual'. Others, however, are concerned that whether articulated as intimate or sexual citizenship the emphasis remains on personal life, which, although arguably it need not be so, risks leading to a (re)privatization of sexual citizenship. Following this argument over the construction of sexual citizenship as located in 'the private', various writers have focused on the meaning of sexual citizenship in *public* spheres, which, for some, also incorporates a concern to give greater consideration to sexual practices (see, for example, Bell and Binnie, 2000).

A growing number of writers have raised concerns not only over the use of specific meanings, but also over the conceptual utility of sexual citizenship. This includes asking questions about who it includes (and excludes), which can be read as both a limit to, as well as a conceptual limitation of, sexual citizenship. The concept of sexual citizenship as currently imagined may have less purchase in looking at lower-income societies and groups, especially where basic legal, political and/or welfare rights have not yet been attained. We might then ask: is sexual citizenship a distinctly Western concept? Although we need to recognize that 'the West' is itself a problematic term, especially when used in relation to rights claims in relation to sexual orientation. Plummer rightly recognizes this point, drawing attention to how ideas of sexual and intimate citizenship with their predominant emphasis on the *right to choose* – your partner; whether to marry or not; to have gender reassignment surgery; have a child or not; your sexual activities – need to be situated as emerging from debates within particular socioeconomic and geopolitical contexts. For many people, women in particular, in many parts of the world these are unintelligible as 'choices'. Indeed, in many countries the injustices carried out against sexual and gender minorities are seen as 'morally justified' rather than as forms of inequality. He states:

> Once low income societies and the poor of rich societies are brought into the picture the concept of intimate citizenship starts to demand further clarification. Looking at issues of abject poverty, forced marriages, sexual slavery, the commodification of bodies etc, intimate citizenship takes on wider meanings. For here are people who often have little control over their bodies, feelings, relationships; little access to representations, relationships, public spaces etc; and few socially grounded choices about identities, gender experiences, erotic experiences. (Plummer, 2005, p. 25)

This does not necessarily mean abandoning the notion of sexual or intimate citizenship as a 'luxury' concept. What it does mean, however, is that there is a need to develop conceptual understandings beyond what has so far been an emphasis upon a 'politics of choice', detailing what both enables and constrains how people experience intimate lives across different societies and different groups within these, and the ways in which gender and sexuality intersect in relation to citizenship, as discussed in Richardson and Monro (2012).

The conceptual limitations of, and limits to, sexual citizenship are at one and the same time political issues. Theoretical frameworks shape the ways in which issues of equality and citizenship rights are addressed (or not as the case may be); equally, as Wilson (2009) observes, political activism can drive forward social and political theory. In this respect, Wilson urges caution in what she sees as conceptual developments arising out of the 'fashionable' use of citizenship and 'human rights' in the field of sexual politics, especially uses of the term sexual citizenship that fail to recognize power dynamics involved in articulating specific claims for rights and the conferring of citizenship by the state. This takes a number of forms: an oversight of continuing inequalities regarding people of different sexualities (for example, partnership rights), as well as new forms of lesbian and gay citizenship status are associated with 'citizenship requirements', which can serve as a means for establishing new boundaries in relation to sexuality, ones that are constitutive of 'other' sexualities that can be figured as problematic and in need of control (Seidman, 2002). For instance, according to some, this new 'othering' might include women and men who form intimate associations and family relationships that are not based on traditional gender and familial norms (Phelan, 2001). As well as 'gay marriage' and civil partnerships, some have suggested that access to parenting rights may divide lesbians and gay men as 'respectable' normative LGBT citizens (Barker, 2006). Another issue concerns the uneven benefits of sexual citizenship. Yvette Taylor, for instance, considers the significance of class as well as gender to these new forms of sexual citizenship that have been rendered possible through state recognition (Taylor, 2011). In a similar vein, Priya Kandaswamy (2008), in a US context, draws attention to the differential benefits of rights enabled through same-sex marriage within a welfare state that is racially stratified. It is, then, important to acknowledge how discourses of equality may not only conceal continuing inequalities, but also produce new ones. A further issue is whether the 'turn to citizenship' in LGBT politics is a narrowing of political space that fails to adequately address wider transformations that feminist and queer writers seek (Lustiger-Thaler et al., 2011).

A final theme, which cuts across many areas of citizenship, is that of normalization, which includes the reduction or eradication of forms of difference that are ascribed to people that render them devalued citizens. Since the 1990s there has been a gradual move towards focusing on identity- and relationship-based rights claims (Richardson, 2000b). Arguably, lesbian and gay politics in prioritizing civil recognition of domestic partnerships and a desire for recognition by the state are drawing on what the state also desires in the form of state-sanctioned and -regulated desires. This is the self-regulating homosexual subject who chooses stable cohabiting relationships. This aspect of the contemporary sexual citizenship agenda has been subject to considerable critical debate (for example, Weeks, 2008). However, what is of relevance to the discussion here is that there would appear to be a new partnership at work between activists and policy-makers, in sharing common goals and political language. Indeed, in the context of a neoliberalism's policy agenda for 'rolling back' the state it is possible to see how governments might well be motivated to introduce civil recognition of lesbian and gay relationships insofar as these are seen as a form of private welfare, providing economic interdependency and support. In this respect, one might argue that there is a convergence occurring between contemporary lesbian and gay politics and neoliberal state practices (Cooper, 2002; Richardson, 2005).

For both gender and sexual citizenship then a number of critiques are apparent concerning the focus of citizenship, and more broadly, the utility of the concept itself. The critiques outlined above serve to highlight some of the 'growing edges' of the field of citizenship studies, for instance the ways in which people's gendered and sexual citizenship are structured by factors such as race, socioeconomic class and nationality, with a number of factors contributing to citizenship status (see Richardson and Monro, 2012). The next section, which looks at the universalism–particularism debate, forms another area in which citizenship studies will continue to develop.

Universalist or Particularist Forms of Sexual Citizenship?

Paralleling debates in citizenship studies more generally is the focus on the question of whether to theorize gendered and sexual citizenship in terms of a universalistic notion of 'women', or 'the sexual citizen' or through a differentiated or particularist model that would allow for a specific notion of, say, lesbian citizenship, or that is located in particular contexts. Some scholars focus on particularist approaches. For example, Elzbieta Oleksy et al. (2011) take a position that, while recognizing broad trends concerning the gendering of citizenship, focuses on different levels (from universal to particular, and encompassing public and private); they contend that '[t]hough it is often constructed in a universal way, it is not possible to interpret and indeed understand citizenship without situating it within a specific political, legal, cultural, social, or historical context' (Hearn et al., 2011, p. 3, in Oleksy et al., 2011). Oleksy et al. (2011) draw on intersectionality theory (McCall, 2005), where attention is paid to the complex ways in which different social forces intersect, shaping the experiences of individuals and the social and political structures within particular nation-states, in their approach to gendered citizenship. In other words, following these authors, there is a need for complex citizenship analysis that is grounded in the context of specific populations and societies. This theoretical shift coincides with the demands outlined above for a destabilization of Western-centric gendered and sexual citizenship analysis. The particularist turn in citizenship studies can take a number of trajectories, focusing on site-specific (e.g., national-level) analysis, or analysis concerning identity-based communities such as migrants, sex workers, or mothers. For this type of analysis, a gender- (or sexual-)differentiated approach is taken, in which the specifics of individual's concerns are addressed (see Lister, 2011). Of course, differentiated approaches are problematic because group-based analysis becomes impossible if the unit of analysis is based on an individual, so that some way of developing commonalities of concern must be arguably found, such as country-based or identity-group–based. This is not to say that analysis based on the experience of one individual cannot generate important insights, as Roseneil (2013) has demonstrated in her research with Zainab, a British Pakistani woman, which enables an exploration of agency and citizenship in post-colonial contexts where experiences of belonging and attachment are spread across continents and are structured by immigration authorities.

Particularist or differentiated country-based analysis include work concerning ethnic minority women in Norway (Predelli, 2011) and transgender people in the UK (Monro, 2011), but studies of transnational migration in relation to specific groups can also take a contextualized, grounded approach (see, for instance, Rosenberger and Sauer, 2011). Identity-based particularist approaches include those concerning transgender citizenship (Monro and Warren, 2004; Monro, 2005, 2011; Aizura, 2006; Hines, 2007, 2009) and intersex citizenship (Grabham, 2007). Clearly, different gender-diverse groupings have different citizenship issues, the details of which are outside the scope of this short chapter. Some examples include birth certificate change as a crucial issue for transsexuals, and, as requested by some intersex people, the abolishment of unnecessary surgery on intersex babies (see Dreger, 2000). Cross-dressers are more likely to emphasize consumer models of citizenship – the rights to access accessories, as well as calling in some cases for the rights to cross-dress in public and to freedom from abuse and harassment. Lesbian, gay and bisexual identities form another basis for particularist approaches; the work concerning lesbian and gay citizenship has been indicated above. However, it worth pointing out that there is little discussion within the literature of bisexual citizenship (for a notable exception see Evans, 1993). Monro (2005) began to lay the foundations for developing a Western notion of bisexual citizenship, arguing that:

> [b]isexual citizenship can be seen to be unique because bisexual identities are different from lesbian, gay, and heterosexual identities in a number of ways. Bisexuality typically includes the experience of fluid and multiple desires. Some bisexual people are attracted to people on the basis of characteristics other than sex, others desire men, women and others simultaneously, others shift in cycles between desire for women and men. Bisexuality is subjectively different from monosexuality [same-sex or opposite-sex desire, which is the norm for lesbians, gay men and heterosexuals]. (Monro, 2005, pp. 155–6)

Bisexual citizenship claims concern the recognition of bisexuality as a valid identity (because this is denied by some people), the acceptance that desire can be fluid, which entails support for lesbian and gay rights but also an understanding that sexuality can be changeable and that people with more fluid or complex identities and multiple (rather than monogamous) relationship forms also require citizenship rights. Western models of bisexual citizenship come with the caveat that in countries – or localized communities – where homosexuality is illegal or heavily sanctioned, people's methods of managing their sexualities are likely to be very different. Rather than seeking recognition for their sexual identities via citizenship claims, bisexuals (and indeed lesbians and gay men) may opt for staying in the closet and surviving, placing their sexualities firmly in the private sphere (Richardson and Monro, 2012).

Hearn et al. (2011) warn against, however, falling into a purely particularist approach; they argue that the concept of citizenship is broad enough to include both the universal (which they see as being the level at which equality claims are made) and the particular (the level at which claims for the recognition of differences are made). There are strong arguments for a universalist approach to gender and sexual citizenship, including, for example, the political utility of claiming equal allocation of gendered citizenship rights regardless of gender (see Lister, 2011). Universalism is also important for sexual citizenship rights. The framing of LGBT politics that is increasingly dominant in numerous national settings is in terms of human rights discourse (Kollman and Waites, 2009), grounded in the liberal democratic tradition with its universalist rhetoric (Phillips, 2006), as opposed to the kind of particularist stances described above where specific identities are used as a basis for rights claims. Drawing on such discourses would imply the adoption of a universalistic rather than a differentiated model of sexual citizenship, as is illustrated both by the adoption of the umbrella term LGBT and the emphasis in LGBT claims for equality on being 'ordinary' citizens' the same as anyone else. As Lister (2011) suggests, a 'differentiated universalism' 'which attempts to capture the idea that the achievement of the universal is contingent upon attention to difference and the particular, as a way of working with the creative tension between the two' (2011, p. 30) may be the most useful approach.

The discussion developed above indicates that a complex approach is needed for the future development of both gender and sexual citizenships; one that takes into account different levels of analysis, and the intersection of diverse social characteristics. There will continue to be a need for interaction between mainstream political citizenship approaches and those associated with both gender, and sexual citizenship, with a need for mainstream approaches to question theory and political interventions with respect to possible masculine bias and heterosexism. There is a particular gap at present in the scholarship concerning sexualities and politics; this includes both LGBT politics and the representation of people with diverse sexual identities and interests via democratic structures and processes. The field of sexual citizenship more broadly has developed swiftly over the last few years but there is more literature available concerning Western LGBT sexual citizenships than there is concerning, first, Southern LGBT (and other non-heterosexual) citizenship, and, second, sexualities more broadly (for example, the sexual citizenship rights and obligations of teenagers). For the field of gender and citizenship, there is a very large amount of scholarship concerning the citizenship issues of women, but much less concerning those of other groups, specifically transgender and intersex people, and there is also a relative absence of citizenship studies that specifically address the citizenship of disenfranchised men (for example, refugees and asylum seekers) in relation to the insights provided by masculinity studies. Last, new fields of sexual and gender citizenship studies will develop around broader social changes, including those associated with migration and climate change.

REFERENCES

Adam, B., J.W. Duyvendak and A. Krawel (eds) (1998), *The Global Emergence of Gay and Lesbian Politics: National Imprints of a Worldwide Movement*, Philadelphia, PA: Temple University Press.

Aizura, A.Z. (2006), 'Of borders and homes: the imaginary community of (trans)sexual citizenship', *Inter-Asia Cultural Studies*, 7(2), 289–309.

Altman, D. (1993), *Homosexual Oppression and Liberation* (first edition, 1971), New York: New York University Press.

Altman, D. (2001), *Global Sex*, Chicago, IL: University of Chicago Press.

Andrijasevic, R. (2010), *Migration, Agency and Citizenship in Sex Trafficking*, Houndmills, UK: Palgrave Macmillan.

Angelides, S. (2001), *A History of Bisexuality*, Chicago, IL: University of Chicago.

Atluri, T. (2012), 'The prerogative of the brave: Hijras and sexual citizenship after orientalism', *Citizenship Studies*, 16(5–6), 721–36.

Ault, A. (1994), 'Hegemonic discourse in an oppositional community: lesbian feminist stigmatization of bisexual women', *Critical Sociology*, 20(3), 107–22. Reprinted in B. Beemyn and M. Eliason (eds), *Queer Studies. A Lesbian, Gay, Bisexual and Transgender Anthology*, New York: New York University Press.

Barker, N. (2006), 'Sex and the civil partnership act: the future of (non) conjugality', *Feminist Legal Studies*, 14(2), 241–59.

Beaumont, C., M. Hill, L. Labe and L. Ryan (2009), 'Becoming citizens in Ireland: negotiating women's suffrage and national politics', in I. Sulkunen, S. Nevala-Nurmi and P. Markkola (eds), *Suffrage, Gender and Citizenship: International Perspectives on Parliamentary Reforms*, Newcastle-upon-Tyne: Cambridge Scholars Publishing.

Bell, D. and J. Binnie (2000), *The Sexual Citizen: Queer Politics and Beyond*, Cambridge, UK: Polity Press.

Berlant, L. (1997), *The Queen of America Goes to Washington City: Essays on Sex and Citizenship*, Durham, NC/London: Duke University Press.

Bondi, L. (1998), 'Sexing the city', in R. Fincher and J.M. Jacobs (eds), *Cities of Difference*, New York: Guilford Press.

Brown, M. (1997), *RePlacing Citizenship: AIDS Activism and Radical Democracy*, New York: Guilford Press.

Bussemaker, J. and R. Voet (1998), 'Citizenship and gender: theoretical approaches and historical legacies', *Critical Social Policy*, 18(3), 278–307.

Carver, T. and V. Mottier (eds) (1998), *Politics and Sexuality: Identity, Gender, Citizenship*, London/New York: Routledge.

Childs, S. (2008), *Women and British Party Politics: Descriptive, Substantive and Symbolic Representation, Routledge Advances in European Politics*, Milton Park, UK/New York: Routledge.

Cooper, D. (2002), 'Imagining the place of the state: where governance and social power meet', in D. Richardson and S. Seidman (eds), *Handbook of Lesbian and Gay Studies*, London: Sage.

Cooper, D. (2004), *Challenging Diversity: Rethinking Equality and the Value of Difference*, Cambridge, UK: Cambridge University Press.

Cooper, D. (2006), 'Active citizenship and the governmentality of local lesbian and gay politics', *Political Geography*, 25(8), 921–43.

Cossman, B. (2007), *Sexual Citizens. The Legal and Cultural Regulation of Sex and Belonging*, Stanford, CA: Stanford University Press.
Council of Europe (2011), *Discrimination on Grounds of Sexual Orientation and Gender Identity in Europe*, Strasbourg, Cedex: Council of Europe Publishing.
Crow, B. and G. Longford (2000), 'Digital restructuring: gender, class and citizenship in the information society in Canada', *Citizenship Studies*, **4**(2), 207–30.
Daly, G. and H. Cowan (2000), 'Redefining the local citizen', in L. McKie and N. Watson (eds), *Organizing Bodies*, London: Palgrave Macmillan.
Delanty, G. (2000), *Citizenship in a Global Age. Society, Culture, Politics*, Buckingham, UK: Open University Press.
D'Emilio, J. and E. Freedman (1988), *Intimate Matters. A History of Sexuality in America*, New York: Harper & Row.
Dreger, A.D. (2000), *Intersex in the Age of Ethics*, Hagerstown, MD: University Publishing Group.
Durose, C., F. Gains, L. Richardson, R. Combs, K. Bromme and C. Eason (2011), *Pathways to Politics*, Research Report No. 65, Manchester: Equality and Human Rights Commission.
Epstein, S. (1999), 'Gay and lesbian movements in the United States: dilemmas of identity, diversity, and political strategy', in B.D. Adam, J.W. Duyvendak and A. Krouwel (eds), *The Global Emergence of Gay and Lesbian Politics: National Imprints of a Worldwide Movement*, Philadelphia, PA: Temple University Press.
Erel, U. (2011), 'Reframing migrant mothers as citizens', *Citizenship Studies*, **15**(6–7), 695–709.
Evans, D. (1993), *Sexual Citizenship: The Material Construction of Sexualities*, London: Routledge.
Franchescet, S. and L. Macdonald (2004), 'Hard times for citizenship: women's movements in Chile and Mexico', *Citizenship Studies*, **8**(1), 2–23.
Fuller, S., P. Kenshaw and J. Pulkingham (2008), 'Constructing active citizenship: single mothers, welfare and the logics of voluntarism', *Citizenship Studies*, **12**(2), 157–76.
Gökalp, D. (2010), 'A gendered analysis of violence, justice and citizenship: Kurdish women facing war and displacement in Turkey', *Women's Studies International Forum*, **33**(6), 561–9.
Gozdecka, D.A. (2009), 'Catholic family values versus equality – Polish politics between the years 2005–2007: envisioning the role of women', in I. Sulkunen, S. Nevala-Nurmi and P. Markkola (eds), *Suffrage, Gender and Citizenship: International Perspectives on Parliamentary Reforms*, Newcastle-upon-Tyne: Cambridge Scholars Publishing.
Grabham, E. (2007), 'Citizen bodies, intersex citizenship', *Sexualities*, **10**(1), 29–48.
Halsaa, B., S. Roseneil and S. Sümer (2012) (eds), *Remaking Citizenship in Multicultural Europe: Women's Movements, Gender, and Diversity*, Houndmills, UK: Palgrave Macmillan.
Hearn, J. (1992), *Men in the Public Eye: The Construction and Deconstruction of Public Men and Private Patriarchies*, London/New York: Routledge.
Hearn, J., E.H. Oleksy and D. Golańska (2011), 'Introduction: the limits of gendered citizenship', in E.H. Oleksy, J. Hearn and D. Golańska (eds), *The Limits of Gendered Citizenship: Contexts and Complexities*, New York/London: Routledge.
Hemmings, C. (2002), *Bisexual Spaces: A Geography of Sexuality and Gender*, London: Routledge.
Herzog, H. (2008), 'Revisioning the women's movement in Israel', *Citizenship Studies*, **12**(3), 265–82.
Hines, S. (2007), *Transforming Gender: Transgender Practices of Identity, Intimacy and Care*, Bristol: The Policy Press.
Hines, S. (2009), 'A pathway to diversity? Human rights, citizenship and politics of transgender', *Contemporary Politics*, **15**(1), 87–102.
Hobson, B. (ed.) (2000), *Gender and Citizenship in Transition*, Houndmills, UK: Palgrave Macmillan.

Jackson, S. (2008), 'Families, domesticity and intimacy: changing relationships in changing times', in D. Richardson and V. Robinson (eds), *Introducing Gender and Women's Studies*, 3rd edition, Houndmills, UK: Palgrave Macmillan.

Kandaswamy, P. (2008), 'State austerity and the racial politics of same-sex marriage in the US', *Sexualities*, **11**(6), 706–25.

Katz, J.N. (1992), *Gay American History: Lesbians and Gay Men in the U.S.A.*, revised edition, New York: Penguin Books Ltd.

Kirk, K. and E. Heath (1984), *Men in Frocks*, London: Gay Men's Press.

Kollman, K. and M. Waites (2009), 'The global politics of lesbian, gay, bisexual and transgender human rights: an introduction', *Contemporary Politics*, **15**(1), 1–17.

Leonard, S.T. and J.C. Tronto (2007), 'The genders of citizenship', *American Political Science Review*, **101**(1), 33–46.

Lewis, G. (2005), 'Same-sex marriage and the 2004 presidential election', *PS: Political Science and Politics*, **38**(2), 195–9.

Lister, R. (1997), *Citizenship: Feminist Perspectives*, London: Palgrave Macmillan.

Lister, R. (2003), *Citizenship: Feminist Perspectives*, 2nd edition, London: Palgrave Macmillan.

Lister, R. (2011), 'From the intimate to the global: reflections on gendered citizenship', in E.H. Oleksy, J. Hearn and D. Golańska (eds), *The Limits of Gendered Citizenship: Contexts and Complexities*, New York/London: Routledge.

Lombardo, E. and P. Meier (2011), 'EU gender equality policy: citizen's rights and women's duties', in E.H. Oleksy, J. Hearn and D. Golańska (eds), *The Limits of Gendered Citizenship: Contexts and Complexities*, New York/London: Routledge.

Lustiger-Thaler, H., J. Nederveen-Pieterse and S. Roseneil (eds) (2011), *Beyond Citizenship: Feminism and the Transformation of Belonging*, Houndmills, UK: Palgrave Macmillan.

Lynch, K., J. Baker and M. Lyons (eds) (2009), *Affective Equality: Love, Care and Injustice*, London: Palgrave Macmillan.

Maloutas, M.P. (2006), *The Gender of Democracy: Citizenship and Gendered Subjectivity*, London/New York: Routledge.

Marshall, T.H. (1950), *Citizenship and Social Class*, Cambridge, UK: Cambridge University Press.

McCall, L. (2005), 'The complexity of intersectionality', *Signs*, **30**(3), 1771–800.

McEwan, C. (2005), 'New spaces for citizenship? Rethinking gendered participation and empowerment in South Africa', *Political Geography*, **24**(8), 969–91.

Minton, H.L. (2002), *Departing From Deviance: A History of Homosexual Rights and Emancipatory Science in America*, Chicago, IL: University of Chicago Press.

Monro, S. (2005), *Gender Politics: Citizenship, Activism, and Sexual Diversity*, London: Pluto Press.

Monro, S. (2006), 'Sexualities initiatives in local government: measuring success', *Local Government Studies*, **32**(1), 19–39.

Monro, S. (2011), 'Introducing transgender citizenship: the UK case', in E.H. Oleksy, J. Hearn and D. Golańska (eds), *The Limits of Gendered Citizenship: Contexts and Complexities*, New York/London: Routledge.

Monro, S. and L. Warren (2004), 'Transgendering citizenship', *Sexualities*, **7**(3), 345–62.

Mousavi, M. (2009), 'Women parliamentarians in Iran: a show of power?', in I. Sulkunen, S. Nevala-Nurmi and P. Markkola (eds), *Suffrage, Gender and Citizenship: International Perspectives on Parliamentary Reforms*, Newcastle-upon-Tyne: Cambridge Scholars Publishing.

Nash, K. (2010), 'Feminism and contemporary liberal citizenship: the undecidability of "women"', *Citizenship Studies*, **5**(3), 255–68.

Oleksy, E.H. (ed.) (2009), *Intimate Citizenships. Gender, Sexualities, Politics*, London: Routledge.

Oleksy, E.H., J. Hearn and D. Golańska (2011) (eds), *The Limits of Gendered Citizenship: Contexts and Complexities*, New York/London: Routledge.

Ong, A. (1999), 'Muslim feminism: citizenship in the shelter of Islam', *Citizenship Studies*, **3**(3), 355–71.
Pateman, C. (1988), *The Sexual Contract*, Palo Alto, CA: Stanford University Press.
Phelan, S. (2001), *Sexual Strangers. Gays, Lesbians and Dilemmas of Citizenship*, Philadelphia, PA: Temple University Press.
Phillips, A. (2006), *Which Equalities Matter?*, Cambridge, UK: Polity Press.
Plummer, K. (1995), *Telling Sexual Stories. Power, Change and Social Worlds*, London: Routledge.
Plummer, K. (2003), *Intimate Citizenship. Private Decisions and Public Dialogues*, Seattle, WA/London: University of Washington Press.
Plummer, K. (2005), 'Intimate citizenship in an unjust world', in M. Romero and E. Margolis (eds), *The Blackwell Companion to Social Inequalities*, Oxford: Wiley Blackwell.
Predelli, L.N. (2011), 'Ethnic minority women and political influence in Norway', in E.H. Oleksy, J. Hearn and D. Golańska (eds), *The Limits of Gendered Citizenship: Contexts and Complexities*, New York/London: Routledge.
Puar, J.K. (2002), 'Circuits of queer mobility: tourism, travel and globalization', *GLQ: A Journal of Lesbian and Gay Studies*, **8**(1/2), 101–38.
Puar, J.K. (2007), *Terrorist Assemblages: Homonationalism in Queer Times*, Durham, NC: Duke University Press Books.
Ramet, S. (1997), *Gender Reversals and Gender Cultures: Anthropological and Historical Perspectives*, London/New York: Routledge.
Rayside, D. (1998), *On the Fringe: Gays and Lesbians in Politics*, Ithaca, NY: Cornell University Press.
Reddy, V. (2009), 'Queer marriage: sexualising citizenship and the development of freedoms in South Africa', in M. Steyn and M. van Zyl (eds), *The Prize and the Price: Shaping Sexualities in South Africa*, Cape Town: HSRC Press.
Richardson, D. (1996), 'Heterosexuality and social theory', in D. Richardson (ed.), *Theorising Heterosexuality*, Buckingham, UK: Open University Press.
Richardson, D. (1998), 'Sexuality and citizenship', *Sociology*, **32**(1), 83–100.
Richardson, D. (2000a), 'Claiming citizenship? Sexuality, citizenship and lesbian/feminist theory', *Sexualities*, **3**(2), 255–72.
Richardson, D. (2000b), 'Constructing sexual citizenship: theorizing sexual rights', *Critical Social Policy*, **20**(1), 105–35.
Richardson, D. (2005), 'Desiring sameness? The rise of a neoliberal politics of normalisation', *Antipode*, **37**(3), 515–53.
Richardson, D. (2007), 'Patterned fluidities: (re) imagining the relationship between gender and sexuality', *Sociology*, **41**(3), 457–74.
Richardson, D. and S. Monro (2012), *Sexuality, Equality and Diversity*, Houndmills, UK: Palgrave Macmillan.
Richardson, D. and S. Seidman (2002), 'Introduction', in D. Richardson and S. Seidman (eds), *Handbook of Lesbian and Gay Studies*, London: Sage.
Riggle, E.D.B. and B.L. Tadlock (eds) (1999), *Gays and Lesbians in the Democratic Process: Public Policy, Public Opinion, and Political Representation*, New York/Chichester, UK: Columbia University Press.
Rosenberger, S. and B. Sauer (2011), 'Governing Muslim headscarves: regulations and debates in Europe', in E.H. Oleksy, J. Hearn and D. Golańska (eds), *The Limits of Gendered Citizenship: Contexts and Complexities*, New York/London: Routledge.
Roseneil, S. (ed.) (2013), *Beyond Citizenship? Feminism and the Transformation of Belonging*, Houndmills, UK: Palgrave MacMillan.
Ryrie, I., S.M. McDonnell and K. Allman (2010), *Experiences of and Barriers to Participation in Public and Political Life for Lesbian, Gay, Bisexual and Transgender People*, Report to the Government Equalities Office, London: Office for Public Management.
Saeidi, S. (2010), 'Creating the Islamic Republic of Iran: wives and daughters of martyrs and acts of citizenship', *Citizenship Studies*, **14**(2), 113–26.

Sedgewick, E.K. (1991), *The Epistemology of the Closet*, Berkeley, CA: University of California Press.
Seidman, S. (2002), *Beyond the Closet: The Transformation of Gay and Lesbian Life*, New York/London: Routledge.
Steyn, M. and M. van Zyl (2009) (eds), 'The prize and the price: shaping sexualities in South Africa', Cape Town: HSRC Press.
Sulkunen, I. and P. Markkola (2009), 'Introduction', in I. Sulkunen, S.-L. Nevala-Nurmi and P. Markkola (eds), *Suffrage, Gender and Citizenship: International Perspectives on Parliamentary Reforms*, Newcastle-upon-Tyne: Cambridge Scholars Publishing.
Sulkunen, I., S.-L. Nevala-Nurmi and P. Markkola (eds) (2009), *Suffrage, Gender and Citizenship: International Perspectives on Parliamentary Reforms*, Newcastle-upon-Tyne: Cambridge Scholars Publishing.
Taylor, Y. (2011), 'Lesbian and gay parents' sexual citizenship: recognition, belonging and (re) classification', in J. McLaughlin, P. Phillimore and D. Richardson (eds), *Contesting Recognition*, Houndmills, UK: Palgrave Macmillan.
Terry, J. (1999), *An American Obsession. Science, Medicine and Homosexuality in Modern Society*, Chicago, IL: University of Chicago Press.
Thomas, C., J.O. Aimone and C.A.F. MacGillivray (eds) (2000), *Straight with a Twist: Queer Theory and the Subject of Heterosexuality*, Champaign, IL: University of Illinois Press.
Tremblay, M., D. Paternotte and C. Johnson (2011) (eds), *The Lesbian and Gay Movement and the State: Comparative Insights into a Transformed Relationship*, Farnham, UK/Burlington, MA: Ashgate Publishing Ltd.
Turner, B. (1993), 'Contemporary problems in the theory of citizenship', in B.S. Turner (ed.), *Citizenship and Social Theory*, London: Sage.
Vasiljevic, S. (2009), 'European citizenship in the context of gender equality legislation in Eastern European countries: the case of Croatia', in I. Sulkunen, S. Nevala-Nurmi and P. Markkola (eds), *Suffrage, Gender and Citizenship: International Perspectives on Parliamentary Reforms*, Newcastle-upon-Tyne: Cambridge Scholars Publishing.
Walby, S. (1994), 'Is citizenship gendered?', *Sociology*, **28**(2), 379–95.
Weeks, J. (1998), 'The sexual citizen', *Theory, Culture and Society*, **15**(3–4), 35–52.
Weeks, J. (2008), *The World We Have Won. The Remaking of Erotic and Intimate Life*, London: Routledge.
Wilchins, R.A. (1997), *Read My Lips: Sexual Subversion and the End of Gender*, Ann Arbor, MI: Firebrand Books.
Wilson, A.R. (2009), 'The "neat concept" of sexual citizenship: a cautionary tale for human rights discourse', *Contemporary Politics*, **15**(1), 73–85.

5. Multicultural citizenship
Narzanin Massoumi and Nasar Meer

INTRODUCTION

It is a sign of our times that it seems clichéd to state that minorities have increasingly 'challenged' the rights and status conferred upon them by various programmes of democratic citizenship. In this chapter we elaborate why this is so and how multicultural political theory and social movements literature can be brought together to provide an account that helps us to understand this. There is, of course, already a very deep and expansive body of literature on the idea and practice of citizenship, something that reflects an incredible variety in its philosophical, legal, social and political relevance. Our objective in this chapter is to discuss how citizenship has been framed and challenged, and the ways in which this relates to prevailing liberal and multicultural philosophies, as well as broader political struggles and social activism. Having established this we conclude with a consideration of how multicultural and social movement literature can be synthesized in the theorization of contemporary citizenship, and what the limitations are in doing so.

THE CHALLENGE OF CITIZENSHIP

'It is hard to find a democratic or democratizing society these days that is not the site of some significant controversy over whether and how its institutions should better recognize the identities of cultural and disadvantaged minorities'. So declared Amy Gutmann (1994, p.3), nearly two decades ago.[1] In many respects this trend has continued, for contestations surround the separation of public and private spheres (Parekh, 2000), the way in which a country's self-image is configured (Uberoi and Modood, 2013), or emerge in what can either be conceived as mundane or politicized calls for dietary or uniform changes in places of school and work (Meer, 2010). What these all share in common is the view that citizenship cannot ignore the internal plurality of societies that play host to 'difference' (Modood, 2013). As Benhabib (2002, p.vii) has argued: 'Our contemporary condition is marked by the emergence of new forms of identity politics around the globe. The new forms complicate and increase centuries-old tensions between the universalistic principles ushered in by the American and French Revolutions and the particularities of nationality, ethnicity, gender, "race", and language'. Another way of putting this is to state that while citizenship takes a legal form, this is never settled because it also operates socially through the reciprocal balance of rights and responsibilities that confer upon its bearers a civic status that affords those bearers equal opportunity, dignity and confidence. To appreciate what is meant by this we need to register how the very idea of citizenship has contained, since it earliest formulations, a dialectical tension between notions of inclusion and exclusion, for the citizenship of certain types of people implies the non-citizenship of others. This is to say that citizenship is a relational idea that is identified as much by what it is not as by what it is. Simultaneously, just as this tension is evident *within* citizen and non-citizen distinctions, so it is *across* citizen distinctions. This requires some elaboration, for what is being argued is that ideas and practices of citizenship need not be fixed in one mould or another. Quite the contrary – through forms of contestation, programmes of citizenship can change and develop.

In the Western tradition, citizenship was born of an Athenian city-state participatory model in which political engagement (in a male-only public sphere) was the highest form of activity (Aristotle, 1986, pp.61–2). In this formulation it was anticipated that a group who united to make laws for the common good, and who would freely consent to be being bound by these laws, could create order from chaos in behaving rationally as citizens. These qualities are proclaimed in Pericles' apocryphal funeral oration commemorating Athenian soldiers lost to Sparta during the Peloponnesian Wars. It is an account that famously illustrates how by 'establishing a rule of law within and without' (Castles and Davidson, 2000, p.29), the Athenians were able to conceive of themselves as a *citizenry*, in contradistinction to their barbarous neighbours. In Athens, Pericles insisted, 'the freedom we enjoy in our government extends also to our ordinary life' so that 'far from exercising a jealous surveillance over each other, we do not feel called upon to be angry with our neighbour for doing what he likes. . . We throw open our city to the world, and never by alien acts exclude foreigners from any opportunity of learning or observing' (Thucydides, 1964, pp.116–17).

It is worth remembering how this very noble formulation – in which it was proclaimed that 'no-one, so long as he has it to be of service to the state, is kept in political obscurity' (ibid.) – restricted participation by excluding women, those without property, slaves, newcomers to Athens, and so forth. Recalling this helps illustrate how although the idea of citizenship can contain a powerful democratic and inclusive thrust, 'the speed of its progress towards...inclusion will depend upon the openness of its rules of admission' (Castles and Miller, 2000, p.31). This is returned to below, and specifically how during the Enlightenment a justification of subjecthood precipitated notions of consent and contract, opening the way to liberalism's language of individual rights: a component of contemporary accounts of both citizenship *and* belonging presented in formulations of *jus soli* (territory of birth) and *jus sanguinis* (origin through lineage). Of course, these later formulations were themselves only made possible by the development of the idea of citizenship as a juridical concept of legal status (by another Western tradition, specifically the Roman need to incorporate very disparate groups within a single empire; Dynesson, 2001).

This discussion, while brief, implores us to consider, first, whether contemporary citizenship continues to reflect tensions arising from its exclusionary aspects, and how this may be particularly evidenced around sociological cleavages of gender, sexuality, class, race, ethnicity, and religion and so forth. Second, it reminds us that an inclusive citizenship capable of challenging or overcoming these cleavages – through contestation – is a relatively recent development in accounts of citizenship and civic status.

MARSHALL AND BEYOND: EQUALITY AND CULTURE

Taking up the question of civic status in his landmark essay, *Citizenship and Social Class* ([1950] 1997), T.H. Marshall insisted that the central feature of citizenship should be 'a status bestowed on all those who are full members of the community' (ibid., p.300), and formulated a conception of citizenship that was both a right *and* a duty. This prospect of membership through citizenship undoubtedly heralded an increase in the rights enjoined by all (see Meer, 2010: Chapter one). For example, Marshall identified a tripartite taxonomy of citizenship made up of the civil, the political and the social. While the *civil* element was composed of 'rights necessary for individual freedom – liberty of the person, freedom of speech...the right to own property and conclude valid contracts, and the right to justice' (Marshall [1950] 1997, p.294), the *political* referred to an extension of the franchise and the 'right to participate in the exercise of political power, as a member of a body invested with political authority or as an elector of the members of such a body' (ibid.). The third *social* element described a 'right to a modicum of economic welfare and security to the right to share in the full social heritage and to live the life of a civilized being according to the standards prevailing in the society' (ibid.).

To maintain this sort of citizenship 'contract' the state would guarantee such rights while the individual is duty bound to pay taxes and obey the law and so forth. The tension, however, in Marshall's account arises from his focus on the majority (in his case the British white working class) in a way that prevented him from seeing cultural minority rights as a factor in full citizenship. That is to say that Marshall's approach is a classic, though nuanced, illustration of an account of citizenship that simultaneously upholds the promise of formal (and in many important respects substantive) equality while passing over the sources of inequality that require an account of cultural differences.

It would be unreasonable to make this a specific charge against Marshall without appreciating the period in which he was writing. Indeed, it is arguable that Marshall proposed a progressive formulation of citizenship that advanced the philosophical conceptions of John Stuart Mill, the 'new Liberals' T.H. Green and L.T. Hobhouse, and economists such as Alfred Marshall and John Maynard Keynes. These figures cumulatively contributed to the idea that citizenship should constitute a positive freedom that would supplement the minimum of 'Life, Liberty, and Property' that had been advocated since at least the seventeenth century by classical liberals who:

> [s]aw such rights as limited, for the most part opposing even the public provision of education, under the period of the welfare state the entitlement to membership and participation also came to embody rights to work, to health, and to security. As such, *a universal citizenship* expressed the new positive role of the state as the embodiment of social democracy. (Olssen, 2004, p.180; emphasis added)

Nevertheless, and while his conception of citizenship was a relative advance that marked an important progress on earlier settlements, Marshall's conception of citizenship embodied a central feature of liberalism to be found in its 'universalism'. Criticisms of this tendency have been mounted from various quarters, not least in recent years from those engaged in the 'multicultural turn' (May et al., 2004, pp.1–19). Authors from this tradition have argued that one problem with the liberal conception of universal citizenship, is that it is blind to the injustices that might arise from treating people marked by social, cultural and political differences in a uniform manner. As Squires (2002, p.117) has argued, however, it is imperative to distinguish *this* complaint from a rejection of universal social and political inclusion per se. So that what is being advocated is 'a differentiated universalism as opposed to the false universalism of traditional citizenship theory'. It is to this that we now turn.

LIBERALISM, RECOGNITION AND MULTICULTURALISM

To some commentators the staple issues that multiculturalism seeks to address, such as the rights of ethnic and national minorities, group representation and perhaps even the political claims-making of 'new' social movements, are in fact 'familiar long-standing problems of political theory and practice' (Kelly, 2002, p.1). Indeed, some hold this view to the point of frustration:

> Liberals have had to recognize that they need to create a better account of what equal treatment entails under conditions of diversity... If we take a very broad definition of multiculturalism so that it simply corresponds to the demand that cultural diversity be accommodated, there is no necessary conflict between it and liberalism... But most multiculturalists boast that they are innovators in political philosophy by virtue of having shown that liberalism cannot adequately satisfy the requirements of equal treatment and justice under conditions of cultural diversity. (Barry, 2002, p.205)

The first part of Barry's statement is perhaps more conciliatory than might be anticipated from an author admired for his argumentative robustness and theoretical hostility toward multiculturalism, while the second part poses more of an empirical question. Beginning with the first part, Barry's view is by no means rejected by those engaged in the 'multicultural turn'. Modood (2007, p.8), for instance, locates the genesis of multiculturalism within a 'matrix of principles that are central to contemporary liberal democracies', in a manner that establishes multiculturalism as 'the child of liberal egalitarianism, but like any child, it is not simply a faithful reproduction of its parents'. A more Hegelian way of putting this is to state that as a concept, multiculturalism is a partial outgrowth of liberalism in that it establishes 'a third generation norm of legitimacy, namely respect for reasonable cultural diversity, which needs to be considered on a par with the [first and second generation] norms of freedom and equality, and so to modify policies of "free and equal treatment" accordingly' (Tully, 2002, p.102).

Our interest is with the political implication of this 'third generation norm of legitimacy' for a concept of citizenship, which includes the recognition that social life consists of individuals and groups, and that both need to be provided for in the formal and informal distribution of powers (Modood, 2013). What we are describing is not a deontological activity. Third generation norms of legitimacy are also borne out of earlier political struggles for equality (Young, 1990, p.157). For example, radical feminists, starting with the motto 'the personal is political', began to challenge the distinction between the private and the public sphere, rejecting the idea that politics were confined to public institutions. In contrast to the liberal feminism of the nineteenth-century women's suffrage movement, who sought to open up the public sphere to women, by enabling women to exhibit more masculine traits, this group of feminists sought to challenge the private/public distinction altogether, by seeking to gain respect for women's differences as women. They claimed that women's individual experience in personal relationships, school or work were all subject to male domination, which therefore rendered these spaces important sites of political struggle. Kate Millett's *Sexual Politics* (1970) was a landmark in this view, and outlined the main tenants of this new politics. The domain of politics was no longer restricted to institutions in the public sphere but pervaded every aspect of individual and social life. A new political strategy emerged for feminists, of consciousness raising, where women would, through discussion with other women, analyse the seemingly personal problems of their everyday life, as actual political problems (Kauffman, 2001, p.28). Similarly, the struggle for ethnic and racial equality began with the colour-blind humanism of Martin Luther King, but later shifted towards black pride and black nationalism (Modood, 2009, p.485). The Black Panther Party had a ten-point programme (1966) that sought self-determination for the black community in America. Political claims were made on the basis of difference, such as seeking the right for blacks to be tried by a black jury (Austin, 2006).

Picking up the second part of Barry's earlier statement, to what extent then do we have an established 'canon' of multiculturalism as an intellectual tradition – one that persuasively distinguishes it from varieties of liberalism? It seems only wise at this stage to offer the intellectual health warning that multiculturalism as a concept is – like very many others – 'polysemic', such that multiculturalist authors cannot be held entirely responsible for the variety of ways in which the term is interpreted. This is something noted by Bhabha (1998, p.31) who points to the tendency for multiculturalism to be appropriated as a 'portmanteau term', one that encapsulates a variety of sometimes contested meanings (see, for example, Meer and Modood, 2009). In this respect, the idea of multiculturalism might be said to have a 'chameleonic' quality that facilitates its simultaneous adoption and rejection in the critique or defence of a position (Smith, 2010). One illustration of this is the manner in which multiculturalism is simultaneously used as a label to describe the fact of pluralism or diversity in any given society, and a moral stance that cultural diversity is a desirable feature of a given society (as well as the different types of ways in which the state could recognize and support it). Some have turned to this variety in meaning and usage of the term as an explanation of the allegedly 'widely divergent assessments of the short history and potential future of multiculturalism' (Kivisto and Faist, 2007, p.35). Either way, it is certainly the case that the political struggle for group-differentiated citizenship that became prominent in the 1960s and 1970s, in the form of feminist, anti-racist and gay liberation movements, brought group-based mobilizations, and what would become known as '*new* social movements' (NSMs), into normative conceptions of citizenship (Touraine, 1981; Melucci, 1989, 1996).

NEW SOCIAL MOVEMENTS AND RECOGNITION STRUGGLES

New social movement theorists distinguished the variety of movements in the 1960s and 1970s that were based on status as well as ideology and values from movements of the late nineteenth and early twentieth century (Bernstein, 2005, p.54). Viewing these as historically new, they explain the development of such movements as a result of changes in the form of modernization, as a product of post-material values resulting from macro structural changes to a post-industrial society (Touraine, 1981; Melucci, 1989, 1996). They saw these movements as seeking to struggle for democracy and control rather than economic survival, aiming at expanding freedom rather than achieving it. As a result, the focus of much social movement activity is on expressing identity, a new 'moral concern' that seeks to gain recognition for new lifestyles and new identities (Melucci, 1996, p.24). These movements challenged dominant narratives and cultural codes. More specifically, mobilizations seeking to rectify the devaluation or misrecognition of particular identities were forging new meanings about the way in which 'difference' is dealt with (Melucci, 1996).

In his seminal work, *Nomads of the Present*, Alberto Melucci (1989) claims that social movements 'operate as signs, in the sense that they translate their actions into symbolic challenges to the dominant codes' (ibid., p.12), emphasizing the procedural aspects of social movements – the ways they produce meanings, communicate and make decisions. Theorizing social movements in this way, Melucci (1989) claims that visibility is not the main strength of a social movement; movements are only visible at times of public conflict. It is what goes on behind the scenes of these movements that is more important 'in the everyday network of social relations, in the capacity and will to reappropriate space and time, and in the attempt to practice alternative life-styles' (ibid., p.71). These 'submerged networks', in their creation of new political cultures, hold the greatest potency for change.

The emergence of these so-called new social movements marked an important shift in the theorization of social movements. They enabled a shift towards a more positive understanding of movements not as 'irrational' or a result of strain in society but as rational political actions by actors who did not have access to the main channels of the political system (McAdam, 1982, p.23). Previously, classical theories of social movements developed during the 1950s using grievance or strain models. Such theories, influenced by the empirical realities of fascism and Stalinism, were dominated by the collective behaviour tradition, which understood social movements as a result of some form of 'dysfunction' or breakdown of social order due to rapid social change such as industrialization (McAdam, 2002, p.3; see, also, for example, Turner and Killian, 1957; Smelser, 1962). In this view, movements are a result of an increase in general levels of discontent, social marginality or isolation, hence, owing more to psychological than political or economic motivations. Resource mobilization theory (RMT), developed in opposition to the collective behaviour models, shifting from psychological to political and strategic understandings of collective actions and social movements (McCarthy and Zald, 1977). They shifted the focus onto the organizational resources that actors draw on in mobilization. In this view, social movements are an extension of politics by other means; this meant that they could be understood in terms of a conflict of interests taking place between groups, like other forms of political struggle, rather than an expression of irrationality.

New social movement theory (Touraine, 1981; Melucci, 1989, 1996) was the first concerted theoretical attempt to develop an analysis of the role of identity within social movements, sparking a 'cultural turn' in the analysis of social movements. This provoked the more rationalist strand of social movement theory, such as resource mobilization and political process theory, to develop an understanding of identity and culture. For resource mobilization theorists, identity plays a role in social movements in providing solidary incentives (Klandermans, 1984), a collective sense of mutual solidarity that can motivate people to participate in collective action and overcome the 'free rider' problem (Olson, 1965). The contribution of political process will be discussed further below.

While new social movement theory offers a 'bottom up' understanding of politics – including the role of everyday subversive practices in collective action – it neglects politics in the wider sense, by relying on a false separation between culture as opposed to politics and political economy. Movements for recognition should not be simply conceptualized as aimed at cultural and expressive goals in contradistinction to movements aimed at political and economic change (Bernstein, 2008, p.286; see also Bernstein, 2005). In their attempt to challenge the state-centredness of political process theories, new social movement theorists only attribute transformative value to the expressive dimensions of social movements. However, if we adopt a 'pluralistic conception of oppression', as operating through interlocking systems, movements formed on the basis of the politics of difference are not simply engaging in cultural politics, but are actually engaged in political action where the goal is to challenge decision-making processes, division of labour and evaluation of worth in society (Young, 1990). That means that in order to understand why movements are seeking recognition of a devalued identity, we must understand that identities are linked to structure and interest (Fraser, 1997; Bernstein, 2008, p.286).

MULTICULTURAL CITIZENSHIP AND SOCIAL MOVEMENTS THEORY

So how can we bridge the literatures of multicultural political theory and social movement theory? As we have seen, a predominant approach to multicultural citizenship has been grounded in normative political theories of justice and democracy. Such theories rely on defining inclusion, rights and membership of political communities. In this tradition, variation exists in terms of how different outcomes are conceived, such as the extent of participation in social, political and economic spheres, the redistribution of resources, and the opening or closing of geographical, social, political and economic spaces (Hobson, 2003, p.3). While these questions concern national-level institutions, social movement theories are focused on subnational organizational processes. These theories address questions as to what generates a social movement, examining the resources and opportunities, the dynamics and cycles of protest, the relationship to identity formation, and the mobilizing structures and networks that bring people together in a collective. However, social movement theories have paid less attention to the outcomes with regard to distribution and access to power and resources (ibid.).

There are two approaches within social movement thought that can provide a bridge between social movement literatures and multicultural political theory in theorizing citizenship. The first is the 'collective identity approach' and the second is the 'political process model'. The collective identity approach offers an understanding of the relationship between oppression and mobilization that can help explain the development of political struggles seeking group-differentiated citizenship, while the political process model enables an understanding of what forms of mobilization can emerge within specific political conditions. The collective identity approach offers an opportunity to consider how social groups mobilize within the context of everyday patterns and practices, rooted in social structures of domination that deny social groups participatory membership; while the political process model can consider political mobilization in relation to the political cultures and the institutional political context.

Collective Identity and Recognition Struggles

While the empirical and historical claims of new social movement theory remains contested (Calhoun, 1993; see Pichardo, 1997 for a review); the collective identity approach has been taken up across the field of social movement analysis (Gamson, 1992; Hunt et al., 1994; Hunt and Benford, 2004). The merits of new social movement theory lies less in its role as a theory of social movements, but more as a method for analysing features that are shared by many contemporary social movements (Johnston et al., 1994, p.6). Therefore, scholars adopting the collective identity approach (Taylor and Whittier, 1992; Laraña et al., 1994) suggest that collective identity construction is crucial to all forms of collective action, not just new social movements. Therefore, whether the movement is organized on the basis of class, animal rights, environmentalism, gay and lesbian rights, the processes of maintaining those identities are similar (Polletta and Jasper, 2001; Bernstein, 2005, p.59).

In this analytical definition, the meaning of collective identity is influenced by social psychological, symbolic interactionist and social constructivist approaches: the social psychological influence inspires social movement scholars to examine the motivational factors that link the individual to the collective; the symbolic interactionist influence points to the interaction among movement participants; and the social constructionist influence stresses the process-based, self-reflexive and constructed manner in which collective actors define themselves (Johnston et al., 1994, p.17). However, these theories do not differentiate between the procedural aspects of collective identity created within social movement activity and those relatively stable forces of domination and subordination that are historically constituted and deeply entrenched within institutions and values of society. This is what Iris Marion Young called:

> systematic institutional processes which prevent some people from learning and using satisfying and expansive skills in socially recognized settings, or institutionalized social processes which inhibit people's ability to play and communicate with others in order to express their feelings and perspectives on social life in contexts where others can listen. (Young [1990] 2011, p.49)

Our argument is that there is a tendency to underemphasize social structural phenomena. Social movement analysis is subject to the biases of symbolic interactionism and social constructionism, whereby the analytical concepts of emergence, social construction, negotiating, framing and identity work emphasize the complex social processes and interactions that take place in social movements. This bias towards *process* means that there is not enough emphasis on enduring social relations informed by both naked and symbolic power (Morris and Braine, 2001, p.24). Thus, it is necessary to pay attention to issues of domination and subordination while maintaining a focus on the fluid processes of social construction and symbolic constructions of meaning. For example, Aldon Morris (1984) in his work on the black civil rights movement in the USA, demonstrated how a pre-existing institutional and cultural skeleton of opposition existed, which developed and matured into full-scale protest. He demonstrated how the groundwork for social protest had been laid by insurgent ideas in churches, voluntary associations, music and collective memories. He claimed that such ideas lie dormant within institutions, cultures and lifestyles of oppressed groups but come to the fore through political struggle (Morris, 1992, p.370).

The question as to the extent in which existing, inherited identities form the basis of mobilization, solidarity and continuity of struggle over time is important. Morris and Braine (2001) argue that the presence of an already existing oppositional culture means that the task for movement leaders is different from that of social movements whereby movement leaders need to create a collective identity from scratch. Amongst oppressed populations, there are already existing forms of collective identities and interpretative frames. The existence of these collective identities and interpretative frames of opposition amongst oppressed groups does not mean that they are always easily translated into collective action, however. Alongside these cultures of opposition, is the presence of cultures of subordination. As oppressed groups seek to survive within a system of domination and oppression, they devise strategies to help them cope; some of these include oppositional and critical ideas that challenge the dominant devaluation of them as a group, while other aspects of this culture can be submissive and subordinating, internalizing the devaluation of their group. This means that amongst the cultures of oppressed groups, an internal contest takes place between oppositional and subordinating elements. Social movement leaders seeking to mobilize such a constituency try to elevate the oppositional elements, rendering it an effective tool for protest (Morris and Braine, 2001, p.22).

The collective identity approach can be qualified to show how systems of domination and subordination play a role in creating oppositional cultures. While new social movement theorists classify movements based on ideology and values and those based on challenging a devalued social status as the same, Morris and Braine (2001) differentiate types of social movements according to their relationship to enduring systems of human domination. They produce a typology of three movement forms: (1) liberation, (2) equality-based special issue and (3) social responsibility movements:

1. The 'liberation movements' are aimed at overthrowing a particular system of domination and are comprised mostly of groups whose lives are (negatively) shaped by such a system. Members of such groups are often differentiated from dominant groups, on the basis of race, gender, ethnicity and/or class position. Liberation movements develop from the infrastructure offered by the already existing oppositional cultures; social movement leaders refine and shape a pre-existing consciousness (ibid., p.35).
2. The 'equality-based special issue movements' are special issue movements that mobilize pre-existing liberation ideologies and oppressed groups in a struggle against a specific mechanism of group oppression. In these movements, the task for leaders and organizers is to align the grievances and interpretations of the movement with those of liberation movements, such that they can adopt the legitimacy and cultural capital of such movements (ibid., pp.36–7).
3. Finally, 'social responsibility movements' seek to make individuals, corporations or governments act in a specific way that is socially responsible. This includes movements such as environmental movements and peace movements. The fundamental difference in this sort of movement, in comparison to the previous two movement types, is that a member of such a movement chooses to assume and internalize the appropriate movement identity. Participants in 'social responsibility movements' must make considerable effort to create the collective identities necessary to sustain activism within such movements. This means they must educate themselves and learn their identities centred around the particular cause the movement is engaged in.

The role of collective identities in a process of mobilization for group-differentiated citizenship is therefore both a rediscovery of traits suppressed by a system of cultural and political domination and the result of creative process based on ongoing interpretative work of the movement. The question remains, however, of how much of each and under what circumstances do these specific forms of struggle emerge (Mueller, 2003, p.274).

Institutional and Discursive Opportunities for Minority Claims-making

The political process models highlight the importance of the broader political systems in structuring the opportunities for collective action (McAdam et al., 1996, p.2), firmly placing the emphasis on a link between institutionalized politics and social movements (see Tilly, 1978; McAdam, 1982; Tarrow, 1983). Outcomes, of social movement activity, are measured through a combination of policy change and access to the structure of political bargaining (Bernstein, 1997, p.534). Forms of political action are shaped by the opportunities offered by the environment. As the political environment changes, movement strategies adapt accordingly. Hence, for Tilly (1978), forms of collective action will be affected by 'political coalitions' and 'the means of actions built into the existing political organization' (ibid., p.167). These 'political opportunities' include the opening of access to participation, the availability of influential allies, and cleavages among elites (Bernstein, 1997, p.534; cf. Tarrow, 1996; Kriesi, 2008).

In this understanding, the development of social movements seeking group-differentiated citizenship will depend on the opportunities and constraints offered by the environment in which it develops. Tilly (2002) argues that the historical, political and cultural contexts provide the basis for recognizing certain classes of identities as valid political actors. For example, countries may differ in the way they recognize ethnic minorities as specific groups; the categories that form the basis of their economic, political and cultural recognition will influence the categories around which the groups will mobilize (Statham, 1999; Koopmans et al., 2005).

This work is exemplified in the work of Koopmans et al. (2005) who explain the mobilization of ethnic minority political formations through opportunity structures. They illustrate that different conceptions of national identity as well as citizenship models act as opportunities and constraints, leading to different forms of minority mobilizations. Institutional opportunities and constraints determine formal access to citizenship and the institutional resources and channels available for participation, for example, voting, party representation of interests. The discursive side comprises the cultural notions of citizenship and national identity that affect the idea of what constitutes a member of the political community. This dimension comprises the cultural obligations that the state places on access to citizenship and amount of cultural difference and group rights allowed, defining what is a legitimate political actor, as well as the understandings around the relationship between minority and majority relations (ibid., p.6). By including this cultural dimension of political opportunities into the framework of analysis, this model answers critiques that claim that the political process model neglects cultural factors in analysing the forms and development of collective action (Goodwin and Jasper, 1999; Armstrong and Bernstein, 2008). By considering both discursive and political opportunities, the state is understood in both symbolic and material terms as an enforcer of rights and obligations as well as a producer of meaning (Armstrong and Bernstein, 2008, p.92).

This work has been comparative, examining the distinct political and discursive contexts across different national frameworks for minority claims-making. For example, Cinalli and Giugni (2013), in a study on Muslim claims-making across five European countries (Britain, France, Germany, the Netherlands and Switzerland), apply the criteria developed by Koopmans et al. (2005) specifically to those that impact on Muslims as a group, and conclude that the political context accounts for the main variation in Muslim claims-making across the different countries. This addresses earlier criticisms that suggest the political process model lacks the specificity to analyse why and under what conditions movements choose certain forms of collective action (Bernstein, 1997, p.534).

POLITICAL IDENTITY FRAMEWORK

Bernstein offers a synthesis between the collective identity and political process models by offering a framework that can consider the variety of possibilities for the political use of identity – both in form (goal or strategy) and in content (sameness and difference). This means situating the political uses of identities that are based on social location within the political environment in which it takes place (Bernstein, 1997, 2008).

Identity is considered to operate in social movements at three levels. First, identity is considered at the level of empowerment, that is, the collective identity that movements create in order to mobilize a collective group and translate individual interests into a group-based collectivity. Second, identity operates at the level of goal, whereby identity becomes the target of change sought by movement. For example, movements may challenge the stigma attached to certain identities, challenge the restrictive categories of certain identities or seek recognition for new identities altogether. Third, identity is considered to be a strategy, such that the movement deploys certain identities in order to achieve certain goals (Bernstein, 1997, p.537).

Massoumi (forthcoming) adapts this approach to understand the ways in which Muslim activists develop their political subjectivities within the movement against the 'War on Terror'. This movement, in forging opposition to the War on Terror, can be classified as a 'social responsibility' movement (Morris and Braine, 2001), whereby the collective identities, organizations and forms of 'oppositional consciousness' would have to be developed from scratch. However, the War on Terror disproportionately targeted Muslim minorities, and in forging opposition to this the movement mobilized significant numbers of Muslim individuals and groups. The study showed that in creating the collective identity against the War on Terror, the movement was heavily influenced by the position of Muslims within the existing systems of domination and subordination. The movement aligned with the mobilizing efforts of many Muslim groups, and emphasized the disproportionate impact of the War on Terror on these groups. The movement incorporated goals particular to Muslim groups, including their struggle for acceptance in Britain, and seeking wider politicization of this constituency.

The movement confronted a range of different targets. This included both political and cultural dimensions, including the wars against Iraq and Afghanistan, anti-terror legislation, campaigns against the civil liberty, violations of prisoners detained as terrorists, as well as challenges to discursive representations of Muslims. In order to achieve these goals, the movement strategically deployed both a liberal Muslim identity that emphasized the compatibility between forms of Muslim political participation and liberal British citizenship, alongside a critical anti-imperialist Muslim identity that transcended the radical/liberal divisions of Muslim identities. However, the study showed that the movement varied its deployment of such forms of Muslim identity according to the opportunities and constraints offered by the political environment, the type and nature of interaction with other social and political actors, and the audience targeted at different points of movement activity (Massoumi, forthcoming).

KNOWN KNOWNS AND KNOWN UNKNOWNS

The public policies that have resulted from political struggles for citizenship, and the relationship these bear to the social, economic and political advancement of minorities, are not easy things to measure because some countries do not collect the appropriate kinds of data (e.g., ethnicity-specific statistics and monitoring) to be able to carry out the necessary research. Inevitably, therefore, we need to concentrate on what is available and where, and for cross-national questions this is sometimes easier to assess through attitude surveys. Beginning with a more identity-centred approach, Berry et al. (2006) use the International Comparative Study of Ethnocultural Youth (which focuses on 13 countries and takes in 5000 young people) to argue that policies and discourses of multiculturalism (e.g., plural national identities, equal opportunity monitoring, effective anti-discrimination legislation and enforcement), encourage a more successful and deeply established integration in those settings. This is consistent with the wider summary of Kymlicka (2012, p.48) who states that 'many studies have shown that immigrants do best, both in terms of psychological well-being and socio-cultural outcomes, when they combine their ethnic identity with a new national identity'. In the British case, this is supported by Heath and Roberts (2008, p.2), who in their analyses of the UK Government's Citizenship Survey, report: 'We find no evidence that Muslims or people of Pakistani heritage were in general less attached to Britain than were other religions or ethnic groups. Ethnic minorities show clear evidence of "dual" rather than "exclusive" identities'. They point instead to 'hyphenated identities',[2] in showing that 43 per cent of Muslims belong 'very strongly' to Britain and 42 per cent say that they belong to Britain 'fairly strongly', and taken together these figures are higher for Muslim respondents than they are for Christians and those of 'no religion'. This is now widely accepted and is reiterated by Wind-Cowie and Gregory (2011):

> Our polling shows that 88 per cent of Anglicans and Jews agreed that they were 'proud to be a British citizen' alongside 84 per cent of non-conformists and 83 per cent of Muslims – compared with 79 per cent for the population as a whole. [p.39]... This optimism in British Muslims is significant as – combined with their high score for pride in British – it runs counter to a prevailing narrative about Muslim dissatisfaction with and in the UK. While it is true that there are significant challenges to integration for some in the British Muslim community – and justified concern at the levels of radicalism and extremism in some British Muslim communities – overall British Muslims are more likely to be both patriotic and optimistic about Britain than are the white British community [p.41].

Elsewhere, there is a robust debate on the position of minorities in the Netherlands, where the dispute centres on the role of a relatively closed labour market (for minorities) (Duyvendak and Scholten, 2011). Another study shows us that when we are able to control for other factors, when the same ethnic minority group (with the same pre-arrival characteristics) enters two different countries at the same time, the group who are in the multicultural context fare much better (Bloemraad, 2006). In her study, Bloemraad (2006) compared the integration of two Vietnamese groups in Toronto and Canada respectively, and then repeated this for Portuguese minorities. According to Kymlicka (2012, p.46), in these cases Canada's proactive multicultural policies 'sent a clear message that Vietnamese [and Portuguese] political participation is welcome, and have also provided material and logistical support for self-organization and political representation of the community'.

FUTURE DIRECTIONS

Since '9/11' the fate of multiculturalism has become intertwined with political debates about Muslim integration, but these political debates have wider implications for the place of religion in plural societies. In some places this question has turned into a radical reform and prohibition, for example, the 2004 parliamentary ban in France on the wearing of 'ostentatious' religious symbols, primarily the hijab (headscarf), in public schools. Yet, as Modood and Meer (2013) remind us, in most if not all European countries there are points of symbolic, institutional, policy, and fiscal linkages between the state and aspects of Christianity. Secularism has increasingly grown in power and scope, but a historically evolved and evolving compromise with religion is the defining feature of European, especially North-Western European secularism, rather than the absolute separation of religion and politics. Secularism today enjoys hegemony in Western Europe, but it is a moderate rather than a radical secularism (Modood, 2013). What this means is that while the appeal of multiculturalism as a public policy has suffered considerable political damage, the intellectual and policy argument that multiculturalism is a valuable means of remaking public identities in order to achieve an equality of citizenship that is neither merely individualistic nor premised on assimilation, remains powerful and unlikely to be erased. Indeed, appeals to multiculturalism have emerged more diffusely in arguments that favour interculturalism, inclusive national identities, community cohesion, and so forth. What needs to be kept mind, therefore, is that multiculturalism is not concerned with creating silos; quite the opposite in fact, for it has both been a concept both intellectually and politically concerned with synthesis, and politically has promoted the idea of integration as a mutual outgrowth of its constituent parts.

CONCLUSIONS

In this chapter we have set out how, while citizenship takes a legal form, it also operates socially through the reciprocal balance of rights and responsibilities that confer upon its bearers a civic status that affords those bearers equal opportunity, dignity and confidence. As such it represents a field in which 'political and social rights, and cultural obligations [can be] contested by collective action' (Statham, 1999, p.599), often with the aim of overcoming frames that make formal citizenship 'exclusive in practice'. In seeking 'a differentiated universalism as opposed to the false universalism of traditional citizenship theory' (Squires, 2002, p.117), we considered, first, how contemporary citizenship continues to reflect tensions arising from its exclusionary aspects, and how this may be particularly evidenced around sociological cleavages of gender, sexuality, class, race, ethnicity, religion, and so forth. Second, we explored how an inclusive citizenship capable of challenging or overcoming these cleavages – through contestation – is a relatively recent development in accounts of citizenship and civic status. Drawing together both multicultural political theory and new social movements literature, our argument is that if we adopt a 'pluralistic conception of oppression', as operating through interlocking systems, then movements formed on the basis of the politics of difference are not simply engaging into cultural politics, but are actually engaged in political action where the goal is to challenge decision-making processes, division of labour and evaluation of worth in society. The role of collective identities in a process of mobilization for group-differentiated citizenship is therefore both a rediscovery of traits suppressed by a system of cultural and political domination and the result of creative process, based on ongoing interpretative work of the movement. This forever renews the 'challenge' of citizenship.

NOTES

1. This section draws on Meer (2014).
2. Ethno-cultural dual identity.

REFERENCES

Aristotle (1986), *The Politics*, trans. T. Saunders, Harmondsworth: Penguin.
Armstrong, E.A. and B. Bernstein (2008), 'Culture, power, and institutions: a multi-institutional politics approach to social movements', *Sociological Theory*, **26**(1), 74–99.
Austin, C.J. (2006), *Up Against the Wall: Violence in the Making: An Unmaking of the Black Panther Party*, Fayetteville, AR: University of Arkansas Press.
Barry, B. (2002), 'Second thoughts; some first thoughts revived', in P. Kelly (ed.), *Multiculturalism Reconsidered*, Cambridge, UK: Polity.
Benhabib, S. (2002), *The Claims of Culture: Equality and Diversity in a Global Era*, Princeton, NJ: Princeton University Press.
Bernstein, M. (1997), 'Celebration and suppression: the strategic uses of identity by the lesbian and gay movement', *American Journal of Sociology*, **103**(3), 531–65.
Bernstein, M. (2005), 'Identity politics', *Annual Review of Sociology*, **31**(1), 47–74.
Bernstein, M. (2008), 'The analytic dimensions of identity: a political identity framework', in J. Reger, D. Myers and R. Einwohner (eds), *Identity Work in Social Movements*, Minneapolis, MN: University of Minnesota Press, pp.277–302.
Berry, J.W., J.S. Phinney, D.L. Sam and P. Vedder (2006), *Immigrant Youth in Cultural Transition*, Mahwah, NJ: Lawrence Erlbaum.
Bhabha, H.K. (1998), 'Culture's in between', in D. Bennett (ed.), *Multicultural States: Rethinking Difference and Identity*, London: Routledge.
Bloemraad, I. (2006), *Becoming a Citizen: Incorporating Immigrants and Refugees in the United States and Canada*, Berkeley, CA: University of California Press.

Calhoun, C. (1993), '"New social movements" of the early 19th century', *Social Science History*, **17**(3), 385–427.
Castles, S. and A. Davidson (2000), *Citizenship and Migration*, Houndmills, UK: Palgrave Macmillan.
Cinalli, M. and M. Giugni (2013), 'Political opportunities, citizenship models and political claims-making over Islam', *Ethnicities*, **13**(2), 147–64.
Duyvendak, W.G.J. and P.W.A. Scholten (2011), 'The invention of the Dutch multicultural model and its effects on integration discourses in the Netherlands', *Perspectives on Europe*, **40**(2), 39–45.
Dynesson, T.L. (2001), *Civism: Cultivating Citizenship in European History*, New York: Peter Lang.
Fraser, N. (1997), *Justice Interruptus: Critical Reflections on the 'Postsocialist' Condition*, London: Routledge.
Gamson, W. (1992), *Talking Politics*, Cambridge, UK: Cambridge University Press.
Goodwin, J. and J.M. Jasper (1999), 'Caught in a winding, snarling vine: the structural bias of political process theory', *Sociological Forum*, **14**(1), 27–54.
Gutmann, A. (1994), 'Introduction', in A. Gutmann (ed.) (1994), *Multiculturalism. Examining the Politics of Recognition*, Princeton, NJ: Princeton University Press.
Heath, A. and J. Roberts (2008), *British Identity, Its Sources and Possible Implications for Civic Attitudes and Behaviour*, London: HMSO.
Hobson, B. (2003), 'Introduction', in B. Hobson (ed.) (2003), *Recognition Struggles and Social Movements: Contested Identities, Agency and Power*, Cambridge, UK: Cambridge University Press, pp.1–17.
Hunt, S.A. and R. Benford (2004), 'Collective identity, solidarity and commitment', in H. Kriesi, D.A. Snow and S.A. Soule (eds), *Blackwell Companion to Social Movements*, Oxford: Blackwell, pp.433–57.
Hunt, S.A, R.D. Benford and D.A. Snow (1994), 'Identity fields: framing processes and the social construction of movement identities', in E. Laraña, H. Johnston and J.R. Gusfield (eds), *New Social Movements: From Ideology to Identity*, Philadelphia, PA: Temple University Press, pp.185–208.
Johnston, H., E. Laraña and J.R. Gusfield (1994), 'Identities, grievances, and new social movements', in E. Laraña, H. Johnston and J.R. Gusfield (eds), *New Social Movements: From Ideology to Identity*, Philadelphia, PA: Temple University Press, pp.3–35.
Kauffman, L.A. (2001), 'The anti-politics of identity', in B. Ryan (ed.), *Identity Politics in the Women's Movement*, New York/London: New York University Press.
Kelly, P. (2002), 'Between culture and equality', in P. Kelly (ed.), *Multiculturalism Reconsidered*, Cambridge, UK: Polity.
Kivisto, P. and T. Faist (2007), *Citizenship: Discourse, Theory, and Transnational Prospects*, Oxford: Blackwell.
Klandermans, B. (1984), 'Mobilization and participation: social-psychological expansions of resource mobilization theory', *Annual Sociological Review*, **49**(5), pp.583–600.
Koopmans, R., P. Statham, M. Giugni and F. Passy (2005), *Contested Citizenship: Immigration and Cultural Diversity*, Minneapolis, MN: University of Minnesota Press.
Kriesi, H. (2008), 'Political opportunity context', in H. Kriesi, D.A. Snow and S.A. Soule (eds), *Blackwell Companion to Social Movements*, Oxford: Blackwell, pp.67–90.
Kymlicka, W. (2012), 'Multiculturalism: success, failure, and the future', in Migration Policy Institute (ed.), *Rethinking National Identity in the Age of Migration*, Bielefeld: Verlag Bertelsmann Stiftung.
Laraña, L., H. Johnston and J.R. Gusfield (eds) (1994), *New Social Movements: From Ideology to Identity*, Philadelphia, PA: Temple University Press.
Marshall, T.H. ([1950] 1997), *Citizenship and Social Class and Other Essays*, Cambridge, UK: Cambridge University Press.
Massoumi, N. (forthcoming), *Muslim Women, Social Movements and the 'War on Terror'*, Houndmills, UK: Palgrave Macmillan.

May, S., T. Modood and J. Squires (2004) (eds), *Ethnicity, Nationalism, and Minority Rights*, Cambridge, UK: Cambridge University Press.
McAdam, D. (1982), *Political Process and the Development of Black Insurgency 1930–1970*, Chicago, IL: University of Chicago Press.
McAdam, D. (2002), 'Beyond structural analysis: toward a more dynamic understanding of social movements', in M. Diani and D. McAdam (eds) (2002), *Social Movements and Networks: Relational Approaches to Collective Action*, Oxford: Oxford University Press, pp.281–98.
McAdam, D., J. McCarthy and M.N. Zald (eds) (1996), *Comparative Perspective on Social Movements: Political Opportunities, Mobilising Structures, and Cultural Framings*, Cambridge, UK: Cambridge University Press.
McCarthy, J. and M. Zald (1977), 'Resource mobilisation and social movements a partial theory', *American Journal of Sociology*, **82**(6), 1212–41.
Meer, N. (2010), *Citizenship, Identity and the Politics of Multiculturalism*, Houndmills, UK: Palgrave Macmillan.
Meer, N. (2014), *Race & Ethnicity*, London: Sage.
Meer, N. and T. Modood (2009), 'The multicultural state we're in: Muslims, "multiculture", and the civic re-balancing of British multiculturalism', *Political Studies*, **57**(1), 473–9.
Melucci, A. (1989), *Nomads of the Present: Social Movements and Individual Needs in Contemporary Society*, London: Hutchinson.
Melucci, A. (1996), *Challenging Codes: Collective Action in the Information Age*, Cambridge, UK: Cambridge University Press.
Millett, K. (1970), *Sexual Politics*, Garden City, NY: Doubleday.
Modood, T. (2007), *Multiculturalism: A Civic Idea*, Cambridge, UK: Polity.
Modood, T. (2009), 'Ethnicity and religion', in M. Flinders, A. Gamble, C. Hay and M. Kenny (eds), *The Oxford Handbook of British Politics*, Oxford: Oxford University Press, pp.484–99.
Modood, T. (2013), *Multiculturalism*, Cambridge, UK: Polity.
Modood, T. and N. Meer (2013), 'Multiculturalism', in J. Krieger (ed.), *The Oxford Companion to Comparative Politics*, Oxford: Oxford University Press.
Morris, A. (1984), *The Origins of the Civil Rights Movement*, New York: Free Press.
Morris, A. (1992), 'Political consciousness and collective action', in A. Morris and M. Mueller (eds), *Frontiers of Social Movement Theory*, New Haven, CT: Yale University Press.
Morris, A. and N. Braine (2001), 'Social movements and oppositional consciousness', in J. Mansbridge and A. Morris (eds), *Oppositional Consciousness: The Subjective Roots of Social Protest*, Chicago, IL: Chicago University Press, pp.20–37.
Mueller, C. (2003), '"Recognition struggles" and process theories of social movements', in B. Hobson (ed.), *Recognition Struggles and Social Movements: Contested Identities, Agency and Power*, Cambridge, UK: Cambridge University Press, pp.274–91.
Olson, M. (1965), *The Logic of Collective Action: Public Goods and the Theory of Groups*, Cambridge, MA: Harvard University Press.
Olssen, M. (2004), 'From Crick report to Parekh report: multiculturalism, cultural difference, and democracy – the re-visioning of citizenship education', *British Journal of Sociology of Education*, **25**(2), 179–91.
Parekh, B. (2000), *Rethinking Multiculturalism*, Houndmills, UK: Palgrave Macmillan.
Pichardo, N.A. (1997), 'New social movements: a critical review', *Annual Review of Sociology*, **23**, 411–30.
Polletta, F.J. and J. Jasper (2001), 'Collective identity and social movement', *Annual Review of Sociology*, **27**(1), 283–305.
Smelser, N. (1962), *Theory of Collective Behaviour*, London: Routledge & Kegan Paul.
Smith, K. (2010), 'Research, policy and funding – academic treadmills and the squeeze on intellectual spaces', *The British Journal of Sociology*, **61**(1), 176–95.
Squires, J. (2002), 'Culture, equality and diversity', in P. Kelly (ed.), *Multiculturalism Reconsidered*, Cambridge, UK: Polity.

Statham, P. (1999), 'Political mobilisation by minorities in Britain: a negative feedback of "race relations"?', *Journal of Ethnic and Migration Studies*, **25**(4), 597–626.

Tarrow, S. (1983), *Struggling to Reform: Social Movements and Policy Changes During Cycles of Protest*, Ithaca, NY: Cornell University.

Tarrow, S. (1996), 'States and opportunities: The political structuring of social movements', in D.McAdam, J.D. McCarthy, M. Zald (eds), *Comparative Perspectives on Social Movements*, Cambridge, UK: Cambridge University Press.

Taylor, V. and N. Whittier (1992), 'Collective identity in social movement communities: lesbian feminist mobilization', in A.D. Morris and M. Mueller (eds), *Frontiers of Social Movement Theory*, New Haven, CT: Yale University Press, pp.104–30.

Thucydides (1964), *The Peloponnesian War*, Harmondsworth, UK: Penguin.

Tilly, C. (1978), *From Mobilisation to Revolution*, Reading, MA: Addison-Wesley.

Tilly, C. (2002), *Stories, Identities, and Political Change*, Lanham, MD: Rowman & Littlefield.

Touraine, A. (1981), *The Voice and the Eye: An Analysis of Social Movements*, Cambridge, UK: Cambridge University Press.

Tully, J. (2002), 'The illiberal liberal', in P. Kelly (ed.), *Multiculturalism Reconsidered*, Cambridge, UK: Polity.

Turner, R. and L. Killian (1957), *Collective Behaviour*, Englewood Cliffs, NJ: Prentice-Hall.

Uberoi, V. and T. Modood (2013), 'Inclusive Britishness – a multiculturalist advance', *Political Studies*, **61**(1), 23–41.

Wind-Cowie, M. and T. Gregory (2011), *A Place for Pride*, London: Demos.

Young, I.M. (1990), *Justice and the Politics of Difference*, Princeton, NJ: Princeton University Press.

Young, I.M. ([1990] 2011), *Justice and the Politics of Difference*, Princeton, NJ: Princeton University Press.

6. Ecological citizenship
Sherilyn MacGregor

Perhaps more than any other social movement, environmentalism has succeeded in changing the way citizenship is theorized. Until the 1960s few political scientists acknowledged the relevance of the natural environment. Today most contemporary texts on citizenship cite transboundary environmental problems like toxic pollution and climate change as reasons for why traditional liberal and nation-state–based understandings of citizenship have become outdated. Environmental issues are increasingly placed at the centre of arguments for conceiving a post-liberal citizenship on a global scale and for the development of institutions of world governance. The concept of 'ecological citizenship' has become a key theme in green political thought, as growing numbers of theorists argue that an 'ecological democracy' is a better means of averting the environmental crisis than the authoritarian strategies favoured by earlier theorists. There is now a sizable body of 'green' literature on citizenship that stands firm on the point that the only political arrangement that will work in conditions of radical uncertainty – such as the ecological crisis – is a democratic one where the voices of as many citizens as possible participate in public debate, and where citizens accept responsibility for improving human–nature relationships. However, the definition and contours of the concept of ecological citizenship remain deeply contested within the discipline.

In addition to becoming a topic of debate among green political theorists, the concept of ecological citizenship is increasingly being deployed by governments and environmental non-governmental organizations (ENGOs) as part of an institutional environmental agenda. With growing concern over global warming and the need to reduce carbon emissions by changing consumption choices, the role of individual citizens has been placed at the centre of strategies for climate change mitigation and adaptation. The promotion of 'pro-environmental behaviour' has become at least as important as, and possibly more important than, the regulation of markets, industries and institutions. It remains to be seen whether the end result will be a public-spirited green citizen who challenges the neoliberal marketization and de-politicization of environmental change or a green citizen-consumer who shops their way out of the crisis. But on this point most will agree: the ecological citizen will be at the centre of environmental governance at all levels for the foreseeable future.

This chapter provides a review of where the academic discussion of ecological citizenship has come from and where it may be going, with a consideration of troublesome potholes and scenic vistas along the way. The journey begins with a short account of the emergence and evolution of the concept and then provides an overview of three major currents of thinking about ecological citizenship within the environmental politics literature: liberal, republican and (post-)cosmopolitan theoretical approaches. Examining these different approaches unavoidably leads to a set of debates among them over definitions and emphases, a discussion of which appears in the third section. Most theoretical debates include a call for further research, so in the fourth section the focus turns to the small but growing body of empirical research that has used ecological citizenship as a framework for analysing people's values and actions. We then consider the views of the critics: those who have raised important challenges to some of the visions of ecological citizenship from perspectives outside the main theoretical tent: ecofeminism, environmental justice and critical environmental sociology. Some thoughts about important new questions that are being asked and future directions for the concept of ecological citizenship in a 'post-political' world are provided in the concluding section of the chapter.

THE GREENING OF CITIZENSHIP: A SHORT HISTORY OF AN IDEA

It is difficult to give a precise starting point for when the greening of citizenship began, but the mid-1990s is a best estimate. One of the first essays to consider the connection between citizenship and the environment was written by Fred Steward in 1991. He uses the phase 'citizenship of planet earth' to capture his vision of a new, globalized understanding of citizenship. By virtue of living on this planet, he argues, citizens have a 'right to a common human inheritance regardless of nation' to the 'the earth's planetary resources of atmosphere, ocean, genetics'. They also 'owe a duty of care to the planet in terms of minimizing resource consumption and pollution' (Steward, 1991, pp. 74–5). For Steward, the concept involves recognizing the need for the regulation of industry in order to curb environmental degradation, 'which itself entails a necessary foregoing of some elements of local and national sovereignty' (ibid., p. 75). These early ideas were explored and expanded throughout the 1990s by a number of political theorists from Europe (e.g., Van Steenbergen, 1994; Newby, 1996; Smith, 1998; Barry, 1999), North America (e.g., Curtin, 1999; Torgerson, 1999) and Australia (e.g., Christoff, 1996; Eckersley, 2004). It is fair to say that the literature on ecological citizenship still comes almost exclusively from the affluent world, largely from the UK, the USA and Canada, Australia, Spain and Sweden.

Since the early 2000s, there has been an explosion of publications on ecological and environmental citizenship, mostly notably with the publication of Andrew Dobson's *Citizenship and the Environment* in 2003 and the edited collection *Environmental Citizenship* (Dobson and Bell, 2006), which have become the most widely cited volumes to date. The pages of *Environmental Politics* (*EP*) journal (established in 1992) has been a forum for discussion and development of the concept, with a special issue on the topic in 2005 and about 30 articles published since then. Interestingly, the first article to appear in *EP* was Eric Darier's (1996) Foucaultian critique of the Government of Canada's Green Plan (1990), the first government document to use the phrase 'environmental citizenship' and perhaps even the first to coin it.[1] Although there seems to have been a decline in published monographs in recent years, there continues to be a regular stream of manuscript submissions to *EP* on the topic.[2] Manuel Arias-Maldonado (2012) calls ecological citizenship the 'most recent and promising development in green political thought' (p. 159), however, it remains very much 'a fresh arrival' (Latta and Garside, 2005) and 'an infant concept' (Melo-Escrihuela, 2008a) that is 'under construction' (Arias-Maldonado, 2012, p. 161).

Why did this new concept take off when it did? The most obvious reason is that it was part of a wider revival of citizenship as a concept in political theory. As Derek Bell observes, it was the environmentalist contribution to 'the many new forms of adjectival citizenship, which have emerged since the resurgence of interest in citizenship theory' in the latter years of the twentieth century (2005, p. 179). It should not be surprising that citizenship became a focus of new work in the environmental politics field, because green political thinkers have engaged in critique and re-visioning of all institutions of liberal democracy. Moreover, environmental politics as a field is devoted to reformulating the discipline of politics 'as if nature mattered' (Carter, 2004). For most of its history, political theorists, and political scientists more generally, have failed to acknowledge the relevance of 'nature', or the biophysical environment, to the sphere of politics. The transboundary nature of environmental problems (climate change, most obviously) provides a good reason for why traditional understandings of citizenship are insufficient. Recognition of this point initiated a process of rethinking both the spatial and temporal constructions of citizenship as being confined to people living in the here and now in nation-states. As we shall see in the next section, green political theorists have gone further than this to develop a literature on citizenship that transforms the traditional meaning of citizenship to accommodate green concerns. At the same time, the turn to citizenship arguably represents recognition that instead of state-imposed strategies (e.g., fiscal measures) 'sustainability requires shifts in attitudes at a deep level', meaning at the level of individuals (Dobson and Bell, 2006, p. 4).

Another question to ask as part of this short history has to do with the name itself: is it environmental or ecological citizenship? Some authors use these terms interchangeably (cf. Latta and Garside, 2005). Dobson (2003) has distinguished between environmental citizenship, which he associates with a liberal reformist approach, and ecological citizenship, which comes from a more radical, cosmopolitan tradition (see also Dobson, 2007; Van Steenbergen, 1994 makes a similar distinction). There are some who opt to dodge this debate by using 'green' as a catch-all term (e.g., Dean, 2001; Trachtenberg, 2010) and others who have offered new labels altogether, such as 'sustainability citizenship' (which has thus far not caught hold; Barry, 2006). A recent survey of the literature suggests that more academics are now using ecological rather than environmental citizenship, perhaps because they wish to respect Dobson's distinction and to avoid lying in the same bed as environmental managers and bureaucrats. Many theorists criticize the institutional invocation of environmental citizenship in policy discourse, while wanting to imagine what a 'real' green ecological citizenship might entail. There is an obvious desire to align the work in this field of green political thought with environmentalism as a social movement that is counter-hegemonic and able to resist the dominant, neoliberal paradigm.

Before moving to an explanation of the different currents of thinking on this topic, it is helpful to answer a third question: why green *citizenship*? Or, asked another way, why have green thinkers elected to make citizenship a key part of their political vision? To some, citizenship may seem more conventional and less radical than the activism and collectivism that have animated the green movement since the 1960s. The origins of the concept of ecological citizenship lie in the turn, in the early 1990s, to democracy and, more specifically, to direct and deliberative democracy in environmental politics (Bookchin, 1992; Latta and Garside, 2005). For serious change to happen, environmentalism had to move from margins to mainstream and bring more people together from a wider population than the counter-culture. What is more, it was recognized that moving towards a 'sustainable society' (or a less unsustainable one) will require answers to fundamentally political questions: how should people live together and distribute finite resources fairly to meet needs? Unless a Leviathan-style authoritarian ruler comes along to 'save us' (which most people agree is an undesirable prospect), it will be necessary to involve citizens democratically in the process of eco-social change. The argument is that citizen involvement will not only enable good policies, but will also ensure the consent of all concerned. And people with pro-environmental values must have their interests represented if there is to be a democratic transition to a sustainable society. This is what Robyn Eckersley (2004) means by an ecological democracy in a green state. And this vision of a political move towards a just and democratic sustainable society requires ecological citizens.

ECOLOGICAL CITIZENSHIP THEORY: DEFINITIONS AND DEBATES

That ecological citizenship is a normative concept that is 'under construction' (Valencia Sáiz, 2005) is due in large part to the fact that even though many theorists accept a general definition of what it entails, few want to prescribe a blueprint and thereby put an end to the process of debating its precise contours. There is a diversity of different interpretations of the relationship of ecological citizenship to traditional definitions of citizenship. It is important to take stock briefly of three main currents of thought that have dominated the academic development of the concept of ecological citizenship – liberal, republican and (post-)cosmopolitan[3] – before sketching out the patch of common definitional ground that exists today. These approaches to citizenship were already established before an ecological challenge came along: each one attempts to apply central traditional features to an understanding of ecological citizenship. In the case of liberals and republicans, it is a matter of giving rights, responsibilities and actions a 'green tinge'. In the case of cosmopolitans, however, the challenge to traditional citizenship is arguably more fundamental (Dobson, 2003, 2006a, 2006b) and more controversial as a result.

Liberal Environmental Citizenship: Participatory and Substantive Rights

A number of green political theorists have offered an immanent critique of liberal conceptions of citizenship at the same time as offering a definition of liberal environmental citizenship. Bell (2005), for example, offers a liberal interpretation of what it might mean, theoretically, to be 'a citizen of an environment'. He starts from a position of wanting to address the weaknesses of liberal theory on matters environmental, primarily that it sees the biophysical world as mere property as opposed to providing basic needs for human survival. The recommended reform of liberal citizenship involves the addition of an environmental dimension to the traditional framework of civil, political and social rights (Hailwood, 2005). Unsurprisingly, the main issue that interests liberals is the environmental rights that individuals are owed by virtue of having the legal status of a citizen as conferred by the state. Few liberals offer much beyond a minimal definition that provides maximum scope for individual freedom. The reason for this is that if one is to be loyal to the meaning of political liberalism, then it is necessary to maintain state neutrality and to avoid a substantive definition of the common environmental good or 'the good life'. Keeping the definition open to 'reasonable disagreement' via democratic deliberation among citizens is key to a liberal understanding of environmental citizenship.

The theoretical case for the liberal environmental rights of citizens is made by Tim Hayward (2005) who argues that the substantive right to a clean and liveable environment should be included in the constitutions of all modern democracies. Substantive environmental rights may be understood as resembling T.H. Marshall's (1950) argument for social rights: the state has a duty to provide citizens with the conditions for exercising their political and civil rights. In a similar way, it is argued that adequate environmental quality is a necessary condition for human functioning and therefore should be protected by law. Hayward (2005, p. 5) argues that neither treating environmental rights as social rights (and lumping them in with social policy) nor restricting them to procedural rights is good enough. In his view, for environmental rights to 'have teeth' they need to be binding rights on a par with human rights and they need to be included in constitutions. In fact, many countries have officially recognized the rights of citizens in environmental matters. Prompted by Agenda 21 (UNCED, 1992), the most common manifestation of environmental rights comes in the form of procedural rights, meaning rights to participate in environmental decision-making. The most important example is the Aarhus Convention, which came into force in the European Community in 2001 to give citizens the right to access to information, participation in decision-making and access to justice on local, national and transnational environmental issues. Civil society organizations and individual citizens can invoke their Aarhus rights in order to challenge government decisions when it is suspected that they have not followed fair and transparent procedures.

Although Arias-Maldonado (2012) suggests, perhaps rightly, that rights-based liberal environmental citizenship may be the most practical approach in the face of contemporary socio-political realities (i.e., that most environmental arguments are made within existing liberal democracies), there remains reluctance to accept this comparatively minimalist position on the part of most green political theorists. In fact, one may detect a renewed anti-liberalism in the face of climate change and other pressing 'existential threats' (Porritt, 2013). That is to say, more environmentalists are currently more interested in how to compel people to act in pro-environmental ways than in how to preserve individual liberty and freedom. It is probably fair to say that the liberal position is in the minority of contemporary work on ecological citizenship and comes up against the most resistance of any of the currents. There are several ways in which liberalism seems fundamentally incompatible with environmentalism. The liberal emphasis on citizen rights has been drowned out by the majority of theorists writing about ecological citizenship who choose to emphasize virtues, duties and responsibilities over rights. These are the republican and the (post-)cosmopolitan greens.

Republican Ecological Citizenship: Individual Green Virtues

The second major current of ecological citizenship theory shares a commitment to participatory rights and liberal democratic ideals, but is not content simply to reform liberal democratic institutions to include environmental concerns. A much more radial reorganization at the level of the state and changes to individual citizens' character are necessary if a sustainable society is to be achievable. For example, Mark Smith (1998) defines the green citizen as 'an individual who recognizes their duties in relation to the environment and takes responsibility to act in line with those duties' (p. 281). Consistent with the civic republican tradition, the emphasis here is on deliberative democracy and the cultivation of individual virtues of responsibility and stewardship among the participants in this system. In fact, the deliberative arena is itself the place where citizens may learn to be green and virtuous.

For green republicans, an important type of pro-environmental behaviour is 'having a say' through civic participation. John Barry (2006), for example, advocates the cultivation of active ecological citizenship in civil society rather than compelling people to follow the rules devised by the state. He argues that ecological citizens have a duty to participate so that they might challenge environmentally destructive development and demand the kinds of changes that would bring about sustainability. So not only do they have the right to participate (as enshrined, for example, in the Aarhus Convention), they also have a civic duty to participate in the political process, as ecological citizens. This participation ranges from getting involved in public consultations on environmentally risky proposals to engaging in non-violent direct action to try to stop development from going ahead. Barry (2006) goes as far as to suggest that ecological citizenship might include a form of 'compulsory sustainability service' (pp. 28–9) similar to national (military) service. This proposal stems from his view that civic participation is good not only because it ensures that the path to sustainability is democratic but also because, consistent with republicanism, it is an end in itself. It is in active citizenship that humans fulfil their true potential.

Unlike liberals who refuse to sign up to a normative end state, the idea of the common good and 'the good life' figure prominently in republican conceptions of ecological citizenship (Barry, 1999, 2006, 2008; Dean, 2001; Smith, 2005). There is a belief in both individual duty to the common good (including the health of the ecosystem) and in the need for a vibrant participatory politics that can challenge the detrimental forces of greed and corruption in a capitalist state (Cannavò, 2012). At the same time, ecological citizenship offers the hope that, through political participation, people will adopt the kind of values and characteristics that will prompt them to bring about the radical transformation of society towards a more ecologically rational nature–society relationship (Barry, 1999). However, there is an obvious problem: as is often noted about republican politics, there is no guarantee that democratic process will lead to the desired outcomes. For those who are concerned with sustainability, there is a paradox: 'citizens might democratically decide to keep on sustaining the unsustainable' (Melo-Escrihuela, 2008a, p. 119).

(Post-)Cosmopolitan Ecological Citizenship: Global Responsibilities

Many of the early conceptions of ecological citizenship from the middle 1990s were prompted by an awareness of the transnational nature of environmental concerns and the concomitant desire to see all people as citizens of one planet with one 'common future'. Since then, a global conception of ecological citizenship has developed that regards citizenship as not tied strictly to the nation-state or territory; in other words, as being both post-national and global. Global ecological citizenship is typically defined as including the right to a non-polluted environment and the responsibility both to refrain from harming the environment and to participate in its preservation and rehabilitation (Jelin, 2000). It demands an understanding of environmental problems as global in scope and a realization that acting locally – although necessary – will not be sufficient for solving them. While local loyalties are not ruled out, global environmental citizens must also hold allegiance to 'our planet, the shared environment of humanity and fellow creatures' (Attfield, 1999, p. 1). In that it departs from exclusively nation-state–based notions of citizenship and supports universal virtues and ethical principles that may improve intra-human as well as human–nature relationships, this approach might be given the name 'green cosmopolitanism'. International ENGOs that promote international solidarity and cooperation on environmental policy issues provide evidence that this approach is already being practised. For example, the Earth Charter may be seen as a global citizen initiative that supports and promotes a cosmopolitan environmental vision. It reads: 'we must recognize that in the midst of a magnificent diversity of cultures and life forms we are one human family and one Earth community with a common destiny' (Earth Charter Commission, 2002, Preamble). In the face of ecological crisis, the Earth Charter seems to be saying, we citizens are all in the same boat and so should row together to stay afloat.

Finding such cosmopolitan talk of universal humanity and common responsibilities inappropriate in the face of inequalities and asymmetries in a globalized world, Andrew Dobson (2003) makes a case for a 'post-cosmopolitan' notion of ecological citizenship. While in agreement with some aspects of cosmopolitan citizenship (namely its non-territoriality and focus on virtue), he proposes an approach to ecological citizenship that rejects idealist, pre-political notions of world community and instead conceives of citizens acting in 'ecological space' that is 'produced by the metabolistic and material relations of individual people with their environment' (p. 106). The obligations of the ecological citizen are asymmetrical and non-reciprocal: those who occupy more than their fair share of ecological space have a greater duty to care than those whose labour and land have been exploited. 'Only those who occupy ecological space in such a way as to compromise or foreclose the ability of others in present and future generations to pursue options important to them owe obligations of ecological citizenship', he writes (p. 120). For him, being a good ecological citizen entails the *responsibility to take responsibility* both for one's causal role in environmental injustice and for ensuring a more just distribution of ecological space. Importantly, justice as fairness is the first virtue of ecological citizenship; sentiments like care and compassion are secondary virtues that can be put at the service of justice. And the pursuit of justice can involve actions in both the public and private spheres of life, as long as they are actions that help to define and realize a more sustainable society. In his most recent publication on the topic, Dobson gives the following definition of ecological citizenship: 'pro-environmental practice, in public and in private, driven by a belief in fairness of the distribution of environmental goods, in participation, and in the co-creating of sustainability policy' (2012, p. 522).

Dobson's work is by far the most widely cited and has made the most indelible marks on this growing field. Most scholars who write about ecological citizenship refer or respond to his particular approach and definition. As a result, while there are differences and debates among green political theorists of different shades, most will agree with Dobson that ecological citizenship is a distinct form of citizenship. Whereas in the non-green citizenship literature, liberals and non-liberals often disagree about the appropriate balance between rights and responsibilities, most proponents of ecological citizenship would choose to emphasize citizen responsibilities and duties to protect the environment and to engage in pro-sustainability actions. This may be seen as a response to the dominance of rights in theories of citizenship over the past two centuries. In recent years, some have argued that too many rights and entitlements have led to a breakdown in community bonds as well as to a crisis of ecological unsustainability (Smith and Pangsapa, 2008). Because people in affluent countries have been socialized into prioritizing their own material interests and claiming their 'just deserts' from the state, they are less inclined to consider how their own actions contribute to, or detract from, the common good. If we are to move towards a more sustainable society, the argument tends to go, then there needs to be a dramatic change in the way people understand their relationships to the state and to fellow inhabitants of the planet.

Ecological citizenship has become prominent in the literature because many green political theorists are sceptical of the idea that the liberal democratic state should take the lead in bringing about environmental change (Eckersley, 2004). Although there is ample evidence to suggest that environmental regulation can lead, and has led, to important incremental changes (such as laws banning aerosol use or making recycling mandatory), most theorists of ecological citizenship place greater emphasis on the adoption of environmental values – and hence lifestyles – by individuals. For example, Dobson and Bell (2006) suggest that ecological citizenship is a preferable alternative to government policies that use 'carrots and sticks' (such as subsidies and taxes) to actively influence or control people's behaviour. Instead, they insist it should be about individual citizens voluntarily adopting more sustainable practices *because they believe it to be the right thing to do*. If people do things because they are compelled by the state, then the prospects for long-term, fundamental social change are minimal. What is needed is a change in societal attitudes. Proponents may debate what these should be, but they share the view that people need to adopt the kinds of pro-environmental values, virtues and attitudes that make the exploitation of nature unacceptable. The key virtues listed include 'resourcefulness' (Hayward, 2006a), 'self-reliance' and 'self-restraint' (Barry, 1999, p. 228) and 'justice' (Dobson, 2003). For Dobson (2003), justice is the primary virtue: when a citizen recognizes that he or she has taken more than his or her fair share of ecological space, justice demands that he or she reduces and redistributes resources so that others have a chance of a decent quality of life.

Good environmental citizens not only simply hold green values and take action to demand policy change, perhaps even more importantly they also 'do their bit' for their environment in their everyday lives. The kinds of responsibilities that are commonly listed under the banner of ecological citizenship include a range of practices that reduce environmental impact and improve the quality of degraded ecosystems, such as reducing energy consumption and growing one's own food. Breaking with the traditional understanding of politics, many theorists of ecological citizenship believe that it is in the private sphere that the most meaningful changes can take place. This move fundamentally changes the notion of citizenship as strictly related to the public sphere. As Dobson and Bell (2006, p. 7) note: 'one key environmental point has always been that "private" actions can have important public consequences. Decisions...as to how we heat or cool our homes, or how and what we choose to consume in them, are decisions that have public consequences in terms of [their] environmental impact'.

In sum, then, even though it is contested and under construction, the concept of ecological citizenship is different from and challenges traditional citizenships by being non-territorial, non-reciprocal and not confined to the public-political domain. It is more about individual values and duties than about rights, and it challenges the traditional emphasis on the individual by locating citizens in a larger community that is global, unequal and dependent on the natural world.

Looking back at the decade since he first published *Citizenship and the Environment* (2003), Dobson (2012) has recently identified and responded to the main debates that have been sparked by his work. Some debates and criticisms seem easily put to one side, while others are worth further consideration and research. Each of these is too complex to discuss in detail here, but there are several unresolved debates that continue to raise questions and the attention of researchers that are worth mentioning. First is the debate over the definition of the polity or political community and the criteria for membership in that community. Some traditionalists have resisted the idea that citizenship can be anything other than a legal status that attaches to human members of a political community of a nation-state (Hayward, 2006a, 2006b). By stressing that ecological citizenship is an activity rather than a status, Dobson emphatically sets aside these protestations. Whether non-humans can be members – as citizens – is a related question than has not yet been resolved. For liberals, environmental rights as part of green citizenship tend to equate only to the entitlements of *human citizens* to a clean and liveable environment. Since only human citizens can claim their rights through existing political and legal processes, it is difficult to imagine a practical way of extending environmental rights to animals or the rest of the biotic community. Although it has received considerable attention elsewhere (e.g., in environmental philosophy), the debate over animal rights has thus far not been central to the literature on environmental citizenship.[4] Peter Christoff (1996) was an early proponent of extending rights to non-citizens (non-human, future generations and aliens), to make ecological citizenship an instrument of inclusion that improves the political representation of all things. Although academic discussion of these issues has gone relatively quiet in recent years, a global social movement for the rights of nature has gained momentum since Ecuador and Bolivia granted rights to the natural world (or 'Mother Earth') in their national constitutions in 2008 and 2011 respectively (York, 2014).

There is another debate about how best to promote ecological citizenship, whether it can or should be taught in schools (and thus promoted by the state) or whether it is better arrived at experientially. Dobson (2003) originally advocated schools and universities as among the best sites for fostering pro-environmental values and actions, but now stresses that lived experience is preferable to formal textbook learning (Dobson, 2012). Those who believe ecological citizenship to be a prime means to the democratic production of a sustainable society tend to favour a more proactive approach: 'ecological citizens will not emerge spontaneously; they have to be created' (Melo-Escrihuela, 2008a, p. 128). A variety of state-based and participatory strategies rooted in civil society have been considered, but the issue remains seriously under-explored (Van der Heijden, 2007; Melo-Escrihuela, 2008a). As explained in the next section, research recently has been conducted that claims to provide 'hard empirical evidence' that ecological citizens already exist – and that they can be 'made'.

A further debate exists over whether the line can or should be erased between public and private without doing violence to the specificity of citizenship as a public practice. Consumption, traditionally not seen as an act of citizenship but as an exchange between buyer and seller in the marketplace, is now central to visions of environmental citizenship. Sustainable consumption is a growing field of research that examines why people make choices to buy certain products and not others and how these decisions might be influenced by particular values (Seyfang, 2005). While most greens want people in the affluent world to reduce their consumption, the past decade has also seen the emergence of a trend toward ethical and green consumerism where people decide to purchase goods that are fair trade, organic and low on carbon emissions and embedded resources (energy, water, and so on). It is worth debating, however, whether consumer demand is bringing about the greening of capitalism or whether businesses are simply capitalizing on a fashionable trend (or both?).

With a disproportionate emphasis on individual choice in the realm of consumption, there are further questions to be asked about the extent to which ecological citizenship obscures key questions of fairness, power and social inequality. Many people regard 'going green' as a lifestyle choice accessible only to those with middle class incomes and post-materialist values. Without taking these issues into account, the practice of ecological citizenship as private duty will not be possible for all people and therefore may be limited as a means to the end goal of sustainability (more on this point below).

Of course we have not considered the question of whether ecological citizenship is a form a citizenship in its own right at all. There are observers of the rise of ecological citizenship who want to deny its uniqueness (see, for example, Isin and Wood, 1999) because it does not fit a classic definition of citizenship as found in a Marshallian framework of civil, political and social rights (see Valencia Sáiz, 2005, p. 173). Perhaps the best representative of this position is Tim Hayward (2006a, 2006b) who resists the kind of conceptual transformation Dobson advocates, wishing to preserve a classical understanding. Providing a summary of the various arguments and criticisms is beyond the scope of this chapter, but it seems important to challenge the idea – in a handbook on political citizenship and social movements – that political concepts like citizenship are or should be preserved in aspic. That they are themselves political and transformable by political processes of deliberation and action seems an important position to defend. The feminist movement fought for women to be considered full and equal citizens, thereby changing forever the meaning of the concept. The same can be said for the civil rights movement and perhaps, depending on where things go next, the animal rights movement. Unlike Hayward, whose philosophical objections may be logical and valid at some level, Dobson's contribution to the conversation has opened up many new areas for theoretical and empirical inquiry, in addition to activism in the political arena, and in so doing has helped to make ecological citizenship a dynamic and exciting subject of research.

STUDYING THE ECOLOGICAL CITIZEN: FORAYS INTO EMPIRICAL RESEARCH

It is clear that the theoretical work on ecological citizenship as a normative idea is dominant in the environmental politics literature. Dobson (2012) observes that his work was purely normative and that he never expected to have the ideas 'tested in the field' (p. 522). Although empirical studies remain relatively scarce, in recent years there have been efforts to 'operationalize' the concept in order to find hard evidence of the existence of the sociological (as opposed to conceptual) ecological citizen (Arias-Maldonado, 2012, pp. 161, 165). Some research is exploratory and sociological, while some is more geared to contributing answers that might be policy relevant: how 'to make' people become ecological citizens (Goodwin et al., 2010). This section offers an overview of the small but growing body of empirical research that uses ecological citizenship as a framework for analysing people's actions and values in everyday life.

The primary approach is to search for evidence that people act as ecological citizens, by engaging in what has come to be called 'pro-environmental behaviour', even if they themselves do not use the word to describe themselves or say specifically that they are engaged in forms of ecological citizenship. Researchers identify a set of characteristics found in the theoretical literature (often using Dobson, 2003 as a reference), such as feelings of solidarity and responsibility towards the ecosystem and distant others and willingness to engage in or actual performance of green practices, and then look for signs of these characteristics in a sample population. Some researchers have used comprehensive quantitative data to scrutinize the existence of ecological citizenship values and ideals among the general public (e.g., Berglund and Matti, 2006; Jagers, 2009; Jagers and Matti, 2009; Martinsson and Lundqvist, 2010). For example, Sverker Jagers (2009) uses a quantitative approach with a large-N to go 'in search of the ecological citizen'. His results provide some support for the idea that ecological citizens, as described in the theoretical literature, exist in Sweden. Moreover he is able to provide this interesting description:

> Who is the typical ecological citizen? The typical ecological citizen is a young (15–29 years old) well-educated woman living in one of the largest cities and sympathizing with either the Green or the Left Party. She comes from a middle-class home, has strong faith in Swedish politicians and is a member of various environmental, humanitarian and cultural organizations. She does not have children, never or rarely drives a car, but does pray to a God. (Jagers, 2009, p. 32)

More recently, Jagers and his colleagues have attempted to make the ideals of ecological citizenship 'operational' in order 'to measure their existence and strength among the general public' (Jagers et al., 2013). They used a survey of over 3000 adult Swedes, which asked respondents about their values and practices in order to perform multivariate regression to test the overall effects of green citizenly ideals on pro-environmental behaviour. Their results indicate that about one in five Swedes can be considered ecological citizens. They also suggest that individuals who hold the ideas advocated by green political theorists are more likely to behave in an environmentally friendly way in their daily lives than 'average people' (ibid., p. 15[5]).

A great many more researchers have conducted smaller, qualitative studies with people engaged in forms of environmentalism and pro-environmental actions (e.g., Seyfang, 2005; Horton, 2006; MacGregor, 2006b; Carolan, 2007; Flynn et al., 2008; Wolf et al., 2009; Kennedy, 2011). These studies tend to explore rather than try to test. Here again the researchers review the theoretical literature on ecological citizenship, develop a list of characteristics, and then set off in search for signs of these among their participants. In one such study, Wolf et al. (2009) conducted interviews and focus groups with 38 residents of two communities in British Columbia, Canada, analysed the data in light of four established characteristics, and found 'strong evidence that practising ecological citizenship motivates individuals' responses to climate change' (p. 519). In fact, they also argue that their study serves to support Dobson against Hayward (2006a, 2006b) in their debate over the polity, justice/ethics distinction and membership questions. Similarly, Kennedy (2011) conducted ethnographic interviews with 26 families in Alberta, Canada in order to investigate how ecological citizenship may be situated in neighbourhood-level networks. Rather than go in search for them, Kennedy takes their existence as given and explores the ways in which empirical research challenges the overly individualistic nature of the theoretical literature by giving evidence of the role of networks in enabling people to engage in pro-environmental practices. Taking a different approach to the topic, Swaffield and Bell (2012) interviewed 36 designated 'climate champions' in large companies based in the UK to see if they could be considered potential environmental citizens. They found that while these individuals sought to promote pro-environmental practices within their companies, they were best characterized as 'neoliberal environmental citizens' because they did not seek to challenge liberal individualism or the capitalist status quo. Their research is unique in yielding evidence of a completely different, and perhaps, counter-intuitive, type of ecological citizen than has been elucidated in the literature to date.

These are but a few of the examples of the research being done to give life to the 'actually existing' ecological citizen. Overall, it seems that the results of empirical research are mixed, inconclusive and contradictory. Some have yielded results that appear to confirm the existence of living-breathing ecological citizens (Jagers, 2009; Wolf et al., 2009; Kennedy, 2011), while others have suggested that there is no compelling evidence to support such a claim (Flynn et al., 2008; Martinsson and Lundqvist, 2010). This mixed picture may be a result of methodological differences (and complexities) in the way the research has been conducted and the different definitions being 'operationalized'. There is as yet no accepted method for 'searching for the ecological citizen' (Jagers, 2009) and most studies conclude with a call for further investigation. In spite of the rather large degree of ambivalence, Dobson (2012) argues that the body of empirical research conducted so far suggests that, at the very least, more research should be undertaken with larger sample sizes and in a larger number of places and cultures around the world (he surmises that findings from Canada and Sweden may not be generalizable to the rest of the world's population). At the same time, he cautions that it would be wrong to judge the potential of ecological citizenship on the basis of whether or not we can find it working 'out there'. It is a concept that is worth promoting regardless, so that ecological citizens can be created, thereby contributing to transformative socio-political change.

CRITICISMS FROM THE MARGINS

Dobson (2006a) identifies cosmopolitanism and feminism as two approaches that have important ideas to contribute to a theory of ecological citizenship from outside what he calls the traditional citizenship 'tent', meaning the space occupied by liberal and republican scholars. The account offered in this chapter differs from his view in that the (post-)cosmopolitan approach has not been categorized as a tent-outsider, due to the impact of Dobson's own 'tent-shifting' contribution to the field. Most literature reviews on ecological citizenship put liberal, republican and (post-)cosmopolitan versions at the centre. The outsiders working from the margins are: (1) feminism (still, because little more than lip service is ever paid to it in mainstream reviews), (2) environmental justice and (3) what may be called 'critical environmental sociological' approaches that look at connections between citizenship and social practices. Each is reviewed briefly below.

Most green political scholars acknowledge – to some degree – the relevance of feminist theories for the development of the concept of ecological citizenship. The main contribution involves the feminist critique of the historical divide between the public and private spheres. Dobson (2003) draws on feminist theories of citizenship to make the case for a blurring of the traditional boundaries between public and private, so that private acts (like recycling) count as acts of ecological citizenship. And he suggests that so-called feminine virtues (e.g., care and compassion) ought to sit alongside the traditional liberal ones (e.g., justice, autonomy and courage) in informing a post-cosmopolitan approach. He devotes considerable space in his book to considering how (the admittedly debated) feminist ethics of care and qualities associated with women's roles as carers and mothers might inform his version of ecological citizenship (see also Dean, 2001). Dobson and Dean are unique among green thinkers in bringing these feminist debates about the ethics of care to the discussion of ecological citizenship. However, their treatment of care lacks a critical assessment of the kinds of cultural, social and economic changes that will be needed if care is to be politicized, de-feminized and de-privatized (MacGregor, 2006a, 2006b). This feminist criticism arguably can be made of how caring appears in the discourse of green citizenship more generally.

Beyond hoping that citizens will 'care about' the environment, few scholars make explicit connections between citizenship and the practice of 'caring for' in the context of environmental policy (MacGregor, 2011). Those working from a feminist environmental (or ecofeminist) perspective analyse the exclusion of care from the realm of politics and the gender roles and assumptions that shape social constructions of care (MacGregor, 2006a, 2006b). Feminists are interested in care because it is performed mostly by women, an association that has contributed to the devaluation of women throughout history. Cross-national data show that even with changes in laws and cultural norms, women still do a disproportionate amount of unpaid caring, serving the needs of children and dependent adults as well as the domestic work involved in managing households (Ferrant, 2014). Meanwhile, in most countries 'men are not culturally expected to make a productive contribution to the social product by fulfilling a reasonable share of care duties' (Kershaw, 2005, p. 161). Most feminists see care as a feminized form of labour that is made up of a range of practices that together are called 'social reproduction' (Di Chiro, 2008). Social reproduction involves the provision of services upon which the economy, the state and individual citizens depend for survival. Moreover, those who do 'provisioning work' (Langley and Mellor, 2002) make it possible for people to act as citizens. Provisioning work in the private sphere is also deeply implicated in visions of a more environmentally sustainable society. There is a long list of ways that people might green their households (e.g., recycling, pre-cycling, self-provisioning, etc.). These green practices can be rewarding, giving people who care about the environment a tangible sense of doing their bit to 'save it'. However, they can also be time-consuming and inconvenient chores in societies where the physical infrastructure, services, funding, education and dominant norms have not yet caught up with the green vision. Private sphere activities ensure the ongoing reproduction and maintenance of life and yet, traditionally, have been 'ignored or trivialized in mainstream political, economic and environmental analyses' (Di Chiro, 2008, p. 281). We saw above that they are now becoming central to the definition of environmental citizenship.

However non-feminist green theorists of citizenship (most of whom are white men, it must be noted) tend to work with a one-dimensional understanding of the private sphere, describing it as primarily a place of consumption and giving little or no consideration to the division of labour within it. This is worrying for feminists because when household activities are seen in gender-neutral terms, environmental policies that address them are usually aimed at people in general with no specific recognition of the gender-specific roles they play. The emphasis on individual lifestyle change as central to environmental citizenship has prompted feminist critics to warn against the privatization and feminization of environmental responsibility (Littig, 2001; MacGregor, 2006a, 2006b; Vinz, 2009). In other words, a gender-blind approach to ecological citizenship carries a serious risk of perpetuating existing gender inequalities.

Deeper still, down to the level of the individual human body, feminist theorists have criticized dominant concepts of ecological citizenship for failing to recognize the fact that humans are both *embodied* and inescapably *embedded* in 'differing social and natural contexts that shape subjectivity and condition our collective agency' (Gabrielson and Parady, 2010, p. 374). Citizenship as a Western political concept rests on the same set of assumptions that sustain the dualisms of culture/nature, public/private, man/woman, mind/body that in turn arguably have led to the devaluation of nature and all things female; they are also the dualisms that celebrate the free, rational and masculine subject as the prime agent in political life. To the extent that ecological citizenship reproduces an abstract, universal and fundamentally Western construction of citizenship, Gabrielson and Parady (2010) argue, it not only excludes recognition of social difference but it also perpetuates the myths of human independence and invulnerability. Of course, Dobson (2003, p. 50) acknowledges 'material embeddedness' in his book, but there is no sustained interrogation of the corporeality of ecological citizens in the mainstream literature; rather it is the exclusive offering of a small number of feminist scholars who have participated in the discussion (Reid and Taylor, 2000; Gabrielson and Parady, 2010). It remains a vastly under-explored theme.

Gabrielson and Parady (2010) identify an important point at which feminist criticisms of ecological citizenship intersect with those of environmental justice scholars. They, along with Latta (2007), argue that green political theorists have conceptualized ecological citizenship in ways that deny both active citizenship and epistemological agency to residents of the non-Western world. The criticisms of ecological citizenship literature from an environmental justice perspective boil down to a concern that dominant conceptions of ecological citizen fail to consider questions of equity and justice (see also Agyeman and Evans, 2006; Clarke and Agyeman, 2011).

Ecological citizenship 125

Although they see it as an important dimension of sustainability policy, environmental justice scholars have expressed concern that the dominant emphasis on obligations and duties reflects the need to change lifestyles in the affluent, minority world while overlooking the fact that the majority of people on the planet do not 'have access to the basic human right of a environment fit for their health and well-being' (Clarke and Agyeman, 2011, p. 1776). For Clarke and Agyeman (2011), it is important to make rights a focus, but not in a political liberal way. An environmental justice or 'just sustainability' (Agyeman, 2005) framing of citizenship puts the experiences of poor and ethnically marginalized people at the centre and resists the cosmopolitan 'everyone in the same boat' approach (something about which Dobson, 2003 is also critical, as noted earlier). Environmental rights ensure justice for those who historically have been denied rights because of structural misrecognition; the claiming of protection and entitlements is an important political move (see Clarke and Agyeman, 2011 for a detailed discussion). Moreover, because there is a disproportionate emphasis on individual duty, and a more narrow understanding of 'the environment' than most non-Western people would recognize, Agyeman and Evans (2006) have said that it is not 'a particularly useful term on which to base political action' (p. 186) (see also Latta, 2007, pp. 385–6). Although very little empirical research has been done to investigate this issue, one preliminary study based in the UK has found that few people in minority ethnic communities express a sense of shared responsibility for environmental problems, but they do engage in rights-based discourse and activism at the community level, particularly to present their claims to local government (Clarke and Agyeman, 2011, pp. 1793–4).

The third critique from outside the ecological citizenship 'tent' comes from what might be called 'critical environmental sociology'. This is a body of theoretical and empirical work that challenges the instrumental aims and the methodological individualism found in much of the ecological citizenship research and theorizing. There is a sense of scepticism of the way in which the ecological citizen has become synonymous with the sustainable consumer in the environmental 'behaviour change' discourse. This is arguably a discourse that emphasizes the role of consumers in meeting government targets and that has been taken up by policy-makers in affluent countries such as the UK. Providing a critique of the processes by which the identity and practices of citizenship have become less related to the state and more related to the market under neoliberalism, scholars working from this perspective call for greater sophistication in the way citizenship is deployed in the environmental politics literature (cf. Seyfang, 2005; Shove, 2010; Barr et al., 2011a, 2011b; Evans, 2011). The most important theoretical framework for these analyses broadly can be called the social practice approach (Spaargaren, 2003; Spaargaren and Mol, 2008), which, inspired by Giddens's (1984) theory of structuration, views people's actions as situated in particular local contexts, shaped by relationships and social structures, and as irreducible to individual rational choices (Middlemiss, 2010; Hards, 2011). For example, David Evans (2011) argues that 'ecologically damaging patterns of consumption cannot be reduced to a problem of human behaviour because individual acts of consuming certain things and in certain ways need to be contextualized in relation to the ordering of social practices' (p. 110). Critical of the focus on 'attitudes, behaviour and choices' (or the 'ABC') of individuals (Shove, 2010), these scholars are keen to point out the dangers of ecological citizenship being taken over by economic and behavioural psychology and thereby marginalizing other perspectives on consumption and social change (Evans, 2011). What is more, the instrumental use of citizenship as a way of internalizing appropriate green attitudes and behaviours, such as seen in 'nudge' approaches to policy (reviewed and criticized in Dobson, 2010), can be criticized as examples of neoliberal governmentality (Slocum, 2004) or 'environmentality' (Darier, 1996; MacGregor, 2006a, 2006b).

There have for many years been critics of the individualized nature of environmental politics and citizenship, and of the centrality of consumption in the green political agenda, which can be seen as a symptom of a 'flight from politics' (Maniates, 2001). For example, as far back as 1989 Murray Bookchin warned that:

> [i]t is inaccurate and unfair to coerce people into believing that they are personally responsible for present-day ecological disasters because they consume too much or proliferate too readily. This privatization of the environmental crisis, like the New Age cults that focus on personal problems rather than on social dislocations, has reduced many environmental movements to utter ineffectiveness and threatens to diminish their credibility with the public. If 'simple living' and militant recycling are the main solutions to the environmental crisis, the crisis will certainly continue and intensify. (Bookchin, 1989, pp. 19–23, quoted in Maniates, 2001, p. 38)

As Bookchin may have predicted, the blurring of the boundary between the public and private, the political and personal, seems to have diminished the potential for ecological citizenship to be a positive force in green politics. There remains in the literature, both from within and outside the tent, a persistent disconnection of the concept of ecological citizenship from the idea of collective social movement in civil society. The more the focus is placed on (studying and changing) the behaviour of citizen-consumers, the less attention is paid to the fundamental point that citizens are always part of a collective – a political community. And environmental movement organizations are '*the* vehicle to add a collective dimension to the concept of individual environmental citizenship' (Van der Heijden, 2007, p. 161; original emphasis). Perhaps it is inevitable that in a neoliberal context we should fail to see the forest for the trees: the forest of civil society is neatly obscured to keep the trees complacent and consenting. This is a pessimistic view that offers very little hope for the future of environmentalism or, indeed, of ecological citizenship.

CONCLUSION: WHAT FUTURE FOR ECOLOGICAL CITIZENSHIP?

Environmentalism is at a crossroads, both as an idea and as one of the key new social movements of the twentieth century. After nearly 50 years, it is not so 'new' anymore. One can observe the blunting of its edges by its being adopted by mainstream institutions and by its reduction to rote behaviours like recycling and using reusable shopping bags. Some have suggested that it may be dying or dead, due to its co-optation by dominant interests and its failure (in the USA at least) to achieve legislation to tackle the root causes of environmental crisis (Nordhaus and Shellenberger, 2007). What is more, in the contemporary context of scepticism or fear about climate change, of fiscal austerity and the internalization of neoliberal ideas, some have lamented the symptoms of a 'post-political turn', particularly within environmentalism in the Global North (Swyngedouw, 2010; Catney and Doyle, 2011). Ecological citizenship may offer great promise – as an ideal – for a reinvigoration of the planet's only collective movement for socio-ecological transformation, where the goals of democracy, justice and sustainability are integrated at its core, but even the greenest of greens rarely call themselves 'ecological citizens'. And claims that there are ecological citizens 'out there' are difficult to prove. Many who study it would agree that ecological citizenship is largely a normative concept that is difficult to find in the world around us.

What role does the concept of ecological citizenship play in the future of the environmental movement? If it is to play any meaningful role, then it must be presented and theorized in a way that resists individualism. In Robyn Eckersley's words, it must be seen as 'shared activity, united around collective problems' (2004, p. 184). Whether ecological citizens are active in a 'green public sphere' (Torgerson, 1999), a 'green state' (Eckersley, 2004) or an urban civil society (Melo-Escrihuela, 2008b), what is important is that they are acting collectively to bring about an *ecological democracy*, rather than acting alone to green their lifestyles without challenging the principles and practices of liberal democracy. It is highly unlikely that the most pressing collective problem of all – global climate change – stands a chance of being solved unless citizens can see beyond their immediate concerns and engage in (what is now considered) old-fashioned social movement politics.

Finally, ecological citizenship must be seen as a position from which to *resist* neoliberalism and its ability to present individual choice and the pursuit of self-interest as natural and inevitable. This requires both an opening up of political space that has been shut down by the rhetoric of crisis and 'existential threats' and a return to genuine collectivism and publicity (public spiritedness). There is a desperate need for public spaces that enable citizens to act *qua* citizen, where they enact *being a citizen* as something distinct from being a parent, worker and consumer. Resisting the conflation of citizen and consumer seems necessary in order to reclaim the democratic impulse within environmentalism and to understand citizenship as a site of political contest. It seems important, moreover, to open up discussion about 'how nature can be politicised a part of the politics of citizenship and vice versa' (Latta, 2007, p. 382). Only then may the concept of ecological citizenship be rescued from the clutches of neoliberalism so it may offer hope for its democratic *re-politicization*. Increasing its relevance to people with a broader set of concerns in the majority worlds seems the best way to keep environmentalism alive and kicking in these uncertain times (Catney and Doyle, 2011). Whether ecological citizenship is a normative ideal that is worth fighting for is an open question. One thing that is certain, however, is that it will continue to be a subject of debate and research within the field of environmental politics for many years to come.

NOTES

1. The Canadian Ministry of the Environment is regularly credited with coining the phrase 'environmental citizenship' in its Green Plan (1990) in the literature on this topic (cf. Szerszynski, 2006; Melo-Escrihuela, 2008a).
2. The author is an editor of *Environmental Politics* and therefore has access to this information.
3. One might also include as a main current the communitarian approach to ecological citizenship that has been articulated by Deane Curtin (1999). Arguing that the ecological crisis is a crisis of citizenship he sets out an approach to environmental ethics that roots moral knowledge in community and calls for people to become native to a place. Although his book, *Chinnagounder's Challenge: The Question of Ecological Citizenship*, gestures toward rather than spells out his conception of citizenship (a conception that seems to be more ethical than political), Curtin believes that true democracy begins at the level of community. This theoretical approach to ecological citizenship seems to have gone quiet over the years, but it is nonetheless worth mentioning here as part of a full

sweep of the field. In fact, one might predict a resurgence of such views in light of the growing Transition Town movement in the UK and other affluent Western countries.
4. However, there has been some movement towards granting rights to non-human great apes. The Great Ape Project has been advocating the extension of legal rights (to life, to individual liberty and freedom from torture) since 1993 (http://www.projetogap.org.br/en/). In 2008 Spain became the first country to give rights to these animals on the grounds that humans share approximately 99 per cent of their active genetic material with non-human primates.
5. Page number from unpublished manuscript that has been accepted for publication in *EP*.

REFERENCES

Agyeman, J. (2005), 'Alternatives for community and environment: where justice and sustainability meet', *Environment*, **47**(6), 10–23.
Agyeman, J. and B. Evans (2006), 'Justice, governance and sustainability: perspectives on environmental citizenship from North America and Europe', in A. Dobson and D. Bell (eds), *Environmental Citizenship*, Cambridge, MA: MIT Press, pp. 185–206.
Arias-Maldonado, M. (2012), *Real Green: Sustainability after the End of Nature*, Farnham, UK: Ashgate.
Attfield, R. (1999), *The Ethics of the Global Environment*, Edinburgh: Edinburgh University Press.
Barr, S., A. Gilg and G. Shaw (2011a), 'Helping people make better choices: exploring the behaviour change agenda for environmental sustainability', *Applied Geography*, **31**(2), 712–20.
Barr, S., A. Gilg and G. Shaw (2011b), 'Citizens, consumers and sustainability: (re)framing environmental practice in an age of climate change', *Global Environmental Change*, **21**(4), 1224–33.
Barry, J. (1999), *Rethinking Green Politics*, London: Sage.
Barry, J. (2006), 'Resistance is fertile', in A. Dobson and D. Bell (eds), *Environmental Citizenship*, Cambridge, MA: MIT Press, pp. 21–48.
Barry, J. (2008), 'Towards a green republicanism', *The Good Society*, **17**(2), 1–12.
Bell, D. (2005), 'Liberal environmental citizenship', *Environmental Politics*, **14**(2), 179–94.
Berglund, C. and S. Matti (2006), 'Citizen and consumer: the dual role of individuals in environmental policy', *Environmental Politics*, **15**(4), 550–71.
Bookchin, M. (1989), 'Death of a small planet', *The Progressive*, **53**(8), 19–23.
Bookchin, M. (1992), *Urbanization Without Cities: The Rise and Decline of Citizenship*, Montreal, QC: Black Rose Books.
Canada, Government of (1990), *Canada's Green Plan – Canada's Green Plan for a Healthy Environment*, Ottawa, ON: Minister of Supply and Services.
Cannavò, P.F. (2012), 'Ecological citizenship, time, and corruption: Aldo Leopold's green republicanism', *Environmental Politics*, **21**(6), 864–81.
Carolan, M.S. (2007), 'Introducing the concept of tactile space: creating lasting social and environmental commitments', *Geoforum*, **38**, 1264–75.
Carter, N. (2004), 'Politics as if nature mattered', in A. Leftwich (ed.), *What is Politics?*, Cambridge, UK: Polity.
Catney, P. and T. Doyle (2011), 'The welfare of now and the green (post) politics of the future', *Critical Social Policy*, **31**(2), 174–93.
Christoff, P. (1996), 'Ecological citizens and ecologically guided democracy', in B. Doherty and M. de Geus (eds), *Democracy and Green Political Thought: Sustainability, Rights and Citizenship*, London: Routledge, pp. 151–69.
Clarke, S. and J. Agyeman (2011), 'Shifting the balance in environmental governance: ethnicity, environmental citizenship and discourses of responsibility', *Antipode*, **43**(5), 1773–800.

Curtin, D. (1999), *Chinnagounder's Challenge: The Question of Ecological Citizenship*, Indianapolis, IN: Indiana University Press.
Darier, E. (1996), 'Environmental governmentality: the case of Canada's Green Plan', *Environmental Politics*, **5**(4), 585–606.
Dean, H. (2001), 'Green citizenship', *Social Policy and Administration*, **35**(5), 490–505.
Di Chiro, G. (2008), 'Living environmentalisms: coalition politics, social reproduction and environmental justice', *Environmental Politics*, **17**(2), 276–98.
Dobson, A. (2003), *Citizenship and the Environment*, Oxford: Oxford University Press.
Dobson, A. (2006a), 'Citizenship', in A. Dobson and R. Eckersley (eds), *Political Theory and the Ecological Challenge*, Cambridge, UK: Cambridge University Press, pp. 216–31.
Dobson, A. (2006b), 'Ecological citizenship: a defence', *Environmental Politics*, **15**(3), 447–51.
Dobson, A. (2007), *Green Political Thought*, 4th edition, New York: Routledge.
Dobson, A. (2010), *Environmental Citizenship and Pro-environmental Behaviour: Rapid Research and Evidence Review*, London: Sustainable Development Research Network.
Dobson, A. (2012), 'Ecological citizenship revisited', in P. Dauvergne (ed.), *Handbook of Global Environmental Politics*, 2nd edition, Cheltenham, UK and Northampton, MA, USA: Edward Elgar Publishing Ltd, pp. 520–29.
Dobson, A. and D. Bell (eds) (2006), *Environmental Citizenship*, Cambridge, MA: The MIT Press.
Earth Charter Commission (2002), *Earth Charter: Values and Principles for a Sustainable Future*, accessed 6 May 2014 at http://www.earthcharter.org.
Eckersley, R. (2004), *The Green State: Rethinking Democracy and Sovereignty*, Cambridge, MA: The MIT Press.
Evans, D. (2011), 'Consuming conventions: sustainable consumption, ecological citizenship and the worlds of worth', *Journal of Rural Studies*, **27**(2), 109–15.
Ferrant, G. (2014), 'Time use as a transformative indicator for gender equality in the post-2015 agenda', OECD Development Centre. Accessed 23 June 2014 at http://www.oecd.org/dev/poverty/Time%20use%20_final_2014.pdf.
Flynn, R., P. Bellaby and M. Ricci (2008), 'Environmental citizenship and public attitudes to hydrogen energy technologies', *Environmental Politics*, **17**(5), 766–83.
Gabrielson, T. and K. Parady (2010), 'Corporeal citizenship: rethinking green citizenship through the body', *Environmental Politics*, **19**(3), 374–91.
Giddens, A. (1984), *The Constitution of Society: Outline of the Theory of Structuration*, Cambridge, UK: Polity Press.
Goodwin, M.J., S. Greasley, P. John and L. Richardson (2010), 'Can we make environmental citizens? A randomised control trial of the effects of a school-based intervention on the attitudes and knowledge of young people', *Environmental Politics*, **19**(3), 392–412.
Hailwood, S. (2005), 'Environmental citizenship as reasonable citizenship', *Environmental Politics*, **14**(2), 195–210.
Hards, S. (2011), 'Social practice and the evolution of personal environmental values', *Environmental Values*, **20**(1), 23–42.
Hayward, T. (2005), *Constitutional Environmental Rights*, Oxford: Oxford University Press.
Hayward, T. (2006a), 'Ecological citizenship: justice, rights and the virtue of resourcefulness', *Environmental Politics*, **15**(3), 435–46.
Hayward, T. (2006b), 'Ecological citizenship: a rejoinder', *Environmental Politics*, **15**(3), 452–3.
Horton, D. (2006), 'Demonstrating environmental citizenship? A study of everyday life among green activists', in A. Dobson and D. Bell (eds), *Environmental Citizenship*, Cambridge, MA: MIT Press.
Isin, E.F. and P.K. Wood (1999), *Citizenship and Identity*, London: Sage.
Jagers, S.C. (2009), 'In search of the ecological citizen', *Environmental Politics*, **18**(1), 18–36.
Jagers, S.C. and S. Matti (2009), 'Ecological citizens: identifying values and beliefs that support individual environmental responsibility among Swedes', *Sustainability*, **2**(4), 1055–79.

Jagers, S.C., J. Martinsson and S. Matti (2013), 'Ecological citizenship: a driver for pro-environmental behaviour?', *Environmental Politics*, forthcoming [published online 31 October 2013], DOI: 10.1080/09644016.2013.835202.
Jelin, E. (2000), 'Towards a global environmental citizenship?', *Citizenship Studies*, **4**(1), 47–63.
Kennedy, E.H. (2011), 'Rethinking ecological citizenship: the role of neighbourhood networks in cultural change', *Environmental Politics*, **20**(6), 843–60.
Kershaw, P. (2005), *Carefair: Rethinking the Responsibilities and Rights of Citizenship*, Vancouver, BC: University of British Columbia Press.
Langley, P. and M. Mellor (2002), 'Economy, sustainability and sites of transformative space', *New Political Economy*, **7**(1), 49–65.
Latta, A. (2007), 'Locating democratic politics in ecological citizenship', *Environmental Politics*, **16**(3), 377–93.
Latta, A. and N. Garside (2005), 'Perspectives on ecological citizenship: an introduction', *Environment*, **33**(3), 1–8.
Littig, B. (2001), *Feminist Perspectives on Environment and Society*, Harlow, UK: Pearson Education Ltd.
MacGregor, S. (2006a), 'No sustainability without justice: a feminist critique of environmental citizenship', in A. Dobson and D. Bell (eds), *Environmental Citizenship*, Cambridge, MA: MIT Press, pp. 101–26.
MacGregor, S. (2006b), *Beyond Mothering Earth: Ecological Citizenship and the Politics of Care*, Vancouver, BC: University of British Columbia Press.
MacGregor, S. (2011), 'Citizenship and care', in T. Fitzpatrick (ed.), *Understanding the Environment and Social Policy*, Bristol: Policy Press, pp. 271–90.
Maniates, M. (2001), 'Individualisation: plant a tree, ride a bike, save the world?', *Global Environmental Politics*, **1**(3), 31–52.
Marshall, T.H. (1950), *Citizenship and Social Class: And Other Essays*, Cambridge, UK: Cambridge University Press.
Martinsson, J. and L.J. Lundqvist (2010), 'Ecological citizenship: coming out "clean" without turning "green"?', *Environmental Politics*, **19**(4), 518–37.
Melo-Escrihuela, C. (2008a), 'Promoting ecological citizenship: rights, duties and political agency', *An International E-Journal for Critical Geographies*, **7**(2), 113–34.
Melo-Escrihuela, C. (2008b), 'Towards an urban ecological citizenship', *From Climate Change to Environmental Justice. Special Issue of Re-public: Re-imagining Democracy*, **1**, 27–30.
Middlemiss, L. (2010), 'Reframing individual responsibility for sustainable consumption: lessons from environmental justice and ecological citizenship', *Environmental Values*, **19**(2), 147–67.
Newby, H. (1996), 'Citizenship in a green world: global commons and human stewardship', in M. Bulmer and A. Rees (eds), *Citizenship Today: The Contemporary Relevance of T.H. Marshall*, London: UCL Press, pp. 209–21.
Nordhaus, T. and M. Shellenberger (2007), *Breakthrough: From the Death of Environmentalism to the Politics of Possibility*, New York: Houghton Mifflin Co.
Porritt, J. (2013), 'The unknowable future', Public Lecture at Keele University, 12 February 2013.
Reid, H. and B. Taylor (2000), 'Embodying ecological citizenship: rethinking the politics of grassroots globalization in the United States', *Alternatives*, **25**(4), 439–66.
Seyfang, G. (2005), 'Shopping for sustainability: can sustainable consumption promote ecological citizenship?', *Environmental Politics*, **14**(2), 290–306.
Shove, E. (2010), 'Beyond the ABC: climate change and theories of social change', *Environment and Planning A*, **42**(6), 1273–85.
Slocum, R. (2004), 'Consumer citizens and the Cities for Climate Protection campaign', *Environment and Planning A*, **36**(5), 763–82.
Smith, M.J. (1998), *Ecologism: Towards Ecological Citizenship*, Buckingham, UK: Open University Press.

Smith, M.J. (2005), 'Obligation and ecological citizenship', *Environments*, **33**(3), 9–23.
Smith, M. and P. Pangsapa (2008), *Environment and Citizenship: Integrating Justice, Responsibility and Civic Engagement*, London: Zed Books.
Spaargaren, G. (2003), 'Sustainable consumption: a theoretical and environmental policy perspective', *Society and Natural Resources*, **16**(8), 687–701.
Spaargaren, G. and A. Mol (2008), 'Greening global consumption: redefining politics and authority', *Global Environmental Change*, **18**(3), 350–59.
Steward, F. (1991), 'Citizens of planet earth', in G. Andrews (ed.), *Citizenship*, London: Lawrence and Wishart, pp. 65–75.
Swaffield, J. and D. Bell (2012), 'Can "climate champions" save the planet? A critical reflection on neoliberal social change', *Environmental Politics*, **21**(2), 248–67.
Swyngedouw, E. (2010), 'Apocalypse forever? Post-political populism and the spectre of climate change', *Theory, Culture and Society*, **27**(2), 213–32.
Szerszynski, B. (2006), 'Local landscapes and global belonging: toward a situated citizenship of the environment', in A. Dobson and D. Bell (eds), *Environmental Citizenship*, Cambridge, MA: The MIT Press, pp. 75–100.
Torgerson, D. (1999), *The Promise of Green Politics: Environmentalism and the Public Sphere*, Durham, NC/London: Duke University Press.
Trachtenberg, Z. (2010), 'Complex green citizenship and the necessity of judgement', *Environmental Politics*, **19**(3), 339–55.
UNCED (1992), *United Nations Conference on Environment and Development – Agenda 21*, accessed 6 May 2014 at http://sustainabledevelopment.un.org/content/documents/Agenda21.pdf.
Valencia Sáiz, A. (2005), 'Globalisation, cosmopolitanism and ecological citizenship', *Environmental Politics*, **14**(2), 163–78.
Van der Heijden, H.-A. (2007), 'Book review of *Environmental Citizenship* by Andrew Dobson and Derek Bell (eds)', *Environmental Politics*, **16**(1), 160–61.
Van Steenbergen, B. (ed.) (1994), *The Condition of Citizenship*, London: Sage.
Vinz, D. (2009), 'Gender and sustainable consumption: a German environmental perspective', *European Journal of Women's Studies*, **16**(2), 159–79.
Wolf, J., K. Brown and D. Conway (2009), 'Ecological citizenship and climate change: perceptions and practice', *Environmental Politics*, **18**(4), 503–21.
York, S. (2014), 'The rights of nature movement gains momentum at Ecuador conference', *Earth Island Journal*, February 17. Accessed 23 June 2014 at: http://www.earthisland.org/journal/index.php/elist/eListRead/the_rights_of_nature_movement_builds_momentum_at_ecuador_conference/.

7. Urban citizenship
Patricia Burke Wood

INTRODUCTION: A CRITICAL AND POLITICAL APPROACH TO CITIZENSHIP

'Urban citizenship' encompasses many phenomena and approaches. It may refer to a form of citizenship in terms of its scale of governance and belonging, distinguishing itself from national citizenship. It may also refer to a particular type of citizenship and belonging that is cosmopolitan and civic in nature, rather than 'national' in an ethnic sense. This cosmopolitan citizenship is often rooted in a vision of such citizenship as a political subjectivity that is produced by the diversity of the city as it continually draws and renews its population from elsewhere and/or the city as a 'difference machine' (Isin, 2001; Bauböck, 2003). It can refer to the ways in which citizenship is in and of the city, and thus specifically and inherently urban, such as through the use of public space for protest or through technologies of discipline and surveillance. While these distinctions matter, these forms all overlap. 'Urban citizenship' often focuses on social movements within the city, and in turn may refer to three related and often coinciding practices: struggle for rights within the city, struggle that employs the city as an instrument or platform, and struggle for the 'right to the city' in a Lefebvrian sense (discussed further below). Broadly, 'urban citizenship' may also describe the ways in which new, mass struggles have restructured the politics of activism, in terms of the nature of claims, spaces and technologies of protest and policing, new alliances and solidarities, and new ways of thinking about citizenship in terms of scale and territory.

For many, citizenship is historically a product of the city, and the fates of the two are inseparable (ibid.). This is such a fruitful and frustrating combination, pursued down a great number of academic alleys, that it would be a challenge to consider 'urban citizenship' as an organized field of study with clear delimitations. Scholarship related to this subject arises in the study of constitutional law, government, public policy, politics and political theory, human rights, borders and security, migrants and refugees, civil rights, education, technology, social movements, identity politics, political economy, infrastructure, municipal politics, urban networks and globalization, architecture, urban and regional planning, housing and homelessness, social policy, culture and the arts, landscape and urban form, processes of urbanization and suburbanization, and scales of governance and law. Urban citizenship nests in this rich and wide-ranging landscape of shifting urban forms and discourses, changing political structures and policies, and ever-evolving scholarly literatures. The scholar of citizenship studies must understand critical urban theory and develop a rich sense of the structure and workings of cities, and the urbanist must likewise engage with a critical approach to 'citizenship'.

In particular, we must come to terms with the active tension and even conflict embedded in both the city and in citizenship. 'Urban citizenship', as a concept and as a practice, brings together two conflictual and even contradictory relationships. On the one hand, the city and citizenship can be coercive and disciplinary; on the other, they can also be empowering and emancipatory. The tensions, contradictions and conflicts within each give shape to the discourse and landscape of the city and to the institution and practice of citizenship.

Let us begin with citizenship. It is now well established that citizenship exists as a form of official membership, as a bundle of rights and responsibilities, and as a set of formal and informal political practices (Isin and Wood, 1999). Many are enthusiastic about the legal-political order and rights protection embedded in the formal status of citizenship, and in an associated 'citizen culture' (Crick, 2001) in which the 'citizen' is politically active and publically takes up the cause of 'ethics' and justice. However, Dalton argues that '[b]y almost any measure, public confidence and trust in, and support for, politicians, political parties, and political institutions has eroded over the past generation' (Dalton, 2004). In response to concerns that citizens have become disenchanted with or even disengaged from politics (as evidenced, for example, by falling rates of voter turnout), many seek a stronger and more central role for ordinary citizens. Barber (1984), for example, advocates moving away from 'politics as zookeeping' and towards 'politics as a way of living' and 'politics as a social being'. Dalton specifies that while there is an increasing lack of trust in government, the same citizens remain critically engaged with political issues and supportive of democracy as a political form (Dalton, 2004; Dalton and Welzel, 2013). For Dalton, the end of unquestioning allegiance or 'duty citizenship', and the emergence (or re-emergence) of 'engaged citizenship' is the product of a generational change related to many factors, including secularization (Dalton, 2009). However, Schudson (1998), in his history of American citizenship, has also exposed the nostalgia for an 'active' or 'informed' citizen that never was, or was more problematic than we now appreciate. Engagement is also a burden of time and information acquisition, and Schudson notes that, ironically, the age of the deferential, uninformed citizen was also a period of some of the highest rates of citizens' political involvement.

There is the promise of emancipation in citizenship: the official political status offers a commitment to and a practice of social equity; this discourse of its constitutions, charters and bills of rights and freedoms promises to act as the great equalizer, to guard our civil, social and political rights, and to provide freedom from discrimination. Even as 'different dimensions of citizenship – rights, entitlements, a state, territoriality, etc...[become] disarticulated from each other, and articulated with diverse universalizing norms defined by markets, neoliberal values, or human rights' (Ong, 2006, p. 500), faith in the capacity of 'citizenship' to effect progressive change remains. For Crick (2001) and others, the central argument revolves around the fundamental idea of democracy serving to hold government accountable. In addition to local and national movements, others make an argument for 'global citizenship' in which mobilization across borders might tackle challenges that thus far stymie or are ignored by national governments. For global citizenship advocates (see, for example, Held, 2002; Sassen, 2009), the hope is to transcend the limits of the overly bureaucratic or, at other times, neoliberal 'hollowed out' national government and its territorialization of political identity (Wood, 2008).

Out of a similar frustration at the limitations of the national state, Barber (2013) has taken his ideas regarding citizenship and democracy to what might be seen as their logical conclusion in an argument for a particular form of urban citizenship: for mayors to 'rule the world':

> Today, after a long history of regional success, the nation-state is failing us on the global scale. It was the perfect political recipe for the liberty and independence of autonomous peoples and nations. It is utterly unsuited to interdependence. The city, always the human habitat of first resort, has in today's globalizing world once again become democracy's best hope. (Barber, 2013, p. 3)

For Barber, today's nation-state is too large for meaningful political participation and too small to deal with the challenge of global crises such as climate change, terrorism and pandemics. He envisions instead a network of mayors forming a 'global parliament of cities', taking as a starting point the United Cities and Local Governments and similar organized global networks of cities (ibid., p. 16). While Bauböck remains 'skeptical to the idea that urban citizenship could simply bypass the national level and become a basis for building institutions of global democracy', he too advocates for a stronger city government emancipated in part from its national counterpart (Bauböck, 2003, p. 156). I have reservations about Barber's endorsement of the municipal government as the most pragmatic and action-oriented ('Presidents pontificate principle; mayors pick up the garbage' – Barber, 2013, p. 6). Scales of government are not neatly discrete, and municipal governments are as vulnerable to corruption and incompetence as any other level. Local elites and other scales of government (and their party politics) may intervene in local politics to produce leaders that are beholden not to the city as a whole, but to the interests of the privileged, local or otherwise.

For Crick, Barber, Bauböck and others who advocate for grassroots engagement and local government, Purcell's (2006) reservation regarding the 'local trap' is warranted. In a cautionary appendix to literature on urban citizenship generally, and on 'the right to the city' more specifically, Purcell notes that critiques of neoliberal processes of globalization and their impact on cities and processes of urbanization have (intentionally and inadvertently) privileged local governance as an ideal form of citizenship. For Purcell, the 'local trap' 'equates the local with "the good"; it is preferred presumptively over non-local scales' (p. 1924) despite 'the empirical fact that local-scale arrangements do not always result in more democratic or more just outcomes' (pp. 1924–5). He warns that 'it is dangerous to make any assumption about any scale. Scales are not independent entities with pre-given characteristics. Instead, they are socially constructed strategies to achieve particular ends' (p. 1921; see also Marston, 2000). As Magnusson has also argued, 'We should be skeptical about a political logic that suggests that the only solution to a problem is to re-pose the problem on a different scale or in a different form' (Magnusson, 2002, p. 119). Purcell further argues that Lefebvre's advocacy for the right to the city did not privilege the urban as a scale, but rather emphasized that the rights of *inhabitants* not be diminished or extinguished in favour of *owners*.

Barber presents a similar critique and motivation as those espousing 'global citizenship', and indeed, both a 'cosmopolitan' sensibility (what he calls 'glocality') and an actual global network for governance are part of his vision. Isin and Turner (2007) have critiqued such a focus on scale as both problem and solution, and the associated faith placed in the 'global citizen'. For Ong as well, this is unsatisfying: 'the rhetoric of ethical globalization operates at too vast a scale to deal with specific milieus of exclusion and endangerment' (Ong, 2006, p. 504). Nevertheless, some of the grappling for a new framework is legitimate, as citizenship has become at least partly dislodged, in discourse and in practice, from its moorings in the nation-state. Critical scholarship unpacking the very idea of 'scale' has mirrored the disassembling of scales of citizenship and governance. Dismantling any idea that scale has an objectively fixed spatial form, Cox has reframed the question in terms of practices, focusing on 'spaces of engagement' and 'spaces of dependence' (Cox, 1998). Similarly, Jones (1998) has posited scale as a way of knowing or apprehending that is thus strategic and political, shaping what we see and are able to know. In this light, a clearer framework to bring to the consideration of citizenship is Isin's (2007) distinction between the 'local' as *actual*, and the national and other 'scales' as *virtual*, recognizing that the virtual becomes actual as it intervenes in or occupies local space. In this way, scales of governance and citizenship are not absolute, nor do they nest in a hierarchy, but rather intersect and overlap as they take actual form (see also M.P. Smith, 2001).

To the above scholarship regarding frustrations with citizen disengagement and citizenship's reconfigurations, we could add the critique of the depoliticizing effects of technological innovation (Barney, 2007). Defining citizenship as 'the practice of political judgment' Barney sounds a strongly cautionary note: 'There are many ways in which technology...can be as much a means of anti-citizenship as it is of citizenship' (ibid., pp. 20–21). While new technologies, particularly the internet, provide easier access to ever-greater amounts of information as well as the facilitation of communication and networking, 'the internet also surpasses its predecessors as an integrated medium of enrolment in the depoliticized economy and culture of consumer capitalism' (p. 21), and thus impedes our ability to exercise that political judgment, especially to make technology itself an object of political judgment. Instead, technology uses us as much as we use technology. Similar to many of the scholars above, Barney's sharp critique of the politics of technology leads to advocacy for greater citizen involvement in the face of a 'liberal, capitalist, technological society' that implicitly purports to have established 'the best way to live' (p. 40). A continuing commonality amongst many of these scholars is their positing citizenship as empowerment, as the embodiment of democracy and as inherently liberating.

For all the promise of its discourse, citizenship emerged in the modern era as a means to privilege certain classes, such as landowning middle-class men, not as a tool of equality. The modern state developed as part of a broader 'market society', in whose development it also participated actively, supporting the interests of capital and a 'self-regulating market' (Polanyi [1944] 2001). According to Schudson (1998), even in the United States, the founding fathers of its democracy never had any intention of establishing political rights for all inhabitants. In all Western democracies, the state strategically allocated particular rights (and not others) to particular groups (and not others) in the discipline of the population it claimed to govern, especially with an eye to management of the labour force (Marshall, 1950; Isin, 2001; Guarnizo, 2012; Wood, 2013). In the face of activism and articulate statements regarding the inherent injustice of such exclusion, governments in Western democracies repeatedly refused to give women and minorities suffrage, property rights and equal legal protection from violence. Furthermore, citizenship has proven to be no shield against mistreatment by the state as, for example, US and Canadian citizens of Japanese origin discovered during World War II (Adachi, 1976; Roy, 2002; Ngai, 2005). Citizenship is a technology of governance on the part of the state, used to discipline both the included and the excluded (Isin and Wood, 1999; Isin, 2001).

As Guarnizo has noted:

> While citizenship is fundamentally a mechanism of state control and rule, both analysts and activists tend to emphasize its role as a membership institution and thus see it as a ticket to gain access to rights and entitlements. This tendency, paradoxically, obscures the significance of today's citizenship as a tool of *governmentality* (Foucault, 1988), behind which socioeconomic inequality is reproduced and maintained. By emphasizing rights and entitlements without addressing the power relations mediated by the institution of citizenship, activists and analysts have, however inadvertently, displaced the focus of their advocacy. (Guarnizo, 2012, p. 12; original emphasis)

I would take Guarnizo's observations still further and quibble with both his use of 'today's' and 'paradoxically'. Citizenship as a formal status bestowed by the state has always served as a tool of governmentality to privilege and discipline. More significantly, not only does 'citizenship' function as 'a mechanism of state control' but the institution itself is the means by which another message of 'democracy, freedom and equality' masks the inequality protected and enabled by the state. Far from 'paradoxical' this strategic management of the state's legitimacy and authority is part of citizenship itself (Wood, 2008), and Isin (2001) has argued that the creation of 'outsider' is central to its purpose. Despite the state's assertion of the authority to define its citizens and citizens' behaviour, its efforts to regulate, exclude and discipline regularly collide with citizens' claims and desires. Citizenship is, necessarily, an agonistic relationship between the governors and the governed. Moreover, just as formal citizenship status does not guarantee equal treatment, Smith has documented clearly that formal status is not required for successful political action, within and across borders (M.P. Smith, 2001). A broad understanding of who constitutes the 'governed' and will thus make a claim against the 'governor' is necessary in order to appreciate how each party defines itself and the other.

Foucault's theory of governmentality, the 'conduct of conduct' (Foucault, 1988) rests on his ideas of discipline and of modern government as biopower, 'the subjugation of bodies and the control of populations' (Foucault, 1978, p. 140). Including disciplinary measures regarding the compulsion of certain behaviour, biopower also encompasses the mobilization of power/knowledge to manage health and welfare through individual choice. Forms of surveillance then discipline the context of that choice; in the extreme of Foucault's carceral panopticon, the goal is an architecture of perceived surveillance that will 'induce in the inmate a state of conscious and permanent visibility that assures the automatic functioning of power... [I]n short, that the inmates themselves should be caught up in a power situation of which they are themselves the bearers' (Foucault, 1995, p. 201). Neoliberal governmentality is characterized by 'technologies of subjectivity' whereby knowledge acquisition enables 'self-government' and increased personal responsibility, and by 'technologies of subjection' that organize people and space efficiently on a larger scale (Ong, 2006; see also Harvey, 1989; Hackworth, 2006). Some of this governmentality is overtly produced: for example, citizenship tests, guides for new immigrants, and public information campaigns encouraging everything from flu shots to recycling, construct ideal behaviour that extends beyond obeying the law to include private responsibilities, public manners, dress and hygiene (see White, 2006). Other aspects result from the discursive blurring of the identities of citizen and consumer, which has been enabled and encouraged by both governments and corporations. The citizen under neoliberal frameworks is commonly recast as the taxpaying consumer of rights and (more often) privileges, framed in the language of markets that are 'efficient, just and natural'; similarly, the actions of the consumer-as-activist conflates purchasing power with political power (Antony and Broad, 1999; Somers, 2008).

Citizenship is not a synonym for activism. If we celebrate 'citizenship' as a purely positive and liberating institution, we participate in the disciplinary work such a positive discourse of 'citizenship' performs, and we risk losing a critical, political edge to our analysis. As the terms of political and economic reference continue to churn and change, citizenship remains, for the state, 'a key tool to govern under conditions of high global mobility and acute inequality' (Guarnizo, 2012, p. 2). Nor is citizenship a 'thing' in and of itself, but rather a relationship. The dynamic between the governor and the governed is always present – and our understanding of that dynamic as a process of governmentality and its response (or, equally fairly, as a process of claims and the governor's response) is only further enriched by the careful and thoughtful inclusion of all forms of governance, not only that of formal government and official policing. The compliance sought by corporations, the manipulation of our desires and identities by advertising, the disciplining of our behaviour by community – these all have their impact on citizens' capacity to be political. Both analysts and activists, to borrow Guarnizo's phrase, must appreciate the unavoidable clash of the governed with the governor and be mindful of the power struggle embedded not only in the open conflict, but also in the quiet order.

WHAT IS URBAN ABOUT CITIZENSHIP?

Much of the previous discussion concerns urban citizenship as a question of scale; the city's relationship to citizenship has many further manifestations. The profound changes to the city and urban space that have occurred since the emergence of the nation-state and the rise of industrial and post-industrial capitalism have transformed urban space, steadily turning the city into an instrument of capital. 'Cities, [Lefebvre, Castells and Harvey] argued, are major basing points for the production, circulation, and consumption of commodities, and their evolving internal sociospatial organization, governance systems, and patterns of sociopolitical conflict must be understood in relation to this role' (Brenner et al., 2012, p. 3). In parallel to this capitalization of the urban is the urbanization of capital, as the processes of capital accumulation, surplus, consumption and reinvestment were wired through both cities and newly networked and monitored places, and all space thus became increasingly 'urban' (Harvey, 1985; Lefebvre [1974] 1991).

The city is not neutral space. We must therefore bring an equally critical approach to the study of the city and processes of urbanization as we have done with citizenship. As Brenner has noted, 'critical urban theory emphasizes the politically and ideologically mediated, socially contested and therefore malleable character of urban space – that is, its continual (re)construction as a site, medium, and outcome of historically specific relations of social power' (Brenner, 2012, p. 11). Following Lefebvre's conceptual triad, urban space includes perceived space (spatial practices), conceived space (representation of space) and lived space (space of representation) – and the dynamic among them (Lefebvre [1974] 1991, pp. 33–9). The specific, embodied, lived experience of the city and the struggle for it remains at the heart of such analysis, which must be able to 'grasp the concrete' (p. 40). In Harvey's summary of Lefebvre's idea of the right to the city, he reminds us that it does not originate among intellectuals, but 'primarily rises up from the streets, out from the neighbourhoods, as a cry for help and sustenance by oppressed peoples in desperate times' (Harvey, 2013, p. xiii). Similarly, for Marcuse, critical urban theory should be drawn from what can be learned from existing, actual resistance and the effort to realize a more progressive potential; 'critical theory is intended to illuminate and inform the future course of such practice' (Marcuse, 2012, p. 25).

The city is a place of struggle, with the potential for extraordinary emancipation *and* oppressive surveillance and control. For many, the city is a refuge and a place of empowerment. This can manifest itself in small, everyday ways or in large-scale, public ways. It could be a one anonymous house in which to hide or it could be a formal City of Sanctuary. The city is a big, busy, ever-innovating place, with freedom from tradition, freedom from others' predetermined idea of oneself, freedom from being known (Boone, 1996). For example, women (Stansell, 1987; Strange, 1995), blacks (Stovall, 1998; Boittin, 2010; Hine and McCluskey, 2012) and queer communities (Chauncey, 1995; Boone, 1996) have all sought and found freedoms in the public space of the city unavailable to them in rural areas or in the private space of home. In a nice parallel to the ideals embedded in ideas of citizenship, Berman finds in the city the potential for nothing less than the pinnacle for human civilization, arguing for the centrality of the city throughout history and the connection between its renewal and the renewal of human society and culture (Berman, 1996). Harvey also notes the utopian hopes and dreams long embedded in the idea of the city and its possibility for social, cultural and political change, in part because, in keeping with Lefebvre, 'there are already multiple practices within the urban that themselves are full to overflowing with alternative possibilities' (Harvey, 2013, p. xvii).

The possibilities for refuge, activism and empowerment, like the city and citizenship, are all ever in motion, and they are each relational to each other and to other things. The city's public space and the reach of urban media allow for the city's greatest opportunity for citizen activism. The accessibility of large space where a collective may gather and the visibility of central streets together enable the possibility of an elemental democratic political order in which giving public voice to dissent was expected. Indeed, the practice of using the city's public space for protest is fundamental to its shape and history. Historically, ordinary citizens have considered common public space to be theirs for giving voice to protest (Goheen, 1993), and, for some communities, riots have been more effective at producing change than any formal political action (Greenberg, 1992). The streets remain a critical arena for political mobilization, particularly of the marginalized (Holston, 1998), and thus the physical shape of the city and the physical, social and legal accessibility of its space remain key to the practice of citizenship. 'It is clear that certain environmental characteristics are more conducive to rebellious protest than others – such as the centrality of squares...the more easily barricaded street' (Harvey, 2013, p. 117). Here the city definitively distinguishes itself from non-urban space that lacks the visibility, accessibility and collectivity needed for political acts.

But the city is also 'the grid', a space produced for specific purposes of efficient capital accumulation, and the biopolitical management of the population, often with the consequence of the erasure of a sense of place (Sennett, 1990; Scott, 1998; Cresswell, 2006). The bureaucracy and technology of the urban reaches through and beyond the city to link individuals and potentially track their comings and goings, activities and purchases. Movement through the city is surveilled, with cameras monitoring car-parks, storefronts, sidewalks, traffic light violations, highway congestion. On the street, police commonly stop and question (and even frisk) 'suspicious' persons, who are frequently racialized youth. Far from liberating, the city for many is restricting, suffocating, incarcerating (Harris, 1997; Wortley, 2004; Brunson, 2007; Weber and Bowling, 2012). Part of the fundamental dynamic of the city is the tension and conflict between the desire to control or regulate, and the desire to disrupt or break free. For the more radical, 'the just city will not be built by planners or other power holders, it will be conquered from them' (Uitermark, 2012, p. 201).

The city is a particular kind of place: both a sociological phenomenon and a geographic (social, ecological and territorial) one. For Mumford, 'a city in the sociological sense [is] a place in which the social heritage is concentrated, and in which the possibilities of continuous social intercourse and interaction raise to a higher potential the activities of men' (Mumford, 1938, p. 161). The city is caught up in the actions of actors who live, work and play there, but also those who pass through it or are entirely beyond it. All of these also shape the city and produce its space. For all the particulars of its assemblages, the city is always, by definition, the centralization and concentration of resources, the production of goods and services, and a site of consumption and administration (Filion and Bunting, 1991). It has an ecological, economic and social diversity and complexity that smaller and less dense places do not. A driving factor of the production of its landscape is the nature of its economy, which is, critically, interdependent and thus fundamentally distinct from a rural economy (Lefebvre, 1996). The city hosts a density of built and social landscapes. Cities put things and peoples close together – not because their residents choose to do so, and often because non-residents chose to construct it so. Each generation inherits the political, social and built infrastructures of its predecessors, which limit and drive vectors of mobility, communication, opportunity, identity formation and knowledge production. They may be changed and overcome, but their durability must be acknowledged.

Today's critical scholarship has its roots in the responses to urban crises in the 1960s. One of the earliest critiques of the state-led capitalist transformation of the post-war city came with Jacobs's challenge to modernist planning, *The Death and Life of Great American Cities* ([1961] 1993). Lefebvre's 'The Right to the City' (1968, in Lefebvre, 1996) and other urban writings appeared in the wake of the 1968 student uprising in France; the theoretical crystallization of his thinking, *The Production of Space*, was then published (in French) in 1974 (Lefebvre [1974] 1991). From here, the literature on urban citizenship divides loosely into two approaches (though there have been efforts to move through and beyond this framing; see Goonewardena et al., 2008): the first is a broadly structuralist focus on capital and class struggle. Lefebvre's student Castells published *The Urban Question: A Marxist Approach* in 1972 (1977 in English), and Harvey's *Social Justice and the City* appeared in 1973 (Harvey [1973] 2009). The renewed engagement with Marxism and other radical theory in urban studies also reconnected the metropolis to the hinterland in a new and critical way. Harvey's student Neil Smith in particular took on the Chicago School's earlier approach to the city, underscoring the ways in which the revolutionary struggle had returned to the city as a whole. Whereas previous struggles arose in the factory within the city, now the entire city itself had become a platform for the circulation of capital and the accumulation of profit, through both public and private resources, reproducing in the city the socially and geographically uneven development that had been observed at regional and national scales (N. Smith, 1979). Critical studies of contests over the use and control of particular public sites in cities (for example, N. Smith, 1990, on Tomkins Square Park; Mitchell, 2003, on People's Park) have documented the ways in which local battles over the gentrification and 'renewal' of the city directly result from a larger effort of capital to control urban space. Lees et al. have argued that gentrification is a global phenomenon reaching well beyond the inner city and is nothing less than the 'leading edge of neoliberal urbanism' (2008, p. xvii). Neoliberalizing forces in the city, especially the move towards privatization of resources and space, have increasingly commodified fundamental needs such as housing and masked them in discourses of rationality and choice, in what Somers has termed 'the fear and loathing of the public sphere' and for Mitchell is the 'annihilation' of public space (N. Smith, 1996; Mitchell, 2003; Slater, 2006; Somers, 2008, p. 254).

The second approach (which also builds on the first) draws more directly on feminist/post-structuralist/post-colonial theory and argues that the city through a critical lens must also recognize the intentional patriarchal, heteronormative and racialized ordering of social and economic space (Peake, 1993). Much of this literature pays closer attention to the lived experience of the city (the 'concrete' of Lefebvre) than the first approach, as it substantiates the theory of the city as a 'difference machine', producing identities by which to make distinctions in order to privilege and create 'others' (Isin, 2001). The exclusion of women from the public sphere is embedded in the processes of urbanization and capital reviewed above. Enshrined in law and social norms, the effort to regulate women in public has been no less focused or violent than that of class struggle; as Ryan has observed, it has even 'provok[ed] a military order aimed at controlling the behavior of one sex' (Ryan, 1992, p. 3). As women began to achieve some urban freedoms, processes of suburbanization followed in the wake, explicitly creating 'appropriate' and separate space for women to reinstate their domestic role in the private sphere, outside the city (Mackenzie, 1988). Racialized populations have equally been marked and violently regulated through the city, and processes of urbanization (particularly 'urban renewal') have also been employed as a strategy for defining and controlling those communities (D.M. Smith, 1992; Boittin, 2010). The segregated spaces for women and for minorities that endure, in formal, legal codes, and the social monitoring, segregation and exclusion from public space that continues today – women, racialized communities, religious minorities (particularly those with distinct forms of dress), youth, the homeless, and so on – continue to perpetuate and normalize unequal access and opportunity. As Smith has summarized, 'socially divided societies reproduce their forms of social difference in geographical space and, by corollary, that hierarchically produced geographies reaffirm and reproduce social differences' (N. Smith, 2005, p. 895).

The patterns of uneven development and unequal social relations are not new to the neoliberal city, having been forged in many capital cities in their days as imperial metropoles (Driver and Gilbert, 1999; Boittin, 2010). However, new urban networks, the development of a new type of 'global city' and accompanying urban forms have given rise to a situation where politically, socially and economically, 'global society is drastically out of balance' (Somers, 2008, p. 3). The class struggle inherent in the geography of the modern city is exacerbated in global cities, which are in some ways at war with themselves (Sassen, 1997; Isin, 2001). As a network and space of flows, '[t]he global city is not a place, but a process' (Castells, 1996, p. 386). Nonetheless, these flows of capital and people that arrive there find places in the city in which to settle. Indeed, global cities thrive on the diverse and increasing immigration – on the diversity of ideas and the exploitation of immigrant labour, especially those who are undocumented or in a similarly precarious state. Yet, at the same time, the global city's elite also resists that diversity in its drive to stabilize and improve its capital into gentrified neighbourhoods, enclaves behind gates, concierges and security codes (Isin, 2001; Lees et al., 2008). Despite the need for workers to maintain the city, the unhindered economic pursuits of the wealthy lead to an increasing refusal to make space for affordable housing, transit and social space for those workers, often in the guise of renewal and order (Mitchell, 2003).

Notwithstanding cities' overarching commonalities of neoliberalism and flows of global capital, the argument is simultaneously made that the city is produced on the ground, and the actions of its residents constantly shape and reshape the city in particular space/time constellations that make each city unique. Cities are not *only* urban; they are not congruent and synonymous in their form and content. Each city is specific as any place is, contingent to climate, topography, history, personalities and coincidence. The complexity and dynamism of the city, generally, intensifies the particularity of each city, specifically. Attention to such detail is the 'concrete' of the struggle to which Lefebvre referred, and from which scholars must draw theoretical and political insight. There are significant questions about who is able to organize and create an institution to represent and lobby for a constituency and thus have the capacity to speak politically (that is, to be heard) in the city (Basu, 2007). Moreover, processes of public consultation, previously 'a tool for empowering urban citizens', have become 'a tool for grounding political authority in the context of urban decline' (McQuarrie, 2013, p. 143; see also Basu, 2007; Hamel, 2011). The city of the streets, the city of inhabitants, the city as it is lived, must continually be distinguished from the city as represented, especially in its formal political spaces.

The active disruption of the order and rhythm of the city remains a key strategy of resistance (Holston and Appadurai, 1999). Lefebvre argued that any intervention that disturbed the efficient capitalist production of space necessarily had an impact and produced a ripple effect, just as every act of spatial planning had in the first place (Lefebvre [1974] 1991; Chiodelli, 2009). In recent years, a strategy has (re)emerged of the occupation of urban space that complements yet moves away from (but does not replace) the temporariness of protest marches and rallies, as well as away from confrontational strategies involving the direct challenge of police forces or damage to property. The Arab Spring, Spain's *acampadas*, and the 'Occupy' movement are examples. The city shapes the form and character of activism and is shaped by it in turn; the mass occupation of urban space has continued to challenge the normative shape and place of politics (Magnusson, 2012) away from formal sites of political engagement, such as voting.

Occupations have had a variety of targets and produced a variety of results. The occupation of Cairo's Tahrir Square from 25 January 2011 played a central role in the revolution that led to the military's removal of President Hosni Mubarak from power. A chain of protests resulted in a change of government in Libya and Yemen (and a second change in Egypt in 2013), and brought political reform to Morocco and Jordan. Other uprisings have been crushed by the state; some protests continue to the present; and Syria collapsed tragically into civil war. Spain's *acampada* movement, under the banner of 'Democracia real YA!' (Real Democracy NOW!) used social media to organize and encourage mass protest against austerity measures in 61 cities across the country, leading to encampments with assemblies with set meeting times, and collective kitchens with meal provision. As a 1 May 2011 blog post on their website explained, the banks had provoked the economic crisis but took no responsibility for those harmed as a consequence: 'We blame the political and economic powers for our precarious situation and insist on a change of course' ('*Acusamos a los poderes políticos y económicos de nuestra precaria situación y exigimos un cambio de rumbo*'; Democracia real YA! website, 2011). In a move that would be replicated by many similar movements, Democracia real YA! refused all partisan political alliances and mobilized in the name of the poor, the unemployed, the evicted, the homeless and the outraged.

In July 2011, the Vancouver activist group, Adbusters, posted a blog inviting a massive occupation of 'Wall Street': 'On September 17, we want to see 20,000 people flood into lower Manhattan, set up tents, kitchens, peaceful barricades and occupy Wall Street for a few months', in what they hoped would be 'a fusion of Tahrir with the acampadas of Spain' (Adbusters, 2011). Activists set up a camp in New York City's Zuccotti Park, and quickly transformed it into a habitation, complete with meal support and a public lending library. Within a few weeks, similar urban protest encampments in the name of 'the 99%' were established by local activists in cities around the world, many of which connected with local social services or became one, helping to feed and house homeless persons. At the height of the movement, there were over 600 encampments across the United States and in almost 1000 cities in 82 countries, on every inhabited continent.

This form of urban activism has many antecedents (Harvey, 2013, pp. 115–16), drawing as it does on strategies of sit-in protests in civil rights struggles, commonly organized around an axis of identity marked for exclusion. While there are some new aspects to these protests in the technologies of social media and smartphones that may facilitate mobilization, occupying urban space has a long history. There is extensive documentation, especially in the feminist/post-colonial literature, of these movements and their implicit or explicit theorization of the city. From early points of contact, indigenous peoples have occupied city space as a way of becoming more visible to the state (Wood, 2006), or to insist on territorial claims, perhaps most dramatically exemplified by the occupation of the island of Alcatraz from 1969 to 1971 (Johnson, 1996). Women challenged the gendered segregation of the public/private divide by 'occupying' social spaces in the city unaccompanied by men, where sometimes just walking down the street after dusk was a transgression (Stansell, 1987; Ryan, 1992; Strange, 1995). In the American civil rights movement, the Congress of Racial Equality deliberately strategized direct action campaigns where African Americans employed the occupation of public urban space – the bus, the lunch counter – to challenge segregation and exclusion (Meier and Rudwick, 1973).

However, there is a key difference in the current strategy. For nineteenth- and twentieth-century women's movements and the civil rights movement, the issue was a literal exclusion from particular public places. Occupation of such spaces was an assertion of their right to be where they were told, by law and by social norms, that they were not allowed. Today, the issue is access to 'public space' more broadly, a 'right to the city' that takes literal shape but whose object is Lefebvre's more abstract idea of society and the ability to participate. It is as much about process as place, about transparency, accessibility and accountability in democracy and the economy, in both public and private institutions. As such it is not simply a challenge to particular exclusions, but an assertion of a reconfiguration of the polity and citizenship rights. Encampment in urban public space is a successful disturbance of the order of 'the grid' *and* all that it represents.

The disappearance of that urban public space is its own issue. It occurs through the privatization or commercialization of space (Mitchell, 2003), and also through the development of urban form that does not provide it. Today the dominant form of city building is the 'in-between city'. The term (*Zwischenstadt* in the original German), coined by German planner, Thomas Sieverts, captures the phenomenon of development at the outskirts of the formal city boundaries driven by global flows of people and capital: major transport infrastructure (highways, railways, trucking depots, airports), large-scale housing for immigrants and large-scale commercial and industrial development, located there for easy access to large, open space at low rents, access to transport infrastructure for international shipping and delivery and local distribution. It is characterized by a high degree of spatial differentiation and poor relationships between its social and other landscapes, with a car-friendly transit infrastructure surrounding either high-density apartment housing (often public housing) or wealthy residential enclaves. It is neither city nor suburb, as we have traditionally understood them, and cannot be transformed into either (Sieverts, 2003).

The in-between city often gives the appearance of a lack of planning or even neglect, whereas the reality is a landscape of competition or even conflict, producing winners and losers but little coherence overall (Grant, 2011). It is the result of 'uneven distribution of infrastructures in the current global, neoliberal urban environment' in which access to resources is increasingly divided and made more exclusive to those with capital (Keil and Young, 2009, p. 490), a process Graham and Marvin (2001) have termed 'splintering urbanism'. Like the splintered city, it is also a landscape of segregation, particularly via residential enclaves or other privileged access to space. 'Unevenness is the nature of capitalist investment in cities always, but the in-between city represents access problems (to participation in social and economic life) in the extreme' (Young et al., 2011, p. 250). In its near-paradoxical rhythm, the fragmentation and splintering of the city produced through privilege and exclusion may in turn create spaces for community organizing and solidarity (Lustiger-Thaler, 1994), but these areas of the in-between city are an example of how urban form may foreclose possibilities for acting politically. Without collective and visible public space, the possibility for any political act of engaging the state is frustrated, and potentially eliminated (Wood, 2013).

CONCLUSION

The idea and practice of urban citizenship presents several distinct forms of citizenship, whose agonistic relationships are inherent in the fundamental political struggle (Mouffe, 1993) that necessarily constitutes citizenship and in the geographic context of that struggle. Unlike the specific goals of 'environmental citizenship' or 'queer citizenship', the vision of urban citizenship in the eyes of many scholars and activists is not simply a transformed city, though it hopefully includes that. In the Lefebvrian theorization of 'the right to the city', urban citizenship is one that uses the city because of what it is and what it represents, to strike a blow for something much larger, and at times a much less articulate or specific goal. As Marcuse has argued, 'Lefebvre is quite clear on this: it is not the right to the existing city that is demanded, but the right to a future city, indeed not necessarily a city in the conventional sense at all, but a place in an urban society'. Citing Lefebvre directly, he adds, '"[The right to the city] can only be formulated as a transformed and renewed right to urban life...thus from this point on I will no longer refer to the city but to the urban"' (Marcuse, 2012, p. 35).

However, in practice, 'urban citizenship' is also the production (and curtailing) of political subjectivity where city space is used to discipline and surveil its inhabitants. The city is a landscape saturated with commercial advertising and security cameras, and this impacts the meaning and practice of political subjectivity. The urban technologies of the internet and smartphones that link us to a global network of information and encounter in turn monitor and process our activities to better profile us as consumer targets. Urban behaviour is governed through traditional legal measures such as anti-vagrancy laws and through urban street architecture that discourages sleeping in public. And most significantly, urban protest in any form, from graffiti to protest to encampment, is met with an increasingly militarized police response (L. Wood, 2014).

Urban citizenship is an inherently agonistic area of study and practice. The battles for the city and for the right to have rights are both dynamic relationships of contested claims (Isin, 2001; Somers, 2008; see also Mouffe, 1993). Massive urban mobilization that seeks either to use the city as platform or to target the city itself for transformation constitutes a new public that crosses lines of political identity, producing new solidarity, but also challenges of competing interests and strategies. These new claims challenge the form of the city and access within it; they also strike at the heart of 'citizenship' itself, as the practice of being political is de-territorialized and unbound from membership in a given polity and from the spaces of formal politics (Sassen, 1997, 2009; Isin, 2001; Ong, 2006; Magnusson, 2012). The mass mobilizations in urban public space that we have witnessed in the last few years merits fuller attention. Some scholars have begun to raise interesting questions about the significance of the Occupy movement for the future of place-based urban activism, for social movements and alliances (Hedges, 2012; Hugill and Thorburn, 2012). Nevertheless, much remains to be done to document the stories of the encampment movements, both in terms of their occupation of city space and subsequent new networks and activism, and in terms of the response by the state and its allies.

Much also remains to be done to bring neoliberal and (neo)colonial theories of citizenship and the city into conversation with each other, and to engage non-Western literature on citizenship and the city in the process (a significant limitation of this chapter itself). The particular and the broad historical production of urban landscapes and networks make each city a palimpsest of architectures of governance and resistance, built into its form and discourse. Despite efforts to sustain 'an imagined epochal break between colonial past and non-colonial present' (Hugill and Toews, 2014, p. 77), the lived reality at the local level and embedded in global networks that continue to follow imperial paths from previous centuries, reveals a more complex experience.

Neither is urban citizenship singular in its meaning or practice. The city as site, the city as platform, and the city as emblem for and manifestation of society at large all figure in the transformation of the urban and the political in the face of neoliberal urbanism. Strategies of activists and governors each work to push the meaning, possibilities and space of politics in new directions. The ever-growing list of mechanisms of policing, securitization and enclosure is met with a multiplicity of tactics, from voter drives to community gardens to public occupations. Each space claimed is an unfinished victory, as practices of the governors and the governed continue to change the city and the practice of politics.

REFERENCES

Adachi, K. (1976), 'The enemy that never was: a history of the Japanese Canadians', Toronto, ON: McClelland and Stewart.
Adbusters (2011), '#OCCUPYWALLSTREET: a shift in revolutionary tactics', accessed 24 February 2014 at https://www.adbusters.org/blogs/adbusters-blog/occupywallstreet.html.
Antony, W. and D. Broad (eds) (1999), *Citizens or Consumers? Social Policy in a Market Society*, Halifax, NS: Fernwood.
Barber, B.R. (1984), *Strong Democracy: Participatory Politics for a New Age*, reprinted 2004, Berkeley, CA/Los Angeles, CA/London: University of California Press.
Barber, B.R. (2013), *If Mayors Ruled the World: Dysfunctional Nations, Rising Cities*, New Haven, CT: Yale University Press.
Barney, D. (2007), *One Nation Under Google: Citizenship in the Technological Republic*, Toronto, ON: Hart House, University of Toronto, accessed 24 February 2014 at http://www.mcgill.ca/files/arts/barney_2007HartHouseLecture.pdf.
Basu, R. (2007), 'Negotiating acts of citizenship in an era of neoliberal reform: the game of school closures', *International Journal of Urban and Regional Research*, **31**(1), 109–27.
Bauböck, R. (2003), 'Reinventing urban citizenship', *Citizenship Studies*, **7**(2), 139–60.
Berman, M. (1996), 'Falling towers: city life after urbicide', in D. Crow (ed.), *Geography and Identity: Exploring and Living Geopolitics of Identity*, Washington, DC: Maisoneuve Press, pp. 172–92.
Boittin, J.A. (2010), *Colonial Metropolis: The Urban Grounds of Anti-Imperialism and Feminism in Interwar Paris*, Lincoln, NE/London: University of Nebraska Press.
Boone, J.A. (1996), 'Queer sites in modernism: Harlem/the Left Bank/Greenwich Village', in P. Yaeger (ed.), *The Geography of Identity*, Ann Arbor, MI: University of Michigan Press, pp. 243–72.
Brenner, N. (2012), 'What is critical urban theory?', in N. Brenner, P. Marcuse and M. Mayer (eds), *Cities for People, Not for Profit: Critical Urban Theory and the Right to the City*, London/New York: Routledge, pp. 10–23.
Brenner, N., P. Marcuse and M. Mayer (2012), 'Cities for people, not for profit: an introduction', in N. Brenner, P. Marcuse and M. Mayer (eds), *Cities for People, Not for Profit: Critical Urban Theory and the Right to the City*, London/New York: Routledge, pp. 1–9.
Brunson, R.K. (2007), '"Police don't like black people": African American young men's accumulated police experiences', *Criminology & Public Policy*, **6**(1), 71–102.
Castells, M. (1977), *The Urban Question*, London: Arnold.
Castells, M. (1996), *The Rise of the Network Society*, Oxford: Blackwell.
Chauncey, G. (1995), *Gay New York: Gender, Urban Culture and the Making of the Gay Male World, 1890–1940*, New York: Basic Books.
Chiodelli, F. (2009), 'La cittadinanza secondo Henri Lefebvre: urbana, attiva, a matrice spaziale', *Territorio*, **51**, 103–9.
Cox, K. (1998), 'Spaces of dependence, spaces of engagement and the politics of scale, or: looking for local politics', *Political Geography*, **17**(1), 1–23.
Cresswell, T. (2006), *On the Move: Mobility in the Modern Western World*, New York/London: Routledge.
Crick, B. (2001), 'Introduction', in B. Crick (ed.), *Citizens: Towards a Citizenship Culture*, Oxford: Blackwell, pp. 1–9.
Dalton, R.J. (2004), *Democratic Challenges, Democratic Choices: The Erosion of Political Support in Advanced Industrial Democracies*, Oxford: Oxford University Press.
Dalton, R.J. (2009), *The Good Citizen: How the Young are Reshaping American Politics*, revised edition, Washington, DC: Congressional Quarterly Press.
Dalton, R.J. and C. Welzel (eds) (2013), *The Civic Culture Transformed: From Allegiant to Assertive Citizens*, Cambridge, UK: Cambridge University Press.
Democracia real YA!, accessed 2 January 2014 at http://www.democraciarealya.es.
Driver, F. and D. Gilbert (1999), *Imperial Cities: Landscape, Display and Identity*, Manchester, UK/New York: Manchester University Press.

Filion, P. and T.E. Bunting (1991), 'Introduction: perspectives on the city', in T.E. Bunting and P. Filion (eds), *Canadian Cities in Transition*, 2nd edition, Oxford: Oxford University Press, pp. 2–22.
Foucault, M. (1978), *The History of Sexuality: An Introduction*, Vol. 1, New York: Random House.
Foucault, M. (1988), 'Technologies of the self', in L.H. Martin, H. Gutman and P.H. Hutton (eds), *Technologies of the Self: A Seminar with Michel Foucault*, Amherst, MA: University of Massachusetts Press, pp. 16–49.
Foucault, M. (1995), *Discipline and Punish: The Birth of the Prison*, 2nd edition, trans. A. Sheridan, New York: Vintage.
Goheen, P. (1993), 'The ritual of the streets in mid-19th-century Toronto', *Environment and Planning D: Society and Space*, **11**(2), 127–45.
Goonewardena, K., S. Kipfer, R. Milgrom and C. Schmid (eds) (2008), *Space, Difference, Everyday Life: Reading Henri Lefebvre*, New York: Routledge.
Graham, S. and S. Marvin (2001), *Splintering Urbanisms: Networked Infrastructures, Technological Mobilities and the Urban Condition*, New York: Routledge.
Grant, J. (2011), 'The fight for (sub)urban form: urbanizing or privatizing the suburban realm?', in D. Young, P.B. Wood and R. Keil (eds), *In-Between Infrastructure: Urban Connectivity in an Age of Vulnerability*, Kelowna, BC: Praxis (e)Press, pp. 101–14.
Greenberg, C. (1992), 'The politics of disorder: reexamining Harlem's riots of 1935 and 1943', *Journal of Urban History*, **18**(4), 395–441.
Guarnizo, L.E. (2012), 'The fluid, multi-scalar, and contradictory construction of citizenship', in M.P. Smith and M. McQuarrie (eds), *Remaking Urban Citizenship: Organizations, Institutions, and the Right to the City*, New Brunswick, NJ/London: Transaction Publishers, pp. 11–35.
Hackworth, J. (2006), *The Neoliberal City: Governance, Ideology, and Development in American Urbanism*, Ithaca, NY: Cornell University Press.
Hamel, P. (2011), 'Collective action on infrastructure and the decentred metropolis', in D. Young, P.B. Wood and R. Keil (eds), *In-Between Infrastructure: Urban Connectivity in an Age of Vulnerability*, Kelowna, BC: Praxis (e)Press, pp. 225–36.
Harris, D. (1997), 'Driving while black and all other traffic offences: the Supreme Court and pretextual traffic stops', *Journal of Criminal Law and Criminology*, **87**(2), 544–82.
Harvey, D. (1985), *The Urbanization of Capital: Studies in the History and Theory of Capitalist Urbanization*, Baltimore, MD: Johns Hopkins University Press.
Harvey, D. (1989), 'From managerialism to entrepreneurialism: the transformation in urban governance in late capitalism', *Geografiska Annaler. Series B, Human Geography*, **71**(1), 3–17.
Harvey, D. ([1973] 2009), *Social Justice and the City*, revised edition, Athens, GA/London: University of Georgia Press.
Harvey, D. (2013), *Rebel Cities: From the Right to the City to the Urban Revolution*, London: Verso.
Hedges, C. (2012), *Days of Destruction, Days of Revolt*, New York: Nation Books.
Held, D. (2002), 'Law of states, law of peoples: three models of sovereignty', *Legal Theory*, **8**(1), 1–20.
Hine, D.C. and J. McCluskey Jr (eds) (2012), *The Black Chicago Renaissance*, Chicago, IL: University of Illinois Press.
Holston, J. (1998), 'Spaces of insurgent citizenship', in L. Sandercock (ed.), *Making the Invisible Visible: A Multicultural Planning History*, Berkeley, CA: University of California Press, pp. 37–56.
Holston, J. and A. Appadurai (1999), 'Introduction: cities and citizenship', in J. Holston (ed.), *Cities and Citizenship*, Durham, NC: Duke University Press, pp. 1–18.
Hugill, D. and E. Thorburn (2012), 'Reactivating the social body in insurrectionary times: a dialogue with Franco "Bifo" Berardi', *Berkeley Planning Journal*, **25**(1), 210–20.
Hugill, D. and O. Toews (2014), 'Born again urbanism: new missionary incursions, aboriginal resistance and barriers to rebuilding relationships in Winnipeg's North End', *Human Geography*, **7**(1), 69–84.

Isin, E.F. (2001), *Being Political: Genealogies of Citizenship*, Minneapolis, MN: University of Minnesota Press.
Isin, E.F. (2007), 'City.state: critique of scalar thought', *Citizenship Studies*, 11(2), 211–28.
Isin, E.F. and B.S. Turner (2007), 'Investigating citizenship: an agenda for citizenship studies', *Citizenship Studies*, 11(1), 5–17.
Isin, E.F. and P. Wood (1999), *Citizenship and Identity*, London: Sage.
Jacobs, J. ([1961] 1993), *The Death and Life of Great American Cities*, New York: Random House.
Jones, K.T. (1998), 'Scale as epistemology', *Political Geography*, 17(1), 25–8.
Johnson, T.R. (1996), *The Occupation of Alcatraz Island: Indian Self-Determination and the Rise of Indian Activism*, Chicago, IL: University of Illinois Press.
Keil, R. and D. Young (2009), 'Fringe explosions: risk and vulnerability in Canada's new in-between landscape', *Canadian Geographer*, 53(4), 488–99.
Lees, L., T. Slater and E. Wyly (2008), *Gentrification*, New York/Milton Park, UK: Routledge.
Lefebvre, H. ([1974] 1991), *The Production of Space*, trans. D. Nicholson-Smith, Oxford: Blackwell.
Lefebvre, H. (1996), 'The right to the city', in E. Kofman and E. Lebas (eds and trans.), *Writings on Cities*, Oxford/New York: Wiley-Blackwell.
Lustiger-Thaler, H. (1994), 'Community and social practices: the contingency of everyday life', in V. Amit-Talai and H. Lustiger-Thaler (eds), *Urban Lives: Fragmentation and Resistance*, Toronto, ON: McClelland and Stewart, pp. 20–44.
Mackenzie, S. (1988), 'Building women, building cities: toward gender sensitive theory in the environmental disciplines', in C. Andrew and B.M. Milroy (eds), *Life Spaces: Gender, Household, Employment*, Vancouver, BC: University of British Columbia Press, pp. 13–30.
Magnusson, W. (2002), 'On the universal and the particular: sovereignty and the urban global', in W. Magnusson and K. Shaw (eds), *A Political Space: Reading the Global Through Clayoquot Sound*, Montreal, QC/Kingston, ON: McGill-Queen's University Press, pp. 113–20.
Magnusson, W. (2012), *Politics of Urbanism: Seeing Like a City*, New York: Routledge.
Marcuse, P. (2012), 'Whose right(s) to what city?', in N. Brenner, P. Marcuse and M. Mayer (eds), *Cities for People, Not for Profit: Critical Urban Theory and the Right to the City*, London/New York: Routledge, pp. 24–41.
Marshall, T.H. (1950), *Citizenship and Social Class*, Cambridge, UK: Cambridge University Press.
Marston, S.A. (2000), 'The social construction of scale', *Progress in Human Geography*, 24(2), 219–42.
McQuarrie, M. (2013), 'No contest: participatory technologists and the transformation of urban authority', *Public Culture*, 25(1), 143–75.
Meier, A. and E.M. Rudwick (1973), *CORE: A Study in the Civil Rights Movement, 1942–68*, New York: Oxford University Press.
Mitchell, D. (2003), *The Right to the City: Social Justice and the Fight for Public Space*, New York: Guilford Press.
Mouffe, C. (1993), *The Return of the Political*, London/New York: Verso.
Mumford, L. (1938), *The Culture of Cities*, New York: Harcourt, Brace & Co.
Ngai, M.M. (2005), *Illegal Aliens and the Making of Modern America*, Princeton, NJ/Oxford: Princeton University Press.
Ong, A. (2006), 'Mutations in citizenship', *Theory, Culture, and Society*, 22(3), 499–503.
Peake, L. (1993), '"Race" and sexuality: challenging the patriarchal structuring of urban social space', *Environment and Planning D: Society and Space*, 11(6), 415–32.
Polanyi, K. ([1944] 2001), *The Great Transformation: The Political and Economic Origins of Our Time*, 2nd edition, Boston, MA: Beacon Press.
Purcell, M. (2006), 'Urban democracy and the local trap', *Urban Studies*, 43(11), 1921–41.
Roy, P.E. (2002), 'Lessons in citizenship, 1945–1949: the delayed return of the Japanese to Canada's Pacific Coast', *The Pacific Northwest Quarterly*, 93(2), 69–80.

Ryan, M.P. (1992), *Women in Public: Between Banner and Ballots, 1825–1880*, Baltimore, MD/London: Johns Hopkins University Press.
Sassen, S. (1997), 'Whose city is it? Globalization and the formation of new claims', *Public Culture*, **8**(2), 205–23.
Sassen, S. (2009), 'Incompleteness and the possibility of making: towards denationalized citizenship?' in J. Go (ed.), *Political Power and Social Theory*, Vol. 20, pp. 229–58.
Schudson, M. (1998), *The Good Citizen: A History of American Civic Life*, Cambridge, MA: Harvard University Press.
Scott, J.C. (1998), *Seeing Like a State: How Certain Schemes to Improve the Human Condition Have Failed*, New Haven, CT: Yale University Press.
Sennett, R. (1990), *The Conscience of the Eye: The Design and Social Life of Cities*, New York: Knopf.
Sieverts, T. (2003), *Cities Without Cities: An Interpretation of the Zwischenstadt*, New York: Routledge.
Slater, T. (2006), 'The eviction of critical perspectives from gentrification research', *International Journal of Urban and Regional Research*, **30**(4), 737–57.
Smith, D.M. (ed.) (1992), *The Apartheid City and Beyond: Urbanization and Social Change in South Africa*, London/New York/Johannesburg: Routledge.
Smith, M.P. (2001), *Transnational Urbanism: Locating Globalization*, Malden, MA/Oxford: Blackwell.
Smith, N. (1979), 'Toward a theory of gentrification: a back to the city movement by capital not people', *Journal of the American Planning Association*, **45**(4), 538–48.
Smith, N. (1996), *New Urban Frontier: Gentrification and the Revanchist City*, New York: Routledge.
Smith, N. (2005), 'Neo-critical geography, or, the flat pluralist world of business class', *Antipode*, **37**(5), 887–99.
Somers, M.R. (2008), *Genealogies of Citizenship: Markets, Statelessness, and the Right to Have Rights*, Cambridge, UK/New York: Cambridge University Press.
Stansell, C. (1987), *City of Women: Sex and Class in New York, 1789–1860*, Chicago, IL: University of Illinois Press.
Stovall, T. (1998), *Paris Noir: African Americans in the City of Light*, Boston, MA: Houghton Mifflin.
Strange, C. (1995), *Toronto's Girl Problem: The Perils and Pleasures of the City, 1880–1930*, Toronto, ON: University of Toronto Press.
Uitermark, J. (2012), 'An actually existing just city?', in N. Brenner, P. Marcuse and M. Mayer (eds), *Cities for People, Not for Profit: Critical Urban Theory and the Right to the City*, London/New York: Routledge, pp. 197–214.
Weber, L. and B. Bowling (eds) (2012), *Stop and Search: Police Power in Global Context*, London: Routledge.
White, M. (2006), 'The dispositions of good citizenship: character, symbolic power and disinterest', *Journal of Civil Society*, **2**(2), 111–22.
Wood, P. (2006), 'The "Sarcee War": fragmented citizenship and the city', *Space and Polity*, **10**(3), 229–42.
Wood, L. (2014), *Crisis and Control: The Militarization of Protest Policing*, Toronto, ON: Between the Lines.
Wood, P. (2008), 'The impossibility of global citizenship', in M. O'Sullivan and K. Pashby (eds), *Citizenship Education in the Era of Globalization: Canadian Perspectives*, Rotterdam and Taipei: Sense Publishers, pp. 27–40.
Wood, P. (2013), 'Citizenship in the in-between city', *Canadian Journal of Urban Research*, **22**(1), 111–25.
Wortley, S. (2003), 'Hidden intersections: research on race, crime and criminal justice in Canada', *Canadian Ethnic Studies Journal*, **35**(3), 99–117.
Young, D., P.B. Wood and R. Keil (2011), 'From critique to politics and planning', in D. Young, P.B. Wood and R. Keil (eds), *In-Between Infrastructure: Urban Connectivity in an Age of Vulnerability*, Kelowna, BC: Praxis (e)Press, pp. 249–60.

8. European citizenship
Espen D.H. Olsen

INTRODUCTION

European citizenship is a peculiar construct. It is citizenship of a 'non-state'. Moreover, it is not based on exclusive individual membership of the EU polity; rather, it is derived from national citizenships of EU member states (Closa, 1992) and it was linked already from the first treaties to EU-specific rights to free movement and non-discrimination based on nationality (Plender, 1976; Evans, 1984; Maas, 2007; Olsen, 2008). Not only that, it has been – and still is – hotly contested among academics and politicians alike. This is, of course, not surprising as citizenship is often seen as one of the crucial ideas, statuses and institutions of the nation-state. Is 'European' citizenship then not an oxymoron, a veritable 'pie in the sky' (D'Oliveira, 1995) that has little to do with citizens' real lives and more to do with the utopian visions of overzealous political leaders and cosmopolitan academics?

This chapter charts the vast research field on European citizenship that has blossomed since citizenship became 'official' in European integration through so-called Union citizenship in the Maastricht Treaty. In so doing, the chapter focuses primarily on the political science literature with certain forays into political philosophy and European law where needed. As this volume deals with political citizenship and social movements, specific emphasis is put on different strands of research that focus on the meaning of European citizenship and its development as a specific kind of citizenship institution 'beyond' the nation-state.

In the next section, three main approaches to the study of European citizenship are charted with special emphasis on their different notions of what parts of citizenship politics in the EU are worthy of scholarly attention. Citizenship is politically contested, historically developed, and imbued with normative ideas. As such, it is not surprising, then, that the three main approaches to the study of European citizenship in political analysis have focused on theoretical questions regarding its viability, historical and institutional accounts of its incremental development, and finally normative issues as to the desirability of forging citizenship outside the nation-state. While these different approaches diverge on issues raised and methods, and produce manifold conclusions on the meaning of European citizenship, one can nevertheless distil a certain core of European citizenship as a political and historical phenomenon. The continued struggles over European citizenship and its composite array of rights are then addressed in the final section of the chapter on prospects for future research. I argue that the recent Euro-crisis highlights the link between the rights of European citizenship and social movements. The concluding section thus focuses on this link, with special emphasis on the potential of political and social mobilization of citizens in times of crisis.

THREE APPROACHES TO EUROPEAN CITIZENSHIP

As a preliminary sign of a certain viewpoint in the literature, the following statement is useful: '[T]here are no such animals as "European citizens". There are only French, German, or Italian citizens' (Aron, 1974, p. 653). This conclusion is taken from one of the first articles that discussed European citizenship explicitly. The core of political sociologist Aron's argument has resonated in several later studies of what European citizenship entails, as well as what it can or should be. But the research and thinking on European citizenship is, of course, not one-sided. As will become evident in this chapter, not all scholars are sceptical towards a viable concept of citizenship beyond the nation-state. On the contrary, it is argued by several students of European integration that it is both theoretically possible and normatively desirable to promote a European citizenship different from that of the paradigmatic model of nation-state citizenship. In addition, historical and institutionalist contributions have illuminated the evolving and contested character of citizenship in the European polity. Nevertheless, the main argument of this chapter is that most research done on European citizenship has certain shortcomings, such as relying exclusively on a nation-state model, conversely postulating the linear evolution of citizenship away from the nation-state form, or emphasizing only one dimension such as rights or identity. These problems are particularly important for the broader empirical research field of political citizenship and social movements. An additional aim of the literature review of this chapter is therefore to highlight both problems and merits of different approaches as a prelude to the chapter's final part on future research trajectories and their link to the diverse social movement literature.

Theoretical Research: Essentialist vs Constructivist Ideas on the Viability of European Citizenship

Crudely speaking, most theoretical ideas on citizenship tend to fall either within an essentialist or constructivist vein. 'Essentialists' highlight citizenship as having some kind of natural 'habitat' within the frame of the territorially and culturally confined nation-state. 'Constructivists' hold that citizenship is historically contingent as an institution; it is shaped by specific political, economic, social and cultural forces. In this first section focused on theoretical endeavours to make sense of citizenship outside the nation-state, these two strands are used as guides to different understandings of European citizenship.

That the sceptical and essentialist thrust of Raymond Aron's (1974) seminal article on the prospect of what he called 'multinational' citizenship in many ways marks the advent of an extensive literature on the possibilities of citizenship beyond the nation-state is not surprising. The European project of unification was, at the time when his critical remarks were published, very much imbued with ideas of economic integration and had yet to reach a more political level (Gillingham, 2003; Dinan, 2004; Hix, 2005). Further, as has been shown to be the case in the European setting, explicit citizenship politics prevailed within nation-states (Bellamy et al., 2004). Its practices diverged horizontally between states, and citizenship was not perceived to be involved in a vertical relationship between states and the supranational institutions of the EU. In addition, there seems to have been agreement in conceptual terms that the meaningful domain of individual membership and political community was to be situated within the boundaries of the nation-state form of political organization (see Walzer, 1983, p. 34; Rawls, 1993, pp. 12, 40ff; for retrospective commentaries on the literature, see, e.g., Turner, 1994; Beiner, 1995; Kymlicka and Norman, 1995). Hence the view of citizenship as relevant only in connection to one nation-state naturally follows.

Aron (1974, p. 638) clearly picks up on this when he asks the rhetorical question: 'How could a citizen possibly belong to several political entities at once?' Aron does indeed acknowledge the development of economic rights in the EU from the Treaty of Rome in 1957, but a specific theoretical view of citizenship stands in the way of a broader assessment of what kind of status was in the making in the early developments of European integration futile. Thus he contends that '[t]he notion of multinational citizenship has a primary sense which is of no immediate philosophical import to us' (ibid., p. 644). Citizenship is seen as inherently unitary, and 'multiple' citizenship is denied as a possibility between any political communities or levels. In the end this is connected to an analysis where political rights are seen as unequivocally national in character; and separated from other types of rights in their significance for the ethos of citizenship (ibid., pp. 642ff, 651). Anthony Smith (1992, p. 62) argues in similar fashion by linking the exercise of citizenship to the nation as a political community that 'embodies a common culture and a common social will'. Privileging political rights linked to political community in this way is akin to the Hegelian distinction between *Bürger* and *citoyen*, between private and public aspects of citizenship. The private character of the *Bürger* was to facilitate participation in the economic life of civil society, while the *citoyen* was recognized by active participation in the political life of the community (see Hegel [1821] 1952, p. 124ff).

Indeed, Aron was correct in pointing out the predominantly economic character of the EU in relation to its citizens in the beginning of the 1970s (ibid., p. 647ff; see also Everson, 1995; Gillingham, 2003, p. 82ff). His point is that this did not amount to a citizenship politics proper given the lack of a political dimension (Aron, 1974, p. 647ff). But, the very specific view of citizenship as tied exclusively to the political dimension of participation in a particular political community stops short of acknowledging the potential novelty of an emerging concept of citizenship in European integration. Aron's own theoretical scheme and historical determinism stands in the way of making sense of developments that go against the model of national citizenship. They are simply not conceptually possible from Aron's account. There is as such a clear tendency in this line of thinking to essentialize a certain historical practice of citizenship – the nation-state practice – as the ultimate theoretical yardstick for an appraisal of contemporary developments.

Shore (2004; see also 2000) has provided more recent contributions to deal with the problem of European citizenship. This body of work is especially interesting as its explicit aim is to interpret European citizenship from the standpoint of political anthropology. Although he does not engage directly with Aron's analysis, Shore clearly shares some of its predominant features. One of the key questions resembles Aron's rhetorical question underlined above: 'How can one be a citizen of a non-state?' (Shore, 2004, p. 32). In asking the question of how feasible the idea of post-national citizenship is, Shore (ibid.) emphasizes citizenship as designated through membership of 'a state', further highlighting the citizen as 'a native or naturalized person' – points on which 'most legal scholars agree'. The concept of citizenship is frozen within a certain frame: it 'belongs firmly to the lexical set of "nation", "state" and "peoplehood"' (Williams, 1976). What is paradoxical is that Shore here relies on predominantly legalistic definitions of citizenship even though he emphasizes the need for going beyond the legal reading of (European) citizenship, to 'focus less on

158 *Handbook of political citizenship and social movements*

its legal content than on the political and symbolic uses of citizenship and its functions as a classificatory device and identity-marker' (ibid., p. 28).

Indeed, Shore does ask theoretically interesting questions regarding the feasibility of constructing citizens of a non-state; of where a genuine European demos (common populace) can stem from. But, what is ultimately problematic with a study in this vein is that the aim of a discursive, non-legalistic study of European citizenship does not acknowledge the possibility of European citizenship taking on a logic of its own in the unprecedented process of European integration and polity building. The commendable search for clues regarding the viability of creating European citizens gets lost in a specific position where the concept of citizenship is tied to a specific nation-state–oriented model of citizenship. It ends in a purely theoretical exercise, showing the inconsistencies of an emerging conception against a specific view of citizenship as tied to exclusive community building in a state. The reason for this is that rather than relying on a more dynamic approach of studying how citizenship is conceptualized in European integration, it falls back on a theoretical critique of the process at the outset. Shore's emphasis on the theoretical connection between citizenship and the state is similar to Aron's rhetorical conclusion and perhaps all the more problematic if this is the case, as Meehan (1993, p. 4) has argued that 'his evidential judgment about lack of support for the transformation that would be necessary to be able to speak of European citizenship has not stood the test of time'. European citizen 'animals' might have emerged in the 40-odd years since Aron's sceptical analysis and this is seemingly not invoked in Shore's attempt at a critical appraisal of EU citizenship discourse.

What I argue is that there is not much room for further theoretical reflection in work of this vein. One merely ends up with a statement on the impossibility of different practical realizations of a phenomenon that is already reified in theory (see Brubaker, 1996, p. 16). It is important to state that the point here is not to claim that theorizing on the viability of European citizenship is futile. What this critique of the sceptical contributions to the study of European citizenship shows is that the theoretical perspectives by which one deals with such an unprecedented phenomenon need to be comprehensive in the sense that they will not at the outset deny a certain interpretation on the grounds that the practice is theoretically unfeasible. The theoretical framework should provide the ability to acknowledge institutional and conceptual novelty. A theory that starts out postulating that citizenship is only feasible within a specific level of political order is then reductive against possibly new institutional practices. As Wessels (1997, p. 292) has emphasized: '[W]e are confronted with realities and challenges that might be outside our traditional categories'. There is then a need to adjust the theoretical lenses through which a phenomenon such as citizenship is typically assessed and categorized.

Studies based on constructivist perspectives are evident in what is often dubbed the post-national literature on European citizenship. In his writings on the European experience, both on the nation-state and EU levels, Habermas (1992, 1996, 1998, 2000) has emphasized the historically contingent character of the link between the idea of national identity and the institution of citizenship. Shaw (2001, p. 76) emphasizes that post-nationalism is a concept designed to get at the dynamic elements of European integration as a 'process of polity formation'. Given this dynamism, the broad idea of this literature is that the 'link implied by nationalism between cultural integration and political integration can be prised open' (Curtin, 1997, p. 51). In this light, the gradual development of integrative measures in the EU as well as the explicit adoption of the concept of citizenship is interpreted as evident of a possibly new phase in modern citizenship politics; the phase when citizenship rids itself of its national 'accomplice' (ibid.; Habermas, 1996, p. 505ff; Preuss, 1998, p. 149; Gerstenberg, 2001, p. 299).

Reflecting further on these developments, Preuss (1998, p. 139) points out that European citizens 'enjoy rights...which do not originate in their respective national parliaments'. This serves to counter the so-called 'disabilities of alienage', meaning the basic gap between citizen and alien (ibid., p. 145ff); or the hierarchy between different loyalties, the belief that the loyalty to the nation-state is always necessarily the most important (Preuss, 1995, p. 280). Further, the argument is that this is indicative of a broadening of the space for the exercise of rights against political entities. It is no longer tied exclusively to the citizen as an author of the law through the use of political rights of participation within his or her specific political community (Preuss, 1996, p. 159). The distinction between insider and outsider – the classical view of membership – is blurred and citizenship is seen as taking on a new meaning within the post-national literature (Neveu, 2000, p. 122). Here one clearly sees the contrast with the sceptical analyses of Aron and Shore. Given Preuss's comments and the initial theoretical analysis of other authors, the post-national perspective is able to advance the view that European integration fundamentally questions the exclusive relationship between nationality and citizenship, meaning that elements of citizenship are only available from a national frame.

Yet, there are also some problems with the post-nationalist analysis of European citizenship. The separation of the national perspective from citizenship on the EU level often overlooks the grounding of a European political community of citizens in the exclusive membership decision of each member state. In this reading, citizenship ultimately remains dependent on nation-state institutions (Aziz, 2002, p. 5). There is clearly also a point at which 'we' end and 'they' begin within the European polity. This boundary is visible in the exclusion of third-country nationals from the rights enjoyed by European citizens (Kostakopoulou, 2001b, p. 181). The exclusionary aspect of the European polity is in fact recognized within the post-national camp (Preuss, 1998, p. 140ff). It does, however, not stop many of the theorists within this literature from claiming an almost linear evolutionary perspective on citizenship where it necessarily will or should transcend the national and mark a new phase in its history. The argument goes that by eroding state monopoly powers and harbouring an identity built on human rights and procedures of a universal character – that is, that transcend the pre-political dimension of cultural group identity – citizenship as membership and rights can be decoupled from nationality (see, e.g., Curtin, 1997, p. 52; Gerstenberg, 2001, p. 299ff). Yet, in terms of citizenship practice, this claim is not corroborated through an explicit empirical appraisal of the links between institutional developments, policy trends and the conception of citizenship in the system. As such, the critique of this evolutionary perspective is similar to the critique above of the tendency in several sceptical studies to reify the nation-state as the sole locus of a viable model of citizenship (see also Habermas, 1998, p. 159). The post-national critique is in danger of actually flipping itself on the head through essentializing its own preferred model as the only possible outcome of the ongoing process of citizenship discourse in the EU.

Connected to this quest for a 'new' model of citizenship – in which they locate the separation of nationality and citizenship – post-nationalists also tend to overlook the possibility of a different practical realization of citizenship on the European level, for instance a cultural conception of citizenship emerging. Many post-nationalists emphasize rights and membership while overlooking sites of 'enacting' citizenship (see Saward, 2012) politically, socially or culturally. With the possibility of a European nation in the making, the concepts of nationality and citizenship would then not be divorced, but rather 'remarried' on a new level of political order.

This possibility of a new exclusivist citizenship register is indeed highlighted by Hansen and Hager (2010) in their 'critical political economy' of European citizenship. Based on a constructivist notion of citizenship as discursively produced by specific institutional power configurations, Hansen and Hager focus especially on what they argue to be the capitalist core of European citizenship. Individual rights and later institutionalized citizenship were according to their analysis firmly based on the idea of the productive European market citizen. While inclusionary in terms of free movement, this market citizenship can be turned on its head to institute exclusionary measures against 'unproductive' insiders as well as outsiders that seek inclusion in European society. The authors especially argue that such exclusionary citizenship politics have been on the rise in the EU since the events of 9/11, in recent debates on multiculturalism in Europe, as well as in the aftermath of the Euro-crisis.

Also focusing on mobility, Aradau et al. (2010) take a different approach while still reaching similar conclusions to those that moderate the post-national thrust of European citizenship. They focus not on the institutional grounding of European citizenship but rather on what they call 'the acts through which it is created' (ibid., p. 946). In so doing they show how the post-national potential of citizenship in the EU falls prey to a territorial or culturalist version of citizenship where the nation-state framing of territorial boundaries as the 'first mover' in citizenship construction is scaled up to the EU level. The further aim of the authors is to highlight mobility not as always contingent on physical border crossings, but as a specific 'mode of sociality' that can condition political acts of citizenship that do not necessarily support predetermined practices based on institutionalized norms of European citizenship. In other words, Aradau et al. bring forward not only a theoretical framework for studying so-called 'acts' of citizenship, but also a critical programme for when citizenship enactment can have normative impact on the constitution of European citizenship. This theme is moreover developed in a series of case studies on enactment of citizenship in trans-border relations and practices of different groups of 'outsiders' on the inside in the EU polity (Isin and Saward, 2013).

The more critical works reviewed toward the end of this section thus speak to the tendency to equate the development of European citizenship with a linear evolution away from the register of the nation-state. Such thinking may overlook the dynamism and open-ended character of the EU that post-nationalists, in fact, often take as a starting point for the critique against the national position on citizenship. As such this strand of the literature often does not take into account complex (counter-)developments of European citizenship. This is not only due to specific theoretical views, but also to an inherent normativity in much of this literature, implying that the national model of citizenship is undesirable and problematic in the present stage of modern political organization.

Normative Research: On the Desirability, Problems and Possibilities of European Citizenship

Citizenship is indeed a concept infused with normativity. As citizenship is closely linked to notions of political community, identity and mechanisms for inclusion and exclusion, normative questions such as 'Who should be seen as citizens?', 'What distinguishes our political community from others?', or 'What should be the character of political participation?' clearly enter the picture. It is then not surprising that much research within the field engages in normative critique or defence of European citizenship.

There is a strand of the literature that on normative grounds is critical of constructing citizenship on the EU level.[1] The main claim of the so-called no-demos thesis is that European citizenship is neither desirable nor feasible given the lack of a proper popular basis for it (Grimm, 1995).[2] At the outset, this seems to be merely an empirical statement: there is no European demos comparable to the nation-state experience and thus it is not likely that democracy and citizenship can evolve in the EU. But, at the heart of this reasoning there is clearly a normative idea of what constitutes the demos and consequently the basis for a viable political community. As Miller (1995, p. 162) puts it, 'shared national identity is the precondition for achieving political aims'. According to this view, the points made by Preuss regarding the abolishment of 'disabilities of alienage' through individual rights on the EU level have nothing to do with citizenship itself (see Miller, 2000, p. 92). The institution, let alone the concept of citizenship cannot surpass the particularity of the popular national identity that lays the ground for a functioning political community within historically relevant boundaries (Miller, 1995, pp. 22ff, 59). Whether this community is 'real', 'constructed' or 'imagined' is according to Grimm (1995, p. 297) beside the point. What matters is that the only meaningful container for citizenship is found in the clearly demarcated sphere of the nation-state. In this sense political community takes on a specific normativity based on its historical particularity.

This is further understood as closely connected with the means of communication of a political community (Miller, 1995, p. 137ff). With regard to the EU the sceptical argument goes that the normative prerequisites for the integration of a political community are not available, as there is no common language leading to a 'weakly developed collective identity and low capacity for transnational discourse' (Grimm, 1995, p. 297; see also Aron, 1974; Shore, 2004). And, 'the prerequisites cannot simply be created' (Grimm, 1995, p. 294) or 'it cannot be simply conjured up ex nihilo' (Miller, 2000, p. 96). Thus, from the viewpoint of the sceptical literature, citizenship in the EU is normatively problematic at the outset. It can simply never amount to a meaningful concept of citizenship. As with the literature focusing on the theoretical viability of European citizenship, the scepticism of Grimm and Miller leaves a lot to be desired in terms of acknowledging the contested and dynamic character of citizenship. I argue that it is problematic to base a study of European citizenship and its conceptual trajectory on a preceding analysis that takes the very specific understanding and practice of citizenship qua national for granted.

In stark contrast to the more negative normative assessments, Linklater (1998a, 1998b) puts forward a normative defence of European citizenship as a building block of an emerging cosmopolitan citizenship.[3] The main thrust of this work is the normative stance that advancing universalistic cosmopolitan citizenship will be conducive to 'the widening of the moral boundaries of political communities' (Linklater, 1998a, p. 2). Acknowledging that citizenship is a dynamic and contested concept historically and normatively, Linklater (ibid., p. 197) argues that citizenship could and should be detached from its exclusive association with the state. It is further argued that this normatively desirable development is partly visible on the EU level (ibid., p. 199). As Gerstenberg (2001, p. 312) states, the EU delivers '[a] promise to release the ideas of citizenship and democracy from territorial sovereignty and shared nationality'. Political citizenship is, then, not to be confined to the borders of sovereign nation-states, but can also flow freely across them. This argument is based on a cursory interpretation of the impact of establishing Union citizenship in the Maastricht Treaty. The legal provisions and rights of this citizenship are seen as indicative of a process 'towards uncoupling citizenship from sovereignty' (Linklater, 1998a, p. 200). As a normative vision this might suffice. Yet, this argument is backed up by conjectures on actual developments. This does, however, not rest on sufficient empirical evidence of how European integration has affected citizenship. Hence, we cannot rule out that closer empirical scrutiny of the EU citizenship process will yield a different picture, and render the normative vision, if not futile, so in need of a more realistic foundation in its empirical claims.

Bellamy (2001) also brings forward a positive analysis and normative vision for EU citizenship construction, albeit from a republican background. Envisaging citizenship as a continuously reflexive practice (ibid., p. 41ff), rather than taking the development of rights provisions as a point of departure, his normative plea is for a neo-republican type of citizenship where the content of European citizenship is to be built in an everyday process of struggle between different citizens and beliefs in the EU as a political community (ibid., p. 42). Bellamy clearly counters the study of European citizenship that emphasizes its legal and political framework of treaties and verdicts from the European Court of Justice. As a prescriptive strategy of how citizenship should be practised by the citizens in the EU this might be plausible, but for empirical purposes it does not take into account the citizenship problematic in the practice of policy- and constitution-making. Given that the status of the EU as a polity is unclear – as Snyder (2003, p. 67) states 'EU boundaries are problematic, flexible, permeable, often situationally defined and frequently negotiable' – the study of how it has affected the status of individuals within the system should focus not only on citizen-to-citizen struggles, but also on the very discourses where the meaning of the EU has been at stake.

Much of the problem with the normative literature presented here is not its normativity as such. It is rather that it further leads to assessments of actual practices from a frame originally focused exclusively on the normative status of the evolving phenomenon. This is visible in the stance of Grimm and Miller who normatively claim that citizenship cannot function without a common language conducive to meaningful deliberation in a democratic political community. This is not available on the European level and hence, the development of a European citizenship is deemed normatively undesirable since it cannot work at the outset. The problems of such normative 'freezing' of citizenship are also visible in the strand of the literature that advocates the fostering of European citizenship as the most prominent site for dissociating the concepts of nationality and citizenship. The work of Linklater is astute in its normative ideals of universalism and the widening of political communities, but this does not add much to the empirical study of how citizenship is conceptualized in the EU. The normativity of Linklater's analysis stops short of addressing the conceptual implications of a European citizenship that a priori cannot be expected to be less particularistic than its national 'counterpart'.[4] The problem here is not the normative claim as such, rather that it sets obstacles for further investigation into what kinds of conceptions of citizenship that have emerged. Perhaps a different kind of citizenship is emerging in the EU? In what ways does it differ from or emulate the nation-state experience? Does it transform political community as we know it or does it rather profess the development of a specific European political community akin to that of the nation-state? The investigation of such questions can further inform the highly interesting normative debate on its wider implications for the functioning of political community. In this sense, these perceived flaws of the normative strand of the literature point to the need for a more practically and conceptually sensitive methodology when studying citizenship in the EU.

This is partly provided by legal scholar Joseph Weiler in his book *The Constitution of Europe* (1999). In his treatment of European citizenship, Weiler takes an explicitly normative position, albeit not one that aims to defend or oppose it as such. Taking the actual institutionalization of Union citizenship as his point of departure, he seeks, rather, to discuss the normative meaning of European citizenship – 'not what it means, but what it ought to mean' (ibid., p. 324) – seen against questions regarding the vocabulary of citizenship, nationality and peoplehood (ibid., p. 327).

As has been highlighted, several studies of European citizenship have emanated from the template of a specific statist model of citizenship. Indeed, Weiler (ibid.) points out that the introduction of the concept of citizenship into the discourse of the European integration process is problematic at the outset if one assumes that 'the traditional, classical vocabulary of citizenship is the vocabulary of state, the nation and peoplehood'. As he further states, the question is whether there is a drive toward centralization inherent in the concept of European citizenship, that is, a change in the raison d'être of European integration from a focus on the peoples of Europe to one people of Europe. However, rather than studying the process of citizenship discourse empirically, Weiler engages in a theoretical and normative analysis of the meaning of European citizenship. This is done on the backdrop of supranationalism as a specific challenge to the codified expressions and cultural excesses of the concept of nationality (ibid., p. 342). In doing so, Weiler's methodology is still more grounded than much of the normative theorizing discussed in this chapter, as it posits the normative questions against actual developments, and not principally through a 'top-down' approach to what European citizenship is or should be. In this sense, his contribution is clearly more fruitful than those of Aron, Miller or Linklater.

Still, this does not mean that one should be completely local in the study of citizenship, something that Weiler is not. Citizenship is imbued with contested values and normative aspects. It is clearly connected to questions of boundaries, identity and demos. In his normative discussion, Weiler thus focuses on these questions, however, without taking the nation-state model for granted. Rather, he seeks to readdress the question of European citizenship normatively through a concept of coexisting multiple demoi where there is simultaneous belonging on the part of citizens to different levels of political community (ibid., p. 344). This is connected to the question of whether introducing citizenship 'to the conceptual world of the Union could be seen as just another step...towards a statal, unity vision of Europe' (ibid.). Weiler's normative stance opposes this 'unity' vision of the EU. Thus, his normative discussion of European citizenship seeks to rescue it from the broader vision of statehood as the *finalité* of European integration.

Another contribution that avoids normative trench wars and overly optimistic or pessimistic visions of European citizenship is Bauböck's (2007) work on clarifying different normative approaches to supranational union in Europe. Bauböck's (2007, p. 455ff) approach is to ask the question of how liberal democracies should respond to membership claims that do not fit with the nation-state framework. In so doing, he outlines different types of polities that can be discerned from the complex integration process of Europe and how these relate to each other. Given the nested character of European citizenship (national and European), different polity models can be normatively defended when the issue of deciding on membership and access to rights are at stake. On a scale of weakened centralism in terms of EU citizenship, Bauböck fruitfully outlines a statist, unionist and pluralist model of multilevel citizenship politics on the European level. Each model corresponds to different solutions to the problem of the multilevel membership claim and correspondingly to different ideas of what kind of polity the EU is and should be. While relying on normative reasoning based on an ideal-typical model of the EU as some kind of regional federation, this approach opens up the Pandora's box of supranational citizenship by highlighting different possible trajectories for this unprecedented experiment in citizenship politics. As such, it eschews the endless debates on whether European citizenship is good or bad: or just as frequently whether it can and should be called 'citizenship' in the first place. Such open normative theorizing is thus closer to historical and institutionalist research as it takes European citizenship seriously, despite whatever shortcomings – normative or legal – it may be argued to encompass.

Historical and Institutionalist Research: On the Emergence of Citizenship as a Policy Field in European Integration

The review of the literature in the two preceding sections referred to a frequent quandary in many studies of European integration and the problem of citizenship – that of not looking beyond the 'old language' of citizenship and statehood – when studying the phenomenon of citizenship on the supranational level. This is less evident in the more historically and institutionally oriented literature on the development of European citizenship. Warleigh (2001), for example, provides an institutionalist account of the struggle over Union citizenship in and after the process of the Maastricht Intergovernmental Conference. In fact, he claims that it is 'a key battleground in the struggle over European integration' (ibid., p. 19). The main argument of the study is that the provisions of Union citizenship served both instrumental and normative purposes in the integration process: 'the facilitation of the single market and the Council's need to rectify the democratic deficit' (ibid., p. 27). But, the study does not offer a further historical or conceptual analysis of the meaning of citizenship in the EU once introduced directly in its treaties and subsequently developed in ensuing practices of the EU system. The implications of citizenship are only ascertained in connection to the different EU institutions and their use of the concept in the ongoing struggle over the direction of European integration, rather than in itself. It does not, for example, discuss the extent to which European citizenship is not only an institutional battleground as such, but also involves a struggle over the ethos of the European polity through the concept of citizenship.

In a more historical and conceptual appraisal, Eder and Giesen (2001, p. 2) have indeed recognized that European citizenship discourse can be understood as 'an attempt towards defining who is an insider and who is not'. They also emphasize that it can be seen as an attempt at defining a demos for a polity beyond the nation (ibid.); it is a question of political citizenship beyond the borders of nation-states. The question of an emerging European demos has also been raised more comprehensively by Kostakopoulou (2001a). This question is related to an analysis of the kind of European identity that has emerged in the wake of direct and indirect citizenship politics in the EU, mainly on the institutional level (ibid., p. 14ff). This study is commendable in its emphasis on studying the ongoing discourse of citizenship and for stressing that citizenship is a contested concept (ibid., p. 84). Still, this is surprisingly not heeded in the establishment of what Kostakopoulou (ibid.) calls 'a theory of European citizenship'. Here, the study explicitly takes the nation-state framework for granted in order to provide an analytical frame that can overcome what is perceived as limitations in the EU's policy on European citizenship and identity.

This seems to be connected to a further normative aim of the study, which is to provide a so-called 'constructive' theory of citizenship in the EU (ibid., p. 101ff; see also Kostakopoulou, 2005, 2008). The normative model brought forward emphasizes the highly political and contested character of identity questions in a multi-faceted polity such as the EU. In locating the question of identity empirically in the integration process, Kostakopoulou (2001a, p. 40) argues that the overcoming of the sectorial approach in the European Coal and Steel Community (ECSC) through the Treaty of Rome signalled and affirmed the political character of European integration. It was, 'a stage in the process towards political union' (ibid.). Kostakopoulou seeks to empirically trace and explain, and ultimately normatively criticize the development of what she calls European identity within the integration process. She locates this institutionally in the treaties, institutions and policies of European integration. So far, so good, but it seems that there is a constant search for affirming 'the political' already in the first treaties regarding what she calls the construction of European identity. There is thus a clear tendency to force a normative programme, so to speak, on the empirical reality one investigates. The more appropriate puzzle would be to ask what kind of identity and individual membership was implied in a Community whose first phase was predominantly marked by economic integration and market-making (see Gillingham, 2003; Dinan, 2004). The theorization of citizenship as a specific kind of political identity thus leads to the failure to notice elements of citizenship that might not be conducive to the a priori model of what citizenship should be.

Another historically oriented approach is evident in Elisabeth Meehan's (1993) comprehensive study of the emergence of a concept of citizenship after the triple summits of Paris and Copenhagen in 1972–74. In fact, this study starts out with a critique of Aron's perspective on the viability of European citizenship. The core of the argument is that 'a new kind of citizenship is emerging that is neither national nor cosmopolitan' (ibid., p. 1). This argument is, however, not founded on a purely theoretical discussion on the feasibility of European citizenship. Rather, it is based on a historically oriented methodology in the study of citizenship. This means that Meehan employs a research strategy where the historical process of European integration and the development of citizenship discourse is mapped and traced. There is a clear merit in this kind of approach as it provides a broader account of European citizenship as a novel phenomenon of citizenship politics. As was shown to be the case with much of the theoretical and normative literature, Meehan's study does not presuppose that European citizenship is a 'mission impossible', but, rather, takes it seriously as a developing institution within the integration process.

But to the extent that Meehan's broad historical and institutional outlook is something to be brought forward in the study of European citizenship, her study is not comprehensive in its theoretical framework. The theoretical discussion starts out with the understanding of citizenship as a contested concept characterized by different realizations in historical practice and ideas in theory (ibid., p. 4ff). In setting out her theory, however, Meehan takes the three-fold division of civil, political and social rights for granted (ibid., p. 6ff). In a sense, this fixes the meaning of citizenship (rights) at a specific point, that is, in the nation-state of the twentieth century (see Marshall [1950] 1992), contrary to Meehan's own statement that 'the meaning of citizenship is neither fixed in time nor the same in different societies' (Meehan, 1993, p. 17). Further, in the actual analysis of what citizenship in the EU entails, the emphasis is clearly social rights. This is, however, not only a product of the empirical analysis, it is also a conscious choice on the part of the author. Arguing that social rights indeed are a part of citizenship against Aron's emphasis on political rights as its ultimate defining feature, Meehan (ibid., p. 21) goes on to postulate that European citizenship involves a different ordering 'of the acquisition of a triad of citizenship rights'. In this sense, it is more a specific study of the development of the social rights of European citizenship, than a comprehensive interpretation of what it means broadly speaking, that is, how it is conceptualized within the European integration process. This is surely not only oriented towards social rights?[5] In fact, Leibfried and Pierson (2000, p. 268ff) have emphasized that social rights remain weakly developed on the European level, despite several efforts to further their harmonization. The absence of a thorough theoretical and empirical discussion concerning aspects of identity and belonging further attests to the somewhat narrow focus.

Meehan thus tends to fall into the same trap as Aron in reifying one specific understanding of citizenship and using this as a template for the empirical study of its practice. Scattered throughout the study is also a tendency to act as a futurologist ('it may happen in future developments') as well as furthering a normative agenda of the primacy of social rights to citizenship, without making this an explicit stance of the study at the outset (Meehan, 1993, p. 26). These weaknesses notwithstanding, the relatively early study by Meehan (written before the Maastricht Treaty was finalized) has clearly furthered our understanding as regards the development of a vocabulary of citizenship in the EU by emphasizing its place within the policy process and institution building. Additionally, in methodological terms the study is laudable in its convincing argument of overcoming the reifying aspects of much research on citizenship. But, the clear emphasis of a particular dimension – social rights – indicates the need for broader empirical studies taking more aspects and nuances of citizenship into account.

Antje Wiener focused on a more comprehensive set of citizenship elements in her historical-institutionalist account of the emergence of citizenship practice as a policy field within European integration (Wiener, 1998: see also Wiener, 1997; Wiener and Della Sala, 1997). Also taking the contested character of citizenship as a point of departure, this study takes a different theoretical route to Meehan. Rather than focusing merely on (social) rights, Wiener's approach is to outline a more general theory of citizenship by which she studies the development of European citizenship from the 1970s onwards. The basic theoretical point of the study is that citizenship is comprised of rights, access and belonging as three historical elements (ibid., p. 24ff). With this theoretical model as a yardstick it then investigates the process of citizenship building for the combinations of these historical elements. The main finding of the study is that a fragmented citizenship practice between different levels of political organization and community – where legal, institutional and socio-historical dimensions were crucial – has emerged in EU policy-making (ibid., p. 293ff).

This approach comes closer than any of the earlier discussed studies to taking European citizenship seriously in itself. The theoretical design rendered possible findings that would fall by the wayside of traditional nation-state–oriented models of citizenship. Wiener's analysis argues that the unitary character of national citizenship is not emulated on the EU level. Such a finding would be deemed either unfeasible or undesirable if the methodologies of many studies of European citizenship had been put to use: 'The fragmented character of "European" citizenship thus posed a challenge to conceptualizations of citizenship as universal' (ibid., p. 294).

Wiener (1998, p. 44) focused explicitly on different policy areas as 'a way of filling the time "lags" between "history-making" decisions'. Focusing on policy-making within different areas and how these affect the concept of citizenship makes sense. There is, however, a possibility of escaping the larger picture by focusing exclusively on policy. It simply overlooks the fact that the so-called 'history-making' decisions can provide further clues to the place of citizenship within the political system of the EU.

On a more theoretical level, Wiener's study is exclusively oriented towards institutional aspects of European citizenship practice. That is, in concluding each part of the case study, the emphasis is laid on illuminating how the citizenship issue has developed from informal resources such as ideas and broad political goals to institutionalized practices of the system. In doing this, it overlooks the question of how the vocabulary of citizenship as such has evolved; and how this links to other issues of modern political order, such as political participation and cultural identity. This is a highly relevant puzzle given the diverging interpretations of European citizenship in the literature.

In his historically innovative work, Willem Maas (2005, 2007) has done exactly this. Taking an explicitly institutionalist but also actor-oriented stance, Maas charts the development of European citizenship discourse even from the period before the first major treaty that formed the ECSC. Maas highlights how the seeds of European citizenship were sown and its main building block of free movement was constructed at the intersection between ideals of European unification and the harsh realities of post-war political and economic reconstruction.

This intersection has been highlighted in other diachronic approaches. Shaw (2007) is a comprehensive piece of research on the institutionalization of political rights and citizenship in the EU setting. Shaw's work highlights how the multilevel system of EU governance has created nested political citizenship where both the supranational and national levels matter in terms of securing and implementing political rights for EU citizens. This in-between character of European citizenship is also argued for in Olsen's (2012) book on transnational citizenship in the EU. The argument in this book is, moreover, that despite numerous supranational reform efforts and promotion of post-national ideas, European citizenship continues to be placed firmly between its basis on member state nationality and border-crossing free movement. The normative and theoretical approaches tend to continue the fight over labelling and the status of European citizenship as 'citizenship proper'. In contrast, the growing body of work that is historically oriented and empirically based underlines the embedded character of European citizenship between philosophical ideas, legal rules and institutional practices of EU governance; and the historical legacies of citizenship 'as we know it' in the nation-state. It is in this specific condition that the prospects for future research linking political citizenship in the EU and the social movement literature is situated and confronted with specific challenges as well as possibilities.

EUROPEAN CITIZENSHIP AND SOCIAL MOVEMENTS: PROSPECTS FOR FUTURE RESEARCH

Citizenship in the EU is simultaneously constructed upon rights derived from the idea of free movement and border crossing, and on nationality as its main building block. From the founding treaties to the most recent efforts of constitution-making, a 'right to have rights' in second countries of the EU has remained at the core of European citizenship. Despite the existence of European-level voting rights in elections to the European Parliament, the supranational dimension of direct relations between the individual and political institutions at the EU level is much weaker than in analogous relations of nation-state citizenship (Olsen, 2012). Transnational citizenship rights in the EU facilitate cross-border relations between citizens of the member states, but do 'very little to create a distinctive attachment to the EU itself' (Bellamy, 2008, p. 598). The weak supranational dimension of European citizenship is, in this sense, highlighted by the lack of research linking the political side of citizenship to the broader debate on EU democracy. Low voter turnout and disinterest in European elections are often used as but one example of the EU's democratic deficit. Yet, little focus has been put on different modes of 'acting out' political citizenship in different societal spheres including those of European elections. In what ways is European citizenship politicized by individual citizens and different kinds of social movements? Is European citizenship a resource for or an impediment to tackling the perils of crisis-ridden Europe? These are some questions that can be raised and highlight the fertile ground for social movement research to explore the dynamics of voting rights and political citizenship; and especially so in times of crisis.

The reality of European citizenship as a special status of individual rights 'beyond' the nation-state is indeed put to question in the current struggle of Europe to contain the economic bust of recent years. It is not unlikely that this will be the major source of struggle and debate over European citizenship in the coming years. As such, it may lead to a shift in citizenship discourse from the conceptualization of citizenship in itself to its linkage to the effects of broader trends in European integration. The tension between intergovernmental and supranational visions of the EU polity might no longer be as important. Rather, the meaning of citizenship is likely to come increasingly into play as member states seek to find short-term solutions to shifting problems. It is not the vision that will matter, but rather the 'everyday' management of policies that will be at the forefront. The Danish suspension of free movement in the Schengen Agreement is a case in point (Olsen, 2013). Such symbolic acts of re-nationalizing control over borders and political communities are not unlikely to occur more often in the future. European citizenship became an explicit agenda of European institutions in a time of optimism after the end of the Cold War; in the coming years it might turn into a scapegoat when the tide has turned and Europe go from crisis to crisis.

This is further linked to the exercise of political citizenship and social movement developments. In the countries that are most heavily affected by the crisis, there has been a surge in political activism and organizing of crisis-specific protest movements. Greece and Spain are the most notable examples. The question is whether these forms of political resilience toward the effects of crisis are linked exclusively to the national agenda or if they also link these to their political and social rights as EU citizens. The crisis is transnational in character while the effects on citizens are felt 'at home'. Do political activists and social movements primarily 'go native' in this situation or do we see the rise of a politically active transnational citizenry that take advantage of rights on different levels of political order. This is an important research avenue as the Euro-crisis has led to increased questioning of the legitimacy of EU institutions and increasing popular dissent with policy-making, while European citizenship opens the possibility for citizens to act not only within their 'own' country but also to utilize EU rights in their struggles to cope with the crisis.

The transnational core of European citizenship presupposes a modicum of solidarity between member states and their respective citizenries. This solidarity goes beyond membership in the political community of a member state. This is indeed the core transnationality of citizenship in the EU: you get access to rights and benefits in other countries by virtue of your European status. Membership of the political community as defined by territoriality or nationality is no longer necessary to be granted civil, social, and even political rights. The states and their populations that are on the 'receiving end' of this mobility space must accept this and follow European regulations even where this might go against national interests or traditions. European citizens that move to another country within the EU should not be discriminated against. But is this solidarity strong enough to sustain further inroads to the value of exclusive political membership and citizenship in European welfare states? Are elites, peoples and social movements alike willing to retain the core of solidarity in the European project? Has the 'cosmopolitanism' of rights attribution gone too far with recent cases from the European Court of Justice? As welfare states face structural problems for the foreseeable future, it is not unlikely that this will become a new battleground of European integration in general and political citizenship more specifically. Member states might try to circumvent their obligations to European citizens, paving the way for a situation where it is again only the Eurostars – the educated and cosmopolitan elites (see Favell, 2008) – that can really benefit from transnational citizenship in the EU.

NOTES

1. Clearly, many of the studies presented in this section offer not only normative assessments of European citizenship, they also engage in reasoning on theoretical grounds. The reason I specifically focus on normativity here is that these studies show an additional side of the predominantly theoretical literature on European citizenship. That is, they employ a specific normative frame of what citizenship should be and thereby offer a normative interpretation of the developments on the EU level regarding citizenship.
2. Grimm (1995) is not an explicit study of European citizenship. It is focused on the (non-)possibility of a European Constitution. But, I argue that it can also be read as a normative and theoretical critique of the idea and institution of citizenship beyond the nation-state.
3. For discussions on cosmopolitan citizenship on a more general level, see, for example, Delanty (2000), Falk (1994), Heater (2004), and Chapter 9 by Tijsterman in this volume.
4. Granted, Linklater (1998a, p. 2) does acknowledge the 'danger' of particularism in many cosmopolitan theories of ethics and political community, but this is not sufficiently addressed as a possible obstacle to his analysis of European, or what he calls 'post-Westphalian' citizenship.
5. The point here is not to say that the three-fold division of rights has no meaning for European citizenship; rather, it is to emphasize that this should not be taken for granted. The perception and idea connected to rights within a specific discourse on citizenship will give evidence to conception(s) of citizenship. Indeed, Bauböck (1994, p. 211) has underlined that the list of citizenship rights in fact is open-ended and has tended to vary within and between different political traditions, structural conditions and cultural backgrounds. Focusing on only one dimension (i.e., social rights) might then lead to skewed interpretations of a citizenship practice where this dimension is not present. Is a conception where social rights are not considered as part and parcel of it less of a citizenship? Or, can it not be interpreted as a specific conception of citizenship, that is, one devoid of a social dimension?

REFERENCES

Aradau, C., J. Huysmans and V. Squire (2010), 'Acts of European citizenship: a political sociology of mobility', *Journal of Common Market Studies*, **48**(4), 945–65.
Aron, R. (1974), 'Is multinational citizenship possible?', *Social Research*, **41**(4), 638–56.
Aziz, M. (2002), 'EU citizenship: spheres of belonging and the politics of dispossession', EUI Working Papers No. 2002/68, Florence: EUI/Robert Schuman Centre for Advanced Studies.
Bauböck, R. (1994), *Transnational Citizenship*, Aldershot, UK and Brookfield, VT, USA: Edward Elgar.
Bauböck, R. (2007), 'Why European citizenship? Normative approaches to supranational union', *Theoretical Inquiries in Law*, **8**(2), 453–88.
Beiner, R. (1995), 'Introduction: why citizenship constitutes a theoretical problem in the last decade of the twentieth century', in R. Beiner (ed.), *Theorizing Citizenship*, Albany, NY: State University of New York Press.
Bellamy, R. (2001), 'The right to have rights: citizenship and the political constitution of Europe', in R. Bellamy and A. Warleigh (eds), *Citizenship and Governance in the European Union*, London: Continuum.
Bellamy, R. (2008), 'Evaluating Union citizenship: belonging, rights and participation within the EU', *Citizenship Studies*, **12**(6), 597–611.
Bellamy, R., D. Castiglione and E. Santoro (eds) (2004), *Lineages of European Citizenship. Rights, Belonging and Participation in Eleven Nation-States*, Houndmills, UK: Palgrave Macmillan.
Brubaker, W.R. (1996), *Nationalism Reframed: Nationhood and the National Question in the New Europe*, Cambridge, UK: Cambridge University Press.
Closa, C. (1992), 'The concept of citizenship in the treaty on European Union', *Common Market Law Review*, **29**(6), 1137–69.
Curtin, D. (1997), *Postnational Democracy. The European Union in Search of a Political Philosophy*, The Hague: Kluwer Law.
Delanty, G. (2000), *Citizenship in a Global Age*, Buckingham, UK: Open University Press.
Dinan, D. (2004), *Europe Recast. A History of the European Union*, Houndmills, UK: Palgrave Macmillan.
D'Oliveira, H.U.J. (1995), 'Union citizenship: a pie in the sky', in A. Rosas and E. Antola (eds), *A Citizen's Europe. In Search of a New Order*, London: Sage.
Eder, K. and B. Giesen (2001), 'European citizenship. An avenue for social integration of Europe', in K. Eder and B. Giesen (eds), *European Citizenship between National Legacies and Postnational Projects*, Oxford: Oxford University Press.
Evans, A.C. (1984), 'European citizenship: a novel concept in EEC law', *The American Journal of Comparative Law*, **32**(4), 679–715.
Everson, M. (1995), 'The legacy of the market citizen', in J. Shaw and G. More (eds), *New Legal Dynamics of European Union*, Oxford: Clarendon Press.
Falk, R. (1994), 'The making of global citizenship', in B. van Steenbergen (ed.), *The Condition of Citizenship*, London: Sage.
Favell, A. (2008), *Eurostars and Eurocities: Free Movement and Mobility in an Integrating Europe*, Oxford: Blackwell.
Gerstenberg, O. (2001), 'Denationalization and the very idea of democratic constitutionalism: the case of the European Community', *Ratio Juris*, **14**(3), 298–325.
Gillingham, J. (2003), *European Integration 1950–2003. Superstate or Market Economy?*, Cambridge, UK: Cambridge University Press.
Grimm, D. (1995), 'Does Europe need a constitution?', *European Law Journal*, **1**(3), 282–302.
Habermas, J. (1992), 'Citizenship and national identity: some reflections on the future of Europe', *Praxis International*, **12**(1), 1–19.
Habermas, J. (1996), *Between Facts and Norms*, Cambridge, UK: Polity Press.
Habermas, J. (1998), *The Inclusion of the Other*, Cambridge, MA: MIT Press.
Habermas, J. (2000), *The Postnational Constellation*, Cambridge, UK: Polity Press.

Hansen, P. and S. Hager (2010), *The Politics of European Citizenship. Deepening Contradictions in Social Rights & Migration Policy*, New York/Oxford: Berghahn Books.
Heater, D. (2004), *World Citizenship*, London: Continuum.
Hegel, G.W.F. ([1821] 1952), *Hegel's Philosophy of Right*, trans. T.M. Knox, Oxford: Oxford University Press.
Hix, S. (2005), *The Political System of the European Union*, Houndmills, UK: Palgrave Macmillan.
Isin, E. and M. Saward (2013), *Enacting European Citizenship*, Cambridge, UK: Cambridge University Press.
Kostakopoulou, T. (2001a), *Citizenship, Identity and Immigration in the European Union. Between Past and Future*, Manchester: Manchester University Press.
Kostakopoulou, T. (2001b), 'Invisible citizens? Long-term resident third-country nationals in the EU and their struggle for recognition', in R. Bellamy and A. Warleigh (eds), *Citizenship and Governance in the European Union*, London: Continuum.
Kostakopoulou, T. (2005), 'Ideas, norms and European citizenship: explaining institutional change', *The Modern Law Review*, **68**(2), 233–67.
Kostakopoulou, T. (2008), *The Future Governance of Citizenship*, Cambridge, UK: Cambridge University Press.
Kymlicka, W. and W. Norman (1995), 'The return of the citizen: a survey of recent work on citizenship theory', in R. Beiner (ed.), *Theorizing Citizenship*, Albany, NY: State University of New York Press.
Leibfried, S. and P. Pierson (2000), 'Social policy. Left to courts and markets?', in H. Wallace and W. Wallace (eds), *Policy-Making in the European Union*, 4th edition, Oxford: Oxford University Press.
Linklater, A. (1998a), *The Transformation of Political Community*, Cambridge, UK: Polity Press.
Linklater, A. (1998b), 'Citizenship and sovereignty in the post-Westphalian European state', in D. Archibugi, D. Held and M. Köhler (eds), *Re-Imagining Political Community*, Cambridge, UK: Polity Press.
Maas, W. (2005), 'The genesis of European rights', *Journal of Common Market Studies*, **43**(5), 985–1001.
Maas, W. (2007), *Creating European Citizens*, Lanham, MD: Rowman & Littlefield.
Marshall, T.H. ([1950] 1992), *Citizenship and Social Class*, London: Pluto Press.
Meehan, E. (1993), *Citizenship and the European Community*, London: Sage.
Miller, D. (1995), *On Nationality*, Oxford: Oxford University Press.
Miller, D. (2000), *Citizenship and National Identity*, Cambridge, UK: Polity Press.
Neveu, C. (2000), 'European citizenship, citizens of Europe and European citizens', in I. Bellier and T.M. Wilson (eds), *An Anthropology of the European Union. Building, Imagining and Experiencing the New Europe*, Oxford: Berg.
Olsen, E.D.H. (2008), 'The origins of European citizenship in the first two decades of European integration', *Journal of European Public Policy*, **15**(1), 40–57.
Olsen, E.D.H. (2012), *Transnational Citizenship in the European Union: Past, Present and Future*, New York/London: Continuum.
Olsen, E.D.H. (2013), 'European citizenship: mixing nation-state and federal features with a cosmopolitan twist', *Perspectives on European Politics and Society* [published online 18 March 2013], DOI: 10.1080/15705854.2013.772750, accessed 7 May 2014 at http://www.tandfonline.com/doi/abs/10.1080/15705854.2013.772750#.U2tzmMdgN7w.
Plender, R. (1976), 'An incipient form of European citizenship', in F.G. Jacobs (ed.), *European Law and the Individual*, Amsterdam: North-Holland Publishing.
Preuss, U. (1995), 'Problems of a concept of European citizenship', *European Law Journal*, **1**(3), 267–81.
Preuss, U. (1996), 'Two challenges to European citizenship', in R. Bellamy and D. Castiglione (eds), *Constitutionalism in Transformation: Theoretical and European Perspectives*, Oxford: Blackwell.
Preuss, U. (1998), 'Citizenship in the European Union: a paradigm for transnational

democracy?', in D. Archibugi, D. Held and M. Köhler (eds), *Re-Imagining Political Community*, Cambridge, UK: Polity Press.

Rawls, J. (1993), *Political Liberalism*, New York: Columbia University Press.

Saward, M. (2012), 'The dynamics of European citizenship: enactment, extension and assertion', *Comparative European Politics*, **11**(1), 49–69.

Shaw, J. (2001), 'Post-national constitutionalism in the European Union', in T. Christiansen, K.E. Jørgensen and A. Wiener (eds), *The Social Construction of Europe*, London: Sage.

Shaw, J. (2007), *The Transformation of Citizenship in the European Union. Electoral Rights and the Restructuring of Political Space*, Cambridge, UK: Cambridge University Press.

Shore, C. (2000), *Building Europe*, London: Routledge.

Shore, C. (2004), 'Whither European citizenship? Eros and civilization revisited', *European Journal of Social Theory*, **7**(1), 27–44.

Smith, A.D. (1992), 'National identity and the idea of European unity', *International Affairs*, **68**(1), 55–76.

Snyder, F. (2003), 'The unfinished constitution of the European Union: principles, processes and culture', in J.H.H. Weiler and M. Wind (eds), *European Constitutionalism Beyond the State*, Cambridge, UK: Cambridge University Press.

Turner, B.S. (1994), 'Outline of a theory of citizenship', in B.S. Turner and P. Hamilton (eds), *Citizenship. Critical Concepts*, London: Routledge.

Walzer, M. (1983), *Spheres of Justice*, New York: Basic Books.

Warleigh, A. (2001), 'Purposeful opportunists? EU institutions and the struggle over European citizenship', in R. Bellamy and A. Warleigh (eds), *Citizenship and Governance in the European Union*, London: Continuum.

Weiler, J.H.H. (1999), *The Constitution of Europe. 'Do the New Clothes Have an Emperor?' and Other Essays on European Integration*, Cambridge, UK: Cambridge University Press.

Wessels, W. (1997), 'An ever closer fusion? A dynamic macropolitical view on integration processes', *Journal of Common Market Studies*, **35**(2), 267–99.

Wiener, A. (1997), 'Making sense of the new geography of citizenship: fragmented citizenship in the European Union', *Theory and Society*, **26**(4), 529–60.

Wiener, A. (1998), *'European' Citizenship Practice. Building Institutions of a Non-State*, Boulder, CO: Westview Press.

Wiener, A. and V. Della Sala (1997), 'Constitution-making and citizenship practice – bridging the democracy gap in the EU?', *Journal of Common Market Studies*, **35**(4), 595–614.

Williams, R. (1976), *Keywords*, London: Collins.

9. Global and cosmopolitan citizenship
Sebastiaan Tijsterman

INTRODUCTION

The idea of global, cosmopolitan or world citizenship has accompanied reflection of citizenship from its inception in the Greek polis onwards. Diogenes the Cynic is supposed to have said in the fourth century BCE, when asked where he came from, *'kosmopolites eimi'* ('I am a citizen of the world') (Miller, 2011, p. 6). In his essay 'Perpetual Peace' (1795) Kant highlights cosmopolitan right as the hospitality owed to all fellow humans. Notwithstanding the philosophical and idea-historical importance of these contributions, the notion of cosmopolitan citizenship has been standing for the most part of the history of political thought in the shadow of territorial citizenship. Citizenship referred primarily to the membership of a specific political community, a polis, empire, or – for the last few centuries – a sovereign (nation-)state. The enjoyment of equal rights, political participation and identity were supposed to require political borders. In this setting, cosmopolitan citizenship could draw attention to the moral shortcomings resulting from the exclusiveness that defines territorial citizenship, but did not constitute a self-sufficient alternative.

During the last decades, the idea of global citizenship has been rapidly emancipated from its marginal position. As a consequence of globalization, the key elements of citizenship – identity, moral responsibilities, rights, and political participation – no longer appear to be strictly confined to national political communities. Political identities cut through borders and political activists unite across countries in shared global goals. The number and influence of international governmental and non-governmental organizations have increased enormously. Rights are no longer taken as exclusively inner state affairs. The notion of global citizenship describes this new mode of citizenship. As a *descriptive* concept, it helps to capture the scale and scope of the new non-national practices of citizenship.

The notion of global or cosmopolitan citizenship is also employed *prescriptively*, to express a moral vision towards which political life should move.[1] Cosmopolitan citizenship challenges the belief that individuals' central political commitments are to the nation-state and their fellow national citizens. Rather, citizens and political institutions should take up a universal position, in which each resident of the world carries equal weight. Normative theorizing about citizenship, taking up and elaborating the project that Kant started more than two centuries ago, is presently undergoing a renaissance. The aspirations of present-day advocates of global citizenship have risen considerably in comparison to the Kantian hospitality towards strangers, arguing for the need for building a global political order in terms of global justice and democracy.

In the scholarly literature, the meaning, extent, and necessity of global citizenship are highly contested. Each section of this contribution gives an overview of the current debates from a different angle. The first section takes global citizenship as a *descriptive* concept. Here, the debate centers around the question of whether globalization has undermined national citizenship and has created political practices that we can justifiably refer to as global citizenship. The second section regards global citizenship as a *normative* concept. This section explores the arguments and counter-arguments for cosmopolitan citizenship. The third section explores global citizenship from a *prospective* perspective, which concerns the question of whether global citizenship is likely to be realized. Are conditions for meaningful citizenship present outside of territorial communities? The concluding section contains suggestions for further research.

Before turning to global citizenship, it is helpful to address briefly our understanding of the notion of citizenship. Citizenship refers to what it means to be a political agent. The concept is multi-layered as political agency consists of different dimensions. The citizenship literature offers some variation with regard to these dimensions. Bellamy (2008) and Leydet (2011), for example, distinguish identity (or belonging), rights, and political participation, while Linklater (2002) differentiates citizenship into obligations (or responsibilities or duties), rights, and participation. We combine both approaches, taking citizenship to be made up of identity, duties, rights, and participation. Though we hold that citizenship is based upon the mutual reinforcement of these dimensions, each dimension can be taken separately as an analytical tool for addressing the nature of global citizenship. With regard to our understanding of *global* citizenship, universalism is a crucial feature. In this sense, global citizenship has a more limited meaning than postnational citizenship, which also applies to citizenship experiences based upon non-national and non-universal cultural or religious attachments. European citizenship, therefore, is not global citizenship, though it might include elements of global citizenship, such as support for universal human rights.

THE EMERGENCE OF GLOBAL CITIZENSHIP: EMPIRICAL PERSPECTIVES

The development of global citizenship as an empirical phenomenon is closely related to globalization, which is said to undermine national citizenship and to advance global citizenship. This section investigates whether global citizenship is indeed emerging. We start with a short account of globalization.

Globalization designates 'a set of processes which are reshaping the organization of human activity, stretching political, economic, social and communicative networks across regions and continents' (Held, 2010, pp. ix–x). Globalization's most eye-catching elements concern the economic and financial processes, in which commodities and labor move freely across borders, and that can partly be traced to the agenda of economic liberalization and global market integration (the 'Washington Consensus'). Globalization also involves the growing mobility of people, both as migrants and as tourists, and the ever-faster dispersion of ideas. The effects of globalization are, according to David Held, revolutionary: 'Contemporary globalization represents the beginning of a new epoch in human affairs. . .as profound an impact as the Industrial Revolution and the global empires of the nineteenth century' (cited in Weiss, 2000, p. 807).

A central metaphor to describe globalization is 'liquidity'. Ulrich Beck (2006), for example, uses this concept to express that the fact that boundaries, particularly territorial borders, are becoming blurred, indistinct, and permeable.[2] Liquidity implies the annulment of much of the temporal and spatial distances that used to separate people, due to developments within communication and transportation technology, for example the internet. For Zygmunt Bauman, whose sociology is built upon the metaphor of liquidity, this '"time/space compression" encapsulates the ongoing multi-faceted transformation of the parameters of the human condition' (1998, p. 2). For the globalized individual the difference between 'here' and 'there', 'the proximate' and 'the distant', 'now' and 'then' drops off. The world has increasingly become a single space.

The territorial state is, as a consequence of globalization, to an ever-less degree carrier and instigator of social processes. Though the Westphalian states were also prone to outside influences, they were with respect to their domestic affairs to a large degree autonomous. In the present globalized context, states experience themselves to be ever more dependent upon their global environment. Events and decisions at one end of the world can come to have significant consequences at home. Bauman also points out that the public spaces that generate and negotiate political meaning are moving beyond the territorial state. 'Localities [such as states] are increasingly dependent on sense-giving and interpreting actions which they do not control or influence' (ibid., p. 3). National states have, for example, relatively little grip on religiously inspired political ideologies.

Bauman also points out that globalization entails new deep social divisions. 'Rather than homogenizing the human condition, [globalization] tends to polarize it' (ibid., p. 18). On the one end, a class of people has adapted successfully to the global condition, having acquired skills that are required by global sectors, such as the corporate sector, finance, and trade. Others, however, are on the receiving end of globalization and remain dependent for their means of living and sense of self upon the remaining local structures, which have lost much of their 'meaning and identity-endowing capacity'. According to Bauman (ibid., p. 2), 'neo-tribal and fundamentalist tendencies' are, like the global top class, the understandable outcomes of globalization.

The Decline of Territorial Citizenship?

Richard Falk (2000, p. 7) argued that globalization, in particular economic globalization 'seems likely to produce a decline in the quality and significance of citizenship'. Following the example of Stoker et al. (2011), we will refer to this claim as the 'declinist thesis'. This section starts with the arguments of why globalization would undermine each of the dimensions of citizenship, while assessing their strengths only at the end.

First of all, globalization threatens to undermine the shared political identity that constitutes the backbone of citizenship. In the traditional account of citizenship, the state provides citizens with a sense of who they are. Collective identity is an important condition for effective citizenship as it bolsters the willingness to contribute to the well-being of the state. For the identity of the new globally orientated elites, nationality is rather peripheral. In the literature and the political debate, however, another aspect of globalization affecting political identities has received much more attention: immigration. During the last decades, the populations of Western countries have become much more diverse, as immigrants have brought with them their former religious, cultural, and ethnic attachments, and often also their citizenship. Globalized communication structures and transport possibilities have also rendered the cultivation, even the reinforcement, of these attachments much easier. As a consequence, states are less able to achieve primacy in the political self-definition of their residents (see Castles and Davidson, 2000). The notion of post-national citizenship expresses the disconnection between the location that nourished the actual experience of citizenship and the place of residence and, possibly, of formal citizenship (Soysal, 1994; Bosniak, 2000; Sassen,

2002). Some scholars and politicians fear that this development is at the expense of social cohesion. Post-national scholars themselves generally are not pessimistic as they regard a shared support for human rights more fundamental for social cohesion than a shared political identity. Soysal (2012) draws attention to the paradox that post-national citizens endeavor to foster their cultural rights of difference within national communities by connecting to transnational discourses of human rights.

Second, globalization is thought to impoverish the rights dimension of national citizenship, in particular social rights, such as welfare rights or minimum income. In an influential essay, T.H. Marshall ([1950] 2009) described the inclusion of social rights next to juridical and political rights as the completion of citizenship, as only this ensemble would grant everyone a sense of full membership. Many scholars, such as Cerny (1999), fear that economic globalization instigates a 'race to the bottom', which undermines the capacity of states to provide the public goods and welfare provisions that constitute social citizenship. The economic fate of nations is to an ever-greater degree dependent upon a highly integrated global economy. Governments are hardly able to insulate their citizens from the global market forces, as the current financial crisis demonstrates. Forced to adapt to the exigencies of the global market, states have to increase their competitiveness by lowering of taxes and cutting expenditures, upon which the provision of social rights depends.[3]

Third, globalization is also suspected of having pernicious consequences for the participatory or democratic component of citizenship. Being a citizen means to contribute as a co-legislator to the laws that structure common life. Just as the logic of global capitalism affects the latitude for social rights, it also curbs the scope of popular sovereignty (Benhabib, 2007). Globalization, however, undermines participation in another way as well. The well-being of society in a globalized world is to a large extent dependent upon what happens outside of its national borders. Environmental, educational, economic, scientific, safety, and other issues often have a regional or global dimension, which provokes politics to go beyond the nation-state as well. A system of global governance is developing, made up of transnational networks and multilateral organizations, such as the UN, EU, IMF, World Bank, and WTO. These powerful supranational institutions appear to carry, together with powerful economic players and states such as the USA, China and Russia, the real power in the contemporary world.

From one perspective, these supranational institutions exemplify pooled sovereignty, which enables states to keep control over external forces and maintain popular sovereignty. Habermas, for example, pointed out two decades ago the impotence of national democracy without supranational institutions: 'the idea of popular sovereignty is doomed to decay into a mere chimera if it remains locked in the historical form of the self-asserting sovereign nation-state' (Habermas, 1994, p. 165). From another perspective, global governance diminishes, in particular in small and middle-sized states, citizens' potential for meaningful participation. Economic and financial decisions of the EU or World Bank, for example, have strong impacts upon countries' domestic economic options. National governments have to comply with international agreements, such as the European deficit rules or conform to the standards of good governance (Van Doeveren, 2011). The influence of national electorates upon outcomes is only small, and often obscure as a consequence of its indirect nature. This brings up the question of why citizens would direct their energy on largely impotent national governments. The steady decline of political participation at the national level that authors such as Mair (2006) observe could be interpreted as a logical outcome of the globalization of politics.

Finally, it is feared that globalization undermines the obligations that are part of citizenship. Citizenship contains a willingness to contribute to uphold the law, for example by the payment of taxes, and contribute in other ways to the common good. Citizens are willing to carry the burdens of citizenship because of the benefits it provides: a strong shared identity, a spectrum of rights, and the possibility to influence the state's political course. As globalization undermines each of these other dimensions, it is feared that citizens' loyalty will follow next. Stoker et al., for example, ask whether 'the historic covenant between state and citizen, forged in the long twentieth century, has been seriously destabilized' (Stoker et al., 2011, p. 133).

When considering the impact of globalization, citizenship seems to be unmistakably in decline. As each of these elements reinforces the others, the prospects for national citizenship appear bleak. This condition of citizenship today provoked one scholar to ask the pressing question 'What's left of citizenship?' (Nyers, 2004). At the same time, the relationship between globalization and the nature and quality of citizenship is a more complex story than one of steady, univocal decline. It is questionable at least whether territorial citizenship is destined to become parochial. Counter-arguments can be offered for each of the dimensions. Against the idea of a 'race to the bottom', national states still offer their citizens considerable social rights. The diversity in welfare regimes indicates that globalization does not force states into a single mold, but offers space for political choice. It is not even clear that the best strategy for states is to give up their strong welfare regimes, as social protection is crucial for rendering the openness of globalization in the end politically sustainable

(Rieger and Leibfried, 2003). Even though the state has lost some competences to supranational levels, globalization also provides states with new roles, such as providing security in the face of terrorism. The persistent relevance of the national state also questions the assumed insignificance of political participation. Political activity is still predominantly national, while a large majority of the population strongly identifies with its own polity. The success of populist parties in many Western countries can be interpreted as a process – or at least an attempt – to renationalize politics. Generally, there is little evidence for decreasing loyalty towards the state. Globalization could also reinforce social solidarity. Kymlicka (1999), for example, suggests that French citizens want to confront the challenges of globalization as a national collectivity.

At the same time, these rejoinders are not meant to deny that citizenship undergoes a profound transformation. The point is that we are not sufficiently able to develop a full account of the impact of globalization upon citizenship, when we merely look at citizenship from the perspective of the territorial state. In that case, we observe the world of today from the perspective of yesterday. The idea of decline of citizenship does not sufficiently take into account the new forms of citizenship that are emerging in the wake of globalization. We have already pointed at the emergence of post-national citizenship. Now, we turn to the question of whether something is developing that may be referred to as 'global citizenship'.

Becoming Global Citizens

Most scholars dealing with global citizenship claim that our globalized age does not simply and exclusively erode territorial, national citizenship, but also offers venues for global citizenship (Linklater, 1998, 2002). Global citizenship is not merely seen as an aspiration, but as 'an unfolding reality' (Hudson and Slaughter, 2007, p. 8). For each of the constitutive dimensions of citizenship, we can point to signs that indicate the development of such citizenship.

One of the clearest signs of the emergence of a global citizenship is the development of a global rights regime. Within the Westphalian order, sovereign states were taken to be the exclusive providers of citizens' civil and other rights. Rights were only to be enjoyed by virtue of being a (legal) citizen. In this setting, international law was based upon treaties between states, which refrained from interfering in each other's domestic affairs. The modern world may be on the threshold of a new cosmopolitan age, built upon the idea of cosmopolitan rights. According to Benhabib (2005, p. 86), 'cosmopolitan norms of justice accrue to individuals as moral and legal persons in a worldwide civil society'. Citizens increasingly consider rights as something they have as individuals, as members of the world or as human beings, and not as citizens of a specific state. These universal rights are enshrined in international treaties and agreements. This way, international public law 'binds and bends the will of sovereign nations' to an ever-larger degree as citizens and groups whose rights have been denied can appeal to human rights law (ibid., p. 87). The European Court of Human Rights has acquired a significant role in providing redress for citizens against their own governments. National states in the EU are also to an ever-less degree allowed to treat non-citizens within their territory differently from their own citizens, which limits the values of national citizenship. A different manifestation of the human rights regime is the International Criminal Court, which challenges the principle of sovereign immunity in cases of human rights' violations (Kaldor, 1999, pp. 124–31). According to Dallmayr (2012), this international machinery and legal structure of universal human rights functions in large measure to reinforce, rather than to erode, the institution of citizenship.

At the same time, this picture of global citizenship is not uncontested. Some scholars claim that this perspective overstretches the strength of the global human rights regime and overlooks the relevance of states. Hansen (2009), for example, argues that the formal membership of states is often a prerequisite for having one's human rights protected. European citizenship, for example, has only existence *via* citizenship of one of its member states. Moreover, questions can be asked with regard to the spread of the human rights regimes. Benhabib gives a progressive account, in which cosmopolitan law becomes in a dynamic process ever-more incorporated into the positive law of democratic states (Benhabib, 2006). This raises the question of how we can be sure that the world is going in this direction, as a wide range of events also point in the opposite direction, such as the growing intolerance with regard to the rights of homosexuals in the Russian Republic, the demand of populist parties to curb some of the rights of minorities and EU interventions on their behalf, and the religiously inspired attempt to curtail the freedom of expression. Finally, the question can be raised of whether global and regional human rights regimes really reinforce *citizenship*. Notwithstanding the importance of human rights, citizenship is generally conceived of as much more than upholding human rights. The global human rights regime allows citizens and non-citizens to make claims regarding their juridical and eventually political rights, but much less concerning their social rights, which constitute an important aspect of the rights dimension of national citizenship.

Another sign for global citizenship concerns the emergence of global civil society (see Muetzelfeldt and Smith, 2002). Global civil society represents 'a space for world citizens to debate the experience of globalization and how it can be steered in ways that benefit everyone' (Hensby and O'Byrne, (2012), p. 387). It consists of a wide range of international non-governmental organizations (INGOs), transnational social movements, advocacy networks and citizens groups across national boundaries that mobilize, organize and exercise the power of citizens in the globalized world. Global civil society shows the possibility for citizens to cooperate across national borders in order to pursue common interests, advocate global ends and keep transnational organizations accountable (see Held and McGrew, 2007, Chapter 2). A clearly visible manifestation of global civil society is the yearly World Social Forum in which a wide spectrum of participants discusses themes relating to the future of the world. Global civil society shows that globalization generates channels for meaningful citizen participation vis-à-vis the powers of global governance.

At the same time, global civil society meets skepticism, especially when compared with political participation on a national scale. In distinction to national politics in which a large majority participates in elections, only a small part of the population is able to use the possibilities of global civil society. Moreover, it is not clear to what degree citizens really have influence on world politics (Bowden, 2006). Global citizenship and global civil society can, according to some, be read as a manifestation of hegemonic neoliberal ideas, which ultimately serve capitalistic interests. From this perspective, participants, who fight for causes that the formal global governance institutions address insufficiently, might at the same time implicitly offer legitimacy to the neoliberal global structure (see Armstrong, 2006).

Another indication for the development of global citizenship concerns the ascent of attitudes and identities that are globally orientated. It is increasingly common that people have global identities and are committed to the global goals, such as sustainability and global justice, and experience a responsibility to act. Empirical literature now takes global awareness or cosmopolitanism as an attitude of citizens, which, like, for example, nationalistic orientation, can be used as an explanatory variable. Reysen and Katzarska-Miller (2013), for example, research the effect of political environments upon the development of global awareness. Kriesi employs cosmopolitanism for explaining the development of party positions (Kriesi et al., 2006). Kriesi's study underlines Bauman's idea that the development of cosmopolitan identities is not to be thought of as an unambiguous progress. Global moral and political orientations are, according to Kriesi, limited to the successful segments of society to a large extent, while the other part of society clings to citizenship identities that are willfully non-cosmopolitan.

To conclude, it is hard to deny that globalization transforms our political communities and practices of citizenship. But at the same time, we cannot conceptualize the transformation of the political order simply as a story of decline of national citizenship and the emergence of global citizenship. The rise of global citizenship is ambiguous and complex. For each dimension of citizenship, the signs of an emerging global citizenship practice can be highlighted. At the same time, the scale and strength of the global human rights regime, democratic activity in global civil society, and cosmopolitan identities can be questioned. Similarly, we cannot conclude that globalization brings about the fading of territorial citizenship, or that it remains unaffected. This picture becomes even more ambiguous as in between national and global citizenship post-national and subnational forms of citizenship have been developing, some of which are based upon religious, cultural and ethnic affiliations.

Globalization therefore entails a complex reconfiguration of citizenship. The conception of citizenship associated with the Westphalian world order was monolithic or unitary (Falk, 2000). Citizenship was related to the single domain of the nation-state, while its constitutive dimensions were taken to reinforce each other. In the present constellation, citizenship can be performed at different levels, while the different dimensions of citizenship have become unbundled. Globalization implies the multiplication or pluralization of citizenship practices and understandings (Sassen, 2002, p. 287). Individuals can link their citizenship to different identities and loyalties, to rights claims addressed to different rights regimes, and to participation on different political levels. In this setting, some segments of society turn out to be more globally oriented, while others are more locally oriented. This disappearance of a single shared conception of citizenship threatens to deprive citizenship of its emancipatory potential, for as citizenship becomes optional, moral claims that are based upon shared membership of a particular political unity (a particular state or the world) can now more easily be ignored.

Whether globalization ultimately undermines the quality of citizenship depends in the end upon one's perspective. From the perspective of territorial citizenship, global citizenship is likely to be taken as a confused or just bad imitation of the real thing. Others are more inclined to give credit to the new citizenship practices, arguing that territorial citizenship does not constitute a universal standard but is the historical product of a relatively short period within world history. The third section deals more systematically with the prospects of global citizenship.

THE NEED FOR COSMOPOLITAN CITIZENSHIP: NORMATIVE PERSPECTIVES

The normative question of whether we should foster global citizenship generally goes under the label of cosmopolitan citizenship. Cosmopolitan citizenship does not refer to an existing practice, but constitutes a standard – a moral vision – of how citizenship should be practiced. Its adherents claim that citizens must feel responsible for and act in line with the well-being of the world as a whole. They argue in favor of the creation and strengthening of political institutions that help to take the rights and interests of world citizens equally into account and bring further global justice. Though cosmopolitans applaud developments towards global governance, they are generally critical of the outcomes of globalization, such as the unequal distribution of its burdens and benefits, the degradation of the environment, and a lack of accountability for transnational organizations and global companies. In fact, cosmopolitan citizenship could be taken as a corrective of globalization. The first part of this section explores the features, background, and development of the cosmopolitan argument, while the second part discusses the different ideas of citizenship that cosmopolitan positions entail.

Distinctive for the cosmopolitan position is the belief that humans are part of a common humanity. This belief consists of three interlocking elements: individuality, universality, and generality (Pogge, 2008, p. 175). Cosmopolitans regard persons, individual human beings, as the relevant units of moral and political concern. They tend to hold an individualistic ontology, according to which the political world is, at a fundamental level, made up of individuals, and consequently reject a state-centered perspective of politics. With regard to universality, cosmopolitans hold that each individual has the same moral weight and consequently is entitled to equal concern and respect. Cosmopolitanism rejects moral favoritism, which asserts that people have special, even prime, obligations towards their compatriots, fellow believers or other groups. Finally, cosmopolitans take the realization of universal norms to be of general moral concern. Every violation of human rights pertains to all members of shared humanity.

Cosmopolitan positions are strongly influenced by Kantian political and moral philosophy. Kant's introduction of the idea of a cosmopolitan order is the most obvious reason for this orientation.[4] In the essay 'Perpetual Peace' ([1795] 2007), Kant distinguished three kinds of legal order: civil law (*ius civitatis*) within the state; international law (*ius gentium*) between states; and cosmopolitan law (*ius cosmopoliticum*), which regards individuals as members of a universal community of peoples. As members of this common humanity, all humans are morally related to each other. 'The people of the earth have thus entered in varying degrees into a universal community, and it has developed to the point where a violation of rights in *one* part is felt *everywhere*' (Kant [1795] 2007, pp. 107–8; original emphasis). For the development of cosmopolitanism, Kant's moral philosophy is at least as important, because of his belief in the existence of universal moral norms and in the ability of reason to uncover them.

For the development of the present-day cosmopolitanism, the philosophy of John Rawls is critical. As a post-Kantian, Rawls gave in *A Theory of Justice* (1973) a rational account of the universal political norms with regard to individual freedom (the liberty principle), redistribution (the difference principle) and their relative weight. Rawls called this theory 'justice as fairness'. It was supposed to be realized in sovereign, territorial states, which Rawls at that time took for granted. Later on in *The Law of Peoples* (1999), Rawls expanded his perspective from the bounded political community to a world scale, which involved a restatement of some of its positions. Others before him, however, had already argued for the application of justice as fairness beyond the territorial state. Charles Beitz (1979) claimed that the traditional practice of inter-state law had to be transformed into a cosmopolitan system of cross-culturally binding ethical rules. Thomas Pogge and David Held are important authors that further developed the idea of global justice as a universal norm that ought to regulate politics inside and beyond states. In Europe, Jürgen Habermas reformulated the universalism and rationality of Kant and Rawls in terms of a 'discourse' in which all people affected by the outcome of deliberations would be entitled to participate. Seyla Benhabib (2006) frames her cosmopolitanism in this line as dialogical universalism. Against this background, a large number of authors argue for the necessity of global justice (e.g., Young, 2006; Armstrong, 2011), global democracy (Held, 1995; Archibugi, 2004) and the expansion of global human rights (Charvet, 1998; Pogge, 2008).

The cosmopolitan position has been criticized mainly by communitarians such as David Miller (2002, 2011).[5] The disagreement can to a large degree be explained by reference to each position's understandings of human nature. Cosmopolitans tend to define humans with reference to their ability to reason and to agree on universal moral principles, while communitarians regard humans in terms of their particular cultural identities. From the communitarian perspective, the international sphere is not made up of equal individuals, but of a plurality of cultures and political societies, whose values at some point turn out to be incommensurable. As a consequence, communitarians are skeptical with regard to the application of abstract universal principles, such as human rights or global justice. According to communitarians, political norms only have meaning within the historically developed social fabric of societies and cultures. Though communitarians often concede that humans have some universal *moral* obligations, more aspiring *political* norms, such as redistribution, only succeed when they resonate with the specific culture and affinitive ties of (political) communities. The depth and width of moral and political obligations are according to communitarians on a par with the measure of shared life. The more people affect each other, communicate and hold each other accountable, in short, the more people share a common life, the more obligations they have towards each other. As, according to communitarians, states are in contrast to world spheres of common life characterized by a high level of reciprocity, they must be considered the primary domain for the definition and realization of political goals (Miller, 2011).

Cosmopolitan citizenship has also received criticism from post-modern positions. Post-moderns are suspicious of any account of justice that claims to be impartial and universal. What is being presented as a 'view from nowhere' is in fact a reflection of Western cultural, political, and ethical preferences and prejudices. Post-moderns fear that humanitarian interventions are merely dressed up as cosmopolitan, while hiding the real interests underneath (Zolo, 1997, p. xiv). Cosmopolitans have also been criticized by neo-Marxist positions of complicity with global (neo)liberal governance (for an overview of both neo-Marxist and post-modern critique see Beardsworth, 2011).

Cosmopolitans have been open to some of the elements of the communitarian and post-modern critique. They are generally prepared to acknowledge that the world consists of an irreducible plurality of forms of life and that, to some degree at least, 'moral reasoning is necessarily situated, embedded, and embodied' in cultural structures (Erskine, 2000, p. 567; cf. Benhabib, 1994). Cosmopolitans seldom argue for the abolition of states. In the literature, there is ample attention for the question of how universal cosmopolitan norms relate to local, culturally specific norms and how cosmopolitan norms manage to find acceptance among such diversity of cultural and political orientations. David Held, for example, acknowledges that cosmopolitan norms are not simply to be applied everywhere, but are dependent upon their interpretation in specific public spheres (2010, pp. 77–81). Moreover, cosmopolitan norms should not be considered a comprehensive account of 'the good' (as post-moderns fear), but as open for differences. The presence of this diversity precisely raises the need for cosmopolitan norms that guarantee that cultural diversity is dealt with fairly. At the same time, cosmopolitan norms are not merely procedural, but also material, dealing, for example, with social justice and sustainability (Held, 2010, pp. 73–4). Insofar as local norms go against the contents of cosmopolitan norms, Held gives prevalence to the latter. This duality between, on the one hand, cultural particularity and, on the other, universalism, can also be found in the work of Benhabib (2006). The notion of 'dialogical universalism' expresses that cosmopolitan human rights are not to be declared unilaterally valid, or be imposed from the outside, but only find their acceptance and realization in different cultural settings in a dialectical and dialogical process. At the same time, she also gives priority to cosmopolitan norms. Ultimately, local and cultural contexts are in need of 'moral justification' through universal norms.

Other cosmopolitans move further towards the communitarian position. Toni Erskine (2000), for example, argues for 'embedded cosmopolitanism'. She concedes that citizens are embedded in particular communities and that, as a consequence, they are not in possession of a global or universal viewpoint. At the same time, she rejects the categorical communitarian position according to which the innermost bands of bounded communities define the individual fully. Individuals are also able to expand their perspective, recognize the similarity of others and be susceptible to their claims. For her, cosmopolitanism is situated at 'the point where circles intersect' (2000, p. 567). Also, Bikkhu Parekh (2003) rejects a cosmopolitan position according to which states and national citizenship are merely instruments for universal ends. According to him, we should accept the reality and the value of national political communities, including the loyalty and obligations they evoke with their citizens. Parekh thus rejects the idea of simple global citizenship. 'The cosmos is not yet a polis, and we should not even try to make it one by creating a world state' (2003, p. 12). At the same time, the contemporary world brings forth obligations and responsibilities, which can only be met when national states and citizens overcome their self-interested and parochial orientations. Parekh therefore argues for a 'globally oriented national citizenship' and for internationalism instead of cosmopolitanism. Internationalism is to respect the basic moral impulses lying at the heart of nationalism and cosmopolitanism while avoiding their pathologies. This position reminds us of Walzer, who should clearly be placed at the communitarian end of the spectrum, when he claimed that national (American) citizens should consider themselves 'cosmopolitan Americans' (quoted in Linklater, 2002, p. 319). Finally, Dallmayr (2012, 2013) argues for a 'dialogue of (or among) civilizations'. Dallmayr is particularly interested in cosmopolitanism as a moral attitude or virtue, which, in his account, precedes cosmopolitan politics. This kind of cosmopolitanism is a personal practice, a combination of thought and action, which comes into being in a process of mutual interpretation and dialogue. His point is that cosmopolitanism is always situational. 'What one has to take seriously here is the necessarily situated character of concrete human action and interaction – the fact that practice or conduct always occurs at a certain place, among a determinate and finite group of people' (2012, pp. 182–3). The cosmopolitan practice is not to be considered as the opposite of, but interwoven in local practices. Cosmopolitanism should therefore not grant blanket primacy to the 'universal' at the expense of the particular. Such a 'universal' cosmopolitan mindset lacks in his eyes real and qualitative ethical engagement (ibid.).

A recurrent theme in cosmopolitan literature is a concern for its motivational weakness, which inhibits the practical realization of its norms. The claim of humans being part of a common humanity requires a transformation of narrow (national, ethnic, or religious) self-interest into a willingness to care for the common good of humankind. According to the Kantian rational tradition, the universal position can be inferred by the faculty of reasoning. However, many cosmopolitans assume that the awareness of having 'connected selves' must to be bolstered by a pedagogical program. Nussbaum (1996, 1997) claims that we should try to develop globally oriented virtues or dispositions, and learn to think and act as members of a single global community. She also answers the pressing question of how this change of self-image is to be realized, arguing for cosmopolitan curricula in our schools and universities. Likewise, Dallmayr argues for the strengthening by education of cosmopolitan dispositions, such as generosity, hospitality, mutuality, and striving for justice. According to Andrew Dobson (2006), cosmopolitanism might convey a sense of shared humanity, but this does not translate sufficiently into deeds. In his words (2006, p. 169), 'recognizing the similarity in others of a common humanity might be enough to undergird the principles of cosmopolitanism, to get us to "be" cosmopolitans (principles), but it doesn't seem to be enough to motivate us to "be" cosmopolitan (political action)'. According to Dobson, this impotence is reinforced by the tendency to give a 'thin' account of cosmopolitan obligations, which in the face of post-modern and communitarian critique has recoiled from giving a 'thick' universal account of cosmopolitan obligations. In this setting, the status of cosmopolitan obligations has become largely supererogatory. Like the acts of the Good Samaritan, they are to be applauded, but are not in a moral sense necessary. Dobson wants to turn these 'Samaritan' relations of beneficence into relations of justice, but he does not argue this requires a thick top-down account of cosmopolitan norms or a commitment to humanity as a whole. Instead, he points at the connectedness of the present globalized world, which, for example, for environmental issues, reveals an ever-greater dispersion of causal links between behavior in one place and effects elsewhere. As a consequence of globalization, we have become part of 'a single community of fate'. These relations according to Dobson thicken the ties that bind us to strangers and create a new kind of political space, in which obligations are not a matter of our identification with humanity as a whole, but a matter of justice. Dobson takes up somewhat paradoxically the communitarian argument that political principles require a common life for sustaining cosmopolitan norms.

The remainder of this section explores the understanding of citizenship – the 'politan' – in cosmo*politan* arguments. Cosmopolitan arguments all share a concern for universalism, but do not share the same conception of citizenship that is to realize this ideal. One group of arguments regards cosmopolitan citizenship first of all as a matter of personal moral obligation. The realization of global justice and other cosmopolitan ends is taken to be dependent upon the attitude of citizens. Cosmopolitan citizens should undergo some kind of moral conversion and widen their moral community beyond their co-nationals to include the species as a whole. A wide range of examples fits this conception of world citizenship, such as consumer activism (e.g., Beck, 2007) or charities based upon transnational solidarity. The argument for personal responsibility is particularly strong with regard to environmental sustainability (Caney, 2005). Inhabitants of industrialized or industrializing countries should refrain from consuming in a way that cannot be extended to all without causing ecological catastrophes (the idea of a global footprint). Next to performing actions in line with a conception of global justice, cosmopolitan citizens should also develop virtues that enable them to interact with strangers (see Dallmayr, 2013). This kind of argument for cosmopolitanism can be referred to as 'ethical cosmopolitanism'. Citizenship is then understood primarily as *moral* agency.

The second kind of cosmopolitan argument is primarily focused upon strengthening transnational political institutions for bringing global public goods closer, such as global justice or sustainability. Because of this focus, this argument can be labeled 'institutional cosmopolitanism'. This cosmopolitan argument takes nation-states to be ill-equipped for meeting global challenges. As many issues are collective action problems and states tend to favor their own interests, strong transnational institutions are necessary.[6] Effective global regulatory institutions could drive back unequal treatment of citizens with regard to their rights and bring about a fair distribution of natural resources around the world. Most institutional cosmopolitans do not favor the creation of a world state, but do applaud the dispersion of state sovereignty. Institutional cosmopolitans argue for sustaining, strengthening, and extending existing international and transnational organizations beyond the nation-state, such as the United Nations and the World Bank. Also, regional institutions such as the European Union can be helpful for realizing global ends, for example in enforcing environmental policies or granting similar rights to citizens of different states.

This kind of argument for cosmopolitanism regards citizenship in terms of having rights, entitlements and shares in global public goods. Citizens are primarily the objects of law. Cosmopolitan citizenship implies that all individuals, irrespective of nationality, should have equal weight. Citizenship in this fashion attributes individuals as objects of global justice a particular (not necessarily formal) status. This clearly differs from ethical cosmopolitanism, which takes citizenship as a subjective attitude. Subjective attitudes on themselves are according to institutional cosmopolitans insufficient to safeguard equal standing. The other way round, Dallmayr and Dobson argue for the limited value of global institutions without subjective citizenship support. At the same time, the institutional and moral dimensions of citizenship are clearly related to one another. Individuals that *subjectively* desire the realization of global norms, must also want to support the *institutions* that bolster these norms (Dower, 2000). Jones (2002, pp. 68–9) points out that as individuals often find themselves unable to protect rights-holders against deprivation of their rights and to provide aid to those in need, it is their *moral* responsibility to sustain the creation of institutions with the relevant capabilities. The presence of global institutions in their turn might help to foster cosmopolitan attitudes.

Third, cosmopolitan arguments can also emphasize the need for extending the democratic project of self-government beyond national frontiers. This argument is often based upon the normative principle that individuals have a moral right to be consulted about any decisions that may affect or harm them wherever these decisions may be made. As individuals are touched in the global context by decisions that are not taken by their own government, new venues for democratic participation must be created. As Archibugi has put it, 'the rights of the world citizen are radically incomplete unless they include rights of representation or participation in global institutions' (quoted in Linklater, 2002, p. 328). This argument regards citizens not merely as moral agents, or as the objects of law, but primarily as *political* agents. Global citizenship refers to a situation in which citizens are involved on a global scale as equal participants in the process of setting political ends.

Some cosmopolitans consider the institution of a world parliament (and consequently a world state) necessary for achieving global democracy (for an overview see Lu, 2006). In the third (2006) edition of his *Models of Democracy*, David Held introduces his model of cosmopolitan democracy. In the short term, Held argues, a UN second chamber should be created, following an international constitutional convention. For the long-term, Held pleads in favor of a global parliament (with limited revenue-raising capacity) connected to regions, nations, and localities (Held, 2006, p. 308).

Generally, advocates of global democracy search for participation somewhere between a world state and the nation-state. Individuals continue to be 'citizens of their immediate political communities' but also of 'the wider regional and global networks which impacted upon their lives' (Held, 2010, p. 102). Cosmopolitans argue that that we should move toward a kind of citizenship that can be referred to as 'multiple'. In international affairs, citizens should have a voice and be represented in parallel with and independently of their own governments. This requires a democratization of the instruments of global governance, such as the WTO, the United Nations, and so on. Another strategy is to strengthen global civil society, populated by international non-governmental organizations, in order to enable citizens to exercise influence upon global governance. The idea of multiple citizenships raises questions with regard to the relationship between the citizenships. Pogge (2008, p. 184) conceives the ideal of multiple citizenship as a setting whose members are 'citizens of, and govern themselves through, a number of political units of various sizes, without any one political unit being dominant'. Cosmopolitans are aware that in practice different citizenship levels can easily conflict, in particular between national and global citizenship. According to Held, restructuring global institutions both inside and outside the framework of the United Nations could attenuate this tension, connecting the global and the local in a mutually complementary or 'dialectical' process.

THE PROSPECTS FOR GLOBAL CITIZENSHIP

Cosmopolitan arguments are not meant to describe how the world ought to be, but as realistic orientations that political reformers should incrementally bring into practice. Because of their belief in the possibility of reordering our political life, Leydet (2011) labels cosmopolitans as 'voluntarists'. This optimism is grounded in the transformation towards global citizenship that cosmopolitans see already happening (see the first section above). Moreover, they tend to emphasize that citizenship is a construct, only contingently linked to the modern nation-state (Anderson, 2006). As the nation-state and national citizenship are only relatively recent phenomena and subject to profound change, why would we not be able to conceive of and pursue citizenship in different political settings?

Against the voluntarists stand skeptics who regard the emergence of global citizenship as unlikely if not impossible. According to them, cosmopolitans undervalue the vigor of the nation-state, which, eventually as a historical construct, determines the way the world turns out to be. The nation-state is the only political structure in which citizens are prepared to overcome their private interests – a core element of citizenship (this standpoint of Miller is discussed in Linklater, 2002, p. 319). A common rejoinder of the cosmopolitans is to criticize their picture of national citizenship as overtly idealized and static. National citizenship is not as successful as the skeptics presuppose, nor do they sufficiently take into account the transformations it is already undergoing. Moreover, the nation-state does not offer an answer to the challenges of the present, globalized era.

The other argument of the voluntarists, the developments that point towards the emergence of global citizenship, do not convince the skeptics either. According to them, these developments do not indicate the appearance of meaningful global citizenship. According to Miller (2011) again, activity within global civil society is not really *political*, which requires more intimate forms of interaction and reciprocity. Real citizenship therefore involves more intense forms of common life. From the left side of the political spectrum, the possibilities for global citizenship also meet skepticism. As addressed in the first section, they regard global citizenship, focused upon individual rights and global markets, as just another manifestation of the neoliberal hegemony characteristic for the modern world. While the nation-state–oriented skeptics regard meaningful citizenship to be dependent upon community (which is absent on the global level), the left-wing skeptics take meaningful citizenship to be dependent upon some kind of liberation from the shackles of the dominant capitalistic power relations.

According to the proponents of global citizenship, skeptics judge global citizenship from a false perspective. Global citizenship should not be conceived as national citizenship written large. Global citizenship is part of a multi-level citizenship constellation, in which citizens not only identify with the world as a whole, but are also part of more local structures. Moreover, this structure is continually evolving and consequently difficult to define precisely and definitively. The ideal picture of fully fledged national citizenship does not provide a fair standard for assessing the prospects of global citizenship. 'Perhaps for Miller the real problem with cosmopolitanism is that it cannot provide a neat account of what citizenship means at this level. But this is no reason to dismiss the idea as on the cutting edge of change – where things are more messy anyway' (Dower, 2000, p. 564).

The emphasis upon the difference of global citizenship from national citizenship and its evolving nature, however, leaves unanswered the legitimate question of whether it can be realized in some meaningful way. Assessing the prospects requires first of all a more precise definition of meaningful cosmopolitan citizenship, which at the same time takes into account its evolving nature and its openness for different institutional concretizations. Such an undertaking takes more space than we can offer here, though we can point at two developments in the present literature.

First of all, the nature of global citizenship has to be defined more precisely. We have addressed that globalization entails the unbundling of monolithic and comprehensive conception of citizenship, but this raises the question of whether each of citizenship's dimensions is sufficient for speaking of 'real' citizenship. According to Stoker et al. (2011, Chapter 8), the concept of citizenship includes the idea of a shared *political* community. From his perspective, citizenship must include the possibility of democratic participation. Global responsibility and global rights are certainly valuable, but do not sufficiently justify the use of the political term citizenship. It is possible to be an ardent supporter of global justice or global ethical responsibilities without employing the notion of citizenship. Singer (2004), for example, makes no reference to citizenship in his arguments about individuals' global responsibilities, including that of consuming responsibly. As Stoker et al. suggest, the introduction of the language of citizenship might be intended to add greater normative or emotive force to claims about our individual responsibilities. But the use of the concept remains largely rhetorical unless the idea of in what way membership of a world community makes normative claims is further explored.

In this line, the possibilities of political participation should be central when assessing the prospects of global citizenship. Political agency on a global level does not have to be on a par with national participation, in which comprehensive constitutions spell out the means for citizens to influence political decision-making. Political agency on a global level is necessarily more fragmented, as it employs the diverse formal means for democratic input to global institutions and the informal or semi-formal venues of civil society. But this fragmentation must not endanger core values of democratic participation, such as (political) equality, effective influence, and meaningful public debate.

In the second place, the relation of global citizenship towards other levels of citizenships has to be defined more precisely. One of the strengths of the recent development of cosmopolitan citizenship theory is that it endeavors to overcome the particularity–universality duality, according to which global citizenship is the complete opposite of national citizenship. Instead, cosmopolitan citizenship does not require leaving behind particular attachments. Citizens do not have to identify with their global identity as strongly as we often conceive of national identity, as the global citizenship does not claim to offer a comprehensive experience of political identity. Instead, the global perspective must become integrated in local citizenship practices. This perspective, however, does not preclude the necessity of some commitment of citizens towards the global level. Even though it is not necessary to substitute the commitments inherent to the local citizenship practices for abstract global commitments, they must be willing to reconsider their local practices in the light of their global ones in order to talk of global citizenship. This minimal requirement implies not only relating the self-interests of a political community to the well-being of the world as a whole, but also qualifying the absoluteness of the cultural norms constitutive for local political life. There is no reason to presuppose that this connection is necessarily harmonious. Some tension between universal and particular citizenship is inevitable. The relevant question for assessing global citizenship's prospects is whether this tension turns into opposition or whether the local and the global keep each other in some kind of dialectical balance.

To sum up, the prospects of global citizenship are dependent upon the possibility for citizens to find meaningful political participation and their ability to bring in and recognize a universal level with regard to their particular interest and concerns. With regard to participation, the challenge for global citizenship does not simply amount to organizing possibilities for participation, but also includes rendering supranational democracy significant for citizens. The European Union, for example, offers extensive possibilities for democratic participation, while citizens only tepidly make use of them. Global civil society offers room to advocate global causes, but this room is to a large degree filled with professional activists (who, to be fair, also find support among average citizens). Even when the idea of a neoliberal hegemony is considered excessive, it is very hard to overcome established interests, which also renders political participation less attractive. Even though these problems also pertain to national citizenship, 'real' global citizenship implies the ability to deal with them satisfactorily. In this respect, theorists have to consider whether meaningful global participation and representation is possible for individuals, or only for members of states that continue to function as intermediary bodies.

The other challenge of global citizenship is to incite citizens to relate their particular identity to global causes. The prospect of global citizenship depends upon the ability to render potentially strong opposition between the local and the global fluid and establish meaningful connections between the different levels. The global and the local should reciprocally implicate each other. The present order does not sufficiently succeed in making these connections. As Bauman explained and Kriesi sustained empirically, those at the losing end of globalization feel threatened by global norms. In comparison to the winners, they are unable to realize how their role as world citizen is in fact related to their particular interests and concerns. Moreover, national politicians are unable, or opportunistically unwilling, to draw out the interdependence of the national and global. This issue is also related to the previous one. As long as citizens are unable to relate to the global sphere, expansion of the means for participation does not bring meaningful citizenship. If global citizenship is said to prosper, it must prove its ability to overcome tensions, which to some degree will always arise between the local and global level.

FURTHER RESEARCH

One of the key issues for future research is to explore the relationship between national citizenship, and other local forms, and global citizenship. With respect to the empirical question of whether global citizenship is emerging, we require more sophisticated accounts, which do not juxtapose territorial and global citizenship but uncover how they also implicate each other. In what sense do global and national citizenship conflict and in what sense do they reinforce each other? Moreover, research into the development of global citizenship would obtain a fuller picture of global participation by taking the global civil society literature addressing the role of global social movements further into account. Conversely, the conception of political agency in global civil society research could be enriched by integrating the citizenship framework of the global citizenship literature.

With respect to the normative questions, it would be useful to make the space for particularistic forms of citizenship vis-à-vis cosmopolitan citizenship more explicit. If cosmopolitan citizenship does not imply simply discarding national citizenship, we need a more precise standard of what forms of national citizenship are compatible with and sustain global citizenship, and which forms are hostile and undermining. Related is the question of whether social bodies and communities that claim allegiances that precede individual choice are legitimate within cosmopolitan citizenship. Normative accounts of cosmopolitan citizenship generally favor an individualistic ontology in which each individual as world citizen has equal weight and democratic rights, independent of their national communities. The liberal idea of individual autonomy seems to be inherent in cosmopolitan citizenship. Does this imply a downright rejection of all non-liberal forms of social life, for example non-liberal religions, or can they somehow be integrated within the cosmopolitan framework? The scope of application of cosmopolitan citizenship also depends upon this question.

NOTES

1. In the literature global and cosmopolitan citizenship (and sometimes world citizenship) are used interchangeably. The notion of cosmopolitan citizenship is more common in normative use and expresses involvement in the long tradition of normative cosmopolitan claims from Diogenes and Kant onwards. The term global citizenship is employed more often in empirical settings, as it conveys a connection to the sociological process of globalization.
2. This does not imply that territorial borders have become in every aspect inconsequential. National borders still constitute a huge obstacle for migration.
3. The retreat of the state brings about a redefinition of citizenship, which emphasizes instead of social rights active citizenship and individual responsibility. Authors such as Lister interpret responsibilization as a decapitation of citizenship's core asset (Lister, 2011). Communitarian approaches of citizenship, however, see possibilities for new meaningful forms of citizenship, for example in the idea of a 'big society' (for a critique, see Kisby, 2010).
4. Before Kant, authors such as Grotius and Pufendorf already argued for the existence of political obligations towards non-citizens.
5. In the field of international relations, the cosmopolitan position stands as an idealist position against realism, which takes states as basic players of the political world. For cosmopolitans, states only have a role as local agents for the global common good, thus undermining the underlying assumption of realists. Realists take such downplaying of the role of the state to be highly unlikely. The cosmopolitan claim, however, is not empirical but normative, challenging the status quo.
6. Ethical cosmopolitanism does not reject institutions, but simply does not regard the absence of cosmopolitan institutions to be the main problem.

REFERENCES

Anderson, B. (2006), *Imagined Communities: Reflections on the Origin and Spread of Nationalism*, London/New York: Verso.
Archibugi, D. (2004), 'Cosmopolitan democracy and its critics: a review', *European Journal of International Relations*, **10**(3), 437–73.
Armstrong, C. (2006), 'Global civil society and the question of global citizenship', *Voluntas*, **17**(4), 348–56.
Armstrong, C. (2011), 'Citizenship, egalitarianism and global justice', *Critical Review of International Social and Political Philosophy*, **14**(5), 603–21.
Bauman, Z. (1998), *Globalization: The Human Consequences*, Cambridge, UK: Polity Press.
Beardsworth, R. (2011), *Cosmopolitanism and International Relations Theory*, Cambridge, UK: Polity Press.
Beck, U. (2006), *Cosmopolitan Vision*, Cambridge, UK: Polity Press.
Beck, U. (2007), 'A new cosmopolitanism is in the air' [online], SightandSound.com, accessed 18 December 2013 at http://www.signandsight.com/features/1603.html.
Beitz, C.R. (1979), *Political Theory and International Relations*, Cambridge, UK: Cambridge University Press.
Bellamy, R. (2008), *Citizenship: A Very Short Introduction*, Oxford: Oxford University Press.
Benhabib, S. (1994), 'In defense of universalism. Yet again! A response to critics of situating the self', *New German Critique*, **62**, 173–89.
Benhabib, S. (2005), 'On the alleged conflict between democracy and international law', *Ethics & International Affairs*, **19**(1), 85–100.
Benhabib, S. (2006), *Another Cosmopolitanism*, Oxford: Oxford University Press.
Benhabib, S. (2007), 'Twilight of sovereignty or the emergence of cosmopolitan norms? Rethinking citizenship in volatile times', *Citizenship Studies*, **11**(1), 19–36.

Bosniak, L. (2000), 'Citizenship denationalized', *Indiana Journal of Global Law Studies*, **7**(2), 447–509.
Bowden, B. (2006), 'Civil society, the state, and the limits to global civil society', *Global Society*, **20**(2), 155–78.
Caney, S. (2005), 'Cosmopolitan justice, responsibility, and global climate change', *Leiden Journal of International Law*, **18**(4), 747–75.
Castles, S. and A. Davidson (2000), *Citizenship and Migration: Globalization and the Politics of Belonging*, Houndmills: Palgrave Macmillan.
Cerny, P.G. (1999), 'Globalization and the erosion of democracy', *European Journal of Political Research*, **36**(1), 1–26.
Charvet, J. (1998), 'The possibility of a cosmopolitan ethical order based on the idea of universal human rights', *Millennium – Journal of International Studies*, **27**(3), 523–41.
Dallmayr, F. (2012), 'Cosmopolitanism: in search of cosmos', *Ethics & Global Politics*, **5**(3), 171–86.
Dallmayr, F. (2013), *Being in the World: Dialogue and Cosmopolis*, Lexington, KY: University Press of Kentucky.
Dobson, A. (2006), 'Thick cosmopolitanism', *Political Studies*, **54**(1), 165–84.
Dower, N. (2000), 'The idea of global citizenship – a sympathetic assessment', *Global Society*, **14**(4), 553–67.
Erskine, T. (2000), 'Embedded cosmopolitanism and the case of war: restraint, discrimination and overlapping communities', *Global Society*, **14**(4), 569–90.
Falk, R. (2000), 'The decline of citizenship in an era of globalization', *Citizenship Studies*, **4**(1), 5–17.
Habermas, J. (1994), *The Past As Future*, Cambridge, UK: Polity Press.
Hansen, R. (2009), 'The poverty of postnationalism: citizenship, immigration, and the new Europe', *Theory and Society*, **38**(1), 1–24.
Held, D. (1995), *Democracy and the Global Order: From the Modern State to Cosmopolitan Governance*, Cambridge, UK: Polity Press.
Held, D. (2006), *Models of Democracy*, Stanford, CA: Stanford University Press.
Held, D. (2010), *Cosmopolitanism: Ideals and Realities*, Cambridge, UK: Polity Press.
Held, D. and A.G. McGrew (2007), *Globalization/Anti-Globalization: Beyond the Great Divide*, Cambridge, UK: Polity Press.
Hensby, A. and D. O'Byrne (2012), 'Global civil society and the cosmopolitan ideal', in G. Delanty (ed.), *Routledge International Handbook of Cosmopolitan Studies*, Milton Park, UK: Routledge, pp. 387–99.
Hudson, W. and S. Slaughter (2007), *Globalisation and Citizenship: The Transnational Challenge*, Milton Park, UK: Routledge.
Jones, C. (2002), *Global Justice: Defending Cosmopolitanism*, Oxford: Oxford University Press.
Kaldor, M. (1999), *New and Old Wars: Organized Violence in a Global Era*, Cambridge, UK: Polity Press.
Kant, I. ([1795] 2007), 'Perpetual peace. A philosophical sketch', in I. Kant, *Political Writings*, Cambridge, UK: Cambridge University Press, pp. 93–130.
Kisby, B. (2010), 'The big society: power to the people?', *The Political Quarterly*, **81**(4), 484–91.
Kriesi, H., E. Grande and R. Lachat et al. (2006), 'Globalization and the transformation of the national political space: six European countries compared', *European Journal of Political Research*, **45**(6), 921–56.
Kymlicka, W. (1999), 'Citizenship in an era of globalization: commentary on Held', in I. Shapiro (ed.), *Democracy's Edges*, Cambridge, UK: Cambridge University Press, pp. 112–26.
Leydet, D. (2011), 'Citizenship', in E.N. Zalta (ed.), *The Stanford Encyclopedia of Philosophy*, accessed 18 December 2013 at http://plato.stanford.edu/archives/fall2011/entries/citizenship.
Linklater, A. (1998), *The Transformation of Political Community: Ethical Foundations of the Post-Westphalian Era*, Cambridge, UK: Polity Press.

Linklater, A. (2002), 'Cosmopolitan citizenship', in E.F. Isin and B.S. Turner (eds), *Handbook of Citizenship Studies*, London: Sage, pp. 317–32.
Lu, C. (2006), 'World government', in E.N. Zalta (ed.), *The Stanford Encyclopedia of Philosophy*, accessed 18 December 2013 at http://plato.stanford.edu/archives/fall2012/entries/world-government.
Mair, P. (2006), 'Ruling the void: the hollowing of western democracy', *New Left Review*, **42**(6), 25–51.
Marshall, T.H. ([1950] 2009), 'Citizenship and social class', in J. Manza and M. Sander, *Inequality and Society*, New York: W.W. Norton and Co., pp. 148–54.
Miller, D. (2002), 'Cosmopolitanism: a critique', *Critical Review of International Social and Political Philosophy*, **5**(3), 80–85.
Miller, D. (2011), 'The idea of global citizenship', *Nuffield's Working Papers Series in Politics*, accessed 8 May 2014 at http://www.nuff.ox.ac.uk/politics/Papers/2011/David%20Miller_working%20paper%202011_02.pdf.
Muetzelfeldt, M. and G. Smith (2002), 'Civil society and global governance: the possibilities for global citizenship', *Citizenship Studies*, **6**(1), 55–75.
Nussbaum, M.C. (1996), *For Love of Country: Debating the Limits of Patriotism*, Boston, MA: Beacon Press.
Nussbaum, M.C. (1997), *Cultivating Humanity: A Classical Defense of Reform in Liberal Education*, Cambridge, MA: Harvard University Press.
Nyers, P. (2004), 'Introduction: what's left of citizenship?', *Citizenship Studies*, **8**(3), 203–15.
Parekh, B. (2003), 'Cosmopolitanism and global citizenship', *Review of International Studies*, **29**(1), 3–17.
Pogge, T.W. (2008), *World Poverty and Human Rights*, Cambridge, UK: Polity Press.
Rawls, J. (1973), *A Theory of Justice*, Oxford: Oxford University Press.
Rawls, J. (1999), *The Law of Peoples: With, The Idea of Public Reason Revisited*, Cambridge, MA: Harvard University Press.
Reysen, S. and I. Katzarska-Miller (2013), 'A model of global citizenship: antecedents and outcomes', *International Journal of Psychology*, **48**(5), 858–70.
Rieger, E. and S. Leibfried (2003), *Limits to Globalization: Welfare States and the World Economy*, Cambridge, UK: Polity Press.
Sassen, S. (2002), 'Towards post-national and denationalized citizenship', in E.F. Isin and B.S. Turner (eds), *Handbook of Citizenship Studies*, London: Sage, pp. 277–92.
Singer, P. (2004), *One World: The Ethics of Globalization*, New Haven, CT: Yale University Press.
Soysal, Y.N. (1994), *Limits of Citizenship: Migrants and Postnational Membership in Europe*, Chicago, IL: University of Chicago Press.
Soysal, Y.N. (2012), 'Post-national citizenship: rights and obligations of individuality', in E. Amenta, K. Nash and A. Scott (eds), *The Wiley-Blackwell Companion to Political Sociology*, Oxford: Wiley-Blackwell, pp. 383–93.
Stoker, G., A. Mason and A.G. McGrew et al. (2011), *Prospects for Citizenship*, London: Bloomsbury Academic.
Van Doeveren, V. (2011), 'Rethinking good governance', *Public Integrity*, **13**(4), 301–18.
Weiss, T.G. (2000), 'Governance, good governance and global governance: conceptual and actual challenges', *Third World Quarterly*, **21**(5), 795–814.
Young, I.M. (2006), 'Responsibility and global justice: a social connection model', *Social Philosophy and Policy*, **23**(1), 102–30.
Zolo, D. (1997), *Cosmopolis: Prospects for World Government*, Cambridge, UK: Polity Press.

PART II

SOCIAL MOVEMENTS: CURRENT APPROACHES AND RECENT DEVELOPMENTS

PART II

SOCIAL MOVEMENTS: CURRENT APPROACHES AND RECENT DEVELOPMENTS

10. Resource mobilization and social and political movements
Bob Edwards and Melinda Kane

INTRODUCTION

The 1960s and early 1970s were marked by dramatic social conflict within most Western societies. The social movement protagonists whose political, social, and cultural challenges often claimed center-stage in those dramas, left a diverse and enduring legacy. In the decades since the 1960s, the political, social, and cultural significance of social movements has become widely recognized. Their agendas and collective action are now integral features of public debate and academic analysis of social change in Europe and North America. Yet, on neither side of the Atlantic did the received academic wisdom of the 1950s and 1960s view social movements in a generally favorable light (Jenkins, 1983; Melucci, 1989). In European analyses were dominated by Marxist conceptions of class conflict in which only the workers' movement truly challenged capitalist injustices, other movements either fragmented the opposition, or were bourgeois and irrelevant to the political agenda of the Left. In the USA, the most hospitable analyses devalued social movements as temporary disequilibria soon to be reintegrated into smoothly functioning social systems.

The renaissance of social movement research on both sides of the Atlantic that began during the 1970s represented a concerted effort by a new generation of scholars to understand the emergence, significance, and effects of the movements of the 1960s. In Europe, this emerging cohort of researchers developed new social movement theory, while their North American counterparts formulated resource mobilization (RM) theory (see Jenkins, 1983; McAdam et al., 1988; Edwards and McCarthy, 2004). Rejecting both the view held by some earlier movement scholars that social movement actors were deviant or anomic, and the pluralist assumption that all parties willing to engage in the political process have a reasonable chance that their grievances will be heard and addressed, resource mobilization scholars sought to understand how rational and often most marginalized social actors mobilized effectively to pursue desired social change goals (Freeman, 1975; Gamson, 1975; McCarthy and Zald, 1977; Tilly, 1978; McAdam, 1982; Morris, 1984; Zald and McCarthy, 1987).

Early formulations of the RM perspective fell into two groups: an organizational, social entrepreneurial variant most closely associated now with McCarthy and Zald (1977) and one more focused on indigenous political processes associated with the work of Tilly (1978). Both approaches viewed social and political movements as goal-oriented extensions of everyday political processes engaged in by various constituencies pursuing desired social change. The social entrepreneurial approach reoriented prevailing theory by taking the analytical insights of organizational sociology and extending them by analogy to movements. This focused analytical attention on the links between the shared social change goals of often marginalized constituencies and their ability to access the resources needed to engage in collective action. It often emphasized the role of social entrepreneurs in accessing resources from outside the aggrieved constituency to found social movement organizations (SMOs) to lead and coordinate collective action. By contrast, the other variant of RM emphasized, among other things, pre-existing organizations, communication networks, and other resources already operating within the movement constituency independent of external support.

In his very influential 1982 book, McAdam articulated the 'political process' model, recasting 'resource mobilization' as a narrow and deficient approach useful in analyses of elite-driven, professionalized reform movements or interest group politics, but not for explanations of confrontational, mass protest movements. Movement scholarship expanded rapidly over the next few decades and has since spread from its 'home front' in sociology across the full spectrum of social science disciplines, with analysts pursuing a wide range of research questions about an equally broad spectrum of movements both reformist and radical (Roggeband and Klandermans, 2007). Despite this diversity, three main approaches are often cited as orienting contemporary social movement analysis: political opportunity, a cultural framework, and resource mobilization (see Travaglino, 2014 for a thorough review). Movement scholarship has largely emphasized the importance of political opportunity and cultural approaches, leading to their regular refinement and development (e.g., Meyer and Minkoff, 2004; Armstrong and Bernstein, 2008; Amenta et al., 2010). In contrast, the lingering perception of RM's limited analytical utility seems to have diminished interest in building and refining the approach among subsequent generations of scholars, leaving it relatively under-developed and under-utilized. Yet, as we will see, the concepts and ideas of RM remain relevant and useful in current research.

We contend that the truncation of RM, though very influential, is unjustified, that the broader RM approach remains very relevant to analyzing the full spectrum of contemporary movements, and strongly recommend that contemporary analysts take a fresh look at it along the lines suggested below. The first major section of this chapter examines how RM has been used in recent research before considering briefly why it has been under-utilized. The second major section articulates a contemporary reformulation of a core portion of RM related specifically to resources. That section begins by differentiating a five-fold categorization of resource types that extends well beyond considerations of money, people, and formal organizations, which have predominated in recent research. We then discuss the analytical importance of two key resource attributes before turning our attention to the broader issue of how movements gain access to resources. Four major mechanisms of resource access characteristic of social and political movements are delineated. Finally, we discuss the important concept of the exchange relationships through which specific movement actors gain access to particular resources and the constraints (or facilitations) that various kinds of exchange relations can place on movements.

CURRENT UTILIZATION OF THE RESOURCE MOBILIZATION APPROACH

We noticed a trend in the social movement literature suggesting that current research tends to under-utilize resource mobilization theory relative to other theoretical explanations. What exactly do we mean? Studies regularly demonstrate the importance of resources in movement emergence, development, strategies, and outcomes, though often without explicitly mentioning the resource mobilization approach. When resource mobilization is explicitly referenced, it is often used as one of many theoretical explanations being examined, rather than a systematic examination of resource mobilization theory itself, or it is used as a series of control variables in studies interested in alternative theoretical explanations. For example, Hewitt and McCammon (2004) find that membership in state suffrage organizations was significantly influenced by the use of fundraising and recruitment strategies, but since the overarching goal of the article was to examine the role of movement frames, the resource measures were essentially treated as controls. Martin and Dixon (2010), in their analysis of modern US union strike activity, find that organizational factors such as the number of unions and the percentage of union members in the state matter, though their primary emphasis is on the influence of threat. Similarly, Johnson and Frickel's (2011) analysis of national environmental movement organization foundings focuses on the role of threat, yet finds that increases in federal government spending on the environment positively predicts increased movement mobilization though they frame this as a political opportunity variable and hypothesized the opposite effect.

One way to interpret this trend is to dismiss resource mobilization theory, deeming it less useful in explaining movements and their activities than alternative approaches. Or, perhaps the research questions central to RM are simply of less frequent interest to social movement researchers than contextual or cultural lines of inquiry. However, we have a very different interpretation, arguing that the current usage of resource mobilization theory actually highlights the centrality of the theoretical perspective. Essentially, resource mobilization tenets and concepts are so ingrained in the social movement literature that they have become taken for granted, and yet, are so fundamental to our understanding of movements that scholars are required to consider them before alternative explanations like frames, threats, and political opportunity can be found to be convincing. Unfortunately, the taken-for-granted nature of resource mobilization has placed limits on the ability of the theory to be successfully developed and refined since many resource mobilization 'results' are essentially under-discussed, under-theorized, and under-compiled.

Using Resources to Explain Movement Development, Strategies, and Outcomes

While resource mobilization theory appears to be under-emphasized in the literature, the concepts that originated within it continue to be used regularly within the study of social movements. As mentioned above, resources are a central defining concept in RM, argued to be the required link between a desire for change (i.e., a grievance) and the ability to mobilize around that desire (Zald and McCarthy, 2002). Current social movement research continues to examine the importance of resources, focusing on three broad types: money, people, and organizations. These resources are used by scholars addressing a wide range of empirical questions including studies of movement emergence and development, movement outcomes, media coverage, and protest frequency, to name a few.

Money

Financial resources have been conceptualized in various ways including the general economic well-being of the population (Fetner and Kush, 2008; Soule and King, 2008), the resources within the aggrieved group (Olzak and Ryo, 2007), access to grants and government funds (Larson and Soule, 2009), as well as organizational budgets and fundraising (McCammon et al., 2001; Andrews et al., 2010). Such financial resources have been empirically linked to the tactics and goals utilized by movement organizations (Olzak and Ryo, 2007), the level of media coverage received by an organization (Barker-Plummer, 2002), and the likelihood of a movement achieving desired outcomes (McCammon et al., 2001). For example, McCammon et al. (2001) consistently find the importance of fundraising on the passage of state-level suffrage for women within the United States. Not surprisingly, money matters.

People
People, as a resource, includes everything from the size of the population that might be receptive to mobilization (Fetner and Kush, 2008), pre-existing networks that facilitate and sustain organizations and the mobilization of members (Edwards and McCarthy, 2004; Kane, 2010, 2013), actual organizational membership (Olzak and Ryo, 2007), as well as active participants and leaders (Andrews et al., 2010). The prevalence of human capital, measured as the proportion of residents with a college degree, has been found to be associated with the spatial distribution and concentration of movement organizations. Organizational and leadership skills acquired by Lithuanian women relegated to work in devalued community institutions during the Soviet era proved crucial in their mobilizing and leading a vibrant rural movement in the decade following independence (Edwards et al., 2009). Similarly, McGurty (2009) found that the presence of experienced civil rights activists accelerated the emergence of the subsequent environmental justice movement.

Organizations
The resource receiving the most attention within the social movement literature is the social movement organization (SMO). Scholarship often examines the importance of just the sheer presence or number of organizations in a given time period or geographic area, usually interpreted as evidence of movement strength and vitality (Kane, 2003; Olzak and Ryo, 2007; Johnson, 2008). Numerous studies have documented the effectiveness of organizations in facilitating subsequent mobilization (Van Dyke et al., 2007), contributing to the achievement of a range of movement outcomes (Greve et al., 2006; Johnson, 2008), gaining media coverage (Andrews and Caren, 2010), and facilitating protest (Van Dyke et al., 2007; Gillham and Edwards, 2011).

While the sheer organizational size of the movement has received significant attention (Edwards and Foley, 2003; Johnson et al., 2009), scholars have also examined the importance of variations in SMO characteristics such as tactics and goals (e.g., Olzak and Ryo, 2007; Johnson, 2008; Soule and King, 2008; Gillham and Edwards, 2011), membership structure

(Rohlinger, 2002; Edwards and Foley, 2003; Johnson, 2008), and the level of formalization (Staggenborg, 1988; Andrews and Edwards, 2004). For example, Rohlinger (2002) argues that the National Organization for Women (NOW) received more media coverage than Concerned Women for America (CWA) partially due to differences in their organizational structures, in particular, the creation of a communications department within NOW specifically to facilitate media coverage.

The Development of Organizations and Resources

Up until this point, our discussion of the current status of resource mobilization has focused on the ways in which commonly examined resources influence a variety of movement characteristics. In other words, we have focused on resources as explanatory factors or independent variables. However, there is also a substantial literature that explores the formation, maintenance, and closure of social movement organizations themselves (Minkoff, 1999; Edwards and McCarthy, 2004; Kane, 2010, 2013; Walker and McCarthy, 2010), as well as their characteristics (Olzak and Ryo, 2007; Soule and King, 2008). Whether labeled a resource mobilization study per se, these projects examine social movement organizations – a core component of RM theory. In fact, within social movement research, the number and size of SMOs has often been used as an empirical proxy for the size of the movement itself, even though theoretical definitions of movements are much broader.

What exactly do these studies do? Scholars examine the formation of individual organizations such as state suffrage organizations (McCammon et al., 2001), campus anti-sweatshop groups (Van Dyke et al., 2007), graduate student labor unions (ibid.), high school gay–straight alliances (Fetner and Kush, 2008), or across the spectrum of SMOs in a single metropolitan area (Blee, 2012). Other researchers are interested in understanding variations or changes in the number of organizations within a specific movement such as the number of state-level LGBT groups (Kane, 2010), the number of environmental organizations nationally (Johnson, 2008) or within a multi-state region (Kempton et al., 2001). More recently scholars have begun to investigate the specific form organizations take, such as Soule and King's (2008) study of the impact of organizational competition characteristics of SMOs, specifically goals and tactics. What these studies have in common is an interest in understanding the formation and characteristics of SMOs, using resources as at least part of the explanation often in conjunction with political opportunity or cultural variables. These studies very much reflect the three tributaries of movement scholarship mentioned above, where the importance of resources, opportunity, and cultural components are all considered.

In contrast, much less attention is paid to the formation, development, and decline of other resource types such as money and members within the movement literature. Notable exceptions exist, such as Andrews et al.'s (2010) study of membership participation in the environmental organization Sierra Club, Olzak and Ryo's (2007) examination of federal civil rights funding, and a recent study by Best (2012) that examines annual changes in government funding for disease research (though both funding studies are framed as studies of social movement outcomes rather than resources). In general, scholars have focused on the impact of these resources on other movement characteristics rather than the ability of movements to generate them.

Why, then, the emphasis on organizations? We believe part of the reason scholars emphasize organizations is because they are much easier to document than other resource types. Gathering data on social movements is difficult, time consuming, and costly (Klandermans and Staggenborg, 2002). Scholars, therefore, often rely upon pre-existing data sources such as organizational directories and non-profit tax filings to provide accessible, somewhat systematic documentation of movement activity (Brulle et al., 2007), putting emphasis on organizations rather than other types of resources. This has even been the case in our own work where Kane (2010) uses the number of SMOs to measure LGBT activism partially because it is the only measure available over time for all 50 US states.

Under-utilizing Resource Mobilization

Clearly, scholars continue to find considerations of both resources and organizations useful in understanding the timing, location, format, and outcomes of social movement and protest behavior. Why, then, isn't RM getting the same attention from scholars as political opportunity or cultural approaches? It's not as if it has been disproven and discarded. Thus, we suggest three reasons why RM has not received the attention it merits. First, early formulations of RM argued strongly that the availability of resources and not the intensification of grievances explained the timing and spatial distribution of movement emergence. By taking the formation of pre-existing grievances, collective identities, and shared social change preferences for granted, RM seemed at odds with new social movement theory and ill-suited to inform core questions in the later cultural turn in social movement analysis (Williams, 2004). Second, during the intervening decades significant macro-level transformations from the end of the Cold War, waves of democratization, the global hegemony of neoliberal capitalism, the significant erosion of 'traditional values' and macro-contextual questions raised by them have captured the imaginations and research agendas of many scholars. Finally, as implied above, RM remains under-theorized by its own proponents, making its enduring vitality difficult to appreciate by a younger cohort of scholars, a problem we begin to rectify in the next section.

THE RESOURCE MOBILIZATION APPROACH

In this next section we articulate a significant portion of a broader RM approach by categorizing relevant resource types, predominant mechanisms of resource access, and the exchange relationships through which movement actors acquire specific resources. Despite the obvious importance of resources to the RM approach, analysts who made resources central to their thinking about movements neglected to specify in much detail the concept of resources, and, especially, they failed to develop clear specification of resource types (McCarthy and Zald, 2001). As the preceding section demonstrates, research in the RM tradition has emphasized three resource types – money, people, and formal organizations – variously defined and operationalized within the constraints of data availability. Yet, more recently RM analysts have benefited from broader developments in social science that have better theorized forms of capital (Bourdieu, 1986; Coleman, 1988; Lin, 2001). This enables the specification and differentiation of five distinct resource types – material, human, social-organizational, cultural and moral – while avoiding the criticism of treating 'everything as a resource' (Edwards and McCarthy, 2004).

Resource Types

Material resources
The category of material resources combines what economists would call financial and physical capital, including monetary resources, property, office space, equipment, and supplies. The importance of monetary resources for social movements should not be underestimated. No matter how many other resources a movement mobilizes, it will incur costs and someone has to pay the bills. Material resources have received much analytic attention because they are generally more tangible, more proprietary, and, in the case of money, more fungible than other resource types. (These resource attributes are discussed below.) In other words, money can be converted into other types of resources (e.g., renting for office space,

organizing events, hiring of picketers, funding documentaries, even paying for celebrity appearances), while the opposite is less often the case.

Human resources
Human resources, similar to material resources, are more tangible and easier to appreciate than the three resource types to be discussed below. This category includes resources like labor, experience, skills, and expertise. We also include leadership in this category because it involves a combination of other human resources included here. Human resources inhere in individuals rather than in social-organizational structures or culture more generally. Thus, a movement's capacity to recruit and deploy personnel is limited by the cooperation of the individuals involved. By deciding whether or not to participate in a movement, event or SMO, individuals exert proprietary control over their labor. This is one reason why voluntary participation on a mass scale, the sheer power of numbers, is an important human resource for movements of all kinds regardless of any particular skills participants may also possess.

Beyond labor, human resources also includes value-added components like experience, savvy, skills, or expertise, known also as human capital (Becker, 1964). Clearly, not all adherents offer the same mix of capabilities. A savvy and seasoned activist is not directly interchangeable with an eager undergraduate, no matter how effective the student may become with additional experience. SMOs often require expertise of varying kinds of human resources and having access to lawyers, web designers, dynamic speakers, organizers, or outside experts when the need arises can be vitally important. A key issue in whether the availability of skilled individuals will enhance movement mobilization hinges on how their expertise fits with movement or SMO needs at a given time. For example, a prominent climate scientist may have less to offer a climate justice group than a savvy intern if an SMO needs to restore its web page after a crash, or recruit six others to monitor police deployments before a protest (Oliver and Marwell, 1992). Similarly, a celebrated musician offers no additional human resource to blockading the entrance of an investment bank than either the tone-deaf academic or the grocery clerk with whom she has linked arms. Yet, from the standpoint of the moral resource contributed by her presence the evaluation would be quite different as discussed below.

Social-organizational resources
Researchers have highlighted several forms of social organization, besides formal organizations, that serve as the mobilizing structures for social movements, including infrastructures, social ties and networks, affinity groups, and coalitions (McCarthy, 1996). These forms clearly vary in

their degree of organizational formalization and bureaucratic structure, yet we wish to emphasize the extent to which access to them can be controlled, or in other words, how proprietary they are. Infrastructures are non-proprietary, relatively open-access social resources. They are the social organizational equivalent of public goods like the postal service, sanitation, the internet or civil infrastructures like roads, sidewalks, and traffic lights that facilitate the smooth functioning of everyday life (McCarthy, 1987). By contrast, access to social networks, including both social media and coalitions, but especially so in face-to-face affinity groups and formal organizations, *can* be limited by insiders through a variety of exclusionary practices, both formal and informal. Thus, resources embedded in them can be hoarded by insiders and denied to outsiders, which often intensifies pre-existing inequalities among groups in their ability to access and utilize crucial resources of other kinds (Tilly, 1998). Since a chief benefit of any form of social organization is to provide access to other resources, we are here raising the issue of uneven access to social-organizational resources among potential social movement constituencies. Such differential access creates further inequalities in access to crucial resources of other kinds, leading to disparities in mobilization capacity across movements.

This resource category includes both intentional and appropriable social organization (Coleman, 1988). Intentional social organization is created specifically to further social movement goals. The form receiving the most scholarly attention is the variety of social movement organizations founded to pursue movement goals (Zald and Ash, 1966; Edwards and Foley, 2003). From named groups of a few activists operating locally with little to no formal structure to fully bureaucratized, formalized organizations deploying hundreds of professional staff across multiple nations (Edwards, 1994), SMOs are both reservoirs of movement resources and a crucial movement tool used to mobilize collective actions of all kinds. By contrast, appropriable social organizations are originally created for non-movement purposes, but movement actors are able to gain access to other types of resources through it. Recruiting volunteers or disseminating information through work, congregation, civic, neighborhood, education, or recreation-based connections are widely cited examples (McCarthy, 1996). The two are further distinguished by the typical means movement actors gain access to them. Resources embedded in appropriable social organization must be *co-opted*, while the exchange relationships providing movement access to intentional social organization are presumably more collaborative and potentially less problematic. In either case, the ease of accessing such resources and the viability of relationships through which resources are exchanged will vary according to the goodness of fit between the specific legitimacy, organizational form, goals and tactics of those groups involved (Gillham and Edwards, 2011).

Both intentional and appropriable forms of social organization have proven crucial in explaining patterns of movement mobilization and access to other resource types. Moreover, that dense levels of pre-existing social organization among movement adherents facilitates the emergence, mobilization, varied activities, and spatial distribution of social movements is one of the most consistent findings to emerge from nearly four decades of social movement research (Edwards and McCarthy, 2004). Social movement researchers seldom discuss these findings in terms of 'social capital'. However, if one reviews that body of work from the vantage point of recent sociological theorizing, it becomes quite apparent that social capital has long been an important element in the analysis of social movements (Diani, 1996; Minkoff, 1997; Edwards, 2013). Conceived as networked access to resources, social capital is a relational and structural concept referring to the ability of individuals, groups or organizations to utilize their social relations and positions in specific social networks to access a variety of resources, and to accumulate a reservoir of viable exchange relationships by consciously investing in social relations (Bourdieu, 1986; Coleman, 1988; Foley and Edwards, 1999; Lin, 2001). Exchange relations are discussed more below.

Cultural resources

Culture is often conceptualized as the tacit and taken-for-granted symbols, beliefs, values, identities, and behavioral norms of a group of people that orient and facilitate their actions in everyday life. Thus, culture is, among other things, a reserve supply of resources ready for use by the individuals, groups, and organizations able to access them and can be usefully understood in much the same way as the kinds of structural resources discussed above (Williams, 1995). Consistent with Bourdieu's concept of 'habitus' as a structural and relational constraint upon access to 'cultural capital' and our emphasis on resource stratification, we stress that cultural resources, though widely available in a given society, are neither evenly distributed (socially or spatially), nor universally accessible to potential movement actors. For example, McGurty (2009) argues persuasively that the rapid emergence and national mobilization in the 1980s of the environmental justice movement among African Americans in the United States benefited greatly from their ready access to cultural, and other, resources produced by the civil rights movement during the 1950s and 1960s. In contrast, predominantly white, working class communities confronting similar issues in the same period mobilized much more slowly, in large part, because they lacked access to cultural resources represented by a resonant collective frame rooted in the civil rights struggle against racial discrimination, and a general unfamiliarity with tactical repertoires they had to learn essentially from scratch (Edwards, 1995). This example makes clear that through decades of sustained resistance to racial injustice African Americans had produced a rich repository of symbols, ideas, rhetorical frames, and behavioral repertoires of protest that could be transferred to the issue of environmental inequality. Over the last 50 years, those cultural resources have entered the public domain and became culturally available and accessible to subsequent social movements.

This category of cultural resources also includes movement or issue-relevant productions like music, literature, blogs, web pages, or films/videos. Such cultural products facilitate the recruitment and socialization of new adherents and help movements maintain their readiness and capacity for collective action. For example, Corte and Edwards (2008) show how the production and marketing of White Power Music by racist activists funded extremist mobilizations, helped create and spread a White Power collective identity, and facilitated the recruitment of new participants. Other cultural resources relevant to social movements include the diffusion into the public domain of taken-for-granted templates for how to accomplish specific tasks like enacting a protest event, holding a news conference, maintaining a tree-sit, or snake-marching through a field of protest to disrupt the police. For example, prior to the 2011 Occupy Wall Street (OWS) movement, the suggestion to use 'the People's Mic'[1] would have been met with perplexed looks and questions about what it was. Yet, because of the widespread use of that face-to-face communication tactic in OWS protest encampments and the attention garnered by the movement, many, though certainly not most Americans would now respond, 'Okay. Yeah, let's do that'. This illustrates that the People's Mic is now a culturally available resource accessible for use by a wide range of individuals and groups.

A key difference between human and cultural resources is that human resources inhere in individuals who possess them, the human resource is portable, and people have proprietary control over who benefits from their labor, skills, knowledge, and talents. By contrast, cultural resources, once they enter the public domain, are more difficult to control by individuals or groups, even those that originally created the resource. For example, Operation Rescue, a radical and confrontational anti-abortion organization in the USA, widely employed non-violent direct action tactics modeled directly and explicitly upon those used during the heyday of the US civil rights movement. They did so without the blessing, and sometimes with the derision, of civil rights organizations and leaders. Undesirable use of cultural resources can be condemned in an effort to undermine the moral authority or legitimacy of that use, but it cannot be prevented. Yet, while cultural resources may be more generally available, their relative accessibility continues to be mediated through patterns of social, economic or spatial stratification, so that some groups and individuals are more able to utilize these resources than others.

Moral resources
Moral resources include legitimacy, authenticity, solidary support, sympathetic support, and celebrity (Cress and Snow, 1996). Of these, legitimacy has received the most theoretical attention. Neo-institutional organizational theorists make strong claims about the importance of legitimacy as a link between macro-cultural contexts and meso- and micro-level organizational processes (Suchman, 1995). Thus, they claim that collective actors who most closely mimic institutionally legitimated features for their particular kind of endeavor gain an advantage relative to groups that do not reflect that template as well (Meyer and Rowan, 1977; Powell and DiMaggio, 1992). The neo-institutional emphasis typically looks to the legitimating power of governmental or culturally hegemonic institutions like the US Internal Revenue Service provision of tax-exempt status to non-profit organizations that agree, among other things, to refrain from certain forms of partisan political activity (McCarthy et al., 1991). Yet, legitimacy takes several forms (Suchman, 1995) and originates from a range of sources (Gillham and Edwards, 2011) beneficial to social and political movements. For example, by endorsing a specific issue campaign, or lending their fame to a particular SMO, celebrities can increase media coverage, generate public attention, open doors to influential allies and generally increase the recipient's ability to access other resources. Similarly, winning awards like the Nobel Peace Prize or receiving public endorsements from widely respected public figures, legitimates recipients to the broader public, while similar endorsement by well-respected issue activists authenticates an SMO or campaign among other activists and can facilitate cross-movement or cross-issue participation.

As discussed, moral resources often originate outside of a social movement or SMO and are bestowed by an external source known to possess them. Nevertheless, some movements succeed in the challenging and long-term task of creating and legitimating moral resources from within. This was clearly the case with the US Southern civil rights movement of the 1950s and 1960s and more recently by a range of other movements including feminism, environmentalism, LGBT rights, and animal welfare. The moral values and ethical practices represented by concepts like 'fair trade', 'sustainable', 'cruelty-free' or 'gay affirming' have been produced and disseminated by social movements. Moreover, such movement-produced moral resources can be conferred upon specific SMOs by credentialing bodies located within civil society. Moral resources are also produced at the organizational level. For example, Pilny et al. (2014) examine the creation of moral resources by formal SMOs and find that their acquisition is influenced by the prior acquisition of social-organizational and material resources, and Corte (2013) finds that the informal interpersonal dynamics in a sub-cultural mobilization depended upon a distinct arrangement of moral, material, and context-dependent 'locational' resources.

Resource Attributes

Before discussing four distinct ways social movement actors access the mix of resources they use, we provide more detail about two important dimensions along which all resource types vary: how 'fungible' they are and how 'proprietary' they are. First, each resource lies somewhere on a continuum between having a use value to social movements that is fully fungible (context-independent) or fully context dependent (idiosyncratic). Second, resources are more or less proprietary, varying in the degree that individual or collective actors can control access to them. The two resource attributes discussed here do not comprise an exhaustive set of potentially useful possibilities. Yet, they are centrally important for specifying the conditions under which resources have greater or lesser use value for movement mobilization. Beyond this, however, these particular attributes incorporate aspects of other resource attributes we have excluded from attention here. Resources that are durable, for example, hold their use value over time and are, thus, fungible across time. By contrast, perishable resources are time bound and thus, more context dependent. Similarly, much has been made of the distinction between public and private goods that, in our terms, can be seen to vary greatly in how proprietary they are. In thinking about such attributes, it is important to focus on attributes of specific resources. For instance, as we have discussed above, resources are distributed unevenly, often exhibiting a geographic or social concentration. These are not attributes of the resources per se, but rather attributes of the distribution of resources. We turn now to a discussion of resource fungibility and proprietarity.

Fungible and context dependent

All resources can be conceptualized along a continuum, ranging from having a fully fungible use value to those whose use value is entirely context dependent. A fully fungible resource would be one that could be transferred easily between persons or organizations. The use value to a social movement of a fully fungible resource would be relatively constant from one social-political context to the next. Money is the most fungible of resources and can presumably be converted into other resources as needs dictate. Therefore, movement actors with a large proportion of fungible resources at their disposal enjoy greater flexibility in the range of strategies and tactics available to them, while the options of their counterparts rich in context-dependent (localized, spatially bound, issue-specific, etc.) resources are more constrained.

The greater fungibility of money compared to other resource types means that money can be converted into other resources through the purchase of equipment, hiring of staff, founding of organizations, organizing events, and in the production of cultural resources. Yet, the fungibility of money clearly has limits, especially with respect to moral resources like legitimacy or authenticity. For example, celebrity endorsements are especially credible when the celebrity commands the details of an issue, shows sincere and long-standing commitment and donates his or her own time. By contrast, the legitimacy or authenticity of an endorsement would suffer if it was perceived that the celebrity participated for purely financial reasons and had a limited grasp of the issues at stake.

At the opposite end of the fungibility continuum are resources with a context-dependent use value limited to specific issues or localized in time and place. The use value of context-dependent resources depends upon a variety of socio-cultural and political factors as well as the type of endeavor for which they will be used. Among the resource types discussed here, the benefits of social-organizational resources are typically confined to the geographical areas in which they are nested. While social-organizational resources would be valuable to social movements in any context, for them to have use value to a social movement they must be accessible and access to them is limited to their social-relational and spatial scope. Similarly, labor per se is less context dependent than the human capital represented by skills, specialized knowledge or technical expertise.

Proprietary

Resources important to social and political movements also vary in the extent to which they are proprietary. They vary on a continuum between being completely proprietary where access to them can be tightly controlled, to those that are broadly accessible in the public domain. Material resources and human labor are both quite proprietary. The decision to participate in a movement or not is a relatively private one and individuals control which movement actors, if any, have access to their labor. By contrast, cultural resources are the least proprietary. Tactical repertoires, organizational templates, and other conceptual tools are culturally available, existing in the public domain usually without proprietary control. Moral resources like formal endorsements or solidary support are proprietary because they are granted through an exchange relationship from one party to another, and can be retracted. Social-organizational resources can be highly proprietary as with those embedded in clandestine organizations or elite social networks where access is tightly controlled, or they can be widely accessible in the public domain as in the case of dense civic networks, the internet, and emerging forms of social media. Whether a resource is proprietary or in the public domain will greatly affect social movement efforts to access it and use it. As we discuss below, the amount of control a resource provider can exert over a recipient's use of the resource relates directly to how proprietary the specific resource is. All resources may have strings attached, but the strings attached to proprietary resources are likely to be stronger, more numerous, and perhaps more constraining.

Mechanisms of Resource Access

Table 10.1 cross-classifies the five resource types described above with four mechanisms of resource access to be discussed next. Each of the 20 cells of Table 10.1 represents a distinct type of exchange relationship through which movement actors gain access to the specific mix of resources described above. Table 10.1 provides representative examples to help clarify the conceptual tools of the RM approach and help researchers use them to formulate more specific and analytically useful research questions. We discuss exchange relationships in more detail below.

Self-production

A fundamental mechanism by which social movements gain access to resources is to produce those resources themselves through the agency of existing organizations, activists, and participants (Edwards and McCarthy, 2004). Movements produce social-organizational resources when they form SMOs, cultivate networks of allies, form issue coalitions, establish communication networks with web pages and blogs, or use social media to maintain Facebook pages and Twitter feeds. They produce human resources by socializing their children into the ways and values of the movement, training participants, mentoring emerging activists and leaders. Movements produce cultural resources when they socially construct ideologies (Williams, 1995) and they produce social capital by establishing movement infrastructures to facilitate communication and cooperation (Minkoff, 1997). Movements like those for civil and human rights have produced out of their struggle a moral authority that is a powerful resource, disseminated, in part, through movement cultural productions like music, literature, and art as well as engaged research and technical expertise. Social movements also produce items displaying significant movement symbols

Table 10.1 Means of social movement and SMO resource access and resource types

Resource Types	Means of Access			
	Self-production	Aggregation	Co-optation/Appropriation	Patronage
Material	Grassroots fund-raising events Conducting 'reality tours' Producing and marketing movement music or art Creating items to sell at events (t-shirts, CDs, coffee mugs, etc.)	Member contributions Bundling financial contributions (Emily's list) Individual donations from non-members Crowd-sourcing, raising money through social media sites like Fundrazer	Use of office space Gaining use of equipment (computers, buses, etc.) WiFi or internet access	Start-up grants Large donations Foundation grants Government grants Service contracts Corporate sponsorship
Human	Raising and socializing children Issue/movement-oriented summer camps Mentoring and training leaders Movement mentors Teaching of women's, environmental studies programs	Recruiting constituents Mobilizing large numbers of participants Recruiting activists with particular skills	Networked recruitment Acquiring a mailing list Having organizational members Bloc recruitment Drawing on members of coalition partners	Providing staff or volunteers Providing technical assistance
Social-organizational	Founding SMOs Starting a task force Launching web pages Maintaining Facebook pages Twitter feeds	Building networks Forming coalitions	Recruiting local affiliates from existing organizations Gaining access to congregations or civic groups for recruitment Mesomobilization	Being loaned the mailing lists and telephone lists of sympathetic individuals

Table 10.1 (continued)

Resource Types	Means of Access				
	Self-production	Aggregation	Co-optation/Appropriation	Patronage
Cultural	Social construction of collective identities
Collective action frames
Producing innovative tactics and repertoires
Issue and movement music
Producing and preserving movement history, oral history	Social movement schools
Movement mentoring organizations
Movement-initiated summits and workshops where groups come together to share advice, information, strategy
Working groups	Providing links on your webpage to materials produced by someone else
Links to someone else's webpage	Excellence awards aimed at competence or effectiveness
Accreditation of fiscal procedures to enhance confidence of supporters and donors
Certification as 'cruelty free', 'gay affirming'
Moral	Moral authority from the effective use of non-violence (e.g., King, Gandhi)
Creation of new moral classifications such as cruelty-free, gay affirming	Compiling lists of endorsers
Recruiting celebrity endorsers
Listing advisory committee members on letterhead
Soliciting statements of support for specific projects	Allying yourself with a well-respected group
Hiring grassroots supporters to lobby office-holders
Company unions
Links to well-respected groups on your webpage without permission	A widely respected person or organization recognizing a group or activist in order to call positive attention to their work
Human rights awards
Nobel Peace Prize
An audience with the Pope

like t-shirts, coffee mugs, posters, and art. At times, they even bake cakes and cookies sold to raise money, or used directly to promote the movement.

Aggregation
Resource aggregation refers to the ways a movement or specific SMO converts resources held by dispersed individuals or groups into collective resources that can be allocated by movement actors. Social movements aggregate privately held resources from a range of supporters in order to pursue collective goals. Monetary or human resources can be aggregated by soliciting donations from broadly dispersed individuals in order to fund group activities or recruit volunteers to help with an activity (Edwards and McCarthy, 2004). Yet, SMOs aggregate other types of resources as well. For example, moral resources held by others are aggregated when groups publicize lists of respected individuals and organizations that endorse the goals and actions of a specific group or event.

Co-optation/appropriation
Social movements often exploit relationships they have within existing forms of social organization that were not formed for explicit movement purposes. Co-optation refers to the transparent, permitted borrowing of resources already under the control of such groups. A large proportion of SMOs include other organizations, more or less formally, among their members. In doing this they are able, to some extent, to co-opt resources previously produced or aggregated by those other organizations. Co-optation carries with it a transfer of some amount of proprietary control over the resources that are co-opted. The extent of proprietary control varies considerably by resource type. Moreover, co-optation usually implies some form of subsequent reciprocity as well as a tacit understanding that the resources will be used for mutually agreeable purposes. Co-optation of resources has received much theoretical attention (McCarthy, 1987) because it has been quite common in many consequential movements including the Southern civil rights movement (McAdam, 1982) and women's liberation (Freeman, 1975), environmental justice (McGurty, 2009), and the Tea Party movement in the USA (Skocpol and Williamson, 2012).

Resource appropriation, by contrast, seems to be a less common practice among social and political movements and has not received as much attention by researchers. Appropriation refers to the surreptitious exploitation of the previously mobilized resources of other groups. Selznick (1960) illustrated the process for the American Communist Party of the 1930s, and a number of student groups active in the 1960s specialized in infiltrating other groups and taking control of their resource base (Isserman, 1987; Miller, 1987).

Patronage

Patronage refers to the bestowal of resources by an individual or organization that often specializes in patronage. In monetary patronage relationships, patrons provide substantial financial support. Patrons typically exercise some degree of proprietary control over how that money can be used and may attempt to influence day-to-day operations and policy decisions. Government contracts, foundation grants, and large private donations are the most common forms of financial patronage and such patrons are typically external to the movement or SMO. Yet, financial patrons can also be internal sources from within the movement, as when a national SMO makes grants to local or state-level SMOs to fund an issue campaign, or when wealthy individuals who are themselves gay, feminist, or environmental activists donate money to particular issue campaigns or SMOs (Edwards and McCarthy, 2004). Such cases are not exempt from seeking to exert influence over how funds are used, but they do originate from within a given movement.

Patronage relationships can also provide some level of human resources including the loan of personnel for periods of time. This kind of patronage is common when coalitions of SMOs field large and complex events, which are often directed by loosely coupled, often temporary, organizations formed specifically for that purpose (McCammon and Van Dyke, 2010). For example, the Washington DC Area AFL-CIO[2] agreed to provide hundreds of individual unionists from its member unions to canvass door-to-door in the Washington DC area to educate residents about global justice issues and recruit them to participate in upcoming protest events planned by the Mobilization for Global Justice coalition (Gillham and Edwards, 2010). Patronage in moral resources occurs when a widely respected individual or organization recognizes a movement actor for positive achievements. Amnesty International's human rights awards and the Nobel Peace Prize are widely known examples, the receipt of which can be an immensely valuable moral resource for recipients, independent of any cash prizes awarded.

Exchange Relationships and Source Constraints

Early formulations of RM emphasized aggregate patterns of resource availability based on the well-founded expectation that the presence of social-organizational resources in a particular locale would increase the overall likelihood of movement mobilization and action in that setting. Much analysis examined associations between aggregate patterns of resource availability (e.g., monetary wealth, the proportion of college graduates within a community, or the number of religious or civic organizations present) and the likelihood of movement mobilization. Yet, recent RM analysts emphasize more explicitly durable patterns of inequality in the social, economic and spatial distribution of resources and seek to understand how movement actors alter that distribution by accessing a range of resources in order to direct them into social and political movements.

Exchange relationships

In order for social movements to use resources generally available in a particular social context, two distinct and necessary components must be present. First, individual or collective actors must perceive that a specific resource is present in their social context. Second, they must have an exchange relationship capable of brokering their access to that resource. Exchange relationships exist between two entities when resources of various kinds are made available and accessed (Blau, 1964). SMOs and other social movement actors typically cultivate, maintain, and preserve numerous exchange relationships through which they gain access to the specific mix of resources supporting its varied endeavors (Aveni, 1979; McAdam, 1982). Exchange relationships are not reducible to network ties or position in a strictly structural sense because a tie, per se, only indicates the opportunity for an exchange, and does not carry with it the social, cultural or ideological meaning of a relationship between entities. Without some knowledge of the content of the exchange relations, and of the specific resources available through them, one cannot assess the import of the exchange relationships movement actors have at their disposal (Gillham and Edwards, 2011).

With respect to SMOs, exchange relationships can be internal or external, vary in the value they provide, and are context dependent. Internal exchange relations refer to those that exist within an organizational body, as when an SMO obtains financial resources through contributions or dues paid by members. External exchange relations refer to those outside of the formal organizational structure, as in receiving foundation grants or patron contributions. Exchange relationships also vary in the value of the resources they make accessible to an SMO. Hence, an SMO wanting to start a campaign that influences a broad base of the American public, or moderate elites, might seek out as an exchange partner a large national organization with the capacity to provide staff, thousands of members, and dollars, rather than a small organization with far fewer resources. In contrast, an organization wishing to engage in a confrontational and disruptive campaign seeking to divide elites may enter into exchange relations with radical groups known for deploying innovative tactics. Finally, the use value of exchange relationships is context dependent, varying by both time and place. For example, valuable relationships with individuals who are elected officials, foundation program officers or leaders in an allied SMO lose substantial use value when such individuals leave their positions or their party is voted out of office. Similarly, the use value of relationships with celebrities or morally authoritative public figures evaporates as careers decline, or a public figure is disgraced by scandal.

Source constraints
Two intertwined debates about resources center around whether social movements obtain their support primarily from indigenous or external sources and the extent to which external support causes SMOs to moderate their goals and tactics (see McAdam, 1982; Cress and Snow, 1996). First, we note that this debate depends entirely upon how one defines a 'social movement' (Diani, 1992), an issue we do not engage here. Second, the long-standing debate over source constraints has been cast very narrowly, focusing almost exclusively on a single exchange relationship – financial patronage. Even SMOs benefitting from financial patronage typically engage in other exchange relationships with various sources. In addition, as indicated above we wish to reframe this debate in a broader and more analytically useful way. From the perspective advocated here this debate becomes a researchable question: to what extent do movement actors moderate their goals and activities in order to preserve existing exchange relationships (or attract new ones) with external supporters? Cast more broadly, we ask what is the range of distinct exchange relationships through which specific movement actors access resources and how do those particular exchange relations constrain (or facilitate) goals, actions, or public statements?

We contend that movement actors simultaneously manage numerous exchange relationships of varying importance and duration with multiple exchange partners. Each exchange relationship brings a reciprocal set of expectations and obligations between the parties, with each relationship having widely varying potential for either social control or facilitation. Thus, the perspective we advocate here encourages analysts to consider the varying mix of facilitation and constraint across the full range of exchange relationships through which specific SMOs, coalitions, issue campaigns, or event organizers mobilize resources.

Their impact on movement actors depends in part upon the specific means of resource access and the type of resource accessed (Gillham and Edwards, 2011). For example, among the 117 organizations actively involved in planning a series of over 30 inter-related Global Justice Week protests in Washington DC in 2001, Global Exchange, Essential Action and the AFL-CIO were all professionalized SMOs. Yet, they had different financial exchange relations. The AFL-CIO depended upon contributions from its member unions, which in turn relied upon dues paid by individual union members. Essential Action depended upon a large grant from another organization, Public Citizen, for most of its operating expenses and had no formal members. Global Exchange self-produced much of its operating funds internally from proceeds collected from coordinating and leading socially conscious 'travel tours' and selling t-shirts, books, and other merchandise. The AFL-CIO has a much larger and broader base of support, which is in many ways a substantial advantage. Yet, the actions it can take without alienating substantial parts of its base are constrained by the very size and diversity of its base. By contrast, as long as Essential Action preserved its core exchange relationship with Public Citizen, it was free to proceed. Clearly, this patronage relationship imposes some constraints on Essential Action. Yet, it also freed Essential Action from the demands of managing multiple and potentially countervailing exchange relationships. For its part, Public Citizen receives no corporate or government support and forgoes the benefits of tax-exempt status in order to operate free of constraints imposed by the US Internal Revenue Service. This enabled the organization to give more free rein to Essential Action. Last, as a self-sufficient SMO, Global Exchange's core financial exchange relationship was internal, and its actions relatively unconstrained by outsiders.

CONCLUSION

The relative lack of systematic attention to the resource mobilization approach makes evaluating the state of the theory difficult. While scholars regularly find evidence that resources matter, there has not been systematic, evidence-based evaluations of the theory that rigorously identify which resource mobilization claims receive consistent empirical support, the tenets that are consistently questioned or undermined, and those that remain unaddressed. There have, for example, been several general, summary examinations of the political process model that have helped to solidify the state of the field (e.g., Amenta et al., 2010). Without a similar analysis for resource mobilization, it is too easy to continue to use the theory and its components in an ad hoc manner, dismissing or ignoring the theory's importance when individual variables in a specific analysis work (or don't work).

We argue that the first step in an RM research agenda should be to find accessible and reliable indicators with which to measure all types of resources and pertinent organizational characteristics. Existing research tends to use a hodge-podge of RM variables based more upon data availability than upon theoretical or empirical grounds. This would not only allow scholars to examine the importance of resources beyond organizations, people, and money, but it would also provide more systematic evaluations of the resources and characteristics that most effectively explain protest strategies, tactics, arguments, and outcomes. The rigorous measurement of RM concepts would also allow scholars to move beyond a consideration of how individual resources work independently to considerations of the combination of resources that are most effective and the conditions under which specific resources matter. For example, are there variations by organizational type, form or size in the importance of specific resources? Research often assumes in the case of financial resources that more is always better. Yet, this might not be true in the case of religious organizations, where dramatic financial resources could undermine the organization's legitimacy, an important cultural resource.

Finally, as mentioned above, while there is a general consensus that resources matter, we have much less information on how resources are accessed, produced, and distributed within and between movements. One way to address this gap is to examine exchange relationships and the extent to which different kinds of exchange relationships with different kinds of exchange partners affect goals, strategies, tactics, outcomes, and framing. To what extent, and in which ways, do exchange relationships facilitate movements or constrain them?

Clearly, we believe that there are still RM questions worth addressing. We also think that RM has the potential to be useful in recent attempts within the social movement literature to broaden the range of activities and targets categorized as movements. Long-standing concerns with the political process model, which has traditionally emphasized movement activity by outsiders targeting the state, were recently crystalized by Armstrong and Bernstein's (2008) multi-institutional approach. Emphasizing that movements involve any challenge to entrenched interests, regardless of the target, participants or type of change desired, Armstrong and Bernstein (2008) call for scholars to examine activism across social institutions to better evaluate the degree to which existing social movement theories can explain the full range of movement activity. While there is a notable lack of attention to resources in their approach, we argue that RM is uniquely positioned to help examine movement activity across the institutional spectrum of social life.

McCarthy and Zald's (1977) original RM definition of a social movement as 'a set of opinions and beliefs in a population which represents preferences for changing some elements of the social structure and/or reward distribution of a society' (pp. 1217–18) is much less restrictive than many other definitions and makes their original concepts and hypotheses applicable to a wider range of movement processes. For example, the original RM definition does not limit social movements to targeting the state. Rather, it is readily applicable to challenges to entrenched authority across the spectrum of cultural, familial, economic, legal, religious, and political institutions. Moreover, in this definition, key movement attributes like level of mobilization, tactics used, ideologies expounded, and organizational forms are all variables to be analyzed both within and across movements rather than defining criteria that unduly limit the field of inquiry. The classic formulations of RM provide important analytical tools, and we strongly encourage researchers to read the original works and not rely upon secondary critiques. Moreover, we contend that the emerging reformulation of RM to which this chapter contributes has great relevance to contemporary trends in social movement research.

NOTES

1. A means for delivering a speech to a large group of people, where people gathered around the speaker repeat what the speaker says, thus 'amplifying' the voice of the speaker without the need for amplification equipment.
2. American Federation of Labor and Congress of Industrial Organizations.

REFERENCES

Amenta, E., N. Caren, E. Chiarello and Y. Su (2010), 'The political consequences of social movements', *Annual Review of Sociology*, **36**, 287–307.

Andrews, K.T. and N. Caren (2010), 'Making the news: movement organizations, media attention and the public agenda', *American Sociological Review*, **75**(6), 841–66.

Andrews, K.T. and B. Edwards (2004), 'Advocacy organizations in the U.S. political process', *Annual Review of Sociology*, **30**, 479–506.

Andrews, K.T. and B. Edwards (2005), 'The organizational structure of local environmentalism', *Mobilization: An International Quarterly*, **10**(2), 213–34.

Andrews, K.T., M. Ganz, M. Baggetta, H. Han and C. Lim (2010), 'Leadership, membership, and voice: civic associations that work', *American Journal of Sociology*, **115**(4), 1191–242.

Armstrong, E.A. and M. Bernstein (2008), 'Culture, power, and institutions: a multi-institutional politics approach to social movements', *Sociological Theory*, **26**(1), 74–99.

Aveni, A. (1979), 'Organizational linkages and resource mobilization: the significance of linkage strength and breadth', *The Sociological Quarterly*, **19**(2), 185–202.

Barker-Plummer, B. (2002), 'Producing public voice: resource mobilization and media access in the national organization for women', *Journalism and Mass Communication Quarterly*, **79**(1), 188–205.

Becker, G. (1964), *Human Capital*, New York: National Bureau of Economic Research/Columbia University Press.

Best, R.K. (2012), 'Disease politics and medical research funding', *American Sociological Review*, **77**(5), 780–803.

Blau, P. (1964), *Exchange and Power in Social Life*, New York: Wiley and Sons.
Blee, K. (2012), *Democracy in the Making: How Activist Groups Form*, New York/Oxford: Oxford University Press.
Bourdieu, P. (1986), 'The forms of capital', in J. Richardson (ed.), *Handbook of Theory and Research for the Sociology of Education*, New York: Greenwood Press, pp. 241–58.
Brulle, R., L.H. Turner, J. Carmichael and J.C. Jenkins (2007), 'Measuring social movement organization populations: a comprehensive census of U.S. environmental organizations', *Mobilization: An International Quarterly*, **12**(3), 255–70.
Coleman, J.S. (1988), 'Social capital in the creation of human capital', *American Journal of Sociology* (Supplement), **94**, S95–S120.
Corte, U. (2013), 'A refinement of collaborative circles theory: resource mobilization and innovation in an emerging sport', *Social Psychology Quarterly*, **76**(1), 25–51.
Corte, U. and B. Edwards (2008), 'White Power music and the mobilization of racist social movements', *Music & Arts in Action*, **1**(1), 3–20.
Cress, D.M. and D.A. Snow (1996), 'Mobilization at the margins: resources, benefactors, and the viability of homeless social movement organizations', *American Sociological Review*, **61**(6), 1089–109.
Diani, M. (1992), 'The concept of social movement', *Sociological Review*, **40**(1), 1–25.
Edwards, B. (1994), 'Semi-formal organizational structure among social movement organizations: an analysis of the U.S. peace movement', *Nonprofit and Voluntary Sector Quarterly*, **23**(4), 309–33.
Edwards, B. (1995), 'With liberty and environmental justice for all: the emergence and the challenge grassroots environmentalism in the USA', in B. Taylor (ed.), *Ecological Resistance Movements: The Global Emergence of Radical and Popular Environmentalism*, Albany, NY: Suny Press, pp. 35–55.
Edwards, B. (2013), 'Social capital and social movements', in D.A. Snow, D. Della Porta, B. Klandermans and D. McAdam (eds), *Wiley-Blackwell Encyclopedia of Social and Political Movements*, Oxford: Wiley-Blackwell, pp. 1173–6.
Edwards, B. and M.W. Foley (2003), 'Social movement organizations beyond the Beltway: understanding the diversity of one social movement industry', *Mobilization: An International Journal*, **8**(1), 85–105.
Edwards, B. and J.D. McCarthy (2004), 'Resource mobilization and social movements', in D.A. Snow, S.A. Soule and H. Kriesi (eds), *The Blackwell Companion to Social Movements*, Oxford: Blackwell, pp. 116–52.
Edwards, B., M. Dillard and A. Juska (2009), 'Gender and leadership in the Lithuanian rural community movement', *Transitions*, **47**(2), 15–28.
Fetner, T. and K. Kush (2008), 'Gay–straight alliances in high schools: social predictors of early adoption', *Youth and Society*, **40**(1), 114–30.
Foley, M.W. and B. Edwards (1999), 'Is it time to disinvest in social capital?', *Journal of Public Policy*, **19**(2), 199–231.
Freeman, J. (1975), *The Politics of Women's Liberation*, New York: McKay.
Gamson, W.A. (1975), *The Strategy of Social Protest*, Homewood, IL: Dorsey Press.
Gillham, P. and B. Edwards (2011), 'Legitimacy management, preservation of exchange relationships, and the dissolution of the mobilization for global justice coalition', *Social Problems*, **58**(3), 433–60.
Greve, H.R., J.E. Pozner and H. Rao (2006), 'Vox populi: resource partitioning, organizational proliferation, and the cultural impact of the insurgent Microradio Movement', *American Journal of Sociology*, **112**(3), 802–37.
Hewitt, L. and H.J. McCammon (2004), 'Explaining suffrage mobilization: balance, neutralization, and range in collective action frames, 1892–1919', *Mobilization: An International Journal*, **9**(2), 147–66.
Isserman, M. (1987), *If I Had a Hammer: The Death of the Old Left and the Birth of the New*, New York: Basic Books.
Jenkins, J.C. (1983), 'Resource mobilization theory and the study of social movements', *Annual Review of Sociology*, **9**, 527–53.

Johnson, E.W. (2008), 'Social movement size, organizational diversity and the making of federal law', *Social Forces*, **86**(3), 967–93.
Johnson, E.W. and S. Frickel (2011), 'Ecological threat and the founding of U.S. national environmental organizations, 1962–1998', *Social Problems*, **58**(3), 305–29.
Johnson, E.W., O. Saito and M. Nishikido (2009), 'The organizational demography of Japanese environmentalism', *Sociological Inquiry*, **79**(4), 481–504.
Kane, M. (2003), 'Social movement policy success: decriminalizing state sodomy laws, 1969–1998', *Mobilization: An International Journal*, **8**(3), 313–34.
Kane, M.D. (2010), 'You've won, now what? The influence of legal change on gay and lesbian mobilization, 1974–1999', *The Sociological Quarterly*, **51**(2), 255–77.
Kane, M.D. (2013), 'LGBT religious activism: predicting state variations in the number of metropolitan community churches, 1974–2000', *Sociological Forum*, **28**(1), 135–58.
Kempton, W., D.C. Holland, K. Bunting-Howarth, E. Hannan and C. Payne (2001), 'Local environmental groups: a systematic enumeration in two geographical areas', *Rural Sociology*, **66**(4), 557–78.
Klandermans, B. and S. Staggenborg (eds) (2002), *Methods of Social Movement Research*, Minneapolis, MN: University of Minnesota Press.
Larson, J.A. and S.A. Soule (2009), 'Sector-level dynamics and collective action in the United States, 1965–1975', *Mobilization*, **14**(3), 293–314.
Lin, N. (2001), *Social Capital: A Theory of Social Structure and Action*, New York: Cambridge University Press.
Martin, A.W. and M. Dixon (2010), 'Changing to win? Threat, resistance, and the role of unions in strikes, 1984–2002', *American Journal of Sociology*, **116**(1), 93–129.
McAdam, D. (1982), *Political Process and the Development of Black Insurgency, 1890–1970*, Chicago, IL: University of Chicago Press.
McAdam, D., J.D. McCarthy and M.N. Zald (1988), 'Social movements', in N. Smelser (ed.), *Handbook of Sociology*, Beverly Hills, CA: Sage, pp. 695–737.
McCammon, H.J. and N. van Dyke (eds) (2010), *Strategic Alliances: Coalition Building and Social Movements*, Minneapolis, MN: University of Minnesota Press.
McCammon, H.J., K.E. Campbell, E.M. Granberg and C. Mowery (2001), 'How movements win: gendered opportunity structures and U.S. women's suffrage movements, 1866–1919', *American Sociological Review*, **66**(1), 49–70.
McCarthy, J.D. (1987), 'Pro-life and pro-choice mobilization: infrastructure deficits and new technologies', in M.N. Zald and J.D. McCarthy (eds), *Social Movements in an Organizational Society*, New Brunswick, NJ: Transaction Press, pp. 49–66.
McCarthy, J.D. (1996), 'Mobilizing structures: constraints and opportunities in adopting, adapting and inventing', in D. McAdam, J.D. McCarthy and M.N. Zald (eds), *Comparative Perspectives on Social Movements*, New York: Cambridge University Press, pp. 141–51.
McCarthy, J.D. and M.N. Zald (1977), 'Resource mobilization and social movements: a partial theory', *American Journal of Sociology*, **82**(6), 1212–41.
McCarthy, J.D. and M.N. Zald (2001), 'The enduring vitality of the resource mobilization theory of social movements', in J.H. Turner (ed.), *Handbook of Sociological Theory*, New York: Kluwer Academic/Plenum Publishers, pp. 533–65.
McCarthy, J.D., D.W. Britt and M. Wolfson (1991), 'The institutional channeling of social movements by the state in the United States', *Research in Social Movements, Conflict and Change*, **14**, 45–76.
McGurty, E.M. (2009), *Transforming Environmentalism: Warren County, PCBs, and the Origins of Environmental Justice*, New Brunswick, NJ/London: Rutgers University Press.
Melucci, A. (1989), *Nomads of the Present*, Philadelphia, PA: Temple University Press.
Meyer, D.S. and D.C. Minkoff (2004), 'Conceptualizing political opportunity', *Social Forces*, **82**(4), 1457–92.
Meyer, J. and B. Rowan (1977), 'Institutionalized organizations: formal structure as myth ceremony', *American Journal of Sociology*, **83**(2), 340–63.
Miller, J. (1987), *Democracy in the Streets: From Port Huron to the Siege of Chicago*, New York: Simon and Schuster.

Minkoff, D.C. (1997), 'Producing social capital: national social movements and civil society', *American Behavioral Scientist*, **40**(5), 606–19.
Minkoff, D.C. (1999), 'Bending with the wind: strategic change and adaptation by women's and racial minority organizations', *American Journal of Sociology*, **104**(6), 1666–703.
Morris, A. (1984), *The Origins of the Civil Rights Movement: Black Communities Organizing for Change*, New York: The Free Press.
Oliver, P.E. and G. Marwell (1992), 'Mobilizing technologies for collective action', in A.D. Morris and C.M. Mueller (eds), *Frontiers in Social Movement Theory*, New Haven, CT: Yale University Press, pp. 251–72.
Olzak, S. and E. Ryo (2007), 'Organizational diversity, vitality and outcomes in the civil rights movement', *Social Forces*, **85**(4), 1561–91.
Pilny, A.N., Y.C. Atouba and J.M. Riles (2014), 'How do SMOs create moral resources? The roles of media visibility, networks, activism, and political capacity', *Western Journal of Communication* [published online 5 February 2014], accessed 9 May 2014 at http://www.tandfonline.com/doi/abs/10.1080/10570314.2013.866689#.U24sScdgN7w.
Powell, W. and P.J. DiMaggio (eds) (1992), *The New Institutionalism in Organizational Analysis*, Chicago, IL: University of Chicago Press.
Roggeband, C. and B. Klandermans (2007), 'Introduction', in B. Klandermans and C. Roggeband (eds), *Handbook of Social Movements Across Disciplines*, New York: Springer, pp. 1–12.
Rohlinger, D.A. (2002), 'Framing the abortion debate: organizational resources, media strategies, and movement–countermovement dynamics', *The Sociological Quarterly*, **43**(4), 479–507.
Selznick, P. (1960), *The Organizational Weapon: A Study of Bolshevik Strategy and Tactics*, Glencoe, IL: Free Press.
Skocpol, T. and V. Williamson (2012), *The Tea Party and the Remaking of Republican Conservatism*, New York/Oxford: Oxford University Press.
Soule, S.A. and B.G. King (2008), 'Competition and resource partitioning in three social movement industries', *American Journal of Sociology*, **113**(6), 1568–610.
Staggenborg, S. (1988), 'The consequences of professionalization and formalization in the pro-choice movement', *American Sociological Review*, **53**(4), 585–605.
Suchman, M.C. (1995), 'Managing legitimacy: strategic and institutional approaches', *The Academy of Management Review*, **20**(3), 571–610.
Tilly, C. (1978), *From Mobilization to Revolution*, Englewood Cliffs, NJ: Prentice-Hall.
Tilly, C. (1998), *Durable Inequality*, Berkeley, CA: University of California Press.
Travaglino, G.A. (2014), 'Social sciences and social movements: the theoretical context', *Contemporary Social Science: Journal of the Academy of Social Sciences*, **9**(1), 1–14.
Van Dyke, N., M. Dixon and H. Carlton (2007), 'Manufacturing dissent: labor revitalization, union summer and student protest', *Social Forces*, **86**(1), 193–214.
Walker, E.T. and J.D. McCarthy (2010), 'Legitimacy, strategy, and resources in the survival of community-based organizations', *Social Problems*, **57**(3), 315–40.
Williams, R. (1995), 'Constructing the public good: social movements and cultural resources', *Social Problems*, **42**(1), 124–44.
Williams, R. (2004), 'The cultural context of collective action: constraints, opportunities, and the symbolic life of social movements', in D.A. Snow, S.A. Soule and H. Kriesi (eds), *The Blackwell Companion to Social Movements*, Oxford: Blackwell, pp. 91–114.
Zald, M.N. and R. Ash (1966), 'Social movement organizations: growth, decay, and change', *Social Forces*, **44**(3), 327–41.
Zald, M.N. and J.D. McCarthy (1987), *Social Movements in an Organizational Society*, New Brunswick, NJ: Transaction Books.
Zald, M.N. and J.D. McCarthy (2002), 'The resource mobilization research program: progress, challenges, and transformation', in J. Berger and M. Zelditch (eds), *New Directions in Contemporary Sociological Theory*, Lanham, MD: Rowman & Littlefield, pp. 147–71.

11. The new social movement approach
Christian Scholl

In contrast to other approaches, the new social movement (NSM) approach stands out, with its complicated language and yet less structured analytical categories. Because it is the first approach to pay extensive attention to the cultural dimension of contentious politics, it is an important theoretical tradition to consider in relation to political citizenship and social movements. It eschews the assumption that social movements are to be directed merely at (national) governments and institutional reform (even political revolution), by explicitly attempting directly to influence society and culture. First, this chapter presents the main arguments made by various contributors to the NSM approach. Second, I summarize the main critiques and debates it has unleashed. Third, I examine recent developments of this approach, specifically in the context of globalization. Fourth, this chapter identifies a number of challenges posed by these developments and makes suggestions for future research. Now, let me historically contextualize the emergence of the NSM approach.

WHY NEW SOCIAL MOVEMENTS?

The theoretical perspective on social movements within the NSM approach establishes an explicit link between broader social changes on the one hand, and the changing patterns of social conflict and political mobilization on the other. Inspired by the 1960s' and 1970s' social movements emerging in many Western, and especially European countries (such as the women's and gay movements, the peace, environmental, anti-nuclear, and urban autonomist movements), it dovetailed with the shift from industrial to post-industrial (Touraine, 1974), from Fordist to post-Fordist, or from material to informational societies (Melucci, 1980). It argues that this shift finds expression in the way the loci within social conflicts move from material values (the 'old' workers' movements focusing on redistributive issues and institutional power) to social ones, especially centring in post-materialist values, such as world peace, gender equality and ecology. One important outcome of this shift is the weakening of traditional class cleavages in favour of searching for new collective identities.

Melucci (1994, p. 110) argues that information societies contribute to the reflexive, artificial and constructed character of social life, making access to knowledge a new terrain of struggle. A new class cleavage emerges that traverses the new middle class, opposing professionals, those who have organizational control (managers, technocrats), and professionals whose work is skills oriented (the social and cultural specialists) (Kriesi et al., 1995, p. xix). Whereas 'old' social movements were concerned with distribution questions, 'new' social movements often focus on recognition and autonomy (Young, 1990). These 'new' movements were seen as examples of a new 'type' of social movements (Kriesi et al., 1995) that differ significantly from 'old' ones (Johnston et al., 1994, pp. 6–7). This is also the reason why they are often considered their own 'social movement family' (Della Porta and Rucht, 1991). In the fourth section I come back to debated questions concerning the novelty of these movements and whether such a metaphor suffices to demarcate them. Many of the 1970s' movements studied by NSM scholars display these characteristics, provoking interesting scholarly questions.

New social movements continued a trend that already started with the 'New Left': anti-war, but especially student movements of the 1960s. These movements almost simultaneously emerged in many countries over the world, that is, not only in the USA and Europe, but also in Mexico, Japan, Pakistan and Czechoslovakia – they were often a reaction to the imperialist war in Vietnam led by the USA and its allies (Katsiaficas, 1987). Besides rejecting Western imperialism, the New Left critiques both technocratic management of liberal democracy and Soviet-communist state bureaucracy. On 17 May 1968, this co-critique of capitalism and bureaucratic structures is captured in a telegram sent from the Committee of the People's Free Sorbonne University to Czech professor Ivan Svitak: 'Humanity won't be happy till the last capitalist is hung with the guts of the last bureaucrat'.[1] In many countries, however, the New Left was eventually dominated by Marxist-Leninist cadre groups that channelled oppositional energies into revolutionary factory-based organizing and alliances with the working class (Touraine, 1971; Epstein, 1993).

Though partly a reaction to that development, the new social movements of the 1970s also resemble the early New Left in three ways: having (1) a majority of young, highly educated new-middle–class participants (often students), (2) a critical stance towards bureaucracy and institutions, in general, including the institutionalized left, because it is perceived as authoritarian, and (3) a demand for a total democratization of every aspect of life. This backgrounds the post-war expansion of consumerist market societies with access to education in many Western countries. Not surprisingly, many student activists in those years enthusiastically picked up central themes of the Frankfurt School (theorists such as Adorno,

Horkheimer, Bloch and Marcuse at the Frankfurt Institute for Social Research in the 1920s and 1930s). Their analysis of the cultural reproduction mechanisms involved in capitalist relations had already inspired a critique of Western consumerism by the Situationist International organization in the 1950s. Indeed, the subversive language used by this anti-art movement, such as in *The Society of Spectacle* by Guy Debord ([1967] 2000), influenced the imagery and discourse of many later movements (see Scholl, 2011).

THE NEW SOCIAL MOVEMENT APPROACH?

Such a title implied a uniform field of research, but this is far from the case; there is no shared approach. As Buechler (1995) points out, we should more rightly speak about a plurality of new social movement approaches. Flesher Fominaya and Cox (2013b, p. 16) argue that the 'canonical account' of new social movement theories also serves the ideological function of demarcating them from Marxism, to integrate identity into the 'strategic' accounts of the 'US paradigm' (resource mobilization and political process theory) without challenging their dominance, and to establish it as an academic sub-discipline of social movement studies and as separate from theorizations of movement activists.

Scholars associated with the NSM approach do not themselves focus exclusively on such 'new' movements, but also have to be seen against the background of other dominant approaches at those times, especially theories about resource mobilization and the political process. Though these approaches contributed major innovations in conceptualizing collective protest and social movements as perfectly rational activity (see Chapter 10 by Edwards and Kane and Chapter 12 by Meyer and Evans in this volume), their analytical frameworks are overly structuralist, leaving little space for the actual agency of, especially less hierarchically organized, activists and activist groups. Whereas the NSM approach is linked to the work of a number of European scholars, resource mobilization and political process are two perspectives largely developed in the USA and, therefore, perhaps too much modelled on the reality and history of social movements there. For this reason, debates between these approaches are often framed as a transatlantic debate between US and European traditions of studying contentious collective action and social movements.

For example, in opposition to these US-based approaches, the NSM approach does not consider social movements as an empirically given entity, looking instead at the process of constructing a collective identity – through giving meaning to the social world and through sharing experiences through action. Rather than explaining emerging movements in terms of political opportunities (as in 'political process' theory) or organizational resources (as in 'resource mobilization' theory), NSM theories look at social movements as themselves carriers of a certain critique of society that challenges social relations and cultural codes. This supersedes protest events, seeing movements as much more than vehicles for political mobilization – functional equivalents of political parties – but as 'submerged networks' that can operate both visibly and covertly (Melucci, 1989).

Very soon, however, US-based scholars picked up a number of central themes emerging in the NSM literature. For their part, many European scholars, especially within political science, worked within the more structuralist frameworks coming from the US tradition. At this point, the NSM approach has been influenced by theories emerging from various international contexts, such as Latin America, where NSM scholar Touraine spent time for research.

By focusing on the cultural aspects of movements, NSM approaches also coincide, theoretically, with a more general 'cultural turn' in the social sciences and other fields (Nash, 2001). Social-constructivist approaches shed light on the social and cultural construction of social relations and hierarchies. Influenced by French philosophers such as Deleuze and Derrida, but also by feminists such as Cixoux, *difference* became a central category for rethinking Enlightenment philosophy and the modernity project: 'In societies that exert strong pressures toward conformity, the appeal to difference has an explosive impact on the dominant logic', as Melucci (1994, p. 119) puts it.

The most important NSM theorists are Alain Touraine (France), Alberto Melucci (Italy), Jürgen Habermas (Germany), and Manuel Castells (Spain). Whereas Habermas's Frankfurt School work (1984, 1987) is largely theoretical in scope, the others have done major empirical work. Castells (1983) focused on urban social movements, which he saw as an increasingly important form of mobilization, focusing on collective consumption provided by the state, cultural identities and community culture, and decentralized political self-management. His experimental method accomplished together with a research team used video-taped sessions with movement participants; those centred around youth, women's, ecology, and what he called 'new-consciousness' movements (self-help groups with some spiritual orientation) in Italy. Through participation of diverse individuals, Melucci tried to unravel the more hidden processes of movement formation. His works that are translated into English are largely theoretical, reflecting on the conceptual underpinnings of his distinctive approach to social movements (Melucci, 1989, 1996).

Together with Hegedus, Dubet and Wieviorka, in the late 1970s Touraine started a research programme on new social movements using a new method: the sociological intervention (Cousin, 2010). Working with several sets of focus groups, comprised of 12–15 different kinds of movement participants (who ideally do not know each other), two sociologists facilitate several sessions where the participants go into debate with various allies and opponents (Dubet and Wieviorka, 1996). The method is intended to foster a process of reflexive self-analysis about the constitution of the group's identity (Touraine, 1981). This fruitful collaboration led, for example, to studies of the student movement (Touraine et al., 1978), the anti-nuclear movement (Touraine et al., 1980), and the Polish Solidarność movement (Touraine et al., 1983). In short, there is a broad diversity of approaches behind the label 'new social movement approach'.

MAIN THEMES AND THEIR THEORETICAL ARTICULATION WITHIN THE NSM PERSPECTIVE

In this section, I introduce and summarize four main themes and arguments that have been foregrounded within the NSM approach. By definition, such a summary cannot be exhaustive, so I am guilty of minimizing some differences between different theorists associated with this approach. Nevertheless, I try to point out major disagreements about certain issues.

Culture and Meaning

The NSM approach links two interconnected themes: culture and meaning. In contrast to the US tradition of relating social movements to the political process (read to political institutions and political reforms), NSM scholars focus on how social movements try directly to influence and change societies, thereby enhancing our conception of the political through this analysis of cultural change. As Rochon (1998) argues, cultural change is the most important outcome of the new social movements in the USA. Touraine (1985) defines social movements in such a way that they necessarily include cultural contestation of society's main orientation.

This different focus arises because in post-industrial societies, material production is replaced by the production of signs, symbols and cognitive schemes. New social movements challenge 'taken-for-granted' norms and meanings, for example, heterosexual norms, the division of roles between men and women, the self-evidence of economic growth. Because, in post-industrial societies, information is seen as the crucial resource, this makes societies more complex and more globally interdependent (Melucci, 1985,

p. 807). Hence, major conflicts emerge around the production and interpretation of signs and symbols. Social movements are carriers of these conflicts. As Melucci's book's title suggests (Melucci, 1996), their role is to 'challenge codes'. Elsewhere, Melucci elaborates: 'The medium, the movement itself as a new medium, is the message. As prophets without enchantment, contemporary movements practice in the present the change they are struggling for: they redefine the meaning of social action for the whole society' (Melucci, 1985, p. 801).

This definition of social movements – as challengers of codes and carriers of cultural change – also removes them from traditional notions of class conflict. According to many NSM scholars, stable social classes no longer exist in post-industrial societies; so, class struggle has lost its privileged position; even actors become more and more temporary. This means that other oppressions around the position of women, the environment, processes of decision-making and so on are no longer subordinate to the class struggle – they are equally if not more important. This move departs from Marxist approaches that see social movements as an expression of their socioeconomically conditioned position (Buechler, 1995). Although class relations are acknowledged, antagonisms for NSM are seen not as the necessary result of the contradictions of capitalism, but rather as struggles over the control of cultural orientations.

As Melucci (1985, p. 797) points out, movements are systems of social relations that function to reveal stakes, to announce to a society that a fundamental problem exists in a given area. He thereby gives movements a somewhat prophetic function. Understanding the stakes they raise helps us to decodify structural conflicts in our present societies. In their book on the anti-nuclear movements, *La Prophétie anti-nucléaire* (*The Anti-nuclear Prophecy*), Touraine et al. (1980) identify the new paradigmatic movement that takes over from the old workers' movement.

Even though this cultural perspective has been picked up by US scholars working within the resource mobilization or political process perspective, they normally incorporate culture into their own models while reproducing their existing structuralist tendencies. For example, McAdam (1982), acknowledging the cultural and constructive processes behind framing processes, speaks about 'cognitive liberation' as the ability of protesters to recognize their collective strength and frame it positively. Others have simply included cultural factors in the political opportunity structure, or else perceive of culture, identities and discourses as specific resources that can be mobilized by movement entrepreneurs (Zald, 1996). Albeit enriching for this literature to include cultural factors in their analytical approaches, I argue that this instrumentalist use of it misses the central considerations of European-based NSM scholars.

(Collective) Identity

The focus on culture and the process of creating meaning among NSM approaches, turned interest to identity construction. Through the shift from a struggle for control over economic production to that over social production, NSM scholars argue that the collective production of an identity becomes a central part of social movements. As Melucci (1989, pp. 177–8) argues, '(t)he freedom to have, which characterized... industrial society, has been replaced by the freedom to be'. In informational societies, conflicts emerge along the lines of the power to make decisions, to influence and to manipulate; hence, individual and collective identities oppose these power configurations.

Just as collective actors in earlier social movements were rooted more clearly in the social condition (e.g., class), the process of identity construction was considered less important and less visible. Once collective identity became recognized as a tool for understanding how people make sense of their world and their actions, scholars turn to the process through which individual participants become a collective, how acting together makes sense for the participants in a social movement. This construction of a collective identity is processual, relational and conflictive.

One of the first scholars who examined the concept of collective identity was an Italian. He, Pizzorno, developed what Cohen (1985) calls a 'pure identity approach'. He argues that the collective action of 'new groups' cannot be explained by instrumental logics of exchange, because their real ends are non-negotiable. This is why he grew interested in the formation of the subject and the construction of identity through collective interaction (Pizzorno, 1978). He opposes this expressive – and defensive – logic of collective action to that strategic-instrumental – offensive – logic. Pizzorno sees a dichotomy of two types of movements split between two logics along this analytical distinction. By foreclosing the analytical possibility of seeing both logics possibly interacting in one and the same movement, Pizzorno's model of identity-oriented movements implies that any strategic dimension is eclipsed.

Moreover, by focusing on the *process* of constructing a collective identity, Melucci critiques any social movements scholarship that approaches social movements as unified ontological essences, as some 'thing' that simply exists: 'what was formerly considered a datum (the existence of the movement) is precisely that what needs to be explained' (Melucci, 1996, p. 70). Rather than seeing collective identities in a static way, his work tries to de-reify this category, recognizing them as a dynamic and self-reflexive process. Collective identity is not an objective condition that defines the place of people in society; people choose who they are and assume responsibility for that choice (Melucci, 1994). This process renders social movements necessarily plural, ambivalent and often contradictory:

> I call collective identity the process of 'constructing' an action system. Collective identity is an interactive and shared definition produced by a number of individuals (or groups at a more complex level) concerning the orientations of their action and the field of opportunities and constraints in which such action is to take place. (Melucci, 1996, p. 70)

Demonstrating its relational and conflictive character, the process of identity construction entails two major tensions: (1) between the self-definition of a group, which can already entail a conflictive process, and its recognition by society; and (2) the fact that the whole society is analogized to a specific category or group (namely, women, gays, people of colour, etc.). These tensions keep the identity construction process dynamic, actuating its urgency. Movement participants actively have to construct their self-definitions in ways that relate to society and to its recognition of this self-definition, so, there is the conflict at stake.

Melucci (1996, p. 71) delineates three key dimensions of the process of collective identity construction: (1) a cognitive process defining means, ends and the field of action; (2) a network of active relationships between actors who interact; and (3) a certain degree of emotional investment. This shows why collective identity construction cannot be separated from individual identity construction. These processes feed into each other. Johnston et al. (1994), therefore, distinguish between individual, collective, *and* public identity (the public perception of the movement) and argue that individual identities, too, change through movement participation.

Like Melucci, Touraine (1985) also sees identity as a field of tensions where actors confront dilemmas. Contra Pizzorno, he stresses that movements are less about defending collective identities than about contesting vested social relationships. This is to say, more than defending the cultural category of 'women', the women's movement contests women–men relationships, thereby challenging the existing 'natural' relationships between men and women. He also recognizes the interaction between individual and collective identities, opposing oppressive power relations within informational societies that include the role of experts or of management elites. For Touraine (1985), movements can be defined by the analytical triangle of identity (definition by the actor), opposition (the definition of the opponent), and cultural totality that defines the field of conflict.

US-inspired social movement approaches have partially appropriated the concept of collective identity, usually in a very rationalist and structuralist fashion (Polletta and Jasper, 2001). That is, they normally pay more attention to the top-down construction of an identity, namely, as a strategic resource, conceptualizing identity as part of these 'cultural opportunities' that movement organizers can tap into for their mobilization efforts. Melucci (1996, p. 70) criticized these reifying approaches of collective identity construction and stressed the bottom-up character of this individual/collective process.

Action, Subjectivity and Experience

Scholars using NSM approaches put actors and their creation of meanings at the centre of their analyses of society. They try to understand the discordant creation of a dynamic society, by grasping the orientation and the meaning of actors capable of producing knowledge. Therefore, it is difficult to grasp the conception of action in the NSM literature without relating it to subjectivity and experience. This underscores how the NSM literature differs from more structuralist accounts. Movements are 'multipolar action systems' (Melucci, 1980). This means we cannot impose one single meaning or orientation onto a movement. There are always varieties of things that movement networks are doing; Melucci refuses to reduce this multiplicity.

Whereas resource mobilization approaches have often exclusively focused on major social movement organizations, NSM scholars give importance to looser and decentralized forms of organization – what Melucci (1989) has called 'submerged networks'. Submerged in these latent and invisible networks, important movement activities take place backstage that prepare for and issue into more visible articulations: 'In fact, when a movement publicly confronts the political apparatus on specific issues, it does so in the name of new cultural models created at a less noisy and less easily measurable level of hidden action' (Melucci, 1994, p. 107). Hence, NSM approaches turn attention to a less spectacular, and often, invisible, realm of action within social movement networks.

In this more hidden realm, the formation of subjectivity plays a major role. In their turn to subjectivity, NSM scholars show not only that social movements are products of structural changes but also actively try to become actors in producing new social relationships. Consciousness-raising groups in the 1970s' women's movement became an important tool for politicizing affairs that were previously considered both private and personal by many women: they fostered autonomous female subjectivities in opposition to the established male-dominated culture. McDonald (2006, pp. 32–3) argues that (post-industrial) network capitalism no longer produces generality but individuality; therefore, subjects become responsible for their self-production. Touraine (2000, p. 145) documents how subjectivity has increasingly become the core of social conflicts: we are less concerned with defending collective identities, which he sees as typical for the industrial age, than with a struggle for coherence of selfhood, 'to make our own existence a meaningful whole'.

Here it is important to understand Touraine's conception of historicity as it pertains to the orientation of societies, the process by which a social order is created. According to Touraine (1981, p. 61), action refers to the capacity of societies to develop and change their own orientations, to produce their own normativity and objectives. Through their capacity to act upon themselves in a self-reflexive way, societies create their own history. For Touraine, movements are active participants in this process; such cultural movements are alternative forms of social integration, preliminary attempts to create a new society. Movements are not seen as reaction to change, but as an orientation towards change. This is how the actions of new social movements receive their prophetic character.

Introducing their cognitive approach to social movements, Eyerman and Jamison (1991) develop further this focus on meaning. They propose conceptualizing social movements as producers of knowledge that challenge cognitive paradigms. It is by creating new ideas, identities and consciousness that social movements transform society, including science. They see a movement's cognitive praxis (its big idea) as not necessarily obvious or explicit to the movement or its intellectuals. Social movements and knowledge creation are alike collective processes.

Autonomy Versus Representation

In new social movements, the rejection of representational forms of politics (such as trade unions and political parties) often goes hand in hand with the quest for autonomy. According to Melucci, the cultural contestations by such social movements create a new space that cross-cuts the liberal distinction between the private and the public:

> A new political space is designed beyond the traditional distinction between state and 'civil society': an intermediate *public space*, whose function is not to institutionalize the movements nor to transform them into parties, but to make societies hear their messages and translate these messages into political decision-making, while the movements maintain their autonomy. (Melucci, 1985, p. 815; original emphasis)

Direct participation is considered to be a good in itself regardless of the results it achieves (Melucci, 1994, p. 123). Bottom-up or grassroots movements are opposed to top-down forms of politics that are seen as another form of (bureaucratic) domination (see also Marcuse, 1964). This means that the process of forming collectivities and practising autonomous forms of politics becomes a central part of social movements. Offe (1985) observes a strong anti-institutionalism among new social movements that explicitly organize as extra-parliamentary forces: '(t)he conflicts and contradictions of advanced industrial society can no longer be resolved in meaningful and promising ways through etatism, political regulation, and the proliferating inclusion of ever more claims and issues on the agenda of bureaucratic authorities' (Offe, 1985, p. 819).

As the discussion between Jo Freeman (2002) and Levine (2002) exemplifies, the quest for autonomy through decentralized forms of organization in the women's movement did not always remain uncontested. Freeman objects that the rejection of any structures is a new form of 'tyranny' of informal leadership structures. But Levine defends the decentralized and horizontal approach as a necessary step to avoid institutionalized hierarchies characteristic of a male-dominated world.

Besides its rejection of institutionalized representative forms of action and the embrace of decentralized and participatory ways of organizing, feminism politicizes everyday life with the attempt to democratize all aspects of life. As Melucci (1989, p. 165) argues, '[i]n different areas of social life, and within institutions and organizations of many kinds, there is taking place a process of transformation of authoritarian regulations into political relationships'. Areas of life, such as sexuality, the household, and child care previously seen as private matters were now perceived as political. De Vries's (1987) work shows how important the slogan, 'the personal is political', was for the second-wave women's movement. Poldervaart (2006) demonstrates how to question all kinds of social hierarchies and experiment with bottom-up democracy in daily life inspired subsequent movements, such as squatters, queers and alter-globalists. Katsiaficas (1987) argues that autonomy and daily life were also a central part of the political project of the urban autonomous movements in Europe. Because this approach to politics starts with the (inter-)personal experiences of living subjects and tries to achieve immediate change of social relations from the position of such a situated subject, this politicization of daily life is sometimes called 'politics of the first person' (Evans, 1979).

As Eder (1993, pp. 107–8) shows, social movements related to modernization historically first sought political participation, then economic justice, but now individual happiness and the 'good life' is primary. Similarly, Raschke (1980) talks about the new 'paradigm of the way of life' as the defining feature of new social movements. As Offe (1985, p. 670) puts it: 'Indeed, many of the actors interpret their actions as attempts to renew a democratic political culture and to reintroduce the normative dimension of social action into political life'.

Habermas theoretically articulates this reorientation of social movements.

In *The Theory of Communicative Action* (Habermas, 1987), he makes an analytical distinction between the system sphere (the market and the state) and the life sphere (culture, personality and social institutions) and he argues that the latter is being subsumed by the former through the rationalist logic of money and power. NSMs try to reverse this process. As Katsiaficas (1987) argues, the 'de-colonization' of the life sphere becomes a central project of new social movements. Habermas's approach, in fact, leads to a very defensive vision of social movements trying to prevent the total colonization of the life sphere. This defensive vision is not shared by all scholars.

For example, others show how the quest for democratizing everyday life goes together with a strong focus on the creation of political as well as personal alternatives. Breines (1982) has called this 'pre-figurative politics': social movements try to pre-figure in a nutshell how the better world they are striving for might look (Maeckelbergh, 2011). In this approach, means and ends largely collide; the internal democratic organization of the movement becomes a goal in itself. Along with autonomous social centres, squatted houses, consciousness-raising groups, work collectives, and collective childcare arrangements, and so on, the practice of alternatives also stood central in a number of protest camps that, long before Occupy, were organized in various countries against planned nuclear power plants, nuclear waste storage facilities, and military basements stocked with nuclear arms (Frenzel, 2012).

Another way of practising autonomy typical for new social movements became direct action and civil disobedience (Cadogan, 1972). In both traditions, mediation by institutionalized actors is largely rejected: social movements are seen as at the centre of change, and a direct conflict – even confrontation – with authorities or power-holders is sought (see also Scholl, 2012, pp. 47–8). Sit-ins, teach-ins, blockades, occupations, and confrontational demonstrations were frequently used action forms (Kriesi et al., 1995). Based on the centrality of participation and personal experience, direct action and civil disobedience reject institutionalized channels for resolving conflicts. Unconventional action repertoires of NSMs relying on civil disobedience and direct action has provoked scholarly interest in the political use of the body and specifically of the category of personal experience for understanding the constitution of political subjectivity (McDonald, 2006).

MAIN CRITICISMS AND DEBATES

NSM approaches have triggered a number of important debates – what follows is an overview of them. The next section presents three key debates that comprise a number of themes. This provides a fair impression of both the contentious and weak points of NSM theories.

New Social Movements?

But what is *really* new about the previously mentioned aspects of 'new' social movements? Precisely this question has sparked quite some debate among social movement scholars. Three questions are at the centre of these debates: (1) do the movements we classify as 'new' really share all the characteristics that supposedly mark NSMs; (2) are there other contemporary movements that do not posit these characteristics or even posit contrary ones; and (3) weren't these supposedly 'new' characteristics also part of 'old' social movements, and hence, isn't the entire distinction between 'old' and 'new' a bit absurd? This section briefly summarizes these debates and notes how Melucci countered these objections.

The first question asks, as does Plotke (1990), whether the newness may not be exaggerated by selectively focusing on the cultural dimensions as distinct from conventional politics. Plotke's question suggests that the cultural dimension was just one of many characteristics and maybe not even the most important one. In some movements labelled as typical new social movement, such as the women's movement, material issues (for example, concerning the payment of equal salaries) still play a huge role. The analysis of NSMs as a separate – cultural – paradigm could be precisely a reaction to the overly narrow focus of existing approaches to instrumental rationality.

Other scholars charge NSM theorists with an exclusive and misleading focus on the middle class (Bagguley, 1992). Scott's (1990) critique of NSM approaches emphasizes the relevance of political aspects and the development of these movements. There are also scholars who, because many of the ascribed characteristics also apply to conservative and right-wing movements (Pichardo, 1997), reject the NSM label itself, demoting it as merely a typology for a small group of radical, middle-class movements of that period.

This raises the second question: don't NSM scholars look at a rather narrow set of social movements within narrow geographical borders – middle-class movements in the Western world? This is refuted when we consider ongoing workers' struggles and other movements (such as landless farmers) in the Southern Hemisphere (e.g., Veltmeyer, 1997), which highlight the role material issues play. For his part, Martin (2002) argues that social movements in the Western world are also confronted with the persistence of material issues and the continuous involvement of institutionalized actors. Kriesi et al. (1995, p. 241) describe the 'non-simultaneity of cleavages in politics and society' to explain how social mobilization around certain issues, which seem politically pacified, still continues.

The third question asks whether the supposed characteristics of new social movements are actually exclusive to them. Calhoun (1993) shows that the supposed 'old' social movements – the workers and socialist movement – display many of these same characteristics. While sharing the critique of restricted and instrumental approaches of social movements as articulated in the NSM literature, Calhoun also proposes a historicizing perspective to avoid falling too easily into glosses about 'post'-industrial or 'post'-modern societies. Like Calhoun, Tucker (1991) also stresses the NSM character of early workers' movements and rejects any exclusive attribution of, for example, decentralized forms of organization to the new social movements. McAdam (1994) argues that all movements are cultural, which reinforces the value of NSM theories for the study of all social movements, not only a sample taken from a specific historical period.

Tarrow (1989) stipulates that every 'new' movement might expose similar characteristics in the early phase of emergence, before they start to enter a trajectory of getting more structured, reformist in orientation and institutionalized in forms of action. This 'culturalization' of new movements by NSM theorists may overlook or minimize the fact that over time most movements have become (by and large) part of 'normal politics' (Kriesi et al., 1995, p. 247). It still can be challenging to divide social movements into such different waves and periods. Tarrow (1989) suggests that NSMs were not a sudden eruption of a unique type of politics, but often the product of previous struggles and already-built organizations. Thus, Cohen (1985, p. 667) prefers to speak instead about contemporary social movements, seeing 'new' as a sequential category ('coming after'), not a qualitative one ('being different from').

In Melucci's response to the nomenclature of 'new', he argues that both critics and proponents of the 'newness' of 'new movements' commit the same epistemological mistake: they see contemporary collective phenomena as unitary empirical objects and seek to define the substance of their newness (Melucci, 1996, p. 5). However, Melucci wants to see collective action not as a point of departure, but as an unfolding result: 'The task of the analyst is to explain how this outcome has been collectively constructed, how it is maintained, and, perhaps, how it alters over time' (Melucci, 1994, p. 106).

When he uses the term 'new', he stresses that this was not to say there was something *essentially* new about a clearly demarcated social phenomenon, but rather, that the meaning of social conflicts was somehow shifting. One of his central observations here is that classes, as real social groups, are withering away (ibid., p. 103), and that this makes the construction of a collective identity a much more central process to the action orientation of social movements. Though this nicely coincides with Inglehart's (1977) observation of a shift at the centre of post-industrial societies from material to post-material values, I wonder if he sufficiently addressed all the criticisms raised against this concept. In any case, the very use of a category – 'new social movements' – has enacted their scholarly categorization, reification as some objectively existing 'thing', exactly what Melucci wanted to avoid.

Strategy Versus Identity

This debate between instrumentalist-structuralist and NSM approaches has also been framed as the two contested theoretical paradigms when we examine either strategy or identity. Hence movements are seen either as being instrumental (strategy-orientated) or expressive (identity-orientated) (Pizzorno, 1978). This way, both approaches and both types of movements focus respectively on strategic interaction or on the defence of a collective identity. They have become incommensurable approaches.

By focusing on cultural processes and identity formation, it is certainly true that many NSM scholars foreclose any consideration of strategic or instrumental aspects of social movements. That NSM approaches consciously leave behind the strategic-instrumental frameworks of US approaches to collective action no doubt reflects a shift made by social movements in those times. As Sanbonmatsu (2004, p. 23) observes:

> Yet the Sixties had nonetheless effected a shift in tone or 'style' in Western praxis, one that decisively privileged emotive and aesthetic expression of an inner, 'radical' nature over considerations of strategy, theoretical coherence, or the patient construction of a counter-hegemonic movement. In the subsequent decades, the 'structure of feeling' of the Sixties – its characteristic elements of impulse, restraint, and tone – later settled in the practices of the social movements and became sediment in the 'baroque' discourses of the academic intelligentsia.

Cohen (1985) shows how, albeit different, both approaches on strategy and identity can fruitfully inform each other, for both share these commitments: that conflictive collective action is normal, that social movements involve organized groups with autonomous forms of communication, and that participants are usually rational members of organizations. Although the instrumentalist approach provided insightful evidence for the organizational and mobilization processes of social movements and the influence of political opportunities, it did not provide satisfying answers to the question as to why people who participate in social movements consider participation a meaningful activity. Such answers can usefully be constructed from NSM approaches.

Cohen recognizes Habermas as a good starting point for the theoretical integration of both traditions. Habermas's (1984, 1987) distinction between strategic and communicative action creates space for both a teleological concept of action and a normative one. Although he never stipulated how both rationalities could inform the practice of social movements, and seemed to see new social movements as particularistic reactions defending the life-world with communicative action, there is potential for conceptualizing social movements as melting pots of strategic and communicative action. In Pleyer's (2010) work on the counter-globalization movement (below), he distinguishes a 'way of reason' and a 'way of subjectivity', an attempt to integrate theoretically.

My point is that the debate around strategy versus identity is not only a scientific endeavour, but also equally transports the normative and strategic preferences of the respective scholar (and scholarly tradition). Social movement theories mirror the social movement of the time in which scholars are living and often involved. They share the same life-world. So questions about strategy, identity, and how to integrate both motivations are not merely theoretical ones for academics, but equally remain important practical ones for activists.

Lifestylism

Another debate concerns what Raschke (1980) calls the 'paradigm of the way of life' in the new social movements. Many scholars and observers critique the 'lifestylism' into which this paradigm had degenerated, especially since corporations discovered the potential of counter-culture and identity politics for (niche) marketing (Klein, 2000). Thornton (1995) analyses how subcultural niches are commodified and transformed into lifestyle commodities to be consumed. Similarly, Kauffman (1990) sees the retreat of the new social movements into lifestyle politics as an 'apolitical introspection mirroring market values' that refrains from engagement with a broader transformative project.

Lifestylism became especially visible in new social movements practising a strong form of 'identity politics' (Young, 1990), for example the women's, black and gay movements. Identity often became something essentialized and set in stone (Adam et al., 1999), again in ways that Melucci conceptually opposed. Besides reifying social groups, norms and behaviours, identity politics also resulted in an increasing fragmentation between struggles. The endless affirmation of difference did not lead to a convergence of struggles. Despite some inspiring attempts by social movements to combine the struggle against various forms of oppression (for example, the environmental justice movement in the USA, which draws together environmental and anti-racists' struggles with a class perspective; see Bond, 2012), there was little or no systematic attention by social movement scholars for how these experiments could produce a viable path for organizing 'unity in diversity'.

Part of reducing social movements to their daily and cultural expressions is the exclusive focus on micro-politics. While backed up by the post-modern turn in cultural and (some) social theories, besides Marxists, many are raising questions about how broader structural changes could be achieved with such a strategy – a 'strategy' just of expressivism. More structuralist approaches show that interaction with elites, political institutions and corporations are an important aspect of social movement's development. In many movements the experimentation with micro-politics has proven to be a very difficult, contradictory and fragile process (Scholl, 2005).

The more rationalist conception of social movements as purposeful actors inspires another critique. Participants in social movements usually want their actions to have consequences. This is in certain contrast to NSM approaches that see social movements as conflating means and ends by engaging in pre-figurative practices – where the here and now becomes more important than a strategic orientation towards future changes. Granted, NSM scholars have pointed out important processes such as identity formation that were not addressed by structuralist or Marxist accounts. But, I wonder, can a movement be just a process that does not choose certain means to gain leverage?

These tensions prompt Kriesi et al. (1995) to distinguish between instrumental, counter-cultural and subcultural wings within social movements. Whereas the environmental movement still relies mainly on an 'instrumental' dynamic (with a small counter-cultural wing, e.g., Earth First!), the squatters' movement is marked more by a 'counter-cultural' dynamic (collective identity formation through confrontational interaction with an opponent), and the women's movement by a 'subcultural' dynamic (collective identity formation through interaction with each other, e.g., consciousness-raising groups).

GLOBALIZATION AND THE NEWEST SOCIAL MOVEMENTS

Because NSM theories are so tightly connected to the social movements emerging in the 1960s and 1970s, why should we bother about them today? For two reasons, as I will show in this section. First, the heritage of the movements emerging in those years still carries on, influencing and inspiring contemporary forms of activism from radical environmentalism to counter-globalization to Occupy movements. Second, themes raised by NSM theorists are further developed by a number of contemporary scholars, especially in relation to globalization. As background for this discussion, I examine what happened to the wave of new social movements throughout the 1980s and 1990s and how this led to what is sometimes called 'the newest social movements' (Day, 2005).

After Institutionalization

As Kriesi et al. (1995) remark, enthusiasm about the cultural/identity paradigm of NSM theorists neglects the fact that by the mid-1990s most of the women's, peace and environmental movements had become part of routinized and institutionalized politics. Throughout the 1980s and 1990s, there was a proliferation of professionalized NGOs that, when successful were surviving, mostly grew in their bureaucratic functionality, and became negotiating partners within institutionalized forms of politics. Many social movement organizations, as Kriesi (1996) shows, either professionalize or else degrade into apolitical support organizations for a clearly defined constituency. The former is most common. Interestingly, despite their divergent action orientations, new social movements seem to follow a similar 'iron law of oligarchy' (Michels, 1962) to earlier workers' movements.

During the 1990s, in reaction to this institutionalization and domestication of new social movements in the Western world, there emerged a radicalization, especially of environmental groups. Earth First! and Earth Liberation Front, both US-based radical environmentalist networks, inspired networks in the UK and other European countries with their direct actions in defence of nature. In the UK, a broad anti-roads movement emerged and, with it, the Reclaim the Streets network that inspired latter counter-globalization movements with its carnivalesque street parades and occupations frequently ending in joyful dance events (Jordan, 2002; Flesher Fominaya, 2013a). Part of the upheaval of grass-roots activism in the UK was due to all kinds of travellers and to dance movements marked by their do-it-yourself culture and direct action orientation (McKay, 1998).

These newest movements call to mind Melucci's idea of 'submerged networks' where alternative ideas and political practices are prepared or survive for many years before they emerge visibly for a larger public. The radicalization of this number of social movements, since the latter 1990s, is not coming out of the blue. Political groups, inter-personal networks, radical movement journals, squats and social centres, and so on, survived from previous waves of activism and then nurtured and facilitated the newest wave. Towards the end of the 1990s, squatted social centres in various European countries were, for example, important meeting spaces for early mobilization of the counter-globalization movement (Membretti and Mudu, 2013).

Entering Global Conflicts

In addition to institutionalization and re-radicalization of social movements, the 1990s also witnessed another angle in public and scholarly debates: globalization. Although definitions differ, there is wide agreement that globalization involves an increasing interconnectedness and interdependence of the world with an increasing awareness about the finitude of the planet (Albrow, 1996). With globalization, new actors emerged, practising new forms of contestations at the global level.

The clearest articulation of emerging global conflicts carried out through global movements is the counter-globalization movement. Opposing neoliberal globalization, this 'movement of movements' (Mertes, 2004) brings a variety of movements, organizations, networks and action groups together. And it shows some clear continuities with (the early phase of) new social movements (see also Scholl, 2012). Maeckelbergh (2009), for example, shows how the movement revived a culture of experimenting with horizontal and decentralized forms of democracy and pre-figurative forms of politics. Sitrin (2006) observes a similar process of a bottom-up democratic practice in contemporary Latin American social movements; she calls this 'horizontalism'. Holloway (2002) and Day (2005) observe an explicit refusal by counter-globalization movements to build up counter-hegemony and take power. Showing clear similarities with the forms of organization and action that many movements in the 1970s employed, these new experiments with affinity groups, consensus-based decision-making, spokescouncils, and civil disobedience add new elements and practices.

Indicated by the term 'newest social movements' (Day, 2005) there is nevertheless also something specific to them. Building on Touraine's work, Pleyers (2010) argues that the counter-globalization movement succeeded in becoming an actor on the global scale. He conceptualizes two paths that have enabled counter-globalization activists to do so: (1) the more advocacy and top-down–oriented way of reason and (2) the experience– and daily-life–oriented way of subjectivity. Each way overlaps and reinforces each other in the daily reality of counter-globalization movements, but they also produce certain contradictions (Pleyers, 2010, p. 181ff).

McDonald (2002) observes how collective identities have destabilized and shifted to a 'public experience of self'. Instead of solidarity he thinks contemporary global movements are based on temporary affinities and fluidity. McDonald (2006, pp. 3–4) conceptualizes the emergence of 'global movements', as 'flows of communication, action and experience' oriented by converging 'grammars of experience' that are 'better understood in terms of cultural pragmatics and personal experience than organization building and collective identity'. This conception chimes very much with the work of the later Touraine (2000, p. 28), where he argues that global flows are accompanied by the search for personal experience.

Perhaps less visible as expressions of emerging global conflicts are local food movements. Looking through the lenses of NSM theories, Starr (2009) argues that we can understand local food practices and reflexive consumerism as social movements proffering new ideas and new collectivities. Pleyers (2011) conceptualizes these movements as a form of critical consumption, a localized and everyday approach to politics.

From Counter-globalization Networks to Indignados and Occupy

If the New Left importantly opened paths for new forms of engagement for the earlier new social movements, the counter-globalization movement opens new forms of global activism. In Europe are clear examples of cross-national mobilizations fed by previous counter-globalization networks, action forms (for example, summit protests and social forums) and discourses ('global justice'), such as the EuroMayDay movement seeking to re-politicize 1 May with rallies for precarious workers (Scholl, 2013).

The climate justice movement clearly demonstrates continuities with the counter-globalization movement (Bullard and Mueller, 2012), even as it introduces a discourse on climate or environmental justice into the social justice-oriented discourse of counter-globalization movements. Within climate justice networks, especially in the Southern Hemisphere under the influence of indigenous movements, the question of the 'good life' ('*buen vivir*') has become a central critique of the existing (capitalist) development paradigm (Walsh, 2010). Together with this articulation of climate justice on the global level goes a broad diversity of local struggles, constructions of alternative lifestyles and communal forms of living.

More recent, and also demonstrating many influences from the counter-globalization movement is the emergence of anti-austerity movements, such as the Spanish Indignados and the Occupy movement. The Occupy movement has explicitly articulated a critique of the established representative party politics system, and opposes to it the practice of horizontal, bottom-up democracy in square encampments and neighbourhood assemblies. Maeckelbergh (2012) shows how these movements not only pick up certain lessons of the alternative democratic practices of counter-globalization movements, but also develop them further by grounding their democratic practices more in neighbourhoods and other pre-existing communities. Rather than opposition and confrontation, questions of the internal process and the construction of alternatives are central to many of these movements.

FUTURE RESEARCH AND CHALLENGES

I conclude by saying that where the US-style approaches of the political opportunity structure and resource mobilization have been overly structuralist, the new social movement approaches suffer from cultural reductionism. By making culture the defining variable for understanding social movements, NSM approaches fall into a tautological argumentation – movements affect cultural change, therefore, culture matters – that is similar to that of the structuralist approaches – everything depends on political context, therefore, context matters.

Though some of its problems are unsurmountable, this theoretical approach has been very innovative and important for understanding social movements in different ways. The most important one is that social movements are not structural equivalents to political parties, above all, directed to political and institutional reforms. NSM approaches understand social movements as non-institutional actors in a broad sense, including culture, everyday life, production of different social relations and collective identities, and experimentation with alternative forms of democracy and living together. This non-reductionist view of the political has been an important counterweight to overly rationalist and structuralist accounts of social movements with its different understanding of social movements as complex and interwoven networks that intervene in the cultural production of societies.

One challenge for NSM approaches is to go beyond deciphering how social movements 'challenge codes' to include the process of seeking more permanent change, but without falling into the trap of structuralist approaches that overemphasize policy-related outcomes of social movements. One possible way to do so is to look at attempts social movements actually take to institute alternative practices on a more continuous level. In this way, the attention brought to daily life, culture and alternative practices by NSM approaches is a helpful starting point here. I would invite future scholars to redress the explicit temporality inherent in many of these perspectives. Since the so-called new social movements (and their followers) enjoy a longer protest history upon which to draw this offers empirical opportunities for longitudinal analysis. Nevertheless, it will be a tricky endeavour, because I believe it raises questions anew regarding the category of success, which was so vehemently refuted by many NSM scholars.

A second challenge for future research has already been indicated: did new social movements in acting upon a different grammar of action open a path for other social movements? How did characteristics of new social movements reappear in latter movements? And how were they transformed and/or recombined with new elements? It would be worthwhile to use and abuse the NSM approaches discussed in this chapter to study contemporary forms of activism, such as the Arab Spring, Occupy and Indignados movements. More interesting still would be to situate new social movements within the development of previous and existing social movements in order to understand how movement practices reconfigure in an increasingly globalized world.

To this historicizing understanding of new social movements, it would be useful to explore combinations of NSM attention to different types of conflict with the political process attention for context. Linking types of conflict to available political opportunities could also tell us whether new social movements choose the cultural way only because other paths were not otherwise available for carrying out the types of conflicts they raise.

NOTE

1. Accessed 20 March 2014 at http://www.bopsecrets.org/SI/May68docs.htm.

REFERENCES

Adam, B., J.W. Duyvendak and A. Krouwel (eds) (1999), *The Global Emergence of Gay and Lesbian Politics: National Imprints of a Worldwide Movement*, Philadelphia, PA: Temple University Press.
Albrow, M. (1996), *The Global Age*, Cambridge, UK: Polity Press.
Bagguley, P. (1992), 'Social change, the middle class and the emergence of "new social movements": a critical analysis', *The Sociological Review*, **40**(1), 26–48.
Bond, P. (2012), *Politics of Climate Justice. Paralysis Above, Movement Below*, Pietermaritzburg: University of Kwazulu-Natal Press.
Breines, W. (1982), *Community and Organization in the New Left, 1962–1968: The Great Refusal*, Boston, MA: Praeger/J.F. Bergin.
Buechler, S.M. (1995), 'New social movement theories', *The Sociological Quarterly*, **36**(3), 441–64.
Bullard, N. and T. Mueller (2012), 'Beyond the "Green Economy": system change, not climate change?', *Development*, **55**(1), 53–62.

Cadogan, P. (1972), 'From civil disobedience to confrontation', in R. Benewick and T. Smith (eds), *Direct Action and Democratic Politics*, London: Allen and Unwin, pp. 162–77.

Calhoun, C. (1993), '"New social movements" of the early nineteenth century', *Social Science History*, **17**(3), 385–427.

Castells, M. (1983), *The City and the Grassroots*, Berkeley, CA: University of California Press.

Cohen, J.L. (1985), 'Strategy or identity: new theoretical paradigms and contemporary social movements', *Social Research*, **52**(4), 663–716.

Cousin, O. (ed.) (2010), *L'intervention sociologique. Histoire(s) et actualités d'une method* [The Sociological Intervention. History(ies) and Relevance of a Method], Rennes: Presses Universitaires Rennes.

Day, R. (2005), *Gramsci is Dead: Anarchist Currents in the Newest Social Movements*, London: Pluto Press.

Debord, G. ([1967] 2000), *Society of the Spectacle*, Detroit, MI: Black & Red.

Della Porta, D. and D. Rucht (1991), *Left-Libertarian Movements in Context: A Comparison of Italy and West Germany, 1965–1990*, Berlin: Wissenschaftszentrum.

De Vries, P. (1987), '"Het persoonlijke is politiek" en het ontstaan van de tweede golf in Nederland 1968–1973' ['The personal is political' and the emergence of the second wave in the Netherlands 1968–1973], in S. Sevenhuijsen, P. de Vries, J. Zipper and J. Outshoorn (eds), *SocFem Teksten*, **10**, 15–35.

Dubet, F. and M. Wieviorka (1996), 'Touraine and the method of sociological intervention', in J. Clark and M. Diani (eds), *Alain Touraine*, London/Washington, DC: Falmer Press, pp. 5–76.

Eder, K. (1993), *The New Politics of Class: Social Movements and Cultural Dynamics in Advanced Societies*, London: Sage.

Epstein, B. (1993), *Political Protest and Cultural Revolution: Nonviolent Direct Action in the 1970s and 1980s*, Berkeley, CA: University of California Press.

Evans, S. (1979), *Personal Politics. The Roots of Women's Liberation in the Civil Rights Movement & the New Left*, New York: Knopf.

Eyerman, R. and A. Jamison (1991), *Social Movements: A Cognitive Approach*, University Park, PA: Penn State University Press.

Flesher Fominaya, C. (2013a), 'Movement culture continuity: the British anti-roads movement as precursor to the global justice movement', in C. Flesher Fominaya and L. Cox (eds), *Understanding European Movements: New Social Movements, Global Justice Struggles, Anti-austerity Protest*, London/New York: Routledge, pp. 109–24.

Flesher Fominaya, C. and L. Cox (2013b), 'Introduction: rethinking European movements and history', in C. Flesher Fominaya and L. Cox (eds), *Understanding European Movements: New Social Movements, Global Justice Struggles, Anti-austerity Protest*, London/New York: Routledge, pp. 7–29.

Freeman, J. (2002), 'The tyranny of structurelessness', in Dark Star (eds), *Quiet Rumours. An Anarcha-Feminist Reader*, Edinburgh: AK Press UK, pp. 54–62.

Frenzel, F. (2012), 'The politics of mobility: some insights from the study of protest camps', in S. Witzgall, G. Vogl and S. Kesselring (eds), *New Mobilities Regimes in Art and Social Sciences*, Farnham, UK: Ashgate.

Habermas, J. (1984), *The Theory of Communicative Action: Reason and the Rationalization of Society*, Vol. I, Boston, MA: Beacon Press.

Habermas, J. (1987), *The Theory of Communicative Action. Lifeworld and System: A Critique of Functionalist Reason*, Vol. II, Boston, MA: Beacon Press.

Holloway, J. (2002), *Change the World Without Taking Power: The Meaning of Revolution Today*, London: Pluto Press.

Inglehart, R. (1977), *The Silent Revolution: Changing Values and Political Styles Among Western Publics*, Princeton, NJ: Princeton University Press.

Johnston, H., E. Laraña and J.R. Gusfield (1994), 'Identities, grievances, and new social movements', in E. Laraña, H. Johnston and J.R. Gusfield (eds), *New Social Movements: From Ideology to Identity*, Philadelphia, PA: Temple University Press, pp. 3–35.

Jordan, J. (2002), 'The art of necessity: the imagination of anti-road protest and Reclaim the Streets', in S. Duncombe (ed.), *Cultural Resistance Reader*, London: Verso, pp. 347–57.
Katsiaficas, G.N. (1987), *The Imagination of the New Left: A Global Analysis of 1968*, Boston, MA: South End Press.
Kauffman, L.A. (1990), 'The anti-politics of identity', *Socialist Review*, **20**(1), 67–80.
Klein, N. (2000), *No Logo: No Space, No Choice, No Jobs*, New York: Picador.
Kriesi, H. (1996), 'The organizational structure of new social movements in a political context', in D. McAdam, J.D. McCarthy and M.N. Zald (1996), *Comparative Perspectives on Social Movements*, New York: Cambridge University Press, pp. 152–84.
Kriesi, H., R. Koopmans, J.W. Duyvendak and M.G. Giugni (1995), *New Social Movements in Western Europe: A Comparative Analysis*, London: UCL Press.
Levine, C. (2002), 'The tyranny of tyranny', in Dark Star (eds), *Quiet Rumours. An Anarcha-Feminist Reader*, Edinburgh: AK Press UK, pp. 63–8.
Maeckelbergh, M. (2009), *The Will of the Many: How the Alterglobalisation Movement is Changing the Face of Democracy*, London/New York: Pluto Press.
Maeckelbergh, M. (2011), 'Doing is believing: prefiguration as strategic practice in the alterglobalization movement', *Social Movement Studies*, **10**(1), 1–20.
Maeckelbergh, M. (2012), 'Horizontal democracy now: from alterglobalization to occupation', *Interface*, **4**(1), 207–34.
Marcuse, H. (1964), *One-dimensional Man: Studies in the Ideology of Advanced Industrial Society*, Boston, MA: Beacon Press.
Martin, G. (2002), 'Conceptualizing cultural politics in subcultural and social movement studies', *Social Movement Studies*, **1**(1), 73–88.
McAdam, D. (1982), *Political Process and the Development of Black Insurgency, 1930–1970*, Chicago, IL: University of Chicago Press.
McAdam, D. (1994), 'Culture and social movements', in E. Laraña, H. Johnston and J.R. Gusfield (eds), *New Social Movements: From Ideology to Identity*, Philadelphia, PA: Temple University Press, pp. 36–7.
McDonald, K. (2002), 'From solidarity to fluidarity: social movements beyond "collective identity" – the case of globalization conflict', *Social Movement Studies*, **1**(2), 109–28.
McDonald, K. (2006), *Global Movements. Action and Culture*, Malden, MA: Blackwell Publishing.
McKay, George (ed.) (1998), *DiY Culture. Party and Protest in Nineties Britain*, London: Verso.
Melucci, A. (1980), 'The new social movements: a theoretical approach', *Social Science Information*, **23**(4/5), 819–35.
Melucci, A. (1985), 'The symbolic challenge of contemporary movements', *Social Research*, **52**(4), 789–816.
Melucci, A. (1989), in J. Keane and P. Mier (eds), *Nomads of the Present: Social Movements and Individual Needs in Contemporary Society*, Philadelphia, PA: Temple University Press.
Melucci, A. (1994), 'A strange kind of newness: what's "new" in new social movements?', in E. Laraña, H. Johnston and J.R. Gusfield (eds), *New Social Movements: From Ideology to Identity*, Philadelphia, PA: Temple University Press, pp. 101–30.
Melucci, A. (1996), *Challenging Codes. Collective Action in the Information Age*, Cambridge, UK: Cambridge University Press.
Membretti, A. and P. Mudu (2013), 'Where global meets local: Italian social centres and the alterglobalization movement', in C. Flesher Fominaya and L. Cox (eds), *Understanding European Movements: New Social Movements, Global Justice Struggles, Anti-austerity Protest*, London/New York: Routledge, pp. 76–93.
Mertes, T. (ed.) (2004), *A Movement of Movements: Is Another World Really Possible?* London/New York: Verso.
Michels, R. (1962), *Political Parties. A Sociological Study of the Oligarchical Tendencies of Modern Democracy*, New York: Collier Books.
Nash, K. (2001), 'The "cultural turn" in social theory: towards a theory of cultural politics', *Sociology*, **35**(1), 77–92.

Offe, C. (1985), 'New social movements: challenging the boundaries of institutional politics', *Social Research*, **52**(4), 817–68.
Pichardo, N.A. (1997), 'New social movements: a critical review', *Annual Review of Sociology*, **23**, 411–30.
Pizzorno, A. (1978), 'Political exchange and collective identity in industrial conflict', in C. Crouch and A. Pizzorno (eds), *The Resurgence of Class Conflict in Western Europe, Vol. 2*, London: Macmillan, pp. 277–98.
Pleyers, G. (2010), *Alterglobalization. Becoming Actors in the Global Age*, Cambridge, UK and Malden, MA: Polity Press.
Pleyers, G. (ed.) (2011), *La Consommation Critique. Mouvements pour une Alimentation Responsable et Solidaire* [Critical Consumption. Movements for Responsible and Solidarian Food], Paris: Desceé de Brouwer.
Plotke, D. (1990), 'What's so new about the new social movements?', *Socialist Review*, **90**(1), 81–102.
Poldervaart, S. (2006), 'The connection between the squatter, queer and alterglobalization movement. The many diversities of multiculturalism', in M. Chateauvert (ed.), *New Social Movements and Sexuality*, Washington, DC: Queer Bulgaria Foundation and Woodhull Freedom Foundation.
Polletta, F. and J. Jasper (2001), 'Collective identity and social movements', *Annual Review of Sociology*, **27**, 283–305.
Raschke, J. (1980), 'Politischer Paradigmenwandel in den westlichen Demokratien' [Political paradigm shift in Western democracies], in T. Ellwein (ed.), *Politikfeld-Analysen 1979: wissenschaftl. Kongressder DVPW, 1.–5. Okt. 1979 in Augsburg*, Opladen: Westdeutscher Verlag, pp. 284–99.
Rochon, T. (1998), *Culture Moves: Ideas, Activism, and Changing Values*, Princeton, NJ: Princeton University Press.
Sanbonmatsu, J. (2004), *The Postmodern Prince: Critical Theory, Left Strategy, and the Making of a New Political Subject*, New York: Monthly Review Press.
Scholl, C. (2005), 'Feministische lessen voor de andersglobaliseringsbeweging. Over de mogelijkheden van een feministisch radicaal-democratisch project' [Feminist lessons for the alter-globalization movement. The potentialities of a feminist radical-democratic project], *Tijdschrift voor Genderstudies*, **8**(4), 28–43.
Scholl, C. (2011), 'Bakunin's poor cousins? Engaging art for tactical interventions', in B. Firat and A. Kuryel (eds), *Theorizing Cultural Activism: Practices, Dilemmas and Potentialities, Thamyris/Intersecting: Place, Sex, Race* series, Amsterdam/New York: Rodopi, pp. 157–78.
Scholl, C. (2012), *Two Sides of a Barricade. (Dis)order and Summit Protest in Europe*, Albany, NY: Suny Press.
Scholl, C. (2013), 'Europe as contagious space. Cross-national diffusion through EuroMayDay and climate justice movements', in C. Flesher Fominaya and L. Cox (eds), *Understanding European Movements: New Social Movements, Global Justice Struggles, Anti-austerity Protest*, London/New York: Routledge, pp. 127–42.
Scott, A. (1990), *Ideology and the New Social Movements*, London: Unwin Hyman.
Sitrin, M. (2006), *Horizontalism*, Oakland, CA: AK Press.
Starr, A. (2009), 'Local food: a social movement?', *Cultural Studies <=> Critical Methodologies* [published online 13 June 2010], accessed 9 May 2014 at http://csc.sagepub.com/content/early/2010/06/10/1532708610372769.
Tarrow, S. (1989), *Struggle, Politics and Reform: Collective Action, Social Movements and Cycles of Protest*, Ithaca, NY: Cornell University Press.
Thornton, S. (1995), *Club Cultures: Music, Media and Subcultural Capital*, Cambridge, UK: Polity.
Touraine, A. (1971), *The May Movement; Revolt and Reform: May 1968 – The Student Rebellion and Workers' Strikes – the Birth of a Social Movement*, trans. L.F.X. Mayhew, New York: Random House.
Touraine, A. (1974), *The Post-Industrial Society*, London: Wildwood House.

Touraine, A. (1981), *The Voice and the Eye. An Analysis of Social Movements*, Cambridge, UK Cambridge University Press.
Touraine, A. (1985), 'An introduction to the study of social movements', *Social Research*, **52**(4), 749–87.
Touraine, A. (2000), *Can We Live Together? Equality and Difference*, Cambridge, UK: Polity.
Touraine, A., F. Dubet, Z. Hegedus and M. Wieviorka (1978), *Lutte étudiante* [Student Struggle], Paris: Seuil.
Touraine, A., F. Dubet, Z. Hegedus and M. Wieviorka (1980), *La Prophétie anti-nucléaire* [The Anti-nuclear Prophecy], Paris: Seuil.
Touraine, A., W. Michel, F. Dubet and J. Strzelecki (1983), *Solidarity – the Analysis of a Social Movement: Poland 1980–81*, Cambridge, UK: Cambridge University Press.
Tucker, K.H. (1991), 'How new are the new social movements?', *Theory, Culture & Society*, **8**(2), 75–98.
Veltmeyer, H. (1997), 'New social movements in Latin America: the dynamics of class and identity', *The Journal of Peasant Studies*, **25**(1), 139–69.
Walsh, C. (2010), 'Development as *buen vivir*: institutional arrangements and (de)colonial entanglements', *Development*, **53**(1), 15–21.
Young, I. (1990), *Justice and the Politics of Difference*, Princeton, NJ: Princeton University Press.
Zald, M.N. (1996), 'Culture, ideology, and strategic framing', in D. McAdam, J.D. McCarthy and M.N. Zald (1996), *Comparative Perspectives on Social Movements*, New York: Cambridge University Press, pp. 261–74.

12. Citizenship, political opportunities and social movements
David S. Meyer and Erin Evans

It's barely a stretch to observe that social movements are all about citizenship. Movements struggle to extend citizenship to new actors (e.g., women, ethnic minorities), or limit such access; to define the privileges and responsibilities of citizenship (e.g., suffrage, taxation, access to education or health care); and to find additional ways to exercise leverage on political decisions (e.g., stop or start war or pollution). More than that, the form of political action is defined by the rules and routines of citizenship.

As Marshall's (1950) classic essay explained, the struggles of citizenship, including the very terms of citizenship, have been the subject of political contention, beginning, in his stylized scheme, with civil rights, that is, protections from abuse by government. Political rights followed, in which those judged qualified for membership were granted tools and opportunities to influence governance. The final struggle in Marshall's scheme, social rights, involved the provision of benefits and protections from the market for those granted membership in the polity.

The content and form of social movements reflect the boundaries and bargains comprising the various dimensions of citizenship. Civil rights afford the dissatisfied with the political space needed to express the concerns and grievances, to find others who might agree, and to make claims on authorities. Without this space, dissent would be limited to episodic eruptions and direct resolution of claims. Hungry people, for example, would seize grain, rather than petition for welfare payments (Tarrow, 1998). Social rights provide a variety of resources to those who seek to make claims on authorities, ranging from the symbolic legitimation of claims (justice, equality) to concrete assets for staging collective action, not least of these being sufficient education to read leaflets or understand how governance is supposed to work. Broadly stated, the citizenship bargain structures the social movements that emerge in its wake. Movements may alter that bargain, which then structures subsequent politics.

The most useful analytical framework for making sense of this relationship, between state structures, including mainstream politics, and organized dissent, is generally described as a 'political process' approach. The core insight of this approach is that politics within mainstream political institutions is closely tied to movement politics, or politics outside. A stark division between mainstream politics and movement politics thus distorts more than it enlightens. Claims and claimants can move across through both institutional and extra-institutional venues, and the forms of contention in movement politics reflect the nature of political opportunities in conventional politics, comprising alternative approaches to achieving similar goals.

In this chapter we will discuss citizenship through social movement theory, specifically theories that use political opportunities to explain the emergence and effects of movements. First, we will discuss the relationship between citizenship and social movements. Then we will review the evolution of theory and empirical scholarship on political opportunity structures and the political process approaches. Finally we will show how using political process theory can help explain the causes, forms, and outcomes of social movement activity. We show how dramatic and disruptive protest can generate incremental reforms that many activists are likely to view as inadequate. But these reforms, providing new resources and opportunities for subsequent activism, can effectively provide footholds for subsequent cycles of movement-based claims-making and policy reform. In this model, social movements become critical resources, and often promoters, of democracy.

SOCIAL MOVEMENTS AND CITIZENSHIP

Scholars offer a wide range of definitions of social movements (McAdam et al., 2001; Snow, 2004; Snow et al., 2004); although most definitions seem to refer to the same set of empirical phenomena, competing definitions draw attention to different elements of movement politics. For example, some emphasize opinion and belief, while others emphasize action; some emphasize a departure from conventional politics and the presence of particular tactics, such as rallies and demonstrations; while others offer less strict tests of action. And some emphasize political struggles in relation to some established authority, most frequently the state, while others are agnostic about the necessity of politics to the existence of a movement. In this chapter, we see social movements as any collective, sustained effort to challenge (or defend) the status quo through institutional *and* extra-institutional means (Meyer, 2006). This definition is broad and inclusive, but it excludes some sorts of advocacy organizations, like trade associations, for example, which eschew broad claims and extra-institutional action in favor of institutionally focused action and non-public politicking to win narrow policy advantages. It includes, however, advocacy organizations that participate in or support other kinds of collective action. Importantly, challenges on matters of policy can take place through mostly conventional channels, including elections and moral suasion through argument, and can exploit state-endorsed channels of influence, like open hearings. They may also include extra-institutional actions, like civil disobedience, rallies, or street theater. Effective movements in liberal politics generally contain both sorts of action, and the challenge for activists is finding ways to develop, maintain, and exploit connections between institutional and extra-institutional politics. All of these influence strategies require the mobilization of resources, including money, information, and organizational support, and require the mobilization of people on behalf of their efforts. Generally, activists seek to cultivate as much support as possible, recruiting the largest number of people possible to the cause. Of course, organizers run the risk of diluting or softening a message in order to do so.

Movements are an important component to understanding the workings of citizenship. First, citizenship bargains structure the form, claims, and influence of social movements. And movements often grow around a citizenship struggle. Think, for example, of the suffrage movement in the United States, whose partisans enjoyed some of the civil protections that Marshall (1950) identifies, but not the political rights and responsibilities that would follow. Achieving suffrage afforded activists, indeed, women more generally, additional tools in making subsequent claims. Other extensions of the franchise, to the unpropertied, to ethnic minorities, or to youth, trace a relatively similar story. Expanding membership in the polity entails an expansion of legitimate claims as well as actors. Once recognized, women, for example, can make direct demands about the necessity of reproductive rights. Expanding the citizenry necessitates expanding the scope of governance and, ultimately, state capacity.

Such citizenship movements were so central in the vision of many of the major social movement scholars that those scholars defined the influence of movements primarily in those terms. Gamson (1990), for example, offered a polity model in which those who staged social movements were located 'outside' the polity, struggling for inclusion (see also Tilly, 1978); in a simple reading, inclusion as a normal contender within the polity marked a success, and consequently, the decline of the need for a social movement.

But social movements generally don't have such neat and delimited goals and starting and stopping points. As social movements develop, political figures compromise; they take ostensibly achievable reforms, while putting a broader agenda off for a later day. At the same, a successful political movement inspires activists within and others without about the possibilities of politics outside, and ways in which they might pursue new goals. There are both direct and crooked lines of influence across apparently dissimilar movements (Meyer and Whittier, 1994); American suffragists, for example, were divided about whether to oppose the United States' entry into World War I, but the anti-war movement was enlivened by the presence of those women's movement activists who worked against the war. Movements in liberal polities don't display sharp boundaries separating them from mainstream politics, or even other movements.

Moreover, social movements are not completely the province of those without other viable strategies for influence. In the past few decades, constituencies with apparent access to more conventional political strategies have employed movement tactics, including demonstrations and civil disobedience. Farmers, middle-class people and ethnic majorities, and even the well-off, have used movement strategies to augment political influence, as the social movement form has been legitimated and diffused broadly, creating a 'social movement society' (Meyer and Tarrow, 1998). Political process scholars examine movements as engaged in ongoing and recursive relationships with political systems. As the social movement form becomes more commonly employed by a broader range of constituencies, we find a state that is less able to adjudicate competing claims and make policy. Winning a metaphoric seat at the table doesn't necessarily produce the desired policy reforms that inspired mobilization in the first place. Some of the classic texts on social movements viewed institutionalization as the end of effective advocacy. Piven and Cloward (1977), employing a fairly conventional Marxist framework, argued that poor people were poorly positioned to benefit from any politics beyond disruption and advised activists to devote all of their efforts toward disruptive mobilization. Lowi (1971), offering an institutionalist framework, came to a similar conclusion about all constituencies, and argued that making peace with conventional politics meant the end of political influence. But other scholars have found that institutionalization changes the institution as well as the constituency, suggesting that establishing footholds in politics can lead to policy gains over a longer period of time, often in ways that surprise both activists and authorities (Meyer, 1990; Amenta, 2006). Questioning established verities that romanticize the protest act and investigating whether institutionalization improves the prospects for subsequent gains is a critical area of inquiry for scholars of contemporary politics and citizenship.

Movements also change society through their actions by building social capital and citizenship. In mobilizing activism and building networks to coordinate collective action, movements train citizens and build organizations that can facilitate political activism over an extended period of time (Staggenborg, 1988). Organizers educate the activists they mobilize, not only about the issues of concern, but also about the way politics works. In this way, they build civic capacity and stronger and more active citizens. The educational impact of movements, of course, is not limited to those who participate, but also extends to those who observe participation and its outcomes. Social movements create a demonstration effect for society, encouraging participation on alternate concerns; they educate the public as well as their partisans.

Social movements also connect individuals through both formal organizations and less formal networks. When would-be mobilizers attend community meetings, knock on doors, or plan activities, they come into closer contact with neighbors and potential allies who might be mobilized in the future for other concerns. The network that facilitates the sale of tickets for a bus ride to a national demonstration can be reactivated to mobilize voters for participation in an election or to create a picket line to prevent unwanted development. In this way, social movements promote social movements, but much more than that – movements promote and extend citizenship.

The third important relation of movements to citizenship is how this shared knowledge of tactics and forms of civic engagement trains a large part of the movement to engage and master specific institutional forms and routines. Citizens are afforded access to institutions in exchange for adaption to the rules of those institutions. The state both directly and indirectly trains citizens to pursue their interests institutionally, channeling concerns into conventional politics through parties, interest groups, and/or governance structures. Movements, as a reflection of their ongoing relationship with these structures, also train activists to pursue these institutional in-roads in specific ways. These in-roads are political opportunities, which come both in the form of intentional pathways into political decision-making, like the public referenda system, and unintentional pathways such as the pandering to movements that occurs when there are shifts in partisan dominance. As movement organizations each refine their tactical repertoire to access political institutions, they develop a constituency that also becomes trained in that repertoire. Movements train and build constituencies that participate in specific tactics that are adapted to political opportunities.

It is much like training ivy to climb a building in a uniform and monitored way, but the climbing affords opportunities to become a part of that structure in ways that are expected and unexpected. Scholars conceptualize this relationship as a political process that influences movements and is likewise influenced by movements. Next, we will review the development of theories on political opportunity structures and the political process approach to explaining movements. We will highlight how issues of citizenship are important to the explanations that political process theories afford.

It's critical to realize that states can also train citizens and citizen activists. Both formally through schools and civic programs, and informally through culture, rituals, and social interactions, states cultivate certain kinds of engagement and stigmatize others. States and societies legitimate some expectations while undermining others, underscoring and encouraging voting, for example, while punishing and discouraging political violence. When successful, states cultivate the kind of politics authorities can respond to comfortably. Less successful regimes create an opposition that can threaten public order and their own survival. Recognizing that states and social movements both work to cultivate and train activists, we can see that activists' success is at least partly contingent upon finding messaging and tactics that resonate with broader social norms about politics and participation. For scholars, recognizing the connections between context and contention meant moving beyond earlier paradigms that focused predominantly on individuals who might take action, or on some broad and undifferentiated notion of society.

SCHOLARSHIP BEFORE THE POLITICAL PROCESS APPROACH

Early literature on collective action looked at riots and other activity, such as the labor uprisings of the early twentieth century, as aberrations of human behavior when they are in groups. These studies did not conceptualize these actions as politically motivated or organized, but as the result of groups being under extreme strain and rationally breaking down because of it (Park and Burgess, 1921; Blumer, 1939; Kornhauser, 1959; Park, 1972). Acts of civil disobedience and property destruction that typically accompanied rioting, such as those during the Flint Sit-Down Strike in 1936–37 against General Motors, were characterized as random events that reflected social-psychological causes. These social-psychological causes were seen as losses of rational decision-making that comes with group chaos. This conceptualization of movement uprisings negated the necessity of physical disruptions of public space that were essential for groups that had no power otherwise. These groups included people of color, women, civilians during war, and others most associated with the political upheaval that occurred in the 1960s.

During and following the broad and global protests of the 1960s, scholars found that the tenets of earlier social-psychological approaches didn't stand up to empirical scrutiny. Those most engaged in these movements performed better on tests of psychological health, were more likely to be engaged in a range of organizations and even more likely to have good relationships with friends and family members (Keniston, 1968; Parkin, 1968). This work was still rooted in social psychology, but placed activists and their behavior at the center of the analysis, as opposed to the disruptive protest activity, and opened up the literature to the more deep-rooted causes at the foundation of disruptive activity and rioting. This facilitated further work on movements and how they tried to cultivate political influence. Scholars found that protest was not only a viable influence strategy, but – at least for some constituencies – the best political strategy – for political influence. This led to a shift in orientation. Rather than viewing protest action as the sign of a dysfunctional society or the product of alienated individuals, scholars came to see the mobilization of protest as a triumph of organization and the successful accumulation and deployment of a variety of resources (McCarthy and Zald, 1977).

For those excluded from conventional political influence strategies, protest was a viable strategy for expanding the scope of the political conflict, bringing in new actors, and raising the costs of governance (Lipsky, 1968). When successful, protest mobilized outside allies who were better resourced, raised issues, and suggested policy alternatives. The disruptive power of rioting or shutting down businesses created an incentive for the powerful to pay attention to protesters' grievances, and if protest is sustained it created an incentive from at least some targets to meet those demands (Luders, 2010). The analytical focus shifted away from alternative macro- and micro-foci. A macro-focus on social conditions that might lead to protest, as in Marxist frameworks, did little to explain the process of stoking and coordinating protest, thus obfuscating political agency. A micro-focus on the propensity of individuals to join in collective action, correspondingly, ignored the purposive efforts of organizers to reach, educate, mobilize, and direct mobilization efforts. A resource mobilization framework offered insights into the dynamics of organizing, building, and deploying resources (Lipsky, 1968; McCarthy and Zald, 1977). Resource mobilization scholars not only dispelled previous theories on the irrationality of collective action (Jenkins and Perrow, 1977), but also legitimized social movement actors and solidified protest as a political resource and tool.

Resource mobilization theories steered the literature away 'from *why* movements emerge to *how*, they emerge' (Meyer, 2004; original emphasis). Resource mobilization theorists used the means by which activists made claims, including their formation of organizations and interest groups (Wilson, 1977; Walker, 1991) to explain how they emerged and pressured their targets to meet their demands. A good portion of the literature focused on how organizers worked to overcome the 'free-rider' tendency, that is, the reluctance of individuals to join in collective action when they viewed their own participation as potentially costly and extremely unlikely to influence the likelihood of a campaign's success (Olson, 1965).

But circumstances alter individual calculations about the attractiveness, costliness, or likely impact of collective action. Analysts came to see the free-rider problem less as an absolute principle and more as an elastic tendency that was extremely responsive to changes in political circumstances. The sales pitch of an umbrella salesperson matters in making sales, but rain improves the prospects of all those trying to sell umbrellas (Meyer, 2007). Thus, organizers were more likely to succeed in convincing would-be activists to mobilize when their claims were underscored by changes in circumstances making collective action seem more urgent or more promising.

DEVELOPMENT OF A POLITICAL PROCESS APPROACH

Citizens and activists are constrained by, and embedded in, a political context. Activists making claims to the state, or against the state, are especially influenced by the characteristics of their government and by the culture that is related to that government. Through comparative studies scholars saw evidence that the constraint of the political system steers the emergence, strategies, and ultimately the results of social movement activity. Since the late 1970s these scholars have developed this intuition into a larger theory.

Peter Eisinger was the first to use the term 'political opportunity' in a study that sought to explain why some US cities had rioting activity and others did not (Eisinger, 1973). He found that cities that offered a mix of 'open' and 'closed' political structures were most likely to see protest. Cities that were completely insulated from political demands offered little hope to would-be activists, while those that offered numerous access points were likely to pre-empt protest by incentivizing other strategies of influence. The likelihood of riots displayed a curvilinear relationship to the political openness of the authorities targeted. Simply, most people are likely to protest when they believe it is both necessary and potentially effective in helping them get what they want. When less costly and less risky alternatives for politics are available, protest movements are less likely. When there is little sense that anything is likely to affect influence, protest is also less likely. (To be sure, some people, saints and psychopaths, are willing to protest for personal satisfaction or moral witness, but movements are about aggregations of individuals, not exceptional cases.) For instance, in some states there are forms of public referenda systems, wherein citizens, by gathering a required number of signatures and other varying requirements, may create new policies statewide. This kind of political access diverts more disruptive tactics, like protests involving property damage, into more institutional tactics, like letter writing or lobbying. He conceptualized these political access points as opportunities for social movements to make state-based claims. These 'political opportunity structures' channeled and encouraged people to organize around particular interests in patterned ways and at particular times; they were also influential in how these social movements chose strategies and accompanying tactics; and further critical in affecting the extent to which extra-institutional politics would ultimately influence the character of those political structures – and opportunities for subsequent movements.

Tilly (1978, 1995) used this political opportunity framework and applied it to movements operating within European nations (Tilly, 1978, 1993, 1995). He found that broader institutional characteristics steered the qualities of contention both immediately and over longer periods of time. A series of cross-national studies also reflected longitudinal patterns in movement behavior. For instance, some scholars found that movements mobilized in waves, and that they functioned as 'cycles of contention' (Tarrow, 1989), wherein movements rose up against a political system using structural opportunities, gained influence against that system, became institutionalized within the political system, and later a related movement would re-mobilize against a new set of structural constraints.

The institutionalization of movements, in the forms of new laws, federal agencies, formal consultative agreements with organizations like labor unions, or political parties, led to the development of movements to carry somewhat different sorts of claims than those that sought political inclusion. In the 1970s and 1980s, the signal movements in advanced liberal democracies were filled with people who seemed relatively well positioned to get what they wanted through other means. These so-called 'new social movements', including environmentalism, feminism, and peace, really weren't all that new, but rather a continuation and redefinition of earlier political campaigns. Activists did not choose protest tactics because they were blocked from alternative strategies of influence, rather, they used protest movement forms to augment and underscore institutionally oriented efforts (Kriesi et al., 1995). Often, activists were engaged in activism in support of collective goods and culturally based changes, exactly the sort of concerns that Olson (1965) argued would be particularly hard to organize and mobilize around. The increased wealth and education of the society dramatically increased the number of people prepared to engage in movements on behalf of such collective goods.

Evidence for the continuity of so-called new movements with older antecedents is seen not only in the individual activists who organized in the prior waves and also in subsequent waves of mobilization, as with the women's movement in the USA (Banaszak, 2010), but also in the 'abeyance' structures scholars have identified (Taylor, 1989). These structures include organizational structures that persist through waves of mobilization and form foundations for future mobilization. They also include changes in institutions or policies that support the continual development and implementation of movement demands (Amenta et al., 2011). This isn't to say that the new social movements are not distinct in the important ways. These newer waves include important changes in tactical repertoires and the integral role of collective identities (Kriesi et al., 1995), among other distinct traits. But it is important to recognize the continuity we see in abeyance structures or insider tactics so that we may track the often slow process of transformative change. These slow changes include policy reforms and other institutional mechanisms that some activists within a movement, and citizens who may not even identify with a particular movement, can enter and ultimately influence, albeit with certain limitations.

Although activists often focus on individual reform efforts, the concerns that drive such contemporary movements can rarely be satisfied by one discrete political reform. Success in stopping the deployment of a particular missile, for example, is a small part of a peace activist's larger agenda. Enhancing the regulation of toxic discharge from a manufacturing plant or banning a pesticide can be seen as a victory, but hardly the endpoint of a struggle. Movements need to develop structures that coordinate and facilitate ongoing activism (Staggenborg, 1988). In effect, movements seek to chip away at unwanted policies, accreting alternatives at the same time. These iterative efforts require ongoing mobilization whereby a movement's interests become relatively permanent interests within the political system. Scholarship showed the ongoing connections between movement politics and mainstream politics (e.g., Costain, 1992; Banaszak, 2010), and comparative work identified differences in movement tactics and claims depending upon political context in different countries (e.g., Kitschelt, 1986; Kriesi et al., 1995), or in the same countries over time (McAdam, 1982; Meyer, 1993).

Although there has been a broad recognition that the political context sets the broad conditions for social movements, discovering just what tactics are advantaged under what circumstances remains an area of ongoing concern for scholars. Identifying the political openings or closures that influenced movements filled much the research in the mid- to late 1990s (Kriesi et al., 1995; McAdam, 1996). Many of the projects focused on specifying opportunities that made mobilization more likely (McAdam, 1982; Tarrow, 1989; Costain, 1992), and threats or institutional constraints that made extra-institutional protest more likely (Meyer, 1990, 1993; Smith, 1996). The research specified a diverse range of factors that facilitated mobilization (Amenta and Zylan, 1991; Amenta et al., 1994; Meyer and Whittier, 1994; Gamson and Meyer, 1996; Minkoff, 1999; Rohlinger, 2002; Meyer, 2004), but these variables were 'often not disproved, refined, or replace, but simply added' (Meyer, 2004, p. 135). Identifying the expanding range of opportunities that activists exploited was important, but it seemed that any element of the political system could be proven an opportunity for activists. Scholars have also identified opportunities outside of the political system, like discursive opportunity structures (McCammon et al., 2007), or cultural opportunity structures (Koopmans and Statham, 1999). Although each study highlighted an important element of the political system that influenced movements and provided a variety of operationalized mechanisms through which activists made claims, the challenge of cumulating these studies to identify generalizable patterns about opportunities and mobilization remains an important and unfinished project. Moreover, most of the research employing this paradigm was focused on advanced economies and liberal democracies. Of course, the terms of citizenship and political engagement would be different in more repressive and less democratic contexts.

Studies of authoritarian regimes found patterns in movement activity that proved useful for identifying mechanisms through which movements interact with citizens to make claims against the state. In highly repressive regimes, protests are less likely due to the extraordinarily high costs and risks that activists must encounter. For these reasons, activism in authoritarian regimes, when it does emerge, often takes more dramatic, disruptive, and often violent forms (Boudreau, 1996; Almeida, 2003; De la Luz Inclan, 2008). In liberal democracies where protest is institutionalized through structures such as constitutional rights protecting freedom of association and speech, protest is likely to pursue institutional acceptance through reform and incremental incorporation of movement demands (Meyer, 1990). In authoritarian regimes, however, where there are no such institutional in-roads, putative citizens (as movements) are more likely to be pushed into revolutionary tactics and goals to address their grievances, and that mobilization of citizens requires an existing network of bonds between individuals and organization (Alimi, 2009). These potentially strong networks among a country's citizenry highlight an important component to activism, and to studying movement activity against the backdrop of the political context. The most common findings from the political process approach support reiterative and cyclical relationship between movements, the political system, and citizenship.

Scholars have employed a variety of comparative methods and cases, including cases of authoritarian systems to show that movement processes are at least partially explained by variances in political contexts. The political process literature now spans across case studies of individual movements across multiple territories in one nation (McAdam and Boudet, 2012), or across multiple nations (Alimi and Meyer, 2011), or multiple movements within one nation (Amenta et al., 2011). There are also studies that highlight the important processes of transnational movements, or movements that address the globally interconnected nature of political processes that affect citizens. For instance, the World Trade Organization protests that occurred in Seattle in 1999 highlighted not only the interconnected nature of issues within the USA, but how issues of environmentalism, animal rights, or indigenous rights are also connected internationally. The Occupy Movement of 2012 also highlighted how activists engaged in a range of issues within the USA could mobilize together, and how those activists could incorporate global exchange as an element of economic inequality. These are just two movements, which one could argue are also related, that recognize the international bases for the injustice they are addressing.

We highlight these two mass mobilizations to emphasize how transnational activism is also contingent upon the capacity of activists to identify common – or at least related – political opportunities activists. Scholars have looked at transnational political opportunities and found that traits of the modern state, such as membership in the European Union, influence the character of social movements with international goals (Marks and McAdam, 1996). Keck and Sikkink (1998) identified 'transnational advocacy networks' and found that influences such as the national embarrassment that comes with denying the demands of a transnational movement when another country has granted them are important to the consequences of transnational activism. They bring the common opportunities that activists identify across nations and show that may be a kind of burgeoning global culture that is pushed by these transnational advocacy networks. Global networks of activists may isolate 'international political opportunity structures' (Van der Heijden, 2006) to address their demands and develop a growing global citizenship of movement networks who address international concerns. Development of an array of comparative studies is integral to finding patterns that may explain the most of movement processes (McAdam et al., 1996), but attempting to specify a static set of structural components that influence every movement in predictive ways is to try to over-simplify a complicated set of dynamics (McAdam et al., 2001).

Part of this over-simplification is demonstrated in earlier models, such as Gamson's polity model, which conceptualize the inclusion of citizenship as the end of protest politics for a movement (Meyer, 2004). The women's movement did not start and end with suffrage, and the civil rights movement of the 1960s ended with the achievement of formally protected voting rights. Indeed, we find that formal protections and mechanisms of inclusion can offer would-be activists additional levers of potential influence. The consequent process where movement actors may participate in political decision-making, through Congressional testimony or lobbying, induces a recursive and 'interpenetrating' (Wolfson, 2001) relationship between movements and the state.

We use 'interpenetrating' to emphasize the two directional influences between movements (as organized coalitions of citizens) and the state. The state penetrates movements by establishing activists' choices, creating opportunities or constraints that influence tactics and strategies. In this way the state is an inherent element of a movement, especially those with state-based goals. Movements penetrate the state by encouraging policy reform, sometimes participating in policy formation, by having constituents become politicians or creating political parties, or by organizing the citizenry into voting blocs that steer a politician's decision-making. These are all potential outcomes of movement activity. Activists make choices about strategies and tactics that affect mobilization, and states make policies that similarly direct mobilization (Meyer, 2004).

OPPORTUNITIES FOR MOBILIZATION AND FOR POLICY CHANGE

Students of social movements continue to explore the same basic set of questions, particularly: why do movements on particular issues emerge when they do? Why do such movements sometimes effect changes in politics and policies? Studies of movements frequently conflate two outcomes and contexts that are really conceptually different: opportunities for mobilization and opportunities for policy change (Meyer and Minkoff, 2004). The signal case of the American civil rights movement, in which broad-scale social protest mobilization accompanied national policy reform, suggests one model in which opportunities for policy reform and mobilization are aligned. It's clear, however, that this pattern isn't generalizable. Meyer's work (1993) on the anti-nuclear movement found exactly the opposite – that opportunities for mobilization occurred when activists' desired policy reforms were particularly unlikely. Thinking more critically about citizenship may help us make sense of this apparent paradox. It seems likely that movements for the extension of citizenship, as for ethnic minorities and women (e.g., Costain, 1992) seem to align with opportunities for policy reform. In such cases, openness to greater participation of a particular constituency inspires both mobilization and concomitant policy reform. In contrast, movements that organize and mobilize those normally well positioned to get what they want without protest are likely to emerge particularly when chances for influence are weak. In this regard, stopping or slowing unwanted initiatives must be coded as influence, albeit achievements that are extremely hard to assess. And, of course, activism by opposing movements, which represent contrary positions on the same issues, make both the politics and scholarship more difficult (Meyer and Staggenborg, 1996).

There is a large literature on policy reform and on political outcomes. Most of the best of this work emphasizes the contingency of political reforms and policy changes. Such nuanced interpretations may ring true, but finding generalizable principles is extremely difficult. Here, we mean to focus on two critical arguments that demonstrate how movements are efficacious with state-based claims only in so far as they respond to changes in political opportunities and citizenship. Movement outcomes, including policy reforms and other state changes, are only 'successful' in as much as they facilitate further mobilization. Although the literature we use is set in liberal democracies for case studies, the network bonds that are argued to facilitate revolutionary activity in authoritarian regimes may be seen also as bonds that facilitate further activity generally.

In a democracy, citizenship and political participation should influence policy reform, but other forces also influence political decision-making, including public opinion, countervailing mobilization, sometimes in movement forms, and the political environment outside the state. Over the last decade or so scholars have identified forms of change they have empirically linked to movement activity, including policy reform (Meyer, 1990; Banaszak, 1996; Soule et al., 1999), movement influence on funding of federal agencies and programs (Amenta et al., 1994; Andrews, 2004), and practices that are targeted by a movement outside of government (Einwohner, 1999; Gupta, 2008; Halfmann and Young, 2010). Much of this research is based on comparative analyses that find causality through deductive reasoning across regions, meaning that scholars take one movement across many regions in one national territory, and trace the types of movement activity across regions.

Using this approach, scholars have found that strong organizational foundations are linked to the most substantive outcomes, especially after a state-based change has occurred that requires enforcement afterward. Rohlinger (2002) found that organizations with strong infrastructures designed to work with media gained increased positive media coverage. Related to the importance of organizational strength, Andrews (2001) found that areas where the civil rights movement had strong organizational infrastructures saw increased funding for educational programs designed for historically disadvantaged groups (Andrews, 2001). Organizational participation and strength both increases the immediate effect of movements, but also increases the impact of a movement success later. Organizational participation through intra-movement and inter-movement coalitions also sustain movement visibility between periods of mobilization (Van Dyke, 2003; Soule and King, 2008; Clemens and Minkoff, 2009; Banaszak, 2010).

These periods and the importance of organizational strength speak back to the previous discussion of Gamson's polity model versus Tarrow's social movement society model, whereby movements do not start and stop with one demand and one goal, but persist through waves of mobilization. Political reform involves compromises with state actors. Activists who push a particular policy reform would be terribly naive to think that their ideal policy will be written, debated, and passed without any watering down of initial demands. Savvy activists pursue political goals that are attainable, facilitate further mobilization, and will not cause negative unintended consequences. The attention to further mobilization is particularly important because movements, in themselves, are comprised of coalitions of various organizations and participant citizens who strategically adapt to the context in which they function (Stepan-Norris and Zeitlin, 1991; Meyer, 2006; Taylor and Van Dyke, 2009). We see how the mutually exclusive use of political opportunity theories to explain mobilization versus explaining outcomes is erroneous, because the most substantive outcomes will result in increased mobilization.

CONCLUSION: MOBILIZATION OF THE CITIZENRY AND POLITICAL OPPORTUNITY

Movements adapt to change contexts, altering their claims, tactics, and the alliances they cultivate. This is a function of political opportunities. The citizenship bargain is a critical component of political opportunities, both in formally outlining routes for political influence and participation, and in informally setting norms and expectations about both potential grievances and remedies and about political engagement. Social movements often enjoy long and variegated careers, punctuated by often distinct episodes focused on proximate goals. Achievement of such a goal, even a partial achievement alters the opportunities for mobilization, and activists need to readjust to these new circumstances. Sometimes, reforms provide a foundation for subsequent mobilization. Such a complicated trajectory makes simple evaluations of success and failure largely inappropriate, but we can identify a few important principles.

Reforms can make it harder or easier for movements to establish a more permanent organizational presence. Such a presence, particularly when well resourced, makes it easier for organizers to act opportunistically, that is, to exploit proximate changes in politics and policy to advance their agendas. In dealing with the prospect of reform then, activists face the difficult task of being able to bank wanted reforms without sacrificing the legitimacy of their claims and the resources they need to continue activism.

We see how the ongoing process of state-based movement activity involves training large coalitions of organizations and the citizenry to use the political system in a way that is iterative and recursive. The ivy is trained to climb the building in predictable ways, but rogue limbs entering the cracks and creating further openings also changes the building. In authoritarian regimes newly formed citizenry that result of mobilization, such as the citizenry formed during the Arab Spring, is trained to address grievances and make claims against the state through specific access points. We can imagine that in the USA this has occurred over the last several hundred years, where citizens of the revolutionary states have been trained over time to use even protest in certain sanctioned and predictable ways. We have a citizenry trained in organized and institutional resistance. Figuring out which changes break the cracks open is the next phase of social movement research.

The most promising methodology for finding these transformative changes is longitudinal analysis that spans relatively long periods of time, extending over at least a decade or two. For instance, Jenkins and Jacobs's (2003) work on African-American Protest from 1948 to 1997 sheds an incredible light on how political processes influence protest (Jenkins and Jacobs, 2003), but we would benefit from analyses that examine how movements influence political institutions recursively. This comes with a barrage of difficulties and complications that have been well documented in literature on movement consequences (Amenta et al., 2011). Scholars should devote more time to dealing with these difficulties and examining the slow, institutional changes that movements have induced. By examining those changes we may track and isolate those that have impacted a movement's constituency in positive and in negative ways. Positive changes, such as the most recent Supreme Court decision that affirms same-sex marriage, or the recent National Institutes of Health moratorium on chimpanzee research, are changes in federal institutions upon which the respective movements have mobilized for decades. Empirically connecting the successes with movements and tracking the institutional processes that lead to those successes will help scholars create a road map for how activists use political opportunities to break open the cracks of social justice.

REFERENCES

Alimi, E.Y. (2009), 'Mobilizing under the gun: theorizing political opportunity structure in a highly repressive setting', *Mobilization: An International Quarterly*, **14**(2), 219–37.
Alimi, E.Y. and D.S. Meyer (2011), 'Seasons of change: Arab Spring and political opportunities', *Swiss Political Science Review*, **17**(4), 475–9.
Almeida, P.D. (2003), 'Opportunity organizations and threat-induced contention: protest waves in authoritarian settings', *American Journal of Sociology*, **109**(2), 345–400.
Amenta, E. (2006), *When Movements Matter: The Townsend Plan and the Rise of Social Security (Princeton Studies in American Politics)*, Princeton, NJ: Princeton University Press.
Amenta, E. and Y. Zylan (1991), 'It happened here: political opportunity, the new institutionalism, and the Townsend movement', *American Sociological Review*, **56**(2), 250–65.
Amenta, E., N. Caren and J. Stobaugh (2011), 'Political reform and the historical trajectories of U.S. social movements in the twentieth century', *Social Forces*, **90**(4), 1073–100.
Amenta, E., K. Dunleavy and M. Bernstein (1994), 'Stolen thunder? Huey Long's "share our wealth" political medication, and the second New Deal', *American Sociological Review*, **59**(6), 678–702.
Amenta, E., N. Caren, E. Chiarello and Y. Su (2011), 'The political consequences of social movements', *American Review of Sociology*, **36**, 287–307.
Andrews, K.T. (2001), 'Social movements and policy implementation: the Mississippi civil rights movement and the war on poverty, 1965 to 1971', *American Sociological Review*, **66**(1), 71–95.
Andrews, K.T. (2004), *Freedom is a Constant Struggle*, Chicago, IL: University of Chicago Press.
Banaszak, L.A. (1996), *Why Movements Succeed or Fail: Opportunity, Culture, and the Struggle for Woman Suffrage*, Princeton, NJ: Princeton University Press.
Banaszak, L.A. (2010), *The Women's Movement Inside and Outside the State*, New York: Cambridge University Press.
Blumer, H. (1939), 'Collective behavior', in R.E. Park (ed.), *Principles of Sociology*, New York: Barnes & Noble, pp. 219–88.
Boudreau, V. (1996), 'Northern theory, Southern protest: opportunity structure analysis in cross-national perspective', *Mobilization: An International Quarterly*, **1**(2), 175–89.
Clemens, E.S. and D.C. Minkoff (2009), 'Beyond the iron law: rethinking the place of organizations in social movement research', in D.A. Snow, S.A. Soule and H. Kriesi (eds), *The Blackwell Companion to Social Movements*, Oxford: Blackwell, pp. 157–70.
Costain, A.N. (1992), *Inviting Women's Rebellion: A Political Process Interpretation of the Women's Movement*, Baltimore, MD: Johns Hopkins University Press.
De la Luz Inclan, M. (2008), 'From the !Ya Basta! to the Caracoles: Zapatista mobilization under transitional conditions', *American Journal of Sociology*, **113**(5), 1316–50.
Einwohner, R.L. (1999), 'Practices, opportunities, and protest effectiveness: illustrations from four animal rights campaigns', *Social Problems*, **46**(2), 69–186.
Eisinger, P. (1973), 'The conditions of protest behavior in American cities', *American Political Science Review*, **67**(1), 11–28.
Gamson, W.A. (1990), *The Strategy of Social Protest*, 2nd edition, Belmont, CA: Wadsworth.
Gamson, W.A. and D.S. Meyer (1996), 'Framing political opportunity', in D. McAdam,

J.D. McCarthy and M.N. Zald (eds), *Comparative Perspectives on Social Movements*, Cambridge, UK: Cambridge University Press.

Gupta, D. (2008), 'Small victories and social movements: how incremental progress affects social movement support and strategy', paper prepared for the 49th International Studies Association Conference, San Francisco, 26–29 March 2008.

Halfmann, D. and M.P. Young (2010), 'War pictures: the grotesque as a mobilizing tactic', *Mobilization: An International Quarterly*, **15**(1), 1–24.

Jenkins, J.C. and D. Jacobs (2003), 'Political opportunities and African-American protest, 1948–1997', *American Journal of Sociology*, **109**(2), 277–303.

Jenkins, J.C. and C. Perrow (1977), 'Insurgency of the powerless: farm worker movements (1946–1972)', *American Sociological Review*, **42**, 249–68.

Keck, M.E. and K. Sikkink (1998), *Activists beyond Borders*, Ithaca, NY: Cornell University Press.

Keniston, K. (1968), *Young Radicals*, New York: Harcourt Brace.

Kitschelt, H.P. (1986), 'Political opportunity structures and political protest: anti-nuclear movements in four democracies', *British Journal of Political Science*, **16**(1), 57–85.

Koopmans, R. and P. Statham (1999), 'Ethnic and civic conception of nationhood and the differential success of the extreme right in Germany and Italy', in M. Giugni, D. McAdam and C. Tilly (eds), *How Social Movements Matter*, Minneapolis, MN/London: University of Minnesota Press, pp. 66–96.

Kornhauser, W. (1959), *The Politics of Mass Society*, New York: Free Press.

Kriesi, H., R. Koopmans, J.W. Duyvendak and M. Giugni (1995), *New Social Movements in Western Europe: A Comparative Analysis of Social Movements, Protest, and Contention*, Minneapolis, MN/London: University of Minnesota Press.

Lipsky, M. (1968), 'Protest as political resource', *American Political Science Review*, **62**(4), 1144–58.

Lowi, T.J. (1971), *The Politics of Disorder*, New York: Basic Books.

Luders, J. (2010), *The Civil Rights Movement and the Logic of Social Change*, New York: Cambridge University Press.

Marks, G. and D. McAdam (1996), 'Social movements and the changing structure of political opportunity in the European Union', *West European Politics*, **19**(2), 249–78.

Marshall, T.H. (1950), *Citizenship and Social Class, and Other Essays*, Cambridge, UK: Cambridge University Press.

McAdam, D. (1982), *Political Process and the Development of Black Insurgency, 1930–1970*, Chicago, IL: University of Chicago Press.

McAdam, D. (1996), 'Political opportunities: conceptual origins, current problems, future directions', in D. McAdam, J.D. McCarthy and M.N. Zald (eds), *Comparative Perspectives on Social Movements*, Cambridge, UK: Cambridge University Press.

McAdam, D. and H.S. Boudet (2012), *Putting Social Movements in their Place: Explaining Opposition to Energy Projects in the United States, 2000–2005*, New York: Cambridge University Press.

McAdam, D., J.D. McCarthy and M.N. Zald (1996), *Comparative Perspectives on Social Movements: Political Opportunities, Mobilizing Structures, and Cultural Framings*, Cambridge, UK: Cambridge University Press.

McAdam, D., S. Tarrow and C. Tilly (2001), *Dynamics of Contention*, New York: Cambridge University Press.

McCammon, H.J., C.S. Muse, H.D. Newman and T.M. Terrell (2007), 'Movement framing and discursive opportunity structures: the political successes of the U.S. women's jury movements', *American Sociological Review*, **72**(5), 725–49.

McCarthy, J.D. and M.N. Zald (1977), 'Resource mobilization and social movements: a partial theory', *American Journal of Sociology*, **82**(6), 1212–41.

Meyer, D.S. (1990), *A Winter of Discontent: The Nuclear Freeze and American Politics*, New York: Praeger.

Meyer, D.S. (1993), 'Protest cycles and political process: American peace movements in the nuclear age', *Political Research Quarterly*, **46**(3), 451–79.

Meyer, D.S. (2004), 'Protest and political opportunities', *Annual Review of Sociology*, **30**, 125–45.
Meyer, D.S. (2006), *Politics of Protest*, Oxford: Oxford University Press.
Meyer, D.S. (2007), *The Politics of Protest: Social Movements in America*, New York: Oxford University Press.
Meyer, D.S. and D.C. Minkoff (2004), 'Conceptualizing political opportunity', *Social Forces*, **82**(4), 1457–92.
Meyer, D.S. and S. Staggenborg (1996), 'Movements, counter-movements, and the structure of political opportunity', *American Journal of Sociology*, **101**(6), 1628–60.
Meyer, D.S. and S. Tarrow (eds) (1998), *The Social Movement Society*, Lanham, MD: Rowman & Littlefield.
Meyer, D.S. and N. Whittier (1994), 'Social movement spillover', *Social Problems*, **41**(2), 277–98.
Minkoff, D.C. (1999), 'Bending with the wind: strategic change and adaptation by women's and racial minority organizations', *American Journal of Sociology*, **104**(6), 1666–703.
Olson, M. (1965), *The Logic of Collective Action*, Cambridge, MA: Harvard University Press.
Park, R.E. (1972), *The Crowd and the Public, and other Essays*, Chicago, IL: University of Chicago Press.
Park, R.E. and E.W. Burgess (1921), *Introduction to the Science of Sociology*, Chicago, IL: University of Chicago Press.
Parkin, F. (1968), *Middle-class Radicalism: The Social Bases of the British Campaign for Nuclear Disarmament*, Manchester: Manchester University Press.
Piven, F. and R. Cloward (1977), *Poor People's Movements: Why They Succeed, How They Fail*, New York: Pantheon Books.
Rohlinger, D.A. (2002), 'Framing the abortion debate: organizational resources, media strategies, and movement countermovement dynamics', *Sociological Quarterly*, **43**(4), 479–507.
Smith, C. (1996), *Resisting Reagan: The U.S. Central America Peace Movement*, Chicago, IL: University of Chicago Press.
Snow, D.A. (2004), 'Social movements as challenges to authority: resistance to an emerging conceptual hegemony', *Research in Social Movements, Conflicts and Change*, **25**, 3–25.
Snow, D.A., S.A. Soule and H. Kriesi (2004), 'Mapping the terrain', in D.A. Snow, S.A. Soule and H. Kriesi (eds), *The Blackwell Companion to Social Movements*, Oxford: Blackwell.
Soule, S.A. and B.G. King (2008), 'Competition and resource partitioning in three social movement industries', *American Journal of Sociology*, **113**(6), 1568–610.
Soule, S.A., D. McAdam, J.D. McCarthy and Y. Su (1999), 'Protest events: cause or consequence of state action? The U.S. women's movement and federal Congressional activities, 1956–1979', *Mobilization: An International Quarterly*, **4**(2), 239–56.
Staggenborg, S. (1988), 'The consequences of professionalization and formalization in the pro-choice movement', *American Sociological Review*, **53**(4), 585–605.
Staggenborg, S. (1996), 'The survival of the women's movement: turnover and continuity in Bloomington, Indiana', *Mobilization: An International Quarterly*, **1**(2), 143–58.
Stepan-Norris, J. and M. Zeitlin (1991), '"Red" unions and "bourgeois" contracts?', *American Journal of Sociology*, **96**(5), 1151–200.
Tarrow, S. (1989), *Democracy and Disorder: Protest and Politics in Italy, 1965–1975*, Oxford: Clarendon.
Tarrow, S.G. (1998), *Power in Movement*, 2nd edition, Cambridge, UK: Cambridge University Press.
Taylor, V. (1989), 'Social movement continuity: the women's movement in abeyance', *American Sociological Review*, **54**(5), 761–75.
Taylor, V. and N. van Dyke (2009), '"Get up, stand up": tactical repertoires of social movements', in D.A. Snow, S.A. Soule and H. Kriesi (eds), *The Blackwell Companion to Social Movements*, Oxford: Blackwell.
Tilly, C. (1978), *From Mobilization to Revolution*, New York: Random House.

Tilly, C. (1993), 'Contentious repertoires in Great Britian, 1758–1834', *Social Science History*, **17**(2), 253–80.
Tilly, C. (1995), *Popular Contention in Great Britain*, Cambridge, MA/London: Harvard University Press.
Van der Heijden, H.-A. (2006), 'Globalization, environmental movements and international political opportunity structures', *Organization & Environment*, **19**(1), 28–45.
Van Dyke, N. (2003), 'Crossing movement boundaries: factors that facilitate coalition protest by American college students, 1930–1990', *Social Problems*, **50**(2), 226–50.
Walker, J.L. (1991), *Mobilizing Interest Groups in America: Patrons, Professions, and Social Movements*, Ann Arbor, MI: University of Michigan Press.
Wilson, J.Q. (1977), *Political Organizations*, Princeton, NJ: Princeton University Press.
Wolfson, M. (2001), *The Fight Against Tobacco: The Movement, the State, and the Public's Health*, New York: Aldine de Gruyter.

13. Post-structuralism, social movements and citizen politics
Steven Griggs and David Howarth

INTRODUCTION

There is no independent and self-contained post-structuralist theory of social movements that is comparable, for example, to 'resource mobilization theory' (e.g., Oberschall, 1973; Tilly, 1978) or the 'political process approach' (e.g., Tarrow, 1978). At best, certain post-structuralist motifs and concepts are reflected in various theoretical frames and perspectives. Such themes include the role of identities, values, and changing subjectivities in the emergence and operation of multiple movements, as well as general theoretical reflections on the character of social structures and their connection to agency, human subjectivity, power and domination. The emancipatory potentials and effects of assemblages of various types are also investigated and evaluated by post-structuralist thinkers, as are their negative and oppressive impacts, though post-structuralists have tended to eschew traditional forms of normative theorizing in favour of genealogical and critical histories of particular struggles and campaigns.

Yet these introductory remarks still beg a number of tricky questions about the nature of post-structuralism itself. Can it be viewed as a discrete social and political theory, or is it a broad approach? Does it even exist as a coherent body of theoretical discourse? Who counts as a post-structuralist theorist or researcher? In our view, post-structuralism is best defined and understood as a particular *style* of theorizing in social and political theory, which is informed by a distinctive *ethos*, where both the style and the ethos are predicated on a specific set of ontological postulates (e.g., Hacking, 1985; Howarth, 2013). More precisely, researchers working within the post-structuralist tradition of inquiry question the completion and closure of social structures, as well as totalizing forms of human subjectivity, identity and reason. Such assumptions flow from an anti-essentialist and anti-foundationalist orientation, which presupposes the radical contingency and historicity of all meanings and social relations, while foregrounding the role of power and political exclusion in the formation of discourses, institutions and systems. They also affirm the role of difference, plurality and pluralization, both to explain and criticize the social world, and to sketch out alternatives to existing relations of domination and oppression. In short, in our view 'post-structuralism' is a name that refers to a way of addressing questions pertaining to the relationships between social structure and human subjectivity, power and agency, and identity and identification (Howarth, 2013).

But this is not to say that the post-structuralist style of theory is unconnected to the emergence, impact and functioning of groups and social movements. On the contrary, social movements form an important focus of attention. This is partly because post-structuralist theorizing was intimately connected to the 'May events' of 1968 in Paris, when students and workers brought down the De Gaulle government led by Prime Minister, Georges Pompidou. As is well documented, such protests soon spread to other countries and contexts. But it is also because many post-structuralist theorists have maintained an on-going dialogue with the so-called 'new social movements', which were strongly connected to this seminal moment in post-war political life (Boggs, 1986; Caute, 1988). Indeed, post-structuralists like Judith Butler, William Connolly, Gilles Deleuze, Jacques Derrida, Michel Foucault, Felix Guattari, Julia Kristeva, Ernesto Laclau and Chantal Mouffe, to name but a few, were strongly inspired by the form, content and diversity of the feminist, environmental, peace, gay liberation, urban and anti-racist movements, and they have in turn sought to furnish concepts, strategic support and normative orientation to such novel forms of collective action.

More concrete post-structuralist accounts of particular social phenomena, such as the emergence of populist movements in different contexts (e.g., Laclau, 2005; Panizza, 2005), or the intersection of citizen protest and policy-making practices in particular contexts (e.g., Griggs and Howarth, 2013a), come in different shapes and sizes. But they are rooted in the more general assumptions we have mentioned above. In this chapter, we draw inspiration from one important strand of post-structuralist theory – Laclau and Mouffe's innovative concept of discourse analysis, which in turn presupposes the articulation of the ideas of Derrida, Foucault, Antonio Gramsci and Jacques Lacan in a novel synthesis – to provide the resources to explain the role and functioning of social movements and their impact on citizens and citizenship (Laclau and Mouffe, 2001). We begin by setting out the basic assumptions of our approach and then elaborate its implications for social and political analysis in the fields of groups and movements. Finally, we employ the approach to provide an account of social movements, in which we focus on recent struggles to prevent the expansion of airports in France and the United Kingdom (UK).

A POST-STRUCTURALIST PERSPECTIVE

Over the last couple of decades, there has been a considerable interest in the concept of discourse and the methods of discourse analysis in the humanities and social sciences. Our approach goes beyond a minimal and purely ideational conception of discourse, in which discourse is conceived of as another empirical variable that can simply be tested against other variables in the search for causal or statistical explanations. Such approaches often give rise to what we might term 'discourse-lite' forms of explanation and interpretation (Torfing, 2005, p. 25). Instead, we propose a 'thicker' conception of discourse, in which the latter does not just consist of an abstract cognitive system of beliefs and words, but is a constitutive dimension of social relations. Discourse analysis does not merely describe or make known a pre-existing or underlying reality, but serves partly to bring that reality into being for subjects (Gottweis, 2003, p. 252).

Adopting this perspective means that all objects – natural things and physical processes, social and cultural phenomena – acquire their meaning and significance in specific discourses; they are 'discursively constructed' in multiple ways. Although such entities certainly 'exist' independently of any particular discourse, their peculiar import – and thus how they are engaged with by social actors – depends on their positioning and use within particular symbolic frameworks (Howarth, 2000; Laclau and Mouffe, 2001). Post-structuralist discourse theory thus rejects essentialist accounts of social movements and groups, which assume that objects, human subjects, or even social formations, have fixed essences or forms. Such presuppositions are often evident, for example, in the economic determinism and class reductionism of Marxist explanations of social and political change, and in some versions of critical realism, but they actually pervade many mainstream traditions of social and political theory.

Our conception of discourse involves three conceptual displacements. In the first place, we enlarge the purview of traditional discourse theory – the analysis of 'texts and talk in contexts' – so as to embrace social practices and political activities within its ambit. *All* objects and social practices are discursive, in that their meaning and position depends upon their articulation within socially constructed systems of rules and differences (Laclau and Mouffe, 1985; Howarth and Stavrakakis, 2000, p. 3). Second, we base our alternative understanding of discourse on the work of Saussure (1983), and subsequent elaborations of structural linguistics, to develop a relational and differential account of discourse. In this model, four particular kinds of entity – agents (or subjects), objects, words and actions – are individuated and rendered intelligible within the context of a particular practice. Each element acquires its meaning only in specific relation to the others (Howarth, 2009, pp. 311–12). Finally, drawing on post-structuralists like Jacques Derrida (1978, 1982), Michel Foucault (1972, 1981, 1984) and Jacques Lacan (2006), we stress the radical contingency and structural undecidability of discursive structures (Howarth, 2009, p. 312). This arises because we assume that all systems of meaning are, in a fundamental sense, incomplete. By saying that discourses are incomplete, we do not mean that they are simply missing something; it is not synonymous with the fact that we have not seen all the episodes of a television series, or that our glass is not full to the brim. Instead, from our perspective, incompletion denotes the presence of an absence or negativity that structurally prevents the completion of a discourse, thereby indicating its limits. Discourses are thus incomplete systems of meaningful practice, because they are predicated on the active exclusion of certain elements. Yet these excluded elements are required for the very identity of the discourse in question.

In our perspective, then, building on Laclau and Mouffe, discourse is a kind of social practice that links together and modifies heterogeneous elements in changing historical formations (Laclau and Mouffe, 1985, p. 96). The outcomes of such practices are discursive formations, in which the linkages between the elements of these systems are relational and differential. Discursive formations are finite, uneven and incomplete. Both as a practice and as an incomplete system of related moments, discourse also presupposes a world of contingent elements – linguistic and non-linguistic, social and natural – that can be linked together in various ways. This perspective is consistent with a minimal realism that acknowledges the existence of the objects and processes that we think about, though our practices of reflection are never external to the lifeworlds into which we are thrown. Indeed, it is only within such symbolic orders that we encounter such objects.

More technically, the elements or components of a discourse are best conceived as floating signifiers, which can in certain circumstances be articulated by rival political projects seeking to fix their meaning and import, whereas moments are those elements that are firmly positioned in a particular discourse. Nodal points are those privileged points of signification within a discourse that partially fix the meaning of practices and institutional configurations, while empty signifiers provide the symbolic means to represent these essentially incomplete orders. The function of the latter is to incarnate the 'absent fullness' of an essentially incomplete discursive system. Put differently, floating signifiers are ideological elements that are not securely fixed in a particular discourse, and can thus be constructed in diverse ways, whereas empty signifiers are points of symbolic fixation, which provide the representational resources that can hold together multiple and even contradictory demands in a precarious unity (Laclau, 1990, 1995).

What does this mean for the study of social movements? To begin with, it provides an effective way of criticizing certain aspects of the dominant theories of groups and social movements, which all tend to focus on the presumed existence of groups, movements and parties operating in a particular political system. Post-structuralists also raise questions about the tendency to emphasize *either* the role of interests and material incentives, *or* the salience of identities and values in explaining the function and impact of groups and movements. On the contrary, post-structuralists are wary of binary oppositions that privilege one or other of the terms over the others, and they seek instead to deconstruct and reconstruct in less essentialist and exclusionary ways (Derrida, 1976, 1981). Finally, those working within the post-structuralist tradition, not unlike rational choice theorists in this instance, are sceptical about a necessary and automatic connection between interests and agency. Sharing a common interest does not necessarily lead social actors to become agents who are intent on mobilizing others, or joining groups or movements.

Post-structuralism thus provides resources for researchers to exercise a critical function in relation to existing group and movement theory. But equally its proponents seek to go beyond a purely negative form of critique by providing an alternative grammar of concepts and logics with which to explain and evaluate social movements. They are also inclined at times towards elaborating interim visions, which can inform the goals and objectives of particular movements or coalitions. The key concepts here are the notion of a demand and the idea of a hegemonic practice, which can either link demands into more or less stable equilibria, or on the other hand decouple demands into singular entities. These two concepts are allied to a reworking of the relationship between interests and identities, and thus a focus on the role of subjectivity, agency and identification in the construction and operation of collective assemblages of various types. We flesh out these propositions in the next section.

GROUPS, SOCIAL MOVEMENTS AND CITIZEN ENGAGEMENT

There are two major strands of theorizing that deal with extra-parliamentary and non-parliamentary forms of collective action, political mobilization and interest articulation: what we shall call 'group theory' and 'movement theory' respectively. As is well documented, classical theories of groups – pluralist, corporatist, Marxist and those associated with the New Right – along with their many internal variations, differ in their understandings of the distribution of power, the nature of groups involved in the political process and the character of government and the state, especially in capitalist democracies. Pluralists, for example, argue that power in democratic societies is dispersed and that many groups can influence and ultimately affect decision-making processes, whereas Marxists focus on the strongly uneven distribution of power, which is rooted in the asymmetrical relations of production characteristic of class-divided societies. On the other hand, corporatist accounts argue that certain institutional frameworks such as the state, facilitate (and constrain) group formation and mobilization, while New Right theorists focus on the deleterious effects of groups on policy-making and state intervention.[1]

Classical theories of social movements, by contrast, whether of a structural functionalist (Smelser, 1962) or Marxist type (Castells, 1977), explain movements by reference to general theoretical laws of society and history. Such approaches tend to subsume the historically specific meanings and practices of movements under higher-order causal propositions, and thus fail to account for the diversity of identities and agencies associated with contemporary movements, especially those pertaining to environmental concerns (Howarth, 1998). More recent discussions of social movements revolve around the differences between resource mobilization perspectives and accounts of the 'new social movements' (e.g., Foweraker, 1995; Della Porta and Diani, 1999). The former approach is closely connected to rational choice theory, and hence with the importance of individual rationality, interests and material incentives, whereas the latter are more concerned with the role of subjective identities and values, which are situated within wider and more complex structural contexts.

Alain Touraine's 'sociology of action' approach occupies a central position in this regard. As against functionalist and structuralist paradigms, his concept of 'action' refers to 'the behaviour of an actor guided by cultural orientations and set within social relations defined by an unequal connection with the social control of orientations' (1981, p. 61), and 'social movements' are defined as 'the organized collective behaviour of a class actor struggling against his class adversary for the social control of historicity in a concrete community' (ibid., p. 77). Social movements thus contain three important elements: the identity of the actor, the definition of an opponent and the 'stakes' of the conflict, which are equivalent to the 'cultural totality'. According to Touraine (1985, pp. 760–61), such elements crystallize the central conflict of any given societal type. More substantively, social movements in Touraine's approach represent ideal typical forms of social conflict in any particular societal type, such that all others are viewed as partial or disintegrated variants. What he names 'post-industrial' or 'programmed' societies, which is the dominant contemporary form, are defined 'by the technological production of symbolic goods which shape or transform our representation of human nature and of the external world', and are characterized by four main components: research and development; information processing; biomedical science and techniques; and mass media (1985, p. 783). It is against the logics of programmed societies that contemporary social movements are said to organize, and Touraine presents the stakes of the conflict as that between an all-encompassing and technocratic state, and a potentially democratic and libertarian civil society.

In a related vein, theorists like Alberto Melucci, who in turn draws upon the work of Habermas, concentrate on the role of collective identities and subjectivities, in which social movements in late capitalist societies engage in various kinds of symbolic struggle designed to prevent the pathological features of modernity and capitalism. Habermas had positioned the new social movements in the socio-cultural sphere, where they resist the dangers of colonization posed by the state and instrumental rationality by elaborating new identities and forms of life (Habermas, 1981, 1987). Opposing overly structuralist and individualistic styles of research, Melucci's more intermediate approach analyses the way individuals 'recognize what they have in common and decide to act together' (Melucci, 1988, p. 339). More substantively, contra traditional forms of collective action, like the workers' movement, new social movements do not desire more state intervention, but seek to deflect the encroachment of dominating systems like the state by defending personal autonomy and creating innovative spaces and networks of interaction (Della Porta and Diani, 1999, pp. 12–15).

Touraine and other theorists of the new social movements, such as Alberto Melucci, thus go some way in overcoming and reorientating the subsumptive and narrow positions of the classical tradition. But their reformulations also raise questions. For one thing, Touraine does not reject the backdrop of a macro-theoretical sociological synthesis with which to explain and evaluate contemporary social movements. Indeed, his notion of a 'programmed society' operates as a grand synthetical backdrop with which to judge whether or not movements are, in his terms, successful or not. Second, Touraine emphasizes the cultural and ideological dimensions of social movements, both for his evaluation of their success in achieving 'progressive' effects, and by stressing the importance of their own self-understandings as the key to explaining their emergence and formation. But as Scott (1990) correctly argues, this precludes the analysis of the different strategies movements may articulate in pursuing their goals, as well as the political context – what resource mobilization theorists call the political opportunity structure – which mediate and channel their demands. Also, on a conceptual level, though Touraine and others highlight the importance of identity and ideology in their analyses, the concepts themselves are not properly clarified. Finally, while Touraine works hard to develop a distinctive sociology of action, he tends not to explore and develop the multi-dimensional character of action, especially the role of instrumental action, which is of particular importance for rational choice theorists.

Groups, Movements and Demands

More recently, there have been attempts to bring the Anglo-American and European traditions closer together, so that questions of interests and resource mobilization are related to questions of identity values and subjectivity. Post-structuralists have also endeavoured to deepen this development in theories of groups and movements. As we have intimated, those adopting a post-structuralist style of theorizing begin by deconstructing the essentialist assumptions that underlie the dominant theories. In the first place, notwithstanding the important substantive and methodological differences in the existing theories and approaches, they all tend to accept the *givenness* of the groups and movements involved in the political process. Post-structuralists, by contrast, tend not to assume that groups or movements, or indeed individuals, simply exist, as this would fall foul of their anti-essentialist and constructivist orientations. Instead of focussing on groups, movements, political parties, or individual actors as the privileged units of analysis, they hone in on the role of demands and the hegemonic practices that come into play around such demands. In other words, they concentrate on the emergence and discursive construction of demands, as well as the various ways in which the latter are either combined into more complex wholes, or disaggregated and decomposed by multifarious practices and processes.

So as to add some more conceptual content to this formal framework, we shall start by analysing the notion of a demand. In our view, building upon Laclau's discussion in his *On Populist Reason* (Laclau, 2005), a 'social demand' is intimately related to a subject's experience of contingency, which is usually engendered by the occurrence of a dislocatory event, coupled with the way that a particular subject responds to it. It is, of course, possible that an objective occurrence or decision that affects a community or subject is not constructed as a dislocatory event, in which case the situation remains more or less unchanged. But, if it is constructed as dislocatory, then one immediate reaction by a subject might be to constitute the experience of contingency as a 'grievance'. In other words, the matter might be constructed as an issue affecting a group or community, whose response can then be articulated as a 'request' in the public domain. If the relevant public authority can process the request in a satisfactory way, then the matter is likely to end there. But the failure of the relevant authority to respond adequately to a request, at least from the perspective of the aggrieved subject, can lead to its hardening into a demand (Laclau, 2005, pp. 73–4). Indeed, if this demand publicly challenges the norm of a practice or regime, which is usually manifested in terms of a particular public policy, then it takes on a political character. In short, then, a demand is political to the extent that it publicly contests the norms of a particular practice or policy regime in the name of a principle or ideal (Glynos and Howarth, 2007, pp. 115–16).

Our strong emphasis on the role of demands as a mechanism to capture the operation of groups and movements is also allied to a novel theory of hegemony. More precisely, working within the post-structuralist perspective, we delineate two dimensions of hegemony that are crucial in developing a viable approach to the study of social movements and their impact on policies, rights and the distribution of goods.[2] On the one hand, hegemony is a type of rule or governance that captures the way in which a regime, practice or policy holds sway over a set of subjects by a particular entwining of consent, compliance and coercion. On the other hand, hegemony is a practice of politics that involves the linking together of disparate demands to forge hegemonic projects or 'discourse coalitions' (Hajer, 1995). Such assemblages can contest a particular form of rule, practice or policy by articulating an alternative discourse (Howarth, 2009, p. 317).

The process of connecting demands involves the interacting logics of equivalence and difference, in which elements are either rendered the same, and thus their particularity annulled, through the negation of a common enemy, or they can be neutralized, accommodated or transformed by being incorporated into projects or coalitions that they contest – in the case of the latter, they become a difference within it. In practice, of course, the two aspects of hegemony are intimately related. Hegemony as a form of rule presupposes various practices of transformism, negotiation, compromise and bargaining, while the struggle to develop counter-hegemonic movements presupposes certain forms of rule or an order that the movements challenge and seek to transform. Only for analytical purposes – and not for ontological reasons – can they be separated. The same is true for the logics of equivalence and difference: they continuously interact and intersect in order to compose and decompose the various demands that are constructed in particular spaces.

Adopting this approach means that entities like political parties, social movements, groups, coalitions and networks do not have distinct essences that tell them apart. Rather, they are better seen as contingent assemblages of elements – more or less sedimented and organized – which operate in different, though sometimes overlapping, spaces, where the latter offer varying degrees of freedom and constraint to the agents organizing or participating in them. The voicing of demands by subjects and their connection or disconnection via the logic of hegemony serve as the bedrock for the analysis of sociological phenomena like movements or groups. But this does not mean that such entities do not share some family resemblances, and that such labels are redundant. On the contrary, as Donatella Della Porta and Mario Diani correctly note, it is still possible to discern at least four general features of social movements, which enable us to distinguish in a loose and pragmatic fashion between different complexes of collective action. In their view, which we share, social movements comprise 'informal networks' that are predicated on 'shared beliefs and solidarity', where the latter are mobilized around antagonistic issues by the repeated use of protest actions (Della Porta and Diani, 1999, p. 16). Social movements thus differ from 'more structured' complexes like political parties and interest groups, which exhibit greater degrees of organization and sedimentation, as well as particular campaigns or protests, temporary alliances and ad hoc coalitions, which tend to focus on single issues.

Conceiving of social movements as 'contingent assemblages of related elements', or as 'networks of interaction between different actors', enables us to trace the interactions and overlappings between different sorts of collective action. Movements may operate within political parties or established groups to bring about internal cultural and ideological change, as well as wider policy shifts. They may also involve the orchestration of coalitions and temporary alliances to bring about particular goals. Movements comprise participants and activists, and not the traditional members of parties and groups; their organization tends to be more fluid and shifting, and thus more precarious, than parties or groups; and their strategies and tactics may vary considerably in the pursuit of their goals. Finally, movements are different in our view from social movement organizations, which are generally more sedimented, formal and hierarchical, and they tend to be rooted and operate in civil society, though they frequently interact with government and the state.

Group Formation and Collective Mobilization

One further difficulty with mainstream accounts concerns the way in which groups, movements, or parties are constituted in the first place, as well as the obstacles that may prevent the mobilization and organization of their members in campaigns and struggles. Just as it cannot be assumed that groups or movements simply exist, so it cannot be assumed that rational individuals will organize or join groups to advance their interests. From a rational choice point of view, this issue is neatly captured by what Mancur Olson (1965) calls the 'collective action problem', which turns on the existence of 'free-riders' who question the rationality of joining groups because the costs of membership are likely to exceed the benefits they obtain regardless of their involvement. Such difficulties arise because groups emerge and mobilize in pursuit of public goods, which are by definition indivisible and once attained not excludable.[3] In Olson's words, *'rational self-interested individuals will not act to achieve their common or group interests'* (1965, p. 2; emphasis in original). Unless the potential size of a group is small, thereby facilitating the monitoring of potential free-riders, or unless the group can employ negative and/or positive sanctions against potential free-riders, no groups are likely to emerge in pursuit of their common interests. In Olson's words:

> Only a *separate* and *'selective' incentive* will stimulate a rational individual in a latent group to act in a group-oriented way. In such circumstances group action can be obtained only through an incentive that operates, not indiscriminately, like the collective good, upon the group as a whole, but rather *selectively* toward the individuals in the group. (Olson, 1965, p. 51; emphasis in original)

Insights like this furnish an important starting point for rethinking the logics of group formation and mobilization. Not only does it raise key questions concerning the relationship between individuals and groups, as well as the internal dynamics of groups, it problematizes the crucial concept of interests, and how the latter can be conceived. Olson and others thus argue that latent groups may be undermobilized or not formed at all, while also suggesting a number of 'supply side' solutions to these structural impediments. Such remedies include the availability of selective material incentives, the interventions of political entrepreneurs and political movers, and the possibility of groups 'piggy-backing' on existing organizations, or drawing upon state or governmental resources, all of which diminish the overall costs of collective action (Oberschall, 1973, p. 159; Dowding, 1996, pp. 38–41). Finally, the classical rational choice model goes some way in explaining the internal structuring of groups, and the cycle of institutionalization and de-institutionalization characteristic of cause groups (particularly environmental groups), as they often result in organizational hierarchy, the relativity passivity of group members, and corporatist entanglements with the state.

Nevertheless, as post-structuralists argue, there are some shortcomings with the *assumptions* of the classical model. First, the classical model tends to operate with a 'fixed' set of preferences from which rational actors choose. Apart from imposing such preferences on agents, this assumption also precludes the possibility that preferences can be altered in the light of changing contexts and circumstances. Second, though rational choice theorists are able to model strategies using game theory, they find it more difficult to account for the 'context dependence' of strategies, and the changing nature of strategic interaction over time. Finally, the classical model tends to assume that the 'identity' of the agent is that of a self-interested 'utility maximizer'. But, as Hirschman claims (1982, p. 85), this suggests that the subjects of their analyses 'are without a history', and implies that critical questions about the 'identities' of agents, as well as their 'agency' in relation to social structures, are not addressed and analysed.[4] In short, orthodox rational choice theory overemphasizes the role of material selective incentives; fails to develop the full implications of its supply-side solutions; neglects the role of group identities and social networks in helping to overcome the collective action problem; and omits to examine 'non-rational' sources of motivation, which may help us to explain why people get involved with environmental groups and movements in the first place.

In response to these concerns, some within the rational choice framework have endeavoured to supplement Olson's framework either by stressing the role of group identities, or by broadening the rational actor model to incorporate 'non-rational' motivations for action. Dunleavy endeavours to *complete* Olson's initial problematic by introducing the concept of a 'group identity', which captures 'the something more' necessary for those deciding whether or not to join a group. In his words, 'unless a rational actor accepts that she has a subjective interest which is shared by others, she has no basis for contributing to the group's activities because of its collective benefits' (1991, p. 55). While Dunleavy aims to complete Olson with his group identity model, Dennis Chong (1991) argues that alongside the role of selective material incentives and benefits motivating people to join groups, some activists and leaders perceive the process of participation and the feelings of solidarity such participation engenders, as reward in itself (Byrne, 1997, p. 42). Such 'expressive' benefits can themselves be regarded as selective incentives (in the Olsonian sense).

The stress that Dunleavy and Chong place on the role of group identities and expressive benefits to explain why people join groups, and why they join the *particular* groups they do, carries the possibility of relativizing the classical rational choice models, because they view instrumental behaviour as only *one* way of accounting for collective action. But they also inject other explanatory logics to explain group formation and mobilization. For example, Michael Taylor argues that 'non-rational' instances of collective behaviour, evident, for example, in the actions of some radical environmentalists, may require us to consider the role of 'normative, expressive and intrinsic motivations and social identification, and [. . .] the conditions in which they are mobilised' (Taylor, 1995, p. 223). In his words, such acts are 'facilitated by community, by social networks, by repeated interaction in a stable group, by ongoing social relationships' (1995, p. 232). Stated bluntly, then, what we might call heterodox rational choice theory, and resource mobilization theory more generally, begin to converge with sociological accounts of groups and collective action, though in sociological discourse the latter are usually considered under the heading of social movements. Indeed, such convergences have enabled the elaboration of synthetic theories of groups and movements, which endeavour to articulate issues of interest and identity, while also connecting concerns with redistribution and recognition, which have tended to be associated with resource mobilization approaches and sociological models respectively.

Interests and Identities, Identification and Agency

Although in our view this is the right move, we are not convinced that the relationships between interests and identities, structure and agency have been correctly articulated in synthetic accounts. Instead, drawing on post-structuralist assumptions, we have endeavoured to develop a clearer conceptualization of interests and identity, and to connect them together in a way that does not reduce one to the other. As against those views that present interests and identities as fixed, essential or primordial, we start by insisting that from a post-structuralist perspective both interests and identities are best understood as contingent and political constructs with precise discursive conditions of existence (Laclau and Mouffe, 1990, p. 118). Moreover, interests are better conceptualized as relative to the identities of agents who are positioned in certain socially constructed places. This means that to define and constitute interests is a political project in two senses. In the first place, interests cannot be assumed to pre-exist agents (whether as subjective preferences, or real entities imputed on agents by external observers), as they are constructed politically and discursively through a whole series of hegemonic practices and interventions. But at the same time social agents are themselves historical and political products whose identities are contingent upon their relation to other identities. It may seem obvious, but interests are always the interests of particular agents, and both the identities, and the interests that are relative to them, can never be assumed, but are strategic outcomes.[5]

This rudimentary account requires us to elaborate our particular conception of identity. Borrowing from Stuart Hall and others, identities can be viewed as those 'points of temporary attachment to the subject positions which discursive practices construct for us. They are the result of a successful articulation or "chaining" of the subject into the flow of discourse' (Hall, 1996, p. 6). In this approach, identities are relational entities whose significance and positioning depend on a system of differences within which any particular identity is defined and marked. Indeed, identities in our view are always differentiated in a twofold manner. On the one hand, they are marked by a set of significant differences that exist within and between social agents. Whether they are defined in terms of class, gender, ethnicity, sexuality, nationality, race, religion, occupation role, and so forth, each identity is different from others, and thus acquires its particular meaning and import. On the other hand, identities often emerge and are constructed by being defined against other identities and differences. Here the production and reproduction of social identities involves the creation of frontiers that divide 'insiders' from 'outsiders'; they require the constitution of 'others' or 'scapegoats' that are presented as blocking the full constitution of an agent's self-identity.[6] As we have already noted, the political construction of identity through the creation of boundaries involves the production of empty signifiers, which represent the 'absent fullness' of a group – their lack of unity and community (Laclau, 1990, p. 171). Empty signifiers are thus means of representation that enable the welding together of internal differences, while simultaneously showing the limits of the group identity, and its dependence on the opposition to other groups.[7]

The role of agency is often discussed in the social movement problématique, as movements are intimately connected up with challenges to various relations of domination, and thus the construction of new collective identities and the exercise of political voice, which can change social values and result in the redistribution of resources. In our approach, we connect the question of agency to the moment of dislocation, the formulation of demands, the agglomeration of disparate demands into broader hegemonic projects, and the way subjects come to identify with such demands and act upon them. Our concern with agency is thus bound up with the relationship between social structures, moments of subjective decision and the exercise of power. Structures in this paradigm are in general considered to be incomplete and undecidable entities, in which the latter properties become visible in moments of crisis and contestation, that is, which we have conceptualized as experiences of dislocation. It is here that subjects are no longer 'chained' to the various positions that are relationally made available by social structures, but can become strong subjects that can change their conditions of existence. In our late modern societies, social movements, whether new or old, represent one of the means through which such political agency can be actualized, and it is to some more concrete instances of such complexes that we now turn.

PROBLEMATIZING NEW SOCIAL MOVEMENTS AND CITIZENSHIP

It is important to start by noting that in our view post-structuralism is a problem-driven approach to social and political analysis (Howarth, 2005; Glynos and Howarth, 2007; Howarth, 2013). More precisely, we follow Foucault in emphasizing that meaningful social research begins by problematizing a specific phenomenon in a particular historical context. Any object of study is thus produced out of a mixture of seemingly unrelated events and processes, and these have to be assembled and analysed. Only then may it be possible to discern and name a problem, which can then be situated at an appropriate level of abstraction and complexity. Such tasks are challenging and complicated. But they are made doubly so because in constructing the problem the researcher is also confronted with the multiple problematizations of groups, movements and social actors, who themselves construct the problem in different ways. Problematizing such problematizations is thus complex. At the same time, there are different dimensions or aspects of most social problems: they may concern, for example, the democratic legitimacy of public policy, issues of environmental justice, or questions of political economy. Within each of these dimensions, there is likely to be competing interpretations and so on (Howarth and Griggs, 2012; Griggs and Howarth, 2013a).

With these challenges and complexities in mind, we shall set out one particular problematization of citizen mobilization and social movements. More specifically, we examine the politics of local campaigns against large infrastructure projects, notably proposed airport expansions, where we focus on local campaigns as sites or spaces in which new identities and alliances or political projects can be forged. Such campaigns have brought together local citizens, politicians, national lobbies and direct action campaigners in novel alliances against airport development. In the protest against the second runway at Manchester airport, for example, local residents joined with direct action environmentalists in what was characterized in the media as an alliance of 'Vegans and Volvos' (Griggs and Howarth, 2002). But how are these alliances between different identities forged? What are the conditions for their emergence and reproduction within the context of local political mobilizations? And what challenges do such experiences pose for representative politics and local democracy? In answering such questions, we shall turn our attention to two specific instances of collective mobilization and organization: the campaign against proposals to build a third runway at Heathrow and the campaign against the construction of a new international airport at Notre-Dame-des-Landes.[8]

At the beginning of August 2013, some 8000 citizens, farmers, environmentalists, local politicians and campaigners from across France gathered for a weekend summer festival. They came together for the thirteenth year running to protest against the building of a new international airport on farmland at Notre-Dame-des-Landes, some 30 kilometres outside the city of Nantes in the west of France (AirportWatch, n.d.). Over the course of the weekend, musicians played free concerts, performing on stage behind a huge banner declaring 'An airport at NDDL never!', while lectures, 'open discussions', and workshops on climate change and alternative lifestyles took place across the site. On the Sunday morning of the gathering, in a symbolic act of public dissent, festival-goers flew 1000 kites over the fields of Notre-Dame-des-Landes; they represented, in the words of one local leader of a citizen association, a collective demand 'to say the sky should be kept free, like the ground at Notre-Dame-des-Landes'.[9]

Similarly, some years earlier in 2007, local residents, environmental activists and anti-corporate protesters held a one-week climate action camp in a field near Heathrow airport. The camp aimed to raise public awareness of the contribution of aviation to rising carbon emissions, and oppose the construction of a third runway at London's international hub airport. Equally, the camp activists, some 1500 in number, sought to model sustainable lifestyles, basing their collective organization on democratic modes of consensus decision-making. George Monbiot, a well-known environmental activist and political columnist, wrote of his experience at the camp that 'a system of affinity groups and neighbourhoods, feeding their decisions upwards to general meetings, permitted a genuine participatory democracy of the kind you will never encounter in British public life' (Monbiot, 2007).

Of course, both these gatherings cannot be seen as isolated events. They are but one episode of citizen mobilization in a complex chain of rallies, protests, marches, occupations and publicity stunts that have punctuated campaigns and struggles against plans for development for over 40 years. In fact, after failures to prevent the construction of a fourth and fifth terminal in the 1980s and 1990s, the campaign against the construction of a third runway at Heathrow mobilized a highly effective anti-carbon coalition that managed to link together a range of different actors and issues, especially the problem of climate change and carbon emissions, in a new kind of airport politics. The coalition brought together local residents, notably the local residents' group, HACAN ClearSkies, national environmental lobbies such as Friends of the Earth and the Aviation Environment Federation, a number of local authorities who were organized in the 2M group, as well as direct action environmentalists, in particular the Plane Stupid anti-aviation activist network. Importantly, the coalition imported new strategies and tactics from the anti-roads movement into the more traditional campaigns of local residents against airport expansion. It was to bring about one of the most significant policy reversals in British transport policy when in May 2010 the Coalition government reversed the decision to expand Heathrow and imposed instead a moratorium on airport expansion in the South East of England (albeit that this moratorium is increasingly contested by the aviation industry and its supporters) (Griggs and Howarth, 2013a, 2013b).

Similarly, at Notre-Dame-des-Landes, there has been a sustained campaign against the new airport since plans for its development were first mooted in the 1960s and 1970s, although it must be stressed that the campaign has taken on a renewed intensity since the relaunch of the project in 2000. Like the campaigns at Heathrow and Manchester, it engages citizens in a wide array of different groups, movements and arenas. Its strategic leadership body, the Coordination, which was formed in 2003, brings together over 40 groups against the planned airport, including ADECA – an association of farmers affected by the proposed development – that was established in 1970, and ACIPA – a citizen association that was founded in 2000 – as well as pilots and over 1000 politicians in collectives opposed to the new airport, and over 200 support groups in cities and towns across France.[10] Importantly, the Coordination works to facilitate the engagement of citizen networks with radical activists from across France and Europe who have occupied land earmarked for development, which they have transformed from a 'zone to be developed' into a 'zone to be defended', or the *'zone à défendre'* or 'ZAD' as it is more commonly known. In occupying the land, activists have sought to work alongside local farmers and citizens to 'make use of abandoned spaces to learn to live together, to cultivate the land and to be more autonomous from the capitalist system'.[11]

At the same time, local citizens have continued to invest in traditional forms of lobbying, taking part in one of the first official Public Debates in France, which ran from December 2002 to May 2003, as well as the Public Inquiry that took place in 2007. But they have also undertaken high-profile media-friendly actions such as tractor blockades in city centres, vigils outside public buildings and the formation of human chains around the proposed site of the new airport. In so doing, they have engaged in what may be termed new protests of bodily risk (Doherty, 1999), which in their more extreme form saw local campaigners going on hunger strike in protest at the planned airport. Indeed, the eviction of protesters from the 'ZAD' by police in October 2012 was marked by violent clashes between protesters and the police, which attracted media attention throughout France; it led the government to impose a 'pause' on plans to develop the airport and put in place a Commission of Dialogue.

Taking a broader perspective, this 'new' politics of airport protest is increasingly common across different sites in Europe and elsewhere (see Griggs and Howarth, 2004). For example, in Germany, demonstrations against expansion at Frankfurt airport have regularly attracted between 10 000 and 20 000 people, while similar demonstrations at Berlin and Munich airports have attracted up to 15 000 and 7000 protesters respectively (Sperk, 2012). Beyond the arena of air transport, similar actions have also been undertaken against the building of other large state-led infrastructure projects, including high-speed rail route extensions, the building of nuclear power stations, incinerators and open cast mining. Indeed, in July 2013 the third European forum on 'unnecessary imposed mega-projects' brought together local citizens opposed to high-speed rail extensions, and airport expansion, including the planned airport at Notre-Dame-des-Landes.[12] Such protests may well be typical of a new form of citizen politics and protest that engages local communities and affected residents in new forms of direct action, thus assembling unexpected alliances between local groups, political campaigners and even anti-corporate protesters. But to return to our initial problematization, how are these alliances between different groups with different identities and interests brought together? What holds them together over time? And how do citizens experience such campaigns and become involved in the new strategies and tactics of such movements?

EXPLAINING THE DYNAMICS OF NEW SOCIAL MOVEMENTS AND CITIZENSHIP

Let us begin by revisiting the dynamics of the citizen campaigns against the building of a new airport at Notre-Dame-des-Landes, as well as those against expansion at London Heathrow and Manchester airports. As we argue above, the formation of political demands in these campaigns arose in part because of the dislocatory experiences felt by local residents who faced the construction of a new runway or airport. Such proposals sharply brought into question their particular ways of life, while threatening the preservation of rural villages and the conservation of valued countryside. At Manchester airport, for instance, the planned construction of a second runway was depicted as a looming 'King Kong', which threatened the extension of urban south Manchester into local communities surrounding the airport (Griggs and Howarth, 2002). Airport expansion thus came to threaten the assertion or reproduction of local identities and interests. In a similar fashion, at Notre-Dame-des-Landes, the campaign has been marked by repeated appeals to the dislocatory threats of lost farmland, biodiversity, water basins, and more importantly, the collapse of a valuable form of peasant lifestyle and agriculture, thus conjuring up visions of an encroaching modernization and industrialization. Indeed, one activist, writing of his experience of participating in the campaign, equated the proposed airport as a crime against humanity, for 'to follow the path of industrial development, the devourer of our nourishing lands, can today be compared to a crime against humanity and against the planet Earth' (Paysan Nantais, 2011, p. 4).

Yet it is important to note that the experience of dislocation and the hardening of grievances into political demands cannot be divorced from the failure of 'normal politics' or traditional modes of decision-making to respond to demands for policy change. Consider, for example, the campaign against the fifth terminal at Heathrow. Here local citizens invested heavily in the Public Inquiry on the construction of a fifth terminal. The inquiry, the longest to date in British history, ultimately came out against the protesters, and this failure of the inquiry to legitimize the demands of protesters had a huge dislocatory impact on the mobilization of local campaigners. In particular, it discredited the strategy and tactics of its leadership, and ultimately led to the resignation of the chair of the local resident group, HACAN. Similarly, campaigners at Manchester invested heavily in the Public Inquiry, and lost, thus leading one protester to suggest that 'we won the argument, but lost the decision'. And at Notre-Dame-des-Landes, campaigners bemoaned the lack of democratic decision-making, characterizing the Public Debate in 2004 as being 'without any real debate', while also suggesting that the Public Inquiry 'totally ignored the 80 per cent of contributions opposed to the project' (ibid., p. 3).

The experiences of contingency and dislocation are thus multiple and uneven. But while they may act as a catalyst for mobilization and the renewal of campaign strategies and tactics, they can equally lead to demobilization, thereby triggering the exit of local residents from the campaign. It is at such moments that the work of strategically placed entrepreneurs can exercise a critical role in the outcome of such mobilizations. In the case of Heathrow, for example, the change of leadership in HACAN ClearSkies following the Public Inquiry into the fifth terminal at Heathrow was critical in the transformation of the campaign and the engagement of local residents in new strategies and tactics. John Stewart, the new chair of HACAN ClearSkies, was schooled in the anti-roads movement in the 1980s and 1990s, and brought its broad community-based politics and practices of direct action with him into the new campaign. He was able to articulate such strategies and tactics into a transformative logic, which diversified the strategies of HACAN ClearSkies (Griggs and Howarth, 2013a).

Nonetheless, as we argue in this chapter, new social identities are never simply given but have to be discursively constructed. What is more, this cannot occur solely as a result of the resonance of particular appeals with embedded demands, nor through the simple repetition of these appeals across multiple arenas. Rather, the forging of new identities requires the drawing of new boundaries between insiders and outsiders, and in our perspective the availability of empty signifiers. At Notre-Dame-des-Landes, the anti-establishment rhetoric of campaigners constructs lines of antagonism between, on the one hand, local citizens and protesters, and, on the other hand, the state, civil servants in the Direction of Civil Aviation, and Vinci, the airport developers. Repeated appeals are made to campaigners as 'outsiders', who face a 'denial of democracy', hierarchical abuses of power from state representatives, and the dismissal of local communities in the face of 'money [that] can do everything and justify everything'. Alluding to the increased use of identity controls, helicopter surveillance, and the heavy-handed policing of local villages, campaigners thus foreground how 'the only responses to our questions are an occupation, and even a muscular and violent police repression!' Such populist appeals are further supplemented by campaign rhetoric that condemns the actions of the Prefect, which in the words of local campaigners, 'seek to intimidate and wear out people', coupled with the attempts by the state to 'divide the population' by seeding divisions between local residents and the occupants of the 'ZAD'. These latter protesters are renamed as 'new inhabitants' in efforts to reassert the lines of antagonism that divide the 'enemy' of the French state from the 'friends' opposing the construction of the new airport (ibid., pp. 1–4).

It will be recalled, however, that in our perspective identities are doubly differentiated. This means that the effectiveness of sharp and intense insider/outsider appeals cannot be divorced from the willingness and ability of campaigners to link together disparate demands in the desire to forge wider hegemonic projects, while also at times masking over any internal differences that might impede such objectives. In fact, one of the conditions for the success of the campaign against the third runway at Heathrow was the capacity of campaigners to couple demands against noise, air pollution and airport expansion, on the one hand, to demands for social justice, democratic decision-making, and corporate regulation, as well as the fight against climate change and for climate justice on the other. In so doing, campaigners first brought together local resident groups in a common campaign against airport expansion, thus transforming particular campaigns against expansion at specific sites into a universal campaign against expansion at any airport in the United Kingdom. They subsequently foregrounded the threat of rising carbon emissions from aviation, linking their struggle against airport expansion to that against climate change. They thus systematically extended the breadth of opposition against Heathrow expansion to engage local residents' groups and local authorities, MPs, environmental and conservation lobbies, direct action environmental groups, anti-capitalist activists, global justice movements and high-profile celebrities. In short, once this emergent chain of equivalences had been relatively sedimented, to oppose airport expansion was also to oppose climate change and unsustainable forms of economic growth.

Of course, the linking together of such chains of equivalences between demands is a political judgement and articulation; chains can become over-extended, thereby weakening the credibility of the claims being asserted, and thus the shared identities and interests of those engaged in the campaign. The forging of equivalences requires astute forms of leadership. At the same time, much depends on the availability of empty signifiers that can be deployed as a means of representation that can weld together internal differences, while showing the limits of the group identity, and its dependence on the opposition to other groups. In the campaign against the third runway at Heathrow airport, for example, the signifier of 'demand management' came to fulfil this function, operating as an empty point of signification, which enabled campaigners to draw antagonistic boundaries between themselves and the supporters of expansion. Evoking a Keynesian-style resolution of the problem of airport management also promised an alternative approach to the 'predict and provide' policies of the past (Griggs and Howarth, 2013a).

An integral component of the hegemonic struggle between competing political projects or coalitions is the ongoing endeavour by opposed forces to break up the chains of equivalences that confront them. One way of doing this is for one project to seek to accommodate or incorporate the demands of their rivals and vice versa. Campaigners at Heathrow sought to do just that by undermining the economic case for aviation by challenging the role of aviation as a driver of social progress, while advocating the benefits of high-speed rail as an alternative to air travel. A good case can be made that such strategic appeals provided in part the requisite conditions or 'ideological cover' for the Conservative–Liberal Coalition government to come out against airport expansion as it did in May 2010, while weakening elements of trade union and business support for airport expansion. More recently, however, proponents of expansion have rearticulated the economic arguments in favour of expansion as the need to safeguard the international hub status of British aviation. This continual refocusing of policy debates on the requirement of an international hub, and more specifically the competitiveness of Heathrow airport, poses new challenges for the anti-carbon coalition. Indeed, given the shifting context of the falling political salience of environmental questions and the continuation of economic recession, the reframing of the debate to one of the competitiveness of London as a hub poses the temptation among local campaigners to revert back to more particularistic campaigns over site location (Griggs and Howarth, 2013b).

But it is crucial to note that in making such claims we do not seek to imply that campaign strategies and tactics can simply be translated from one site of contestation to another. It is important to stress that campaigns are invariably located within broader networks of activists and local residents, which operate in distinctive cultural and political settings, and it is through such networks that different practices are usually transferred. What often occurs, therefore, is the emergence of learning across particular struggles, as repertoires of different forms of protest and action 'travel' from campaign to campaign. In our terms, they are thus reiterated: repeated and altered in the displacement. For example, the practice of challenging the economics of aviation expansion has seen both campaigners at Heathrow and Notre-Dame-des-Landes commission CE Delft, an environmental consultancy, to undertake studies on the alleged connectivity benefits from air transport. One aspect of this growing set of interactions can be explained by the veritable Europeanization of aviation policies. But it is also driven by increasing networking between activists, which is often aided and abetted by the tools of social media.

Once again, however, we would stress that the transfer of practices is not merely a case of repetition or resonance, but rests on their rearticulation by campaigners in a specific context. Here the shifting appeals of the campaign against Heathrow expansion and the building of a new airport at Notre-Dame-des-Landes offer further insight into the contextual-dependence of campaigns, that is to say, our claim that campaigns are always constituted within particular historical and social contexts. At Heathrow, as we argue, local residents came to forge equivalences between aviation and climate change, so that to be against airport expansion was to be against climate change. In the struggles at Notre-Dame-des-Landes, however, the demand to reduce emissions from aviation to tackle climate change is not foregrounded in a similar manner. Rather, campaigners persistently characterize the project to construct an international airport as a 'useless project' or a 'project without a future', labelling plans as 'a Pharoah-like project from the last century', which will be abandoned given the constraints of peak oil, for example, on air travel (Coordination, 2011). Such appeals and statements thus foreground an anti-statist discourse against a *dirigiste* French state, which campaigners frequently portray as a source of 'waste', both in terms of public funding and agricultural land (Solidarités Ecologie, 2005; Coordination, 2012). In this particular context, the protection of peasant farming or alternative models of 'slow farming' are tied to a discourse of anti-modernization, which resists an 'outlived logic: always further, quicker, bigger and fatter' (Coordination, 2011). Indeed, within the campaign, the 'ZAD' has come to exercise a symbolic role as a space in which alternative lifestyles can be put into practice through taking over abandoned farms and 'seeding the ZAD'.[13] The campaign against the new airport thus constructs its heritage and tradition through direct appeals to the famous French campaign at Larzac in the 1970s, which gained national attention as local farmers and activists sought to prevent the taking over of some 100 farms by the French army (Paysan Nantais, 2011).

CONCLUSIONS: TRANSFORMATIVE CAMPAIGNS, CITIZENS AND DEMOCRATIC GOVERNANCE

Our chapter has examined the ways in which post-structuralism offers a particular style of theorizing and ethos with which to study citizen mobilization and new social movements. In contrast to most mainstream theories, it starts from the recognition that both interests and identities are contingent and political constructs with precise discursive conditions of existence. In other words, as a style of theorizing, it draws attention to the ways in which shared interests and identities in moments of citizen mobilization are constructed politically and discursively through hegemonic projects. As we have demonstrated, a key element of such endeavours is the linking together of disparate demands and claims via the construction of frontiers between insiders and outsiders, as well as the production of empty signifiers, which enable the welding together of internal differences. Such means of representation also show the limits of the group identity that is forged, as well as its dependence on an opposition to other groups. In this approach, agency is tied to the moment of dislocation, the formulation of demands, the agglomeration of disparate demands into broader hegemonic projects and the way subjects come to identify with such demands and act upon them.

Such assumptions raise particular challenges for the leadership of movements and citizen mobilizations. Local citizen leaders wrestle with the political judgements over how best to reproduce or forge connections between the disparate demands mobilized as part of competing hegemonic projects. On the one hand, extending chains of equivalence by incorporating new demands may appear to strengthen the support behind coalitions. But, on the other hand, as more and more demands are incorporated, equivalential chains risk becoming over-extended, leading to the potential demobilization and alienation of groups of supporters. Indeed, in the case of airport protests, it can be a difficult balancing act for campaign leaderships to accommodate the demands of more conservative local residents against noise and air pollution with the demands of radical activists for anti-capitalist system change. Local residents who signed up for a campaign against airport development may baulk at the prospect of continuing their engagement in campaigns advocating demands for an end to short-haul flights as part of climate change mitigation programmes.

Challenges of this sort make visible the difficulties for campaign leaderships, which emanate from the contingency of movement politics. Movements are susceptible to dislocatory events as well as the counter-strategies of rival political groups. Notably, post-structuralist perspectives point to the absence of a virtuous cycle of success in citizen mobilization and foreground the necessity of transformative leadership within campaigns. In other words, participation does not trigger further participation, as might be assumed in social capital explanations of group mobilization, for example (Griggs and Howarth, 2004). Indeed, campaigns are often most vulnerable at their moments of success, as participants in campaigns appearing to have won their demands can question their engagement in the campaign, with the departure of the few triggering a bandwagon towards 'exit' as more and more campaigners question their involvement (Chong, 1991). Under such conditions, the challenge for campaign leaderships is that of renewal, which demands that they engage in transformative campaigns so as to realign projects with the changing political conditions.

But these emerging coalitions of citizens, lobbies and direct action campaigners also pose new challenges for government, bringing into question traditional modes of democratic governance. The coupling of disparate demands together by such coalition constitutes increasingly 'wicked issues' (Griggs and Howarth, 2013b) that cannot be confined to single-issue dimensions or for that matter a single political arena. As we have demonstrated in this chapter, for example, in the field of aviation policy novel alliances between local residents, farmers and environmentalist activists have transformed issues of aviation expansion into issues not simply of noise and air pollution or land use, but also into questions of social justice, corporate regulation, democratic decision-making and the global threat of climate change. In addition, they have diversified strategies and tactics, so that social dialogues over aviation now take place in multiple and fragmented arenas, beyond the confines of formal consultations and public inquiries. Against this background, the emergence of these new forms of protest and modes of movement politics requires, if nothing else, that governments revisit their traditional practices of governance. Of paramount importance in this regard is how best they can work to engineer political settlements in the face of what are becoming, increasingly, intractable policy controversies.

Finally, such challenges for democratic governance, coupled with the insights that post-structuralist interpretations of the dynamics of social movement campaigns provide, establish the parameters of a new research agenda in citizenship and movement politics. To begin with, the ethos of post-structuralist analysis calls for more 'thick descriptive', longitudinal studies of particular citizen campaigns and movements. It is only by undertaking engaged studies of the logics of citizen engagement, preferably over multiple cycles of protest, that post-structuralist analysts will be able to grasp the complex and shifting practices of identity formation, as well the transformative politics of campaigns and the conditions of their renewal through the formation of new alliances. Second, where desirable and possible, and contrary to the mistaken wisdom of the limits of post-structuralist perspectives, such studies should be comparative. Ideally, they should examine different local campaigns within one policy sector, across different policy sectors, and indeed across different political systems. In our view, comparative forms of analysis offer the opportunity for post-structuralists to explore in meticulous detail how different legacies and histories of campaigns come to make possible and constrain different strategies and tactics, while potentially disclosing novel insights into whether and how campaigns learn from other campaigns, embed new discursive practices into campaigns, and ultimately engage in democratic innovations. Last, by engaging in carefully selected and problematized longitudinal and comparative studies, post-structuralist analysis has the opportunity to demonstrate how its distinctive insights on radical democracy can offer innovative forms of critical evaluation for existing practices of stakeholder engagement, deliberative policy forums and modes of network governance. Such critical evaluations carry the potential of revitalizing our orthodox understandings of local democracy by helping to create new institutional spaces for local decision-making. In contributing to this new agenda of critical research post-structuralists aim to advance the understanding, explanation and imaginings of citizens and social movements.

NOTES

1. John Dryzek and Patrick Dunleavy provide an excellent survey and critical evaluation of these theoretical orientations. See Dryzek and Dunleavy (2009).
2. This section builds upon and develops ideas set out in Howarth (2000, 2009), Howarth and Griggs (2012) and Griggs and Howarth (2013a).
3. Russell Hardin has tightened Olson's original definition of 'public goods'. According to Hardin, Samuelson's definition of public goods centred on benefits that were 'indivisible' and 'non-excludable'; but because of the multiple criteria for inclusion he goes on to argue that 'very few of the goals or goods that groups seek can accurately be described as pure public goods [in Samuelson's terms]. [So] it is probably best not to confuse the analysis of collective action by treating it as a problem in the provision of public goods. [Interest group] goods need to be collective only in the sense that they are collectively provided... Olson's analysis of collective action depends only...on *de facto* infeasibility of exclusion'. See Hardin (1982, p. 19), cited in Dunleavy (1991, p. 31).
4. Olson famously and explicitly rules out explanations based purely on non-material incentives, arguing that these other motivations can be explained by recourse to material selective incentives. See Olson (1985, p. 61, n. 17).
5. In this respect, our analysis shares some affinities with the various sociological critiques of resource mobilization theory put forward. See Castells (1997) and Melucci (1989).
6. This is a central dimension of what Laclau and Mouffe call the construction of antagonistic relations. See Laclau and Mouffe (1985, pp. 122–7).
7. For a fuller analysis and application of this concept, concentrating specifically on the way 'blackness' functioned as an empty signifier, see Howarth (1995) and Griggs and Howarth (2002).
8. Our analysis here draws upon semi-structured interviews and focus groups carried out with local campaigners and protesters engaged in the struggle against airport expansion at London Heathrow and at Notre-Dame-des-Landes.
9. Anne-Marie Chabod, the co-president of ACIPA, an organization that has organized protests on the site for 13 years, accessed 9 December 2013 at http://www.english.rfi.fr/visiting-france/20130804-thousands-protest-against-new-airport-western-france.
10. For a brief history of the campaign, see the website of ACIPA, accessed 15 November 2013 at http://acipa.free.fr/Savoir/savoir.htm.
11. See the website of the ZAD occupation, accessed 14 November 2013 at http://zad.nadir.org/?lang=en.
12. For a discussion of the conference, see the Third European Forum Against Unnecessary Imposed Mega Projects webpage, accessed 14 November 2013 at http://xn--drittes-europisches-forum-xec.de/.
13. See the website of the ZAD occupation, accessed 14 November 2013 at http://zad.nadir.org/spip.php?rubrique44&lang=en.

REFERENCES

AirportWatch (n.d.), 'Notre-Dame-des-Landes: 1000 kites "occupy" the sky', accessed 8 December 2013 at http://www.airportwatch.org.uk/?p=4010.
Boggs, C. (1986), *Social Movements and Political Power: Emerging Forms of Radicalism in the West*, Philadelphia, PA: Temple University Press.
Byrne, P. (1997), *Social Movements in Britain*, London: Routledge.
Castells, M. (1977), *The Urban Question: A Marxist Approach*, London: Edward Arnold.
Castells, M. (1997), *The Power of Identity*, Oxford: Basil Blackwell.

Caute, D. (1988), '*68: The Year of the Barricades*, London: Hamish Hamilton.
Chong, D. (1991), *Collective Action and the Civil Rights Movement*, Chicago, IL: Chicago University Press.
Coordination (2011), *Sortons d'un Projet Sans Avenir!*, pamphlet, March.
Coordination (2012), *Sommes-nous Prêt-e-s à Payer Pour un Grand Projet Inutile et Présenté au Citoyen de Manière si Fallacieuse*, pamphlet, January.
Della Porta, D. and M. Diani (1999), *Social Movements: An Introduction*, Oxford: Wiley-Blackwell.
Derrida, J. (1976), *Of Grammatology*, trans. G.C. Spivak, Baltimore, MD: Johns Hopkins University Press.
Derrida, J. (1978), *Writing and Difference*, trans. A. Bass, London: Routledge.
Derrida, J. (1981), *Positions*, Chicago, IL: University of Chicago Press.
Derrida, J. (1982), *Margins of Philosophy*, Brighton: Harvester Press.
De Saussure, F. (1983), *Course in General Linguistics*, London: Duckworth.
Doherty, B. (1999), 'Paving the way: the rise of direct action against road-building and the changing character of British environmentalism', *Political Studies*, **47**(2), 275–91.
Dowding, K. (1996), *Power*, Buckingham, UK: Open University Press.
Dryzek, J. and P. Dunleavy (2009), *Theories of the Democratic State*, London: Palgrave.
Dunleavy, P. (1991), *Democracy, Bureaucracy and Public Choice*, Hemel Hempstead, UK: Harvester Wheatsheaf.
Foweraker, J. (1995), *Theorizing Social Movements*, London: Pluto.
Foucault, M. (1972), *The Archaeology of Knowledge*, London: Tavistock.
Foucault, M. (1981), 'The order of discourse', in R. Young (ed.), *Untying the Text*, London: Routledge, pp. 48–79.
Foucault, M. (1984), 'Nietzsche, genealogy, history', in P. Rabinow (ed.), *The Foucault Reader*, Harmondsworth: Penguin Books, pp. 76–100.
Glynos, J. and D. Howarth (2007), *Logics of Critical Explanation in Social and Political Theory*, London: Routledge.
Gottweis, H. (2003), 'Theoretical strategies of post-structuralist policy analysis: towards an analytics of government', in M.A. Hajer and H. Wagenaar (eds), *Deliberative Policy Analysis: Understanding Governance in the Network Society*, Cambridge, UK: Cambridge University Press, pp. 247–65.
Griggs, S. and D. Howarth (2002), 'An alliance of interest and identity? Explaining the campaign against Manchester airport's second runway', *Mobilization*, **7**(1), 43–58.
Griggs, S. and D. Howarth (2004), 'A transformative political campaign? The new rhetoric of protest against airport expansion in the UK', *Journal of Political Ideologies*, **9**(2), 167–87.
Griggs, S. and D.R. Howarth (2013a), *The Politics of Airport Expansion in the United Kingdom: Hegemony, Policy and the Rhetoric of 'Sustainable Aviation'*, Manchester: Manchester University Press.
Griggs, S. and D. Howarth (2013b), '"Between a rock and a hard place": the coalition, the Davies Commission and the wicked issue of airport expansion', *Political Quarterly*, **84**(4), 515–26.
Habermas, J. (1981), 'New social movements', *Telos*, **49**, 33–7.
Habermas, J. (1987), *The Theory of Communicative Action, Vol. 2: Lifeworld and System: A Critique of Functionalist Reason*, Cambridge, UK: Polity Press.
Hacking, I. (1985), 'Styles of scientific reasoning', in J. Rajchman and C. West (eds), *Post-Analytic Philosophy*, New York: Columbia University Press, pp. 145–64.
Hajer, M.A. (1995), *The Politics of Environmental Discourse: Ecological Modernization and the Policy Process*, Oxford: Clarendon Press.
Hall, S. (1996), 'Introduction: who needs identity?', in S. Hall and P. du Gay (eds), *Questions of Cultural Identity*, London: Sage, pp. 1–17.
Hardin, R. (1982), *Collective Action*, Baltimore, MD: Johns Hopkins University Press.
Hirschman, A.O. (1982), *Shifting Involvements: Private Interest and Public Action*, Princeton, NJ: Princeton University Press.

Howarth, D. (1995), 'Complexities of identity/difference', *Journal of Political Ideologies*, **2**(1), 55–78.
Howarth, D. (1998), 'Post-Marxism', in A. Lent (ed.), *New Political Thought: An Introduction*, London: Lawrence and Wishart, pp. 126–42.
Howarth, D. (2000), *Discourse*, Buckingham, UK: Open University Press.
Howarth, D. (2005), 'Applying discourse theory', in D. Howarth and J. Torfing (eds), *Discourse Theory in European Politics*, London: Palgrave.
Howarth, D. (2009), 'Discourse, power and policy: articulating a hegemony approach to critical policy studies', *Critical Policy Studies*, **3**(3/4), 309–35.
Howarth, D.R. (2013), *Poststructuralism and After: Structure, Subjectivity and Power*, Houndmills, UK: Palgrave Macmillan.
Howarth, D. and S. Griggs (2012), 'Poststructuralist policy analysis: discourse, hegemony and critical explanation', in F. Fischer and H. Gottweis (eds), *The Argumentative Turn Revisited: Public Policy as Communicative Practice*, Durham, NC: Duke University Press, pp. 305–43.
Howarth, D. and Y. Stavrakakis (2000), 'Introducing discourse theory and political analysis', in D. Howarth, A.J. Norval and Y. Stavrakakis (eds), *Discourse Theory and Political Analysis*, Manchester: Manchester University Press, pp. 1–23.
Lacan, J. (2006), *Écrits*, New York: W.W. Norton.
Laclau, E. (1990), *New Reflections on the Revolution of Our Time*, London: Verso.
Laclau, E. (1995), 'Why do empty signifiers matter to politics?', in J. Weeks (ed.), *The Greater Evil and the Lesser Good*, London: River Oram, pp. 168–77.
Laclau, E. (2005), *On Populist Reason*, London: Verso.
Laclau, E. and C. Mouffe (1985), *Hegemony and Socialist Strategy: Towards a Radical Democratic Politics*, London: Verso.
Laclau, E. and C. Mouffe (1990), 'Post-Marxism without apologies', in E. Laclau (ed.), *New Reflections on the Revolution of Our Time*, London: Verso, pp. 79–106.
Laclau, E. and C. Mouffe (2001), *Hegemony and Socialist Strategy: Towards a Radical Democratic Politics*, 2nd edition, London: Verso.
Melucci, A. (1988), 'Getting involved: identity and mobilization in social movements', in B. Klandermans, H. Kriesi and S. Tarrow (eds), *From Structure to Action: Comparing Movement Participation Across Cultures*, Greenwich, CT: JAI Press, pp. 329–48.
Melucci, A. (1989), *The Nomads of the Present*, London: Hutchinson.
Monbiot, G. (2007), 'Beneath the pall of misery a new movement is born', 21 August, accessed 9 December 2013 at http://www.monbiot.com/2007/08/21/beneath-the-pall-of-misery-a-new-movement-is-born/.
Oberschall, A. (1973), *Social Conflict and Social Movements*, Englewood Cliffs, NJ: Prentice Hall.
Olson, M. (1965), *The Logic of Collective Action*, Cambridge, MA: Harvard University Press.
Panizza, F. (ed.) (2005), *Populism and the Mirror of Democracy*, London: Verso.
Paysan Nantais (2011), 'Dossier: Projet d'Aéroport: Gardons les Terres Nourricières', extract, Issue 1244, 1–4, accessed 13 May 2014 at http://acipa.presse.free.fr/Articles/PaysanNantais201109.pdf.
Scott, A. (1990), *Ideology and the New Social Movements*, London: Allen and Unwin.
Smelser, N. (1962), *Theories of Collective Behaviour*, London: Routledge and Kegan Paul.
Solidarités Ecologie (2005), 'Notre-Dame-des-Landes: Projet Inutile, Nuisible et Ruineux', newsletter, Spring.
Sperk, F. (2012), 'A new third runway at Munich airport?', 12 May, accessed 9 December 2013 at http://www.foeeurope.org/node/896.
Tarrow, S. (1978), 'National politics and collective action: recent theory and research in Western Europe and the United States', *Annual Review of Sociology*, **14**, 421–40.
Taylor, M. (1995), 'Battering rams', *Critical Review*, **9**(1–2), 223–34.
Tilly, C. (1978), *From Mobilization to Revolution*, Reading, MA: Addison-Wesley.
Torfing, J. (2005), 'Discourse theory: achievements, arguments, and challenges', in

D. Howarth and J. Torfing (eds), *Discourse Theory in European Politics*, Houndmills, UK: Palgrave Macmillan, pp. 1–32.

Touraine, A. (1981), *The Voice and the Eye: An Analysis of Social Movements*, Cambridge, UK: Cambridge University Press.

Touraine, A. (1985), 'An introduction to the study of new social movements', *Social Research*, **52**(4), 749–87.

14. Social movements and emotions
Helena Flam

INTRODUCTION

In the US in the 1970s and 1980s, research on social movements equated social movements with political 'challengers' seeking to capture or gain influence over the state in opposition to the 'incumbents' (Tilly, 1978). Or it posited an analogy between social movements and industry: it cast movement leaders as 'movement entrepreneurs' and mobilized individuals as rational actors who seek to realize their goals by choosing between different 'movement organizations' (McCarthy and Zald, 1977). About the same time, the sociology of emotions emerged, but was neither well-known nor appreciated.

This entry starts by presenting early research on emotions and social protest, focusing on the role of anger and loyalty. Thereafter two widely received US approaches to the study of emotions in social movements and the 'emotional turn' receive much attention. Research on single transformative and 'nagging' protest events that tear up the self-congratulatory social and political fabric is presented next. Finally, I highlight emotions emerging during the interactions between social movements and various government institutions, within nation-states, and across state borders. Criticisms and remarks concerning future research directions close this contribution.

PART I

Emotions and Mobilization

In the 1970s a renowned historian and several sociologists looked for the preconditions of individual and mass defiance. They asked what explains the emergence of moral outrage, moving people to rebel against established authorities. Their Locke-inspired answer was: elites breaking socio-economic or political contracts. This answer made mobilization seem both rational and legitimate.

Moore, Jr (1978) drew on the early twentieth-century German working class history to propose that it is a matter of long-term contingent developments, marked by radicalizing and de-radicalizing events and their interpretations, that ultimately decide whether or not *new* standards of justice and condemnation will emerge, the alter-ego will become defined as an opponent who has breached moral norms, and it is concluded that this opponent deserves to be confronted with justified expressions of massive moral outrage. Fireman et al. (1979), based on three encounters and 33 laboratory experiments, similarly argued that processes leading up to the development of moral outrage are time-consuming and highly contingent. Some individuals react with immediate disbelief, anger, and disgust towards transgressions of what they see as widely accepted moral standards by persons in positions of authority. They are quick to feel moral outrage. Others need more time. The experiments showed that individuals randomly assigned to various groups when presented with evident breaches of norms by persons in position of authority engage in symbolic, both oral and bodily, communication to establish whether a breach in fact happened and moral outrage is called for. If so, negotiations begin about who is to lead the protest and how it should be framed and shaped. A collective decision to act on the shared sense of moral outrage is thus presupposed by early successes in delicate bonding processes and initial organizing attempts. Zeroing on 'passionate' protest, Flam (1988, p. 94; 1990, p. 43) pinpointed that it constitutes the *volte face* of political apathy and daily routine.

This rare response to exploitation and marginalization remains an important source of the unexpected in social and political life. Fascinated by the unexpected eruptions of angry protest and its cultural embeddedness, Scott (1990) proposed a hydraulic model of anger. Using many empirical cases as illustrations he argued that the dominated usually hide their anger at being oppressed behind a mask of apathy for fear of repercussions. Instead of openly rebelling, they resort to anonymous or disguised, hard-to-detect, and therefore low-cost forms of resistance, such as poaching, shabby work or irony. The dominated groups when possible create their own defiant cultures with distinct speech and practice patterns. Unexpectedly even to the rebels themselves, their anger explodes in the face of the oppressor. The protests move the frontier between the official culture and the culture of 'hidden transcripts'. Taking up Bakhtin, Scott drew attention to the medieval and contemporary carnivalesque protest forms, launching a debate on whether these 'merely' periodically release anger or have a revolutionary potential. However, neither of these texts on expressions of collective anger became a citational hit. The mere label 'hot cognition' (Gamson, 1992, pp. 7, 31–2) became a citational hit instead.

Dead Ends

In a German-language text Nedelmann (1986) developed a process-focused approach to the study of social movement mobilization and issue cycles. She proposed that when the opposing groups manage to emotionalize and dichotomize the issue by relying on such polarizing slogans as 'No Nukes' or 'Right to Life', successful mobilization and placing the issue on the national agenda become likely. To regain control and neutralize the issue, politicians remove it from the public agenda, delegating it to experts or 'apolitical' investigative commissions who split the issue into ever-finer sub-issues that hinder broad mobilization. The mobilized groups, in their turn, try to block or reverse such attempts and keep the issue hot. Her text found no echo (but see Flam, 1994, p. 18f). In the USA, McAdam's beautifully argued *Freedom Summer* (1988) probably won large numbers of newcomers to the field of social movement research. It vibrated with emotions, but McAdam did not analyze them in their own right (Flam, 2000, pp. 135–6, 144–5).

Most attempts to speak about emotions actually came from the unorthodox economists exploring rational organizations (Hirschman, 1970), rational choice (Olson, 1965), and the soft edges of rationality (see in Flam, 1990). Drawing on these and the work of Simmel and Hochschild, Flam (1990) proposed an emotional model as an alternative to the then prevailing normative and rational models of action. Leaning on theorizing about intentional communities and the burgeoning sociology of emotions, she argued that social movement mobilization starts not only with those acting out of a sense of duty, but also with passionate solidaristic core groups. These intentionally stabilize their own reproduction and lower the costs of joining for the rational, calculating individuals, thus overcoming the problem of high threshold to collective action posited by the rational choice theorists.

In his famous *Exit, Voice and Loyalty*, Hirschman (1970) argued that loyal members play a key role in deteriorating organizations, as they are more likely to voice criticism and stay on despite deterioration, giving reform a chance. In contrast, a political scientist, Pizzorno (1986), pinpointed that the most loyal members, who he dubbed 'identifiers', never leave their organizations. Denying deterioration, they prevent self-administered change (cf. Norgaard, 2011).

While the unorthodox economists favored theorizing supported by fictional examples or discrete pieces of information, a couple of European sociologists pursued similar questions, relying on autobiographic-narrative interviews. Della Porta (1991, 1995) showed that loyalty in the Italian left-wing student movement of the 1960s shaped decisions about 'descending' into the underground following repressive state responses and, later, when some members of the underground were imprisoned, not taking the exit option. Flam (1993; 2005, pp. 31–2) argued that emotions underpin the social order shaping dominant identities, and that therefore not only cognitive liberation (McAdam, 1988) but also emotional liberation has to take place for the individual to adopt a dissenting identity. Comparing Polish and East German dissidents in the Soviet bloc before its demise (Flam, 1998), she showed that loyalty to other dissidents, a pronounced sense of the individual and collective 'honor' helping to overcome repression-related fears, and a collectively developed symbolic world, closed the exit doors for many Polish opposition members. This was not the case in much more individualistic, leader-and-history-averse East German dissident groups whose members quit or left for West Germany when given a chance (see also Adams, 2003; Gould, 2009; Kleres, 2012).

Widely Acknowledged Pioneer Approaches to the Study of Emotions

In the USA, working from a gender and cultural perspective but attentive to emotions, Taylor, along with her PhD students, Whittier (Taylor and Whittier, 1995) and Van Willigen (Taylor and Van Willigen, 1996), and her lifelong associate, Rupp (Taylor and Rupp, 2002), among others, investigated various self-help groups organized by women. They argued that self-help groups should not be seen as merely expressive or cultural groups but be recognized as the political challengers to the prevailing gender, cultural, institutional, and legal-political order. The ongoing neoliberal privatization and professionalization of the public welfare programs and the emerging new services, as they pointed out, intensify stigmatization processes, subjecting individuals to control by the institutions operating with narrow medical, legal, and criminal categories (Taylor and Leitz, 2010). An entire spectrum of emotions compels women who are subject to various forms of victimization or stigmatization to establish or to join self-help groups (Taylor and Van Willigen 1996, pp. 128–33). Faced with the indifference of their absentee husbands, society or the medical profession and the disabling illness, women with breast cancer and postpartum depression that Taylor and Van Willigen studied, suffered from feelings of suppressed anger, sense of injustice, and humiliating disregard, without daring to express these emotions. Self-help groups offered the novelty of individual self-expression. They provided emotional, moral, and informational support. The groups questioned the images and codes attached to femininity, home, motherhood, and sexuality; created new, defiant individual and collective identities, working for the greater acceptance of these innovations by the public; and modified, when successful, definitions of illness as well as laws and practices pertaining to patient treatment and medication. In general, these types of homogeneous self-help movements counter victimization and stigmatization by defining 'new collective identities', drawing new 'boundaries' around and offering compassion to all those with shared emotional experience: they help them to learn to negotiate these boundaries with the public and with various institutions (Bernstein, in Taylor and Leitz, 2010, p. 278; see also Flesher Fominaya, 2010).

This line of research (Britt and Heise, 2000; Gould, 2001) posited negative emotions such as shame, guilt, and self-hate as characteristic of gender, lesbian, homosexual, and other 'stigmatized' identities. These were said to constitute the motivation to join social movements that redefined and improved their self-images, while moving their members to feel angry and proud. The thesis that social movements neutralize debilitating and reinforce empowering self-directed emotions had a strong echo among researchers concerned with stigmatized groups engaged in collective action to redefine their negative public identities and societal status. Since the focus was on the micro-level transformation from shame to anger and pride, leading social movement scholars dismissed its agenda as too narrow for generalists.

Jasper and Poulsen (1995, p. 493) provided another micro-level approach. They introduced the concept of 'moral shocks' to account for the recruitment of newcomers to movements and thus challenged the network-focused accounts of mobilization: while friends and acquaintances can be mobilized relying on the already established networks, 'moral shocks' explain how total strangers become mobilized. Jasper's (1998a, 1998b) contribution was to stress the significance of situations or events that raise:

> such a sense of outrage in people that they become inclined toward political action, even in the absence of network contacts. These are usually public events, unexpected and highly publicized. . . such as the accident at the Three Mile Island. . .nuclear plant. . .but they can also be the experiences of individuals, as the gradual discovery that one's drinking water has been contaminated. (Jasper and Poulsen, 1995, p. 498)

Social movement organizers try to 'generate' moral shocks through their rhetorical appeals. The concept of 'moral shocks' has been widely used as a catchall phrase ever since, ignoring the authors' original definition.

Jasper's (1998a) text on the emotions of protest moved beyond the concept of moral shocks. Taking up key concepts such as blame attribution, frame alignment, collective identity, cognitive liberation, and movement culture, Jasper pointed out that in fact each of these concepts is unthinkable without emotions, as emotions rather than pure cognition or values propel individuals to act (on how emotions interweave with framing, movement cultures, collective identities or opportunity structures, see Ruiz-Junco, 2013). All apart from moral shocks and mobilizing, durable emotions towards nature and family, neighborhood or country, movement members also share negative emotions towards those they blame for injustice or see threatening their lives or lifestyles, and experience reciprocal positive emotions towards movement members. The last two sets of emotions reinforce each other, creating, along with various emotionalizing movement rituals, a basis for collective solidarity.

The Emotional Turn

Research on social movements and emotions took off after Goodwin and Jasper organized meetings on social movements and emotions before, at and after the congress of the American Sociological Association of 1998. Their own publications as well as the organizational initiatives and editorial efforts shared with Polletta (2000, 2004), increased the visibility of emotions in social movement research. The edited volume (Goodwin et al., 2001) includes sparse references to the US sociology of emotions. Among the contributors to this volume we find some post-World War II classics of sociology, such as Randall Collins and Craig Calhoun, and also a classic of the sociology of emotions, Theodore Kemper. They suggested, for example, that we should look at how specific emotion-expressing movement families develop and compete for limited public attention; inspect the emotional, interactional habitus of movements or compare emotions attached to organizations and institutions to those intersubjectively generated in social movements; and refine frame analysis by investigating how differences in the status and power of the bystanders influence their emotions and thus their responses to movement frames and actions. The volume itself echoed and expanded Verta Taylor's and James Jasper's approaches to social movements. Several contributors, writing on protest and social movements in non-Western countries, introduced their own takes on emotions.

Whittier's (2001) contribution stood out. She showed that movement participants reflect, discuss, and promote a mixture of victimization-related and self-assertive oppositional emotions in the movement settings, while strategically adapting their emotional displays to the requirements of public settings. While government agencies providing services to victims call for a display of victimization-related emotions, media and courts responding to professional controversies and counter-movement pressures may require displays of cool rationality. Whittier's text has inspired other researchers to investigate the bifurcation of emotions between movement and public settings (Kenney, 2009). Research explicating complex connections between framing, emotions, and target audiences generated even more complex results (Cadeno-Roa, 2002; Dunn, 2004; Bonds, 2009).

Almost parallel to Goodwin et al. (2001), a special issue of *Mobilization* (2002) devoted to emotions appeared, guest edited by Aminzade and McAdam. The same year, Tilly et al. (2002, pp. 14–50) published a (strikingly atheoretical, ad hoc) chapter on 'Emotions and contentious politics' in an edited volume *Silence and Voice in the Study of Contentious Politics* (Aminzade et al., 2002). These authors referred mostly to their earlier work in which emotions were adjectives or adverbs but never posited as an explicit theoretical concern. These volumes signaled that emotions have become legitimate research objects.

After the XVth congress of the International Sociological Association in Brisbane, Australia that took place in 2002, Flam and King brought out *Emotions and Social Movements* (2005, p. 19), arguing for connecting the micro-politics of social movements to the realm of meso- and macro-politics. Flam in particular called for attention to be paid to the 'cementing' emotions holding up social structures and relations of domination in order to show how social movements attempt to weaken some, such as fear or self-shame, while re-appropriating, redirecting, and intensifying others, such as pride, anger or solidarity, all along specifying the actors to whom they should be attached. Social movements try to affect a transfer of loyalties and trust away from the dominant system. Importantly, emotions – their direction and intensity – become the very stakes of the struggle. The collection innovated by discussing not only the importance of emotions for the initial and continued mobilization but also by investigating the emotional dynamics among and between the protesters and onlookers (Benski, Eyerman, Flam, and Yang), between two different social movements at war within a single policy sector (Hopkins), and between two movements that merged during a reunification of two states (Kleres). It also addressed emotions of movement members that emerged over time (Kleres) and jarred with those prescribed by the movement (King), leading these members to engage in extra-movement 'therapies' (King) or to exit (Kleres). It showed that (and how) online protest visuals (Wettergren) and movement rituals (Summers-Effler; see also Hercus, 1999; 2005, pp. 125–9; Schmidt, 2013) generate emotions.

It was the duo Goodwin and Jasper, sometimes joined by Polletta, rather than the more established authors, who engaged in the entrepreneurship on emotions, turning out several texts on the topic (Goodwin and Jasper, 1999, 2004, 2007a, 2007b; Goodwin et al., 2000, 2001, 2004). They pinpointed that emotions are relevant to every phase of mobilization: recruitment, consolidation, and dissolution.

Under the heading of 'emotional resonance' sophisticated work followed. Robnett (2004) discussed complex dynamics between practices, frames, and emotional resonance: after the initially wished for limited influx of 'whites' into a civil rights organization, the Student Nonviolent Coordinating Committee expanded, and some arrogant and self-assertive newcomers marginalized the burgeoning 'black' leadership. This undermined, painfully for many, the emotional resonance of the racial equality frame, leading to the decision to get rid of the 'whites'. The proposal to formalize gender equality resonated with 'white' but not 'black' women active in this organization.

Texts by Taylor and colleagues have celebrated friendship and solidarity as well as smooth transitions from self-help to politicized groups via oppositional emotions encouraged by the self-exploration settings. Schrock et al. (2004) provided an interesting contrast by highlighting intra-group conflicts and settings in which self-help depoliticizes and skirts real issues (see also Whittier, 2009 or Rousiley and Garcez, 2014). Schrock et al. documented for a transgender (TG) group that its members joined self-help groups to find relief from excruciating and debilitating feelings of isolation, shame, fear, and alienation. They were indeed able, even though in a time- and space-limited way, to enjoy group solidarity. Groups united in rejecting both psychiatric and Christian frames, casting them respectively as pathological and sinful. However, the heterogeneous groups of cross-dressers and transsexuals that accepted therapeutic frames stressing personal authenticity and experience found each other's self-definitions and lifestyles infuriating. This led to internal conflicts detracting attention from the shared oppression. Furthermore experiences of violence and humiliation were turned into a joke. Although emotion work in the support groups helped overcome many debilitating emotions, these groups:

> undermined a more complete emotional transformation. Both the[ir] success and failure... [became] resources for SMOs. SMOs' motivational framing promised to meet the...emotional needs [of the mixed group members] which created the conditions for emotional resonance. SMOs promised potential recruits solidarity and authenticity by constructing a collective identity; promoted pride and self-efficacy by encouraging TG people to stand up for their rights; and validated and stoked TG people's anger at harassers and discriminators. (Schrock et al., 2004, p. 71)

Gould's long-awaited *Moving Politics* (2009, pp. 166–71) offered a series of compelling arguments and empirical material while discussing political opportunity structures, frames or identity-related emotion work. Gould (ibid., pp. 32–42, 106, 119, 427) proposed that social movements have a multifaceted – emotional, cognitive, normative – yet stable habitus. Focal in the book is the emotional habitus: both social movements and their members are self-divided in their emotions about self and society at large – they feel joy and pride at signs of social recognition and shame and anger at too little of it. They feel despair and hope about their own or a specific world condition they are concerned about. The eventful context of the movements' emergence and consolidation shapes their emotional habitus, favoring some emotions while downplaying others. This habitus determines a specific political horizon and a legitimate range of protest activities. In the case of gay and lesbian AIDS-crisis movement the habitus favored moderation. It was first when political events caused widespread moral outrage among movement participants that the leaders offering frames addressing and amplifying anger (and expressing or reviving hope) could achieve substantive mobilizing successes over those urging moderation. Moral outrage, fueled by anger, made for a new political horizon, and with it new – stronger, more militant – forms of protest. Soon thereafter ACT UP – a movement of people 'united in anger' and committed to civil disobedience – staged its first protests (Gould, 2009, p. 131). These were interwoven with the joy of constructing new worlds and planning protests just as much as with intense socializing, erotic excitement and collective fear, euphoria, and effervescence. When the pull and the gravity of the movement is that great, crumbling hopes, intense disappointment, hurt, betrayal or guilt accompany conflicts and quitting.

PART II

Transformative Protest Events

A long, intellectual tradition associates the name of Gustave LeBon, with protesting events, masses and irrationality. Charles Tilly and his collaborators reversed this tradition: protest events constitute confrontations between unequal groups equipped with uneven resources pursuing their interests in opposition to each other. Inspecting the press reports, one can codify and quantify various aspects of protest events to find out whether there is a discernible pattern of contestation over time and any national differences in actor constellations, action repertoires, and state involvement (Tilly et al., 1975). In contrast 'protest event analysis' asks whether specific cycles of protest can be detected, seeking to account for them in terms of political opportunity structures, organizational resources or issue cycles (Moore, 2011, pp. 296–8). Both lines of investigation establish protesters as rational actors.

Departing from these trends from the late 1990s on, several authors brought emotions into the studies of protest events without forsaking the basic idea that protesters are rational actors. They stressed that protest events are generated by long-term structural differences in power between those involved in the conflict. They recognized that what I would like to call 'protest emotions' are context dependent, that is, situated, interactional, and temporal. Their key insight was that protest events entail rapid reconfigurations of feelings and ideas, pushing forward action constitutive of the protest event, and that both protest and protest-evoked emotions have transformative effects. Partaking in the 'cultural', 'narrative', and 'spatial' turns, they all analyzed the role of space, narrative, discourse, and creativity in protest.

A Chicago-based scholar, Sewell (1996, p. 865), took on the category of 'watershed', 'momentous', 'remarkable' emotion-laden protest events. His analysis started with structural dislocation, leading to the duality of powers, tension, and insecurity about which interests, cosmology, morality, and underlining emotions to follow. The momentous, emotion-laden event itself – the taking of the Bastille in Paris, France in 1789 – was not mainly constituted by its inherently exceptional routine-breaking dimensions, but rather by its interpretation as extraordinary by the contenders for power. Although the watershed event already in part determines the winner in the ongoing power struggles, it is its public symbolic-emotional elaboration that seals the outcome, and results in a profound socioeconomic, cultural, and political transformation. Co-constitutive of this particular event as extraordinary was that the General Assembly focused on and creatively signified (cf. Moore, 2011) the taking of the Bastille (rather than any other similar event) as violent but self-restrained revolution against an abusive state, staged by the sovereign people for the sake of national liberty.

Petronijewić (1998) investigated the three-months-long mass protests that started in November 1996 in Belgrade, Serbia against the political rule by Milosević. She innovates by stressing that the protesters had to overcome fear of violent repression to break the silence about their unwilling political subjugation. They did so by taking possession of the means of signification in their own hands to express their status as citizens disdainful and contemptuous of the corrupt political elites. She also innovates by depicting a self-disciplined, peaceful, carnivalesque protest that employed humor and ridicule rather than violence to confront and demand the abdication of the political elite. Petronijewić (ibid., pp. 269–71, 277) focused on the creative use of urban space and artistic forms of symbolic challenge:

the protesters employed eggs, red paint, toilet paper, condoms, and disinfectant to display open animosity, disdain, and contempt towards specific public institutions. Through badges and narratives they expressed admiration for martyrs and heroes of protest, shamed passive bystanders by asking seemingly innocent questions and the police by putting mirrors to their faces. Taking a stroll with a horse or a fish aquarium together with tens of thousands of protesters to stake out the 'democratic topography of Belgrade', the protesters ridiculed the authorities and felt protected against state violence. When the elites resorted to massive violence, the protesters stayed put, taking their toll of killed and wounded. The joy and exaltation were great when, having lost the control of the city, Milosević and his clique realized they had to give up the state as well.

Barker (1986, 2001) analyzed the stockyard strike leading to the emergence of the Polish official trade union movement Solidarność. Countering old crowd theories attributing irrationality to the milling masses, he showed that whenever deep uncertainty prevails about the course of the protest itself – who will join, how to run the protest, what to expect from the opponents – the protesters might very well look like an irrational, volatile crowd. But in fact, during these moments of great moral, emotional, and strategic significance, the activists engage in sense-making and communication, setting the stage for the future. In contrast, the moment of organizational and substantive consolidation is marked by apprehension, seriousness, and concentration. In the final phase either emotions of defeat or the exuberant rejoicing at the unprecedented victory become visible. In this particular case the extraordinary grounds for rejoicing consisted in the official recognition of Solidarność, a promise to release all detainees and to fulfill all of its 21 demands.

Yang's (2000) analysis of the student protest in Tiananmen Square in Beijing in 1989 focuses on the changes in the participants' identities and emotions. Yang's main thesis is that students and their supporters pursued emotional achievement by joining the protest and partaking in the unfolding protest drama. After the first successful protest the students, greatly relieved by the peaceful conclusion of the demonstration, dispersed. A few weeks of frustration with the inconclusive end of the confrontation and boredom (with the socialist routine), compelled them to call for a hunger strike. For most, anxiety and fear of the consequences lost the inner battle against the urge to pursue self-expression and self-validation in heroic protest action. The outpouring of parent support and unprecedented media and large-scale popular display of compassion and bravery greatly encouraged the students. Like these students, farmers flowing into the capital took their chance of joining in the extraordinary. The protesting students persevered against all odds in Tiananmen Square, some until the bitter, death-bringing end. Yang cast emotions as expressing and validating personal and collective identities. He proposed that self-validating emotions press individuals and collectivities to ignore, challenge or break norms pertaining to emotions, the so-called feeling rules, when these call for emotions management that hinders emotional self-expression and validation (ibid., pp. 595–7; see also Yang, 2005). New in Yang's text is the very idea of human emotional intentionality and its particular manifestation: the pursuit of extraordinary, heroic, and collective emotions by individuals and groups. Also new is the stress on the self-conscious communication and dramatization of emotions by the protesters and their allies.

A detailed comparison of the Arab Uprisings (Pearlman, 2013) shows that emotions help focus blame, switch the cost–benefit calculus, and increase the propensity to act on one's values, leading to broad political mobilization. For decades the Arab regimes had cultivated institutions, practices, and discourses instilling dispiriting emotions such as cynicism and pessimism among their citizens. However, once these citizens experienced moral shocks (Tunisia) or neighbor-envy, hurt self-pride, and hope (Egypt), they switched to emboldening emotions such as moral outrage. Even then, the fear was great and had to be overcome, but the tactical mistakes of the power-holders, the accumulated anger at the disdained, corrupt rulers, the empowering joy of acting together and hope that things might improve helped to keep it under control. Pearlman's text meets current utilitarian and value-rational arguments by showing how paying attention to emotions helps to answer questions they cannot.

Disparate protest events each have their own emotional constellation and developments (Flam, 2004, 2005; Benski, 2011) emerging from the interactions with the co-demonstrators, allies, passersby, and the opponent(s). They are marked by long-term structure-generated emotions pertaining to the opponent and potential allies.

'Nagging' Protest Events

The previously depicted protest events had long-term structural causes, were spontaneous and deeply transformative. They contrast with protest events that also have profound structural causes but, although meant to break the silence about taboo issues, do not produce immediate or mid-term political transformation. Yet they do manage to become routinized as an extremely irritating thorn in the social and political fabric, and in the long run contribute to change. There is hardly any research on the contrasts between short protest events and recurring protests. Benski (2005) argues that short protest events call for and call forth very intense emotions, in contrast to recurring protest events associated with moderate emotions.

Mobilized grieving mothers, starting with the pioneering case of Las Madres de Playa de Mayo (the 14 founders marched in Buenos Aires in April 1977), have attempted to break the silence about the regimes responsible for the disappearances, torture, and political killings of their children, or the extremely cruel draft, training, and combat practices of the military (Flam, 2013a). Grieving mothers stage regular 'innocent' protest events, acting the part of haunting memories. They are usually first met with ridicule and repression. When they persevere despite ridicule, harassment, arrests and disappearances decimating their ranks, they grow in numbers and achieve some support, which helps to insure elevated and protected status. Hundreds of grieving mothers' organizations can be found across the globe. The most well known are those in Argentina, Chile, Cuba, El Salvador, Israel, Guatemala, Nicaragua, Russia, China, Kashmir, and Iran.

Just like the Argentinian Las Madres, the Israeli Women in Black (WiB) have served as a model worthy of imitation around the world. The first Israeli WiB vigils took place in 1988; ever since, WiB have conducted silent vigils each Friday against the 'Occupation' in several central locations. Benski (2005) and others characterize the vigils as 'breaching events'. With very modest means they powerfully challenge cultural and political coding of women and of the Israeli state by occupying a central rather than a peripheral place; protesting when they should be preparing for the holy supper; and wearing power- and grief-communicating black dresses. They refuse to show solidarity with the Israeli state, accusing it of aggression instead. Their vigils provoke some supportive responses, but Benski (2005, 2011), focusing on the Haifa WiB, draws attention to the multifaceted verbal and bodily expressions of anger, hate, disgust, and contempt with which – mostly male – car and truck drivers have responded to these regular protest events (for another form of breaking the silence, see Katriel, 2009 and Katriel and Shavit, 2013).

The quilts devoted to the memory of AIDS victims play the part of uncomfortable, haunting memories to those who would rather forget or not know. The NAMES Project AIDS Memorial Quilt, widely known through media reports, enjoys nearly iconic status (Power, 2011, pp. 45–159). Where statistics tire, a colorful quilt personalizes and draws people in by telling a story:

> [by] encouraging viewers to make an empathetic connection to people who have died from AIDS through the details depicted on its panels, the Quilt plays a role in extending the emotional impact of the AIDS epidemic beyond the borders of the gay community... By encouraging an emotional reaction

from its viewers, the Quilt has the potential to recast prejudice towards both gay men and people with HIV/AIDS. (Power, 2011, p. 152)

Some activists argue that the Quilt sanitizes homosexuality and AIDS, and does nothing about deep-seated homophobia and AIDS stigma, yet they acknowledge its capacity to win public support for people with AIDS in particular and the gay community in general. The Australian AIDS Memorial Quilt is also subversive in breaking the taboo on openly grieving one's 'illicit' love. The Quilt helps to gain the recognition that gay people have the right to grieve for and be angry about losing their loved ones.

Challenging and Shaping Policies

Social movement research in the US has just begun to concern itself with the study object variously called the organizational field, policy sector, field of contention or field of strategic action (Martin, 2005; Whittier, 2009; Taylor and Zald, 2010; Fligstein and McAdam, 2011). Some ideas are already in place, but it is a research field still under construction.

As Taylor and Van Willigen (1996) showed early on, the women affected by breast cancer and postpartum depression not only questioned and redefined gender codes, effecting cultural change, but also achieved significant advances in the medical sector. They pressed the male-dominated medical profession to modify their definitions of and views on postpartum depression and breast cancer. The anger and moral outrage mobilized the activists to press for medication, more sensitive and respectful types of medical treatment, and laws pertaining to patient treatment. By following their activists, Taylor and Van Willigen made the first forays into various policy sectors.

Hopkins et al. (2005) focused on the conflict between the Disabled People's Movement (DPM) and the Feminist Movement (FM) in Britain about the type of assistance they should receive. The DPM fought for dignity and autonomy for disabled people by demanding that these should have the option of choosing and paying for their care. It called for a break with past demeaning stigmatization as passive, pitiable, and in need of altruistic help. The FM argued that the DPM was giving in to the neoliberal commercialization of everyday life: by renouncing emotions and interdependence involved in personal care, the DPM deepened the commodification and exploitation of care workers – overwhelmingly comprised of women. The article innovated by focusing on the opposing discourses of two worthwhile movements, highlighting the emotions of the disabled and their caretakers to argue for different institutional policy recommendations. It staked out a promising research path by pointing out that highly appreciated social movements can be pitted against each other rather than just the market or the state.

In her book, *The Politics of Child Sexual Abuse* (2009) Whittier's point of departure is the time when sexual child abuse and incest were unseen, perpetrators dismissed as rare pathological cases, and victims or their mothers given the blame. Between the 1970s and the 1990s several movements concerned with sexual child abuse emerged, each attributing different experiences, emotions, and needs to the focal group. Whittier presents the discourses, practices, and agendas of the patriarchal feminists, the feminist self-help movement, and the single-issue survivors' movement. She highlights how and which of these became captured by the therapeutic, medical, and judicial professions, adopted and modified by the mass media, and countered by the conservatives and the 'false memory' parents' counter-movement (2009, pp. 9, 91, 93, 106, 133–66). Whittier pays homage to the complexity of real-life situations in which an innocent victim of the violence wielded by the pervasive patriarchical power system appears simultaneously as a vulnerable, shame- and guilt-ridden fractured human being in need of healing and an empowered and self-confident survivor breaking the silence about a mass phenomenon that has to be countered. When relating what happened, this victim-survivor is confronted by the insensitivity, mistrust, and hostility of the police, doctors, judges as well as the undesired embraces, hatred, and dismissal of the 'false memory' parents' movement. One great contribution of this book is to show that the feminist movement became involved in knowledge production, national agenda-setting, legal contestation, professionalization, service provision, medical and social innovation, and multifaceted political and policy work, just like the allegedly 'brainier' and instrumental environmental movements. The second great contribution is to highlight an endless number of emotional ties created by both cementing and subversive emotions of shame, guilt, anger, pride, gratitude, solidarity, fear, resentment, envy, and hatred. These at times united and at times pitted against each other various social movements, institutions, and communities, criss-crossed by gender and 'race', merging them all into one large, heavily emotionalized 'issue community'. Whittier's is a truly Simmelian-Tonniesian opus that pays heed to the many ways in which communities are welded by emotions and deeply marked by power.

When Whittier (2009, pp. 16, 182–207) looks at the complex intersections between the policy-makers and various movement organizations entering the mainstream to combat sexual abuse, emotions are not focal. In contrast, Power's (2011) account of the responses to AIDS in Australia pays much attention to emotions. It is based on interviews with activists, politicians, and experts. Her book divides the movement into the phases of fear, anger, and grief. She shows how the fear of homosexuality and AIDS-caused death blocked political and medical interest in AIDS, even among politicians sympathetic to the gay community. The upset and outraged gay community, which soon split up between moderates and radicals, built up its expertise, relying on its own doctors and networks. Later, several investigative and decision-making bodies as well as the medical profession – even if extremely reluctantly – came to rely on this expertise. Mass media campaigns warning about AIDS addressed everybody. The early inclusion of the gay community experts in the consultative, investigative and decision-making bodies led to 'boundary-crossing' (Ariss, in Power, 2011, p. 139), nationwide support for the long overdue drug regulation reforms, and other victories for the gay movement, which affected many policy sectors. The book tells too how emotion-laden, full of suspicion, mistrust and hatred, were the battles for co-determination in medical and administrative matters. Simultaneously the medical profession was glad of research funds that came its way thanks to the militancy of the gay community.

Even further-reaching in its ambition is the undertaking of Kleres (2012). He criticizes the literature on NGOs and the Third Sector for its negative definition of this sector as neither the state nor the market, and the social movement research for its neglect of the question of how social movements and policy-makers interact and why even well-established movement organizations dissolve. He combines autobiographic research on emotions with modified neo-corporatism and neo-institutionalism to understand how a new policy sector emerges where earlier activism prevailed. One of his compelling arguments is that how individuals *feel* about the group they engage for and about the hegemonic power structures, determines the type of civic action they will end up pursuing. Solidarity towards the group combined with the anger and frustration directed towards the hegemonic powers imply militant political activism. Compassion or pity for the 'needy' combined with a belief in active citizenship but no emotions towards the hegemonic powers implies (moderate) voluntarism. Professionalism, cast as a third type of civic action, builds on taking pride in serving or helping others *and* following professional norms and ideals – these call for expertise- and authority-embracing conduct. The same two factors in sum decide (1) which type of civic action individuals are likely to pursue, (2) whether they will envision and try to build a reform- and service-oriented or instead militant and anti-hegemonic movement organization, (3) whether they will welcome, reluctantly engage with or completely reject outside pressures to professionalize, to cooperate or to bid for public resources, and finally (4) whether they will support or reject the dissolution of their organization when it changes.

Looking at the output side, nearly 20 years before these three studies Martin (2005) started investigating the dynamic intersection between the feminist movement and public institutions involved in rape cases, asking to what extent these show sensitivity and compassion to the victims. She took on countering the prevailing feminist view that these institutions had managed to subvert and co-opt the feminist movement almost immediately after it succeeded in putting rape and sexual abuse on the national agenda. For southern Florida Martin demonstrated that the feminist movement greatly improved how the police and crisis center workers, but not how judges and doctors deal with the minds, bodies, and emotions of the rape victims. Not gender or class, but instead organizational goals and work conditions determine whether the personnel take time and display any compassion towards the victims of rape.

States

Research on emotions directed towards the state or its institutions is very scarce and random. However, Berezin (2002) pinpointed that states are inconceivable without strong emotions towards nations that these states allegedly secure, while Barbalet (2002) examined nineteenth-century British conflicts about the secret ballot. He drew attention to the intense emotions playing a key role in these conflicts: the elite fear of the irrationality of the working classes, the bourgeoisie's hatred of the corrupt aristocracy, and the working class solidarity in its struggle for more democracy. His thesis: the introduction of the secret ballot neither reduced corruption nor produced more rationality. Instead it transformed vibrant, debating voting communities into an aggregate of individual voters – lonely, impotent, and estranged. For a later phase of nation-building in Italy, Berezin (1999) researched how Italian Fascists orchestrated grand events on sacred spaces in an attempt to build up a national-fascist collective identity. Their aim was to affect transfer of love from family and region to the nation. Addressing the post-World War II phase in Italian history, Della Porta (1995, pp. 158–61) showed that terrifying police brutality and authoritarian state actions in Italy caused intense hatred among the extreme left-wing students – this helped to legitimate their own reliance on violence.

Focusing on two countries in the Soviet bloc, Flam (1994) demonstrated that the differing relationships of the party members, dissidents, and bystanders to their respective party-state explained contrasts in their regime-related anxieties and fears. In the 'liberal' socialist Poland of the 1970s, anxiety focused mainly on one's life chances, while fear of repression lessened. The intensity with which they were felt and the admiration for the oppositional exemplaries accounted for the party members' decision to leave the state-controlling Communist Party and to join the opposition. In the GDR, where the party-state enjoyed more legitimacy, even though it no longer relied on physical repression in the 1980s, dissent still had no clout: fear and anxiety loomed large, keeping exits from the party and the number of dissenters minimal. Addressing both democratic and authoritarian regimes, Flam (2004, 2005) pinpointed that protest forms depend very much on how movement members feel about their opponent and whether or not they believe they will be met with repression. In democracies, movements may encourage hatred and anger since the chances of repression are small. In repressive regimes and contexts, instead, oppositional leaders try to keep anger under the lid for fear of bloodshed. In assuming responsibility for a myriad of policy areas, democratic Western states have made themselves vulnerable to criticisms and thus more open to social protest:

> [s]ocial movements attempt to shake people out of their routine trust in the authorities and out of their everyday assumption that authorities work towards the public good and therefore deserve their loyalty...[indeed] social movements play a prominent role as social agents who try to instigate fear, suspicion, distrust and anger – a distrust of and anger at authorities, and the fear of their policies and their results...[they] also debate about which principles and feeling rules should apply in a given policy sector. (Flam, 2005, p. 25)

Expanding the emotional cartography of protest mobilization, Blom and Jaoul (2008) devoted a special issue of the *South Asia Multidisciplinary Academic Journal* to 'The Moral and Affectual Dimension of Collective Action in South Asia'. The focus is on the 'outraged communities' pitted against each other or the state. The volume helps to de-orientalize South Asia when the contributors translate collective mobilization and violence into examples of the powerless trying to appropriate anger and defy the powerful groups or the state, daring to make their very first claims to social recognition, inclusion, and equal treatment. The volume also opens new horizons in showing that states set legal rules for the public expression of emotions; victims of outrage multiply and refuse being pinned down; and in explaining in historical and biographic terms why an event becomes an outrage or when an apparent riot is 'really' about communal bonding. Bridging between nation-state and transnational studies, Blom and Jaoul (ibid., p. 68) investigated the emotional microfoundations of a long-distance outrage caused by the Danish cartoons in 2006 in Pakistan to show that the cartoon-related diversity of emotions and the Pakistani state's politics of public emotions together shaped the country's culture of dissent.

On Cross-border Mobilizing Emotions

Research on transnational movements is scarce and little has been done on emotions across borders. However, Taylor and Rupp (2002, pp. 141, 145–52) showed that the international women's movement could survive an overt demobilization phase during the hostilities leading up to World War I only because of its own emotion culture and shared collective identity. These held the movement in abeyance rather than letting it decline (for more on abeyance, see Taylor, 1989). The movement relied on gender-dualistic metaphors and rituals to target women's anger at men, and to reinforce trust and mutual affection for each other across national borders. The letters women exchanged stressed shared joys and sorrows. Employing family metaphors helped to keep alive the mutual bonds and the maternalist pacifist politics threatened by war. Echoing Hochschild the authors proposed that mobilization is akin to emotional labor, since it consists of 'channeling, transforming, legitimating and managing one's own and other's emotions in order to cultivate and nurture the social networks that are the building blocks of social movements' (ibid., p. 142).

Focusing on the obverse processes, Nomiya (2004) documented that the love for one's nation and the memory of the hurt inflicted on it in the past undermined the willingness of the South Korean peace movement to form a coalition with its Japanese counterpart, although both were in a global coalition – World Peace Now. Similarly, Goodman (2009) showed that love for one's nation for some Australians did not contradict but for others proscribed border-defying compassion for refugees, when the 'boat people' crossed Australian borders. In a recent study, Rosenberger and Winkler (2014) explore the emotional ties that moved Austrian families, friends and NGOs to mobilize in support of the refugees threatened by deportation despite a general climate of hostility towards migrants and refugees in their country.

Boltanski ([1993] 1999) and Leebaw (2007), although with very different intensity, investigated currently disappearing contrasts between the humanitarian movement, exemplified by the Red Cross and Doctors Without Borders, and the human rights movement, exemplified by Amnesty International and Human Rights Watch. The first took pride in its neutral stand in the past, and long stood for immediate, urgent compassion for human suffering (Boltanski [1993] 1999, pp. 178, 181–8; Leebaw, 2007, pp. 27–9). It made no distinction between victims and perpetrators. Instead it negotiated, even compromised, with political actors to secure neutral space in which aid could be administered. The second, after appropriate investigation, focused less on compassion for the victims than on curtailing and condemning the political powers responsible for the existence and brutality of the authoritarian and totalitarian regimes. Today they both engage in fact-finding before coming to the rescue of 'true' victims (see also Flam, 2013b).

CRITICISMS, COMMENTS AND CONCLUSIONS

Since these have been focal, let me briefly turn to Jasper's concept of moral shocks and Taylor's more general approach to social movements. I then turn to research gaps and desirable research directions.

Jasper's (1998a) widely used concept of moral shocks contains too many contradictions and ambiguities to be useful as it stands. Moral shocks are both immediate *or* slowly developing responses to events and pieces of information and autonomous subjective responses to events and information *or* an accomplishment of movement activists framing such events. These shocks are equally likely to produce de-mobilizing anxiety, resignation or grief as the mobilizing anger, outrage, hatred or indignation. Moreover, when speaking of moral shocks and discussing blame attribution or frames, Jasper sees mainly negative emotions (ibid., pp. 411–12), such as anger or hatred, as mobilizing. This neglects an early feminist argument that caring, love, and worry are all potent mobilizing forces. The lists of single emotions and their effects ignore that emotions come in bundles and interact (Benski, 2011). They are not inherently positive or negative, but should be assessed as such only in a situation- and actor-dependent manner.

Taylor's efforts to assert the importance of intra-group mutual support, friendship, and solidarity as a means of gaining individual and collective self-confidence, and a step towards the redefinition of an individual and collective self, helping to keep movements in abeyance and effecting cultural and political change, leave out some key movement dynamics. For example, classical texts on friendship ask not only what constituted and sustained it, but also how it was tested, what caused conflicts, and why and how these could be overcome. A complementary research program highlights internal cleavages, investigates the means of their suppression or balancing in order to account for (dis)continued mobilization in terms of suppressed or constructively resolved internal conflicts, all along paying attention to emotions and their unruliness (see Holmes, 2004).

Despite repeated criticisms, there is little new theorizing and much focus on single case studies and a few selected emotions. The question of power and other structural disparities leading to protest is often left out as is the question of what the movement actually accomplished. Theoretical and comparative empirical-theoretical research along the lines indicated in the body of this text would be desirable, focusing on transformative and 'nagging' protest events as well as on national policy-making and transnational movements. Importantly, social movement research should throw a broad net rather than trying to reinvent the wheel. For example, social scientists in general and fellow social movement researchers in particular have already done quite a lot of research on the social movement interactions with communal, regional, and national policy-makers. There is no dearth of governance regime or regulation concepts. These could be imported and modified, instead of re-inventing the wheel, freeing energies to focus on emotions.

The mobilizing power of emotions has hardly been investigated for non-stigmatized groups, such as the past or present nationalist, workers', farmers', temperance, suffrage or nature preservation movements, although their significance is beyond any doubt. It would be fascinating to learn whether their various waves had 'frozen' or developed their emotional language over time. Can one indeed speak of emotional movement families? Before we answer these questions, we have to work on the methods of unearthing emotions (Flam and Kleres, 2015), allowing us to pin down in a systematic manner typical references – discursive and visual – to emotions employed by social movements. Only then can we analyze whether several movements shared them and/or these developed over time. With such instruments in hand we could also investigate whether emotion referencing changes in substance and intensity over issue and movement mobilization cycles. Comparing emotional habitus and emotion referencing for similar movements across strongly contrasting cultural and political systems could highlight to what extent their emotional repertoires are co-determined by their cultural and political contexts.

Moreover, an exciting challenge would be to explicate what research on the role of emotions in protest events and social movements contributes to larger scientific debates. How could our research results bear on the discussion of crowds among historians or philosophers? How could and should it affect the constitution of sociology as a discipline (Borch, 2012)? In what ways can research on emotions and 'frame resonance' take the newest political science theory (Marcus, 2002) to task for positing anxiety as a neuro-psychological factor mobilizing voters? What is the contribution of those investigating the role of emotions in sustaining or breaking individual and collective identities to the broader debates about identity?

REFERENCES

Adams, J. (2003), 'The bitter end: emotions at a movement's conclusion', *Sociological Inquiry*, **73**(1), 84–113.
Aminzade, R.R., J.A. Goldstone, D. McAdam, E.J. Perry, W.H. Sewell, S. Tarrow and C. Tilly (2002), *Silence and Voice in the Study of Contentious Politics*, Cambridge, UK: Cambridge University Press.
Barbalet, J. (2002), 'Secret voting and political emotions', in R. Aminzade and D. McAdam (Guest Editors), *Mobilization*, 'Special Issue on Emotions and Contentious Politics', **7**(2), 129–40.
Barker, C. (1986), *Festival of the Oppressed: Solidarity, Reform and Revolution in Poland, 1980–1981*, London: Bookmarks.
Barker, C. (2001), 'Fear, laughter, and collective power: the making of solidarity at the Lenin Shipyard in Gdansk, Poland, August 1980', in J. Goodwin, J.M. Jasper and F. Polletta (eds), *Passionate Politics. Emotions and Social Movements*, Chicago, IL: The University of Chicago Press.
Benski, T. (2005), 'Breaching events and the emotional reactions of the public: Women in Black in Israel', in H. Flam and D. King (eds), *Emotions and Social Movement*, London: Routledge, pp. 57–78.
Benski, T. (2011), 'Emotion maps of participation in protest: the case of Women in Black against the occupation in Israel', in P. Coy (ed.), *Research in Social Movements, Conflicts and Change, Vol. 31*, pp. 3–34.
Berezin, M. (1999), 'Political belonging: emotion, nation and identity in Fascist Italy', in G. Steinmetz (ed.), *State/Culture*, Ithaca, NY: Cornell University Press, pp. 355–77.
Berezin, M. (2002), 'Secure states: towards a political sociology of emotions', in J. Barbalet (ed.), *Emotions and Sociology*, Oxford: Blackwell.
Blom, A. and N. Jaoul (eds) (2008), 'Outraged communities', in 'The Moral and Affectual Dimension of Collective Action in South Asia', a special issue of the *South Asia Multidisciplinary Academic Journal* (SAMAJ), **2**, accessed 29 April 2013 at http://samaj.revues.org/1912.
Boltanski, L. ([1993] 1999), *Distant Suffering: Morality, Media and Politics*, Cambridge, UK: Cambridge University Press.
Bonds, E. (2009), 'Strategic role taking and political struggle: bearing witness to the Iraq War', *Symbolic Interaction*, **32**(1), 1–20.
Borch, C. (2012), *The Politics of Crowds. An Alternative History of Sociology*, Cambridge, UK: Cambridge University Press.
Britt, L. and D. Heise (2000), 'From shame to pride in identity politics', in S. Stryker, T.J. Owens and R.W. White (eds), *Self, Identity, and Social Movements*, Minneapolis, MN: University of Minnesota Press, pp. 252–68.
Cadeno-Roa, J. (2002), 'Strategic framing, emotions, and SUPERBARIO – Mexico City's masked crusader', *Mobilization*, **7**(2), 201–16.
Della Porta, D. (1991), 'Die Spirale der Gewalt und Gegengewalt; Lebensberichte von Links- und Rechtsradikalen in Italien' [The Spiral of Violence and Counter-violence: Life Stories of Left-wing and Right-wing Extremists in Italy], *Forschungsjournal Neue Soziale Bewegungen*, **4**(2), 53–62.
Della Porta, D. (1995), *Social Movements, Political Violence and the State: A Comparative Analysis of Italy and Germany*, Cambridge, MA: Cambridge University Press.
Dunn, J.L. (2004), 'The politics of empathy: social movements and victim repertoires', *Sociological Focus*, **37**(3), 235–50.
Einwohner, R.L. (1999), 'Gender, class, and social movement outcomes: identity and effectiveness in two animal rights campaigns', *Gender and Society*, **13**(1), 56–76.
Fireman, B., W.A. Gamson, S. Rytina and B. Taylor (1979), 'Encounters with unjust authority', in L. Kriesberg (ed.), *Research in Social Movements, Conflicts and Change, Vol. 2*, Greenwich, CT: JAI Press.
Flam, H. (1988), 'Of interest', *International Review of Sociology*, **2**, 83–132.

Flam, H. (1990), 'Emotional "man": I. The emotional "man" and the problem of collective action', *International Sociology*, **5**(1), 39–56.

Flam, H. (1993), 'Die Erschaffung und der Verfall oppositioneller Identität' [The rise and fall of oppositional identity], *Forschungsjournal Neue Soziale Bewegungen*, **2**(3), 83–97.

Flam, H. (ed.) (1994), *States and Anti-nuclear Movements*, Edinburgh: Edinburgh University Press.

Flam, H. (1998), *Mosaic of Fear: Poland and East Germany before 1989*, New York: East European Monographs distributed by Columbia University Press.

Flam, H. (2000), 'Moral dwarfs and lifesize heroes', in H. Flam, *The Emotional 'Man' and the Problem of Collective Action*, Berlin: Peter Lang, pp. 131–52.

Flam, H. (2004), 'Anger in repressive regimes', in M. Holmes (Guest Editor), *A Special Issue on Anger and Politics. The European Journal of Social Theory*, **7**(2), 171–88.

Flam, H. (2005), 'Emotion's map: a research agenda', in H. Flam and D. King (eds), *Emotions and Social Movement*, London: Routledge, pp. 19–40.

Flam, H. (2013a), 'The politics of grief and the "grieving" mothers', in D.A. Snow, D. della Porta, D. McAdam and B. Klandermanns (eds), *The Wiley-Blackwell Encyclopedia of Social and Political Movements*, Malden, MA: Wiley-Blackwell, pp. 978–83.

Flam, H. (2013b), 'The transnational movement for truth, justice and reconciliation as an emotional (rule) regime?', in J.R. Heaney and H. Flam (Guest Editors), 'A Special Issue on Emotions and Power', *The Journal of Political Power*, **6**(3), 363–83.

Flam, H. and D. King (2005), *Emotions and Social Movements*, London/New York: Routledge.

Flam, H. and J. Kleres (eds) (2015), *Methods of Exploring Emotions*, New York/London: Routledge.

Flesher Fominaya, C. (2010), 'Collective identity in social movements: central concepts and debates', *Sociology Compass*, **4**(6), 393–404.

Fligstein, N. and D. McAdam (2011), 'Toward a general theory of strategic action fields', *Sociological Theory*, **29**(1), 1–26.

Gamson, W. (1992), *Talking Politics*, New York: Cambridge University Press.

Goodman, J. (2009), 'Refugee solidarity: between national shame and global outrage', in D. Hopkins, J. Kleres, H. Flam and H. Kuzmics (eds), *Theorizing Emotions*, New York: Campus, pp. 269–89.

Goodwin, J. and J.M. Jasper (1999), 'Caught in a winding, snarling vine: the structural bias of political process theory', *Sociological Forum*, **14**(1), 27–54.

Goodwin, J. and J.M. Jasper (2004), *Rethinking Social Movements. Structure, Meaning and Emotions*, Lanham, MD: Rowman & Littlefield.

Goodwin, J. and J.M. Jasper (2007a), 'Emotions and social movements', in J.E. Stets and J.H. Turner, *Handbook of the Sociology of Emotions*, New York: Springer, pp. 611–35.

Goodwin, J. and J. Jasper (2007b), *Social Movements. Critical Concepts in Sociology. Vol. 4: Culture and Emotion*, London: Routledge.

Goodwin, J., J.M. Jasper and F. Polletta (2000), 'The return of the repressed: the fall and rise of emotions in social movement theory', *Mobilization*, **5**(1), 65–84.

Goodwin, J., J.M. Jasper and F. Polletta (2001), *Passionate Politics. Emotions and Social Movements*, Chicago, IL: University of Chicago Press.

Goodwin, J., J.M. Jasper and F. Polletta (2004), 'Emotional dimensions of social movements', in D.A. Snow, S.A. Soule and H. Kriesi (eds), *The Blackwell Companion to Social Movements*, Oxford: Blackwell, pp. 413–32.

Gould, D. (2001), 'Rock the boat, don't rock the boat, baby: ambivalence and the emergence of militant AIDS activism', in J. Goodwin, J.M. Jasper and F. Polletta (eds), *Passionate Politics. Emotions and Social Movements*, Chicago, IL/London: University of Chicago Press, pp. 135–57.

Gould, D. (2009), *Moving Politics: Emotion and ACT UP's Fight against AIDS*, Chicago, IL: University of Chicago Press.

Hercus, C. (1999), 'Identity, emotion, and feminist collective action', *Gender & Society*, **13**(1), 34–55.

Hercus, C. (2005), *Stepping Out of Line: Becoming and Being a Feminist*, London: Routledge.
Hirschman, A.O. (1970), *Exit, Voice and Loyalty. Responses to Decline in Firms, Organizations and States*, Cambridge, MA: Harvard University Press.
Holmes, M. (2004), 'Feeling beyond rules: politicizing the sociology of emotions and anger', in M. Holmes (ed.), 'Special Issue on Anger in Political Life', *European Journal of Social Theory*, 7(2), 209–28.
Hopkins, D., L. McKie, N. Watson and B. Hughes (2005), 'The problem of emotion in care: contested meanings from the Disabled People's Movement and the Feminist Movement', in H. Flam and D. King (eds), *Emotions and Social Movements*, London: Routledge, pp. 119–34.
Jasper, J.M. (1998a), 'The emotions of protest: affective and reactive emotions in and around social movements', *Sociological Forum*, 13(3), 397–424.
Jasper, J.M. (1998b), 'The art of moral protest: culture, biography and creativity in social movements', Chicago, IL/London: The University of Chicago Press.
Jasper, J.M. and J.D. Poulsen (1995), 'Recruiting strangers and friends: moral shocks and social network in animal rights and anti-nuclear protests', *Social Problems*, 42(4), 493–512.
Katriel, T. (2009), 'Inscribing narratives of occupation in Israeli popular memory', in M. Keren, M. Holger and H. Herwig (eds), *War Memory and Popular Culture*, Jefferson, NC: McFarland Publishers, pp. 150–65.
Katriel, T. and N. Shavit (2013), 'Speaking out: testimonial rhetoric in Israeli soldiers' dissent', *Versus: Quaderni di Studi Semiotici*, 116, 81–105.
Kenney, S.J. (2009), 'Emotions and the campaign for victims' rights in Canada', *Canadian Journal of Criminology and Criminal Justice*, 51(4), 473–510.
Kleres, J. (2012), 'AIDS organizations as civil society actors', PhD thesis, Leipzig: University of Leipzig.
Leebaw, B. (2007), 'The politics of impartial activism: humanitarianism and human rights', *Perspectives on Politics*, 5(2), 223–39.
Marcus, G.E. (2002), *The Sentimental Citizen. Emotion in Democratic Politics*, Philadelphia, PA: Pennsylvania University Press.
Martin, P.Y. (2005), *Rape Work: Victims, Gender & Emotions in Organization and Community Context*, New York: Routledge.
McAdam, D. (1988), *Freedom Summer*, New York: Oxford University Press.
McCarthy, J. and M.N. Zald (1977), 'Resource mobilization and social movements: a partial theory', *American Journal of Sociology*, 82(6), 1212–41.
Mobilization (2002), 'Special Issue on Emotions and Contentious Politics', Guest Editors, R. Aminzade and D. McAdam, 7(2).
Moore, A. (2011), 'The eventfulness of social reproduction', *Sociological Theory*, 29(4), 294–314.
Moore, B. (1987), *Injustice. The Social Bases of Obedience and Revolt*, Houndmills, UK: Palgrave Macmillan.
Nedelmann, B. (1986), 'Das kulturelle Milieu politischer Konflikte' [The cultural milieu of political conflicts], in F. Neidhardt, M. Rainer Lepsius, J. Weiss, R. König (eds), *Kultur und Gesellschaft, Sonderheft 27 der Kölner Zeitschrift für Soziologie und Sozialpsychologie*, Opladen: Westdeutscher Verlag, pp. 397–414.
Nomiya, D. (2004), 'Linking local-historical memories to global movements: the World Peace Now Movement in Japan', paper presented at the 36th World Congress of the International Institute of Sociology, Beijing, 7–11 July 2004.
Norgaard, K. (2011), *Living in Denial: Climate Change, Emotion and Everyday Life*, Cambridge, MA: MIT Press.
Olson, M. (1965), *The Logic of Collective Action*, Cambridge, MA: Oxford University Press.
Pearlman, W. (2013), 'Emotions and the microfoundations of the Arab uprisings', *Perspectives on Politics*, 11(2), 387–409.
Petronijević, E. (1998), 'Streets of protest. Space, action and actors of protest 96/97 in Belgrade', *Polish Sociological Review*, 123(3), 267–86.
Pizzorno, A. (1986), 'Some other kinds of otherness: a critique of rational choice theory', in

A. Foxley, M.S. McPherson and G. O'Donnell (eds), *Development, Democracy, and the Art of Trespassing: Essays in Honor of Albert O. Hirschman*, Notre Dame, IN: University of Notre Dame Press for the Helen Kellogg Institute for International Studies, pp. 355–73.

Power, J. (2011), *Movement, Knowledge, Emotion: Gay Activism and HIV/AIDS in Australia*, Canberra: Australian National University Press.

Robnett, B. (2004), 'Emotional resonance, social location, and strategic framing', in *Special Issues in Sociological Focus, Social Movements: Approaches and Trends in a New Century in Sociological Focus*, **37**(3), 195–212.

Rosenberger, S. and J. Winkler, 'Com/passionate Protests - Fighting the Deportation of Asylum Seekers', to be presented at the European Consortium for Political Research Conference, September 2014.

Rousiley, M. and R. Garcez (2014), 'Recognition, feelings of injustice and claim justification: a case study of deaf people's storytelling on the internet', *European Political Science Review* (forthcoming).

Ruiz-Junco, N. (2013), 'Feeling social movements: theoretical contributions to social movement research on emotions', *Sociology Compass*, **7**(1), 45–54.

Schmidt, I.B. (2013), 'Perpetual trauma and its organizations: Mothers Against Drunk Driving and drunk driving revisited', *Memory Studies* [published online 12 February 2013], accessed 14 May 2013 at http://mss.sagepub.com/content/early/2013/02/11/1750698012470836.

Schrock, D., D. Holden and L. Reid (2004), 'Creating emotional resonance: interpersonal emotion work and motivational framing in a transgender community', *Social Problems*, **51**(1), 61–81.

Scott, J. (1990), *Domination and the Arts of Resistance: The Hidden Transcript of Subordinate Groups*, New Haven, CT: Yale University Press.

Sewell, W.H. (1996), 'Historical events as transformations of structures: inventing revolution at the Bastille', *Theory and Society*, **25**(6), 841–81.

Taylor, V. (1989), 'Social movement continuity: the women's movement in abeyance', *American Sociological Review*, **54**(5), 761–75.

Taylor, V. and L. Leitz (2010), 'From infanticide to activism. Emotions and identity in self-help movements', in M.N. Zald, J. Banaszak-Holl and S. Levitsky (eds), *Social Movements and the Transformation of American Health Care*, New York: Oxford University Press, pp. 266–83.

Taylor, V. and L.J. Rupp (2002), 'Loving internationalism: the emotion culture of transnational women's organizations, 1888–1945', *Mobilization*, **7**(2), 141–58.

Taylor, V. and M. van Willigen (1996), 'Women's self-help and the reconstruction of gender: the postpartum support and breast cancer movements', *Mobilization*, **1**(2), 123–42.

Taylor, V. and N. Whittier (1995), 'Analytical approaches to social movement culture: the culture of the women's movement', in H. Johnston and B. Klandermans (eds), *Social Movements and Culture*, Minneapolis, MN: University of Minnesota Press, pp. 163–87.

Taylor, V. and M.N. Zald (2010), 'The shape of collective action in the U.S. health sector', in J. Banaszak-Holl, S. Levitsky and M. Zald (eds), *Social Movements and the Transformation of American Health Care*, Oxford/New York: Oxford University Press, pp. 300–17.

Tilly, C. (1978), *From Mobilization to Revolution*, Reading, MA/New York: McGraw Hill.

Tilly, C., L. Tilly and R. Tilly (1975), *The Rebellious Century 1830–1930*, Cambridge, MA: Harvard University Press.

Tilly, C. et al. (2002), 'Emotions and contentious politics', in R.R. Aminzade, J.A. Goldstone, D. McAdam, E.J. Perry, W.H. Sewell, S. Tarrow and C. Tilly (2002), *Silence and Voice in the Study of Contentious Politics*, Cambridge, UK: Cambridge University Press, pp. 14–50.

Whittier, N. (2001), 'Emotional strategies: the collective reconstruction and display of oppositional emotions in the movement against child sexual abuse', in J. Goodwin, J.M. Jasper and F. Polletta (2001), *Passionate Politics. Emotions and Social Movements*, Chicago, IL/London: University of Chicago Press, pp. 233–50.

Whittier, N. (2009), *The Politics of Child Sexual Abuse*, Oxford/New York: Oxford University Press.

Yang, G. (2000), 'Achieving emotions in collective action: emotional processes and movement mobilization in the 1989 Chinese student movement', *The Sociological Quarterly*, **41**(4), 593–614.

Yang, G. (2005), 'Emotional events and the transformation of collective action: the Chinese student movement', in H. Flam and D. King (eds), *Emotions and Social Movements*, London: Routledge, pp. 79–98.

15. The transnationalization of social movements
Movindri Reddy

INTRODUCTION

Before the self-immolation of Mohamed Bouazizi sparked social unrest in Tunisia and spurred conflicts throughout the region, would theorists of transnational social movements have predicted these events? The unlikeliness of this level of predictability is exacerbated by the difficulties that analysts have in grappling with social movements that engage in activism at both the local and global levels, often at the same time and frequently relying on national and transnational networking. Most theories on the transnationalization of social movements take as starting points conventional perspectives of social movements that focus mainly on the national arena and primarily center on the Global North. Here the hegemonic perspective is the political opportunity model, which emphasizes structural reasons for social mobilization; others have emphasized agency to counter this bias. A significant challenge lies in applying these theories to social movements in the Global South where states are more likely to be authoritarian and repressive, and where political changes and reforms are few and not usually experienced as opportunities. The impact that transnational social movements have on the system of states has also complicated these debates. Here propositions about the existence of a global civil society come up against notions of stronger and more insular states. Further, the sea change in technology and communications media have impacted the reach and depth of social movements, but they also tend to replicate the old power divisions that continue to prevail on the global stage.

This chapter will first address the ways in which social movements have been theorized so far in order to show that existing theories fall short in explaining the transnationalization of social movements. In particular the dominant theoretical perspectives are more suited to analyzing social movements in the Global North. Social movements in the Global South react to political changes and transitions in specific ways; they also tend to react to and mobilize around issues pertaining to economic inequalities and changes, which have become less relevant as key mobilization ingredients for movements in the Global North. Moreover, while theorists focusing on movements in the Global North have moved more steadily towards an emphasis on agency, theorists who study movements in the Global South have recognized a need to maintain an emphasis on structure.

Second, the chapter then moves to an analysis of transnational social movements, and here the tensions between the *theoretical* perspectives that attempt to capture the characteristics of these movements, and the actual movements themselves, are highlighted. The challenges posed by transnational social movement on the system of states at both the theoretical and practical level, are pertinent. While all agree that states retain their integrity and power, how states are defined and operate in relation to complex and multilateral relations with transnational economic organizations and social movements, have affected this power and purview.

Third, while some theorists maintain that a global civil society has been established and transnational social movements constitute its social capital; this chapter emphasizes the need for caution. It also recognizes the disjuncture, tension, and contradiction that often plague relations among transnational activists, broadly divided along the lines of the Global North and South, but also along the lines of gender, race, ethnicity, and other markers of identity. The impact of global human rights regimes on the concept of a global civil society is equally significant. The dialogue established by human rights movements often bypasses states and creates strong transnational networks. It has to be recognized however, that even these transnational networks are filtered through the nation-state, and the state retains the power to act in an arbitrary and/or self-interested manner.

The main propositions made in this chapter are that while theorists of social movements have been adept at capturing the characteristics of such movements in the national arena, and have made a concerted effort to make sense of their transnationalization, there has been a tendency to prioritize the Global North, and an inclination to give transnational social movements a coherence and rationality that does not actually exist. Theories that pertain to the Global South, and those that interrogate the notion of a global civil society, take us further in the effort to construct analytical perspectives that capture the dynamism, robustness, and intensity behind the transnationalization of social movements.

THEORIZING SOCIAL MOVEMENTS

While there is no definitive theorist or moment that lays claim to the concept of social movements, Charles Tilly suggests that the concept can be traced to a particular way of pursuing public politics that started in the later eighteenth century, and combined three elements: 'campaigns of collective claims on target authorities', a wide range of 'claim-making performances', and 'public representation of the cause's worthiness, unity, numbers, and commitment' (Tilly and Wood, 2013, pp. 7–8). These themes are prevalent in most theories about social movements. Of relevance to the study of the transnationalization of social movements is the work of theorists who focus on new social movements (NSMs) – those movements that developed from the mid-1960s during the post-industrial period, and that mobilized around rights-based and other concerns. Theorists like Manuel Castells, Alain Touraine, Alberto Melucci, and Jürgen Habermas were reacting to the inadequacies of Marxist theorists to offer explanations for the kinds of social movements that were proliferating. Shifting attention away from class conflicts to political, social, and cultural conflicts in post-industrial systems, NSMs focused on collective action that addressed new relations of domination (see Touraine, 1988, 2000).

For them, the state and market framed and rationalized the private sector, giving rise to new social movements that reflected 'the silent and arbitrary elements of the dominant codes' and publicized 'new alternatives' (Melucci, 1989, p. 3). NSMs emerged out of the 'crisis of modernity and focus on struggles over symbolic, informational, and cultural resources and rights to specificity and difference' (Edelman, 2001, p. 289). Despite wide variations among these writers, they all recognized the 'newness' of the social movements that evolved in the post-industrial period; they were criticized precisely for attempting to define a break from 'old' social movements (see, e.g., Offe, 1985; Plotke, 1997). Steven Buechler says: 'the term new social movements inherently overstates the differences and obscures the commonalities between past and present movements' (Buechler, 1995, p. 449). Other deliberations revolved around the progressive and/or reactive nature of NSMs (see, e.g., Rucht, 1988; Mooers and Sears, 1992), whether these movements were political or cultural (see McAdam and Rucht, 1993), and what the class bases of NSMs were (Wright, 1985; Dalton and Kuechler, 1990).

Critics of the NSM approaches pointed out that the mere existence of discontent among civilians did not explain how, when, and why specific organizations arose. Reacting to this model, a 'resource mobilization' and strategy-orientation perspective emerged that drew attention to 'entrepreneurs' who mobilized resources and organized grievances (McCarthy and Zald, 1977). Collective action could be traced directly to grievances and social cleavages, but required activists to marshal resources, to become aware of and to seize opportunities, and then to frame their demands so that others could join against identified common targets. But in this interest-group perspective, the subjective feelings of camaraderie and solidarity were ignored; success was evaluated on the basis of whether policy objectives were achieved or whether activists were successful in garnering support.

To address the question of why people joined social movements, Sidney Tarrow proposed a 'political opportunity' model. Tarrow explained it as follows: 'Movements are produced when political opportunities broaden, when they demonstrate the existence of allies and when they reveal the vulnerability of opponents. By mounting collective actions, organizers become focal points that transform external opportunities, conventions and resources into movements' (Tarrow, 1994, p. 23). Those writing within this perspective focused on the historical cycles of social movements and conflicts that occurred at similar and different times in the same region (Tilly, 1986; Tarrow, 1989; Gamson, 1990). Critics felt that this model marginalized issues pertaining to identity, gender, and culture. Further, the social construction of political opportunity structures itself were underplayed; its broadly defined parameters included just about anything pertaining to social movements but lacked particular explanatory power (Gamson and Meyer, 1996; Della Porta and Diani, 1999; Beinin and Vairel, 2011). This paradigm came to occupy a dominant position in the field of social movements.

Various aspects of this model were expanded and rearticulated. Political opportunities, for example, came to include moves towards reform, shifts in the ruling alignment, the opening up of different avenues of power, exposure to new possible allies due to divisions among the ruling elite and so on. Charles Tilly introduced the concept of a 'repertoire of contention' in an effort to interrogate how a social movement formed or spread (Tilly, 1986, p. 10). He proposed that they grew out of three kinds of factors: the daily routines of a population and their internal organization, their prevailing rights and system of justice, and the accumulated experience and knowledge of their history of collective action and contention. It also includes the existence of shared meaning prior to mobilization and it offers a range of symbols, rituals, worldviews, that can be accessed (Swidler, 1986; Traugott, 1995). Tarrow added that from the late eighteenth century, similar forms of collective action spread throughout the world – strikes, petitions, demonstrations, barricades, urban insurrection – and he called this a 'modular repertoire' (1994, p. 19). The role of 'social networks' (McAdam, 1983, 1990) and community structures and history were highlighted (Margadant, 1979; Agulhon, 1982), as were investigations as to why individuals join social movements (Gamson et al., 1982; Dawes et al., 2002). All these approaches added to the idea that social networks among smaller groups sustained large collective action groups, adding further evidence to oppose Olson's claim that large groups were doomed to fail.[1] Furthermore, cultural 'framing' was underscored, viewed as enabling sustainable, long-lasting collective action (Klandermans et al., 1988; Morris and Mueller, 1992). Framing involved interpreting and representing the complex environment in simplified, condensed, and selective schemes (Snow and Benford, 1988; Benford and Snow, 2000).

One of the main criticisms of political opportunity approaches was the inherent structural biases and the undermining of subjective constructs. Goodwin and Jasper (1999) proposed a social constructionist approach to understand emotions, personal perceptions, and the meanings that actors attribute to collective action. Viewing emotions as culturally and socially constructed, Goodwin et al. (2001) for example, make a compelling argument for reintegrating sensations like anger and indignation, fear and disgust, and joy and love into political analyses. They contend that the notion of political opportunity structures is too rigid and downplays the particular contexts that pertain to mobilization. In other words an:

> extraordinary large number of processes and events, political and otherwise, potentially influence movement mobilization, and they do so in historically complex combinations and sequences... Such opportunities, when they are important, do not result from some invariant menu of factors, but from situationally specific combinations and sequences of political processes – none of which, in the abstract, has determinate consequences. (Goodwin and Jasper, 1999, pp. 36–9)

Addressing these criticisms McAdam et al. (2001) proposed a more 'relational' perspective in which 'interpersonal networks' are central to mobilization. They emphasized *agency* and changing structures with respect to mobilization, framing, and repertoires of contention. The model was complex and attempted to encapsulate a changing dynamic that was situation specific but also fitted within broad thematic trends. Criticism included the vaguely defined distinction made between processes and mechanisms, and a general weakness in terms of explicating how these two concepts function (Koopmans, 2003). The model was also criticized for using classical categories, albeit adjusted and re-formulated in novel ways.

Can these perspectives be used to analyze social movements in the Global South? The results have been less promising. As Edelman observes, they are less appealing 'because it was difficult especially under authoritarian regimes, to imagine political opportunity as a significant explanatory category', and in those instances where they were used, theoretical frameworks were understated (2001, p. 292). Some of the early adopters of these frameworks were analysts in or studying social movements in Latin America. With the uprising of the Zapatista in Chiapas (1994–2003), they began to study the role of social media and transnational networking.[2] In general, gaps in the social movement literature with respect to understanding organizations in the Global South include studies that emphasize organizations among peasants, and mobilization for right-wing movements. Elizabeth Wood, for example, shows that Salvadorian peasants participated in insurgency movements in El Salvador, not because they benefited from participation or due to widening political opportunities and other conventional explanations, but because it allowed them to assert 'dignity and defiance through the act of rebelling' (2001, p. 288). They were prepared to suffer brutal repression by siding with the FMLN[3] and in the process they developed a new political culture of insurgency based on solidarity and equality (Wood, 2000). Further, instead of an emphasis on political opportunities that seem more relevant in Europe and other Western democracies, there remains a need to analyze the impact of economic inequalities (Edelman, 2001, p. 294). This provides a more useful way of getting to grips with issues pertaining to indigenous groups, barrio[4] dwellers, street children, and other economically disadvantaged groups – these are the subjects of collective action that fall outside the purview of politics but lie at the center of economic policy and (in)action. Once again class divisions (the basis of Marxist analyses) rather than other social and political cleavages gained more explanatory power and instead of a steadfast attachment to new social movement theories, intellectuals began to speak of 'popular' movements (Foweraker, 1995).

Those theorists who study Africa and the Middle East have shown that classical social movement theories are not neatly applicable to states where authoritarian rule makes few, if any, political opportunities available. Social movements form within a context of scarce resources, relying on informal networks, family and community connections, and they employ 'innovative repertoires to mobilize' (Beinin and Vairel, 2011). Perceptions of threats or the subjective feeling of being under attack can and do give rise to collective action – political opportunities are not clearly visible or in fact available.

How actors mobilize resources and the kinds of resources they access also differs in the developing world.[5] Some have argued for the need to focus on informal networks, social movement communities, and social and political histories and contemporary circumstances (Snow et al., 1980; Buechler, 1990; Taylor and Whittier, 1992). However, this can lead to an under-appreciation of the discontinuities and fragile consensus within such social movements. Moreover, the emphasis on visible social movements underplays attention on hidden forms of resistance that are rife and consistent in the Global South (Scott, 1985).

Beinin and Vairel add that under authoritarian states in much of North

Africa and the Middle East, people do not mobilize to take advantage of political opportunities, but rather because they are reacting to threats when they 'feel their sense of justice and morals, their basic rights, or the possibility of offering decent living conditions to their children, are being attacked' (2011, p. 22). Activists rely on informal networks for everyday survival as well as for collective mobilization. These are the reasons why 'undercurrents of anger and dissatisfaction' can be marshaled for organization, and why mobilization is an 'episodic phenomenon' that is unlikely to be sustained over a long period of time. Further, when social movements are mobilized, they might not articulate 'common strategic objectives' (ibid., p. 12). Significantly many networks of former political activism have adopted a human rights platform that is tolerated by oppressive states and rely on a repertoire of contention that provides the basis for mobilization and survival.

In their work on the Iranian revolution of 1979 several theorists added elements to social movement theory that addressed the special circumstances of social movements in the Global South. Misagh Parsa (1989) again elevated the notion that a structural explanation for the revolution was viable – especially the role of the state in determining petroleum prices, the direct role it played in creating the conditions for revolt, and the important part played by mosques in mobilizing social movements. Charles Kurzman (1996) drew attention to agency and perceptions of contention by using a social constructivist perspective. He showed that reforms did not offer new political opportunities, but it also didn't stop participation in organizations. Actors engaged in social mobilization despite adverse conditions – he called this an anti-explanation. Finally, Mansoor Moaddel emphasized the 'broad episodic context' in which revolutionary discourses emerged and the specific character of revolutions as modes of mobilization (1992).

Analysts are beginning to recognize the peculiarities of many countries in the Global South where democratic transitions and globalization have occurred simultaneously. The adoption of the neoliberal economic model and the consequent increased integration with the global economy are situated alongside the policies pursued by nascent democratic states to address the economic and social inequities that prevailed under repressive systems like apartheid (Ballard et al., 2005).

Theorists studying social movements have begun to recognize some of the limitations of theories that were constructed mainly for the Global North. A few of these challenges also remain when these theories are modified to capture the transnationalization of social movements.

Transnational Social Movements

In 1993 Richard Falk coined the phrase 'globalization-from-below' to capture the transnational forces instigated by concerns over the environment, rights, neoliberal economics, multinational corporations, oppression and violence (1993). Transnational social movements began to mobilize around key global events, for example: the global women's meetings sponsored by the United Nations in the 1980s and 1990s, the 1992 Earth Summit, and non-government forums held when the World Bank, International Monetary Fund, and Group of Seven met (see e.g., Adam, 1995; Charlton, 1998; Brecher et al., 2000).

A number of analysts began to focus on the characteristics of these transnational movements. Risse-Kappen focused on how international governance structures support and legitimize transnational activism (1995). Smith et al. tied transnational activism to earlier discussions about collective action and global governance (1997). Waterman used old working-class transnational solidarities to discuss emerging trends (2001). Keck and Sikkink focused on transnational advocacy networks to elaborate on the depth and reach of transnational social movements (1998). What is distinctive about transnational movements in general is that they are 'acephalous, horizontal, loosely networked alliances' (Edelman, 2001, p. 305). They share a vision embedded in the transnational arena (shared networks, information, data, strategies, experiences) and they also share a sense of what Seidman calls 'moral connectedness' and identities that go beyond states (2003). This makes them difficult to analyze.

Overall there are tensions between the transnationalization of social movements on the ground and theories that try to explain them. In terms of the former, the speed, frequency, number, depth, and reach of social movements in the globalized era continue to evolve and proliferate. Theorists have come late to the table and rely heavily on applying classical explanations to new transnational situations. Once again it is possible to broadly see a distinction between those that emphasize structure and those that prioritize agency. Underlining a structural analysis, Sydney Tarrow sees a difference between globalization and 'internationalism', the latter offering a focal point for collective action and resources and opportunities that bring together transnational coalitions and campaigns (2005). He defines internationalism as a 'dense, triangular structure of relations among states, nonstate actors, and international institutions, and the opportunities this produces for actors to engage in collective action at different levels of this system' (ibid., p. 25). Building on past concepts associated with domestic activism, he highlights global framing (use of international symbols to frame domestic conflicts), internationalization (a response to foreign/international pressures within domestic politics), diffusion (transfer of claims from one site to another), scale shift (coordination of collective action at a different level from where it began), externalization (the vertical projection of domestic claims onto international institutions or foreign actors), and transnational coalition formation (horizontal formation of common networks among actors from different countries with similar claims) (ibid., pp. 32–3). Jackie Smith et al. make a similar proposition based on a more nuanced view of the state (1997). Instead of conceptualizing the state as a unitary actor, they see it as a complex process that operates within an international context of cooperating and contending associations; here all non-government organizations are considered part of the global political process. For O'Brien et al. (2000) 'complex multilateralism' represents the transformation in the nature of global economic governance, and this process is a result of the encounter between multilateral economic institutions and global social movements that have shifted attention away from exclusively state-based structures. Others have focused more specifically on structural causal changes and transnational action (Evans, 2005; McMichael, 2005). Finally, there has been a move to capture the internationalization of local and nationally based forms of contention (Guidry et al., 2000; McAdam et al., 2001; Della Porta and Tarrow, 2005; Della Porta et al., 2009). Here Tarrow (2005) relies on the concept of 'rooted cosmopolitans' to show how transnational activists (those rooted in specific national contexts but engage in activism that rely on transnational networks and conflicts) make use of political opportunities that become available at the international level.

Moving away from a structural analysis to emphasize agency are theorists like Margaret Keck and Kathryn Sikkink (1998) who argue that the emergence of transnational advocacy networks helped to instigate and sustain changes between 1968 and 1993. Using the concepts of frames of meaning, access to resources, and opportunity structures, they show how transnational advocacy networks employ the 'boomerang' strategy whereby 'domestic NGOs bypass their state and directly search out international allies to try to bring pressure on their states from outside' (ibid., p. 12). These linkages provide access, leverage, and information to less powerful Third World activists, and for activists in the Global North it offers credence to the claim that they are struggling 'with, and not only for, their southern partners' (ibid., p. 13). Over time transnational networking has become part of the common repertoire of activists.

Theorists of social movements have tended to privilege local organizations and national goals, yet in a globalized world it is short-sighted (and rare) for social movements themselves to either ignore or exclude transnational networks. Social movements consistently draw on international norms to challenge local policies and practices, they regularly appeal to international audiences through the use of shared images, they often use global discourses to challenge and de-legitimize local policy-makers, and they frequently define their identities and participation criteria in terms of international norms and organizations. While theorists define movements in terms of political targets and local goals, activists often do the opposite; they construct programs to appeal to international audiences, they are attuned to universal norms, and they employ these to achieve both local and transnational goals. By focusing on the local, theorists fail to fully explore the transnational side of collective action and social movement mobilization. In other words, to analyze the transnationalization of social movements, we need to figure out what the global and/or transnational side of *all* social movements are, assuming that they are all leveraging political opportunities, mobilizing resources, and framing with both the local *and* global in mind. The lag in theoretical analysis tends to underestimate the transformations that have occurred, and to overestimate the successes and/or failures to win local objectives.

All those who focus on the transnationalization of social movements draw on the notion that domestic structures mediate transnational interactions. Here Risse-Kappen is important in showing how state structures (centralized versus fragmented), societal structures (weak versus strong), and policy networks (consensual versus polarized), impact the way transnational networks evolve (1995, p. 22). Furthermore, the idea of a global civil society has gained traction in some quarters – with increased connectedness brought about by globalization and the concurrent weakening of state borders, it is argued that civil society has become more global (Meyer et al., 1987; Florini, 2000). Others disagree with this notion arguing that it proposes a coherence among transnational movements that doesn't exist, and it presupposes a weakening of states and the institutionalization of international norms (Keck and Sikkink, 1998; Fox, 2000). Tensions among activists between those fighting for local and nationally based issues and those focused on transnational alliances, add further cleavages (Fox and Brown, 1998). Some focus on agency rather than diffusion (as the concept of global civil society tends to portray), even though all recognize that state sovereignty is challenged by transnational activism (Keck and Sikkink, 1998, p. 33). The differences between transnational movements, coalitions, and networks, are complex and require definitional boundaries.

What is the impact of globalization, communication and digital technology on the transnationalization of social movements? At one level it is clear that digital technology has had an indelible impact making it easier to communicate within and across state borders and hence to build both national and international networks. Howard Rheingold, for example, talks about the formation of 'smart mobs' whereby large groups of people act together without knowing each other, and 'netwar' where participants are assembled throughout the world directly impacting specific international or domestic events (2002). Examples where these techniques were used include protests against the World Trade Organization in 1999 in Seattle, the Manila mobilization against the Philippine president Joseph Estrada in 2001, the worldwide support garnered for the Zapatista movement between 1994 and 2003, and the wave of overthrows that occurred in North Africa and the Middle East from 2010 onwards. There are many investigations about the effects of digital media on international activism. Lance Bennett (2003) clearly elucidates some important trends: the formation of loosely structured networks (as opposed to more dense ones of the past), the weakening of the identification of local activists with movements as a whole, the reduction of the influence of ideology on personal involvement in social movements, the decreasing importance of bounded national organizations as the basis of social movements and the strategic importance of resource-poor social movements, the creation of permanent campaigns with changing targets, and combining old, more intimate forms of organization with virtual performances.[6] But these transformations are also affected by the changing economic circumstances of many social activists given the increasing role of transnational corporations and the growing influence of neoliberal economic policies (Polanyi, 2001; D. Harvey, 2007). There is general agreement that technological determinism is problematic – the transnationalization of social movements is mediated by pre-existing cultures of resistance, practices, and organizational routines (see Garrett and Edwards, 2007). Tilly adds to this discourse by focusing on the changing nature of three elements that constitute social movements: (1) 'campaigns', which have increased in frequency and can involve similar targets simultaneously at different sites; (2) 'repertoires' of contention that depend less on expressions of program, identity, and standing claims that 'require physical co-presence' of participants, and favor 'locally clustered performances connected by long, thin strands of communication'; (3) public displays of 'worthiness, unity, numbers, commitment (WUNC)', signaling WUNC to the world but increasingly localized WUNC codes for their local environments (Tilly, 2010, p. 183; Tilly and Wood, 2013).

A high-profile diverse coalition of forces opposing corporate power was the Seattle demonstrations of 1999 against the World Trade Organization. This represented the new wave of demonstrations and transnational organization against global neoliberal policies and dwindling state welfare programs worldwide (Ritchie, 1997; Ayers, 1998; Edelman, 1999). While the challenges of sustaining such organizations are high, transnational activists have become brokers who relay organizational techniques and mobilization tactics for national and local struggles. Opposition movements now have access to international funding and expertise to fight local battles. With new technology and the increasing impact of global economic networks, social movements have become more transnational, and yet they face the same old challenges in terms of group cohesion and dynamics. These include: a growing distance between a small cabal of leaders and others in lower leadership rungs, the distancing of leaders and their followers, tensions among the leadership about goals and objectives, the lack of buy-in from various sectors of the groups, dealing with or ignoring social divisions like class, race, identity, gender and region, and the myriad other problems that social movements experience. With our lenses focused on trying to get to grips with the huge expansion in transnational social movements, or the ways in which all social movements are to some extent transnationalized, attention has moved away from studying the pervasive challenges, disjuncture, and fissures that affect all these movements – we give them a coherence that does not necessarily exist.

Global Governance/Global Civil Society

The pace of transnational social movements indicates that we are witnessing the development of a 'hybrid' form of multilateralism that is the result of changes in the international arena (O'Brien et al., 2000). These changes include more democratic political transitions and the liberalization of economies that included deregulation and globalization in the Global North, and the adoption of neoclassical economics in the Global South encouraged by the structural adjustment programs of the International Monetary Fund and World Bank.

These processes occurred in tandem with changes in information technology that enabled and/or facilitated the rapid movement of goods, money, services, people, and ideas. This created and sustained international networks for finance, multinational corporations and global civil society (including diasporas, migrants, and social movements) (Castells, 2009). The impact of internet technology on transnational movements, especially in terms of organization, information flow, and accessing resources in the short term, cannot be underestimated, but the long-term implications are as yet unclear. Persistent issues remain regarding the sustainability of such movements, their longevity in terms of structure and membership, the ability to sustain interest in a given issue in the face of a multitude of competing interests, and the long-lasting effects of transnational networks on national social movements. Some argue that even if transnational social movements do not generate face-to-face contact among members, they provide infrastructure that facilitates transnational communication and action, they cultivate transnational identities, and develop a global public discourse (Smith, 2007). Most agree that activists do not rely entirely on digital technologies to organize; in fact many organizations still rely on face-to-face contact to mobilize support (Levi and Murphy, 2006).

Global social movements are considered key players in the constitution of global governance – they are active at the local, national, and international spaces. A transnational public sphere is simultaneously national and transnational as activists 'think globally, act locally' (Seidman, 2003, p. 346). They organize and mobilize to push for changes that have a global impact. But such movements are not always progressive; there are a number of conservative groups operating at the transnational level, as are business and financial groups representing a wide range of ideological perspectives and objectives (Khagram and Alvord, 2006). The idea of global civil society needs to include the complex and multi-layered levels that such a concept and entity entails, and the various ideologies and publics.

Theorists have proposed that the transnationalization of social movements creates the social capital for global civil society (Smith et al., 1997; Smith and Johnson, 2002). The definitions and parameters of such a society is fuzzy, but there is some input about its characteristics. There has generally been an emphasis on cultural connectedness and vision, as well as the ways in which transnational social movements are able to mobilize and increase their bargaining power and position vis-à-vis national states or international organizations. For example a connection can be made between this kind of social capital and the rise of ethnic mobilization in that linkages to global civil society empower ethnic minorities and encourage political mobilization (Tsutsui, 2004). Others see world cultural forces as strongly influencing state characteristics; there are remarkable similarities among states on conceptions of statehood and citizenship despite differences in histories and social and political institutions (Meyer and Hannan, 1979; Meyer et al., 1987). These similarities are influenced by, and influence transnational social movements. Given the slim evidence available to substantiate the claim of the existence of global civil society, some prefer the term 'transnational civil society' or international civil society (Keck and Sikkink, 1998, p. 33).

Further, through the transnationalization of social movements, rights activists from various cultural settings are able to share more with each other than their compatriots (Bandy and Smith, 2004). An international dialogue is established that bypasses state institutions, and influences how local movements define their strategies and objectives. For example, indigenous movements that have access to global civil society are more likely to use the 'boomerang process', which enables them to pressure their governments by appealing to international institutions and states outside the targeted government boundaries. The rights language of the global arena has also made some countries more sensitive to their practices, hence making them more vulnerable to claims made by disadvantaged and/or oppressed groups (Risse-Kappen et al., 1999). All these characteristics allude to the existence of a global civil society.

Human Rights and Norms

International norms and human rights regimes have come to play a significant role in global governance. Even when states are unwilling to institute these human rights norms, rights activists have been able to influence and shape policies (Brysk, 2002). Many human rights NGOs are not explicitly transnational (in that they have local objectives), but the power of their arguments is derived from the vocabulary of human rights as defined in the public arena of the transnational space (Ball, 2000). In such instances, through access to transnational knowledge, human rights activists are able to hold their states accountable. Advocacy networks can influence policies at various levels by 'framing debates' to make them part of the larger agenda, 'encouraging discursive commitment from states and other policy actors', causing changes in procedures at the international and local level, 'affecting policy', and by 'influencing behavior changes in target actors' (Keck and Sikkink, 1998, p. 201).

There is also a need to make a distinction between old (first-generation) and new (emergent or second-generation) movements: the former were mainly issue-specific (labor, environment, human rights) and coalesced around NGOs that aimed to change specific policies at the national or international level (Bennett, 2003). Emergent social movements include NGOs but operate in an 'emergent movement environment of large-scale direct activism, multi-issue networks, and untidy "permanent" campaigns with less clear goals and political relationships with targets' (ibid., p. 212). The anti-apartheid movement, for example, was a transnational social movement whereby activists developed a global anti-racist identity that transcended and challenged state borders (Seidman, 2007). While they coalesced around the anti-apartheid struggle in South Africa, they also became part of a transnational anti-racist community.

What is clear is that transnational relations are always filtered or negotiated through the nation-state. It is this reality that produces the binary of local and global in theoretical studies, undermining the impact of the transnational arena and the transnationalization of social movements.

Transnational Social Movement and Challenges to the System of States

Many theorists have generally focused on the impact of globalization on the structures of international politics. Much hinges on the way in which globalization is defined. In narrow terms it includes the increasing volume and speed of the movement of capital, goods, information, ideas, people, and forces across states (Tarrow and McAdam, 2005). In broader terms it has been defined as the compression of time and the transcendence of space, with new transborder spaces encroaching on traditional territorial entities (Katzenstein, 2005). At its basis globalization is about global capitalism, or as Robinson says, it 'denotes a transition from the linkages of national societies predicated on a *world economy* to an emergent transnational or global society predicated on a *global* economy' (1998, p. 563; original emphasis). The term is often misguidedly given a 'contemporary, presentist' frame (Shukla, 2001, p. 554) or it is so loosely defined that it describes 'just about any process or relationship that somehow crosses state borders' (Hannerz, 1996, p. 6). While some theorists see globalization as weakening the nation-state (Walker, 1993; Appadurai, 2002), others have shown how nation-states have reacted by strengthening their orbit of power (Sassen, 2006). Exactly where transnational social movements fit in these multiple framings of globalization is complex, but it can be assumed that while the implications of globalization might cause the rise of social movements at the local level in the national arena, globalization does not necessarily lead to the rise of global social movements. Local activists in local environments organize to protest local implications – this has been the basis of much of the social movement literature that focuses on ways in which they leverage political opportunities, mobilize resources, and frame their demands (McAdam et al., 1996; Tarrow, 2005).

There is a growing recognition that theoretical distinctions must be made between globalization and transnationalism. The latter is the space that has been 'eroding, subsuming, and superseding' national boundaries as the 'locus of social life', a social life that is nevertheless 'filtered through' the nation-state (Robinson, 1998). This is the place in which transnational social movements gain resonance. The core of globalization is based on the free-trade agreements, integration of financial markets, transactions operationalized through the internet and digital media, and the operation of the economy above and below states. These institutions frame the rise of transnational social movements, whether they range from progressive to xenophobic. Such movements are more universalist and value-oriented, coalescing around environmental issues, peace, and rights (Lynch, 1988).

The discipline of International Relations has been most focused on the *system* of states. The foundational paradigms of realism and neo-realism solidified state-centric approaches whereby power, self-interest, security, and the rational action of states are suspended in an anarchic international arena with no central governing body. Challenging this framing, critical theorists emphasized the social basis of international politics, and constructivists stressed norms, identity, and culture in the construction of nations (Lapid and Kratochwil, 1996; Katzenstein, 2005). Others have underscored the order that exists in the international arena with the existence of international norms and international organizations (Ruggie, 1993). Post-constructivists have further added to the debate by showing that rather than viewing the state as the space of security and the international space as the source of insecurity, anarchy, and danger, national security should be analyzed in terms of how a nation produces and reproduces a particular identity (Buzan and Hansen, 2009). State sovereignty and the assumptions of internal security and external danger has been challenged in the post-Cold War world when international relations were affected more regularly by intra-state conflict rather than inter-state conflict (Walker, 1995). With increasing transnational linkages, regional politics, and global economic structures, the system of states is being undermined (Appadurai, 2002). If transnational social movements challenge the 'system of states', we need to figure out what this system is and how the transnational space has changed over time.

The transnational space is a complicated arena made up of institutions that are rooted in states, and of institutions that are transnational and comprised of more nebulous entities like ideas and digital media. It is the latter that has made definitions more difficult. Contrary to a common assumption that globalization is driven by technology, some theorists see it as embedded in historical contingency that might be driven by a technology (Guidry et al., 2000). Further, given that there are many globalizations, the transnational public space is actually composed of many networks and publics, all of which have a broad range of actors, 'formations, functions, political orientations, motivations and capacities', thus making generalization difficult and theoretical paradigms sluggish (Khagram and Alvord, 2006, p. 77).

Transnational Social Movements in Transition States in the Global South

What is distinctive about the Global South in our current period of globalization is that in many countries the globalization of the economy and the transition to democracy has occurred at the same time. In these contexts, social movement theories have neglected to analyze and contextualize the 'marginalization' of these countries and social movements within them (Ballard et al., 2005).

In post-apartheid South Africa, for example, social movements have emerged to oppose government policies, or to focus on the partial failure of the state to deliver services. The shift to neoliberal economic policies by the African National Congress coalition government has led to economic growth and prosperity for a small percentage of the population, but also to increasing economic disparities between the various classes and races. The turn away from a socialist agenda of the ruling Congress of South African Trade Unions (COSATU) and the South African Communist Party (SACP) has created the environment for social mobilization and activism among the poor, marginalized, and under-served. The democratic transition has involved greater economic integration into the global economy, with fewer restrictions and barriers for international investors. While South Africa was the focus of global attention during apartheid, the post-apartheid state experiences equal marginalization in the global arena as transnational investors compete for cheaper and more lucrative investment opportunities throughout the world. Social movements too, once leading the anti-racist global agenda, are also marginalized in global battles against the WTO, IMF, World Bank, and other multinational companies. In terms of theoretical challenges, the South African case forces us to come to terms with the implications of globalization in the developing world, the limitations it places on democratic transitions, and the marginalization of such states and social movements in the global arena.

In both Egypt and Morocco, civil society was shaped by the reciprocal adaptations between reforming authoritarianism and de-radicalizing activists (Beinin and Vairel, 2011, p. 30). In countries that have transitioned from repressive regimes, the ideological character of social movements also changes from socialist or anti-regime, to rights-based objectives that are less antagonistic and more in tune with the agendas of transnational social movements. In Egypt the Kafiya social movement that was once radical and rejected elections, actively participated in preparing and ensuring the outcome for the 2005 elections. Likewise in South Africa, COSATU, once the bastion of revolution and class struggle, is now an active member of the tripartite alliance that supports neoliberal policies that exacerbate class differences. The prevalence and adaptations made by transnational social movements in countries transitioning to democracy and dealing with the institutions of neoliberal global economic organizations require special attention.

Analysts are beginning to recognize the peculiarities of many countries in the Global South where democratic transitions and globalization have occurred simultaneously. The adoption of the neoliberal economic model and the consequent increased integration with the global economy are situated alongside the policies pursued by nascent democratic states to address the economic and social inequities that prevailed under autocratic systems. An issue that is relevant to the North–South divide is the 'extent to which civil society' had come to mirror the 'power and resource structure of globalization' (Naidoo, 2006, p. 61). Activists in the Global North have more access to funds, they are plugged into networks that offer them support in terms of strategy, they have a repertoire of contention about activism on the global stage, and they can more easily access the internet and technological support. This makes them more likely to dominate international events and to speak on behalf of their counterparts from the Global South. The heavy reliance on English and/or French as the lingua franca at many of these international meetings increases their dominance and marginalizes Southern movements. The Global South is also not well represented at the transnational level, with some regions overshadowing others.

Social movements in the Global South have characteristics that are very different from those of the Global North – they usually operate underground, their use of international networks is heavily reliant on individuals who are able to travel or communicate without drawing too much attention from security forces, they can be isolated from the global battles being fought because of the urgency of local issues, and their mode of organization and operation is dependent on a high level of commitment that inevitably leads to a greater reliance on a few personalities (Clark, 2003). All these features are significant when studying transnational social movements as they clearly reflect difference across the globe and impact any notion of global governance/global civil society.

To add to the debate is the question of the characteristics of transnational social movement activists themselves. Success requires some degree of 'education' and know-how in both national and international politics, confidence and knowledge with social media, strong writing (and verbal) skills (usually in the medium of English and/or French), and knowledge of the international scene. The notion of cosmopolitanism perhaps best captures the ideal activist, or more appropriately someone who is a 'rooted cosmopolitan' – deeply engaged in the international arena while firmly rooted in the domestic realm (Tarrow, 2005; Appiah, 2006). The class, caste, gender, and generational implications of these requirements have yet to be thoroughly studied.

CONCLUDING REMARKS

This chapter is not an exhaustive overview of theories on transnational social movements; rather it serves as a provocative framework to stimulate further debate and research. It revolves around several issues that are missing or underdeveloped in the transnational social movement literature:

1. The extraordinary wave of revolutions that began in North Africa and the Middle East in 2010 begs us to ask the following: when do transnational social movements become revolutionary? Or from another perspective, can a transnational social movement become revolutionary? While the fall of several powerful regimes can be attributed directly to the action of national social movements, most of the movements had strong transnational ties. For example, the Muslim Brotherhood of Egypt has branches throughout this region and relies on an ideological reading of Islam that is shared at the transnational level by a number of different social movements. Likewise, the April 6 Youth Movement made connections with the Serbian social movement Otpor! for assistance with strategies and tactics. These social movements were 'transnationalized' with respect to their strategic agendas, mobilization tactics, ideologies, and objectives.
2. Even though it is recognized that transnational social movements challenge but don't necessarily weaken the nation-state, it is a subject that needs more attention. States have reacted to globalization and increasing transnational civic activism by reinforcing their power and purview with more strident immigration laws, greater internal security surveillance measures, and an increasing emphasis on patriotism and belonging. Transnational social movements certainly challenge the 'system of states' that has been conventionally defined by self-interest, economic and political power, and cooperative agreements and norms. How do transnational social movements challenge this system of states? What kind of 'system' are transnational movements constructing?
3. Given the large number of revolutions and democratic transitions that have occurred in the twenty-first century, there is a need to investigate how transnational social movements are affected by and affect new democratic systems. From Eastern Europe through to Southern Africa, transnational social movements mobilize under new conditions. What are the characteristics of transnational social movements that operate under conditions where the nation-state is dealing with the implications of globalization as well as with democratic transition? The institution of neoliberal economic priorities and the changing role of these newly transitioned states have forced transnational social movements to fight their battles on several stages, none of them clearly delineated or easily accessible.

4. With the continuing divisions that exist between the Global North and Global South, it is important to interrogate the dynamics and characteristics of transnational social movements in each sector. Important questions are: what are the implications for transnational social movements in the Global South operating as they do in a globalized and interconnected world? How do they deal with the increasing marginalization (and integration) of their regions? How is the role of transnational social movements in the Global North changing and adapting to cope with more powerful and wealthy states, international organizations, and multinational corporations? How have transnational social movements in the Global South dealt with their increasing reliance on funding and leadership (in the international arena) on movements in the North? How have transnational social movements in the Global North adapted to their role of providing resources and leadership for transnational social movements in the Global South?

NOTES

1. Writing within a rational choice perspective, Mancur Olson (1965) argued that it was self-interest that motivated individuals to join social movements. If the group is fighting for broadly defined public goods, then individuals might decide not to join, taking the low-risk option of free-riders, gaining from collective action but not directly participating in them. In order to get strong group participation selective incentives for active participants motivate group action, or else they are unlikely to sustain support or be successful. Large groups are less likely to act in their common interests than smaller ones, and in the former, a minority who have more selective incentives, might come to dominate the majority.
2. See Castells (1977); N. Harvey (1988); Collier and Quaratiello (1994); Nash (1997); Womack (1999).
3. Farabundo Martí National Liberation Front.
4. A Spanish word meaning an area of a city with a high poverty level.
5. Resource mobilization theory was proposed by many including McAdam (1986, 1990).
6. See Diani (2001); Bennett (2003); Della Porta et al. (2006); Della Porta and Caiani (2007); Juris (2008); Earl and Kimport (2011).

REFERENCES

Adam, B.D. (1995), *The Rise of a Gay and Lesbian Movement*, New York: Twayne Publishers.
Agulhon, M. (1982), *The Republic in the Village. The People of the Var from the French Revolution to the Second Republic*, trans. J. Lloyd, Cambridge, UK/New York: Cambridge University Press.
Appadurai, A. (2002), 'Broken promises', *Foreign Policy*, **132**, 42–4.
Appiah, K.A. (2006), *Cosmopolitanism. Ethics in a World of Strangers*, New York: Norton and Company.
Ayers, J.M. (1998), *Defying Conventional Wisdom: Political Movements and Popular*

Contention Against North American Free Trade, Toronto, ON: University of Toronto Press.
Ball, P. (2000), 'State terror, constitutional traditions, and national human rights movements: a cross-national quantitative comparison', in J.A. Guidry et al. (ed.), Globalization and Social Movements, Culture, Power, and the Transnational Public Space, Ann Arbor, MI: University of Michigan Press.
Ballard, R., A. Habib, I. Valodia and E. Zuern (2005), 'Globalization, marginalization and contemporary social movements in South Africa', African Affairs, **104**(417), 615–34.
Bandy, J. and J. Smith (eds) (2004), Coalitions Across Borders: Transnational Protest and the Neoliberal Order, Lanham, MD: Rowman & Littlefield.
Beinin, J. and F. Vairel (2011), Social Movements, Mobilization, and Contestation in the Middle East and North Africa, Stanford, CA: Stanford University Press.
Benford, R.D. and D.A. Snow (2000), 'Framing processes and social movements: an overview and assessment', Annual Review of Sociology, **26**(1), 611–39.
Bennett, L.W. (2003), 'Communicating global activism. Strengths and vulnerabilities of networked politics', Information, Communication and Society, **6**(2), 143–68.
Brecher, J., T. Costello and B. Smith (2000), Globalization from Below: The Power of Solidarity, Boston, MA: South End.
Brysk, A. (2002), Globalization and Human Rights, Berkeley, CA: University of California Press.
Buechler, S.M. (1990), Women's Movements in the United States: Woman Suffrage, Equal Rights, and Beyond, New Brunswick, NJ: Rutgers University Press.
Buechler, S.M. (1995), 'New social movement theories', The Sociological Quarterly, **36**(D), 441–64.
Buzan, B. and L. Hansen (2009), The Evolution of International Security Studies, Cambridge, UK: Cambridge University Press.
Castells, M. (1977), The Information Age: Economy, Society and Culture, The Power of Identity, Vol. II, Oxford: Blackwell.
Castells, M. (2009), The Rise of the Network Society. The Information Age: Economy, Society, and Culture, Vol. 1, Oxford: Wiley-Blackwell.
Charlton, J.I. (1998), Nothing About Us Without Us: Disability Oppression and Empowerment, Berkeley, CA: University of California Press.
Clark, J. (ed.) (2003), Globalizing Civic Engagement: Civil Society and Transnational Action, London: Earthscan Publications Ltd.
Collier, G.A. with E.L. Quaratiello (1994), Basta! Land and the Zapatista Rebellion in Chiapas, Oakland, CA: Food & Development Policy.
Dalton, R.J. and M. Kuechler (eds) (1990), Challenging the Political Order: New Social and Political Movements in Western Democracies (Europe and the International Order), New York: Oxford University Press.
Dawes, R.M., A.J.C. van de Kragt and J.M. Orbell (2002), 'Not me or thee but we: the importance of group identity in eliciting cooperation in dilemma situations: experimental manipulations', Acta Psychologica, **68**(1–3), 83–97.
Della Porta, D. and M. Caiani (2007), 'Europeanization from below? Social movements and Europe', Mobilization: An International Journal, **12**(1), 1–20.
Della Porta, D. and M. Diani (1999), Social Movements, Oxford: Blackwell.
Della Porta, D. and S. Tarrow (2005), Transnational Protest and Global Activism, Lanham, MD: Rowman & Littlefield.
Della Porta, D., H. Kriesi and D. Rucht (2009), Social Movements in a Globalizing World, New York: Palgrave Macmillan.
Della Porta, D., A. Peterson and H. Reiter (eds) (2006), The Policing of Transnational Protest, Burlington, VT: Ashgate.
Diani, M. (2001), 'Social movement networks: virtual and real', in F. Webster (ed.), Culture and Politics in the Information Age: A New Politics, London: Routledge, pp. 117–28.
Earl, J. and K. Kimport (2011), Digitally Enabled Social Change: Activism in the Internet Age, Boston, MA: MIT Press.

Edelman, M. (1999), *Peasants Against Globalization: Rural Social Movements in Costa Rica*, Stanford, CA: Stanford University Press.
Edelman, M. (2001), 'Social movements: changing paradigms and forms of politics', *Annual Review of Anthropology*, **30**(1), 285–317.
Evans, P. (2005), 'Counterhegemonic globalization: transnational social movements in the contemporary global political economy', in T. Janoski et al. (eds), *The Handbook of Political Sociology: States, Civil Societies, and Globalization*, Cambridge, UK: Cambridge University Press, pp. 655–70.
Falk, R. (1993), 'The making of global citizenship', in J. Brecher, J.B. Childs and J. Cutler (eds), *Global Visions: Beyond the New World Order*, Boston, MA: South End, pp. 39–50.
Florini, A.M. (ed.) (2000), *The Third Force: The Rise of Transnational Civil Society*, Washington, DC: Carnegie Endowment for International Peace.
Foweraker, J. (1995), *Theorizing Social Movements*, London: Pluto.
Fox, J.A. (2000), 'Assessing binational civil society coalition: lessons from the Mexico–US experience', Working Paper, No. 26, Santa Cruz: Chicano/Latino Research Center, University of California.
Fox, J.D. and D.L. Brown (1998), *The Struggle for Accountability: The World Bank, NGOs, and Grassroots Movements*, Cambridge, MA: MIT Press.
Gamson, W.A. (1990), *The Strategy of Social Protest*, 2nd edition, Belmont, CA: Wadsworth.
Gamson, W.A. and D.S. Meyer (1996), 'Framing political opportunity', in D. McAdam, J.D. McCarthy and M. Zald (eds), *Comparative Perspectives on Social Movements*, Cambridge, UK: Cambridge University Press, pp. 275–90.
Gamson, W., B. Fireman and S. Rytina (1982), *Encounters with Unjust Authority*, Homewood. IL: Dorsey Press.
Garrett, K.R. and P.N. Edwards (2007), 'Revolutionary secrets: technology's role in the South African anti-apartheid movement', *Social Science Computer Review*, **25**(1), 13–26.
Goodwin, J. and J.M. Jasper (1999), 'Caught in a winding, snarling vine: the structural bias of political process theory', *Sociological Forum*, **14**(1), 27–54.
Goodwin, J., J.M. Jasper and F. Polletta (eds) (2001), *Passionate Politics: Emotions and Social Movements*, Chicago, IL: University of Chicago Press.
Guidry, J.A., M.D. Kennedy and M.N. Zald (eds) (2000), *Globalization and Social Movements. Culture, Power, and the Transnational Public Space*, Ann Arbor, MI: University of Michigan Press.
Hannerz, U. (1996), *Transnational Connections: Culture, People, Places*, London/New York: Routledge.
Harvey, D. (2007), *A Brief History of Neoliberalism*, Oxford: Oxford University Press.
Harvey, N. (1988), *The Chiapas Rebellion: The Struggle for Land and Democracy*, Durham, NC: Duke University Press.
Juris, J. (2008), *Networking Futures: The Movement against Corporate Globalization*, Durham, NC: Duke University Press.
Katzenstein, P.J. (2005), *A World of Regions: Asia and Europe in the American Imperium*, Ithaca, NY: Cornell University Press.
Keck, M.E. and K. Sikkink (1998), *Activists Beyond Borders. Advocacy Networks in International Politics*, Ithaca, NY: Cornell University Press.
Khagram, S. and S. Alvord (2006), 'The rise of civic transnationalism', in S. Batliwala and D.L. Brown (eds), *Transnational Civil Society: An Introduction*, Bloomfield, CT: Kumarian Press, pp. 65–81.
Klandermans, B., H. Kriesi and S. Tarrow (eds) (1988), *International Social Movement Research, Vol. 1, From Structure to Action: Comparing Social Movement Research Across Cultures*, Greenwich, CT: JAI Press.
Koopmans, R. (2003), 'A failed revolution, but a worthy cause', *Mobilization*, **8**, 116–18.
Kurzman, C. (1996), 'Structural opportunity and perceived opportunity in social movement theory: the Iranian revolution of 1979', *American Sociological Review*, **61**(1), 153–70.

Lapid, Y. and F.V. Kratochwil (1996), *The Return of Culture and Identity in IR Theory*, Boulder, CO: Lynne Rienner.
Levi, M. and G.H. Murphy (2006), 'Coalitions of contention: the case of the WTO protests in Seattle', *Political Studies*, **54**(4), 651–70.
Lynch, C. (1988), 'Social movements and the problem of globalization', *Alternatives: Global, Local, Political*, **23**(2), 149–73.
Margadant, T.W. (1979), *French Peasants in Revolt. The Insurrection of 1851*, Princeton, NJ: Princeton University Press.
McAdam, D. (1983), 'Tactical innovation and the pace of insurgency', *American Sociological Review*, **48**(6), 735–54.
McAdam, D. (1986), 'Recruitment to high-risk activism. The case of freedom summer', *American Journal of Sociology*, **92**(1), 64–90.
McAdam, D. (1990), *Freedom Summer*, Oxford/New York: Oxford University Press.
McAdam, D. and D. Rucht (1993), 'Cross-national diffusion of movement ideas', *Annals of American Academy of the Political and Social Sciences*, **528**(1), 56–74.
McAdam, D., J.D. McCarthy and M.N. Zald (eds) (1996), *Comparative Perspectives on Social Movements: Political Opportunities, Mobilizing Structures, and Cultural Framings*, Cambridge, UK: Cambridge University Press.
McAdam, D., S. Tarrow and C. Tilly (eds) (2001), *Dynamics of Contention*, Cambridge, UK: Cambridge University Press.
McCarthy, J. and M. Zald (1977), 'Resource mobilization and social movements: a partial theory', *American Journal of Sociology*, **82**(6), 1212–41.
McMichael, P. (2005), 'Globalization', in T. Janoski, R.R. Alford, A.M. Hicks and M.A. Schwartz, *The Handbook of Political Sociology. States, Civil Societies and Globalization*, Cambridge, UK: Cambridge University Press, pp. 587–606.
Melucci, A. (1989), *Nomads of the Present: Social Movements and Individual Needs in Contemporary Society*, Philadelphia, PA: Temple University Press.
Meyer, J. and M.T. Hannan (eds) (1979), *National Development and the World System*, Chicago, IL: Chicago University Press.
Meyer, J., J. Boli and G. Thomas (1987), 'Ontology and rationalization in the western cultural account', in G.M. Thomas, J.W. Meyer, F.O. Ramirez and J. Boli (eds), *Institutional Structure: Constituting State, Society, and the Individual*, Newbury Park, CA: Sage, pp. 12–40.
Moaddel, M. (1992), 'Ideology as episodic discourse: the case of the Iranian revolution', *American Sociological Review*, **57**(3), 353–79.
Mooers, C. and A. Sears (1992), 'The new social movements and the withering away of state theory', in W.K. Carroll (ed.), *Organizing Dissent: Contemporary Social Movements in Theory and Practice: Studies in the Politics of Counter-hegemony*, Toronto, ON: Garamond Press, pp. 52–68.
Morris, A. and C.M. Mueller (eds) (1992), *Frontiers in Social Movement Theory*, New Haven, CT: Yale University Press.
Naidoo, K. (2006), 'Claiming global power: transnational civil society and global governance', in S. Batliwala and D.L. Brown (eds), *Transnational Civil Society: An Introduction*, Bloomfield, CT: Kumarian Press.
Nash, J. (1997), 'The fiesta of the word: the Zapatista uprising and radical democracy in Mexico', *American Anthropology*, **99**(2), 261–74.
O'Brien, R., A.M. Goetz, J.A. Scholte and M. Williams (2000), *Contesting Global Governance: Multilateral Economic Institutions and Global Social Movements*, Cambridge, UK: Cambridge University Press.
Offe, C. (1985), 'New social movements: challenging the boundaries of institutional politics', *Social Research*, **52**(4), 817–67.
Olson, M. (1965), *The Logic of Collective Action: Public Goods and the Theory of Groups*, Cambridge, MA: Harvard University Press.
Parsa, M. (1989), *Social Origins of the Iranian Revolution*, New Brunswick, NJ: Rutgers University Press.

Plotke, D. (1997), 'Representation is democracy', *Constellations*, **4**(1), 19–34.
Polanyi, K. (2001), *The Great Transformations: The Political and Economic Origins of Our Time*, 2nd edition, Boston, MA: Beacon Press.
Rheingold, H. (2002), *Smart Mobs. The Next Social Revolution*, Cambridge, MA: Perseus.
Risse-Kappen, T. (1995), 'Bringing transnational relations back in: introduction', in T. Risse-Kappen (ed.), *Bringing Transnational Relations Back In: Non-State Actors, Domestic Structures, and International Institutions*, Cambridge, UK: Cambridge University Press.
Risse-Kappen, T., S.C. Ropp and K. Sikkink (eds) (1999), *The Power of Human Rights: International Norms and Domestic Change*, New York: Cambridge University Press.
Ritchie, M. (1997), 'Cross-border organizing', in J. Mander and E. Goldsmith (eds), *The Case Against the Global Economy: And For a Turn Toward the Local*, San Francisco, CA: Sierra Club Books, pp. 494–500.
Robinson, W.L. (1998), 'Beyond nation-state paradigms: globalization, sociology, and the challenge of transnational studies', *Sociological Forum*, **13**(4), 561–94.
Rucht, D. (1988), 'Themes, logics, and arenas of social movements: a structural approach', *International Social Movement Research*, **1**, 305–28.
Ruggie, J.G. (1993), *Multilateralism Matters: The Theory and Praxis of an Institutional Form*, New York: Columbia University Press.
Sassen, S. (2006), *Territory, Authority and Rights. From Medieval to Global Assemblages*, Princeton, NJ: Princeton University Press.
Scott, J. (1985), *Weapons of the Weak: Everyday Forms of Peasant Resistance*, New Haven, CT: Yale University Press.
Seidman, G. (2003), 'Monitoring multinationals: lessons from the anti-apartheid era', *Politics and Society*, **31**(3), 381–406.
Seidman, G. (2007), *Beyond the Boycott, Labor Rights, Human Rights, and Transnational Activism*, New York: Russell Sage Foundation.
Shukla, S. (2001), 'Locations for South Asian diasporas', *Annual Review of Anthropology*, **30**, 551–72.
Smith, J. (2007), *Social Movements for Global Democracy*, Baltimore, MD: Johns Hopkins University Press.
Smith, J. and H. Johnson (eds) (2002), *Globalization and Resistance: Transnational Dimensions of Social Movements*, Lanham, MD: Rowman & Littlefield.
Smith, J., C. Chatfield and R. Pagnucco (1997), *Transnational Social Movements and Global Politics: Solidarity Beyond the State*, Syracuse, NY: Syracuse University Press.
Snow, D. and R. Benford (1988), 'Ideology, frame resonance, and participant mobilization', *International Social Movement Research*, **1**(1), 197–217.
Snow, D.A., L.A. Zurcher and S. Ekland-Olson (1980), 'Social networks and social movements: a microstructural approach to differential recruitment', *American Sociological Review*, **45**(5), 787–801.
Swidler, A. (1986), 'Culture in action: symbols and strategies', *American Sociological Review*, **51**(2), 273–86.
Tarrow, S. (1989), *Democracy and Disorder: Protests and Politics in Italy 1965–1975*, Oxford: Clarendon Press.
Tarrow, S. (1994), *Power in Movement*, Cambridge, UK: Cambridge University Press.
Tarrow, S. (2005), *The New Transnational Activism*, Cambridge, UK: Cambridge University Press.
Tarrow, S. and D. McAdam (2005), 'Scale shift in transnational contention', in D. della Porta and S. Tarrow (eds), *Transnational Protest and Global Activism*, Lanham, MD: Rowman & Littlefield.
Taylor, V. and N.E. Whittier (1992), 'Collective identity in social movement communities: lesbian feminist mobilization', in A.D. Morris and C.M. Mueller (eds) (1992), *Frontiers in Social Movement Theory*, New Haven, CT: Yale University Press, pp. 104–26.
Tilly, C. (1986), *The Contentious French*, Cambridge, MA: Harvard University Press.
Tilly, C. (2010), *Regimes and Repertoires*, Chicago, IL: University of Chicago Press.

Tilly, C. and L.J. Wood (2013), *Social Movements, 1768–2012*, 3rd edition, Boulder, CO/London: Paradigm.
Touraine, A. (1988), *Return of the Actor: Social Theory in Postindustrial Society*, trans. M. Godzich, Minneapolis, MN: University of Minnesota Press.
Touraine, A. (2000), *Can We Live Together? Equality and Difference*, Stanford, CA: Stanford University Press.
Traugott, M. (1995), 'Recurrent patterns of collective action', in M. Traugott (ed.), *Repertoires and Cycles of Collective Action*, Durham, NC: Duke University Press.
Tsutsui, K. (2004), 'Global civil society and ethnic social movements in the contemporary world', *Sociological Forum*, **19**(1), 63–88.
Walker, R.B.J. (1993), *Inside/Outside: International Relations as Political Theory*, Cambridge, UK: Cambridge University Press.
Walker, R.B.J. (1995), 'International relations and the concept of the political', in K. Booth and S. Smith (eds), *International Relations Today*, Philadelphia, PA: Pennsylvania University Press.
Waterman, P. (2001), *Globalization, Social Movements and the New Internationalisms*, London/Washington, DC: Continuum.
Womack, J. (1999), *Rebellion in Chiapas: An Historical Reader*, New York: New Press.
Wood, E.J. (2000), *Forging Democracy from Below. Insurgent Transitions in South Africa and El Salvador*, Cambridge, UK: Cambridge University Press.
Wood, E.J. (2001), 'The emotional benefits of insurgency in El Salvador', in J. Goodwin, J.M. Jasper and F. Polletta (eds), *Passionate Politics: Emotions and Social Movements*, Chicago, IL: University of Chicago Press.
Wright, E.O. (1985), *Classes*, London: Verso Editions.

16. Social movements and the ICT revolution
Jennifer Earl, Jayson Hunt and R. Kelly Garrett*

Researchers have examined the relationship between social movements and new information and communication technologies (ICTs) for decades, but with exponentially increasing intensity. Scholarship in the area has shifted from emphasizing a small number of high-profile cases to a more theoretically driven body of research that considers a range of technologies, social movements, and outcomes. The number of publications has grown tremendously and today this subfield represents a burgeoning area of research. With this expansion, a number of distinct theoretical questions and positions have emerged, and new research frontiers have been identified.

In this chapter, we review important developments in the field, highlighting central theoretical questions and debates and summarizing key findings. We focus on two levels where theoretical discussion and debate have taken place. First, there have been 'grand'-level debates about whether or not ICT usage has impacts on activism and social movements, and, if so, whether these effects are the product of amplifying well-known social movement processes (e.g., making diffusion happen faster or diffuse farther) or they represent a more fundamental transformation of our models of social movement activity.

Second, theoretical discussion and debate has also taken place within established social movement subfields, such as within research on repression, movement outcomes, and so on. At times these discussions are linked to the grand-level debate we begin with. For instance, we consider at length research examining whether the role of social movement organizations is fundamentally altered by more extensive ICT usage. At other times, ICT-related research focuses on issues that have been long central to social movement subfields without reflecting on the larger animating debate, as is the case with research on repression and the internet.

No matter which of these kinds of theoretical dialogues one focuses on, we argue that it is also critical for researchers to make theoretical distinctions between the forms of internet activism they are discussing and, therefore, the kinds of internet activism to which their findings might generalize. We review various typologies of internet activism so that readers can have a bird's-eye view of meaningful distinctions amongst different kinds of online and offline activity.

Through reviewing both kinds of theoretical dialogues – those occurring at the grand or macro-level, and the numerous more specific debates happening in existing subfields – we provide a relatively comprehensive review of research on ICTs and protest. Our review begins by engaging three top-level and animating topics: (1) early research on ICTs and an examination of how the field has changed over time; (2) typologies for internet activism; and (3) different positions in the grand animating debate over the theoretical ramifications of ICT usage. We then move to more subfield-specific reviews to analyze the impacts of ICTs in particular social movement subfields, including: (a) ICT usage and micro-mobilization and participation; (b) ICT usage in organizing and by organizations (which has important tie-backs to grand theoretical debates); (c) ICTs and collective identity and social movement community; (d) ICTs and transnational social movement action; (e) ICTs and repression; and (f) the consequences of internet activism. We close with reflections on where the field stands and major topics to be addressed by future research.

EARLY AND CONTEMPORARY RESEARCH CASES

Although some of the earliest research on ICTs and protest focused on systems like PeaceNet (Downing, 1989), which was an early email and conferencing system for peace movement organizations, the literature hit its first growth spurt with research on two movements: the Zapatista movement and the anti-globalization (also known as global social justice) movement. The Zapatista movement is a guerrilla movement representing indigenous people in Chiapas, Mexico, which attracted global attention when it forcefully seized a number of cities and villages in 1994 in hopes of beginning a revolution in Mexico. When the Mexican military countered, the Zapatistas turned to the internet to gather support from around the world. Attention, support, and financial donations came rolling in, buoying the movement and constraining the Mexican government's response in the face of an attentive international audience.

Scholars quickly seized on this high-profile case as an example of the promise of internet-enabled technologies for social movements. In analyzing the case, scholars documented the history of the movement (Schulz, 1998), examined how the Zapatistas used ICTs to mobilize weak ties to support the movement, described the broader network of actors on the web connected to the Zapatistas (Garrido and Halavais, 2003; Salter, 2003), and examined particular online tactics used by Zapatista supporters

(Wray, 1999). Other researchers framed the Zapatistas in more militant ways, casting the Zapatistas as waging a 'net war', even while acknowledging that the war was really a war fought through discourse, not conventional weapons (Martinez-Torres, 2001). Yet, even within research on this early case, there were prescient calls to consider issues that are still at the cutting edge of research today, such as theoretical discussions of how movements will need to compete with one another for attention in an increasingly crowded information space (Kreimer, 2001).

Much of the scholarship on the Zapatistas came about around the beginning of the millennium, which also coincided with the rise of the anti-globalization movement, the second major case to push the research area forward. Initial work examined the role of ICTs in supporting offline protests, such as the so-called 'Battle in Seattle' that took place in 1999, through online support and direct action (Cloward and Piven, 2001; Eagleton-Pierce, 2001). Researchers also examined other major global social justice protest campaigns, including the campaign challenging the OECD's Multilateral Agreement on Investments (Ayres, 1999; Smith and Smyth, 2001).

In terms of major findings, work on anti-globalization and internet activism suggested that the quick provision and transfer of information was a key affordance of ICTs for social movements, even if it might sometimes lead to the spread of misinformation (Ayres, 1999). Researchers also saw transformative potential lurking in new capacities brought by social media (Bennett, 2003b), particularly in terms of stressing networks of association and their role in social movement organizing (Bennett, 2003a, 2004b). However, not all commentators saw such a strong upside from the internet. For instance, while Tarrow (1998) recognized that ICTs might spur diffusion, he nonetheless argued that the net impact of ICTs on protest would be limited because of the importance of thick, face-to-face ties.

While much of the work discussed so far focused primarily on offline protests that were facilitated using the web, or online civil disobedience conducted in support of offline protests (e.g., Cloward and Piven, 2001; Eagleton-Pierce, 2001), scholars also used the anti-globalization movement to examine how activism could take place more exclusively online (e.g., Carty, 2002). Scholars interested in movements beyond the Zapatistas and global social justice soon started reporting on other online movements and campaigns. For instance, Earl and Schussman (2003, 2004; Schussman and Earl, 2004) examined the strategic voting movement, which developed during the 2000 US presidential election. Gurak (1997, 1999; Gurak and Logie, 2003) examined a variety of online cases, including battles over the so-called 'Clipper Chip', which would have facilitated government surveillance within the USA. More recent work has examined the digital rights movement (Postigo, 2012), although this work draws on controversies with longer digital histories such as the struggle to make DeCSS[1] scripts available online (Eschenfelder and Desai, 2004; Eschenfelder et al., 2005).

The diversity of cases has only continued to grow over time. Whether one considers cultural tactics such as culture jamming[2] (Madrigal, 2012), hacktivism through distributed denial of service actions (Jordan and Taylor, 2004), or the use of Twitter in social movements (Segerberg and Bennett, 2011), it is clear that the kinds of technologies, tactics, and movements that scholars study only continue to expand.

We suspect that work on the Arab Spring and the role of ICTs, particularly social media use, may become an important anchoring debate in the literature, just as the Zapatistas and the global social justice movement were early touchstones. Early work on the Arab Spring is already shedding light on deeply opposing positions. For instance, Tufekci and Wilson (2012) argue that social media usage, such as Facebook, was critical to the Arab uprisings. One can find scholars who share this view (Ems, 2009; Grossman, 2009; Zhuo et al., 2011) and scholars who hotly contest it (Burns and Eltham, 2009; Morozov, 2009, 2011a; Gladwell, 2010).

TYPOLOGIES OF INTERNET ACTIVISM

As cases became increasingly diverse, a welter of findings began to amass; the diversity of technologies, uses, and movements made discerning clear trends difficult. Two reactions have helped to make sense of so much apparently competing work. First, as this section discusses, scholars have developed a variety of typologies of internet activism that could be used to organize quickly amassing scholarship. Second, as addressed in the following section, scholars have positioned work within a larger, orienting theoretical debate.

Two approaches have been taken to classifying online action in ways that allow the literature to be more easily parsed. First, scholars have created broad theoretical conceptualizations that capture major theoretical fault lines. For instance, Vegh (2003) distinguished between 'internet-enhanced' and 'internet-based' activism: internet-enhanced activism denoted activism made more efficient but not fundamentally changed by internet usage, whereas internet-based activism occurred almost wholly online and often had fundamentally different dynamics. Van Laer and Van Aelst (2010) add a second dimension to this typology, distinguishing between low- and high-threshold actions. This dimension is illustrated in the contrast between 'hacktivism', wherein tech-savvy activists exploit computer networks and security weaknesses as an expression of protest, and online petitions that anyone with a web browser can 'sign'.

Earl and collaborators (Earl et al., 2010) took a different approach by focusing on different styles of use. They distinguish between forms of internet use that are entirely about serving information (which they refer to as brochureware), uses that facilitate offline protest (e.g., online advertising of offline protests), uses that facilitate online participation (e.g., online petitions), and uses that allow entire movements to emerge and thrive online (i.e., online organizing). They found that in terms of empirical prevalence, information provision was the most common activist use of the web (i.e., brochureware sites), but that online forms of participation and organizing were also quite common. However, in contrast to what the literature might otherwise suggest, uses of ICTs to facilitate offline activism were relatively rare.

A second group of scholars have focused on enumerations of potential online tactics, instead of larger classificatory systems. For instance, Wray (1998) discussed five different online tactics (e.g., politicized hacking) as did Lievrouw (2011; i.e., including culture jamming, hacking, participatory journalism, facilitating offline mobilization, and the co-production of knowledge). Other scholars have offered conceptually analogous enumerations of different feature sets that activist websites might include (Della Porta and Mosca, 2009; Stein, 2009). These enumerations help to make the diversity of online protest cases clear, and provide standard feature sets to compare across movements and platforms.

ANIMATING THEORETICAL DEBATES

A second path toward making these myriad findings more interpretable as a whole is to position them within a larger animating debate over whether existing models of movement emergence, maintenance, and success can be applied with little or no adjustment to online cases. In other words, can existing theories designed to explain protest prior to the pervasive use of ICTs be readily adapted to explain online activism and how technologies relate to protest? The stakes that ride on the answer to this question are significant. If extant theories can be easily applied or adapted, then online protest represents only a minor theoretical challenge to the field. If, however, there are numerous circumstances that call for new theorizing because existing models fail to hold – even with modifications – then the field will require a steep learning curve to keep up with new cases.

There are three basic positions in this debate (see the following for more elaboration on this argument: Earl et al., 2010; Earl and Kimport, 2011). First, early scholarship claimed that extant theory could be applied without even modest adjustments. Scholars taking this perspective were primarily concerned with explaining ICT impacts on offline organizing (Van de Donk et al., 2004). They reasoned that since ICTs only provided new methods for outreach, but did not fundamentally change the dynamics of the offline events that were being supported, existing theory could easily accommodate these new cases. This essentially meant that all major existing theories – from resource mobilization (RM) to political process – were thought to be directly applicable to internet activism without any modifications. Most work stressed the importance of offline social relationships to the health and maintenance of social movements, implicitly arguing that ICTs could not be used to develop, maintain, or extend these deep social ties (Tarrow, 1998; Diani, 2000). Other researchers made an even more aggressive argument, asserting that ICTs might actually be harmful, further disadvantaging the already politically disadvantaged (Tilly, 2004).

Over time, this early, hard line position has given way to a second position that argues that online protest can be understood with only minimal adjustments to existing theories. This is still a theoretically conservative position in that it argues that the theoretical status quo needs little adjustment in order to explain protest in the digital world. This approach sees major existing theoretical approaches, such as RM, as still largely informative and relevant. However, scholars from this camp would suggest minor adjustments to these major approaches to accommodate unique or novel aspects of the digital world. For instance, Peckham (1998) argues that RM is already equipped to explain internet activism except that we need to expand the definition of resources to include digital resources such as bandwidth. But, once these minor modifications are made, major existing theories could be readily applied to online settings.

An alternative that is still within this line of work is the argument that ICT usage accelerates, enlarges, or otherwise magnifies existing theoretical expectations. For example, diffusion processes might work the same way processually, but one might expect information to diffuse further, faster, and at lower costs than it would without ICTs (e.g., Ayres, 1999). Earl et al. (2010, p. 428) framed the argument in this way:

> Although the internet may let groups disseminate information quickly (Ayres 1999; Myers 1994), reduce the cost of online communication (Fisher 1998; Peckham 1998), and/or enhance the ability of groups to create and represent broad online coalitions through links to other websites (Garrido and Halavais 2003), it doesn't change who activists are, what activists do, or how they do it in some more fundamental way.

Foot and Schneider (2002) refer to this theoretical approach as a 'scale change' approach because the underlying model is unchanging; only the scale at which it operates is different. One could think of this as similar to a quantitative, but not qualitative, shift in processes. Earl and Kimport (2011) referred to this as a 'super-size' approach, making cultural reference to larger fast food meals offered under the same moniker. The idea being that nothing but the portions changed when a meal was super-sized. Likewise, the theoretical processes of social movements were thought to be unchanged, though they operate across larger geographical areas or at faster paces than they had traditionally. Thus, major approaches such as RM could still be readily applied to understanding internet activism: the processes that RM describes might be amplified or sped up, but they are not fundamentally altered.

A third, and much more radical theoretical position has been that ICT usage within social movements can actually alter underlying dynamics or processes, requiring more significant shifts in our theoretical approaches. For some scholars, theoretical changes are required because fundamental assumptions of extant models no longer hold. For example, Bimber et al. (2005) argue that the free-rider dilemma, which was an important foundational concern for RM, is not theoretically relevant in the information age. This, in turn, implies that RM itself might be less relevant to explaining the rise and fall of some kinds of internet activism. For other scholars, aspects of theories that historically have been treated as constants must now accommodate extreme variation. Earl and Kimport (2011), for instance, argue that although costs have had minor variation historically, when unique affordances of internet-enabled technologies are leveraged, costs for organizing and participating can drop to unprecedented lows. In fact, these costs become so low that basic tenants of RM – such as the importance of social movement organizations to organizing – start to unravel. In fact, Earl and Kimport (2011) go so far as to argue that ICT usage is ushering in a new 'digital repertoire of contention' that reflects these fundamental theoretical shifts. Thus, this approach marks a larger departure from existing major social movement approaches such as RM and political process by arguing that new theories or major redesigns of RM or political process would be needed to explain internet activism.

This brand of theorizing has been referred to as the 'model change' approach by Foot and Schneider (2002) because it requires changes to fundamental models of contention. Earl and Kimport (2011) argue new 'theory 2.0' approaches are required. By analogy, they suggest that while super-size models used a gas combustion engine that increased in size from a four-cylinder to an eight-cylinder engine, the model change approach is more like replacing a gas combustion engine for an electric engine

– its mechanics and principles are different. One could also think of this approach as arguing that there have been qualitative, not just quantitative, changes in how movements emerge, maintain themselves, and succeed.

To summarize, these three camps are very differently positioned in terms of their relationship with major extant theories designed to explain offline social protest. The first line of work sees no need to modify extant theories such as resource mobilization or political process. The second line of work argues that these theories are still largely applicable, but need minor retrofits to maintain their digital relevance, such as adding in new digital resources. The third line of work questions whether the assumptions underlying extant theories – such as the centrality of resources and/or organizations – are still valid and argues that scholars need to break new theoretical ground in order to understand some kinds of online activism. In this way, this approach calls for a paradigm shift in theorizing about the development, maintenance, and success of movements online.

In most of the literature, one does not see this debate playing out as the central argument in any given work. Rather, this larger animating argument is being adjudicated within more discrete debates across a host of meso-level theoretical issues. For instance, do organizations play fundamentally different roles when ICTs are heavily leveraged? In the rest of this chapter, we weave this animating debate through most of our discussions of each more specific theoretical issue. However, we don't discuss this grand debate in every section as a substantial amount of research on ICTs and activism is nested within subfields disconnected from this broader debate.

MICRO-MOBILIZATION AND PARTICIPATION

Research on micro-mobilization has questioned whether ICT usage hurts, helps, or doesn't really affect participation. Studies finding that online support for offline protest has positive impacts on individual political participation are more prevalent than those finding negative impacts. In Boulianne's (2009) meta-analysis of existing work on internet use and civic engagement, there is no support for the assertion that internet use has negative consequences for political participation but there is statistically significant support for a positive relationship (although the effect size is substantively quite small). A number of scholars have found that ICT usage has a positive impact on individual participation in offline protest demonstrations for particular subsets of activists, such as internet-savvy activists (Van Laer, 2010) and individuals lacking traditional organizational and network ties to other activists (Fisher and Boekkooi, 2010).

Norris (2005) concludes that in democratic countries, shifts towards information societies, generated in part by ICTs, lead to increases in cause-oriented and civic forms of offline activism.

Some work on offline mobilization suggests no impact on participation or mixed impacts. Bimber (2001) utilizes survey data on internet use and various forms of political participation to evaluate the long-standing belief that successful attainment of political information translates into increases in the likelihood of political participation. He finds that the only form of participation that is affected by internet use is the likelihood of donating money. Quintelier and Vissers (2008) find no support for the time-replacement hypothesis that proposes that more time spent using ICTs will allow for less time spent on offline political and public participation. Hooghe and colleagues (2010) attempt to understand differences between online and face-to-face efforts at mobilizing individuals to engage in general, offline political participation, and conclude that the internet can be used effectively to spread knowledge and raise issue salience, but lacks efficacy in creating actual behavioral changes.

Research explicitly comparing factors that contribute to online and offline micro-mobilization is limited. Some scholars assert that online expressive participation strengthens political engagement online and off, and suggest that ICTs support new ways of connecting the personal and political (Bakardjieva, 2009; Rojas and Puig-i-Abril, 2009). Earl and Kimport (2011) find changes in scale when focused on offline mobilization facilitated by the web, but suggest that changes related to online forms of participation are more transformative. Brunsting and Postmes (2002) identify differences in predictors of online and offline political participation, arguing that online participation is determined more by perceived efficacy, while offline participation is more dependent on identification with a cause or movement. The relationship between online and offline mobilization is an important topic, and merits further study.

Scholars have also debated whether internet use promotes inequalities in micro-mobilization and individual participation levels. A number of studies have found that the positive relationship between ICT usage and mobilization only holds for a specific subset of the population, identified by demographic characteristics and varying levels of internet savvy (Krueger, 2006; Van Laer, 2010). In contrast, other studies suggest that online mobilization can reduce participatory inequalities by offering alternative pathways to the political process (Rojas and Puig-i-Abril, 2009), helping to expand our conceptions of what defines civic engagement (Bakardjieva, 2009; Cohen et al., 2012), connecting the otherwise isolated to political causes (Fisher and Boekkooi, 2010), and increasing the voice of those lacking traditional organizational resources (Norris, 2005). Still others suggest that participatory equality is dependent on a number of factors related to how ICTs are used, including the way that the internet is institutionalized in a given country or political environment (DiMaggio et al., 2001; Ganesh and Stohl, 2010).

ORGANIZING AND ORGANIZATIONS

One of the most developed, and also debated, areas of research on internet activism involves the role of individuals, networks, and social movement organizations (SMOs) in organizing. Broadly speaking, one strand of work, associated here with the scale-change perspective, argues that SMOs benefit from technology because they are able to better accomplish existing goals. Another strand of work, which we associate with a model-change approach, argues that organizing without organizations is possible in specific situations and seeks to understand why SMOs may be less critical in these instances. A third strand of work is not easily classified as either scale or model change, as it has elements of each, arguing that technology use is changing organizations and how they behave (which has model change implications) but that organizations are still the central organizers of protest and this is unlikely to change (which is a scale-change, or even no-change argument). We outline each strand below and argue that the approaches are not as incommensurable as many believe.

In terms of scale-change findings, a number of authors have examined organizational ICT usage and found that ICTs allow organizations to work more effectively and/or at lower costs. For instance, Stein (2009) argues that because ICTs allow organizations to engage people with very low costs, they are better able to engage in a variety of activities, such as outreach. In the European context, Della Porta and Mosca (2009) make very similar arguments. Reflecting on similar themes, Zhuo et al. (2011) argue that while ICTs were important to the Arab Spring, existing organizations were foundational and ICTs were only layered on top of those pre-existing ties and organizing structures. Bennett (2003b, 2004a) argues that ICTs can be used to support ideologically thin coalitions between organizations, amplifying meso-mobilization efforts. Garrett and Edwards (2007) make clear that ICTs also can be used to route around repression in some instances, and support movement decision-making and action.

Other researchers, though, have more fundamentally called into question existing theories about organizing and organizations. This work generally examines cases where organizing was accomplished outside of organizations, either through individuals or in networks. Within this area, there is a large amount of descriptive work documenting organizing outside of organizations. For instance, Gurak (1997, 1999; Gurak and Logie, 2003) examined a range of online cases – from protests about the Clipper Chip to GeoCities' web hosting terms of service – that sprung up quickly and without centralized leadership or organizations. Likewise, Eschenfelder and colleagues (Eschenfelder and Desai, 2004; Eschenfelder et al., 2005) examined protest about censorship of DeCSS code, which allowed Linux users to play DVDs on their machines. While there were some organizations, such as the Electronic Frontier Foundation (EFF), which played a role in the DeCSS conflict, there was also substantial organizing that happened outside of organizations. The same can be said of other digital rights struggles, which tend to feature a mix of organization activity (by groups like EFF) and organizing by individuals or small groups outside of formal organizational structures (Postigo, 2012). Other interviewing projects have confirmed the non-organizational infrastructure of various online movements and campaigns (Earl and Schussman, 2003; Earl and Kimport, 2011).

A number of different explanations have been forwarded for why organizing without organizations is increasingly possible using ICTs. One argument, championed by Earl and Kimport (2011), is that with ingenious uses of ICTs, organizing costs can be driven so low that organizational infrastructures are unnecessary. This argument echoes other related claims in the literature (Earl and Schussman, 2003; Benkler, 2006; Shirky, 2008). Further, they argue that online organizing often follows a power law dynamic where only a small number of people need to take significant action in order to enable the effective, but much smaller, efforts of the masses. Others argue that traditional roles for organizations, such as providing selective incentives to prevent free-riding, are no longer required because the costs of action online are so low that free-riding is not a major concern (Bimber et al., 2005). Still others argue that this transition is facilitated by the rise of 'flash activism', which involves massive numbers of people engaging in more ephemeral actions (Bennett and Fielding, 1999). It may also be that leadership can be distributed across a diverse group of individuals such that it no longer needs to be organizationally anchored (Earl, 2007; Beyer, 2011; Howard and Hussain, 2011). Finally, some have suggested that networks may more nimbly route around existing organizations to drive a movement agenda or media coverage of a movement (Bennett, 2003b).

No matter the theoretical rationale, though, these works together represent a powerful model-change argument that suggests that SMOs are no longer ubiquitously needed. But, it is important to note that most of these authors are not arguing that SMOs will never be useful and/or will go extinct. Rather, they are arguing that in some instances, what has been considered a basic assumption of social movements research for three decades – that SMOs are pivotal – may not hold. For instance, Earl and Kimport (2011) argue that SMOs will still play a major role when organizing offline events, even if they may be less necessary to organizing online actions. Bimber and colleagues (Bimber et al., 2012) argue that despite the increasing irrelevance of the free-riding dilemma, there is still significant interest in membership organizations.

Standing outside of this scale-change versus model-change debate, but reflecting elements of each position, is a strand of work examining how organizations themselves might be changing as a result of ICT usage. As Karpf (2012) has put it, this work is interested not in organizing outside of organizations, but rather is interested in organizing through *different* organizations. For instance, Bimber et al. (2012) argue that organizations are not being displaced by the ubiquity of technology, but are instead being reshaped so that organizational form now matters less to patterning member behavior. They argue that in any organization there is a diversity of types of members who use SMO-offered tools, but also other ICTs outside the control of SMOs (such as social networking sites and Twitter) to engage as they wish. Karpf (2012) examines the growth of 'netroots' organizations that often span multiple movements and have come to serve as central anchoring groups for progressives. Likewise, Kreiss (2012) has examined how even institutional politics, including election campaigns, are being redesigned to accommodate ICTs and netroots organizations.

MoveOn is often seen as an archetypical SMO for this kind of 'different' organizing, as evidenced by its wide academic coverage (see the following illustrative examples: Carty, 2011; Bimber et al., 2012; Karpf, 2012). MoveOn is a liberal advocacy group that organizes in pursuit of progressive change and supports political candidates that are supportive of such change. The organization's relevance to this body of literature is largely a product of its popularity in the United States and its utilization of ICT platforms and multimedia to facilitate communication between members and provide them with protest tools. Also included in this 'different organizing' line of work is research arguing that networks are playing an increasing infrastructural role in movements (e.g., Chadwick, 2007) and research arguing that organizational changes are also altering the meaning of membership within SMOs (Earl and Schussman, 2003; Schussman and Earl, 2004; Bennett et al., 2008; Earl and Kimport, 2011; Bimber et al., 2012).

While many see these strands of work in tension with one another, we argue that all three approaches are probably correct but describe complementary parts of the organizing story. There is strong evidence that organizing is happening, by virtue of ICT usage, outside of organizations (although this trend has received too little research attention and deserves more). But, even though we regard evidence of organizing outside of organizations to be strong, we do not believe that this means that SMOs will fade away. Rather, we suspect that SMOs that have more distant patron–client relationships with their members will be able to use ICTs in ways consistent with the super-size arguments reviewed above. Members will not seek major reorientations and SMOs will appropriate ICTs to achieve existing goals more efficiently. SMOs whose members are more actively engaged are likely to feel more pressure to contribute to movements in new ways, which will lead to changes within organizations, or organizing by 'different' organizations.

It is important to note, though, that technological change and technology use are not the only factors contributing to a changing role for SMOs. Questions about the primacy of centralized organizations to social movements' success predate widespread adoption of the internet, and there are numerous examples of loosely interconnected activist networks existing without the aid of sophisticated digital communication (e.g., Gerlach and Hine, 1970; Gerlach, 2001). Indeed, the notion that formal organizations are not required for mobilization is one of the defining features of new social movement (NSM) theory (Buechler, 1995), a model-change argument grounded in social, not technological, transformations. Although NSM theory has been vigorously critiqued (e.g., Pichardo, 1997) few scholars dispute the existence of decentralized movements. Instead, critics question whether NSMs are in fact new, suggesting that the unique characteristics of these movements, including their fluid organization, are actually part of a larger cyclic pattern for which there are numerous historical precedents. To the extent that organizing within social movements is changing, however, it is possible also that technology-enabled capabilities are operating in tandem with other socioeconomic changes to promote these new forms (Castells, 1997; Inglehart and Welzel, 2005), as post-modernization theory would suggest. The precise nature of this relationship remains relatively unexplored as recent research has tended to focus on the significance of technology alone.

ONLINE COLLECTIVE IDENTITY AND COMMUNITY

Examinations of collective identity and community in the online context sought to determine what impact, if any, involvement online had on social and community involvement offline, which might be negative, positive, or model changing. The majority of early work warned that increases in internet use would lead to offline decreases in community engagement and maintenance (Sassi, 1996; Lockard, 1997; Doheny-Farina, 1998). Much of this initial work raised doubts about the ability of individuals, groups, and organizations to foster and maintain an online collective identity. By comparing a feminist group whose members primarily interact with one another online to a feminist group whose members primarily interact with one another offline, Ayers (2003) concluded that the online group lacked the very things that fostered a collective identity. Nip (2004) found that while the internet group she studied was able to foster a sense of belonging and shared opposition to the dominant order, they were unable to generate and maintain a collective consciousness and failed in establishing a collective identity.

This early trend of skepticism in the literature is somewhat surprising considering evidence of the positive effects of emergent technologies on mobilization and collective identity historically. For example, Roscigno and Danaher (2001) conclude that radio played an important role in shaping the collective identity and shared understandings of political opportunity among textile workers in the US South during the late 1920s and early 1930s.

That said, there were some that asserted that online communities strengthened offline communities or expanded offline themselves (Rheingold, 1993; Elkins, 1997; Wellman and Gulia, 1999). More recent scholarship has confirmed this less skeptical view and has come to accept the instrumental role that ICTs can play in collective identity formation and maintenance. Kavanaugh et al. (2008) find that the ability to gather information and create relationships online strengthened political ties in a local community computer network, to which Haythornthwaite and Kendall (2010) add that such ties can persist even after offline links are severed. For these scholars, online community and communication can reinforce already existing collective identities and maintain them solely online even after offline contact stops.

Others have explained the importance of ICTs to activist collective identities for those disadvantaged by both distance and repression. Work by Arquilla and Ronfeldt (2001) demonstrates that for cyber-terrorists and civil society activists alike, ICTs can strengthen collective identity even in the absence of physical or geographical proximity. Reid and Chen (2007) claim that for extremist Middle Eastern groups who are not able to meet or communicate publicly, the internet offers a private, mediated way for individuals to find a sense of belonging, even if done under the condition of anonymity. It is clear that this research finds both that collective identity is important to social movements and collective action mobilization and that the internet can be leveraged to strengthen identity formation and maintenance by increasing communication and interpersonal ties, making geographic distance insignificant, and providing safe places for people to connect.

Moving beyond these positive versus negative effect debates, other scholars have questioned whether collective identity is always as important for online mobilization as extant research suspects. For instance, Earl and Kimport (2011) argue that ICTs enable collective action without a physical co-presence among participants, which changes participants' sense of others' participation. As such, they posit that the social processes driving collective identity, or collective identity itself, will change in online contexts, possibly forcing us to change our understandings of the sources of collective identity and how it impacts mobilization. Bennett et al. (2008) reach a similar conclusion, claiming that recent, dramatic increases in the speed and scale of mobilization efforts is a product of a transformation of SMOs that is typified by looser ties with members and allows for more widespread mobilization as participants rely on much denser, personal political networks. The development of the 'networked individualism' perspective (Zhuo et al., 2011; Rainie and Wellman, 2012), which proposes fundamental changes to our conceptual models of collective identity, is consistent with what Earl and Kimport (2011) call for.

TRANSNATIONAL SOCIAL MOVEMENTS AND ICT USAGE

Transnational social movement activity has been impacted more by ICT usage than domestic protest because changes in the time, distance, and cost constraints of mobilization and organization are more influential among transnational movements. Globally connected internet-based communication allows the rapid diffusion of tactics (Van Laer and Van Aelst, 2010); facilitates the coordination of massive demonstrations simultaneously around the world (Smith, 2001; Kahn and Kellner, 2004; Bennett et al., 2008); enhances and eases collective identity formation (Van Aelst and Walgrave, 2002; Reid and Chen, 2007; Matsuzawa, 2011); speeds the growth of transnational protest (Nico Verhaegan, in Van Aelst and Walgrave, 2002); and alters political networks across borders (Bennett et al., 2008). The repertoire of contention may also be changing as activists experiment with adapting existing tactics to the digital environment, capitalizing on the speed and reach of the network (Ayres, 2005).

Changes in time, cost, and geographic constraints have also impacted organizational and networking processes. The internet allows for looser and more fluid transnational organizational structures to remain effective across great distances without being highly formalized (Smith et al., 1997; Bennett, 2003a). In their work on Egypt during the Arab Spring, Zhuo et al. (2011) echo research done on the Zapatistas (Schulz, 1998; Garrido and Halavais, 2003), arguing that established activist organizations were aided in their efforts by a geographically dispersed network of allies, maintained at low costs with the use of ICTs. Similarly, Matsuzawa (2011) highlights the ways in which the internet can enable local groups, often lacking in resources, to become 'translocal' by connecting them to non-hierarchical transnational activist networks.

REPRESSION

In comparison to other areas, far less work has been done on repression online. What work does exist can largely be divided into work on repression in authoritarian versus democratic contexts. Work on repression in authoritarian contexts has examined online censorship levels with remarkably sophisticated technical designs (e.g., Deibert et al., 2008, 2010). While much of that work points to the effectiveness of authoritarian governments in censoring, research does suggest that some repressive regimes are not as effective at online repression as they are at offline repression (Alexanyan et al., 2012). A few researchers have also examined how activists might try to use ICTs to circumvent surveillance and/or censorship (Roberts et al., 2010). However, it is worth noting that work on censorship has not been well integrated into the literature on repression, although Earl (2011a) argues that scholars must work on bridging this gap.

Other work on authoritarian contexts has examined the use of ICTs as surveillance tools, particularly in Arab countries and in relation to the Arab Spring (Howard and Hussain, 2011; Lynch, 2011). Morozov (2011a) has been the most ardent critic of ICTs because of their repressive potential. In addition to arguing that ICTs can be used effectively by state agents to monitor and repress, he argues that the entertainment uses of ICTs can sap the will of the masses and limit the likelihood of mobilization. In contrast, others have argued that repressive attempts have backfired, and, for instance, emboldened Arab protesters (Mourtada and Salem, 2011). Online organizing may also make repression more difficult for states because bottom-up organizing is harder to monitor and suppress than centralized, bureaucratic organizing (Etling et al., 2010).

Work examining repression online in democratic contexts examines these issues in parallel. For instance, Chadwick (2006) is concerned with surveillance, even in democratic contexts, and Earl et al. (2013) note that police may use Twitter for surveillance. Concerns about access to online activism in democratic states also exist: Earl (2012) notes that because so much protest happens on private servers in democratic spaces, there is little actual protection for online protest (see DeNardis, 2012 for a related point). Similarly, Peckham (1998) argues that even private actors can repress online, as when Scientology tried to limit the offline and online resources of anti-Scientology activists. Moreover, just as backfire from repression was observed in more authoritarian contexts, backfire has also been a common response in democratic contexts (Earl and Schussman, 2004; Krueger, 2005; Postigo, 2012; Earl and Beyer, 2013). However, censorship broadly construed as blocking access to information in general has not been the subject of research in democratic contexts.

THE CONSEQUENCES OF INTERNET ACTIVISM

It has been popular to argue that online activism is of little consequence, although we take issue with this conclusion. One version of this argument assumes that 'real' activism must inevitably play out in the streets, and so online activism is, at best, a gateway to this more important form of activism, and, at worst, a distraction. Noted popular writers such as Gladwell (2010), as well as respected social movement scholars such as Tarrow (1998), have made such claims. A second version of this argument indicts online activism as too easy to be effectual, implicitly tying effectiveness to difficulty. Karpf (2012) repeatedly makes this claim, and notes that his skepticism reflects a consensus about the futility and unimportance of so-called 'slacktivism' or 'clicktivism', activities that he sees as 'bemoaned by scholars and public intellectuals' (p. 29). A final version of this argument is that even when there are positive aspects of internet activism, the downsides (e.g., heightened surveillance and repression) are larger and/or organizers (or supportive governments) are not clever enough to accomplish heavy democratic lifts with these tools. Morozov (2011a) makes this argument most strongly in his aptly titled book, *The Net Delusion*. He notes: 'The "delusion" that I am attacking in the title of my book refers not only to our tendency to view the internet as the "ultimate liberator" but also to our false belief that the internet is a tool that Western policy-makers can wield at will and without consequences' (Morozov, 2011b).

Much of the recent debate over the consequences of online engagement has been fanned by research on the Arab Spring. A number of scholars have argued that ICTs were important to Arab Spring mobilizations (Aday et al., 2010; Zhuo et al., 2011; Tufekci and Wilson, 2012) but other researchers have questioned this finding (Gladwell, 2010; Morozov,

2011a; Aday et al., 2012). Whatever research ultimately reveals about the role of ICTs in the Arab Spring, we do not think this will resolve the outcome's controversy.

In fact, we argue that the debate up to this point has been far too simplistic and that research and theorizing (with a few notable exceptions) has been far too unsystematic for any substantial conclusions to be reached. Perhaps most importantly, research has tended to be grounded on untested assumptions about effectiveness (e.g., Gladwell, 2010) or anecdotes and isolated cases (e.g., Morozov, 2011a) instead of on more systematic surveys of social movement consequences. This means we know little about impacts that is generalizable. Research has also been structured around 'straw man' debates where authors defend or contest the uniform irrelevance of online activism. We think these kinds of simplistic arguments hide the more likely outcome of long-term empirical research, which we suspect will show that online activism is effective for certain kinds of goals and under certain circumstances, but is neither universally effective nor universally ineffective (which, incidentally, is no different from findings on offline activism).

Furthermore, research has failed to engage the same wide set of social movement consequences that research on offline activism has, including research on the biographical, cultural, and policy-agenda–setting impacts of internet activism, among others (see Earl, 2011b for more on this point). Thus, there are many untouched research frontiers in this area. Just as researchers have elsewhere failed to distinguish between dynamics associated with different types of 'internet activism' (Earl et al., 2010), so too have scholars failed to organize the debate using precise conceptualizations of technology use. This means that scholars tend to make grand claims about the consequences of ICT-facilitated protest, instead of carefully tailoring to the kinds of technology usage about which findings may generalize. Finally, scholars have failed to distinguish between alternative models of power that are at work in long-term offline social movements versus flash activism. While long-term activism works on a model of power through sustained influence, flash activism works on a flash-flood model in which ephemeral rushes of participation can have serious consequences. Although this distinction has been discussed in the literature, it has not been imported into research and theorizing on the impact of internet activism (Earl, 2011b). We hope to see more development in this area, as it is a critical and hotly contested research frontier.

CONCLUSION

Clearly, research on the relationship between ICTs and protest and social movements has come a long way over the last several decades. From humble early examinations of activists' Usenet bulletin boards and the Zapatistas, the literature has grown to examine different forms of 'internet activism' across the globe. In reviewing this ever-growing body of work, we have cautioned readers that it is critical to always remember that not all 'internet activism' is the same – there are important conceptual differences, and differences in findings, associated with online facilitation of offline action versus fully online participation. When scholars ignore this distinction, the generalizations drawn from research are suspect.

We have also outlined a grand debate over the general theoretical impact of ICTs on protest: does ICT usage have no effect on fundamental underlying theoretical processes, does it accelerate known processes or otherwise enlarge them, or are those processes fundamentally altered through ICT use? We have shown throughout the review that when scholars study offline mobilization that is supported online, no effects or scale-changing 'super-size' effects are most likely. This is apparent across all subfields reviewed. On the other hand, when *online participation* in activism is examined, researchers tend to find more model-changing consequences of ICT usage. This is true whether one examines work on organizing and organizations or collective identity. This suggests that scholars who tend to make grand conclusions about the consequences of ICT-facilitated protest are likely to be overplaying their hand. Instead, theoretical findings need to be tailored to the kind of activity and technology usage under study. Future research needs to be much more sensitive to this issue and researchers need to do a better job of discussing what kinds of cases findings might generalize to. Moreover, researchers need to spend more time examining online forms of activism because the offline facilitation of online activism has thus far received the lion's share of research attention, despite being empirically rare (Earl et al., 2010).

This review has summarized major research themes at the intersection of social movements and new ICTs, highlighting current and continuing controversies in the field. Inevitably, we have had to make difficult choices about what to omit. In a longer review, we would also have discussed work on diffusion or networks online, however, these rich areas of research are simply beyond the scope of this review. Nonetheless, the chapter presents a portrait of a compelling research area and shines a light on a number of important open questions. We anticipate important advances in the next decade.

NOTES

* We would like to thank Heidi Reynolds-Stenson for her research assistance.
1. One of the first free computer programs capable of decrypting content on a commercially produced DVD video disc.
2. Used by anti-consumerist social movements to disrupt media culture and mainstream cultural institutions, and exposing supposedly questionable political assumptions behind commercial culture, for example by refiguring logos and product images.

REFERENCES

Aday, S., H. Farrell, M. Lynch, J. Sides and D. Freelon (2012), 'Blogs and bullets II: new media and conflict after the Arab Spring', Washington, DC: United States Institute on Peace, accessed 15 May 2014 at http://www.usip.org/publications/blogs-and-bullets-ii-new-media-and-conflict-after-the-arab-spring.

Aday, S., F. Henry, M. Lynch, J. Sides, J. Kelly and E. Zuckerman (2010), 'Blogs and bullets: new media in contentious politics', Washington, DC: United States Institute of Peace, accessed 15 May 2014 at http://www.usip.org/publications/blogs-and-bullets-new-media-in-contentious-politics.

Alexanyan, K.A, V.R. Barash, B. Etling, R. Faris, U. Gasser, J. Kelly, J. Palfrey and H. Roberts (2012), 'Exploring Russian cyberspace: digitally-mediated collective action and the networked public sphere', Cambridge, MA: Berkman Center for Internet & Society at Harvard University.

Arquilla, J. and D. Ronfeldt (2001), *Networks and Netwars: The Future of Terror, Crime, and Militancy*, Santa Monica, CA: RAND.

Ayers, M.D. (2003), 'Comparing collective identity in online and offline feminist activists', in M. McCaughey and M.D. Ayers (eds), *Cyberactivism: Online Activism in Theory and Practice*, New York: Routledge, pp. 145–64.

Ayres, J.M. (1999), 'From the streets to the internet: the cyber-diffusion of contention', *The Annals of the American Academy of Political and Social Science*, **566**(1), 132–43.

Ayres, J.M. (2005), 'Transnational activism in the Americas: the internet and innovations in the repertoire of contention', *Research in Social Movements, Conflicts and Change*, **26**, 35–61.

Bakardjieva, M. (2009), 'Subactivism: lifeworld and politics in the age of the internet', *The Information Society*, **25**(2), 91–104.

Benkler, Y. (2006), *The Wealth of Networks: How Social Production Transforms Markets and Freedom*, New Haven, CT: Yale University Press.

Bennett, D. and P. Fielding (1999), *The Net Effect: How Cyberadvocacy is Changing the Political Landscape*, Merrifield, VA: e-advocates Press.

Bennett, W.L. (2003a), 'Communicating global activism: strengths and vulnerabilities of networked politics', *Information, Communication and Society*, **6**(2), 43–168.

Bennett, W.L. (2003b), 'New media power: the internet and global activism', in N. Couldry and J. Curran (eds), *Contesting Media Power*, New York: Rowman & Littlefield, pp. 17–37.

Bennett, W.L. (2004a), 'Communicating global activism: strengths and vulnerabilities of networked politics', in W. van de Donk, B.D. Loader, P.G. Nixon and D. Rucht (eds), *Cyberprotest: New Media, Citizens and Social Movements*, New York: Routledge, pp. 123–46.

Bennett, W.L. (2004b), 'Social movements beyond borders: understanding two eras of transnational activism', in D. della Porta and S. Tarrow, *Transnational Protest and Global Activism*, New York: Rowman & Littlefield, pp. 203–27.

Bennett, W.L., C. Breunig and T. Givens (2008), 'Communication and political mobilization:

digital media and the organization of anti-Iraq War demonstrations in the U.S.', *Political Communication*, **25**(3), 269–89.
Beyer, J.L. (2011), 'Youth and the generation of political consciousness online', PhD dissertation, Washington, DC: Department of Political Science, University of Washington.
Bimber, B. (2001), 'Information and political engagement in America: the search for effects of information technology at the individual level', *Political Research Quarterly*, **54**(1), 53–67.
Bimber, B., A.J. Flanagin and C. Stohl (2005), 'Reconceptualizing collective action in the contemporary media environment', *Communication Theory*, **15**(4), 365–88.
Bimber, B., A.J. Flanagin and C. Stohl (2012), *Collective Action in Organizations: Interaction and Engagement in an Era of Technological Change*, Cambridge, UK: Cambridge University Press.
Boulianne, S. (2009), 'Does internet use affect engagement? A meta-analysis of research', *Political Communication*, **26**(2), 193–211.
Brunsting, S. and T. Postmes (2002), 'Social movement participation in the digital age: predicting offline and online collective action', *Small Group Research*, **33**(5), 525–54.
Buechler, S.M. (1995), 'New social movement theories', *The Sociological Quarterly*, **36**(3), 441–64.
Burns, A. and B. Eltham (2009), 'Twitter-free Iran: an evaluation of Twitter's role in public diplomacy and information operations in Iran's 2009 election crisis', *Communications Policy & Research Forum 2009*, Sydney: University of Technology.
Carty, V. (2002), 'Technology and counter-hegemonic movements: the case of Nike Corporation', *Social Movement Studies*, **1**(2), 129–46.
Carty, V. (2011), *Wired and Mobilizing: Social Movements, New Technology, and Electoral Politics*, New York: Routledge.
Castells, M. (1997), *The Power of Identity*, Oxford: Blackwell.
Chadwick, A. (2006), *Internet Politics: States, Citizens, and New Communication Technologies*, Oxford: Oxford University Press.
Chadwick, A. (2007), 'Digital network repertoires and organizational hybridity', *Political Communication*, **24**(3), 283–301.
Cloward, R.A. and F.F. Piven (2001), 'Disrupting cyberspace: a new frontier for labor activism?', *New Labor Forum*, **8**, 91–4.
Cohen, C.J., J. Kahne, B. Bowyer, E. Middaugh and J. Rogowski (2012), *Participatory Politics: New Media and Youth Political Action*, Chicago, IL: MacArthur.
Deibert, R.J., J.G. Palfrey, R. Rohozinski and J. Zittrain (2008), *Access Denied: The Practice and Policy of Global Internet Filtering*, Cambridge, MA: MIT Press.
Deibert, R.J., J.G. Palfrey, R. Rohozinski and J. Zittrain (2010), *Access Controlled: The Shaping of Power, Rights, and Rule in Cyberspace*, Cambridge, MA: MIT Press.
Della Porta, D. and L. Mosca (2009), 'Searching the net: web sites' qualities in the global justice movement', *Information, Communication & Society*, **12**(6), 771–92.
DeNardis, L. (2012), 'Hidden levers of internet control', *Information, Communication & Society*, **15**(5), 720–38.
Diani, M. (2000), 'Social movement networks virtual and real', *Information, Communication and Society*, **3**(3), 386–401.
DiMaggio, P., E. Hargittai, W.R. Neuman and J.P. Robinson (2001), 'Social implications of the internet', *Annual Review of Sociology*, **27**, 307–36.
Doheny-Farina, S. (1998), *The Wired Neighborhood*, New Haven, CT: Yale University Press.
Downing, J.D.H. (1989), 'Computers for political change: PeaceNet and public data access', *Journal of Communication*, **39**(3), 154–62.
Eagleton-Pierce, M. (2001), 'The internet and the Seattle WTO protests', *Peace Review*, **13**(3), 331–7.
Earl, J. (2007), 'Leading tasks in a leaderless movement: the case of strategic voting', *American Behavioral Scientist*, **50**(10), 1327–49.
Earl, J. (2011a), 'Political repression: iron fists, velvet gloves, and diffuse control', *Annual Review of Sociology*, **37**, 261–84.

Earl, J. (2011b), 'Protest online: theorizing the consequences of online engagement', *Outcomes of the Social Movements and Protest Conference*, Wissenschaftszentrum, Berlin.

Earl, J. (2012), 'Private protest? Public and private engagement online', *Information, Communication & Society*, **15**(5), 591–608.

Earl, J. and J. Beyer (2013), 'The dynamics of backlash online: anonymous and the battle for WikiLeaks', unpublished manuscript.

Earl, J. and K. Kimport (2011), *Digitally Enabled Social Change: Activism in the Internet Age*, Cambridge, MA: MIT Press.

Earl, J. and A. Schussman (2003), 'The new site of activism: online organizations, movement entrepreneurs, and the changing location of social movement decision-making', *Research in Social Movements, Conflicts, and Change*, **24**, 155–87.

Earl, J. and A. Schussman (2004), 'Cease and desist: repression, strategic voting and the 2000 presidential election', *Mobilization*, **9**(2), 181–202.

Earl, J., H.M. Hurwitz, A.M. Mesinas, M. Tolan and A. Arlotti (2013), 'This protest will be tweeted: Twitter and protest policing during the Pittsburgh G20', *Information, Communication & Society*, **16**(4), 459–78.

Earl, J., K. Kimport, G. Prieto, C. Rush and K. Reynoso (2010), 'Changing the world one webpage at a time: conceptualizing and explaining "internet activism"', *Mobilization*, **15**(4), 425–46.

Elkins, D.J. (1997), 'Globalization, telecommunication, and virtual ethnic communities', *International Political Science Review*, **18**(2), 139–52.

Ems, L. (2009), 'Twitter use in Iranian, Moldovan and G-20 summit protests presents new challenges for governments', CHI 2009 Conference, Boston, MA, 4–9 April 2009.

Eschenfelder, K.R. and A.C. Desai (2004), 'Software as protest: the unexpected resiliency of U.S.-based DeCSS posting and linking', *The Information Society*, **20**(2), 101–16.

Eschenfelder, K.R., R.G. Howard and A.C. Desai (2005), 'Who posts DeCSS and why? A content analysis of web sites posting DVD circumvention software', *Journal for the American Society for Information Science and Technology*, **56**(13), 1405–18.

Etling, B., R. Faris and J. Palfrey (2010), 'Political change in the digital age: the fragility and promise of online organizing', *SAIS Review*, **3**(2), 37–49.

Fisher, D.R. (1998), 'Rumoring theory and the internet: a framework for analyzing the grass roots', *Social Science Computer Review*, **16**(2), 158–68.

Fisher, D.R. and M. Boekkooi (2010), 'Mobilizing friends and strangers: understanding the role of the internet in the Step It Up day of action', *Information, Communication & Society*, **13**(2), 193–208.

Foot, K.A. and S.M. Schneider (2002), 'Online action in Campaign 2000: an exploratory analysis of the U.S. political web sphere', *Journal of Broadcasting and Electronic Media*, **46**(2), 222–4.

Ganesh, S. and C. Stohl (2010), 'Qualifying engagement: a study of information and communication technology and the global social justice movement in Aotearoa New Zealand', *Communication* Monographs, **77**(2), 51–74.

Garrett, R.K. and P.N. Edwards (2007), 'Revolutionary secrets: technology's role in the South African anti-apartheid movement', *Social Science Computer Review*, **25**(1), 13–26.

Garrido, M. and A. Halavais (2003), 'Mapping networks of support for the Zapatista movement: applying social-networks analysis to study contemporary social movements', in M. McCaughey and M.D. Ayers (eds), *Cyberactivism: Online Activism in Theory and Practice*, New York: Routledge, pp. 165–84.

Gerlach, L.P. (2001), 'The structure of social movements: environmental activism and its opponents', in J. Arquilla and D. Ronfeldt (eds), *Networks and Netwars: The Future of Terror, Crime, and Militancy*, Santa Monica, CA: Rand, pp. 289–310.

Gerlach, L.P. and V.H. Hine (1970), *People, Power, Change: Movements of Social Transformation*, Indianapolis, IN: Bobbs-Merrill.

Gladwell, M. (2010), 'Why the revolution will not be tweeted', *New Yorker*, 4 October 2010, accessed 15 May 2014 at http://www.newyorker.com/reporting/2010/10/04/101004fa_fact_gladwell?currentPage=all.

Grossman, L. (2009), 'Iran protests: Twitter, the medium of the movement', *Time*, accessed 15 May 2014 at http://content.time.com/time/world/article/0,8599,1905125,00.html.

Gurak, L.J. (1997), *Persuasion and Privacy in Cyberspace: The Online Protests over Lotus MarketPlace and the Clipper Chip*, New Haven, CT: Yale University Press.

Gurak, L.J. (1999), 'The promise and the peril of social action in cyberspace', in M.A. Smith and P. Kollock (eds), *Communities in Cyberspace*, London: Routledge, pp. 243–63.

Gurak, L.J. and J. Logie (2003), 'Internet protests, from text to web', in M. McCaughey and M.D. Ayers (eds), *Cyberactivism: Online Activism and Theory and Practice*, New York: Routledge, pp. 25–46.

Haythornthwaite, C. and L. Kendall (2010), 'Internet and community', *American Behavioral Scientist*, **53**(8), 1083–94.

Hooghe, M., S. Vissers, D. Stolle and V.-A. Mahéo (2010), 'The potential of internet mobilization: an experimental study on the effect of internet and face-to-face mobilization efforts', *Political Communication*, **27**(4), 406–31.

Howard, P.N. and M.M. Hussain (2011), 'The role of digital media', *Journal of Democracy*, **22**(3), 35–48.

Inglehart, R. and C. Welzel (2005), *Modernization, Cultural Change, and Democracy: The Human Development Sequence*, Cambridge, UK: Cambridge University Press.

Jordan, T. and P. Taylor (2004), *Hacktivism and Cyberwars: Rebels with a Cause*, New York: Routledge.

Kahn, R. and D. Kellner (2004), 'New media and internet activism: from the "Battle of Seattle" to blogging', *New Media & Society*, **6**(1), 87–95.

Karpf, D. (2012), *The MoveOn Effect*, Oxford: Oxford University Press.

Kavanaugh, A., B.J. Kim, M. Perez-Quinones, J. Schmitz and P. Isenhour (2008), 'Net gains in political participation: secondary effects of internet on community', *Information, Communication & Society*, **11**(8), 933–63.

Kreimer, S.F. (2001), 'Technologies of protest: insurgent social movements and the First Amendment in the era of the internet', *University of Pennsylvania Law Review*, **150**(1), 119–71.

Kreiss, D. (2012), *Taking Our Country Back*, Oxford: Oxford University Press.

Krueger, B.S. (2005), 'Government surveillance and political participation on the internet', *Social Science Computer Review*, **23**(4), 439–52.

Krueger, B.S. (2006), 'A comparison of conventional and internet political mobilization', *American Politics Research*, **34**(6), 759–76.

Lievrouw, L.A. (2011), *Alternative and Activist New Media*, Cambridge, UK: Polity Press.

Lockard, J. (1997), 'Progressive politics, electronic individualism and the myth of virtual community', in D. Porter (ed.), *Internet Culture*, New York: Routledge, pp. 219–31.

Lynch, M. (2011), 'After Egypt: the limits and promise of online challenges to the authoritarian Arab state', *Perspectives on Politics*, **9**(2), 301–10.

Madrigal, A.C. (2012), 'The new culture jamming: how activists will respond to online advertising', *The Atlantic*, accessed 15 May 2014 at http://www.theatlantic.com/technology/archive/2012/05/the-new-culture-jamming-how-activists-will-respond-to-online-advertising/257176/.

Martinez-Torres, M.E. (2001), 'Civil society, the internet, and the Zapatistas', *Peace Review*, **13**(8), 347–55.

Matsuzawa, S. (2011), 'Horizontal dynamics in transnational activism: the case of Nu River anti-dam activism in China', *Mobilization*, **16**(3), 369–87.

Morozov, E. (2009), 'Iran: downside to the Twitter revolution', *Dissent*, Fall, 10–14, accessed 15 May 2014 at http://www.dissentmagazine.org/article/iran-downside-to-the-twitter-revolution.

Morozov, E. (2011a), *The Net Delusion: The Dark Side of Internet Freedom*, New York: Public Affairs.

Morozov, E. (2011b), 'Response to Philip N. Howard's review of *The Net Delusion: The Dark Side of Internet Freedom*', *Perspectives on Politics*, **9**(4), 897.

Mourtada, R. and F. Salem (2011), *Civil Movements: The Impact of Facebook and Twitter*, Dubai: Dubai School of Government.

Myers, D.J. (1994), 'Communication technology and social movements: contributions of computer networks to activism', *Social Science Computer Review*, 12(2), 251–60.

Nip, J.Y.M. (2004), 'The Queer Sisters and its electronic bulletin board: a study of the internet for social movement mobilization', *Information, Communication & Society*, 7, 23–49.

Norris, P. (2005), 'The impact of the internet on political activism: evidence from Europe', *International Journal of Electronic Government Research*, 1(1), 20–39.

Peckham, M.H. (1998), 'New dimensions of social movement/countermovement interaction: the case of scientology and its internet critics', *Canadian Journal of Sociology*, 23(4), 317–47.

Pichardo, N.A. (1997), 'New social movements: a critical review', *Annual Review of Sociology*, 23, 411–30.

Postigo, H. (2012), *The Digital Rights Movement*, Boston, MA: MIT Press.

Quintelier, E. and S. Vissers (2008), 'The effect of internet use on political participation: an analysis of survey results for 16-year-olds in Belgium', *Social Science Computer Review*, 26(4), 411–27.

Rainie, L. and B. Wellman (2012), *Networked: The New Social Operating System*, Cambridge, MA: MIT Press.

Reid, E. and H. Chen (2007), 'Internet-savvy US and Middle Eastern extremist groups', *Mobilization*, 12(2), 177–92.

Rheingold, H. (1993), *The Virtual Community: Homesteading on the Electronic Frontier*, Reading, MA: Addison-Wesley.

Roberts, H., E. Zuckerman, R. Faris and J. Palfrey (2010), *2010 Circumvention Tool Usage Report*, Cambridge, MA: Berkman Center for Internet & Society at Harvard University.

Rojas, H. and E. Puig-i-Abril (2009), 'Mobilizers mobilized: information, expression, mobilization and participation in the digital age', *Journal of Computer-Mediated Communication*, 14(4), 902–27.

Roscigno, V.J. and W.F. Danaher (2001), 'Media and mobilization: the case of radio and southern textile worker insurgency, 1929 to 1934', *American Sociological Review*, 61(1), 21–48.

Salter, L. (2003), 'Democracy, new social movements, and the internet: a Habermasian analysis', in M. McCaughey and M.D. Ayers (eds), *Cyberactivism: Online Activism in Theory and Practice*, New York: Routledge, pp. 117–44.

Sassi, S. (1996), 'Network and the fragmentation of the public sphere', *Electronic Journal of Communication*, 6(2), 25–41.

Schulz, M.S. (1998), 'Collective action across borders: opportunity structures, network capacities, and communicative praxis in the age of advanced globalization', *Sociological Perspectives*, 41(3), 587–616.

Schussman, A. and J. Earl (2004), 'From barricades to firewalls? Strategic voting and social movement leadership in the internet age', *Sociological Inquiry*, 74(4), 439–63.

Segerberg, A. and W.L. Bennett (2011), 'Social media and the organization of collective action: using Twitter to explore the ecologies of two climate change protests', *The Communication Review*, 14(3), 197–215.

Shirky, C. (2008), *Here Comes Everybody: The Power of Organizing Without Organizations*, New York: Penguin Press.

Smith, J. (2001), 'Globalizing resistance: the Battle of Seattle and the future of social movements', *Mobilization*, 6(1), 1–20.

Smith, J., R. Pagnucco and C. Chatfield (1997), 'Social movements and world politics: a theoretical framework', in J. Smith, R. Pagnucco and C. Chatfield (eds), *Transnational Social Movements and Global Politics: Solidarity Beyond the State*, Syracuse, NY: Syracuse University Press, pp. 59–77.

Smith, P.J. and E. Smyth (2001), 'Globalization, citizenship and technology: the multilateral agreement on investment meets the internet', in F. Webster (ed.), *Culture and Politics in the Information Age: A New Politics?*, London: Routledge, pp. 183–206.

Stein, L. (2009), 'Social movement web use in theory and practice: a content analysis of US movement websites', *New Media and Society*, **11**(5), 749–71.

Tarrow, S. (1998), 'Fishnets, internets, and catnets: globalization and transnational collective action', in M.P. Hanagan, L.P. Moch and W. te Brake (eds), *Challenging Authority: The Historical Study of Contentious Politics*, Minneapolis, MN: University of Minnesota Press, pp. 228–24.

Tilly, C. (2004), *Social Movements, 1768–2004*, Boulder, CO: Paradigm Publishers.

Tufekci, Z. and C. Wilson (2012), 'Social media and the decision to participate in political protest: observations from Tahrir Square', *Journal of Communication*, **62**(2), 363–79.

Van Aelst, P. and S. Walgrave (2002), 'New media, new movements? The role of the internet in shaping the "anti-globalization" movement', *Information, Communication & Society*, **5**(4), 465–93.

Van de Donk, W., B.D. Loader, P.G. Nixon and D. Rucht (2004), 'Introduction: social movements and ICTs', in W. van de Donk, B.D. Loader, P.G. Nixon and D. Rucht (eds), *Cyberprotest: New Media, Citizens and Social Movements*, New York: Routledge, pp. 1–22.

Van Laer, J. (2010), 'Activists online and offline: the internet as an information channel for protest demonstrations', *Mobilization*, **15**(3), 347–66.

Van Laer, J. and P. van Aelst (2010), 'Internet and social movement action repertoires', *Information, Communication & Society*, **13**(8), 1146–71.

Vegh, S. (2003), 'Classifying forms of online activism: the case of cyberprotests against the World Bank', in M. McCaughey and M.D. Ayers (eds), *Cyberactivism: Online Activism and Theory and Practice*, New York: Routledge, pp. 71–95.

Wellman, B. and M. Gulia (1999), 'Net surfers don't ride alone: virtual communities as communities', in B. Wellman (ed.), *Networks in the Global Village*, Boulder, CO: Westview Press.

Wray, S. (1998), 'Electronic civil disobedience and the World Wide Web of hacktivism: a mapping of extraparliamentarian direct action net politics', World Wide Web and Contemporary Cultural Theory Conference, Drake University.

Wray, S. (1999), 'On electronic civil disobedience', *Peace Review*, **11**(1), 107–12.

Zhuo, X., B. Wellman and J. Yu (2011), 'Egypt: the first internet revolt?', *Peace Magazine*, 6–10, accessed 15 May 2014 at http://peacemagazine.org/archive/v27n3p06.htm.

PART III

CONTEMPORARY SOCIAL MOVEMENTS

17. The environmental movement
*Hein-Anton van der Heijden**

INTRODUCTION

There is strong evidence that the environmental movement has been the most influential of all social movements of the past half-century, at least in Western countries. If we make a distinction between substantive, procedural, structural, and sensitizing impacts, this argument could be firmly buttressed.

As for substantive impacts, no movement has so decisively influenced political decision-making at the subnational, national, and transnational levels. Examples include law-making with respect to the pollution of air, water, and soil; preventing the construction of highways through pristine nature reserves; diminishing the role of nuclear energy; restricting the use of genetically modified organisms; and so on. Without environmental movements the world would have looked unrecognizably different.

Procedural impacts refer to the access a social movement or social movement organization (SMO) has to the subnational, national, and transnational political systems, for instance, by their participation in consultation or negotiation procedures. Examples include the formal recognition of environmental movement organizations (EMOs) in local, regional, and national decision-making procedures; the frequent meetings of the ten most important Europe-level EMOs ('G10') in Brussels with the Cabinet of the Environmental Commissioner and even with the President of the European Commission; and the involvement of transnational EMOs in the negotiations on multilateral environmental agreements (MEAs) with respect to, for instance, climate change and biodiversity protection.

Structural impacts, the changing of specific institutional structures due to movement or SMO activities, include the foundation of government departments for the environment in almost every country, as well as the foundation of Green parties that have decisively changed the political landscape of countries like Germany. Sensitizing impacts, finally, means that a social movement or SMO is able to put an issue on the public or political agenda or that, due to the movement's efforts, the attitudes of the public regarding a specific issue change significantly. Public opinion surveys at the national, transnational (Eurobarometer), and global level (e.g., World Values Survey) time and again reveal the high degree of environmental awareness of the national, transnational, and global publics and, to a certain extent, their readiness to change part of their environmental behavior (e.g., with respect to consumption, recycling, transport, and so on).

Despite all these impacts, environmental movements have little reason to be complacent. During the past half-century, environmental problems have developed from relatively easily manageable pollution problems at the local and national levels, via an alarming but equally easily soluble global problem (the depletion of the ozone layer due to human-made propellants in spray cans and refrigerators), to a range of complex, multi-dimensional and mutually reinforcing global problems like deforestation, desertification, and, first of all, climate change. Despite all endeavors of environmental movements and EMOs at different territorial levels, the condition of the global environment is worse than ever before, and the picture of the future looks rather gloomy indeed.

In this chapter a theoretically informed analysis of the contemporary environmental movement will be provided. Although a history of more than 50 years of environmentalism would suggest a diachronic analysis, in this chapter the synchronic rather than the historical dimension will be emphasized. Numerous environmental problems have developed from local to global ones, but their root causes seem to have remained the same. As Saurin (1993) has convincingly argued: environmental problems should be seen as one of the 'routine consequences' of modernity and, one could specify, of modernity's four interconnected institutional features: capitalism, industrialism, surveillance, and military power (cf. Giddens, 1990). It is my contention that the uniqueness of (some parts of) the environmental movement has always been in the fact that it explicitly challenges these very institutional features of modernity ('diagnostic framing'), and thus shows a glimpse of what a green world could look like ('prognostic framing').

FROM NATURE PROTECTION TO ENVIRONMENTALISM: THE ENVIRONMENTAL MOVEMENT FROM THE LATE NINETEENTH CENTURY TO THE 1960s

The history of the environmental movement and/or its constituting branches and discourses in different parts of the world has been told numerous times (e.g., Eckersley, 1992; Dalton, 1994; Guha and Martinez-Alier, 1997; Rootes, 1999, 2004; Brulle, 2000; Guha, 2000; Doherty, 2002; Gottlieb, 2005; Dobson, 2007; Montrie, 2011).[1] In these studies a large number of different concepts and categorizations have been used, and it is important to remind ourselves that concepts and categorizations cannot by judged by their truth or falsity, but only by their theoretical utility at a certain time and place.

In European environmental movement research, until the 1980s an influential distinction has been the one between conservationism, environmentalism, and ecologism (Rootes, 2004, p. 619), based on the radicalness or range of the goals of the different strands of the movement. Another way to understand the movement is to arrange its different currents on a continuum between the two poles of anthropocentrism and ecocentrism. At this continuum, Eckersley (1992, p. 34ff) distinguishes between five different positions: resource conservation, human welfare ecology, preservationism, animal liberation, and ecologism, each of which has its own EMOs.

Robert Brulle, analyzing the environmental movement in the United States, distinguishes between 11 distinct 'discursive communities' of EMOs, each based on a specific worldview: wildlife management, conservation, preservation, reform environmentalism, deep ecology, environmental justice, environmental health, ecofeminism, ecospiritualism, animal rights, anti-globalization/Greens (Brulle, 2000, pp. 96–9).

Most of the environmental organizations in Europe and the USA that were founded before 1960 belong to Brulle's categories of wildlife management, conservation, and preservation, and, in Eckersley's terms, each of them could be called anthropocentric rather than ecocentric. Wildlife management intends no more than to secure adequate supply of game and fish to provide for the recreational use of humans in terms of hunting and fishing. According to the conservation frame, on the other hand, natural resources should be technically managed from a utilitarian perspective in order to realize the greatest good for the greatest number of people. Preservationism, finally, propounds that the continued existence of wilderness and wildlife, undisturbed by human action, is necessary because nature is an important component in supporting both the physical and the spiritual life of humans (Brulle et al., 2007, p. 200).

Many of the present day wildlife management, conservation, and preservation organizations date from the nineteenth century.[2] In the USA, preservationist John Muir was not only pivotal in the foundation of the first national park in 1890 (the Yosemite National Park), but he also helped to establish the Sierra Club in 1892, one of the oldest, largest and most influential environmental organizations in the USA. Other early-founded EMOs in the USA include the National Audubon Society (1905), the National Parks and Conservation Association (1919), the Wilderness Society (1935), and the National Wildlife Federation (1936) (Dunlap and Mertig, 1992, p. 13).

Also in Europe until the 1960s, the environmental movement almost exclusively dealt with wildlife management, conservation, and preservation issues (Dalton, 1994), and, like in the USA, several of its EMOs were already founded around the second half of the nineteenth century. The French National Society of Nature Protection dates from 1854, the British National Trust from 1895, and the German League for Bird Protection from 1899 (ibid., pp. 29–31). An insightful comparative analysis of the history of nature protection organizations in France, Germany, Italy, the Netherlands, Norway, Poland, Sweden, the UK, and the USA is provided by Van Koppen and Markham (2007), whereas Markham (2008) wrote a detailed genealogy of the German nature protection and environmental movement.

THE NEW ENVIRONMENTAL MOVEMENT

Reform environmentalism, the fourth 'discursive community' as distinguished by Brulle, states that nature is an ecological system, a web of interdependent relationships of which humanity is a part. Human health is vulnerable to disturbances in the ecosystem, and this animates actions to identify and eliminate the physical causes of environmental degradation.

The new environmental movement emerging from the mid-1960s onwards was strongly influenced by a number of scientific publications, all of which challenged the hidden assumptions between modernization, technological progress, and 'blind' economic growth. In *Silent Spring* Rachel Carson called attention to the negative effects of the use of DDT and other pesticides. Carson's book (1962) not only addressed DDT, but also described ecological cycles and chain reactions, and hence provided a frame of reference and a scheme of interpretation for the emerging environmental movement that was also relevant for a number of other environmental problems. The global ecological model as developed in the Club of Rome's report *The Limits to Growth* (Meadows et al., 1972) was a cybernetic model in which formerly isolated categories like natural resources, population growth, capital, food production, and pollution were being connected for the first time. In *The Costs of Economic Growth* (1967), another influential scientific publication, Mishan broke down the consensus on the desirability of economic growth at any price, and thus paved the way for both Schumacher's philosophy of 'thinking small', as well as for a Marxism-based 'political ecology'. Schumacher perceived small-scale, self-sufficient communities as an alternative for a growth-oriented world, whereas political ecology considered the capitalist economic structure as the main cause of environmental problems (Van der Heijden et al., 1992, pp. 4–5).

The emergence and flowering of the new environmental movement in Western Europe, the USA, and other 'First World' countries is one of the best documented episodes in the history of environmental movement research. Country and region studies include, among several others, Diani (1995) on Italy; Hayes (2002) on France; Jamison et al. (1990) on Sweden, Denmark, and the Netherlands; Rucht and Roose (1999) and Markham (2008) on Germany; Doherty (1999), Wall (1999), and Doherty et al. (2002) on radical environmentalism in Britain; Van der Heijden et al. (1992) and Dalton (1994) on Western Europe; Dunlap and Mertig (1992), Gottlieb (1993), Dowie (1996), Brulle (2000), and Montrie (2011) on the USA; Hutton and Connors (1999) and Doyle (2000) on Australia; Downes (2000) on New Zealand; Broadbent (1999) and Mason (1999) on Japan.

In the first years of its existence in most countries the new environmental movement was not yet clearly separated from other new social movements like the women's movement, the students' movement, urban social movements, and the Third World solidarity movement, with all of which it often constituted a joint broad 'countercultural' undercurrent (Jamison et al., 1990; Dalton, 1994, pp. 36–7; Rootes, 2004, p. 14).

In most Western countries the new environmental movement started as a number of dispersed grassroots groups struggling against, for instance, a polluting factory, the construction of a new motorway, the pollution of a lake or a river, the extension of an airport or the destruction of an old, low-rent inner-city neighborhood in favor of office buildings and skyscrapers. During the 1960s and early 1970s thousands of local environmental groups all over Western Europe and the USA were formed, and in some countries, most of all in Germany, they remained an important feature of the environmental movement. In the early 1990s, for instance, in Berlin there were 115 local environmental groups, in Konstanz 62, and in Cologne 60 (Rucht and Roose, 1999, p. 64). In sum the German environmental movement consists of over 9000 local groups (Rootes, 2004, p. 628).

From the early 1970s onwards, in all Western countries, new, national-level environmental organizations were founded, partly intended to coordinate and support the activities of grassroots groups, but also to enforce national legislation with respect to, for instance, pollution of air, water, and soil, and the protection of valuable natural areas.[3] Examples of these new environmental organizations include, first of all, the national branches of three transnational EMOs: WWF, Greenpeace, and Friends of the Earth (FoE) (Dalton, 1994, p. 81). Apart from specific differences at the national level, basic distinctions between WWF, Greenpeace, and FoE did and do exist with respect to organizational structure, action repertoire, and the ways environmental problems are being framed (diagnostic, prognostic, and motivational) (Doherty, 2002).

The World Wildlife Fund (WWF, now the World Wide Fund for Nature), founded in 1961, started as a conservation organization with hundreds of conservation projects mainly in Southern countries, like, for instance, the restoration of orangutan habitats and the establishment of nature reserves. In the last three decades WWF has broadened its mission to stopping the degradation of the planet's natural environment, resulting in the coverage of topics like pollution and climate change (reform environmentalism). However, contrary to Greenpeace and FoE, WWF never applies unconventional and confrontational action strategies, and in most countries its constituency could be called 'donators' or 'supporters' rather than 'members' or 'activists' (Van der Heijden, 2000, p. 30).

The origin of Greenpeace (1971) is in both the peace and the environmental movement (Zelko, 2013). Its very first target was the United States testing of nuclear devices in Amchitka, Alaska, and nuclear weapons and nuclear energy have been topics of contention ever since. Greenpeace has played a pivotal role in the adoption of a ban on toxic waste exports to less-developed countries, a moratorium on commercial whaling, and bans on the dumping at sea of radioactive and industrial waste. Greenpeace tries to reach its goals by lobbying, by scientific research, and, most of all, by its unconventional action repertoire with a large role for 'professional activists' rather than for grassroots members. Due to its sophisticated communication strategy, Greenpeace has been very successful in environmental consciousness raising (Van der Heijden, 2000, pp. 111–14).

Friends of the Earth was founded in 1969 in the USA by David Bower, a former Sierra Club official who quit his job after the Sierra Club refused to share his view on the necessity of opposing nuclear energy. FoE is an international confederation of environmental movements with, contrary to Greenpeace, a high degree of autonomy for individual member groups, both at the national and the local level (Doherty, 2006). FoE challenged and, in some countries, still challenges the prevailing model of neoliberal economic and corporate globalization. In order to protect the earth against further environmental degradation, FoE aimed and, in some countries, still aims to increase public participation and democratic decision-making, and to stimulate grassroots activism. All these features constitute the core of what could be called 'political ecology', a branch within environmentalism in which environmental degradation was seen as one of the consequences of capitalism. One of the most sophisticated forms of political ecology was forwarded by the Danish EMO NOAH (FoE Denmark). In a number of publications NOAH not only criticized the Club of Rome report *Limits to Growth* as being too mechanical and too deterministic, but also published a discussion between left-wing intellectuals like Marcuse, Mansholt, and Gorz about ecology and class struggle (Jamison et al., 1990, p. 88), a discussion that would strongly influence the debate on the relationship between capitalism and environmental degradation. Similar debates took place between the 'organic intellectuals' of the environmental movement in countries like France, Germany, Italy, and the Netherlands.

Also in the USA a number of new, national environmental organizations were founded, among which were the Environmental Defense Fund (1967), and the Natural Resources Defense Council (1970) (Dunlap and Mertig, 1992, p. 13). However, earlier than in Western Europe, in the USA a deep cleavage developed between national organizations, the grassroots environmental movement, and radical environmentalism, a cleavage that we will come back to later.

THE NUCLEAR ENERGY CONFLICT

One of the decisive contributions of the environmental movement to reshaping politics and to challenge the prevailing belief in the relationship between progress and technology has been its role in the conflict over nuclear energy. The movement's action campaigns not only resulted in a fundamental rethinking of nuclear technology as one of the strategic technologies of post-war modernity, but also in a basic reconsideration of the very institutions of modernity itself: capitalism, industrialism, surveillance, and military power (Van der Heijden, 2014). Apart from this, the anti-nuclear movement has also strongly contributed to the emergence of a completely new type of political parties: Green parties (structural impact).

The history of the anti-nuclear movement has been widely documented (Downey, 1986; Rudig, 1990; Flam, 1994; Van der Heijden, 2014), and anti-nuclear movement research has significantly contributed to a deeper insight in the relationship between social movements and political opportunity structures (Kitschelt, 1986; Flam, 1994; Koopmans and Duyvendak, 1995; Kolb, 2007). In most Western countries, resistance against nuclear energy emerged at the local level in the early 1970s, whereas the decisive confrontations with the government took place at the end of that decade (Rudig, 1990; Flam, 1994). The 1960s and early 1970s had been an era of 'technological progress optimism'. Japan, the United States, and Western Europe had experienced a long period of economic growth that demanded, however, ever more energy. In major countries nuclear energy was seen as the very option to cover future energy demands. The French government, for instance, claimed that by the year 2000 France would operate 170 nuclear reactors, supplying 85 per cent of all national electricity.

In many countries the anti-nuclear movement could be considered as the very archetype of a 'new social movement'. It was a decentralized network of grassroots groups, using a new, unconventional action repertoire, a core feature of which was that activists deliberately deployed their own bodies. This occurred, for instance, in physical confrontations with the police, but also in non-violent mass demonstrations, blockades, and site occupations (Rudig, 1990; Flam, 1994).[4]

In the United States a similar pattern could be observed. In 1977 the New England-based Clamshell Alliance received national recognition for its use of consensual decision-making and non-violent civil disobedience during a two-week incarceration following an attempted occupation of the Seabrook nuclear plant (Downey, 1986, p. 357; Epstein, 1991). After the 1979 Three Mile Island accident, also in the USA numerous mass demonstrations took place, including a New York City protest that attracted 200 000 demonstrators.

In the 1970s the reasons why people opposed nuclear energy were very divergent, and in the literature not less than seven different 'diagnostic frames' or definitions of nuclear energy have been distinguished, often occurring complementary to one another. These seven definitions included a local, an anti-technological, an anti-industrial, an anti-authoritarian, an anti-capitalist, a pacifist, and a rational definition/rejection of nuclear energy (Van der Heijden, 2014). Whereas, for instance, farmers in remote villages embraced a local definition because they considered a nuclear plant to be an ultimate threat to the particular character of their local community (Rudig, 1990, p. 125), Marxist students embraced an anti-capitalist definition, as they considered nuclear energy to be an important instrument of corporate capitalism, and pacifists, in their framing of the issue, perceived an intimate relationship between 'peaceful' nuclear energy on the one hand, and nuclear weapons on the other.

In the early 1980s the conflict about nuclear energy slowly died out, and so did the anti-nuclear movement (Rudig, 1990; Flam, 1994). Due to favorable political opportunity structures, in some countries the movement had been very successful (e.g., in Sweden), whereas in other countries (e.g., in France), hardly any substantive result was achieved (Kitschelt, 1986). Then, on 26 April 1986, the world's worst nuclear power accident thus far occurred at Chernobyl in the former USSR (now Ukraine). In Western Europe, the Chernobyl catastrophe led to a renaissance of the anti-nuclear protest in some countries (Germany, Italy), whereas the level of crisis intensity in countries like Belgium, France, the Netherlands, Sweden and Switzerland remained extremely low (Koopmans and Duyvendak, 1995, p. 238; Kolb, 2007, p. 214). In addition, in the years following the Chernobyl disaster, in Germany a number of national EMOs as well as local campaign networks raised nuclear issues, whereas in Britain anti-nuclear protests were mostly the preserve of one single organization – Greenpeace – whose actions were more oriented towards putting pressure on the government and corporations by getting the attention of mass media than toward stimulating mass protest (Rootes, 2003, p. 240).

On 11 March 2011, 15 years after Chernobyl, a series of equipment failures and nuclear meltdowns in the Japanese Fukushima nuclear station led to the release of huge quantities of radioactive material into the atmosphere as well into ground and ocean water. In Japan, the Fukushima catastrophe led to a real revival of the anti-nuclear movement, culminating in numerous demonstrations and a nuclear rally in Tokyo on 16 July 2012, in which 170 000 protesters demanded the government to end the use of nuclear power. In Germany, one day after the beginning of the Fukushima disaster, 60 000 Germans formed a 45-km human chain from Stuttgart to the Neckarwestheim nuclear power plant. Two days later 110 000 people protested in 450 other German towns; the day after Angela Merkel announced the temporary closing down of seven nuclear power plants that went on line before 1980 (Van der Heijden, 2014).

In other European countries Greenpeace and FoE rather than grass-roots groups articulated the fear and the anger of large parts of the European population. In its report *Lessons from Fukushima* (2012), Greenpeace argued that although the Japan earthquake and the following tsunami triggered it, the key causes of the Fukushima accident lie in the institutional failures of political influence and industry-led regulation. According to Greenpeace, the Fukushima accident not only marks the end of the 'nuclear safety' paradigm, it also exposes the deep and systemic failure of the very institutions that are supposed to control nuclear power and protect people (Van der Heijden, 2014).

THE INSTITUTIONALIZATION OF THE ENVIRONMENTAL MOVEMENT AND ITS CONSEQUENCES

Whereas the protests against nuclear energy, especially in the 1970s and 1980s, were mainly grassroots based, from the early 1980s onwards a process of institutionalization of the environmental movement has occurred. Institutionalization is the process by which originally individual norms, expectations, goals, and values tend to form a collective pattern, a pattern by which interactions and communications are regulated and structured. Institutionalization occurs in varying degrees; three dimensions could be distinguished: (1) organizational growth: the growth of the number of SMOs of a social movement, and the growth of their number of members or supporters (and, consequently, the amount of financial resources SMOs have at their disposal); (2) internal institutionalization in the form of professionalization and centralization; (3) external institutionalization; a shift in the way a social movement acts, in favor of conventional rather than unconventional forms of action (Van der Heijden, 1997, pp. 31–2).

All three forms of institutionalization of the environmental movement have been largely documented and discussed (Dowie, 1996; Jordan and Maloney, 1997; Van der Heijden, 1997; Bosso, 2000), but the points of view of these studies are very different. Bosso, analyzing the American movement at the end of the 1990s, suggests that environmentalism in the USA has become an 'interest group community' (Bosso, 2000). Dowie tries to analyze the consequences of institutionalization for the very power of the US environmental movement, but Jordan and Maloney don't even accept the existence of any 'environmental movement' at all, and rather try to explain 'public interest groups' like FoE and Greenpeace from an Olsonian rational choice perspective. Still other (comparative) studies stress the relationship between institutionalization and political opportunity structures in individual countries (Van der Heijden, 1997; Dryzek et al., 2003).

As for organizational growth, in the United States between 1979 and 1990 the National Audubon Society, a US organization dedicated to conservation, doubled its membership from 300 000 to 600 000, the Sierra Club grew from 346 000 to 560 000 (Dunlap and Mertig, 1992, p. 13), whereas at the zenith of its membership explosion (1985–90) Greenpeace USA grew from 800 000 to 2.35 million (Jordan and Maloney, 1997, p. 12).[5] In the USA, in 1995 over 10 000 EMOs with a combined membership of over 41 million were counted (Brulle, 2000, pp. 102–3).

For Western (Continental) Europe similar figures could be provided. Between 1980 and 1995 the joint membership of four national EMOs (FoE, Greenpeace, WWF, and the most important national conservation organization) in four countries (France, Germany, the Netherlands and Switzerland) grew from 1 200 500 to 5 104 000 (Van der Heijden, 1997, p. 38). The largest grower was Greenpeace, which multiplied its membership from 22 500 in 1980 to 1 258 000 15 years later.[6]

The most important way to attract new members or supporters in the USA, and to a lesser extent also in Western Europe, is direct (e-)mail. Every year many millions of environmental (digital) begging letters are being sent. The resulting large numbers of new members or supporters provide 65–70 percent of the income of the national environmental organizations in the USA, but the drawback is that this kind of money increasingly sets the agenda, the strategy, the targets, and the priorities of national environmental organizations (Dowie, 1996, p. 41). Another consequence is that national environmental groups are increasingly being homogenized.

Dowie argues that until the mid-1980s there was some noticeable variety among the large national American groups. One could distinguish a Sierra Club hiker from a National Wildlife Federation hunter, an Audubon bird watcher from a National Resources Defense Council biochemist. Each organization had its own priorities and its own projects. By the mid-1980s, however, the distinctions had blurred and groups began to look and sound alike. Staff, direct mail campaigns, rhetorics and politics – even wardrobes – became homogenized (Dowie, 1996, p. 60).

How could these developments be explained? According to Dunlap and Mertig (1992) the common American distinction between different branches of environmentalism is based on the radicalness of their strategies and tactics. Environmental organizations have different tactical options at their disposal, among which are policy reform and direct action. The preferred tactical choice of the national organizations (Sierra Club, National Wildlife Federation, etc.) has been policy reform. Lobbying, publicity campaigns, and litigation are the most important tactics, but increasingly many of the organizations entered national politics by establishing political action committees (PACs) to fund favored candidates (Dunlap and Mertig, 1992).

In Western Europe a similar emphasis on policy reform could be observed, albeit with a stronger theoretical underpinning: ecological modernization. Ecological modernization has been defined as the discourse that recognizes the structural character of environmental problems but nevertheless assumes that existing political, economic, and social institutions can internalize care for the environment (Hajer, 1995). Consequently, however, ecological modernization requires cooperation rather than structural resistance from the side of the environmental movement (Van der Heijden, 1999), internal institutionalization being both a cause and a consequence.

External institutionalization, finally, the moderation of the action repertoire of the environmental movement, appears to be connected with a country's political opportunity structure (Van der Heijden, 1997, pp. 43–4; Dryzek et al., 2003), but all over Western Europe, with the partial exception of Britain and Germany, conventional forms of action predominated during the 1990s (Rootes, 2003). In the USA, conventional forms of action (e.g., lobbying) have become by far the most important form of action of the national environmental groups, thus excluding almost any possibility for structural change of the social and economic system.[7]

The institutionalization of the American environmental movement has had several important consequences. From the perspectives of numerous grassroots activists, the national organizations seem to be more interested in protecting animal species from extinction than in protecting children from toxic pollutants in their own backyards. Many thousands of local community organizations constituted the foundation of what could be called 'the grassroots environmental movement', whose direct actions could be considered as a challenge to the prevalent belief that economic growth is good per se and ultimately benefits everyone (Dunlap and Mertig, 1992). The emergence of grassroots environmentalism within minority communities will be addressed below.

Radical environmentalism, another reaction to the institutionalization of American environmentalism, is primarily concerned with wilderness and wildlife (Earth First!, the Sea Shepherd Conservation Society). The action repertoire of radical environmentalism includes ecotage,[8] guerrilla theater,[9] and other unconventional or radical forms of action (ibid.). Radical environmentalism has been the topic of Rik Scarce's *Eco-Warriors* ([1990] 2005). In this book, Scarce not only pictures groups like Earth First!, the Sea Shepherd Conservation Society, the Animal Liberation Front, and the Earth Liberation Front from within, but also sketches their ideological background, going back to Gandhi and the Luddites. In *Green Rage: Radical Environmentalism and the Unmaking of Civilization* Christopher Manes (1990) goes even further by claiming that 'ecotage' – the sabotage of equipment, for instance by arson, to prevent further ecological damage – is a legitimate means to challenge the ethics of modern industrial society and to assert the right of the natural world to blossom, evolve, and exist for its own sake.

Also in Western Europe the institutionalization of the environmental movement has resulted in the emergence of radical forms of environmentalism, although the differences from the institutionalized national EMOs have never been as great as in the USA. Doherty (1999) contends that sustained protests against the building of new roads in Britain since the early 1990s signal the emergence of a new social movement dimension to British environmentalism. The growth of direct action has occurred outside the existing environmental pressure groups, and the radical environmental activists of Earth First! – also active in Australia, Ireland, Germany, France, the Netherlands, and Eastern Europe – have played a leading role in this respect (Wall, 1999). Direct environmental action is not restricted to road building but also addresses issues like car culture, genetically modified organisms/foods (GMOs), consumerism, and global finance institutions. Doherty and his collaborators, analyzing the identities and the 'new tribalism' of these 'eco-warriors' as well as the strategies and tactical innovations in their action repertoire, argue that direct action has undermined the assumption that the power of politics and big business cannot be contested (Doherty et al., 2002). In ideological terms, especially in the USA, radical environmentalism could also be labeled as 'deep ecology', the fifth of Brulle's 11 discursive communities in the American environmental movement as discussed earlier (Brulle, 2000, pp. 203–7).[10]

THE EUROPEAN UNION AND THE TRANSFORMATION OF EUROPEAN ENVIRONMENTALISM

From the last quarter of the twentieth century onward, environmentalism increasingly developed a transnational dimension. Whereas in the early 1970s the European Union started to play a modest role in environmental policy-making, this role strongly expanded during the 1980s and 1990s. Environmental problems were increasingly defined as problems of multi-level governance in which different levels of policy-making were being involved (the EU, national governments, but also the subnational level). Parallel with this development we can observe the emergence of 'multi-level environmentalism': EMOs organizing themselves at different territorial levels in order to improve their potential influence.

The growing importance of the European level is reflected in the number of environmental organizations with an office in Brussels (Webster, 1998; Roose, 2003; Mazey and Richardson, 2005; Van der Heijden, 2010). Most environmental groups, however, still consider the national level as their natural habitat, and resistance to changing existing resource allocation strongly conditions how much activity at the EU level an EMO will undertake (Roose, 2003).

The first EMO in Brussels was the 1974-founded European Environmental Bureau (EEB), a European federation of environmental groups that, at present, represents 143 umbrella organizations from 31 countries all over Europe. These umbrella organizations, in their turn, represent some 14 000 member organizations, ranging from the UK National Trust, national branches of FoE, Greenpeace, and WWF, to the Germany-based European Union Against Aircraft Nuisances. In sum the EEB represents more than 15 million individual EMO members and supporters (Van der Heijden, 2010, p. 62).

Until 1988 the EEB was the only EU-level EMO (Webster, 1998). From that year onward, a number of other environmental umbrella organizations established themselves in Brussels, including Birdlife International, CEE Bankwatch Network, Climate Action Network Europe, the European Federation for Transport and Environment, Friends of the Earth Europe, Greenpeace, the Health and Environmental Alliance, International Friends of Nature, and WWF. In sum these ten groups represent a collective membership of more than 20 million (Greenwood, 2007, p. 132), and employ a Brussels-based staff of over 100 (Van der Heijden, 2010, p. 63), supplemented by the potential resources of over 1000 staff in individual European countries (Greenwood, 2007, p. 132). From 1988 onwards, these groups began to coordinate their activities and increasingly acted as a single lobby group (the Group of Four, later Group of Ten) within the European environmental arena (Webster, 1998, p. 184). They have institutional access to the European Directorate for the Environment; most of them, except Greenpeace, receive EU funding; and often they are able to express a genuinely European view, which is, of course, very attractive to the European Commission (Mazey and Richardson, 2005, p. 114). However, their organizational structure and their relationship to their 'mother EMO' largely differs from one case to another (Webster, 1998, pp. 179–81; Van der Heijden, 2010, pp. 67–9).

The most common instrument of European environmental politics are environmental 'Directives', laws that are 'binding as to the result to be achieved', while the 'choice of form and method' is left to the national authorities. Examples of Directives include the Birds Directive, the Emissions Trading Directive, and the Directive regulating the possible approval of GMOs. Whereas Brussels-based EMOs try to influence the substance of these different Directives, national and local-level EMOs campaign on all kinds of issues related to their implementation ('multi-level environmentalism').

As European environmental politics to a large extent structures the form and content of national environmental politics, European environmental politics has deeply changed the structure and organizational form of European environmentalism. For instance, EU politics with respect to GMOs has contributed to the emergence of the European NGO Network on Genetic Engineering (GENET) as well as the European GM-Free Regions Network (Van der Heijden, 2010, pp. 135–8). Similar examples could be given of EMO networks with respect to, for instance, pesticides, toxic waste, transport, climate change, nature protection, and biodiversity. One example of the substantive impact of this kind of 'multi-level environmentalism' is the Birdlife-initiated largest ever petition presented to the European Parliament (2 million signatures), aimed at stopping the modification of the Birds Directive to extend hunting seasons, resulting in the withdrawal of the proposal by the European Commission (Greenwood, 2007, p. 136).

GREEN PARTIES

With the 1970s turning into the 1980s, and with the settlement of the nuclear energy conflict in most countries, an increasing number of environmental activists and groups came to the conclusion that grassroots activism, spirituality, and/or EMO lobbying were no longer sufficient alternatives to parliamentary politics. In numerous countries Green parties were founded, and many of them would develop into serious electoral competitors to the more traditional political parties (Mueller-Rommel, 1989).

The very first Green party in the world was founded in 1972 (the Values Party in New Zealand), and in 1979 the very first national Green member of parliament was elected (Daniel Brélaz in Switzerland) (Richardson and Rootes, 1995, p. 4). In many cases, however, establishing a Green party turned out to be highly controversial within the environmental movement. Could a political party really be an adequate means to bring about the 'new society' as envisioned by the environmental movement of the 1970s? How could and should a movement with grassroots democracy, anti-parliamentarism and the need for radical change as their core business, deal with concepts like party organization, coalition building, and strategic negotiations? In many countries the relationship between Green movements and Green parties was quite uneasy. The overall solution to the different dilemmas was often found in the hybrid concept of 'movement party': by simultaneously being a movement *and* a political party, the Greens tried to combine the best of the radical and the reformist tradition.

Ideologically, at least in the 1980s and 1990s, the new Green parties substantially differed from one another. In countries like the UK where, due to the electoral system, the possibilities to exert political influence were very limited, the ideology was 'dark green' and heavily influenced by the ideas of deep ecology. In countries like Germany with a more favorable electoral opportunity structure, the ideology could rather be called 'light green'. In this respect a continuum could be sketched, ranging from 'deep ecology green' (Les Verts in France and the Ecology Party in Britain), via a mix of ecology and environmentalism (e.g., Ecolo in the Walloon provinces of Belgium) to 'Red–Green', like Die Grünen in Germany (Richardson and Rootes, 1995).

Green parties have been the topic of numerous research endeavors. Mueller-Rommel (1989) and Richardson and Rootes (1995), for instance, both analyze the development and successes of Green parties in a number of European countries. Doherty (1992) analyzed and compared the occurrence of 'green fundamentalism' and 'green realism' in four European countries: France, Germany, Italy, and the United Kingdom. More recent, and broader in geographic scope, is Frankland et al. (2008), who, rather than focusing on ideology, distinguish between Green parties with government experience (Belgium, Finland, France, Germany, and Ireland); Green parties with national parliamentary relevance (Austria, the Netherlands, Sweden, and Switzerland); and Green parties with little or no parliamentary experience (Australia, Canada, New Zealand, United Kingdom, the USA). With respect to the EU level, the issues, visions, strategies, and electoral performances of the Greens throughout the years are assessed by Bomberg (1998). The journal *Environmental Politics* regularly reports about the electoral performance and other experiences of Green parties all over the world.

Of all countries, Germany is the one in which the Greens have most decisively influenced national politics. Early studies of the German Greens include, among several others, Kitschelt (1989), Frankland and Schoonmaker (1992), Poguntke (1993), and Wiesenthal (1993). With the coming to power of the Red–Green coalition in 1998, a long process of social movement politics was rounded off. The Greens now had a Minister of Foreign Affairs (Joschka Fischer) and a Minister for the Environment who was able to steer environmental politics in Europe's largest economy. The volume *The German Greens; Paradox between Movement and Party*, edited by Margit Mayer and John Ely (1998), is an insightful assessment of the transformation of the Greens from a social movement into a pragmatic parliamentarian party, and of the eternal attempts to find a means to bring movement politics into party politics. It reveals the gradual changes in Green definitions of politics and the changes in radical discourse that result from the pressures of parliamentarism and party competition. The volume includes chapters on the roots of the Green party in the anti-nuclear movement, on Green feminism in parliamentary politics, on grass-roots democracy within the Green party, and on the paradox of the party presenting itself as an 'anti-party'.

THE ENVIRONMENTAL MOVEMENT IN EASTERN EUROPE

Up to 1989, strong differences existed between environmental movements in Western Europe and those in the Eastern part of the continent, due to basically different resources, political opportunity structures, and cognitive frames. After the fall of the Berlin Wall these differences gradually declined, but never completely disappeared. From the early 1990s onward, numerous research reports on different aspects of environmental movements in Eastern Europe and the former Soviet Union have been published in journals like *Environmental Politics*, the *Journal of Communist Studies*, and *Voluntas*, and in a number of country- or region-specific books (e.g., Carmin and Fagan, 2010 and Jancar-Webster, 1993 on Eastern Europe as a whole; Hicks, 1996 on Poland; Pickvance, 1998 on Hungary and Russia; and Dawson, 1995, Yanitsky, 1999 and 2012, and Henry, 2010 on post-Soviet Russia). Most of them stress the importance of political opportunity structures for explaining and/or comparing the action repertoires, organizational forms, and impacts of environmental movements.

Up to the early 1980s in most East European countries only an 'official' state-licensed environmental movement did exist. In the former Soviet Union, for instance, the largest organization was the Pan-Russian Nature Conservation Society with a constituency of over 30 million. A common way these organizations used to support the state, whilst at the same time engaging the broader population, was through the formation of so-called 'brigades' that performed activities like managing forests, cleaning up litter from rivers, and maintaining inventories of plant and animal species (Carmin and Fagan, 2010, p. 92). From the early 1980s onward, the legitimacy of East European regimes began to crumble, but political freedom did not yet exist. Environmental protection was often seized as a vehicle for striving for autonomy or national independence, especially in Bulgaria (Ecoglasnost), Hungary, and Czechoslovakia. In the mid-1980s, protest emerged against the construction of two hydroelectric power stations on the Danube River, one at Gabčikovo in (Czecho-)Slovakia, and one at Nagymaros-Visegrád in Hungary. The struggle over the dams brought many disparate groups temporarily together: reform-minded communists, socialists, social-democrats, liberals, Christian-democrats, nationalists, and environmentalists. In October 1988, 40000 people marched in Budapest against the dam (Jancar-Webster, 1993, p. 193), and the anti-dam movement made a substantial contribution to undermining the legitimacy of the Hungarian political regime.

In the Soviet Union, after the 1986 Chernobyl nuclear accident, the anti-nuclear movements in Lithuania and Armenia performed the same function as the environmental movements in Bulgaria and Hungary. Their objective was not only the closing down of nuclear plants, but also national independence of the two republics (Dawson, 1995). About the same time, however, in October 1988, the first all-Union umbrella environmental organization – the Socio-Ecological Union – was established on the basis of a network uniting over 250 environmental groups across the Soviet Union and even some from the United States.

Like one or two decades earlier in the West, environmental protest in Eastern Europe in the 1980s strongly emphasized the directly tangible pollution of air, water, and soil, and its consequences for public health. An infamous example was the notorious region of Bohemia, the south-eastern part of the former GDR, Silesia and Ostrava, with its extended brown coal mines, its massive Nowa Huta steelworks and associated industries. Most scholars agree that such environmental problems were the products of intrinsic features of decaying communist political regimes (centralization, growth-oriented planning system, lack of democratic control, lack of information and participation) (Jancar-Webster, 1993).

Almost immediately after the fall of the regimes, environmental organizations all over Eastern Europe and the former Soviet Union were confronted with the challenges of self-administration. They not only had to respond to new preferences and expectations in society, but also deal with issues of staffing, program administration, fundraising, and financial management (Carmin and Fagan, 2010, p. 697). During this period, political parties and environmental organizations from Western countries generously sponsored the newly emerging civil society in Eastern Europe, in which environmental movements had initially played such an important role. Professional knowledge and other resources for environmental groups were also provided by the Regional Environmental Center for Central and Eastern Europe (REC) in Budapest, founded by Hungary, the European Commission, and the United States.

A next stage in the development of environmental movements in Eastern Europe formally started in 2004, when the Czech Republic, Estonia, Hungary, Latvia, Lithuania, Slovakia, Slovenia, and Poland joined the European Union, three years later followed by Bulgaria and Romania. One consequence of this Europeanization was the incorporation of East European EMOs within EU-wide epistemic communities and green networks such as the Brussels based 'Green-10'. However, whereas this part of the East European environmental movement has captured most attention of environmental movement scholars, Carmin and Fagan point out that professionalized NGOs still represent only a small percentage of all active EMOs in the region (Carmin and Fagan, 2010, p. 698). In Central and Eastern Europe environmental activism has usually taken the form of intense local campaigns, and national EMOs have been weak (Rootes, 2004, p. 630).

In Russia, the democratic upsurge and the high level of environmental mobilization in the early 1990s abruptly ended with the shooting at the federal Parliament building in 1993 and the beginning of authoritarian rule. This authoritarian rule severely curtailed the influence of civil society, among which grassroots environmentalism. Though Yeltsin personally had proclaimed an ecologically oriented economy, the logic of wild capitalism meant its development by way of over-exploitation of nature (Yanitsky, 2012, p. 929). Under the conditions of bureaucratic capitalism the Russian environmental movement could only survive by becoming a set of professional NGOs, although grassroots groups and government-affiliated organizations remained to exist as individual categories (Henry, 2010). After the collapse of the 1988 founded Socio-Ecological Union, there were no other umbrella organizations capable of offering a unified agenda for all Russian environmentalists. Environmental protest in the 1990s was mostly directed against the massive construction of trans-Russian gas and oil pipelines that could be disastrous to local and regional ecosystems. In the most recent period, as the system crisis deepened, Russian environmentalists also struggled against the construction of cottages and town houses for the rich within the protective greenbelts around Moscow and other cities. As Yanitsky observes, today it is practically impossible to separate ecological demands from social and political ones (Yanitsky, 2012, pp. 936–7).

At the end of the 1980s global EMOs like WWF and Greenpeace started working in Russia. In 1988 WWF began small-scale projects for the protection of rare species, and also provided technical assistance to nature reserves. In 1995 WWF officially established an office in Moscow. The Russian branch of Greenpeace has, at present, about 5000 financial contributors and 200 000 volunteers and online activists. Targets of action include the protection of Lake Baikal, the drilling of oil on the Arctic shelf by Gazprom, and genetically modified organisms. Greenpeace Russia's action repertoire is not basically different from the one that has become its hallmark in Western countries – climbing chimneys, activists walking through the streets disguised as garbage cans, and so on. However, the reaction of the police is much more repressive, and to a large extent the authorities have succeeded to frame 'Western' environmental organizations as basically anti-Russian ones. A 2012 Russian law required NGOs with any foreign funding to register as 'foreign agents', and in 2013 30 activists of the Greenpeace ship *Arctic Sunrise* were arrested and imprisoned. According to Yanitsky the Russian environmental movement has to work in an ever more hostile context, and the movement's response – NGO-ization, bureaucratization, Westernization – has led to the loss of its ability to function as a producer and distributor of environmental values (Yanitsky, 1999, p. 157).[11]

THE TRANSNATIONALIZATION OF THE ENVIRONMENTAL MOVEMENT

The transnationalization of the environmental movement is related to three different aspects: the transnationalization of environmental problems; the emergence of a transnational 'polis', intended to address environmental and other transnational social problems; and, finally, the transnationalization of environmental activism itself. Between the mid-1960s and the late 1980s, the way environmental problems and their solutions were defined in Western countries gradually developed from the local via the national to the transnational and even global level.[12] In the 1960s environmental problems were 'discovered' at the local and regional level, in the 1970s national environmental legislation was developed, in the 1980s the EU became deeply involved in environmental policy-making, and the 1992 United Nations Conference on Environment and Development (UNCED) in Rio de Janeiro emphasized the global character of environmental problems like climate change, deforestation, desertification, and biodiversity loss, and, consequently, the need for global solution strategies ('sustainable development'). These global solution strategies were embedded in a large number of multilateral environmental agreements and regimes and the accompanying organizational structures, together constituting the environmental part of what could be called a 'transnational polis'. The development of environmental activism closely follows this trend (1) by the foundation of a large number of new, transnational EMOs (Arts, 1998; Keck and Sikkink, 1998; Chasek et al., 2010); (2) by the emergence of several hundreds of (digital) transnational environmental networks (Keck and Sikkink, 1998, p. 132); (3) by the organizing of parallel summits at UN summits on topics like climate change and biodiversity, attended by thousands of activists (Princen and Finger, 1994; Friedman et al., 2005; Andrée, 2007). As for the foundation of new, transnational environmental movement organizations, in 1973 17 such EMOs were counted, whereas in 2000 that figure had risen to 167 (Doherty and Doyle, 2006, pp. 698–9).

The three most important international mass membership organizations remain Greenpeace, WWF, and Friends of the Earth International (FoEI). At present Greenpeace has branches in 42 countries, and a total constituency of over 2.5 million. Among its largest branches are the Dutch and the German ones, each with more than 500 000 supporters, as well as the British and the North American branches (each has about 250 000 supporters). WWF is the world's largest conservation organization with a joint constituency of over 5 million spread over more than 90 countries. Contrary to Greenpeace, WWF never applies unconventional or confrontational action strategies, and it frequently cooperates with business on specific environment-related projects. Friends of the Earth International is the world's largest grassroots environmental network, uniting 69 national member groups and some 5000 local activist groups on almost every continent. FoEI has more than 2 million members and supporters worldwide; among its largest branches are the German, the British and the Dutch ones.

Although, due to Western dominance in defining the rules of the game transnationalization has a strong Western color, the Global South has also generated a number of transnational environmental movements and EMOs, including the Green Belt Movement. The Green Belt Movement was founded by Wangari Maathai, winner of the 2004 Nobel Peace Prize. It provides income and sustenance to millions of people in Kenya through the planting of trees. It also conducts educational campaigns to raise awareness about women's rights, civic empowerment, and the environment throughout Kenya and Africa (Chasek et al., 2010).

Present day international environmental networks partly flourish due to the extensive use of ICT. Examples include those against the international trade in toxic waste, the destruction of tropical rainforests, climate change, and GMOs. Although most actions take place at the local, regional or national levels, these actions are typically coordinated by international or global networks: the Basel Action Network (BAN), the Rainforest Action Network (RAN), the Climate Action Network (CAN), and Genetic Resources Action International (GRAIN).

One well documented further example of the increasing globalization of environmental activism is the transnational anti-dam movement (Khagram, 2004). In their struggle against big dams, Khagram argues, transnational NGOs, grassroots groups, and social movements have jointly altered the political economy of development in Third World countries, as behind the struggles over big dams lie deep struggles between competing visions and models of development. Khagram's book not only gives a meticulous analysis of the history of the anti-dam movement in India, including the struggles against the Narmada Valley projects, but also a comparative historical cross-country analysis of anti-dam activity in Brazil, Indonesia, South Africa, and China (ibid.).

The influence of environmental activism and EMOs in transnational environmental politics and at UN summits (sometimes called 'global civil society': Friedman et al., 2005) has been the subject of numerous studies. Examples include Andrée (2007) on GMOs and biosafety; Arts (1998) on biodiversity and climate change; Betsill and Corell (2008) on climate change, biodiversity, desertification, whaling, and deforestation; Friedman et al. (2005) on the UNCED; Keck and Sikkink (1998) on deforestation; Princen and Finger (1994) on international water quality, the ivory trade, and the protection of Antarctica; Van der Heijden (2006) on the influence of international political opportunity structures on transnational environmentalism.

Reflecting on these developments, Tamiotti and Finger observe a trend of changing roles and functions of international EMOs in global environmental politics. Apart from consciousness raising, lobbying, environmental education, and facilitating grassroots activism, international EMOs are increasingly involved in the decision-making, but also in the implementation and monitoring of multilateral environmental agreements (Tamiotti and Finger, 2001, p. 62).

THE ENVIRONMENTAL JUSTICE MOVEMENT AND THE ENVIRONMENTALISM OF THE POOR

In the 1980s environmental activists in the USA, but also in Global South countries, increasingly became aware that environmental pollution did not harm everybody in the same way, but disproportionally affected people of color. 'Environmental racism' refers to the disproportionate input of environmental hazards, particularly toxic waste dumps and polluting factories, on people of color. The experience of this specific form of discrimination has given birth to the environmental justice movement. The befalling of this movement is documented in a number of studies: Szasz (1994); Schlosberg (1999, 2007); Bullard (2000, 2005); Cole and Foster (2000); and Pellow (2007), to mention just a few.[13]

One of the earliest studies that describes the rapid development of the movement from a myriad of local, community-based anti-toxic waste dump groups into a rich infrastructure of stable social organizations, is provided by Szasz (1994). In *Dumping in Dixie: Race, Class and Environmental Quality*, Robert Bullard (2000) chronicles the efforts of five African-American communities, empowered by the civil rights movement, to link environmentalism with issues of social justice. In *From the Ground Up: Environmental Racism and the Rise of the American Justice Movement* Cole and Foster (2000) document similar case studies across the USA. Five years later Bullard (2005) edited a book in which not only local, but also national and global movements against environmental injustice were addressed. This book, *The Quest for Environmental Justice*, gives an overview of the early environmental justice movement in the USA and emphasizes the key leadership roles played by women activists. It also examines the lives of people living in so-called 'sacrifice zones': toxic corridors such as Louisiana's infamous 'Cancer Alley', where high concentrations of polluting industries are found. In the second half of the book the focus shifts from the USA to the global level. The relationship between human rights and global justice issues is examined by means of an analysis of South Africa's legacy of environmental racism and the corruption and continuing violence plaguing the oil-rich Niger delta.

Global environmental injustice and the movements resisting it is also the topic of Pellow's path-breaking *Resisting Global Toxics* (2007). The starting point of this book is that nations and corporations in the 'Global North' every year produce millions of tons of toxic waste. These hazardous materials, linked to high rates of illness and death and widespread ecosystem damage, are frequently exported to communities of color all over the world. Pellow traces this transnational waste trade from its beginnings in the 1980s to the present day, from global garbage dumping, via the toxic pesticides that are the legacy of the Green revolution in agriculture, to today's scourge of dumping and remanufacturing high-tech and electronic products. Subsequently, Pellow analyzes the emergence of transnational environmental justice movements to challenge and reverse these practices. Waste dumping across national boundaries from rich to poor countries, Pellow argues, should be conceived as a form of transnational environmental inequality that reflects North/South divisions in a globalized world, and must be theorized in a context of race, class, nation, and environment. This is also the starting point of one of the recent branches in environmental movement research, 'the environmentalism of the poor', a topic to which we turn now.

In this chapter so far, the different branches of the environmental movement have been analyzed according to their position on the spectrum between anthropocentrism and ecocentrism (Eckersley, 1992), as well as according to their belonging to one of the 11 'discursive communities' of EMOs (Brulle, 2000). In their ground-breaking 1997 *Varieties of Environmentalism*, however, Ramachandra Guha and Juan Martinez-Alier contend that environmental movement research has been (too) heavily biased towards First World countries.[14] According to the authors, a strong relationship exists between the urban notion of 'environmental justice' as used in the USA, and the rural Third World notion of 'the environmentalism of the poor'. In *The Environmentalism of the Poor* (2002) Martinez-Alier explicitly uses the two terms as synonyms, as opposed to what he calls the two other main currents in environmentalism: 'the cult of wilderness' and 'the gospel of eco-efficiency' (ibid., p. vii). 'The environmentalism of the poor' thus refers to the environmental justice groups in the USA as well as to the myriad of movements in the Third World that struggle against the environmental impacts that threaten poor people (who are in many countries a majority of the population). Case studies in

The Environmentalism of the Poor from all parts of the world address the preservation of mangroves against shrimp farming; resistance to dams and disputes over underground water; movements against oil or gas extraction in tropical areas; struggles against the import of toxic waste; conflicts over the appropriation of genetic resources; conservation of fisheries against external use; complaints against tree plantations; and also urban environmental conflicts over land use, water availability, transport systems, and air pollution. Also due to its connections to the global justice movement, 'the environmentalism of the poor' seems to be a very promising branch of environmentalism and of environmental movement research.

CONCLUSION: THE FUTURE OF ENVIRONMENTALISM

In the social sciences environmental movements have predominantly been researched from a Western point of view, and also in this chapter more words have been spent on environmentalism in the Global North than in Third World countries. 'Global environmental justice' and 'the environmentalism of the poor', however, are concepts that also include a 'Global South' perspective.

Reflecting on the history of five decades of environmental activism, it is not difficult to conclude that present day environmentalism has a Janus face. On the one hand there are the large, professionalized Western EMOs like the Sierra Club and Greenpeace with millions of contributors (although those numbers are decreasing), but only a limited amount of grassroots mobilization. These EMOs keep playing an indispensable role in consciousness raising, professional activism and lobbying, but their solution strategies (prognostic frames) often do not go beyond the thresholds of present day capitalism. Apart from Germany, at present the Western environmental movement is largely a demobilized and institutionalized one. On the other hand, there are the global environmental justice movement, the recently emerged 'climate justice movement', and the innumerable movements and groups in the Global South, jointly coined 'the environmentalism of the poor', and jointly constituting a vast 'community of fate'. Whereas the large institutionalized EMOs in the Global North have defined global issues like climate change, deforestation, and biodiversity loss predominantly as environmental issues, in the Global South they have been framed primarily as sustainable development issues, whose solutions are seen as inseparable from larger issues of poverty, trade, and globalization. Climate change, deforestation and biodiversity loss are sometimes articulated with 'anti-globalization', thus connecting them with North/South economic relations, whereas others frame them as issues of environmental justice, pointing to the hugely disproportionate impact of pollution and ecological degradation on poor and/or black communities. This analysis is not completely new, as it recalls the 'political ecology' branch within the Western environmental movement of the 1970s. Consequently, it is no surprise that environmental groups and networks affiliated with the political ecology frame (for instance, Friends of the Earth) try to be intermediaries not only between Northern and Southern environmentalism, but also between environmental and other social movements that challenge global neoliberalism.[15]

One sophisticated theoretical underpinning of this kind of environmental activism is provided by Robyn Eckersley. In her 2004 book *The Green State*, Eckersley argues that the global environmental movement is confronted with three core challenges that jointly constitute the root causes of environmental degradation: the 'anarchistic' character of the system of sovereign states; capitalist accumulation; and the democratic deficits of the liberal democratic state (Eckersley, 2004, p. 14). Multilateral environmental agreements, ecological modernization, and environmental advocacy are partial responses to these three challenges (ibid., pp. 14–15), but, at the time of writing, it seems unlikely that these responses will ever operate in mutually reinforcing ways. Whereas most Western EMOs nevertheless stick to these solution strategies, global environmental justice groups explicitly articulate global environmental degradation with the three core challenges as mentioned by Eckersley.

In 1989 Robert Paehlke contended that environmentalism had the potential to become the first original ideological perspective to develop since the middle of the nineteenth century (Paehlke, 1989, p. 3), but his analysis had a strong US-bias. Twenty-five years later one could argue that political ecology as defined by the global environmental justice movements and their allies has not only the potential to become the first new ideological perspective as mentioned by Paehlke, but also the very action perspective to revolutionalize present day global capitalism. 'Committed' and detailed analysis of these movements, their frames, organizational structures, networks, and action repertoires, should become a core task of environmental movement research in the years to come. Equally important, however, is research into the question of what role Western environmentalism could play in breaking the present neoliberal impasse, both at the national and transnational level.

NOTES

* The author would like to thank Brian Doherty and John Grin for their helpful comments on an earlier draft of this chapter.
1. In the literature the term 'environmental movement' is often used in the plural ('environmental movements', e.g., Rootes, 1999), and the movement itself is sometimes subdivided into, or contrasted with, other movements like, for instance, the conservation movement, the anti-nuclear movement, the environmental justice movement, and the animal rights movement. This last movement will be addressed in Chapter 22 of this book; the other movements are being conceived as branches of the environmental movement. In some other studies the terms 'green' or 'ecology' movement rather than environmental movement are being used (e.g., Doherty, 2002). For a discussion on these and other categorizations see, for instance, Van der Heijden et al. (1992); Rootes (2004).
2. The most important (relative) newcomer is the 1951-founded Nature Conservancy.
3. In England, the Clean Air Act of 1956 was an early and direct response to the 4000 deaths attributed to the London smog of December 1952 (Rootes, 2004, p. 613).
4. Rudig, however, observes that some forms of action were more dominant in some countries than in others. Local opposition, site occupations, and mass demonstrations played a central role in France and West Germany, whereas participation in hearings and public inquiries was the main course of action pursued in the USA and the UK (Rudig, 1990, p. 7).
5. However, between 1990 and 1998 the membership of Greenpeace USA declined from 2.35 million to 350 000 (Bosso, 2000).
6. The accompanying increases in budgets and staff (professionalization: internal institutionalization) have also been charted meticulously (Dunlap and Mertig, 1992, p. 13; Dalton, 1994, pp. 92–7; Dowie, 1996, pp. 40–41; Jordan and Maloney, 1997, pp. 15, 20; Van der Heijden, 1997, pp. 40, 42).
7. During the mid-1980s the ten largest American environmental organizations issued a series of blueprints and agenda documents including, for instance, *An Environmental Agenda for the Future* (Cahn, 1985). These agenda documents were focused on maintaining and moderately extending the environmental policy system that had been primarily crafted during the 1970s (Gottlieb, 2005).
8. Direct action/sabotage by environmentalist groups.
9. Spontaneous surprise performances in public spaces to an unsuspecting audience to get a message across.
10. Due to space restrictions it is not possibly to separately address each of Brulle's remaining 'discursive communities'. Valuable introductions to environmental health, ecofeminism, and eco-spiritualism are, respectively, Warren (1997), Brown (2007), and Dobson (2007). Anti-globalization and the Greens are addressed elsewhere in this chapter, whereas the animal rights movement is addressed in Chapter 22 of this volume.
11. The bureaucratization of the movement's core, however, has also led to the emergence of new, more radical EMOs, like Eco-Defense and the Rainbow Keepers (Yanitsky, 1999, p. 167).
12. In one respect, however, the impact of national political cultures appears persistent. In Italy, Spain, and Greece, the characteristic localism of Southern European political cultures has been fully reflected in the character of environmental protest. In Greece, 90 percent of protests in the period 1988–97 were local mobilizations around local issues, although half of them were targeted at national authorities (Rootes, 2004, p. 622). For an excellent review of research on environmentalism in Southern Europe see Kousis (2001).
13. In his *Environmental Justice and the New Pluralism* Schlosberg (1999) argues that the environmental justice movement and new pluralist theories represent a considerable challenge to both conventional pluralist thought and the practices of the mainstream groups in the US environmental movement. The myriad ways people define and

experience 'the environment' has given credence to a form of environmentalism that takes difference seriously. The environmental justice movement, with its base in diversity, networked structure, and its communicative practices and demands, is an example of an attempt to design political practices beyond what one would expect from a standard interest group in the conventional pluralist model. In *Defining Environmental Justice* Schlosberg (2007) explores how the term is used in both self-described environmental justice movements and in theories of environmental and ecological justice.
14. For an overview of environmental movements in individual 'Third World' countries see, for instance, Haynes (1995); Lee and So (1999); Xie (2009).
15. An in-depth analysis of the history, the organizational structure and the transnational identity of FoEI is provided by Doherty (2006).

REFERENCES

Andrée, P. (2007), *Genetically Modified Diplomacy. The Global Politics of Agricultural Biotechnology and the Environment*, Vancouver, BC: UBC Press.
Arts, B. (1998), *The Political Influence of Global NGOs. Case Studies on the Climate and Biodiversity Conventions*, Utrecht: International Books.
Betsill, M. and E. Corell (eds) (2008), *NGO Diplomacy: The Influence of Nongovernmental Organizations in International Environmental Negotiations*, Cambridge, MA: MIT Press.
Bomberg, E. (1998), *Green Parties and Politics in the European Union*, London: Routledge.
Bosso, C. (2000), 'Environmental groups and the new political landscape', in N. Vig and M. Kraft, *Environmental Policy*, Washington, DC: CQ.
Broadbent, J. (1999), *Environmental Politics in Japan: Networks of Power and Protest*, Cambridge, UK: Cambridge University Press.
Brown, P. (2007), *Toxic Exposures: Contested Illnesses and the Environmental Health Movement*, New York: Columbia University Press.
Brulle, R. (2000), *Agency, Democracy and Nature: The US Environmental Movement from a Critical Theory Perspective*, Cambridge, MA: MIT Press.
Brulle, R., H.H. Turner, J. Carmichael and J.C. Jenkins (2007), 'Measuring social movement organization populations: a comprehensive census of U.S. environmental movement organizations', *Mobilization*, **12**(3), 195–211.
Bullard, R. (2000), *Dumping in Dixie: Race, Class and Environmental Quality*, Boulder, CO: Westview Press.
Bullard, R. (ed.) (2005), *The Quest for Environmental Justice: Human Rights and the Politics of Pollution*, Berkeley, CA: University of California Press.
Cahn, R. (1985), *An Environmental Agenda for the Future*, Washington, DC: Island Press.
Carmin, J. and A. Fagan (2010), 'Environmental mobilisation and organisations in post-socialist Europe and the former Soviet Union', *Environmental Politics*, **19**(5), 689–707.
Carson, R. (1962), *Silent Spring*, Boston, MA: Houghton Mifflin.
Chasek, P., D. Downie and J.W. Brown (2010), *Global Environmental Politics*, Boulder, CO: Westview Press.
Cole, L. and G. Foster (2000), *From the Ground Up: Environmental Racism and the Rise of the Environmental Justice Movement*, New York: New York University Press.
Dalton, R. (1994), *The Green Rainbow. Environmental Groups in Western Europe*, New Haven, CT/London: Yale University Press.
Dawson, J. (1995), 'Anti-nuclear activism in the USSR and its successor states: a surrogate for nationalism?', *Environmental Politics*, **4**(3), 441–6.
Diani, M. (1995), *Green Networks. A Structural Analysis of the Italian Environmental Movement*, Edinburgh: Edinburgh University Press.
Dobson, A. (2007), *Green Political Thought*, London: Routledge.

Doherty, B. (1992), 'The Fundi-Realo controversy: an analysis of four European Green parties', *Environmental Politics*, **1**(1), 95–120.
Doherty, B. (1999), 'Paving the way: the rise of direct action against road building and the changing character of British environmentalism', *Political Studies*, **47**(2), 275–91.
Doherty, B. (2002), *Ideas and Action in the Green Movement*, London: Routledge.
Doherty, B. (2006), 'Friends of the Earth International: negotiating a transnational identity', *Environmental Politics*, **15**(5), 860–80.
Doherty, B. and T. Doyle (2006), 'Beyond borders: transnational politics, social movements and modern environmentalisms', *Environmental Politics*, **15**(5), 697–712.
Doherty, B., M. Paterson and B. Seel (2002), *Direct Action in British Environmentalism*, London: Routledge.
Dowie, M. (1996), *Losing Ground. American Environmentalism at the Close of the Twentieth Century*, Cambridge, MA: MIT Press.
Downes, D. (2000), 'The New Zealand environmental movement and the politics of inclusion', *Australian Journal of Political Science*, **35**(3), 471–91.
Downey, G. (1986), 'Ideology and the Clamshell identity: organizational dilemmas in the anti-nuclear power movement', *Social Problems*, **33**(3), 337–73.
Doyle, T. (2000), *Green Power: The Environmental Movement in Australia*, Sydney: University of New South Wales Press.
Dryzek, J., D. Downes, C. Hunold and D. Schlosberg (2003), *Green States and Social Movements. Environmentalism in the United States, United Kingdom, Germany, & Norway*, Oxford: Oxford University Press.
Dunlap, R. and A. Mertig (eds) (1992), *American Environmentalism. The US Environmental Movement 1970–1990*, Philadelphia, PA: Taylor & Francis.
Eckersley, R. (1992), *Environmentalism and Political Theory. Towards an Ecocentric Approach*, London: UCL Press.
Eckersley, R. (2004), *The Green State. Rethinking Democracy and Sovereignty*, Cambridge, MA: MIT Press.
Epstein, B. (1991), *Political Protest & Cultural Revolution. Nonviolent Direct Action in the 1970s and 1980s*, Berkeley, CA: University of California Press.
Flam, H. (ed.) (1994), *States and Anti-nuclear Movements*, Edinburgh: Edinburgh University Press.
Frankland, E. and D. Schoonmaker (1992), *Between Protest and Power. The Green Party in Germany*, Boulder, CO: Westview Press.
Frankland, E., P. Lucardie and B. Rihoux (eds) (2008), *Green Parties in Transition. The End of Grassroots Democracy?*, Farnham, UK: Ashgate.
Friedman, E., K. Hochstetler and E. Clark (eds) (2005), *Sovereignty, Diplomacy and Global Civil Society. State–Society Relations at UN World Conferences*, Albany, NY: State University of New York Press.
Giddens, A. (1990), *The Consequences of Modernity*, Cambridge, UK: Polity Press.
Gottlieb, R. (1993), *Forcing the Spring: The Transformation of the American Environmental Movement*, Washington, DC: Island Press.
Gottlieb, R. (2005), *Forcing the Spring: The Transformation of the American Environmental Movement*, revised edition, Washington, DC: Island Press.
Greenwood, J. (2007), *Interest Representation in the European Union*, Houndmills, UK: Palgrave Macmillan.
Greenpeace (2012), *Lessons from Fukushima*, accessed 15 May 2014 at http://www.greenpeace.org/international/Global/international/publications/nuclear/2012/Fukushima/Lessons-from-Fukushima.pdf.
Guha, R. (2000), *Environmentalism: A Global History*, New York: Longman.
Guha, R. and J. Martinez-Alier (eds) (1997), *Varieties of Environmentalism. Essays North and South*, London: Earthscan.
Hajer, M. (1995), *The Politics of Environmental Discourse. Ecological Modernisation and the Policy Process*, Oxford: Oxford University Press.

Hayes, G. (2002), *Environmental Protest and Policymaking in France*, Houndmills, UK: Palgrave Macmillan.
Haynes, J. (1999), 'Power, politics and environmental movements in the third world', *Environmental Politics*, **8**(1), 222–42.
Henry, L. (2010), *Red to Green: Environmental Activism in Post-Soviet Russia*, Ithaca, NY: Cornell University Press.
Hicks, B. (1996), *Environmental Politics in Poland. A Social Movement between Regime and Opposition*, New York: Columbia University Press.
Hutton, D. and L. Connors (1999), *A History of the Australian Environmental Movement*, Cambridge, UK: Cambridge University Press.
Jamison, A., R. Eyerman and J. Cramer (1990), *The Making of the New Environmental Consciousness: A Comparative Study of the Environmental Movements in Sweden, Denmark and the Netherlands*, Edinburgh: Edinburgh University Press.
Jancar-Webster, B. (1993), 'The East European environmental movement and the transformation of East European society', in B. Jancar-Webster (1993), *Environmental Action in Eastern Europe. Responses to Crisis*, Armonk, NY: Sharpe.
Jordan, G. and M. Maloney (1997), *The Protest Business? Mobilizing Campaign Groups*, Manchester: Manchester University Press.
Keck, M. and K. Sikkink (1998), *Activists Beyond Borders. Advocacy Networks in International Politics*, Ithaca, NY: Cornell University Press.
Khagram, S. (2004), *Dams and Development. Transnational Struggles for Water and Power*, Ithaca, NY/London: Cornell University Press.
Kitschelt, H. (1986), 'Political opportunity structures and political protest: anti-nuclear movements in four democracies', *British Journal of Political Science*, **16**(1), 57–85.
Kitschelt, H. (1989), *The Logics of Party Formation. Ecological Politics in Belgium and West Germany*, Ithaca, NY: Cornell University Press.
Kolb, F. (2007), *Protest and Opportunities. The Political Outcomes of Social Movements*, Frankfurt/New York: Campus.
Koopmans, R. and J.W. Duyvendak (1995), 'The political construction of the nuclear energy issue and its impact on the mobilisation of anti-nuclear movements in Western Europe', *Social Problems*, **42**(2), 235–51.
Kousis, M. (2001), 'Competing claims in local environmental conflicts in Southern Europe', in K. Eder and M. Kousis (eds), *Environmental Politics in Southern Europe. Actors, Institutions and Discourses in a Europeanizing Society*, Dordrecht: Kluwer Academic Publishers.
Lee, Y. and A. So (eds) (1999), *Asia's Environmental Movements*, Armonk, NY: Sharpe.
Manes, C. (1990), *Green Rage. Radical Environmentalism and the Unmaking of Civilization*, Boston, MA: Little, Brown.
Markham, W. (2008), *Environmental Organizations in Modern Germany*, New York: Berghahn Books.
Martinez-Alier, J. (2003), *The Environmentalism of the Poor. A Study of Ecological Conflicts and Valuation*, Cheltenham, UK and Northampton, MA, USA: Edward Elgar Publishing.
Mason, R. (1999), 'Whither Japan's environmental movement? An assessment of problems and prospects at the national level', *Pacific Affairs*, **72**(2), 187–207.
Mayer, M., J. Ely and M. Schatzschneider (eds) (1998), *The German Greens; Paradox between Movement and Party*, Philadelphia, PA: Temple University Press.
Mazey, S. and J. Richardson (2005), 'Environmental groups and the European Community: challenges and opportunities', in A. Jordan (ed.), *Environmental Policy in the European Union. Actors, Institutions and Processes*, London: Routledge, pp. 106–23.
Meadows, D., D.L. Meadows, J. Randers and W. Behrens (1972), *Limits to Growth*, New York: New American Library.
Mishan, E.J. (1967), *The Costs of Economic Growth*, London: Staples Press.
Montrie, C. (2011), *A People's History of Environmentalism in the United States*, London/New York: Continuum.
Mueller-Rommel, F. (ed.) (1989), *New Politics in Western Europe. The Rise and Success of Green Parties and Alternative Lists*, Boulder, CO: Westview Press.

Paehlke, R. (1989), *Environmentalism and the Future of Progressive Politics*, New Haven, CT: Yale University Press.
Pellow, D. (2007), *Resisting Global Toxics: Transnational Movements for Environmental Justice*, Cambridge, MA: MIT Press.
Pickvance, K. (1998), *Democracy and Environmental Movements in Eastern Europe: A Comparative Study of Hungary and Russia*, Boulder, CO: Westview Press.
Poguntke, T. (1993), *Alternative Politics. The German Green Party*, Edinburgh: Edinburgh University Press.
Princen, P. and M. Finger (1994), *Environmental NGOs in World Politics. Linking the Local and the Global*, London: Routledge.
Richardson, D. and C. Rootes (eds) (1995), *The Green Challenge. The Development of Green Parties in Europe*, London: Routledge.
Roose, J. (2003), *Die Europäisierung von Umweltorganisationen: die Umweltbewegung auf dem langen Weg nach Brüssel* [The Europeanization of the Environmental Movement. Environmental Organizations on the Long Road to Brussels], Wiesbaden: Westdeutscher Verlag.
Rootes, C. (ed.) (1999), *Environmental Movements: Local, National and Global*, London: Frank Cass.
Rootes, C. (ed.) (2003), *Environmental Protest in Western Europe*, Oxford: Oxford University Press.
Rootes, C. (2004), 'Environmental movements', in D. Snow, S. Soule and H. Kriesi (eds), *The Blackwell Companion to Social Movements*, Oxford: Blackwell, pp. 608–40.
Rucht, D. and J. Roose (1999), 'The German environmental movement at a crossroads?', *Environmental Politics*, **8**(1), 59–80.
Rudig, W. (1990), *Anti-nuclear Movements. A World Survey of Opposition to Nuclear Energy*, Harlow, UK: Longman.
Saurin, J. (1993), 'Global environmental degradation, modernity and environmental knowledge', *Environmental Politics*, **2**(4), 248–66.
Scarce, R. ([1990] 2005), *Eco-warriors. Understanding the Radical Environmental Movement*, Chicago, IL: The Noble Press.
Schlosberg, D. (1999), *Environmental Justice and the New Pluralism: The Challenge of Difference for Environmentalism*, Oxford: Oxford University Press.
Schlosberg, D. (2007), *Defining Environmental Justice: Theories, Movements and Nature*, Oxford: Oxford University Press.
Szasz, A. (1994), *EcoPopulism: Toxic Waste and the Movement for Environmental Justice*, Minneapolis, MN: University of Minnesota Press.
Tamiotti, L. and M. Finger (2001), 'Environmental organizations: changing roles and functions in global politics', *Global Environmental Politics*, **1**(1), 56–76.
Van der Heijden, H.A. (1997), 'Political opportunity structure and the institutionalisation of the environmental movement', *Environmental Politics*, **6**(4), 25–50.
Van der Heijden, H.A. (1999), 'Environmental movements, ecological modernization and political opportunity structures', *Environmental Politics*, **8**(1), 199–221.
Van der Heijden, H.A. (2000), *Tussen Aanpassing en Verzet. Milieubeweging en Milieudiscours* [Between Adaptation and Resistance. Environmental Movement and Environmental Discourse], Amsterdam: Ambo.
Van der Heijden, H.A. (2006), 'Globalization, environmental movements and international political opportunity structures', *Organization & Environment*, **19**(1), 28–45.
Van der Heijden, H.A. (2010), *Social Movements, Public Spheres and the European Politics of the Environment. Green Power Europe?*, Houndmills, UK: Palgrave Macmillan.
Van der Heijden, H.A. (2014), 'The great fear. European environmentalism in the atomic age', in M. Armiero and L. Sedrez (eds), *Tales from Planet Earth. The History of Environmentalism in Seven Stories*, London: Continuum, pp. 185–211.
Van der Heijden, H.A., R. Koopmans and M. Giugni (1992), 'The West European environmental movement', in M. Finger (ed.), *The Green Movement Worldwide*, Greenwich, CT: JAI Press, pp. 1–40.

Van Koppen, C. and W. Markham (2007), *Protecting Nature: Organizations and Networks in Europe and the USA*, Cheltenham, UK and Northampton, MA, USA: Edward Elgar Publishing.
Wall, D. (1999), *Earth First! and the Anti-Roads Movement. Radical Environmentalism and Comparative Social Movements*, London: Routledge.
Warren, K. (ed.) (1997), *Ecofeminism; Women, Culture, Nature*, Bloomington, IN: Indiana University Press.
Webster, R. (1998), 'Environmental collective action: stable patterns of cooperation and issue alliances at the European level', in W. Greenwood and M. Aspinwall (eds), *Collective Action in the European Union*, London: Routledge, pp. 176–95.
Wiesenthal, H. (ed.) (1993), *Realism in Green Politics. Social Movements and Ecological Reform in Germany*, Manchester: Manchester University Press.
Xie, L. (2009), *Environmental Activism in China*, London: Routledge.
Yanitsky, O. (1999), 'The environmental movement in a hostile context. The case of Russia', *International Sociology*, 14(2), 157–72.
Yanitsky, O. (2012), 'From nature protection to politics: the Russian environmental movement 1960–2010', *Environmental Politics*, 21(6), 922–40.
Zelko, F. (2013), *Make it a Green Peace! The Rise of Countercultural Environmentalism*, Oxford/New York: Oxford University Press.

18. The women's movement
Jo Reger

Ferree and Mueller begin their essay on the women's movement by stating that it 'is not new, not only Western, and not always feminist' (2004, p. 577). In doing so, they provide a useful synopsis that captures much of past research and at the same time illustrates the complexity of women's organizing in national, transnational, and global contexts. In this chapter, I draw upon their synopsis to explore some of the most significant scholarship and to examine theoretical contributions emerging from the study of women's movements. To do so, I use the United States, the national context that I research, as a case study to illustrate the development of concepts and theories from women's movements. I do so not to reiterate a Western-only focus on social movements but to further elaborate ideas, concepts, and debates about women's movements and to show the development of theories from scholarship. By focusing on the United States, I explore some of the mid-range theories and concepts that have been applied and expanded because of this work. While scholarship on social movements has influenced how women's movements have been studied, women's movements have also influenced the field of social movements. Important theoretical concepts and frameworks have emerged from the study of women's movements that shape not only social movement research but sociological research in general. In particular, I argue that the concepts of abeyance, the critique of 'waves' of protest, and the expansion of notions of mobilization and movement outcomes are important to all movement research. In addition, feminist work on the intersectionality of social identities and the need to develop beyond Western thinking are critical ideas in all sociological scholarship. I conclude with a short sketch on the future theoretical and empirical developments on women's movements in feminist and social movement scholarship. In order to contextualize my discussion, I begin with a short history of the US women's movement and then return to Ferree and Mueller's argument that women's movements are enduring, do not always embrace feminism as an ideology, and happen in a variety of national, international, and global contexts. For each of these statements, I illustrate the development of important theoretical ideas to the study of social movements.

THE US WOMEN'S MOVEMENT

In the United States the women's movement emerged in the 1800s as the result of women's organizing in a variety of contexts including other movements. Outraged at being shut out of the abolition movement, Lucretia Mott and Elizabeth Cady Stanton held the Seneca Falls Women's Rights Convention on 14 July 1848 (DuBois, 1978; Buechler, 1990). At this convention, male and female activists drafted a Declaration of Sentiments and 12 resolutions demanding women's rights particularly in areas of the law, marriage, employment, and the Church. It is then that a women's movement began to mobilize and eventually developed multiple organizations and networks focused on women's rights with a goal of passing suffrage. Working on suffrage and other issues, the movement went through a series of divisions over tactical and ideological questions from 1869 to 1890, before merging organizations. In 1920, activists succeeded in obtaining suffrage, and feminists from one of the major groups, the National Women's Party, then turned their focus to the passage of an Equal Rights Amendment (ERA), a constitutional amendment guaranteeing equal rights for the sexes (Giele, 1995). However, in the decades following the passage of suffrage, the climate grew increasingly hostile to feminism and the amendment got little attention. By the late 1940s and early 1950s, images of the domestic role of women dominated American culture, feminists were vilified and once vibrant women's movement organizations went into a state of the 'doldrums' (Rupp and Taylor, 1987).

However, it is also at this time that women increased their labor force participation and educational attainment and also began to experience a series of life changes, including marrying younger, having more children, and experiencing more divorce. For white women in particular, increased employment and educational opportunities conflicted with constraining domestic roles. These changes resulted in the rise of a social phenomenon Betty Friedan labeled, 'the problem which has no name' (1963). This was also a time of upheaval for young women in the New Left (i.e., civil rights, anti-war, students' rights) when they began to articulate the sexism they experienced in these movements (Evans, 1980; Ferree and Hess [1985] 1995). These different experiences coalesced into a resurgence of the movement in the late 1960s. The movement at this stage is often divided into two different strands. One strand was composed of women's rights organizations such as the National Organization for Women (NOW), Women's Equity Action League, and the National Women's Political Caucus, which are all formally organized organizations with national offices. These groups were characterized as the bureaucratic strand, with mostly older professional women who were also members in organizations such as the President's Commission on the Status of Women, state commissions, and groups such as Business and Professional Women and trade unions. A second strand of organizing emerged from the movements of the New Left when young women activists experienced exclusion and ridicule within the civil rights, students' rights and anti-war movements of the time as well as in the emerging women's rights organizations (Evans, 1980). As a result, women's liberation groups or the 'collectivist' strand was made up of young women college students who drew on networks and organizing skills acquired in other movements. The emphasis on social networks in recruiting and the ideology of radical feminism led to the development of organizations that discouraged the development of leaders and hierarchical structure.

These two strands experienced a peak of activity between the years of 1972 and 1982 and each had their successes. The women's rights strand succeeded in the passage of Title IX that banned sex discrimination in publicly funded educational institutions, and the passage of *Roe* v. *Wade*, a US Supreme Court decision legalizing abortion, among other victories. Women's liberation groups were successful at drawing national media attention to the movement and were a source of art, music, literature, and critical analyses of women's lives (Taylor and Whittier, 1997). Just as the earlier movement created, merged, and dissolved organizations and networks, so did strands of the movement in the 1960s and 1970s. Over time, the women's liberation groups began to dissolve, and activists from both sides came together, mobilized in particular by the struggle to ratify the ERA. The ERA campaign soon encountered opposition from anti-feminist organizations and by 1982 the amendment had not met the ratification deadline for Congress and was defeated (Mansbridge, 1986).

While some strands of the movement, made up mostly of white women activists, experienced decline and diminishing accomplishments during this period, scholars argue that other strands of the movement continued to grow and thrive (Thompson, 2002; Roth, 2004; Nadasen, 2010). Becky Thompson argues that the often-told trajectory of the US women's movement ignores how women of color organized in separate organizations and around a diverse array of interests that did not always include white women (2002). In addition to separate organizing, women of color along with other groups of women began to break off from the movement around issues of privilege and marginalization based on race, ethnicity, class, and sexual orientation in the movement. This is at a time when politically the movement faced a conservative backlash against feminism, giving rise to what has been called the 'post-feminist era' in the United States (Faludi, 1991). Despite the hostile environment, activists continued to accomplish their goals with the successes such as the growth of women's studies programs in colleges and universities. It is the successes of the past, such as women's studies and the development of feminist organizations, that keep the movement mobilized with contemporary feminists continuing to join the movement (Reger, 2012). Contemporary feminists work in organizations founded by past generations such as NOW, National Abortion Rights Action League (NARAL), and Planned Parenthood. They also founded their own national organizations such as the Third Wave Foundation, a group focusing on direct action, education, and leadership training for young women.

In sum, although brief, this history tells of a movement that endures, grows, and declines in response to the social context of the times. It experiences organizational growth, mergers, and divisions. It also tells of generations of sustained challenges and groups of activists with different identities and ideologies who sought a variety of outcomes and goals. In addition, these activists came from different positions of privilege and marginalization in American society and struggled to find a way to coexist and work together in the movement. With this history in mind, I return to Ferree and Mueller's synopsis on women's movement and the theoretical ideas that accompany their ideas.

WOMEN'S MOVEMENTS ARE 'NOT NEW'

Ferree and Mueller argue that women's movements are often long lived and 'are among the most enduring and successful of all social movements of the modern period' (2004, p. 576; see also Ferree and Hess [1985] 1995; Rupp and Taylor, 1987; Taylor, 1989). They note, 'Overall, across classes and countries, the history of feminist claims and women's movement mobilizations stretches back in to the earliest formation of nation-states, political parties and democratic institutions' (Ferree and Mueller, 2004, p. 584). As noted in the brief history, the contemporary US women's movement has its roots in the 1800s and was centered on questions of citizenship and freedom, particularly around suffrage and slavery. As evidence to their importance in the formation of nations, political parties, and government institutions, women's movements exist across the globe. Scholars and commentators have documented the existence of women's movements in a variety of global contexts, often over multiple generations, including Canada (Rebick, 2005; Staggenborg and Lecomte, 2009) and Western Europe (Katzenstein, 1987) with a focus on Germany (Ferree et al., 2002; Guenther, 2010), Ireland (Smyth, 1988), France (Jenson, 1987), and Italy (Beckwith, 1987; Hellman, 1987). These studies extend out of the Western context with case studies of countries such as Guatemala

(Borland, 2006, 2010), India (Ray, 1999; Desai, 2002), and Israel (Herzon, 2008) among many, many others.

Despite their widespread nature, longevity, and continuity, women's movements, particularly those in the United States, are constantly being questioned by those hostile to movement gains. As such the US women's movement, as well as women's movements in other countries, is often declared dead and/or non-functional. Mary Hawkesworth, a feminist scholar, calls this the 'premature burial' of a movement because it mounts a significant challenge to the social order (2004). Katzenstein in her examination of both the United States and Western Europe agrees that the 'obituary is premature'. She notes that examinations of the structure of women's movements contained only in large, established organizations can lead to the conclusion that a movement is in decline (1987, p. 1). Adding to the constant call for the decline of women's movements is the cultural repression of their goals and ideologies. While women's movements are not commonly repressed through violence, Ferree (2004) notes that women's movements that seek to change the status quo of a society often face 'soft repression' in the form of ridicule or dismissal of the movement's goals and tactics. One example is the media focus and ridiculing of the Riot Grrrl underground feminist punk rock movement in the United States that started in the 1990s. The media scrutiny was so intense that eventually leaders of feminist punk groups refused to speak to the press (Marcus, 2010), which contributed to the conclusion that this feminist activism had waned. To counter the constant call for the women's movement's 'obituary', scholars have examined how women's movements go through stages of mobilization, contributing to our knowledge of all social movements.

Continuity, Abeyance, and 'Waves' within Movements

In the study of continuity, scholars often draw upon two main theoretical frameworks – structural explanations through resource mobilization and political process theories, and more cultural explanations through new social movement theory. The resource mobilization and political process model argues that centralized and formal social movement organizations are key to movement longevity (McCarthy and Zald, 1977; Tilly, 1989; Staggenborg, 1991; Minkoff, 1993). New social movement theory adds another dimension to the examination of continuity, arguing that there is a cultural basis to movement mobilization. Continuity in this view is due to the development of a collective identity that keeps activists in a movement, even when the movement suffers setbacks. Instead of organizations and the external environment supporting the mobilizing of the movements, new social movement theorists see movements as continuing cultures that develop where activists share a group identity and work to keep the movement alive in hostile times (Rupp and Taylor, 1987; Taylor, 1989; Staggenborg, 1998). As a result of new social movement theory, scholars have examined the role of submerged networks and movement cultures in continuity.

By merging these theoretical frameworks and examining organizations, culture, and networks, scholars of the women's movement offer a more complex understanding of social movement continuity. Verta Taylor and Lelia Rupp argue that in the case of the United States, the movement entered a period of abeyance in the late 1940s and 1950s only to reinvigorate in the 1960s as other social movements flourished in the national context (Rupp and Taylor, 1987; Taylor, 1989). This view countered the idea that the movement had died in the 1920s only to be reborn in the 1960s. They argue that submerged networks embedded in a movement organization during a period of the 'doldrums' from 1945 to 1960 played an important role in the resurgence of the women's movement. As noted in the US movement's history, during this hostility to feminism period the formally organized National Woman's Party sustained a community of white, middle-class, older feminists focused on passing the ERA through the creation of submerged networks. Taylor (1989) describes these networks as holding the movement in abeyance, or a holding pattern, until social conditions were right for its re-emergence. The abeyance structures of this time period gave activists pre-existing networks, a repertoire of goals and tactics, a collective identity, and a consciousness from which to draw on in the re-emergence of the movement in the late 1960s. Abeyance structures are an important concept in understanding how movements continue when they are not visible through large national organizations or protests. For example, Staggenborg and her co-authors draw on the idea of abeyance in their examination of a feminist music festival and argue that the relationships that are created through social networks, feminist spirituality groups, feminist bars, and lesbian-feminist communities extend outside the festival and promote mobilization (1993–94).

By understanding that rates of mobilization can vary and that abeyance can occur without the movement ceasing to exist opens the study of movements to one of generations of activists and organizations that continue for long periods of time. In the case of the US women's movement, the longevity of the movement spans multiple generations of feminist activists who are embedded in networks or organizations that transition to new generations or serve as a bridge between generations. Social movement scholars have conceptualized movement mobilization as cyclical (Tarrow, 1994; Koopmans, 2004), often characterized as 'waves' within the USA and other women's movements. Waves are conceptualized as times of intense mobilization followed by slower periods of mobilization and abeyance. In the United States, the movement is characterized by the first wave beginning in the 1860s, the second wave beginning in the 1960s, and a third wave conceptualized as emerging in the 1990s. Nancy Hewitt argues that the 'master narrative' of the wave began in the US women's movement in the 1800s and was adopted by feminists again in the 1960s as a way to identify themselves and differentiate between generations of activists (2010, p. 15). As such, the wave model has become the dominant way of identifying women's movement history.

While the wave model provides a useful way to capture the history of social movements, in particular women's movements, it has not been without critique. Scholars who study activism by women of color have argued that the wave model 'whitewashes' activist histories, often focusing on white women's organizing and ignoring other forms. Instead scholars argue that women of color, lesbians, and poor women often organized in different strands and experienced different rates of mobilization than what is captured in a predominantly white and 'mainstream' movement. As noted, these critiques include the work of Roth (2004), Thompson (2002), and Nadasen (2010) who envision a history that is much more complicated than singular waves of activism (or cycles) rising and crashing. In addition, Cathryn Bailey (1997) argues that the metaphor presupposes a clear beginning and ending to each 'wave' of feminism, something difficult to determine. A related critique has been that the wave model only focuses on the evident history at the national level, ignoring grassroots and community activism that continues over time (Reger, 2012). This view draws on Taylor's ideas of abeyance and a focus on community versus national-level mobilization.

These critiques of the wave model (along with others),[1] have led women's movement scholars to expand our understanding of movement continuity. Nancy Whittier (1995, 1997) in her study of radical feminist activism moves the discussion from waves of activism to instead, political generations. Building on Karl Mannheim's work (1952), Whittier argues that political generations enter into movement contexts in a series of micro-cohorts that respond to and shape the movement context differently from each other. Other scholars, such as Ednie Garrison (2000, 2005) take up the critique and argue that the form and shape of women's movements is more along the lines of radio waves (rather than ocean waves) that coexist, intermingle, and separate from each other. Switching the focus from the national level, Reger and Staggenborg (2006) argue that movement mobilization is not only connected to national or broad-scale societal change but also occurs at grassroots level when social movement organizations embrace a range of internal dynamics and strategies. We argue that organizations with steady leadership, who adopt a range of mobilizing tactics and have a set organizational structure, are able to draw on external factors to increase their mobilization, independent of national organization activities.

In sum, understanding the enduring nature of women's movements creates an opportunity for scholars to examine the ways in which activism surges and wanes and how activists within a movement often have a variety of goals, strategies, and tactics that do not always align with each other. This conceptualization of activism expands both resource mobilization and new social movement theories, adding new dimensions to the study of movement continuity.

WOMEN'S MOVEMENTS ARE 'NOT ALWAYS FEMINIST'

Ferree and Mueller state that they 'explicitly refrain from defining all women's movements as feminist' (2004, p. 579). Instead they argue that there is a distinction between seeing women as a movement's constituency and the foundation of organizational strategies versus adopting a belief in feminism that critiques and seeks to challenge gender inequality. Women's movements often emerge around a variety of issues that address the rights of women and children. Women's movements have focused on a variety of issues including those pertaining to ownership and control of the body such as reproductive rights and abortion, trafficking, rape, and domestic violence, as well as issues of citizenship and sex equity, such as the fight to obtain suffrage, fair and legal employment standards, and constitutional and legal protections. The struggle for these issues can be visible on the national level such as the effort in the United States for constitutional amendments such as the ERA or at the community level on issues such as poverty (Naples, 1998) or neighborhood safety (Pardo, 1998). Taking a global perspective illustrates how women's movements also address a range of citizenship and societal concerns such as globalization and militarism (Enloe, 2007), social justice (Wilson, 2007), and labor in the global economy (Moghadam, 2005) among others such as colonialization, immigration, racism, and urbanization. The addressing of these issues varies by political culture, making each women's movement unique in its goals, activist identities, and ideologies (Ferree, 1997; Ray, 1999).

Despite the wide range of goals embraced by women's movements, scholars argue that women's movements flourish in periods of generalized social upheaval (Chafe, 1977; Taylor and Whittier, 1997; Staggenborg,

1998) with changes in the social structure sparking women's activism (Huber and Spitze, 1983; Klein, 1984; Chafetz and Dworkin, 1986). These changes include factors such as increase in labor force participation and educational attainment, women's ability to control their reproduction and fertility and/or changes in the shape and structure of the family (Klein, 1984; Ferree and Hess [1985] 1995; Chafetz and Dworkin, 1986). As Basu notes, as women's lives change they are able to organize collectively against injustice and oppression in their lives and communities (1995). The popular media has also confirmed this idea with the work of reporters Nicholas Kristof and Sheryl WuDunn, who argue that women who gain control over their lives are able to collectively work to challenge societal conditions such as slavery, female circumcision, and illiteracy (2010).

While not all women activists identify as a feminist, the transformational nature of many of the goals of women's movements places them on a continuum that may move toward feminist ideologies even when feminist identities are not adopted. Ferree and Mueller write of their distinction between women's movements and feminist movements: 'This broader definition takes explicitly into account that many mobilizations of women as women start out with a nongender directed goals, such as peace, antiracism or social justice and gradually acquire explicitly feminist components' (2004, p. 577).

This shifting dynamic between women as a constituency and a feminist movement is noted in the work of scholars. For example, Nancy Naples (1998) documents women's activism centered in neighborhood networks that emerged as a result of the US War against Poverty. She argues that these women activists drew on feminist ideologies and strategies, even when they did not identify as feminists or label their work as 'political'. Mary Pardo (1998) finds a similar dynamic in her examination of the neighborhood of east Los Angeles where women's networks drew on ideologies of gender inequality to stop state and commercial projects near their neighborhoods. In a similar vein, Mary Katzenstein (1987) argues that even within a women's (or feminist) movement there is a diversity of action and ideology that eludes easy characterization. She argues that feminist movements are 'a political force that even in a single country has broad ideological variety and range of organizational expressions' (1987, p. 5). She continues, 'One reason for the diversity of feminism is the fact that the women's movement is a potentially transformational social movement and thus [it] draws supporters with a range of different agendas' (ibid.). This range of goals, participants, and ideologies often makes the distinction between a feminist and a women's movement problematic. In sum, while not all women's movements are feminist, there is often an intermingling of ideologies, actions, and goals that complicates women's activism, particularly when it engages other social movements.

Since women's movements are largely enduring and often embrace a wide range of ideologies, they can shift in the goals and types of activism over time. The US women's movement provides an example of a movement that has shifted through generations of activists. In the twenty-first century, women and men come to feminism in a society dramatically shaped by the feminist generations that came before them. As children they may have read gender-neutral children's books, attended summer camps organized around gender equity, and entered universities and colleges offering women's and/or gender studies classes. Two contemporary feminist US writers note, 'For our generation, feminism is like fluoride, we scarcely notice that we have it – it's simply in the water' (Baumgardener and Richards, 2000, p. 17). As a result, contemporary feminists in the United States continue to work in the formal organizations started by the previous generation but also embrace new forms of feminist activism often embedded in their everyday routines and activities (Reger, 2012).

Mobilization and Outcomes

Appreciating that women's movements embrace a variety of ideologies from feminist to seeing women as a constituency, as well as noting how multiple generational movements shift over time, opens the way for scholars to conceptualize new ways of seeing movement mobilization and outcomes. As noted, women's movements are often seen as being in decline when they do not align with traditional conceptions of movement mobilization and outcomes. Katzenstein, writing on Western Europe and US movements documents this dynamic:

> Unlike the civil rights movement, moreover, whose strength was measured in large part by its very public protests and demonstrations, the women's movement even at the outset made less use of the 'orthodox' tactics of disorder. It has instead pursued its often very radical agenda in less visible ways through consciousness-raising groups, collectives, caucuses, and local organizations. (Katzenstein, 1987, p. 3)

The move from seeing movements as only engaging with the state to viewing more submerged and cultural tactics has been developed by women's movement scholars. For example, Suzanne Staggenborg and Verta Taylor (2005) critique the 'contentious politics' approach (Tarrow, 1994; Tilly, 2004) to social movements and agree with Katzenstein that women's movements do not always fit with traditional social movement conceptualizations. The contentious politics approach focuses political action and protest events, particularly those targeting elites and other power holders in society. Staggenborg and Taylor argue that this view of social movements contributes to the notion that the US women's movement is in decline. They write:

> In a long-term, widespread movement such as the women's movement, however, public actions and interactions with targets may appear more sporadic than sustained, and ideological support for the feminist struggle against women's political and social subordination is created and maintained through less visible actions in various venues. (2005, p. 41)

Instead, Staggenborg and Taylor argue that women's movements often embrace a range of tactics, from state-focused actions to cultural tactics, broadening the ways in which movements can be viewed. They advance that an alternative perspective on the US women's movement reveals the maintenance and growth of women's organizations, the breadth of tactical repertoires, and the spread of feminist culture and identities. They include in their analysis Katzenstein's (1990) work on 'feminist unobtrusive mobilization' within mainstream institutions such as religion and the military. Unobtrusive mobilization is a form of 'invisible' mobilization within institutions, such as the Catholic Church or the US armed services, where women engage in everyday resistance, working for long-term gains such as women's ordination and the recruitment and integration of women into the military. By expanding and critiquing the contentious politics approach, Staggenborg and Taylor illustrate how concepts of movement mobilization and outcome are made more complex through the study of women's movements.

In sum, understanding the diversity of women's movements from 'women as a constituency' to 'women as feminist activists' expands conceptualizations of activism as well as how movements shift in their ideologies and goals, adopt multiple strategies and tactics, and often work in ways such as unobtrusive mobilization. While building upon concepts and ideas in social movement theories, women's movement scholars have also challenged the way in which ethnocentrism can color the study of social movements.

WOMEN'S MOVEMENTS ARE 'NOT ONLY WESTERN'

Another powerful critique of the way in which women's movements have been studied is through the recognition of an ethnocentric lens that sees Western women's movements as a 'guide' for understanding all women's movements. This view has been critiqued by a variety of scholars who take researchers to task for employing 'Western goggles' when viewing non-Western women's activism. One of the most important voices on this subject is Chandra Mohanty who argues that non-Western women are often created as a monolithic category through 'assumptions of privilege and ethnocentric universality' and 'inadequate self-consciousness' by Western feminist scholars and activists (1986, p. 335). She argues that this scholarship creates an image of a woman with little to no agency who is the opposite of a Western woman. She writes:

> This average third world woman leads an essentially truncated life based on her feminine gender (read: sexually constrained) and being 'third world' (read: ignorant, poor, uneducated, tradition-bound, domestic, family-oriented, victimized, etc.). This, I suggest is in contrast to the (implicit) self-representation of Western women as educated, modern, as having control over their own bodies and sexualities, and the freedom to make their own decisions. (1986, p. 337)

The result of this for the study of women's movements is the construction of 'Third World' women as 'victims' of social patterns, structures, and systems and seldom as actors with agency. In a similar vein, Hawkesworth (2006) divides the globe into the privileged North and the less privileged South and argues that Northern liberal feminism often ignores many of the issues faced by women of the Global South such as imperialism, colonialism, and development. Mohanty writes, 'The analysis of specific historical differences becomes impossible, because reality is always apparently structured by divisions – two mutually exclusive and jointly exhaustive groups, the victims and the oppressors' (1986, p. 340). In other words, when the particular circumstances of women's lives are flattened into just being 'oppressed' there is no room for the examination of their instances of agency and resistance. In addition, this reinforcement of binary divisions between 'Third World' women and 'Third World' men ignores the ways in which women's movements have often incorporated men into their struggles. For example, Obioma Nnaemeka argues that in many African cultures what it means to be a feminist is different from the Western definitions. She argues that instead of an individualized, self-empowerment model that sees men as the enemy, many forms of African feminism embrace 'nego-feminism' which means to negotiate with no ego and writes, 'By not casting a pall over men as a monolith. African women are more inclined to reach out and work with men in achieving set goals' (2005, p. 209). The idea that women's movement activist identities do not reflect (or exist in opposition) to a Western model and vary depending on socio-historical context contributes to the employing of two important social movement concepts – collective identity and intersectionality.

Identity Construction and Intersectionality

A core concept in new social movement theory, collective identities are shared activist identities that emerge from interaction in a community or organization (Melucci, 1989). Collective identities construct a shared and politicized view of the social world, the group's experiences, goals, and the movement's opponents (Melucci, 1989; Taylor, 1989; Taylor and Whittier, 1992; Johnston et al., 1994). While the concept of collective identities is not new, having its roots in disciplines such as anthropology, work on the women's movement allowed for new understandings of the workings of collective identities within movements. In their examination of lesbian-feminist communities, Taylor and Whittier (1992) argue that three dynamics are essential in the construction of collective identities: boundary construction, the development of consciousness, and negotiation with internal and external forces. For example, they argue that in lesbian feminism of the United States in the 1970s and 1980s, the drawing of boundaries between male and female promoted the kind of oppositional consciousness necessary for organizing one's life around US feminism and the formation of an activist community. These communities did not construct impenetrable boundaries between themselves and society but found ways to interact with the groups and institutions they sought to change. This process of negotiation – or practices of everyday life that affirm the identities embraced by participants – contributed to the formation of a shared group consciousness. In sum, it is through work on women's movements that scholars have come to understand that identities are continuously negotiated and revised and are context-specific. Women's movement scholarship has also shown how collective identities within a movement are not singular. For example, my work (Reger, 2002) illustrates how within a national social movement organization, grassroots groups can develop different feminist identities based on personal experiences, community context, and organizational environment. In an examination of two NOW chapters, I find that the ideology of motherhood is interpreted two ways, as a social status with political ramifications, and as the act of caring and taking responsibility for relationships. These different interpretations of the core female identity of motherhood resulted in the construction of distinct feminist identities. This work confirms the view of Mohanty by illustrating the importance of placing activists within their own socio-historic contexts. In addition, by conceptualizing the shifting nature and multiplicity of feminist identities, women's movement scholars create more complex frameworks for the study of all social movements.

It is also through women's movements that another concept complicating how we understand identity has emerged. Feminist activists and scholars, such as the Combahee River Collective (1978), Deborah King (1988), and Patricia Hill Collins (1991), conceptualized an intersectional feminist paradigm that views race-ethnicity, class, gender, and sexuality as interlocking systems of oppression, forming a 'matrix of domination' in which one social identity cannot be understood completely without considering all aspects of a person. The matrix of identity experienced by activists mutually influence interactions, opportunities, and access to resources (hooks, 1989; Collins, 1991). Intersectionality was conceived through the work of US black feminist theorists and activists to address the racism, classism, and homophobia of the earlier feminists with the goal of dismantling the concept of universal womanhood. In particular, black feminists argued that they could not be understood as either black or women but as both. The concept of intersectionality is at the core of much research on women's movements, allowing scholars to conceptualize activists in their own socio-historic periods and their own contexts (as advocated by Mohanty) as well as understanding the complexity of identity development within movements (as advocated by collective identity scholars).

Transnational Mobilization and Global Connections

By undoing binaries between Western and non-Western, men and women, powerful and powerless, Mohanty argues for 'building a noncolonizing feminist solidarity across borders' (2002, p. 503). One response to this call is transnational feminist thought developed in the early 1990s that complicates the ways in which women's movements are viewed (Patil, 2011). Vrushali Patil writes:

> In a 'traditional' arena of feminist concern such as violence against women within practices such as female genital cutting, sati, and women's involvement in the sex industry, they [transnational feminist theorists] have advanced considerations of colonial and neo-colonial legacies in the construction of knowledge of the 'other,' politico-economic inequalities, cross-cultural hierarchies, and women's agency. (2011, p. 541)

A result, she argues, is the expansion of the scope of feminist activism. Ara Wilson in her study of the 2005 and 2006 World Social Forum, a gathering of international social justice activists, provides evidence of this scope and notes that while the meetings are not overtly feminist, feminist organizing and ideology is present (2007). As indicated by the World Social Forums, not only have women organized in their communities and their countries, they also reach across borders to work together. While transnational feminist theory is relatively new, transnational connections are not. For example, in 1878, the first international women's congress convened in Paris, bringing together women from different European cultures (Taylor and Rupp, 2002). The bringing together of national women's movements in the nineteenth century created a transnational activist discourse that continues into contemporary times. Valentine Moghadam argues 'global feminism and transnational feminist networks' are the result of 'material, social and economic forces and factors [that] have given rise to new identities, discourses, values and forms of organization led by women' (2005, p. 20). Patil notes that this focus on 'networks, communities and opportunity structures' (2011, p. 545) is part of a growing trend in social movement studies with work such as Ferree and Tripp (2006) that examines the opportunities and constraints faced by transnational women's movements. Rupp and Taylor note that one of the important developments in the creation of international feminism was the construction of a feminist collective identity (1999) and transnational emotion culture (Taylor and Rupp, 2002).

In sum, by acknowledging that not all women's movements are Western in origin or ideology, scholars expand and construct micro-level concepts such as collective identities and intersectionality that have an impact on the macro-level conceptualizations of transnational movements through theories of networks, community, opportunity structures and their relationship to social forces and significantly shape sociology and interdisciplinary works.

FUTURE DEVELOPMENTS AND RESEARCH TOPICS

While I have used these three characterizations of women's movements – not new, not only Western, and not only feminist – as evidence of the direction and breadth of women's movement research, they also serve as the foundation of future research topics and developments within the field. While the study of women's movements expands our empirical knowledge, it also creates a context to refine, develop, and correct theoretical assumptions about movements. In our article on the relationship between women's movements and social movement research, we write:

> Like the scholarship on women's movements that blossomed over the past three decades, this newer work should not only engage with mainstream thinking in social movement theory but criticize and expand existing models that fail to capture the distinctive features of women's movements. In this way, the symbiotic relationship between research on the women's movement and social movement theory will persist. (Reger and Taylor, 2002, p. 114)

As we note, much of the research to come will continue to develop out of a disjuncture between what women's movement scholars and activists know and what social movement theories afford in terms of explanations in their frameworks. However, the future of women's movement research is not just in the expansion of theoretical frameworks but also in the ways in which social movements are studied. Feminist and community action researchers draw on the ideas of post-colonial and black feminist theorists to find ways to move past ethnocentric, Western-focused notions of research and objectivity and to engage the researcher and the researched in collaborative, co-researcher relationships. I detail these future theoretical and methodological directions in women's movement research below.

Theoretical Expansions

Reger and Taylor (2002) argue that to understand women's movements as long lived, with multiple generations of activism in shifting political contexts, allows researchers to develop a deeper understanding of the relationship between these movements and the ways in which gender is understood within a society. McCammon et al. (2001) call this a 'gendered political context' that links the movement and its activism to the culture and structure of a society. In addition, by understanding how women's movements endure over time, the links between these movements and others in society, and the way in which the movements 'spill over' into each other (Meyer and Whittier, 1994) can be teased out empirically. This is particularly true of women's movements that focus on issues such as citizenship, social justice, immigration, and others that connect to other movements within the same social context. Future research will continue to tease out the specifics of movement connections within a society. Focusing on movements and their contexts can illuminate how different strands, groups, tactics, strategies, and ideologies within a movement can coexist, adding to the complexity of movement characterizations. Patil (2011) notes that these conversations in sociology are at the beginning stages regarding transfeminist movements. She sees the future of this work in investigating not just 'women' as a category but expanding frameworks to view the body, sexualities, and genders as they interact with large social dynamics such as globalization. In addition, future scholarship will continue to integrate ideas of intersectionality with the concept of the 'transnational', creating a complex understanding of activist identities and locations.

Future research will also continue to address long-lived movements that encompass multiple generations of activists and will complicate simple characterization of women's movements as happening in 'waves' or cycles of protest. As Reger and Taylor (2002) point out, examining the complexity of interaction within and outside of the movement has the benefit of adding to concepts such as social movement outcomes and moves the focus on social movements from more than engagement with the state. We write:

> It is important for scholars of the women's movement to maintain a critical stance toward mainstream theories of social movements in order to provide historical specificity to the field as well as to restore its attention to the diversity of modern social movements and the role of social movements as sources of equality and of meaning, identity, and community in complex modern societies. (2002, p. 113)

Expanding the Means of Study

The work of post-colonial feminists, such as Mohanty and Patil, directs researchers of all movements to explore ways in which their power can be a barrier in the study of subjugated people. To address this dynamic, some scholars advocate utilizing a community action research approach to research within a community, identify the main issues its residents face, and then to collaborate on solutions. For example, M. Briton Lykes and Alison Crosby, whose work is primarily in Mayan communities in Guatemala, write:

> Through our research, we seek to explicitly problematize the encounter between the Western self and the colonized Other, and to contest power and acknowledge systemic privilege, as well as oppression. Such an approach requires attention to the interlocking and intersecting relations of power, including gender, racialization, class, sexuality and ability. (2013, p. 146)

By adopting this approach, community action research blurs the lines between the activism and research of women, particularly those in non-Western contexts by paying attention to how Western ideas provide ethnocentric understandings instead of relativistic and socio-historic examinations. This methodological approach to research addresses power differential between researcher and those being researched and seeks to create a collaborative relationship where community members identify issues or social problems and then with the researcher create ways of addressing them. This research is often accomplished through the use of photography, oral histories or autobiographical writing by the community members who are the subject and also 'authors' of study. This research, meant to aid in the transformation of communities, moves past the traditional social science model and stands as an example of a research direction in this future.

In sum, focusing on the ways in which women's movements have been characterized in the literature and then working to undo the assumptions that limit our knowledge is both a theoretical and methodological journey. Women's movements have many commonalities; they emerge in times of social upheaval that prompts gender role change and often focus on gender dynamics and the transformation of a society. However, for all the commonalities there are also differences. Women's movements are not always based in an ideology of feminist or gender transformation or follow Western liberal feminist pathways. Women's movements may construct men as the opposition or, as I note in the case of some forms of African feminism, they may view men as allies. Women's movements happen around the world and as Mohanty (1986) notes they may vary considerably by history and context and may differ from Western expectations. Women's movements, often characterized in movement 'waves' or cycles also may be more complex with multiple strands of activism intertwining and separating throughout history, experiencing different rates of mobilization. These dynamics remind scholars that to understand women's movements, theoretical frameworks need to be flexible and open to departures from expected trajectories and that new methods of engaged research may be necessary to truly understand the dynamics of research.

NOTE

1. In 2010, the journal *Feminist Formations* dedicated almost 60 pages of essays by feminist historians critiquing the wave metaphor.

REFERENCES

Bailey, C. (1997), 'Making waves and drawing lines: the politics of defining the vicissitudes of feminism', *Hypatia*, **12**(3), 17–28.
Basu, A. (ed.) (1995), *The Challenge of Local Feminisms: Women's Movements in Global Perspective*, Boulder, CO: Westview Press.
Baumgardener, J. and A. Richards (2000), *Manifesta: Young Women, Feminism and the Future*, New York: Farrar, Straus & Giroux.
Beckwith, K. (1987), 'Response to feminism in the Italian parliament: divorce, abortion and sexual violence legislation', in M.F. Katzenstein and C.M. Mueller (eds), *The Women's Movements of the United States and Western Europe: Consciousness, Political Opportunity, and Public Policy*, Philadelphia, PA: Temple University Press, pp. 153–71.
Borland, E. (2006), 'The mature resistance of Argentina's Madres de Plaza de Mayo', in H. Johnston and P. Almeida (eds), *Latin American Social Movements: Globalization, Democratization, and Transnational Networks*, Boulder, CO: Rowman & Littlefield, pp. 115–30.

Borland, E. (2010), 'Crisis as a catalyst for cooperation? Women's organizing in Buenos Aires', in N. van Dyke and H.J. McCammon (eds), *Strategic Alliances: Coalition Building and Social Movements*, Minneapolis, MN: University of Minnesota Press, pp. 241–65.

Buechler, S. (1990), *Women's Movements in the United States*, New Brunswick, NJ: Rutgers University Press.

Chafe, W.H. (1977), *Women and Equality: Changing Patterns in American Culture*, New York: Oxford University Press.

Chafetz, J.S. and A.G. Dworkin (1986), *Female Revolt: Women's Movements in World and Historical Perspective*, Totowa, NJ: Rowman & Allanheld.

Collins, P.H. (1991), *Black Feminist Thought: Knowledge, Consciousness, and the Politics of Empowerment*, Boston, MA: Unwin Hyman.

Combahee River Collective (1978), 'The Combahee River Collective Statement', copyright © Z. Eisenstein, accessed 1 July 2013 at http://circuitous.org/scraps/combahee.html.

Desai, M. (2002), 'Multiple meditations: the state and women's movements in India', in D.A. Meyer, N. Whittier and B. Robnett (eds), *Social Movements: Identity, Culture and the State*, Oxford/New York: Oxford University Press, pp. 66–84.

DuBois, E.C. (1978), *Feminism and Suffrage: The Emergence of an Independent Women's Movement in America 1848–1869*, Ithaca, NY: Cornell University Press.

Enloe, C. (2007), *Globalization and Militarism: Feminists Make the Link*, Lanham, MD: Rowman & Littlefield.

Evans, S.M. (1980), *Personal Politics: The Roots of Women's Liberation in the Civil Rights Movement & The New Left*, New York: Vintage Books.

Faludi, S. (1991), *Backlash: The Undeclared War Against American Women*, New York: Crown Publishers.

Ferree, M.M. (1997), 'Patriarchies and feminisms: the two women's movements of post-unification Germany', in L. Richardson, V. Taylor and N. Whittier (eds), *Feminist Frontiers IV*, New York: McGraw-Hill, pp. 526–36.

Ferree, M.M. (2004), 'Soft repression: ridicule, stigma, and silencing in gender-based movements', in D.J. Myers and D.M. Cress (eds), *Authority in Contention, Research in Social Movements, Conflict and Change*, Boston, MA: Elsevier, pp. 85–101.

Ferree, M.M. and B.B. Hess ([1985] 1995), *Controversy and Coalition: The New Feminist Movement Across Three Decades of Change*, New York: Twayne Publishers.

Ferree, M.M. and C.M. Mueller (2004), 'Feminism and the women's movement: a global perspective', in D. Snow, S.A. Soule and H. Kriesi (eds), *The Blackwell Companion to Social Movements*, Oxford: Blackwell, pp. 576–607.

Ferree, M.M. and A.M. Tripp (eds) (2006), *Global Feminism: Women's Activism, Organizing and Human Rights*, New York: New York University Press.

Ferree, M.M., W.A. Gamson, J. Gerhards and D. Rucht (2002), *Shaping Abortion Discourse: Democracy and the Public Sphere in Germany and the United States*, Cambridge, UK: Cambridge University Press.

Friedan, B. (1963), *The Feminine Mystique*, New York: W.W. Norton and Co.

Garrison, E.K. (2000), 'US feminism – grrrl style! Youth (sub)cultures and the technologies of the third wave', *Feminist Studies*, **26**(1), 141–70.

Garrison, E.K. (2005), 'Are we on a wavelength yet? On feminist oceanography, radios and third wave feminism', in J. Reger (ed.), *Different Wavelengths: Studies of the Contemporary Women's Movement*, New York: Routledge, pp. 237–56.

Giele, J.Z. (1995), *Two Paths to Women's Equality: Temperance, Suffrage and the Origins of Modern Feminism*, New York: Twayne Publishers.

Guenther, K.M. (2010), *Making Their Place: Feminism after Socialism in Eastern Germany*, Stanford, CA: Stanford University Press.

Hawkesworth, M. (2004), 'The semiotics of premature burial: feminism in a postfeminist age', *Signs: Journal of Culture and Society*, **29**(4), 961–86.

Hawkesworth, M. (2006), *Globalization and Feminist Activism*, Lanham, MD: Rowman & Littlefield.

Hellman, J.A. (1987), 'Women's struggle in a worker's city: feminist movements in Turin', in M.F. Katzenstein and C.M. Mueller (eds), *The Women's Movements of the United States and Western Europe: Consciousness, Political Opportunity, and Public Policy*, Philadelphia, PA: Temple University Press, pp. 111–31.

Herzon, H. (2008), 'Re/visioning the women's movement in Israel', *Citizenship Studies*, **12**(3), 265–82.

Hewitt, N.A. (2010), 'From Seneca Falls to suffrage: reimagining a "master" narrative in US women's history', in N.A. Hewitt (ed.), *No Permanent Waves: Recasting Histories of US Feminism*, New Brunswick, NJ: Rutgers University Press, pp. 15–38.

hooks, bell (1989), *Talking Back: Thinking Feminist, Thinking Black*, Boston, MA: South End Press.

Huber, J. and G. Spitze (1983), *Sex Stratification: Children, Housework and Jobs*, New York: Academic Press.

Jenson, J. (1987), 'Changing discourse, changing agendas: political rights and reproductive policies in France', in M.F. Katzenstein and C.M. Mueller (eds), *The Women's Movements of the United States and Western Europe: Consciousness, Political Opportunity, and Public Policy*, Philadelphia, PA: Temple University Press, pp. 64–88.

Johnston, H., E. Laraña and J.R. Gusfield (1994), 'Identities, grievances, and new social movements', in E. Laraña, H. Johnston and J.R. Gusfield (eds), *New Social Movements: From Ideology to Identity*, Philadelphia, PA: Temple University Press, pp. 3–35.

Katzenstein, M.F. (1987), 'Comparing the feminist movements of the United States and Western Europe: an overview', in M.F. Katzenstein and C.M. Mueller (eds), *The Women's Movements of the United States and Western Europe: Consciousness, Political Opportunity, and Public Policy*, Philadelphia, PA: Temple University Press, pp. 3–22.

Katzenstein, M.F. (1990), 'Feminism within American institutions: unobtrusive mobilization in the 1980s', *Signs: Journal of Culture and Society*, **16**(11), 27–54.

King, D. (1988), 'Multiple jeopardy, multiple consciousness: the context of a black feminist ideology', *Signs: Journal of Culture and Society*, **14**(1), 42–72.

Klein, E. (1984), *Gender Politics*, Cambridge, MA: Harvard University Press.

Koopmans, R. (2004), 'Protest in time and space: the evolution of waves of contention', in D. Snow, S.A. Soule and H. Kriesi (eds), *The Blackwell Companion to Social Movements*, Oxford: Blackwell, pp. 19–46.

Kristof, N.D. and S. WuDunn (2009), *Half the Sky: Turning Oppression into Opportunity for Women Worldwide*, New York: Vintage.

Lykes, M.B. and A. Crosby (2013), 'Feminist practice of action and community research', in S. Hesse-Biber (ed.), *Feminist Research Practice: A Primer*, Thousand Oaks, CA: Sage Publications, pp. 145–81.

Mannheim, K. (1952), 'The problem with generations', in P. Keckemeti and P. Keegan (eds), *Essays on the Sociology of Knowledge*, London: Routledge, pp. 276–320.

Mansbridge, J.J. (1986), *Why We Lost the ERA*, Chicago, IL: University of Chicago Press.

Marcus, S. (2010), *Girls to the Front: The True Story of the Riot Grrrl Revolution*, New York: Harper.

McCammon, H., K. Campbell, E.M. Granberg and C. Mowrey (2001), 'How movements win: gendered opportunity structures and US women's suffrage movements, 1866 to 1919', *American Sociological Review*, **66**(1), 49–70.

McCarthy, J. and M. Zald (1977), 'Resource mobilization and social movements: a partial theory', *American Journal of Sociology*, **82**(6), 1212–41.

Melucci, A. (1989), *Nomads of the Present: Social Movements and Individual Needs in Contemporary Society*, Philadelphia, PA: Temple University Press.

Meyer, D.S. and N. Whittier (1994), 'Social movement spillover', *Social Problems*, **41**(2), 277–98.

Minkoff, D. (1993), 'Organization of survival: women's and racial-ethnic voluntarist and activist organizations, 1955–1985', *Social Forces*, **71**(4), 887–908.

Moghadam, V. (2005), *Globalizing Women: Transnational Feminist Networks*, Baltimore, MD: Johns Hopkins University Press.

Mohanty, C. (1986), 'Under western eyes: feminist scholarship and colonial discourses', *Boundary*, **2**(3), 333–58.
Mohanty, C. (2002), '"Under western eyes" revisited: feminist solidarity through anticapitalist struggles', *Signs: Journal of Women in Culture and Society*, **28**(2), 499–535.
Nadasen, P. (2010), 'Expanding the boundaries of the women's movement: black feminism and the struggle for welfare rights', in N.A. Hewitt (ed.), *No Permanent Waves: Recasting Histories of US Feminism*, New Brunswick, NJ: Rutgers University Press, pp. 168–92.
Naples, N. (1998), *Grassroots Warriors: Activist Mothering, Community Work, and the War on Poverty*, New York/London: Routledge.
Nnaemeka, O. (2005), 'Nego-feminism', in J. Lorber (ed.), *Gender Equality: Feminist Theories and Politics*, Los Angeles, CA: Roxbury Publishing Co., pp. 208–12.
Pardo, M. (1998), *Mexican American Women Activists: Identity and Resistance in Two Los Angeles Communities*, Philadelphia, PA: Temple University Press.
Patil, V. (2011), 'Transnational feminism in sociology: articulations, agendas and debates', *Sociology Compass*, **5**(7), 540–50.
Ray, R. (1999), *Fields of Protest: Women's Movements in India*, Minneapolis, MN: University of Minnesota Press.
Rebick, J. (2005), *Ten Thousand Roses: The Making of a Feminist Revolution*, Toronto, ON: Penguin.
Reger, J. (2002), 'Organizational dynamics and the construction of multiple feminist identities in the National Organization for Women', *Gender & Society*, **16**(5), 710–27.
Reger, J. (2012), *Everywhere and Nowhere: Contemporary Feminism in the United States*, New York/Oxford: Oxford University Press.
Reger, J. and S. Staggenborg (2006), 'Patterns of mobilization in local movement organizations: leadership and strategy in four national organization for women chapters', *Sociological Perspectives*, **49**(3), 297–323.
Reger, J. and V. Taylor (2002), 'Women's movement research and social movement theory: a symbiotic relationship', *Research in Political Sociology*, **10**, 85–121.
Roth, B. (2004), *Separate Roads to Feminism: Black Chicana and White Feminist Movements in America's Second Wave*, New York: Cambridge University Press.
Rupp, L. and V. Taylor (1987), *Survival in the Doldrums: The American Women's Rights Movement, 1945 to 1960s*, New York: Oxford University Press.
Rupp, L. and V. Taylor (1999), 'Forging feminist identity in an international movement: a collective identity approach to twentieth century feminism', *Signs: Journal of Culture and Society*, **24**(2), 363–86.
Smyth, A. (1988), 'The contemporary women's movement in the Republic of Ireland', *Women's Studies International Forum*, **11**(4), 331–41.
Staggenborg, S. (1991), *The Pro-Choice Movement: Organization and Activism in the Abortion Conflict*, New York: Oxford University Press.
Staggenborg, S. (1998), 'Social movement communities and cycles of protest: the emergence and maintenance of a local women's movement organization', *Social Problems*, **45**(2), 180–204.
Staggenborg, S. and J. Lecomte (2009), 'Social movement campaigns: mobilization and outcomes in the Montreal women's movement community', *Mobilization: An International Journal*, **14**(2), 163–80.
Staggenborg, S. and V. Taylor (2005), 'Whatever happened to the women's movement?', *Mobilization: An International Journal*, **10**(1), 37–52.
Staggenborg, S., D. Eder and L. Sudderth (1993–94), 'Women's culture and social change: evidence from the National Women's Music Festival', *Berkeley Journal of Sociology*, **38**, 31–56.
Tarrow, S. (1994), *Power in Movement: Social Movements and Contentious Politics*, Cambridge, UK: Cambridge University Press.
Taylor, V. (1989), 'Sources of continuity in social movements: the women's movement in abeyance', *American Sociological Review*, **54**(5), 761–75.
Taylor, V. and L.J. Rupp (2002), 'Loving internationalism: the emotion culture of

transnational women's organizations, 1888–1945', *Mobilization: An International Journal*, **7**(2), 125–44.

Taylor, V. and N. Whittier (1992), 'Collective identity in social movement communities: lesbian feminist mobilization', in A.D. Morris and C.M. Mueller (eds), *Frontiers in Social Movement Theory*, New Haven, CT/London: Yale University Press, pp. 104–29.

Taylor, V. and N. Whittier (1997), 'The new feminist movement', in L. Richardson, V. Taylor and N. Whittier (eds), *Feminist Frontiers IV*, New York: McGraw Hill, pp. 544–61.

Thompson, B. (2002), 'Multiracial feminism: recasting the chronology of second wave feminism', *Feminist Studies*, **28**(2), 337–60.

Tilly, C. (1989), *From Mobilization to Revolution*, New York: Random House.

Tilly, C. (2004), *Social Movements, 1768–2004*, Boulder, CO: Paradigm Publishers.

Whittier, N. (1995), *Feminist Generations: The Persistence of the Radical Women's Movement*, Philadelphia, PA: Temple University Press.

Whittier, N. (1997), 'Political generations, micro-cohorts, and the transformation of social movements', *American Sociological Review*, **62**(5), 760–78.

Wilson, A. (2007), 'Feminism in the space of the World Social Forum', *Journal of International Women's Studies*, **8**(3), 10–27.

19. The international human rights movement
Ann Marie Clark and Paul Danyi

The human rights idea, that governments should honor the physical integrity and inherent dignity of all persons, has inspired millions of people to work to translate the ideal into political reality. Although the concept of rights has a history that reaches back centuries, the concept of human rights is relatively new, and it has sparked a high level of organized transnational action from the mid-twentieth century to the present. Numerous studies by historians, sociologists, anthropologists, and political scientists chart the origins of human rights (e.g., Lauren, 2003; Cmiel, 2004; Ishay, 2004; Hunt, 2007; Quataert, 2009; Moyn, 2010; Neier, 2012), and so we focus mainly on later developments as the human rights movement emerged and flourished. We begin with a brief discussion of the early articulation of human rights principles after World War II and then address the transnational aspects of the human rights movement: its members and structure; its distinctive frames and repertoires; and the political opportunities available to the movement at the global level. Finally, we review some of the questions that have been posed by researchers about the identity, politics, and effects of the transnational movement for human rights.

THE TWENTIETH-CENTURY BEGINNINGS OF THE MODERN HUMAN RIGHTS MOVEMENT

Non-governmental organizations (NGOs) based in the United States were among those who pushed for the inclusion of human rights in the United Nations (UN) Charter. Many of them were invited to attend the 1945 founding conference of the UN in San Francisco as 'consultants' to the US delegation. No other delegation included NGOs. They pushed for an ongoing consultative role at the UN's Economic and Social Council (ECOSOC). That role became what we now know as 'consultative status' and set a procedural path for NGOs' ongoing involvement at the UN. In addition, some lobbied for the inclusion of human rights in the UN Charter. The groups advocating human rights included the Commission to Study the Organization of Peace, the Federal Council of Churches, the

American Association for the United Nations, and the American Jewish Committee (Korey, 1998, pp. 30–33). These groups also pushed for a 'Bill of Rights' to be drafted for the UN (ibid.). The Universal Declaration of Human Rights (UDHR; United Nations, 1948) was the result.

The UDHR outlined 30 basic articles of human rights and was intended to provide the basis for a more binding global treaty. The rights enumerated in the Declaration were elaborated in two different treaties that finally saw the light of day in 1966, when the International Covenant on Civil and Political Rights (ICCPR) and the International Covenant on Economic, Social, and Cultural Rights (ICESCR) were opened for signing. After the required number of states had ratified the Covenants, the treaties entered into force in 1976. However, members of the human rights movement did not wait for those treaties before pushing for wider acceptance of human rights.

In the late 1960s and early 1970s NGOs were developing and testing many of their trademark mobilization techniques as a response to abuses occurring in Greece, Chile, Argentina, South Africa, and elsewhere. Legal advocates working with other activists and like-minded officials and diplomats at the UN also initiated work on more detailed legal standards and procedures to address human rights concerns emerging from these and other countries. Also in the 1970s, foreign aid donor countries including the United States began making some of their foreign aid dependent on the human rights conditions in recipient countries.

THE GROWTH AND DEVELOPMENT OF HUMAN RIGHTS ORGANIZATIONS

Despite NGOs' demonstrated interest in human rights when the UN structure was created, initial political opportunities for human rights advocates were limited at the global level. Consultative status with ECOSOC allowed some observer privileges for NGOs that could meet UN criteria, but more substantive participation was not part of the privilege. As was the custom in diplomatic circles, public political statements within the UN that directly criticized nation-states were frowned upon, whether the authors were states or NGOs. Instead, the most important entrées into global human rights governance for NGOs, such as shadow reporting on governments' human rights records, had to be appropriated or expanded upon by the advocates themselves.

The early human rights movement was kindled by organizational activity around the universal human rights idea. This differs from some social movements that have begun with collective protest. Like several other well-known movements, including the US civil rights movement and the gay liberation movement, the human rights movement began with organizational activity and then moved to more widespread mobilization of individuals. In fact, the organizations' work helped to make protest and collective organizing possible,[1] which seems to be a pattern for successful transnational movements.

Amnesty International (AI) and Human Rights Watch (HRW) are perhaps the largest and best-known members of a worldwide network of domestic human rights advocates and other specialized global and national NGOs working on human rights. Today, HRW and AI have very similar goals, but their individual methods and organizational structures still retain some of the early characteristics that made them distinctive.

Wong (2012) notes that transnational organizations tend to be more successful when they set the agenda centrally and then decentralize implementation of the agenda. She sees Amnesty International (AI), founded in 1961 and headquartered in London, as a prototype. Although AI was centrally organized, from the start its grassroots members carried out most of its advocacy work based on AI's initial identification, largely through news reports, of detained individuals it could help. In fact, AI described itself as a 'worldwide movement' in the front material of many early publications (e.g., Amnesty International, 1980, p. iv). Local groups of AI members 'adopted' specific prisoners assigned to them by AI, with the goal of securing the release of prisoners jailed because of their non-violently-held beliefs – the famous 'Prisoner of Conscience' model. Adoptions were assigned in politically balanced groups of three, to avoid charges of bias. AI also lobbied for all prisoners' well-being and rights.

For several decades now, AI has employed globally orchestrated campaigns in addition to its work on behalf of specific individuals. Since its first Campaign against Torture in 1973, AI has regularly designed and implemented large-scale, thematic advocacy campaigns involving its grassroots membership. Fewer adoptions are initiated, in large part because of changes in governments' techniques of repression, but AI retains a distinctive focus on individuals and their rights and its national sections are still membership governed.

Seventeen years after AI's founding, what would become Human Rights Watch was founded in New York as Helsinki Watch (Snyder, 2011). Helsinki Watch monitored rights in the Soviet Union and Eastern Europe under the Helsinki Accords, relying for information on underground *samizdat* literature exposing violations in the Soviet-controlled states (Laber, 2005, p. 58). Other regional watch groups formed under the 'Watch Committees' banner, and they consolidated as HRW in 1987 (Neier, 2012). Human Rights Watch did not use an explicit member mobilization strategy, nor did it follow AI's membership-governance and funding model. While HRW does seek individual 'member' donations, it has relied extensively on funds provided by wealthy US philanthropic organizations. And, in contrast with AI's early insistence on being an 'apolitical' movement, the Committees and HRW often took explicitly political stands. Americas Watch, for example, has always been outspokenly critical of US foreign policy. HRW also pioneered use of principles of humanitarian law as well as human rights law to critique the human rights effects of situations of internal armed conflict in the Americas. HRW adopted a vantage point broader than but complementary to AI's intense focus on reporting on violations against individuals in that region at a time in the 1980s when AI's organizational focus was more limited (ibid.; also see Baehr, 1994).

REPERTOIRES OF THE HUMAN RIGHTS MOVEMENT

The patterns and methods of activism on behalf of human rights have emerged from decades of effort and experimentation by movement actors. In the language of social movement theory, these patterns and methods are known as repertoires of contention (Tilly, 1979). Because the human rights movement spans the globe, it is characterized by the vibrant creativity of local activists from a multitude of cultures. We separate the movement's repertoires into three categories: bringing human rights violations to light, incorporating human rights concerns and concepts into international law and institutions ('standard setting'), and holding states accountable.

Information and Advocacy: Bringing Violations to Light

Telling the stories of victims of human rights abuses was one of the early action repertoires used by the human rights movement, and it is still one of the most important. Further, human rights NGOs have become the most important conduits for supplying information about human rights abuses and raising awareness both at the UN and more generally, as members of global civil society (Friedman et al., 2005). Dissemination of information about human rights violations raises the awareness of the public – potential movement members – and casts shame on governments both for their own abuses and for inaction in the face of others' abuses. For NGOs, another important reason for sharing information is to support individual victims and their families and to make sure that they are not forgotten by the outside world, as exemplified by AI's earliest campaigning on behalf of 'the forgotten prisoner' (Benenson, 1961).

NGOs and their supporters take the monitoring of violations very seriously. Clark et al. (1998, pp. 21–3) observe that a 'monitoring frame', NGOs' widely held view of their own role as watchdogs of governments, motivates globally active NGOs both in human rights work and other fields. A 'frame' is a way of describing a commonly held set of beliefs about a problem's causes and solutions (Snow and Benford, 1992, p. 137). In the monitoring frame guiding human rights activism, the problems of government secrecy and the inattention of bystanders at home and abroad enable governments to perpetrate violations against their populations with impunity. Bringing violations to light through NGOs' careful fact-finding, advocacy, and use of publicity is a repertoire that enables NGOs to be part of the solution within this frame.

The role of local activists
Although we have noted the importance for the global human rights movement of large, global NGOs, local activists have been essential conduits for information and action, as Sikkink (1993a, 2011) and Keck and Sikkink (1998) have emphasized. Information about violations of human rights begins with local activists. Locals are best situated to gather ongoing information on human rights because they are embedded in the society they are monitoring and have strong connections with other locals and groups. Without the help of local social movement actors, international human rights NGOs would be unable to monitor violations effectively, and their response speed would be greatly diminished (Neier, 2012, p. 12).

The links between local and global actors form a 'transnational advocacy network' of human rights activists that is characterized by durable links and 'dense exchanges of information and services' (Keck and Sikkink, 1998, p. 2). Political repression constrains local groups' ability to broadcast information about human rights conditions within their countries, as well as their avenues for protests. When locals are able to forge links with international NGOs, journalists, politicians, and activists in other countries, they can pass on information and find a broader audience for their concerns. Transnational networks further demonstrate that 'the world is watching' how governments treat their populations, including defenders of human rights at the local level of the network. Amnesty's innovative Urgent Action Network, in which members write letters as quickly as possible on behalf of the human rights and well-being of individuals thought to be in imminent danger, has been operating since 1973. It exemplifies this process of linkage, and has been copied by other international NGOs (Amnesty International, 2013). The urgent messages from members of the network at the global level ask for specific help for named individuals.

Even with a functioning transnational advocacy network, human rights monitoring can be difficult. Since the initiation of bilateral human rights policies in the 1970s that tie foreign aid to human rights performance, mentioned above, some donor governments also monitor human rights conditions. In such cases, NGO monitors can act as a check on and supplement to information gathered by governments. For example, the US State Department's country reports became more accurate because activists and investigators continued to inquire about bias and demand accuracy (Sikkink, 1993b; Clark and Sikkink, 2013). The US State Department now regularly consults with human rights NGOs of many types as it prepares its reports (Clark and Sikkink, 2013).

With the initiation of external governmental monitoring, local people in some countries, such as advocates and family members seeking information on disappeared persons in Argentina in the 1970s and 1980s, learned they could sometimes bring information about abuses to embassy officials as a way of sending information out of the country (Quataert, 2009, p. 133). Institutionalizing the monitoring function in foreign offices expanded these opportunities for advocates and embedded human rights in standard procedures for bureaucrats to follow even if they were previously not part of the human rights movement.

Standard Setting and Institution Building

In addition to using information as a basis for grassroots and diplomatic pressure on governments, human rights organizations have developed repertoires for work within international organizations to develop new legal norms of human rights. Human rights norms – both as legal rules and as shared beliefs about appropriate behavior – complement information gathering since they can serve as reference points in evaluating the actions of governments. Members of the human rights movement use norms to weigh the actions of governments against these standards and point out governments' deficiencies. Institutional and political changes at the domestic level are often required to implement new standards. Here we discuss the role of the movement in articulating new norms, interpreting behavior in light of those norms for publics and governments, and incorporating these standards in institutions.

Articulating new standards
Perhaps the most precarious moment for the human rights movement was in the immediate post-World War II period, when it was unclear

whether new international institutions would become casualties of Cold War politics or useful forums in which to advance the human rights cause. Quataert (2009) argues that human rights in the UN system had little bite until average people and activists mobilized between the late 1940s and the end of the Cold War. She highlights the movements in some of the important cases we have already mentioned: opposition to apartheid in South Africa; focus on disappearances in Argentina; and concern over the Soviet Union's treatment of political dissidents during the Cold War. During these early moments, the human rights movement drew upon but expanded the narrow interpretation of human rights that was orthodoxy at the UN. Activism helped to redefine the role of human rights norms within UN bureaucracy, shifting from a narrow declaratory role to the more active monitoring and reviewing role the UN plays today.

NGOs' modern repertoire of appealing directly to governments for new human rights standards was forged by Amnesty International in the 1970s as it urged states to articulate new formal principles outlawing torture, culminating with the UN Convention Against Torture and Other Cruel, Inhuman or Degrading Treatment or Punishment (United Nations, 1984). In doing so AI relied on the legitimacy it derived from loyalty to human rights principles, political impartiality, the knowledge of human rights conditions affecting detainees that it had learned about in its advocacy for individuals, and the fact that it had grassroots supporters in many countries (Clark, 2001). AI participated in parts of the treaty drafting process before informal collaboration between states and NGOs was widely practiced, and in this context used its carefully cultivated legitimacy to argue for its interpretation of human rights norms as applied to the behavior of states.

Only a few organizations other than AI and the International Commission of Jurists (ICJ), a worldwide organization of lawyers and judges (Tolley, 1994), shared this standard-setting work at the beginning. AI was uniquely able to bring its membership 'audience' to bear in pushing for new norms (Clark, 2001). By 1998, a sizeable majority of human rights NGOs saw establishing new standards of behavior as the primary goal of their work (Smith et al., 1998), and many more international NGOs actively participate in such work today, including Human Rights Watch, Human Rights First, and other smaller, specialized groups.

These efforts have broadened the agenda and the normative impact of the human rights movement. Human rights advocates have participated in the creation of international treaties and other legal norms covering torture, disappearances, treatment of prisoners, racism, women's rights, indigenous rights, children's rights, and disabled people's rights, among others – as well as over a dozen regional conventions reflecting similar principles.

Institution building
Creating and codifying human rights norms has also involved winning the inclusion of human rights principles within international institutions: the UN's Human Rights Council and other parts of the UN's human rights apparatus, regional organizations like the European Commission of Human Rights, and national human rights institutions (Mertus, 2009). Even cities and local communities have been building institutions to enforce compliance with human rights norms (e.g., City of Portland, Office of Human Relations, 2011).

Accounts of more recently formed national and international human rights institutions such as the International Criminal Court (ICC) and criminal tribunals for human rights violators stress the importance of NGOs and individuals (Deitelhoff, 2009; Nettelfield, 2010; Sikkink, 2011). These explanations place the human rights movement at the center of institutional change and stand in contrast to arguments that human rights institutions are outcomes of power politics in which human rights are a tool of the strong states against weaker states (e.g., Morgenthau, 1967). They stress that the organized human rights movement has galvanized national and international opinion and reframed debates over the legitimate treatment of citizens by their governments. Changes have been achieved through appeal to moral principles, finding common ground with similarly interested governments, and through outside pressure. Different members of the human rights movement use a variety of tactics, and some have shifted in their tactics over time. But their work has, in many cases, managed to buttress fledgling human rights institutions and to build institutions where they previously did not exist.

Holding States Accountable

Translating human rights ideas into political practice is the ultimate goal of the human rights movement. Activists have developed several methods through which seemingly weak political actors are able to push governments towards better human rights behavior. We divide these into four categories: using powerful allies, economic leverage, discursive engagement, and domestic accountability.

Reaching out to powerful allies and international institutions
When advocates are able to place an issue on the agenda of a powerful government or international organization, what was previously

a local or national concern can be elevated to an issue of diplomacy and greatly increase the movement's influence. At the UN, the first large NGOs explicitly concerned with human rights – such as the ICJ and AI – learned to connect with governments sympathetic to human rights issues and cooperate with them informally as a way to place their issues on the agenda (Tolley, 1994; Clark, 2001). The Netherlands and Sweden, for example, are among the countries that have a tradition of human rights leadership and collaboration at the global level. However, the human rights movement's political interactions with nation-states are often much more contentious. Human rights activists have learned to coordinate all parts of their networks to apply international pressure when democratic channels for demands are non-existent or are blocked. Keck and Sikkink (1998, p. 24) call this approach the 'boomerang effect'.

Transnational connections enable locals to engage in 'leverage politics', a method of contention in which moral arguments are used either to shame a government into changing its behavior or convince other countries and international organizations to place diplomatic, often material, pressure on violators. Transnational networks afford local activists access to foreign media (Ramos et al., 2007), sympathetic foreign politicians, and international NGOs. In this way, they can communicate and amplify their concerns to powerful international actors. By engendering pressure from outside actors and combining it with sustained domestic pressure from NGOs the movement has been successful in improving respect for human rights (Murdie and Davis, 2012).

Through NGOs the human rights movement also engages international institutions directly. In addition to their work on standard setting, NGOs have accessed international institutions via the UN's human rights treaty review bodies, which scrutinize countries' compliance reports. In this way, the movement's prior standard-setting work and lobbying have helped to create further political opportunities for NGOs within the UN human rights structure. Representatives from NGOs join in workshops prior to a country's review and also participate as observers during reviews. NGOs provide information to the UN about a state's record and may produce 'shadow reports' that can be compared with a home country's own report on its human rights treaty compliance. Shadow reporting has become an institutionalized process at the United Nations and is officially encouraged as a means for NGOs to challenge government reports (e.g., UN, Division for the Advancement of Women, n.d.; Jacobsen, 2008). New human rights bodies at the UN have also encouraged NGOs to provide information. For example, a new Universal Periodic Review (UPR) procedure was adopted in 2006 as a mechanism to review each UN member state's human rights conditions every four years (United Nations, 2006). The UPR makes NGOs' reports and other 'stakeholder' reports one of the primary sources of information to set the agenda when governments come up for review (Sen and Vincent, 2009, p. 16).

Not all efforts by local human rights activists successfully capture the limited attention of powerful allies. Placing a human rights issue on the agenda of the larger transnational movement or established human rights NGOs is in itself a political endeavor in which some causes fit better than others. The human rights network has performed well in focusing on states where human rights conditions are the worst (Ron et al., 2005), but recent research suggests that issue adoption is also influenced by considerations of how well a new issue complements the current network concerns, how a new issue might affect ongoing campaigns, and how compatible a new issue is with the agenda of partners in the network (Bob, 2005; Carpenter, 2007). Wong (2012) argues that hierarchies within human rights networks also shape how human rights are framed.

The research just mentioned identifies and explores the distribution of power within transnational networks, in which more powerful NGOs, or 'gatekeepers', within the network have more influence over which issues find a place on the global human rights agenda and how they are framed when they do emerge. At times, activists find it necessary to form new transnational coalitions when existing networks, international organizations, and NGOs are slow to respond to issues (Tarrow, 2010). However, despite the existing network's sometimes imperfect responses to grievances, 'once the machine starts it cannot be turned off at a stroke' (Guest, 1990, p. 210). That is, once activists do convince international institutions to take up an issue, violating countries can expect sustained attention and pressure.

Economic levers

Lobbying governments to initiate bilateral economic sanctions, or to join multilateral sanctions, has been a key action repertoire of human rights campaigns since the efforts against apartheid in South Africa. Sanctions on South Africa began in the 1950s and progressed slowly to put the country into near complete isolation by the 1980s (Klotz, 1995). The human rights movement has with varying success tugged on the purse strings of governments in the effort to convince states that human rights are more important than material interests in trade or investment (ibid.). Methods include pushing for bans on foreign investment in a target state, shaming firms to prevent them from operating in a country, boycotts, and pushing governments to freeze the assets of a state or its leadership. Strong economic efforts are typically reserved for cases of large-scale violations, often those involving violence or incarceration against innocents or political opposition.

Case studies show that economic sanctions can be effective, primarily as a part of a larger campaign in which activists leverage other forms of pressure on governments to make them sensitive to sanctions (Klotz, 1995; Keck and Sikkink, 1998, p. 201). In the case of South Africa, economic sanctions were accompanied by diplomatic pressure from allies, popular protest, and diplomatic isolation from the world community.

Often, isolating the exclusive impact of economic sanctions is not possible. Sanctions frequently constitute just one tactic among many in a process pushing for reform. Although they are considered important components of human rights campaigns, sanctions alone are rarely a 'sufficient condition for effectiveness' of a campaign (Risse and Sikkink, 1999, p. 38). Research drawing on a large number of cases has argued that employing economic sanctions does not, on its own, improve human rights behavior (Cardenas, 2007), and can actually make conditions worse (Peksen, 2009). This research suggests that elites responsible for violations may simply pass the 'pain' of sanctions on to average citizens. Government leaders then find themselves empowered as they resist responsibility and take on the role of embattled heroes resisting outside influence. To avoid the unwanted dynamics that can result from generalized sanctions, some scholars have advocated 'smart sanctions' that can be targeted more precisely (Cortright and Lopez, 2002). Despite potential drawbacks, because economic sanctions have proven in important cases to be part of an effective campaign for human rights, they are likely to remain an important tool of the movement.

Accountability politics and discourse
In moving governments from violation to compliance, skillful discursive engagement has been an important action repertoire of the human rights movement. Discourse involves all exchanges, both written and verbal, between the movement and governments and includes 'processes of communication, argumentation, and persuasion' (Risse and Sikkink, 1999, p. 13). By coalescing around human rights to frame governmental repression, the human rights movement has helped to create a common set of principles that both governments and citizens use to understand grievances. As governments discuss and defend their human rights records against critics, they can trap themselves in both discourse and a political process that can lead to reform. Risse et al.'s 'spiral model' of the influence of human rights norms stresses that activist pressure can push a state to make minor tactical concessions that set in motion a process of mobilization and intensified debate over a state's behavior (ibid.; see also Risse et

al., 2013). Such concessions can be subtle or more obvious, but rhetoric accepting human rights norms as legitimate basis for argumentation can signal a significant turning point in a government's response to external pressure. For example, governments that might previously have labeled activists and NGOs as 'foreign agents' seeking to do harm to the state may cease to do so, tacitly conceding a measure of legitimacy to movement activities as well as to human rights principles for human rights. In response to the small victory of rhetorical concessions, domestic activists are able to mobilize others to join their efforts. Governments' active engagement in debate with a mobilized global and domestic civil society further legitimates the movement and the legal principles of human rights, ultimately leaving governments with few international or domestic allies to turn to and signaling the beginnings of reform in the best cases. It is hard to know when these kinds of discursive shifts will lead to changes, but positive historical examples suggest that, as with sanctions, persistence by human rights actors is warranted.

Through fact-finding, discussion, and persuasion, human rights NGOs have also been able to reframe existing international debates over rights violations away from prior negotiating frames and towards a frame in which justice and human rights is a primary concern, thus altering resulting state positions (Clark, 2001; Deitelhoff, 2009). Other existing issues including environmental degradation, indigenous rights, and women's rights have also been reframed to varying degrees to take advantage of the perceived global acceptance of human rights language in discussing grievances, thereby also expanding received notions of what human rights means. By focusing on how the environment affects the human right to health and how average people have a right to participate in decision-making, the issue of environmental degradation can be incorporated into the human rights movement (Picolotti and Taillant, 2010). For indigenous peoples, framing the struggle for self-determination culminated in the creation of new international human rights law (Morgan, 2004). NGOs pushing for women's reproductive rights and against forms of violence against women utilized a series of international human rights conferences and expert opinion to combat a lack of consensus concerning women's rights and reframe them as human rights issues (Joachim, 2003; Friedman et al., 2005).

Domestic accountability
Compliance with human rights standards can also come about as an outcome of domestic political processes that are only partially related to international politics. In democratizing countries, institutions of government may be weak, but relatively fluid. This creates opportunities for

local activists to influence the new democratic political agenda (Simmons, 2009). In the same way that a government's accession to human rights discourse legitimates human rights concerns, Simmons (ibid.) argues that the expectations of domestic human rights activists, and their political influence, are enhanced by treaty commitments their government has made, most especially when the government is in transition from authoritarianism to democracy. For example, when a government is party to a human rights treaty, activists can incorporate treaty provisions when bringing suit in domestic courts. Then, 'judges have to think about how [treaty provisions] are interpreted' (ibid., p. 131), and they may look to the international monitoring bodies for guidance. Deploying and interpreting treaty law through domestic litigation builds case law that can be mobilized in the future. Just as the human rights frame does in the global context, it defines for the movement at home the exact nature of a government's failures to live up to its promises and revises the political opportunity structure in domestic institutions.

In sum, the human rights movement has built stable organizations and networks through which sustained activism has altered not only international politics, but also the domestic politics of countries the world over. At this point, the movement can generate information about violations relatively quickly and disseminate it through already-networked activists to allies in international institutions. The movement has also forged legal pathways for advocacy. The full collection of techniques is used to support domestic activists and pressure human rights violators. In the following section, we explore a few of the prominent debates about the international human rights movement and its effects on politics.

DEBATES ABOUT THE HUMAN RIGHTS MOVEMENT

As scholars reflect on the past, present, and future of the international human rights movement, several new and ongoing debates are evident. First, is the international human rights movement unique in its appeals to principle? Although its reliance on the power of principle may be unusual, some scholars see the human rights movement as comparable to other kinds of popular movements that are based on common beliefs. Second, what does the human rights movement represent as a political force in international relations? In addition to introducing a new idea into international politics, the international human rights movement has impacted what citizens expect of governments and international governance. And third, what impact has the human rights movement had internationally?

In this regard, we point to debates over the effects of human rights activism and research on the extent to which governments honor the new human rights rules that the international human rights movement has helped to create.

How Unique is the Human Rights Movement?

The unique power of the human rights idea – both as an idea that attracts activists and provides leverage against violating governments – constitutes a major theme, and occasionally a point of contention, in recent historical and social science scholarship. Of course, the current historical and institutional aspects of human rights are not the only possible expression of respect for human dignity. However, one reason for the conceptual power of human rights may be its resonance with principles enshrined in many of the world's legal, philosophical, and religious traditions (Lauren, 2003), and with practices and norms common to many cultures (Renteln, 1990). Recent scholarly work adds further critical consideration to our understanding of how and why the human rights movement has become so well recognized.

If we view human rights through a power-politics lens, any movement that pits ideas about right and wrong against power and succeeds, even partially, is notable. The evident shift toward governments' increased recognition of human rights as an important principle is, unfortunately, not the same thing as actual compliance.

Critical views of the historical and political trajectory of twentieth-century human rights initiatives have highlighted complexities within the human rights movement. Historians chronicling the beginnings of the movement have placed the individuals and organizations not on a pedestal but in detailed historical context, as Buchanan has done with regard to Amnesty International (Buchanan, 2002, 2004). As human rights become more institutionalized at national and international levels, advocates face pragmatic choices between fierce loyalty to a rather narrow set of principles and issues, such as freedom of expression and physical integrity rights, and calls for the expansion of the very meaning of human rights.

Samuel Moyn exemplifies the historians' reluctance to wax poetic about human rights, although he notes that the human rights movement was remarkable in its 'prominence and survival in the harsh ideological context of the 1970s', when human rights experienced 'a startling spike in cultural prestige. . .after decades of irrelevance' (Moyn, 2010, p. 122). He argues, however, that latching on to a utopian ideal has often hindered successful movement politics, and he applies this criticism to the human rights movement. In his view, advocates' responsibility to get involved in politics in order to truly make a difference in human rights on the ground makes it untenable – and undesirable – for them to maintain a utopian sense of being set apart from power. In a similar vein, Hopgood (2006) likens human rights advocates' devotion, normally seen as a positive and even inspirational quality, to that of a faith community based on belief as much as results.

These observations about pragmatism versus principle are not so different from unresolved arguments that human rights advocates have been having among themselves since the 1960s. Neier (2012, p. 4), who founded HRW and served as its director for 12 years, offers a sharp rebuttal to the idea that human rights provides a 'vision for the organization of society'. Instead, he argues, the historical development that 'mattered most of all was the collapse of prior universalistic schemes, and the construction of human rights as a persuasive alternative to them' (ibid.).

Even when sharing similar principles and goals, activists do differ among themselves on how best to advocate human rights in the face of state resistance. Many differences that domestic activists have with representations of the global human rights movement can be traced to their own national political experiences (see, e.g., Friedman et al., 2001; Bair and Palpacuer, 2012). To some degree, also, NGOs' material resources mirror the positions of their own states in the international political structure, and global movement alliances have been unable to fully close the gaps that exist. Differences between Northern and Southern NGOs are reflected in varying preferences as to repertoires: lobbying versus informal networking, for example (Friedman et al., 2005). At home, human rights activists in many countries have widely adopted the human rights framework, but have also *adapted* international action frameworks to their own purposes. Hertel (2006) identifies these techniques as 'backdoor moves' and blocking tactics. The scholarly analyses of power relations and debates within the networks of activists reflect a maturing and spread of knowledge about human rights work as well as a maturing of the movement.

The Maturation of the Human Rights Movement

Although it is taken for granted today, the practice of human rights, and human rights as a concept, is built in large part on the conceptual evolution of the idea of human rights as a claim on the nation-state. In fact, the politics of international human rights practice have become much more complex. Beitz (2009, p. 33) suggests that 'one way to grasp this complexity' is to look at the number and kinds of 'international and transnational agents' involved with human rights. Power-holders such as corporations, armed opposition groups and organized crime syndicates can markedly affect the quality of human rights in regions where they are active. These power-holders are often transnationally organized, presenting additional challenges to human rights advocates and researchers (Risse et al., 2013).

As outlined above, change over time in the formal and practical realization of human rights is particularly evident in the following areas: the increasing awareness and documentation of human rights violations in the world; the growth of international legal standards that exist on the books; and the application of human rights law to specific violations.

There is little doubt that we know more about human rights violations than in the past, and we find out more quickly about current violations. NGOs and other human rights observers are increasingly adept at documenting violations and sharing information, as described above. Although there are still difficulties associated with contemporaneous human rights reporting, it is not unusual for nation-states returning to democracy after a repressive period to authorize a 'Truth Commission' as a matter of official record. Truth commissions investigate and document the scope, nature, and severity of past violations in a published report. For example, one of the earliest and most famous reports, *Nunca Más* (*Never Again*) (National Commission on Disappeared Persons [CONADEP], 1984) chronicled violations under Argentina's period of military rule between 1976 and 1983. A digital collection of Truth Commission reports listed 33 reports published as of 2013, along with 12 reports by more limited 'commissions of inquiry' (United States Institute of Peace, 2013).

Within societies, post-hoc documentation projects invariably raise questions about the political impact of digging into the past and whether to prosecute violators (Hayner, 2001). Truth Commissions have often initially substituted in some way for prosecutions, because they enable fact-finding without entailing a certainty of politically or legally difficult judicial action. Even so, getting at the facts of human rights violations has been an important goal in itself. Families of human rights victims often have been most outspoken in calling not only for facts, but also for accountability. In many countries, such as Chile and Argentina, legal trials are proceeding years after political transitions and Truth Commissions have been completed (Kim and Sikkink, 2010; Sikkink, 2011). Sikkink (2011) argues that just as in other stages of the human rights movement, without citizen pressure and the leadership of far-sighted individuals who dared to challenge the status quo, the trials would not have happened.

As Truth Commission reports and other information-preservation efforts have become a common part of reckoning with the past, social scientists and legal experts increasingly assist governments, civil society organizations, and intergovernmental organizations with technical aspects of documentation (see, e.g., American Association for the Advancement of Science, AAAS, n.d.). The reports themselves are valuable sources of information as social scientists seek to understand causes and prevention of violations, and techniques for statistical analysis are increasingly being used as more information is gathered. Debates across scholarly disciplines continue about how best to collect, preserve, and interpret such information (Ball, 2001; Chapman and Ball, 2001; Merry, 2011; Clark and Sikkink, 2013). Preservation and information-sharing efforts are a growing concern as the international human rights movement matures, and libraries and NGOs are increasingly building informational and advisory links among scholars, practitioners, and human rights activists as an outgrowth of global human rights advocacy (Columbia University, n.d.; HURIDOCS, n.d.).

In addition, as for many movements, the way that human rights institutions have been built cannot be understood without relating it to the interplay between human rights claims and the political institutions they have been designed to address. Donnelly, a political scientist, argues that rights as they have evolved reflect what has been learned through 'threat and response' between governments and the governed, regarding 'the most necessary protections needed as preconditions for a life of dignity in a world of modern markets and states' (Donnelly, 2013, p. 42). Political scientists have cited, in addition, the usefulness of human rights as a concept that provides legal, discursive, or moral leverage for activists who wish to put pressure on nation-states (Risse and Ropp, 1999; Risse, 2000; Clark, 2001). Quataert, a historian, emphasizes the importance of interactions between local movements and states, but also parts of international organizations, especially the United Nations' human rights apparatus (Quataert, 2009, p. 299).

Taking a long view of the treaty law developed after 1945, Quataert reminds us that 'what...legal coverage meant was determined largely by struggle, by a slow and uneven process of incorporating conflicting individuals and groups...and balancing conflicting claims' (ibid., p. 302). Techniques developed by the human rights movement, and the human rights concepts themselves, have been used by others. Considerable cross-fertilization has occurred between the human rights movement, the global women's movement, and the global environmental movement, for example (Friedman et al., 2005).

The appeal of the international human rights framework also provides a conceptual and legal resource as activists frame initiatives on new issues. As mentioned above, activists have begun to expand the notion and politics of the human rights movement to encompass economic, social, and cultural issues more directly and effectively. For example, human rights have been invoked in poor people's movements in the USA to claim economic rights (Smith, 2008), and by indigenous peoples to link environmental protection to human rights. In another example, women's groups have worked to integrate gender issues and rights claims at multilateral economic institutions such as the World Bank (O'Brien, 2000) and to embed gender within the UN human rights framework and in domestic law as well (Friedman, 2003; Friedman et al., 2005; Htun and Weldon, 2012). Despite Bob's (2005) suggestion that local movements may feel pressure to adapt their causes to the global framework, these kinds of examples seem to show that human rights remains a useful tool for many activists. Although critics worry that by generalizing human rights local concerns may be diminished, Quataert argues that observing the ways individuals apply human rights standards for their own purposes in specific circumstances helps to address the concerns of 'critics of law as a totalizing force' (Quataert, 2009, p. 302). Researchers on newer interpretations of human rights note that social movements seem both to employ and adjust human rights claims in the ways that they find useful in their specific political situations. If so, it suggests that the human rights concept can be flexible and useful in a variety of contexts. Understanding the impact of new members of the movement and the distribution of power within the movement is an area of relatively recent, promising research.

The Impact of the Human Rights Movement

What *effects* or *achievements* of the human rights movement are in evidence? The evidence suggests that advocates have been successful in developing and implementing the methods described above. Scholars have documented the human rights movement's influence in ending the Cold War, both by facilitating the development of trust necessary for general negotiations between the superpowers (Adamishin and Schifter, 2009), and by influencing the course of democratization in Eastern Europe (Snyder, 2011, p. 217). Further examples of positive political change in individual countries can be traced to the activity of the global human rights network (Risse et al., 1999). Despite successes, progress has not been uniform or inevitable, and researchers have identified persistent challenges or roadblocks.

For example, while the standard-setting activity mentioned above has created an important baseline for states, the international enforcement of legal standards by states and intergovernmental organizations is clearly a weak point. There is no doubt in the global community about the legal basis of human rights and states' obligations to implement international norms and provide information about their practices. However, international institutions' investigative powers and enforcement powers, which would require a 'qualitative leap' in the strength of human rights norms, are largely still lacking at the global level (Donnelly, 2013, p. 108). This, incidentally, is largely the point at which action moves out of the hands of activists to dependence on state power and intergovernmental organizations' political will for action. Here advocates face a broad disparity in power between themselves and states, and in many venues lack the status that would grant them access to the institutional tools required for greater efficacy.

Consequently, scholars now debate how best to understand the conditions under which human rights norms and human rights mobilization *do* result in measurable improvements for societies. Recent statistical approaches permit more systematic, if less nuanced, analysis, and this research appears to show that treaties on their own are not the solution to improvement. Research on human rights treaty ratification and international agreements in general supports the contention that states bind themselves most where it costs them the least (Downs et al., 1996; Hathaway, 2002; Von Stein, 2005; see Simmons, 2013 for a summary of the debates). For example, states for which 'costs' are low include democratic and economically developed countries that already accept human rights principles and expect to comply with them (Landman, 2005). Governments for whom ratification might impose heavy compliance costs will likely resist the human rights movement's pressures to ratify.

If this view is correct, we might expect that when ratification results from movement pressure on countries with problematic records, becoming a party to a treaty may be a tactical concession to deflect external pressure or enhance international legitimacy (Hafner-Burton and Tsutsui, 2005). Even so, Simmons (2009) suggests that citizens' mobilization *is* closely linked to human rights improvements in countries that have ratified human rights treaties and are in a period of recent political transition from authoritarianism to democracy. In such cases, she suggests, domestic activists have both the need to pursue human rights demands (because the democratization process may be incomplete) and an expectation (because of their governments' stated treaty commitments) that their democratic governments will respond to their demands.

Several other cross-national studies bear out the importance of democracy and the involvement of citizens' movements in the effectiveness of human rights claims (Landman, 2005; Neumayer, 2005). International human rights groups' external pressure also appears to make domestic publics more critical of deficiencies in their own governments' respect for human rights and to cultivate conditions favorable to domestic protest (Murdie and Bhasin, 2011; Davis et al., 2012). Some evidence exists that focused criticism by the UN after a government has ratified a human rights treaty can be effective whatever a state's government type, suggesting that global human rights advocates should persist in their external monitoring and protection efforts (Clark, 2013).

CONCLUSION

To summarize, the international human rights movement has made itself a lasting political and moral force to be reckoned with, having grown by leaps and bounds since the 1970s. Its tools for influencing states and strengthening human rights are distinctive. Its prominence and development as a long-lasting movement has impressed scholars, whether or not they agree on the reasons for its success.

Some of what the human rights movement has achieved makes future challenges easy to anticipate. After raising awareness and increasing pressure on state violators of human rights, it can be difficult for advocates at the international level to persuade nation-states and international organizations to continue effective monitoring and follow-up (Risse and Sikkink, 1999). Any successful movement eventually sees the institutionalization of its concerns, but that very institutionalization can come up short vis-à-vis the principles that helped initiate it. For that reason, there is a continuing role for human rights advocates once a violator state has acknowledged the validity of human rights norms, but the role is likely to shift to monitoring new and existing institutions. Likewise, attempts to establish durable and effective human rights institutions at the international level are still controlled primarily by states. Although non-governmental groups at the international level have carved out a niche for themselves as an important critical audience for states' human rights performance, they still are not fully vested players in human rights institutions (Friedman et al., 2005).

A final important issue that should be highlighted is that what is recognized as a human rights violation has broadened over time. International human rights advocates are pushing harder for recognition and action in the areas of economic, cultural, and social rights in addition to civil and political rights. However, the human rights effects of governments' economic development strategies, for example, require interpretation by members of the broader movement via a longer, more complex, and possibly ambiguous narrative, and accountability is more diffuse (Clark, 2011). The other side of the coin is that universal human rights seems to be proving a durable basis for local action adapted to economic, social, and cultural specifics, as well as situations where the principal violators are non-state actors such as corporations (see Brysk, 2005; Hertel, 2006; Smith, 2008). With new human rights challenges, the movement will need to continue its proven techniques and come up with new ones as it works to protect and enhance human dignity.

NOTE

1. We thank Rachel Einwohner for this point.

REFERENCES

Adamishin, A.L. and R. Schifter (2009), *Human Rights, Perestroika, and the End of the Cold War*, Washington, DC: United States Institute of Peace Press.
American Association for the Advancement of Science (AAAS) (n.d.), AAAS Scientific Responsibility, Human Rights and Law Program, accessed 16 February 2013 at http://shr.aaas.org.
Amnesty International (1980), *Amnesty International Report 1980*, London: Amnesty International Publications.
Amnesty International (2013), 'Amnesty International marks 40 years of urgent actions', press release, accessed 3 July 2013 at https://www.amnesty.org/en/news/amnesty-international-marks-40-years-urgent-actions-2013-03-19-0.
Baehr, P.R. (1994), 'Amnesty International and its self-imposed limited mandate', *Netherlands Quarterly of Human Rights*, 12(1), 5–21.
Bair, J. and F. Palpacuer (2012), 'From varieties of capitalism to varieties of activism: the antisweatshop movement in comparative perspective', *Social Problems*, 59(4), 522–43.
Ball, P. (2001), 'Making the case: the role of statistics in human rights reporting', *Statistical Journal of the United Nations*, 18(2–3), 163–73.
Beitz, C.R. (2009), *The Idea of Human Rights*, Oxford/New York: Oxford University Press.
Benenson, P. (1961), 'The forgotten prisoners', *The Observer*, 28 May, accessed 12 July 2013 at http://www.guardian.co.uk/uk/1961/may/28/fromthearchive.theguardian.
Bob, C. (2005), *The Marketing of Rebellion*, Cambridge, UK: Cambridge University Press.
Brysk, A. (2005), *Human Rights and Private Wrongs*, New York: Routledge.
Buchanan, T. (2002), ' "The truth will set you free": the making of Amnesty International', *Journal of Contemporary History*, 37(4), 575–97.
Buchanan, T. (2004), 'Amnesty International in crisis, 1966–7', *Twentieth Century British History*, 15(3), 267–89.
Cardenas, S. (2007), *Conflict and Compliance*, Philadelphia, PA: University of Pennsylvania Press.
Carpenter, R.C. (2007), 'Studying issue (non)-adoption in transnational advocacy networks', *International Organization*, 61(3), 643–67.
Chapman, A.R. and P. Ball (2001), 'The truth of Truth Commissions: comparative lessons from Haiti, South Africa, and Guatemala', *Human Rights Quarterly*, 23(1), 1–43.
City of Portland, Office of Human Relations (2011), *Report to the Community, February 2011*, accessed 27 February 2013 at http://www.portlandonline.com/equityandhumanrights/index.cfm?c=54304&a=337920.
Clark, A.M. (2001), *Diplomacy of Conscience*, Princeton, NJ: Princeton University Press.
Clark, A.M. (2011), 'Expanding international standards of justice: Amnesty International's classic strengths and current challenges', in W. de Jonge, B.M. Leyh, A. Mihr and L. van Troost (eds), *50 Years of Amnesty International: Reflections and Perspectives*, Utrecht: SIM and Amnesty International.
Clark, A.M. (2013), 'The normative context of human rights criticism: treaty ratification

and UN mechanisms', in T. Risse, S.C. Ropp and K. Sikkink (eds), *From Commitment to Compliance*, Cambridge, UK: Cambridge University Press.
Clark, A.M. and K. Sikkink (2013), 'Information effects and human rights data: is the good news about increased human rights information bad news for human rights measures?', *Human Rights Quarterly*, **35**(3), 539–68.
Clark, A.M., E.J. Friedman and K. Hochstetler (1998), 'The sovereign limits of global civil society: a comparison of NGO participation in UN World Conferences on the environment, human rights, and women', *World Politics*, **51**(1), 1–35.
Cmiel, K. (2004), 'The recent history of human rights', *American Historical Review*, **109**(1), 117–35.
Columbia University (n.d.), Center for Human Rights Documentation and Research, accessed 16 February 2013 at http://library.columbia.edu/indiv/humanrights/about.html.
Cortright, D. and G.A. Lopez (2002), *Smart Sanctions*, Lanham, MD: Rowman & Littlefield.
Davis, D.R., A. Murdie and C.G. Steinmetz (2012), ' "Makers and shapers": human rights INGOs and public opinion', *Human Rights Quarterly*, **34**(1), 199–224.
Deitelhoff, N. (2009), 'The discursive process of legalization: charting islands of persuasion in the ICC case', *International Organization*, **63**(1), 33–65.
Donnelly, J. (2013), *International Human Rights*, 4th edition, Boulder, CO: Westview Press.
Downs, G.W., D.M. Rocke and P.N. Barsoom (1996), 'Is the good news about compliance good news about cooperation?', *International Organization*, **50**(3), 379–406.
Friedman, E.J. (2003), 'Gendering the agenda: the impact of the transnational women's rights movement at the UN conferences of the 1990s', *Women's Studies International Forum*, **26**(4), 313–31.
Friedman, E.J., K. Hochstetler and A.M. Clark (2001), 'Sovereign limits and regional opportunities for global civil society in Latin America', *Latin American Research Review*, **36**(3), 7–35.
Friedman, E.J., K. Hochstetler and A.M. Clark (2005), *Sovereignty, Democracy, and Global Civil Society*, Albany, NY: State University of New York Press.
Guest, I. (1990), *Behind the Disappearances*, Philadelphia, PA: University of Pennsylvania Press.
Hafner-Burton, E.M. and K. Tsutsui (2005), 'Human rights in a globalizing world: the paradox of empty promises', *American Journal of Sociology*, **110**(5), 1373–411.
Hathaway, O.A. (2002), 'Do human rights treaties make a difference?', *Yale Law Journal*, **111**(8), 1935–2040.
Hayner, P.B. (2001), *Unspeakable Truths*, New York: Routledge.
Hertel, S. (2006), *Unexpected Power*, Ithaca, NY: Cornell University Press.
Hopgood, S. (2006), *Keepers of the Flame*, Ithaca, NY: Cornell University Press.
Htun, M. and S.L. Weldon (2012), 'The civic origins of progressive policy change: combating violence against women in global perspective, 1975–2005', *American Political Science Review*, **106**(3), 548–69.
Hunt, L. (2007), *Inventing Human Rights: A History*, New York: W.W. Norton & Co.
HURIDOCS (n.d.), HURIDOCS: Human Rights Information and Documentation Systems, International, accessed 16 February 2013 at http://www.huridocs.org.
Ishay, M. (2004), *The History of Human Rights: From Ancient Times to the Globalization Era*, Berkeley, CA: University of California Press.
Jacobsen, A.F. (2008), *Human Rights Monitoring: A Field Mission Manual*, Leiden: Martinus Nijhoff/Brill.
Joachim, J. (2003), 'Framing issues and seizing opportunities: the UN, NGOs, and women's rights', *International Studies Quarterly*, **47**(2), 247–74.
Keck, M. and K. Sikkink (1998), *Activists Beyond Borders*, Ithaca, NY: Cornell University Press.
Kim, H. and K. Sikkink (2010), 'Explaining the deterrence effect of human rights prosecutions for transitional countries', *International Studies Quarterly*, **54**(4), 939–63.
Klotz, A. (1995), *Norms in International Relations*, Ithaca, NY: Cornell University Press.

Korey, W. (1998), *NGOs and the Universal Declaration of Human Rights*, New York: St. Martin's Press.
Laber, J. (2002), *The Courage of Strangers*, New York: Public Affairs.
Landman, T. (2005), *Protecting Human Rights*, Washington, DC: Georgetown University Press.
Lauren, P.G. (2003), *The Evolution of International Human Rights*, 2nd edition, Philadelphia, PA: University of Pennsylvania Press.
Merry, S.E. (2011), 'Measuring the world: indicators, human rights, and global governance', *Current Anthropology*, **52**(S3), S83–S95.
Mertus, J. (2009), *Human Rights Matters: Local Politics and National Human Rights Institutions*, Stanford Studies in Human Rights, Stanford, CA: Stanford University Press.
Morgan, R.C. (2004), 'Advancing indigenous rights at the United Nations: strategic framing and its impact on the normative development of international law', *Social & Legal Studies*, **13**(4), 481–500.
Morgenthau, H.J. (1967), *Politics Among Nations*, 4th edition, New York: Knopf.
Moyn, S. (2010), *The Last Utopia*, Cambridge, MA: Belknap Press of Harvard University Press.
Murdie, A. and T. Bhasin (2011), 'Aiding and abetting: human rights INGOs and domestic protest', *Journal of Conflict Resolution*, **55**(2), 163–91.
Murdie, A.M. and D.R. Davis (2012), 'Shaming and blaming: using events data to assess the impact of human rights INGOs', *International Studies Quarterly*, **56**(1), 1–16.
National Commission on Disappeared Persons (CONADEP) (1984), *Nunca Más* [Never Again], Buenos Aires: Editorial Universitaria de Buenos Aires.
Neier, A. (2012), *The International Human Rights Movement*, Princeton, NJ: Princeton University Press.
Nettelfield, L.J. (2010), *Courting Democracy in Bosnia and Herzegovina*, New York: Cambridge University Press.
Neumayer, E. (2005), 'Do international human rights treaties improve respect for human rights?' *Journal of Conflict Resolution*, **49**(6), 925–53.
O'Brien, R. (2000), *Contesting Global Governance*, Cambridge, UK/New York: Cambridge University Press.
Peksen, D. (2009), 'Better or worse? The effect of economic sanctions on human rights', *Journal of Peace Research*, **46**(1), 59–77.
Picolotti, R. and J.D. Taillant (2010), *Linking Human Rights and the Environment*, Tucson, AZ: University of Arizona Press.
Quataert, J.H. (2009), *Advocating Dignity*, Philadelphia, PA: University of Pennsylvania Press.
Ramos, H., J. Ron and O.N.T. Thoms (2007), 'Shaping the northern media's human rights agenda, 1986–2000', *Journal of Peace Research*, **44**(4), 385–406.
Renteln, A.D. (1990), *International Human Rights*, Newbury Park, CA: Sage Publications.
Risse, T. (2000), ' "Let's argue!": communicative action in world politics', *International Organization*, **54**(1), 1–39.
Risse, T. and S.C. Ropp (1999), 'International human rights norms and domestic change: conclusions', in T. Risse, S.C. Ropp and K. Sikkink (eds), *The Power of Human Rights*, Cambridge, UK: Cambridge University Press.
Risse, T. and K. Sikkink (1999), 'The socialization of international human rights norms into domestic practices: introduction', in T. Risse, S.R. Ropp and K. Sikkink (eds), *The Power of Human Rights*, Cambridge, UK: Cambridge University Press.
Risse, T. S.R. Ropp and K. Sikkink (eds) (1999), *The Power of Human Rights*, Cambridge, UK: Cambridge University Press.
Risse, T., S.C. Ropp and K. Sikkink (eds) (2013), *The Persistent Power of Human Rights*, Cambridge, UK: Cambridge University Press.
Ron, J., H. Ramos and K. Rodgers (2005), 'Transnational information politics: NGO human rights reporting, 1986–2000', *International Studies Quarterly*, **49**(3), 557–88.

Sen, P. and M. Vincent (2009), *Universal Periodic Review of Human Rights: Towards Best Practice*, London: Commonwealth Secretariat.
Sikkink, K. (1993a), 'Human rights, principled issue-networks, and sovereignty in Latin America', *International Organization*, **47**(3), 411–41.
Sikkink, K. (1993b), 'The power of principled ideas: human rights policies in the United States and Western Europe', in J. Goldstein and R.O. Keohane (eds), *Ideas and Foreign Policy*, Ithaca, NY: Cornell University Press.
Sikkink, K. (2011), *The Justice Cascade*, New York: W.W. Norton.
Simmons, B. (2009), *Mobilizing for Human Rights*, Cambridge, UK: Cambridge University Press.
Simmons, B. (2013), 'From ratification to compliance: quantitative evidence on the spiral model', in T. Risse, S.C. Ropp and K. Sikkink (eds), *The Persistent Power of Human Rights: From Commitment to Compliance*, Cambridge, UK: Cambridge University Press, pp. 43–60.
Smith, J. (2008), 'Domesticating international human rights norms', in *Social Movements for Global Democracy*, Baltimore, MD: Johns Hopkins University Press.
Smith, J., R. Pagnucco and G.A. Lopez (1998), 'Globalizing human rights: the work of transnational human rights NGOs in the 1990s', *Human Rights Quarterly*, **20**(2), 379–412.
Snow, D.A. and R.D. Benford (1992), 'Master frames and cycles of protest', in A.D. Morris and C.M. Mueller (eds), *Frontiers in Social Movement Theory*, New Haven, CT: Yale University Press, pp. 133–55.
Snyder, S. (2011), *Human Rights Activism and the End of the Cold War*, Cambridge, UK: Cambridge University Press.
Tarrow, S. (2010), 'Outsiders inside and insiders outside: linking transnational and domestic public action for human rights', *Human Rights Review*, **11**(2), 171–82.
Tilly, C. (1979), 'Repertoires of contention in America and Britain, 1750–1830', in M.N. Zald and J.D Mccarthy (eds), *The Dynamics of Social Movements*, Cambridge, UK: Winthrop Publishers.
Tolley, H.B. (1994), *The International Commission of Jurists*, Philadelphia, PA: University of Pennsylvania Press.
United Nations (1948), *Universal Declaration of Human Rights*, G.A. res. 217A (III), U.N. Doc A/810 at 71 (1948).
United Nations (1984), *Convention Against Torture and Other Cruel, Inhuman or Degrading Treatment or Punishment*, G.A. res. 39/46 (annex, 39 U.N. GAOR Supp. [No. 51] at 197, U.N. Doc. A/39/51 [1984]), entered into force 26 June 1987.
United Nations (2006), G.A. res. 60/251 of 3 April 2006 (A/RES/60/251).
United Nations, Division for the Advancement of Women (n.d.), NGO Information Note, accessed 15 May 2014 at http://www.un.org/womenwatch/daw/cedaw/NGO_Information_note_CEDAW.pdf.
United States Institute of Peace (USIP) (2011), Truth Commissions Digital Collection, Washington, DC: USIP, accessed 14 July 2014 at http://www.usip.org/publications/truth-commission-digital-collection.
Von Stein, J. (2005), 'Do treaties constrain or screen? Selection bias and treaty compliance', *American Political Science Review*, **99**(4), 611–22.
Wong, W.H. (2012), *Internal Affairs*, Ithaca, NY: Cornell University Press.

20. Urban social movements
Pierre Hamel

Few observers in the 1970s would have anticipated the extent to which cities have currently become a theatre of global transformation. The numerous disruptions they have witnessed – not just in socioeconomic but also in sociopolitical and urban terms – are once again raising the question of what type of city we want to live in. Socio-spatial segregation and a trend toward privatization of public spaces, for instance, are not new phenomena, yet the practices with which such processes are associated nevertheless hinge on major changes in the scales, spaces and content of economic activity, which some are quick to associate with new urban forms (Sassen, 2011). A related issue is the recent mobilizations in many cities around the world, which have rekindled the debate on the nature of class conflict in capitalism. This was one result of the 2011 'Occupy' movement at any rate. Spreading to '951 cities in 82 countries around the world' (Castells, 2012, p. 4), these struggles shed new light on social inequity and have led, if not to a rethinking, at least to a re-examination of both collective action and the nature and scope of urban social movements.

Although social movements and collective action around certain central urban issues such as housing date back to the late nineteenth and early twentieth centuries (Lawson, 1986), the notion of 'urban social movement' did not appear in the literature until 1972.[1] It was first proposed in France by Manuel Castells (1972) to highlight the political scope of such struggles, which the term encompassed. Theoretically, the social activists who led such struggles were able, albeit under certain conditions – in particular by forging alliances with unions and progressive political parties – to initiate a process of structural change in urban systems. While such movements may reflect the contradictions at work in urban planning, Castells felt that their action was aimed primarily at initiating a 'structural transformation of the urban system' (Castells, 1972, p. 444).

While Castells's thesis generated many criticisms (Pickvance, 1976; Lojkine, 1977; Saunders, 1979), these did not discredit the study of urban movements; rather, they nourished the theoretical debate and, subsequently, spurred numerous empirical studies. Initially, most of these studies occurred in Europe, as well as in Latin and North America (case studies, comparative analyses, ethnographic research). These studies shed light on the diversity and complexity of forms of action, methods of organization, and the contexts typical of collective action on urban issues, whether on a city-wide or a neighbourhood scale. It also helped to reveal the orientations and interests underlying urban planning and development.

Notwithstanding the preceding, research on urban movements was conducted – at least until the mid-1980s – in relative isolation from the theory of social movements (Pickvance, 2003). We will return to this point and the reasons behind it later. And even though the researchers who subsequently began to study urban movements did not hesitate to make use of this theory, their work has occupied a limited, even marginal, position within the field of social movement research (Hamel et al., 2000).[2]

Urban movements have been strongly influenced as much by the nature of urban problems as by local culture. But, as with other social movements, attempts to define them have generated controversies that have called into question not only the analytical processes and study methods used but even the very conceptions of collective action and social movements (Cefaï, 2007). In this respect, the study of urban movements has not been immune to the theoretical conflicts experienced by the sociology of social movements.

Without rehashing the terms of the controversy that opposed the tenants of resource mobilization theory and those of the identity paradigm camp associated with the new social movements approach in the 1980s (Melucci, 1989; Rucht, 1991; Cohen and Arato, 1992; Bash, 1995), it is worthwhile remembering that the study of social movements has been, and continues to be, a highly controversial field. In advancing divergent hypotheses to explain the emergence and unfolding of social action, the various analytical models that developed starting in the 1970s considered the different ranges of collective action – from its roots in class struggle to the emergence of new social conflicts – and its scope with respect to social change. These models helped to highlight the contexts and factors that influence social engagement. They also helped to better identify various underlying aspects of social activism, whether they are concerned with organizational factors, resources, relationships among the various actors (including leadership roles and conflicts with adversaries), or subjective dimensions. However, the question of the deep motivations that lead social actors to embark on a collective process remains open. Ultimately, we still have a poor understanding of the driving force behind the individual and collective engagement of social actors. This is true both for the theory of social movements in general and for the understanding of urban movements specifically. Consequently, given the ability of such movements to furnish a new social understanding of the city, their burgeoning and diversity is something that both social actors and researchers must come to grips with.

This chapter is divided into four sections. In the first, as an introduction to the primary research directions, I review the primary theoretical influences. I then examine the principal results of the research to date, highlighting what I believe to form a consensus in the literature. Third, I delve into the diversity of this field, focusing more on approaches that are complementary to the primary research trends. And finally, based on the previous three sections, I reflect on some possible future research directions.

URBAN SOCIAL MOVEMENTS, CITIES AND THE THEORY OF SOCIAL MOVEMENTS

Contemporary urban movements, like those of the 1960s and 1970s, continue to seek social recognition, demand a 'right to the city' (Harvey, 2012), and build democratic and solidarity-based spaces rooted in local cultures undergoing transformation. Actors in such movements have inherited a tradition of mobilization and social engagement that is reflected in their opposition to urban development models designed by and for the elite (Brenner et al., 2011).

However, in light of their past achievements, the subversive aspect of urban movements nevertheless raises many questions. For instance, their declining presence in public and political discourse has been questioned (Ceccarelli, 1982). Their reformist character has been emphasized, owing to the fact that they have tended to treat class issues within communities – in particular those reflected in the urban crisis – separately from work-related issues (Katznelson, 1981). On several occasions, researchers have criticized their localism (Fainstein and Hirst, 1995), their tendency to split up or fragment (Dupuy and Halpern, 2009) and, in certain circumstances, their conservatism (Miller, 2006). Even their specifically urban scope has been called into question, alleging that while their demands may concern a given territory, they are not essentially 'urban' (Harris, 1987).

Such partial evaluations, however, are influenced by specific historical contexts and conjunctures and are consequently not suitable for making an overall assessment. For while they stimulate a critical outlook, they do not take into account the complexity, the diversity and the transformation of the role played by such actors within a theory of the city that is not itself unified, meaning, that is able to 'explain all of the spatial and social dynamics that govern cities and metropolitan regions' (Judd, 2011, p. 17). Hence, to what extent have such movements transformed cities and urban areas in the past, and continue to do so, in terms of the democratization of public action? How do we identify their social, political and cultural effects? Indeed, how do we first define those effects? Is mobilization that seeks to produce political change or influence the decisions of elected officials the only 'successful mode of political action' (Pickvance, 1976, p. 208)?

Before broaching these questions, we must return to the introduction, and the statement to the effect that, until the mid-1980s, the study of urban movements was conducted in relative isolation from the overall theory of social movements, which had developed considerably starting in the 1970s (Klandermans and Tarrow, 1988). According to Chris Pickvance (2003), there are two reasons for this. First, researchers studying urban movements came to the field from a range of disciplines, of which sociology was only one. As a result, they paid little attention to the theoretical developments inherent to sociology, including those related to social movements. Second, the work of most sociologists studying social movements dealt for the most part with new social movements; urban movements held little interest for them since, given the material nature of their demands, they considered urban movements to be largely associated with traditional social movements.

The consequences of this isolation for the study of urban movements were both positive and negative. On the positive side, researchers examined dimensions that the sociology of social movements had neglected. Hence, they focused on the effects – both urban and political – of these movements; they highlighted their connection with a theory of state that takes into account both local and national scales; and they placed more importance on the context, especially the political context, in which collective action emerges by stressing the scope of local conditions, regardless of whether they were defined in reference to resources or to political opportunities. On the negative side, this isolation meant that little consideration was given to the conflict among interpretations that was driving the theory of social movements. Moreover, before the publication of *The City and the Grassroots* (Castells, 1983), little attention was paid to the identities of the actors and of their importance in how the terms of the action are defined. Finally, a division developed between the study of voluntary associations and their interaction with authorities on one hand, and the study of urban movements on the other (Pickvance, 2003). As Peter Saunders (1979) pointed out, quoting a community activist, this led to an idealization of urban demands, even though most of the time, because of their defensive nature, given that they were reactions to threats from authorities (as was the case with urban renewal projects), they tended to take place within the system:

> Defensive strategies rarely give rise, even potentially, to revolutionary consequences. As one community activist has observed, 'Although community action campaigns may be successful in their own terms, the end result may only be small scale compensatory provision...which, while representing a positive improvement in the situation, does nothing to alter the crucial determinants of the life-styles and life chances of residents'. (Saunders, 1979, pp. 129–30)

Starting in the mid-1980s, the increased importance placed on the theory of social movements within the field of sociology as a whole meant that the study of urban movements could no longer ignore these theoretical and methodological devices. As a result, the study of these movements' collective action not only began to hinge on city and urban theory, it became connected with and in return contributed to, if only in a limited fashion because of its still marginal status, the development of the theory of social movements.

The controversies surrounding the theory of social movements necessarily had repercussions on the study of urban movements. Revolving around not only the positioning of action with respect to historicity (Touraine, 1978) or to political power (Tilly and Tarrow, 2007) but also around the ability of actors to profoundly transform social relationships (Dubet and Martuccelli, 1998) and even around the social and cultural meaning of their action (Melucci, 1996), these controversies immediately called into question the relevance of conceptual and theoretical categories in creating a sociology of collective action. In this respect, three analytical requirements deserve reaffirmation.

The first is to establish from the outset a theoretical status for the concepts of collective action and social movement: 'Social movements are not spontaneously constituted. Neither are they necessarily the starting point of an analysis. They are more the end result, the fruit of a labour of theoretical construction and analytical demonstrations' (Maheu, 1995, p. 11). This position avoids analyses that take an overly movement-centred approach and goes hand in hand with the theoretical view that the discourse and practices of actors must be placed in context within the structures of domination they are in conflict with. However, this view, which attempts to strike a balance between action and system does not resolve all aporias. To do so we must take into account the difficulty of grasping the diversity of emerging practices, especially those that make use of new information and communications technologies (Castells, 2012) or protest practices in institutional settings that underscore the movements' ambivalence (Roth, 1996).

The second requirement is based on a recognition of the prevailing opposition between sociologists who take a sector-based approach to social movements – that is, those who deal with collective action from a sectorial perspective, considering it in the same way that other sectorial sociologies, such as the sociologies of work, family or sport, address their object of study – and those who approach it from the issue of social transformation, with movements constituting an entry point for illuminating an ongoing transformation of social relationships. In this case, collective action should be considered 'as a global process embedded in the structuration of social life' (Maheu, 1995, p. 8). While both perspectives have their advantages and limitations, a tension between the two should prove fruitful. At any rate, this is the hypothesis I subscribe to.

Finally, the third requirement deals with the recognition of the inherent ambivalence of collective action. The collective forces engaged in change or transformation that define modern society pass through multiple channels that may be institutional or societal (Fassin, 2010). In this regard, collective action tends to oscillate between two extremes: one of decomposition, characterized by the defensive conduct of actors who focus on opposing undertakings that threaten their integrity, opting, for example, for subjective withdrawal – phenomena that have been brought to light through analyses related to identity politics (Kruks, 2000) – and one of 'recomposition', in which activists build political, cultural or social perspectives that they use, through conflicts surrounding resources, to promote a world view that contributes to social transformation (Maheu, 2005). This 'dichotomy' and 'oscillation' between decomposition and 'recomposition' are part and parcel of the ambivalence of modern collective action, and they underlie the theoretical perspective I subscribe to in examining research into urban movements.

In this context, I feel that the question of the success of collective action within civil society in democratizing values, norms and institutions – akin to the idea of political culture – reveals a crucial concern. This question was formulated by Jean L. Cohen and Andrew Arato (1992) over 20 years ago and remains just as relevant today. It certainly goes beyond the study of the mere instrumental ends inherent in action, and it should be restated to take into account the structural and institutional changes that have occurred since (Hamel and Maheu, 2001). Do the collective actors involved in social movements reach their objectives despite the constraints limiting their action and given the resources they have access to? For example, are they able to redefine the regulatory and cognitive framework of public action? In this respect, it appears that the ability of social actors not only to challenge relationships of domination but also to contribute to a renewal of action are critical criteria in assessing the significance of their engagement.

At the same time, one might examine the democratic significance of collective action by considering the ability of movements to overcome the limitations that have historically characterized their action. On one hand, this has led to the study of their organizational methods within civil society, in particular, taking into account their 'hybrid character' (Goss and Heaney, 2010) but also the ambivalence that typifies their engagement in public arenas. On the other hand, attempts have been made to understand how these same activists are redefining public and political spheres, while the deepening of democracy – which in many respects can be associated with the 'terms of democratic renewal' (Rosanvallon, 2006, p. 305) – goes hand in hand with a redefinition of citizenship (Zukin et al., 2006, p. 86).

While, in the wake of numerous empirical studies (Gautney et al., 2009), it is clear that in order to understand the scope of collective action we must take into account the complexity of conduct that results in large part from how it fits into social, cultural and geographical contexts, this is not enough. We must also consider the social conflicts arising from relationships of inequality and domination that occur upstream of the conduct. This was the case, for example, with class conflicts that characterized the labour movement of the late nineteenth century. In other words, the ability to redefine the actions that give actors their legitimacy remains highly delineated by the social conflicts within which they arise. But this possibility nevertheless also faces downstream and, in large part, toward public policy. The desire of social actors to influence public choices is inevitably at play. Even if the collective action is not targeted exclusively toward public authorities and the state (Armstrong and Bernstein, 2008) – the state being neither the only source of power nor the only authority that structures social relationships – it is no less concerned with occurrences in the arena of public policy. In this respect, factors such as the autonomy and legitimacy of governments and, in particular, their ability to steer reforms likely to respond to the differentiation and increasing fragmentation of societies, as well as new types of territoriality connected with globalization (Sassen, 2013), are directly involved.

This is not a question of retracing the route of the sociology of social movements over the past 40 years (Buechler, 2000; Snow and Soule, 2010). The model of the political process (Tilly and Tarrow, 2007; Tilly, 2008), despite certain limitations (Armstrong and Bernstein, 2008), has proven to be quite useful in its focus on, among other things, refining the study of the political process, and in its updating of the factors that either promote the emergence and development of collective action or that, on the contrary, tend to discourage it, given the costs that social actors incur. It has afforded a better understanding of how collective action can converge on political spheres, even if it forgoes the issue of its redefinition or at least its relation to a series of prescriptive and cognitive dimensions that are increasingly sought out by public authorities in their attempts to adjust to structural changes. Such dimensions might be involved, for instance, in the redefinition of or changes in public action, dimensions that engage societal values in various spheres (the culture of native peoples, the role of religion, the environment, unionism, cities and metropolitan regions) in which systems or categories of inequality prevail.

Thus far, researchers have explored many avenues in studying collective action and social movements from the perspective of their political reach. Some have called for a review of the bases of democracy and the conditions for its renewal. This is the case with the liberal (Wolfe, 2010) and Marxist (Harvey, 1973) traditions. Others suggest a rejection of the universalist demands of the emancipation project championed by the Enlightenment and modernity, which are found in particular in the major works that have helped convey these demands in their modern form (Escobar, 2008). The priority has now clearly settled on pluralism and the recognition of identities and of diverse and multiple points of view (Young, 1990), which cannot but lead to a certain relativism on occasion. Finally, others (Della Porta, 2005), in the wake of Habermas, are exploring whether deliberative democracy – beyond republicanism and liberalism – can engage in a 'cooperative search of common solutions' (Habermas, 2003, p. 47), reiterating a demand for universality that has always characterized the critical function of philosophy (Habermas, 1988).

Thus far, these different interpretations of politics and democracy have not resulted in a satisfying synthesis. They nevertheless help to create a body of knowledge that can lead to a better understanding of the context within which collective action takes place, on the condition that the perspective from which they are understood is clear. In this regard, as was mentioned above, the hypothesis advanced here is that the central issue of collective action and social movements is one of the renewal of action. It is that collective action effects social and political transformation only insofar as it is able to substantially transform the conditions under which action takes place and its forms of expression. In this respect, it is relevant to reiterate the need for distance from overly sector-based approaches to studying social movements, approaches that focus primarily on the main components of the action, to the detriment of an understanding of their underlying social relationships. From this perspective one might say that the study of social movements serves above all as an entry point into the study of social and – for the purposes of this chapter – urban phenomena. In this sense, it is not possible to separate it from an analysis of the structural constraints of collective action that takes place at various levels, even if those constraints deserve to be considered in relation to the representations and strategies used by social actors and to the organizational means they employ. Moreover, while this conception may be applied to various types of social protest, including claims made by conservative and authoritarian activists, I use it above all to describe collective conduct that is primarily in pursuit of justice and social progress.

WHAT CAN WE LEARN FROM THE STUDY OF URBAN SOCIAL MOVEMENTS?

Research into urban movements has been highly sensitive to the forms that collective actions of protest take. There is generally a very strong link between citizens' concerns and actions undertaken in the face of disruptions to their living conditions, on one hand, and the types of studies developed to better understand them, on the other. From this perspective, the renewal of research into urban movements has been highly influenced by the energy of protests with respect to urban forms and their transformations. This first observation does not, however, eliminate divergences in assessing the effective reach of these movements and their underlying struggles. How effectively are they able to significantly transform cities and social relationships with the urban space? Are they able to radically change the dynamics of power or influence political decisions in the sense, for example, of the 'right to the city' (Harvey, 2012)?

These questions were already underlying the early work of Castells on urban struggles (1972, 1975), and he re-examined them from a different angle in his 1983 work *The City and the Grassroots*. The change in perspective between his work in the 1970s and the 1983 book was significant, and it is necessary at this point to clarify certain ambiguities[3] concerning the study of these movements' reach or effects. In *The Urban Question* (1972), Castells takes a Marxist-structuralist approach, seeing urban social movements as undertakings that can lead to radical social change. The book, in particular with respect to issues of 'collective consumption', presents a crystallization of the contradictions of capitalism in its advanced stages. It posits that insofar as social mobilization surrounding urban issues hinges on political class struggles, they can transform the city.

The study of urban social movements rests, then, on a certain number of central analytical categories: social base (those affected by the issue), social force (those who mobilize), organization, issue, demands, opponents, and effects produced, both urban and political. There is always the risk that these movements be limited to collective consumption when governing authorities cannot come to an understanding with left-leaning forces or political organizations. However, such convergences are possible, as was observed, for example, with the struggles of the Chilean squatters' movement. This was explained by the fact that because the housing problem could not be assaulted directly, the actors decided that the struggle had to move toward the 'electoral conquest of the government' (Castells, 1972, p. 433). In this case, the protest practices were able to overcome the contradictions at play in the economic, political and urban spheres, making them an exemplary model of an urban social movement.

As mentioned earlier, Castells's analysis of urban social movements is not without its critics. He is reproached for not giving enough importance to organizations. These do not serve merely to link together contradictions, as Castells tends to imply. They play an important role in the shape that protests take and in how action takes place (Pickvance, 1976). Castells also takes for granted that any effects stem directly from the collective action. However, it is often difficult to establish whether the source of the observed change is the movements themselves, the local authorities, or other factors (ibid.), and greater caution is warranted when examining this issue. The problem here is the removal of social factors. For all intents and purposes, social factors are present in Castells's analytical model only by way of political factors (1972, p. 14). This is reflected, for example, in his analysis of effects that are defined solely in systemic terms – either urban or political – completely ignoring the various beneficial consequences for the social actors themselves.

This simplistic reading of urban movements was somewhat set aside and indirectly repudiated in *The City and the Grassroots*. Abandoning the Marxist-structuralist approach and making use of grounded theory, Castells (1983, 2006) took the time to explore mobilizations around various issues and in contrasting contexts and cities. Over a 12-year period, he used a case-study approach to examine a series of urban struggles: the *grand ensembles* movements in Paris; neighbourhood mobilization in the San Francisco Mission district, along with the gay movement in the same city; collective action against urban marginality in Latin America, studying conflicts in Lima, Mexico City, Santiago, Chile, and the citizen movement in Madrid. It would appear, then, that even if urban social movements are not able to significantly change society, they are able to change, and even transform, local culture by introducing new 'urban meanings'.[4] This is what occurs when they formulate a point of view that calls into question the structurally dominant meaning with regard to a specific space, as feminists were sometimes able to do to drive urban social change (Castells, 1983, p. 304). In this sense, urban social movements help to question the dominant meanings of the city and, more generally, of urban spaces.

In general, researchers in various fields received this book much more favourably than they did *The Urban Question* (see, among others, Mayer, 2006; Susser, 2006). It also galvanized research into urban movements.[5] Nevertheless, the concept of the urban social movement remains ambiguous and difficult to define. In Castells's work (1972, 1983), we find two definitions: a restrictive one – designating several levels of possible political effects depending on whether simple participation, protest, or an urban social movement is observed – and a generic one that covers all forms of collective action generated by citizens, regardless of the obtained or anticipated effects. 'There was some basis for this ambiguity in Castells's definition of urban social movement which referred to a system of practices whose "development tends objectively towards the structural transformation of the urban system"...i.e. to potential rather than actual effects' (Pickvance, 2003, p. 103).

One might think that the generic definition is preferable, given that the effects of urban movements are difficult to measure with any certainty, not to mention that they have a tendency to occur over the long-term, which is itself difficult to define. But the goal of conflict-based actions is also hard to define. In other words, the ambiguity is related not only to the effects of the movement, but also to its urban nature.

While urban movements are in no way homogeneous in nature – either from a social, organization or ideological standpoint – we must guard against the temptation of lumping them together with all social mobilizations that take place in cities. One cannot qualify a struggle as 'urban' merely because it takes place within a city. Most social conflicts take place in cities, and this is why urban sociologists distinguish between phenomena that take place 'in the city' and those that are 'of the city' (Pickvance, 1989). Only with the latter – which may be related to the planning of the city and its components or to a transformation of its cultural references – can we properly speak of urban movements. Hence, urban movements relate to the city, its management and planning methods, and its cultural references. That said, urban movements can be divided into three categories: (1) those that deal with collective consumption, including local services; (2) those that deal with how local political institutions function; and (3) those that concern territorial defense (Pickvance, 1985). Although this categorization is not exhaustive – for instance, one could add another category dealing with built environments around local economic development – it helps to establish a relationship with the concerns of sociology as they relate to specific urban issues.

Beyond the definition issue, research has helped shed light on the transformation of relationships between actors and urban systems. These relationships have become more diverse because of increased pluralism over the years. This can be explained by the diversity of situations – with respect to the abundance of issues (ranging from housing shortages, to the threats of gentrification, to neighbourhood life and rent prices, to lack of urban services, to the privatization of public spaces) – and of the actors that mobilize, but also by the socio-political contexts within which social mobilizations take place.

In the face of this reality, a consensus has emerged regarding the importance of context. There are no researchers today, as Castells (1972) once implied, who believe that the success of urban movements rests above all on their own unique qualities. The means of action and the results obtained are in large part a function of the constraints imposed by the configuration of the political forces in place and, depending on the political situation, of institutional support of social actors (Nicholls, 2008).

Conflictual relationships between institutions and social actors prevent neither cooperation nor co-opting (Becher, 2010; Lombard, 2013). Indeed, it would appear that any gains made in terms of local democracy – even the democratization of public administration – remain fragile and are frequently temporary. Hence, with respect to conflictual collective actions that continue to promote the right of the city, expressions of collective resistance to the increasing hegemony of neoliberal forces take multiple courses that flow as much through cultural spheres (Long, 2013) as they do through social and political spheres (Friedmann, 2002; Brenner et al., 2011). In this respect, one can observe not only a diversity in the forms and modes of resistance but also a significant divide between what occurs in the cities of the Global North and those of the Global South. Despite similarities between the marginality experienced by the underclass in the ghettos of Western cities (Wacquant, 2006) and the exploitation of workers that prevails in the South, there are differences – especially with respect to interactions with more or less repressive political regimes, the resources available to actors, and the forms taken by collective identities – that require further study by researchers. A better understanding of the similarities and differences between these two worlds could help to better grasp the components and factors of collective action.

Today we have a clearer understanding of the role of context in the success of mobilization, and of the diversity of forms that collective action can assume. These forms may take a variety of avenues: participation with or against local authorities to change cities' spatial layout (De Souza, 2006); engagement with or against institutions to implement and monitor public policy (Silver et al., 2010); convergence of local struggles with global social movements (Köhler and Wissen, 2003); prevalence of diverse cultures of engagement, which are reflected in forms of mobilization and collective organization (Lombard, 2013); and the re-emergence of militancy and the sense of urban activism that promotes autonomy and direct action (Douay, 2012). These are only a few examples of the diversity of urban collective action. They bear witness to the growing complexity of urban systems and their regulation. But above all they reflect a renewed engagement of citizens who do not hesitate to combine traditional and new ways of mobilization to contest dominant models of urbanism and planning.

In that respect, urban movement actors did not hesitate to act both within and outside of institutions. This is why movement leaders and community activists have increasingly agreed to take part in urban governance, even though the risk of their action being channelled by state initiatives remained strong. This has taken place almost everywhere, though with differing results. In Xalapa, a medium-sized city in Mexico, the mechanisms of participation developed by the municipality show that citizens are not necessarily passive actors. At the same time, as Melanie Lombard (2013) underlined, in this case, social marginalization can still occur because of the hierarchy of citizenship included in the bylaw. In terms of the democratization of public policies, the effectiveness of participation is necessarily being compromised by the availability of resources and the tendency to reproduce existing social segregation. While this conclusion may prevail generally for participatory mechanisms in cities of the South, it is no different for cities in the North. Consider what has occurred in the United Kingdom since the 1960s in terms of community participation in the development of policies to combat urban poverty. Community empowerment and its related outcomes remain weak if not actually negative, and the role of civil society actors has often been marginal (Diamond, 2005). However, despite such mixed results, there are also examples where collective action has been more successful. For example, in the late 1960s and early 1970s, popular pressure from tenants' groups in a downtown area of Mexico City (comprising 60 blocks and 100 000 residents) succeeded in opposing a government urban renewal project, preserving the inner city fabric, and making possible the construction of houses that respected community traditions (Eckstein, 1990). Another example is the Slow City 'sustainable living' movement (*Cittàslow*), founded in Italy in 1999. By 2008, the movement had over 100 member towns worldwide. Its primary objective is 'to improve "life quality" in a context of what its leaders see as a homogenising globalisation process' (Pink, 2008, p. 164). This example clearly expresses a different model of organization and action compared with both old and new urban movements. According to Sarah Pink, '[i]t involves a more subtle form of mobilisation and of persuasion through living examples and experiential education rather than by public demonstration and disruption' (2009, p. 463). Even if one might be sceptical of this analysis, *Cittàslow* is at the very least an illustration of the broadening repertoire of collective action taken by current urban movements.

The diversity of forms of collective action cannot be fully understood without taking into account the complexity of the movements themselves, which involves several levels: organizational structures, the repertoire of collective action available to social actors, various phases through which movements tend to evolve, interaction with local political power – especially when facing co-optation by elites – and use of non-political methods of action through, for example, different means of deploying social solidarity. On all of these levels, urban movements employ various modes of action and follow paths that are difficult to predict. The use of context-based strategies to develop projects; the presence of multiple ideological, political and cultural trends among the actors; and tension and conflicts that drive 'hybrid' forms of action are some of the factors that influence actor engagement.

The diversity of social practices is also reflected in the range of theoretical and methodological approaches researchers use to study them. In this respect, sociology and the theory of social movements have developed a panoply of tools to better grasp the interactions that occur both within and between social movements and the contexts within which they operate (Snow and Soule, 2010). As mentioned previously, the study of urban movements began using these tools in the mid-1980s. In doing so, however, they did not escape the tensions running through this field of study subsequent to its being framed in terms of an 'autonomous sector of theory formation and research within the social sciences' (Melucci, 1996, p. 3). In this respect, I can only stress the three analytical requirements stated in the first section of this chapter that lead me to reiterate the focus on the ambivalence of collective action. From this perspective, further emphasis is needed on the relationships between structures and agency. This would allow us to better explain actors' behaviour and, in particular, the subjective dimensions of their action.[6] While in recent years, research on social movements has taken actor subjectivity more into account (Jasper, 1998; Dubet and Lustiger-Thaler, 2004; McDonald, 2006), there is still no consensus on the role it plays in the renewal of action.

Nevertheless, since the 1990s, taking into account the subjectivity of actors has without a doubt introduced new concerns to the study of urban movements. This was expressed, for instance, in the empirical analysis of collective action around local economic development, as highlighted by the case of Montreal (Hamel, 1995). In that instance, community activists found that taking into account individual concerns was a more effective means of advancing community interests. Another example can be seen in women's mobilization around environmental and local issues. Women's organizations in various North American cities (Montreal, Toronto, Vancouver, but also Los Angeles) have encouraged the development of 'women-policies' at the municipal level as a way to fight discrimination and improve the condition of women. Individual women's concerns – even if shared on a collective basis – are clearly at the forefront here: 'A distinguishing feature of women's urban social activity of the 1980s is that women have mobilized on their own behalf *qua* women rather than acting on behalf of others' (Werkele, 1996, p. 139). And finally, another example comes from the direct action of the Reclaim the Streets movement that emerged in London in 1991 in the struggle against a motorway, re-emerging in North London in 1995 to join the general wave of opposition to the Tory rule, and re-emerging yet again in 1999. The general orientation of the movement was based on a reappropriation of the public space by marginalized groups, especially gay activists. The initial intention of participants was to promote 'the capacity of human beings for individual collective acts of resistance' (Brown, 2004, p. 105) against the commoditization of daily life and urban space. At the heart of the movement, the 'carnivalesque spirit' of open experimentation, as promoted by the actors, was embedded in reclaiming everyday life for individuals and for everyone (Brown, 2004).

One final factor that has influenced the primary directions of research on urban movements concerns the globalization of collective action. The links between local struggles and transnational activism can only be considered in reference to the spread of mobilization around the theme of social justice. While this is not a recent concern (Lefebvre, 1968; Harvey, 1973) it has re-emerged in a new, strong and unexpected manner in protests by the 'alter-globalization' movement, by the networked social movements that spread in the Arab world and by the 2011 Occupy movement (Flank, 2011; Gledhill, 2012).

Although alter-globalization is not a unified movement (Della Porta, 2008), especially if one considers the divergent definitions of democratization in the North and South, it has linked the question of justice to the issue of democracy and placed it in a global context (Smith, 2008). With the Occupy movement, the issue of inequality – whether in terms of poverty, employment, workfare, or social exclusion – and its connection to the crisis in capitalism has resurfaced. While the movement is a reiteration of concerns about social justice that the left raised in the 1970s and 1980s in the United States (Kazin, 2011), it is an example of how to overcome both the localism for which urban movements have been criticized in the past (Fainstein and Hirst, 1995) and the fragmentation of class solidarity that their action can lead to (Katznelson, 1981). In these recent social and urban mobilizations, which can be related to a reaffirmation of the right to the city, new alliances between social classes are being forged that help put past urban mobilizations into perspective:

> The right to the city is not an exclusive individual right, but a focused collective right. It is inclusive not only of construction workers but also of all those who facilitate the reproduction of daily life: the caregivers and teachers, the sewer and subway repair men, the plumbers and electricians, the scaffold erectors and crane operators, the hospital workers and the truck, bus and taxi drivers, the restaurant workers and the entertainers, the bank clerks and the city administrators. It seeks a unity from within an incredible diversity of fragmented social spaces and locations within innumerable divisions of labor. (Harvey, 2012, p. 137)

COMPLEMENTARY APPROACHES TO PRIMARY RESEARCH DIRECTIONS

While by the 1980s, the study of urban movements was increasingly being done from the perspective of a general theory of social movements, its connection to urban theory nevertheless remains. This is true as much for work on mobilization around urban issues as it is for other specific movements that have become recognized fields of specialization within the theory of social movements, such as workers', women's or environmental movements. Even though the study of urban movements has contributed only minimally to the theory behind collective action thus far, this could conceivably change in the future, given the increasing importance and strategic role of cities, city-regions and metropolitan areas in the current context of globalization (Sassen, 1999, 2009).

The study of urban movements has highlighted and attempted to define conflicts stemming from the transformation of built environments. This is why research subjects emerge from the transformation of cities and urban forms. It is no coincidence that researchers in the 1970s were primarily interested in mobilizations around renewal projects (Olives, 1972) or urban development, while they turned toward the gentrification of city centres and its negative effects on residents in the 1990s and 2000s (Hackworth, 2002; Franzén, 2005).

Opposition to the model of a functional city defined primarily in relation to exchange values is not new (Harvey, 2012). In the past, such opposition focused on both the construction of infrastructure such as urban highways and the large-scale demolition of housing in working-class neighbourhoods. It is this type of opposition that Jane Jacobs thought necessary to support in order to break with orthodox city planning and improve city performance in promoting diversity. Her book *The Death and Life of Great American Cities* (1961) is frequently cited by urban movement activists. In recent years, opposition to modernist planning has also turned against megaprojects. One example is the fight against 'Stuttgart 21', a highly controversial railway and urban development project (Peters and Novy, 2012). Another is the mobilization and protests against the building of an international airport in Notre-Dame-des-Landes, near Nantes, France, which have undergone a resurgence since 2008.

Social opposition to top-down urban planning occasionally takes forms that, while not completely new, are at least approached in a new way. This was the case with the Occupy movement (Smith and Glidden, 2012; Pickerill and Krinsky, 2012; Uitermark and Nicholls, 2012). This is also what happens when protest occurs as part of global social movements, by opposing the privatization of public services and neoliberal restructuring, and by promoting the empowerment of marginalized citizens (Köhler and Wissen, 2003).

This does not mean that historically crucial issues for urban movements, such as housing, have not endured. They are just as present as always; however, their interpretation by social actors is quite different:

> Social movements mobilizing around housing describe the problems underlying the 2008-present crisis differently: not as the result of the failure of specific mechanisms within financial markets, but as a product of the economic logic underlying these markets. These movements draw a continuum from gentrification to economic crisis by linking both to 'neoliberalism', thereby identifying the source of current housing problems not as the failure of financial markets, but as 'neoliberalism' itself. (Maeckelbergh, 2012, pp. 655–6)

One can liken this analysis to the experience and discourse of actors who have participated in various squatting protests in European and North American cities (Pruijt, 2003). Like other urban struggles, squatters' movements can be considered within the waves and cycles of protest that affect their collective identity. For instance, the M15 movement in Spain, which began in May 2011 to protest neoliberal austerity policies, conferred renewed legitimacy on squatting. Indeed, there was mutual assistance between the squatters and the M15 activists (Martinez-Lopez and Garcia Bernardos, 2012). This assistance was brought into focus from a perspective that highlights diffusion processes 'within and across movements' (Soule, 2004, p. 295).

Two other complementary topics have significantly influenced research on urban movements: citizen participation and citizenship. Considered from the point of view of collective action, and when it is driven by citizens themselves – despite the ever-present risk that public authorities might channel the action – citizen participation can contribute to a democratization of the state (Wolch, 1989). For instance, this was observed recently in low-income neighbourhoods in Xalapa, Mexico (Lombard, 2013). This conclusion must, however, be reconciled with the fact that in other contexts, participation can in fact lead to increased social inequality (Silver et al., 2010). Overall, the research done on participation has brought to light the diversity of approaches and the limitations of initiatives, but also how they can be diverted by the elite. Beyond the institutional forms it may take, citizen participation – including any effects it may have on democratizing public administration – always depends on how it fits into specific contexts, history and the local culture (Beaumont and Nicholls, 2008). The topic of participation is often studied in concert with that of governance (Uitermark and Duyvendak, 2008; Holden, 2011) and that of deliberative democracy (Della Porta, 2005; Tilly, 2007; Offe, 2011).

This work has helped develop more targeted research into how groups of social actors have helped define the content and expression of deliberative democracy. The ways in which social movements operate are experiments – both internally and externally, in their relationships with institutions – with alternative models of democracy that are open to participation, to consensus building, and to the development of horizontal decision-making structures. Hence, the principles of deliberative democracy are part of the organizational ideology of social movements. For instance, Donatella della Porta (2005) studied the example of the global justice movement in Italy. The values it defends are similar to those championed by the new social movements: inclusion, subjectivity and diversity. The ways in which organizations associated with social movements operate thus adhere to the principles of deliberative democracy. However, the level of pluralism within these movements is higher than that generally encountered in public institutions. An openness to identity politics converges with a stronger definition of self-transformation.

The issue of citizenship has been part of the study of urban movements since at least the 1980s. In certain cities such as Jerusalem, citizenship has been called into question by social demands for an affirmation of ethnic identity (Hasson, 1987). Citizenship is concerned not only with social and political inequality, but also with individual rights claimed by members in these groups (Hasson, 1996). Additionally, although nation states give citizens formal rights, such rights are often abstract. Urban movements have helped us understand that citizenship is more related to an open-ended process rather than something set in stone. In this sense, the notion of citizenship has more than ever been shown to be a contested one. As Soledad Garcia (1996) points out, given the transformations that took place in many countries after 1989, the link between national identity and citizenship could no longer be taken for granted:

> The gain of political rights after 1989 has coincided with a reduction of the social rights that existed in the previous non-democratic regimes. Thus new democratic mechanisms appear to undermine those citizens' rights which are enabling, in the sense that they provide both life chances and personal security. (Garcia, 1996, p. 7)

With the increasing immigration that has accompanied globalization, cities have become venues for social and political transformations. Situated as they are within global networks, they have become strategic spaces that not only preside over economic restructuring but also allow immigrants to express 'new forms of citizenship practices and identities' (Sassen, 2002, p. 22). Many 'little ruptures' in the classic definition of Western citizenship are occurring (CitSee, 2012), and we are slowly but surely moving away from Thomas H. Marshall's conception of a range of rights. Rooted in the social sphere, these new forms of citizenship, which coincide with an affirmation of the subjectivity and conduct of minorities – racial and ethnic, but also homosexual – open a breach in the political rationale of liberal rights (Procacci, 2001).[7]

SUGGESTIONS FOR FURTHER RESEARCH

As we have seen, since the 1980s, the study of urban movements has drawn closer to the theory of social movements while at the same time preserving strong ties with urban theory. More recently, by taking up the concerns of movements for global justice, activist engagement has spread beyond the local scene to national and supra-national arenas.

It is difficult to establish with certainty the effects of urban movements and their action on the transformation of the built environment, even if their goals – rent control, the disruption of projects that force out local populations, or the improvement of services in residential areas, for example – are often clearly stated. In this respect, some researchers have rightly concluded that there is a 'mix of failure and success' (Pruijt, 2009, p. 5124). In addition, the actions of urban movements in the public arena in areas ranging from historic preservation to the fight against ethnic, cultural and sexual segregation (Sandercock, 1998) have changed urban culture itself (Castells, 1983).

Despite this, it is hard to determine whether these movements transform the balance of power in any meaningful way. This question, asked by Castells (1972) in the 1970s, continues to underlie more recent work. Today, however, it is formulated in different terms. Although there is a consensus that social change – or the resistance to it – remains an inherent part of the world we live in and that as such its measurement will vary according to context, not everyone agrees on the methods by which it should be analyzed. While for some, the changes are indeterminate, others either limit them to the political arena or broaden them to subjective and cultural dimensions. Emerging as they do out of different analytical intents, these approaches can nevertheless be associated with social conflicts of 'liquid modernity', which are influenced not only by increasingly individualized social relationships but also by reflexivity (Bauman, 2000).

The theoretical and methodological convergence in primary research trends that some have pointed out (Buechler, 2000) does not mean that the divide between studies that use sector-based sociology and those that consider movements as an entry point for the study of social relationships no longer exists. In order to overcome this divide, four factors deserve more attention from researchers in the years to come.

First, the tension between structure and agency that arises within movements is constituent to collective action as defined from the perspective of ambivalence. The goal of studying this tension is to go beyond an understanding of movements that is limited to an examination of the discourse of the social actors and, above all of the leaders that often monopolize the entire arena. Moreover, the need for renewal of action – a useful analytical criterion – requires an update of the action's structural context. In short, I feel that the theoretical requirements presented in the first section of this chapter must be examined in much greater depth in order to develop a sociology of collective action. This perspective deserves reaffirmation to give the study of urban movements a stronger connection with theory and with the sociology of movements in general as well as with urban theories.

Second, more consideration should be given to the inherent subjective aspects of urban movements. Although the organizational aspects of movements' action were a concern (Collectif Chili, 1972), the study of urban movements was initially focused primarily on their external effects, whether urban or political. However, researchers have been slow to study what individuals gain from their engagement on a personal level, whether it be recognition or empowerment with respect to their individuality or to their own identities as individuals. One exception – and it is a recent one – is when the actions of urban movements converge with those of the feminist movement. Research into urban movements from a feminist point of view (Werkele, 1996; Hassin, 2006; Andrew, 2010) have shed light on the experiential nature of collective action, starting with the defense of authenticity for these actors. Urban movements are usually rooted in the very fabric of daily life. Studies examining the contribution of women and their differing definitions of urban issues help to clarify how subjectivity defends against the threats to actors' autonomy by so-called 'objective forces'. Openness to and research into the subjective dimensions of action – whether it be concerned with organizational processes, components of action, or fallouts from it – are essential if we are to determine the conditions that foster the renewal of action.

The third factor relates to structural aspects with regard to the relationship between agency and structure. While the action of urban movements is rooted in the subjectivity of the actors, that does not mean it is not related to social-structuring factors. Structural dimensions are integral to the objective conditions that both limit and enable action. From this perspective, urban movements cannot be studied without also considering the structural factors at play in the transformation of cities. Under the guise of globalization, cities are taking on a polycentric shape, one that hinges on a system of hubs and spheres that are interconnected by an ever-expanding system of highways (Knox, 2008). Compared with the industrial-era city, the contemporary city has incorporated new spatially based logics. Such cities are often in fact urban regions – veritable city-regions (Savitch and Vogel, 2012). While collective action generated by urban movements has already begun to spread on the scale of these city-regions,[8] such examples are few in number. However, they will undoubtedly continue to grow in the years to come and should receive more attention from researchers.

The fourth and final factor relates to one of the crucial aspects of twenty-first-century urban development: the expansion of cities, and in particular the emergence of mega-cities in the Global South and the social, economic and cultural repercussions for their millions of inhabitants. It is not far-fetched to assume that the conflicts and mobilizations that are occurring in such cities may increase in the near future. This can certainly be at least partially confirmed by examples in China, India or Latin American countries.

In recent decades, urban modernization in China has not benefited everyone equally. Many have been forcibly evicted from their rural villages or urban neighbourhoods. According to the Centre on Housing Rights and Evictions – an NGO based in Geneva – up to 40 million farmers have lost their land over the last 20 years due to urbanization and industrialization, while 400 000 inhabitants of Beijing, to take a well-known example, were evicted from their homes due to site-specific requirements for the 2008 Olympic Games (Douay et al., 2012). In addition, these events have given rise to a boycott movement of real-estate developments. Starting in 2010, Chinese Internet users began to use social media tools to map where violence has occurred by creating what has been called a 'Bloody Map' (ibid.).

Mass protests around social and urban issues in China have become more widespread in recent years. But these protests appear 'politically weak' (Yan, 2013, p. 1) despite the large number of people mobilizing.

The fact is that these protests do not represent a threat to the Chinese Communist Party because the motives behind the claims are not 'revolutionary'. Previously, all local issues were at stake and insurgents were targeting local authorities: 'Instead protesting central government policy, as in the run-up to 1989, the current wave of protest is often calling for the implementation of central government policy at the local level' (ibid., p. 6).

After 1990, the political sphere and the economic system in India and other countries were transformed by neoliberal globalization and rampant consumerism (Kumar, 2008). While there may be a new awareness of social justice, this does not mean that there is a prevailing consensus among the population for involvement in or support for collective action. In Delhi, for example, Ravi Kumar made a survey of ongoing protests and mobilizations and observed that the expansion of the middle class – which can be associated with an increasing capacity for collective action – did not lead to support for poor people's concerns and campaigns. The overview he gives is one fraught with heterogeneity, division, and fragmentation: 'It is a collage of merchants protesting for better tax options, house-owners demanding a say on new rent bills, students demanding education to be made more accessible and a vast majority struggling against the displacement of industries, slums and loss of livelihood' (Kumar, 2008, p. 86). But this is not the only concern. Marginalization of poor people has also increased due to the co-optation of segments of the middle classes into the system, either economic or political. Finally, while the reformist character of past struggles continues to apply, the new movements, which are open to subjective concerns, are not targeting a radical social transformation.

In Latin America, Brazil is a good example for understanding collective attempts to change the status quo. The successful struggle in the mid-1960s of *favela* residents in Rio de Janeiro – who opposed eviction and demanded that their settlements be upgraded – has spread to most other Brazilian cities. Even though these groups 'are no longer very relevant actors in most cities' (De Souza, 2006, p. 331) – mainly because their action has been transformed into 'clientelistic' behaviour – since the 1990s, new urban movements, similar to Argentina's *piqueteros*, have emerged in Brazilian cities to combat homelessness by using squatting strategies but, unlike shanty-town residents, these movements pursue political objectives defined around what Marcelo Lopes de Souza calls 'grassroots urban planning'. Space limitations do not allow me to present the main characteristics and collective model of action of the Movimento dos Trabalhadores Sem Teto (Homeless Workers' Movement), but I can mention that their presence in cities like Rio de Janeiro and Sao Paulo has contributed to a redefinition of these cities' spatial organization. These actors have revealed that 'there are not only problems there, but also solutions which are being proposed and to some extent also implemented both by the state and by social movements (sometimes *together with* the local state apparatus, sometimes *despite* the state, sometimes *against* the state)' (ibid., 2006, p. 339; original emphasis).

For urban movements in cities of the Global South, the road to social justice will be a long and arduous one to say the least. The future course of their action remains difficult to predict, though one can assume that conflicts arising from the development of mega-cities will help to bring renewed legitimacy for collective action. In this respect, can we expect a new wave of urban protest? If so, and in light of the examples mentioned above, national contexts may continue to play a major role.

CONCLUSION

The study of urban movements has, among other things, led to a clearer understanding that urban production is not borne solely on the shoulders of architects, engineers, and the political elite but also on those of citizens, whose increasing presence in the public sphere cannot be boiled down to the actions of simple consumers. Castells (2006) stressed this point, but it was also central to Henri Lefebvre's (1968) conception of the city and of urbanity. While we can say that cities 'matter' to social movements (Nicholls, 2008), the opposite is also true. Urban protest and social mobilization around urban issues have helped to transform urban meanings and even, on occasion, spatial forms and their content.

This is less a matter of explaining the rise and fall of urban movements (Pickvance, 1995) than of better understanding their ability to question the propagation of relationships of dominance at play in urban development within the current context of globalization. Hence, the study of these actors and their struggles accords with the concerns of a post-colonial sociology that is open to the urban informality typical of the Global South (Roy, 2011). So how, and to what extent, are the actors in urban movements able to prevent social inequity, either by improving urban infrastructure in impoverished neighbourhoods in order to foster resource redistribution or by combating social exclusion and challenging limited opportunities to participate actively in a given community? How do they shape new forms of social solidarity? How do they contribute to a renewal of action? In many respects, these questions intersect with the theory of social movements. But they also stand apart from it by exploring new avenues for considering the relationships between structure and agency in reference to contemporary cities and their futures.

NOTES

1. It should be mentioned from the outset that the terms 'urban social movement' and 'urban movement' are interchangeable. For example, we do not say ecological or environmental social movement; we simply say environmental movement. In this regard, I completely share the view of Pickvance (2003) who feels that it is preferable to use the term 'urban movement': 'One may ask why the term urban social movement gained currency in place of the more straightforward 'urban movement'. After all, terms like feminist social movement or environmental social movement have never been proposed in place of feminist movement or environmental movement. Strangely, this question does not seem to have been raised.
   In my view the answer to this is in part the influence of Castell's writing, but beyond this it is because the term urban social movement has became a symbol. To use the term was to identify oneself with a group of writers who distrusted established political parties and believed in the potential for radical change of non-institutionalized urban political action. . .' (2003, p. 104). In the rest of this paper I will use 'urban movement' instead of 'urban social movement' except if I want to emphasize Castells' usage.
2. For example, *The Blackwell Companion to Social Movements* by Snow et al. (2004) does not include a chapter dedicated to urban movements.
3. Even if, according to certain researchers (see, in particular, Pickvance, 1985), he introduces new ones.
4. 'We define urban meaning as the structural performance assigned as a goal to cities in general (and to a particular city in the inter-urban division of labour) by the conflictive process between historical actors in a given society' (Castells, 1983, p. 303).
5. This is highlighted by Margit Mayer: 'No work has been as influential as *The City and the Grassroots* in defining urban social movement research. Its definition of urban social movements (USMs) has shaped how subsequent generations of urban scholars—and not merely in Western countries—have perceived their object of study: "urban-orientated mobilizations that influence structural social change and transform the urban meanings" (Castells, 1983, p. 305). While this is a far less loaded concept than his earlier Marxist-structuralist one. . . Castells, still only categorizes as "social" those urban movements which combine struggles for improved collective consumption with struggle for community culture as well as for political self-determination' (2006, p. 202).
6. 'Subjectivity, defined in sociological terms as the main conduit for autonomy and self-assertion, emerges as an essential theme and as the only force capable of opposing the process of rationalization, which expresses itself through the domination of science and technology, or through impassive law of global markets. Rationalization and subjectivity remain nowadays the two central features of modernity. . .and social movements have shown themselves to be one of the privileged arenas where subjectivity can be deepened, besides biographical trajectories as experienced through the fulfillment of professional careers and loving commitments' (Hamel et al., 2012, p. 179).
7. For a more detailed analysis of these aspects, see Chapter 4 in this volume.
8. This is the case when their action converges with that of environmental movements, by opposing, for example, the construction of regional facilities whose effects threaten biodiversity.

REFERENCES

Andrew, C. (2010), 'Récit d'une recherche-action: la participation et le passage de frontières de femmes immigrantes à la Ville d'Ottawa' [Report on action-research: participation and border crossing frontiers among immigrant women in the City of Ottawa], *Sociologie et sociétés*, **42**(1), 227–43.

Armstrong, E.A. and M. Bernstein (2008), 'Culture, power, and institutions: a multi-institutional politics approach to social movements', *Sociological Theory*, **26**(1), 74–99.
Bash, H.H. (1995), *Social Movements*, Atlantic Highlands, NJ: Humanities Press.
Bauman, Z. (2000), *Liquid Modernity*, Cambridge, UK: Polity Press.
Beaumont, J. and W. Nicholls (2008), 'Plural governance, participation and democracy in cities', *International Journal of Urban and Regional Research*, **32**(1), 87–94.
Becher, D. (2010), 'The participant's dilemma: bringing conflict and representation back in', *International Journal of Urban and Regional Research*, **34**(3), 496–511.
Brenner, N., P. Marcuse and M. Mayer (eds) (2011), *Cities for People, Not for Profit. Critical Urban Theory and the Right to the City*, London/New York: Routledge.
Brown, G. (2004), 'Sites of public (homo)sex and the carnivalesque spaces of Reclaim the Streets', in L. Lees (ed.), *The Emancipatory City? Paradoxes and Possibilities*, London: Sage, pp. 91–107.
Buechler, S.M. (2000), *Social Movements in Advanced Capitalism*, New York and Oxford: Oxford University Press.
Castells, M. (1972), *La question urbaine* [The Urban Question], Paris: François Maspéro.
Castells, M. (1975), *Luttes urbaines* [Urban Struggles], Paris: François Maspéro.
Castells, M. (1983), *The City and the Grassroots*, Berkeley and Los Angeles, CA: University of California Press.
Castells, M. (2006), 'Changer la ville: a rejoinder', *International Journal of Urban and Regional Research*, **30**(1), 219–23.
Castells, M. (2012), *Networks of Outrage and Hope. Social Movements in the Internet Age*, Cambridge, UK: Polity Press.
Ceccarelli, P. (1982), 'Politics, parties, and urban movements: Western Europe', in S. Fainstein and N. Fainstein (eds), *Urban Policy Under Capitalism*, Beverly Hills, CA: Sage, pp. 261–76.
Cefaï, D. (2007), *Pourquoi se mobilise-t-on? Les théories de l'action collective* [Why Do We Mobilize? Theories of Collective Action], Paris La Découverte.
CitSee (2012), 'Artisans for incorporation – an interview with Saskia Sassen', Citizenship in Southeast Europe [online] accessed 15 May 2014 at http:// http://www.citsee.eu/interview/%E2%80%98artisans-incorporation%E2%80%99-interview-saskia-sassen.
Cohen, J.L. and A. Arato (1992), *Civil Society and Political Theory*, Cambridge, MA: The MIT Press.
Collectif Chili (1972), 'Revendication urbaine, stratégie politique et mouvement social des *"pobladores"* au Chili' [Urban claim, political strategy, and the *'pobladores'* social movement in Chile], *Espaces et Sociétés*, **3**(6–7), 37–57.
Della Porta, D. (2005), 'Deliberation in movement: why and how to study deliberative democracy and social movements', *Acta Politica*, **3**(40), 336–50.
De Souza, M.L. (2006), 'Together with the state, despite the state, against the state. Social movements as "critical urban planning" agents', *City*, **10**(3), 327–42.
Diamond, J. (2005), 'Revitalisation urbaine et participation communautaire. Les leçons de l'expérience britannique' [Urban revitalization and community participation. Lessons from the British experience], in M.H. Bacqué, H. Rey and Y. Sintomer (eds), *Gestion de proximité et démocratie participative. Une perspective comparative* [Management of Proximity and Participatory Democracy: A Comparative Perspective], Paris: La Découverte, pp. 101–15.
Douay, N. (2012), 'L'activisme urbain à Montréal: des luttes urbaines à la revendication d'une ville artistique, durable et collaborative' [Urban activism in Montreal: from urban conflicts to the revendication of an artistic, sustainable and collaborative city], *Information Géographique*, **76**(3), 83–96.
Douay, N., S. Marta and T. Giraud (2012), 'La carte du sang de l'immobilier chinois, un cas de cyber-activisme' [The Chinese bloody map of real estate, a case of cyber-activism], *Information Géographique*, **1**, 74–88.
Dubet, F. and H. Lustiger-Thaler (2004), 'Introduction: the sociology of collective action reconsidered', *Current Sociology*, **52**(4), 557–73.

Dubet, F. and D. Martuccelli (1998), *Dans quelle société vivons-nous?* [What Kind of Society Do We Live In?], Paris: Editions du Seuil.
Dupuy, C. and C. Halpern (2009), 'Les politiques publiques face à leurs protestataires' [Public policies facing challenges], *Revue Française de Science Politique*, **59**(4), 701–22.
Eckstein, S. (1990), 'Poor people versus the state and capital: anatomy of a successful community mobilization for housing in Mexico City', *International Journal of Urban and Regional Research*, **14**(2), 274–96.
Escobar, A. (2008), *Territories of Difference. Place, Movements, Life, Redes*, Durham, NC/London: Duke University Press.
Fainstein, S.S. and C. Hirst (1995), 'Urban social movements', in D. Judge, G. Stoker and H. Wolman (eds), *Theories of Urban Politics*, London: Sage, pp. 181–204.
Fassin, D. (2010), *La raison humanitaire* [Humanitarian Reason], Paris: Gallimard and Seuil.
Flank, L. (ed.) (2011), *Voices From the 99 Percent: An Oral History of the Occupy Wall Street Movement*, St. Petersburg, FL: Red and Black Publishers.
Franzén, M. (2005), 'New social movements and gentrification in Hamburg and Stockholm: a comparative study', *Journal of Housing and the Built Environment*, **20**(1), 51–77.
Friedmann, J. (2002), *The Prospect of Cities*, Minneapolis, MN: University of Minnesota Press.
Garcia, S. (1996), 'Cities and citizenship', *International Journal of Urban and Regional Research*, **20**(1), 7–21.
Gautney, H., O. Dahbour, A. Dawson and N. Smith (eds) (2009), *Democracy, States, and the Struggle for Global Justice*, London/New York: Routledge.
Gledhill, J. (2012), 'Collecting Occupy London: public collecting institutions and social movements in the 21st century', *Social Movement Studies: Journal of Social, Cultural and Political Protest*, **11**(3–4), 342–8.
Goss, K.A. and M.T. Heaney (2010), 'Organizing women as women: hybridity and grass-roots collective action in the 21st century', *Perspectives on Politics*, **8**(1), 27–52.
Habermas, J. (1988), *Le discours philosophique de la modernité* [The Philosophical Discourse of Modernity], Paris: Gallimard.
Habermas, J. (2003), 'Au-delà du libéralisme et du républicanisme, la démocratie délibérative' [Beyond liberalism and republicanism, deliberative democracy], *Raison Publique*, **1**(1), 40–57.
Hackworth, J. (2002), 'Postrecession gentrification in New York City', *Urban Affairs Review*, **37**(6), 815–43.
Hamel, P. (1995), 'Collective action and the paradigm of individualism', in L, Maheu (ed.), *Social Movements and Social Classes. The Future of Collective Action*, London: Sage, pp. 236–57.
Hamel, P. and L. Maheu (2001), 'Beyond new social movements: social conflicts and institutions', in K. Nash and A. Scott (eds), *The Blackwell Companion to Political Sociology*, Malden, MA: Blackwell, pp. 261–70.
Hamel, P., H. Lustiger-Thaler and L. Maheu (2012), 'Global social movements: politics, subjectivity and human rights', in A. Sales (ed.), *Sociology Today. Social Transformations in a Globalizing World*, London: Sage, pp. 171–94.
Hamel, P., H. Lustiger-Thaler and M. Mayer (eds) (2000), *Urban Movements in a Globalizing World*, London: Routledge.
Harris, R. (1987), 'A social movement in urban politics: a reinterpretation of urban reform in Canada', *International Journal of Urban and Regional Research*, **11**(3), 363–81.
Harvey, D. (1973), *Social Justice and the City*, London: Edward Arnold Publishers.
Harvey, D. (2012), *Rebel Cities. From the Right to the City to the Urban Revolution*, London: Verso.
Hassin, S. (2006), 'The challenges of inclusion and transformation: the women's movement in democratic South Africa', in R. Ballard, A. Habib and I. Valodia (eds), *Voices of Protest. Social Movements in Post-Apartheid South Africa*, Scottsville, SA: University of KwaZulu-Natal Press, pp. 349–70.

Hasson, S. (1987), *Urban Social Movements in Jerusalem*, Albany, NY: State University of New York Press.
Hasson, S. (1996), 'Local politics and split citizenship in Jerusalem', *International Journal of Urban and Regional Research*, 20(1), 116–33.
Holden, M. (2011), 'Public participation and local sustainability: questioning a common agenda in urban governance', *International Journal of Urban and Regional Research*, 35(2), 312–29.
Jacobs, J. (1961), *The Death and Life of Great American Cities*, New York: Random House.
Jasper, J.M. (1998), 'The emotions of protest: affective and reactive emotions in and around social movements', *Sociological Forum*, 13(3), 493–512.
Judd, D.R. (2011), 'Theorizing the city' in D.R. Judd and D. Simpson (eds), *The City Revisited. Urban Theory From Chicago, Los Angeles, New York*, Minneapolis, MN: University of Minnesota Press, pp. 3–20.
Katznelson, I. (1981), *City Trenches. Urban Politics and the Patterning of Class in the United States*, Chicago, IL/London: The University of Chicago Press.
Kazin, M. (2011), *American Dreamers. How the Left Changed a Nation*, New York: Alfred A. Knopf.
Klandermans, B. and S. Tarrow (1988), 'Mobilization into social movements: synthesizing European and American approaches', *International Social Movement Research*, 1, 1–38.
Knox, P.L. (2008), *Metroburbia USA*, New Brunswick, NJ: Rutgers University Press.
Köhler, B. and M. Wissen (2003), 'Glocalizing protest: urban conflicts and global social movements', *International Journal of Urban and Regional Research*, 27(4), 942–51.
Kruks, S. (2000), *Retrieving Experience: Subjectivity and Recognition in Feminist Politics*, Ithaca, NY: Cornell University Press.
Kumar, R. (2008), 'Globalization and changing patterns of social mobilization in India', *Social Movement Studies*, 7(1), 77–96.
Lawson, R. (ed.) (1986), *The Tenant Movement in New York City, 1904–1984*, New Brunswick, NJ: Rutgers University Press.
Lefebvre, H. (1968), *Le droit à la ville* [The Right to the City], Paris: Anthropos.
Lojkine, J. (1977), *Le marxisme, l'Etat et la question urbaine* [Marxism, the State and the Urban Question], Paris: Presses Universitaires de France.
Lombard, M. (2013), 'Citizen participation in urban governance in the context of democratization: evidence from low-income neighbourhoods in Mexico', *International Journal of Urban and Regional Research*, 37(1), 135–50.
Long, J. (2013), 'Sense of place and place-based activism in the neoliberal city', *City: Analysis of Urban Trends, Culture, Theory, Policy, Action*, 17(1), 52–67.
Maeckelbergh, M. (2012), 'Mobilizing to stay put: housing struggles in New York City', *International Journal of Urban and Regional Research*, 36(4), 655–73.
Maheu, L. (1995), 'Introduction', in L. Maheu (ed.), *Social Movements and Social Classes. The Future of Collective Action*, London: Sage, pp. 1–17.
Maheu, L. (2005), 'Mouvements sociaux et modernité avancée: le retour obligé à l'ambivalence de l'action' [Social movements and advanced modernity: a forced return to the ambivalence of action], in L. Guay, P. Hamel, D. Masson and J.G. Vaillancourt (eds), *Mouvements sociaux et changements institutionnels* [Social Movements and Institutional Changes], Québec: Presses de l'Université du Québec, pp. 9–34.
Martinez-Lopez, M.A. and A. Garcia Bernardos (2012), 'Squat the squares, occupy the buildings', paper presented at the Joint Session on Urban Movements, Buenos Aires, Argentina, The Second ISA Forum of Sociology, 1–4 August.
Mayer, M. (2006), 'Manuel Castells' *The City and the Grassroots*', *International Journal of Urban and Regional Research*, 30(1), 202–6.
McDonald, K. (2006), *Global Movements. Action and Culture*, Oxford: Blackwell.
Melucci, A. (1989), *Nomads of the Present. Social Movements and Individual Needs in Contemporary Society*, London: Hutchinson Radius.
Melucci, A. (1996), *The Playing Self. Person and Meaning in the Planetary Society*, Cambridge, UK: Cambridge University Press.

Miller, B. (2006), 'Castells' *The City and the Grassroots*: 1983 and today', *International Journal of Urban and Regional Research*, 30(1), 207–11.
Nicholls, W.J. (2008), 'The urban question revisited: the importance of cities for social movements', *International Journal of Urban and Regional Research*, 32(4), 841–59.
Offe, C. (2011), 'Crisis and innovation of liberal democracy: can deliberation be institutionalised?', *Czech Sociological Review*, 47(3), 447–72.
Olives, J. (1972), 'La lutte contre la rénovation urbaine dans le quartier de la "cité d'Aliarte (Paris)"' [The fight against urban renewal in the neighbourhood of the 'city of Aliarte'], *Espaces et Sociétés*, 3(6–7), 9–28.
Peters, D. and J. Novy (2012), 'Rail station mega-projects: overlooked centrepieces in the complex puzzle of urban restructuring in Europe', *Built Environment*, 38(1), 5–12.
Pickerill, J. and J. Krinsky (2012), 'Why does Occupy matter?', *Social Movement Studies*, 11(3–4), 279–87.
Pickvance, C. (1976), 'On the study of urban social movements', in C.G. Pickvance (ed.), *Urban Sociology: Critical Essays*, London: Tavistock Publications, pp. 198–218.
Pickvance, C. (1985), 'The rise and fall of urban movements and the role of comparative analysis', *Environment and Planning D: Society and Space*, 3(1), 31–53.
Pickvance, C. (1989), 'Urban movements or social movements in cities?' in K. Brown, B. Hourcade, M. Jole, C. Liauzu, P. Slugett and S. Zubaida (eds), *Etat, ville et mouvements sociaux au Maghreb et au Moyen-Orient* [Urban Crises and Social Movements in the Middle East], Paris: L'Harmattan, pp. 72–86.
Pickvance, C. (1995), 'Where have the movements gone?', in C. Hadjimichalis and D. Sadler (eds), *Europe at the Margins: New Mosaics of Inequality*, London: Wiley, pp. 197–217.
Pickvance, C. (2003), 'From urban social movements to urban movements: a review of the field and introduction to a symposium', *International Journal of Urban and Regional Research*, 27(1), 102–9.
Pink, S. (2008), 'Re-thinking contemporary activism: from community to emplaced sociality', *Ethnos*, 73(2), 163–88.
Pink, S. (2009), 'Urban social movements and small places. Slow Cities as sites of activism', *City*, 13(4), 451–65.
Procacci, G. (2001), 'Governmentality and citizenship', in K. Nash and A. Scott (eds), *The Blackwell Companion to Political Sociology*, Oxford: Blackwell, pp. 342–51.
Pruijt, H. (2003), 'Is the institutionalization of urban movements inevitable? A comparison of the opportunities for sustained squatting in New York City and Amsterdam', *International Journal of Urban and Regional Research*, 27(1), 133–57.
Pruijt, H. (2009), 'Urban movements', in G. Ritzer (ed.), *The Blackwell Encyclopedia of Sociology*, Malden, MA: Blackwell, pp. 5123–7.
Rosanvallon, P. (2006), *La contre-démocratie. La politique à l'âge de la défiance* [Counter-Democracy. Politics in an Age of Mistrust], Paris: Seuil.
Roth, R. (1996), 'The institutionalization of new social movements in Germany. Empirical findings at the local level and theoretical perspectives', paper presented at the Conference 'Europe and the United States: Movement Societies or the Institutionalization of Protest', Ithaca, NY: Cornell University, 1–3 March.
Roy, A. (2011), 'Slumdog cities: rethinking subaltern urbanism', *International Journal of Urban and Regional Research*, 35(2), 223–38.
Rucht, D. (ed.) (1991), *Research on Social Movements. The State of the Art in Western Europe and the USA*, Frankfurt/Boulder, CO: Campus Verlag/Westview Press.
Sandercock, L. (1998), *Towards Cosmopolis*, New York: John Wiley & Sons.
Sassen, S. (1999), 'Cracked casings: notes toward an analytics for studying transnational processes', in J.L. Abu-Lughod (ed.), *Sociology for the Twenty-first Century. Continuities and Cutting Edges*, Chicago, IL: The University of Chicago Press, pp. 134–45.
Sassen, S. (2002), 'The repositioning of citizenship: emergent subjects and spaces for politics', *Berkeley Journal of Sociology*, 46, 4–25.
Sassen, S. (2009), 'Cities in today's global age', *SAIS Review*, 29(1), 3–32.
Sassen, S. (2011), 'New spatial formats. Megaregions and global cities', in J. Xu and A.G.

Yeh, *Governance and Planning of Mega-City Regions (An International Comparative Perspective)*, London: Routledge, pp. 101–26.
Sassen, S. (2013), 'When territory deborders territoriality', *Territory, Politics, Governance*, **1**(1), 21–45.
Saunders, P. (1979), *Urban Politics: A Sociological Interpretation*, London: Hutchinson.
Savitch, H. and R. Vogel (2012), 'New state spaces, globalization, and the politics of rescaling', paper presented at the Governing the Metropolis: Powers and Territories. New Directions for Research conference, Paris, 29 November.
Silver, H., A. Scott and Y. Kazepov (2010), 'Participation and urban contention and deliberation', *International Journal of Urban and Regional Research*, **34**(3), 453–77.
Smith, J. (2008), *Social Movements for Global Democracy*, Baltimore, MD: The Johns Hopkins University Press.
Smith, J. and B. Glidden (2012), 'Occupy Pittsburgh and the challenges of participatory democracy', *Social Movement Studies*, **11**(3–4), 288–94.
Snow, D.A. and S.A. Soule (2010), *A Primer on Social Movements*, New York: W.W. Norton & Company.
Snow, D.A., S.A. Soule and H. Kriesi (eds) (2004), *The Blackwell Companion to Social Movements*, Malden, MA: Blackwell.
Soule, S.A. (2004), 'Diffusion processes within and across movements', in D.E. Snow, S.A. Soule and H. Kriesi (eds), *The Blackwell Companion to Social Movements*, Malden, MA: Blackwell, pp. 294–310.
Susser, I. (2006), 'Global visions and grassroots movements: an anthropological perspective', *International Journal of Urban and Regional Research*, **30**(1), 212–18.
Tilly, C. (2007), *Democracy*, Cambridge, UK: Cambridge University Press.
Tilly, C. (2008), *Contentious Performances*, Cambridge, UK: Cambridge University Press.
Tilly, C. and S. Tarrow (2007), *Contentious Politics*, Boulder, CO: Paradigm Press.
Touraine, A. (1978) *La voix et le regard* [*The Voice and the Eye*], Paris: Editions du Seuil.
Uitermark, J. and J.W. Duyvendak (2008), 'Citizen participation in a mediated age: neighourhood governance in the Netherlands', *International Journal of Urban and Regional Research*, **32**(1), 114–34.
Uitermark, J. and W. Nicholls (2012), 'How local networks shape a global movement: comparing Occupy in Amsterdam and Los Angeles', *Social Movement Studies*, **11**(3–4), 297–301.
Wacquant, L. (2006), *Parias urbains. Ghetto, Banlieue, Etat* [Urban Outcasts: A Comparative Sociology of Advanced Marginality], Paris: La Découverte.
Werkele, G.R. (1996), 'Reframing urban sustainability: women's movement organizing and the local state', in R. Keil, G.R. Werkele and D.V.J. Bell (eds), *Local Places in the Age of the Global City*, Montreal: Black Rose Books, pp. 137–45.
Wolch, J. (1989), 'The shadow state: transformation in the voluntary sector', in J. Wolch and M. Dear (eds), *The Power of Geography*, Boston, MA: Unwin Hyman, pp. 197–221.
Wolfe, A. (2010), *The Future of Liberalism*, New York: Vintage Books.
Yan, F. (2013), 'A little spark kindles a great fire? The paradox of China's rising wave of protest', *Social Movement Studies*, **12**(1), 1–7.
Young, I.M. (1990), *Justice and the Politics of Difference*, Princeton, NJ: Princeton University Press.
Zukin, C. et al. (2006), *A New Engagement? Political Participation, Civic Life, and the Changing American Citizen*, Oxford: Oxford University Press.

21. The Tea Party movement
Edward Ashbee

INTRODUCTION

The Tea Party movement emerged shortly after President Obama's inauguration at the beginning of 2009. It drew upon depictions of a bloated governing elite as well as representations of a popular uprising and a citizenry reclaiming its natural rights. Although there have been different claims about the movement's embrace of the term 'tea party', it is usually understood as an allusion to the Boston Tea Party of 1773, so often celebrated as the beginning of the American colonies' rebellion against tyrannical government.

Almost at once the movement galvanized sections of the right that had been dispirited by both the 2008 elections and what some saw as the fiscal recklessness of the Bush years. The two-party system and the relative porousness of those parties enabled it to leverage the Republican Party in a way that would not be possible in many other political systems. The movement drew together those who had backed Alaskan Governor Sarah Palin's vice-presidential campaign, libertarians as well as independent conservatives who were at some distance from the Republican Party 'establishment'. As it began to take a more structured form and movement organizations such as the Tea Party Express emerged, the movement seemed to have either displaced or absorbed the 'religious right' that had been a core Republican constituency from the late 1970s onwards.

The movement also had wider impacts. Although other surveys produced strikingly different results, an NBC News/*Wall Street Journal* poll at the beginning of 2010 suggested that 41 per cent of Americans had a 'positive view' of the movement. In contrast, just 35 per cent had a positive view of the Democrats and only 28 per cent had a positive view of the Republican Party (Brooks, 2010). Certainly, the movement played a major part in shaping the November 2010 mid-term elections. Almost half of the seats in the House of Representatives gained by the Republicans were won by candidates that the Tea Party movement had endorsed. Tea Party favourites, Rand Paul and Marco Rubio were elected to the US Senate (Lerer and Fitzgerald, 2010). At the same time, however, it became evident that identification with the movement could also impose political costs. Some closely associated with the movement went down to defeat in seats that might otherwise have been won by the Republicans. Christine O'Donnell's defeat in the Delaware Senate race has been widely cited. In 2012, Tea Party supporters pulled former Massachusetts Governor, Mitt Romney, the Republicans' presidential candidate, towards political positions that were later to cost him the presidency.

The movement, however, seemed to have reached an impasse by the end of 2012 and President Obama's second-term election victory appeared to reinvigorate those on the right who questioned the movement's strategy, character and direction. Indeed, as 2013 progressed, there were increasingly visible tensions between different sections of the right.

This chapter surveys the Tea Party movement and assesses the different studies and analyses of its growth and development. In subsequent sections, it considers the relationship between these studies and the theoretical approaches pursued in social movement literature over recent decades, the frames and discourses employed by the movement, and its different impacts.

THE TEA PARTY MOVEMENT AS A SOCIAL MOVEMENT

Accounts of Tea Party activism have for the most part been at some distance from the frameworks and approaches that have generally defined the study of social movements. This divide between the literatures is nothing new. Indeed, although there have been periodic overlaps, there has long been a cleavage between surveys of conservative and radical right movements in the USA and studies of social movements.[1]

There are three principal reasons for this. First, there has been an implicit reluctance in much of the social movement literature to acknowledge the authenticity of rightist movements. It is said that they may resemble movements but are, in reality, the offspring of entrenched commercial or ideological interests. At the most, they are quasi-movements. Perhaps to a greater extent than others, the Tea Party movement has been represented as the 'top-down' creation of particular financial interests or policy entrepreneurs. In a celebrated comment, former House of Representatives Nancy Pelosi used the word 'astroturf' to describe the movement. She was invoking a term that had been employed during the 1980s to describe the front organizations established or backed by corporations seeking commercial gain while at the same time concealing their true purposes through talk of a broader public interest (Formisano, 2012, p. 7).

Claims that the movement has an 'astroturf' character have been reproduced in some of the scholarly literature, although, almost always, the emphasis on the part played by elite interests takes a more nuanced form. Anthony DiMaggio rejects the proposition that Tea Party activists constitute a 'movement' by stressing the extent of the weakness of grassroots organizations, structures and networks. He notes that although significant numbers claimed to be active in Tea Party groupings, there were relatively few opportunities for mass participation.[2] Instead, movement organizations were largely the instrument of elite interests. Movement structures, he argues, have had a top-down character. He points to the part played by 'partisan and media elites who are essentially Republican Party operatives' and 'business elites of the Koch variety' (Borchert and DiMaggio, 2011). DiMaggio challenges the representations around which the movement's self-narrative is structured and the assertion that it is based among ordinary citizens: 'the alleged Tea Party "insurgents" who have led the Tea Party "revolution" in Congress are extremely elitist in their policy positions and in terms of their economic backgrounds' (ibid.).

The 'astroturf' commentaries also often focus on the large financial contributions that were given by wealthy individuals and interests so as to develop and build the movement. In particular, the role of David and Charles Koch has attracted considerable attention. The Koch brothers have long been known for their large-scale contributions to libertarian and conservative causes (Mayer, 2010).[3]

Second, where conservative and other rightist movements have been understood in much of the social movement literature as mass rather than elite phenomena, they have been represented as 'counter-movements'. This is partly because they have appeared to emerge only in response to an initial movement or impulse. In other words, they are a function of an original impetus and make 'contrary claims simultaneously to those of the original movement' (Meyer and Staggenborg, 1996, p. 1631). Yet, by treating rightist movements as a function of other movements, such an approach tends to offer a constrained picture of conservatism and the radical right and the dynamics of the movements that emerge from within their ranks.

Rightist movements are not only understood as 'counter-movements' because they emerge as a function of an original movement but because they generally appear as efforts to hold back change and reform and little more. The right itself has often lent credence to these depictions. Many commentators have reproduced William F. Buckley Jr's celebrated description of conservatism as standing 'athwart history, yelling Stop' (quoted in Moran, 2008).[4] In contrast, much of the social movement literature has tended to define social movements as efforts to secure social, cultural and economic change. They are understood as struggles to secure or extend popular 'rights'. As a consequence, there has generally been a focus on the new social movements that emerged in the latter half of the twentieth century and that were for the most part allied with or at least loosely identified with post-materialism and the cultural, political and economic goals associated with secularism, egalitarianism and a faith in greater government interventionism.

Third, many of the studies of the right have been written as journalistic descriptions or narratives rather than theoretical analyses. Indeed, a significant proportion of these accounts of right-wing activists and campaigns are structured as 'journeys' into a seemingly different and alien world. Some such as Kate Zernike and Matt Taibbi's reports have sought out the eccentric and the unusual and rest on extended interviews and participant observation (Taibbi, 2010; Zernike, 2010).

Insofar as there have been overlaps and points of contact between accounts of conservative and radical right movements and the broader literature on social movements, such studies have drawn, at times unconsciously, on the collective behaviour and structural strain theories that held sway during the mid-century years. Research was guided, if only implicitly, by notions of modernization, structural dispossession, interclass cleavages and the generation of 'collective grievances' (Bell, 1963, p. 19). These processes, particularly when allied to particular notions taken from social psychology, laid a basis for 'extremism'.

Seymour Martin Lipset's 1960 book, *Political Man: The Social Bases of Politics*, is representative. It stressed the confluence between structural strain and particular personality types: 'Extremist movements have much in common. They appeal to the disgruntled and the psychologically homeless, to the personal failures, the socially isolated, the economically insecure, the uneducated, unsophisticated, and authoritarian persons at every level of the society' (Lipset, 1960, p. 175). In a celebrated account originally published in 1964, Richard Hofstadter talked in similar terms and emphasized the irrationalist political psychologies of many movement participants. He spoke of 'the paranoid style, simply because no other word adequately evokes the sense of heated exaggeration, suspiciousness, and conspiratorial fantasy' (Hofstadter [1964] 1996, p. 3).[5]

In an echo of these early studies, recent accounts of rightist movements in the USA have also thought in terms of structural maladjustment and dispossession. They have stressed the radical right's associations with particular groupings that feel under siege such as the white South or evangelical Protestants. During the 1990s (and again more recently), the concept of 'angry white men' provided an axis for the study of the Republican right and Christian conservative movements as well as the militia and survivalist movements (Baker, 2012). Seen in this way, movements of the right are a 'hold-out' or 'backlash' against the shifts that are remoulding the USA as a less overtly religious and more racially and ethnically diverse society in which women and minorities play a much more visible and egalitarian role.

Nonetheless, despite the cleavage between studies of the American right and the social movement literature the Tea Party movement and comparable protests should be understood as social movements and placed within the frameworks that have structured the literature. In the article that did much to secure acceptance for resource mobilization theory, John D. McCarthy and Mayer Zald defined a social movement as 'a set of opinions and beliefs in a population which represents preferences for changing some elements of the social structure and/or reward distribution of a society...we view social movements as nothing more than preference structures directed toward social change' (McCarthy and Zald, 1977, pp. 1217–18). Thus, although rightist movements are not often the object of study in the study of social movements, they should be, from this perspective, legitimately understood as such.

More recent definitions of social movements can also be taken to encompass the right as well as the left. As David Snow, Sarah Soule and Hanspeter Kriesi, note, most contemporary definitions draw on at least three of the following characteristics: the undertaking of joint or collective action, 'change-oriented goals or claims', some use of extra or non-institutional collective action, some degree of organization, and a degree of temporal continuity (Snow et al., 2003, p. 3). Approached in this way, social movements may either be challengers or defenders of institutional or cultural authority (ibid., p. 5).

Nonetheless, although the approaches, frameworks, concepts and categories employed in the study of social movements can be utilized so as to consider the emergence and development of the Tea Party movement (and the radical right more broadly), most of the accounts that have been published sit uneasily with the social movement literature. These accounts tend to reproduce the theoretical frameworks that have defined the social movement literature but they do not consciously place themselves within, or even acknowledge, those frameworks.

Of the studies that in contrast to 'astroturf' approaches accept the 'legitimacy' of Tea Party activism as a movement, a significant proportion of these remain within the structural strain perspectives that, as noted above, defined much of the social movement literature during the mid-century years. They echo the arguments found in studies tying the emergence of movements to collective 'deprivation'. At times, these accounts convey the impression that there is an embedded irrationalism in the Tea Party movement's thinking and activities. At other points, however, commentators seem to go beyond notions associated with structural strain and instead suggest that the movement was a rational response to shifts and changes in the structure of political opportunity. There are hints of a political process approach.

Most of these accounts begin by considering the profound economic shifts and labour market changes that have taken place in recent decades and the ways in which they have impacted those who were once the bulwark of the American middle class. In some cases, these accounts are tied to radical and Marxian critiques of market processes. William I. Robinson and Mario Barrera locate the rise of the Tea Party movement within the context of a more generalized analysis of capitalism. They consider the rise of the transnational capitalist class, the crisis of overaccumulation and the structural strains within the neoliberal order that arose towards the end of the twentieth century. From this perspective, the 'Great Recession' from 2007–08 onwards was a 'restructuring crisis'. Like the crises of the 1930s and 1970s, it had 'the potential to become a systemic crisis, depending on how social agents respond to the crisis and on the element of contingency that is unpredictable and always plays some role in historical outcomes' (Robinson and Barrera, 2012, p. 6).

Although there are therefore different ways in which an economic crisis might be assuaged, (through perhaps the pursuit of global neo-Keynesianism or more left-leaning reformist strategies), Robinson and Barrera suggest that 'twenty-first century fascism' may come into play (ibid., p. 8). Such a form of 'fascism' draws upon the classical fascist themes of earlier eras but has a distinct character. Modern fascist repression, they argue, may be compatible with the maintenance of outwardly democratic forms and a two-party system. Within a notionally democratic framework, authoritarianism and new technology can be allied so as to bolster the power and the interests of the transnational capitalist class (ibid., p. 12).

Approached in this way, the Tea Party movement should be considered alongside 'violent hate groups' and the campaigns against immigration. Taken collectively, they pave the way for institutionalized oppression insofar as all are expressions, they argue, of 'the psychopathology of white decline, sharp militarisation and pervasive policing' and have 'fascistic characteristics' (ibid., p. 4).

Other authors also take the state of the contemporary economy as their starting point and associate the Tea Party movement with reaction and elite interests but they locate the movement within more 'normalized' forms of politics. As DiMaggio notes, real median incomes largely stagnated since the economic crises of the 1970s. Whereas some industries had paid a 'family wage' to men during the long post-war boom, households now required two incomes and, in some instances, individuals had to take more than one job. All of this can be tied to Jacob Hacker's notion of a 'great risk shift' (Hacker, 2008). Individuals and families are now much more vulnerable as earnings have become more volatile and as provision for retirement has become increasingly dependent upon semi-private arrangements. Chip Berlet adopts a broadly similar approach by also tying the growth and development of the movement to the structural economic strains facing whites in middle and lower-income groupings:

> [M]uch of what steams the tea bag contingent is legitimate. They see their jobs vanish in front of their eyes as Wall Street gets trillions. They see their wages stagnate. They worry that their children will be even less well off than they are. They sense that Washington doesn't really care about them. On top of that, many are distraught about seeing their sons and daughters coming home in wheelchairs or body bags. With no one appearing to champion their cause, they line up with the anti-Obama crowd, and they stir in some of their social worries about gay marriage and abortion, dark-skinned immigrants, and a black man in the White House. (Berlet, 2010)[6]

Some other studies of Tea Party activism correspond, at least loosely, with the approaches associated with resource mobilization theory insofar as they are directed towards the different resources (whether they be moral, cultural, social-organizational, human, and material) that both elite and mass participants in the movement have utilized (Edwards and McCarthy, 2003, p. 2). These studies acknowledge that many of the ideas and grievances that underpinned the Tea Party protests had a long history within the American right. What changed in 2009 and 2010 was the ways in which such ideas and grievances were mobilized and then brought to the fore.

As Clarence Lo has argued, the material and human resources offered by the established conservative networks were invaluable in taking Tea Party activism beyond an elemental level (Lo, 2012, p. 9). Such networks took shape from the 1970s onwards as the New Right gained an ideational and organizational foothold. Conservative advocacy organizations and thinktanks such as the Heritage Foundation were formed while political entrepreneurs took advantage of direct mailing and the opportunities offered by talk radio. In a further development the Fox News Channel was established in 1996. These initiatives were bound together by quasi-formal networks such as the weekly meetings convened in Washington DC by Grover Norquist of Americans for Tax Reform. These network gatherings bring together conservative activists from all the different layers, clusters and organizations that collectively constitute the conservative right. Their role as a meeting point is captured in the claim made by John Fund, formerly of the *Wall Street Journal*, that it is 'the Grand Central station of the conservative movement' (quoted in Kroft, 2012).

The result of such network gatherings and the interlinking of campaigns, ad hoc organizations and more formal institutions is that there is, as Richard Meagher records, extensive 'cross-pollination' within the right (Meagher, 2012, p. 479). For Meagher, the Tea Party movement is to be understood within this context. Although movement organizations claim to have an autonomous character, there was a close, indeed largely integrated, relationship between Tea Party groupings and pivotal conservative organizers (ibid., p. 483).

The pivotal role of particular conservative organizations and clusters is worthy of note. Americans for Prosperity (AFP) and the Heritage Foundation played an important part in training Tea Party activists (ibid., p. 482). AFP was particularly quick on the uptake. In April 2009, so as to build the Tax Day protests, it employed 34 national office employees and 35 state-level employees (Formisano, 2012, p. 69). Furthermore, in overall terms, the movement's growth and expansion owed much to Fox News and individual conservative commentators such as Glenn Beck and Rush Limbaugh. Indeed, survey data suggested that Tea Party supporters were more likely to rely on Fox News as a source of news than not only the general population but also other Republicans (Disch, 2012, p. 128). Fox News and conservative talk-radio outlets served as both 'cheerleader and megaphone' (Skocpol and Williamson, 2012, p. 121). Clarence Y.H. Lo suggests that Fox News enabled some of the movement's entrepreneurs to engage in 'test marketing' and gauge the ways in which particular Tea Party ideas and themes could be packaged (Lo, 2012, p. 101).

In an account that considers the organizational development of the movement and that is one of a relatively small number that cites social movement literature, Lo distinguishes between a first and second wave of Tea Party mobilizations during 2009. In an echo of the path followed by Students for a Democratic Society (SDS), the leftist movement of the 1960s, it changed its organizational form as it developed. The second wave, which Lo suggests began in mid-April 2009, rested upon 'facilitated mobilization' in which activists utilized established networks. Many of these were tied to the conservative movement and bodies such as the Young Republicans but also included campaign structures, lists of donors to particular candidates and causes, as well as social networking and blogs (ibid., p. 99). The second wave also shaped the organizational character of the movement and gave it a 'decentralized and federated mode of organization'. This enabled the different factions within the movement and social movement organizations to secure a 'marginal autonomy' from both conservative organizations and Republican Party constituencies (ibid.).

The different social movement organizations (SMOs) should be understood within the context of the 'second wave'. The Tea Party Patriots (which seeks 'to attract, educate, organize, and mobilize our fellow citizens to secure public policy consistent with our three core values of Fiscal Responsibility, Constitutionally Limited Government and free markets'[7]) perhaps commands the most extensive support. It claimed 2800 local affiliates in 2010 and, according to a canvass of Tea Party groups conducted by *The Washington Post* in October 2010, this represented almost a third (32 per cent) of local groups (Miller and Walling, 2012, p. 11). The Tea Party Express claimed 200 local affiliates and a membership of 400 000. For its part Tea Party Nation said that it had 445 affiliates and 33 000 members (*Washington Post*, 2010). Forty-two per cent of local Tea Party groups were, however, unaffiliated (ibid.).

Although they enjoy a degree of autonomy, there were ties between these organizations and established interests within the conservative movement. Indeed, a significant proportion of accounts, particularly those that lean towards an 'astroturf' perspective argue that, if only by implication, the different Tea Party groupings should not be regarded as SMOs but instead simply as 'add-ons' or extensions of conservative organizations. They note claims, for example, that the Tea Party Patriots has close ties with FreedomWorks[8] and its parent organization, Americans for Prosperity (AFP) as well as American Solutions for Winning the Future, an advocacy organization established by Newt Gingrich, (the former House of Representatives Speaker who sought the Republican presidential nomination in 2012), and the American Liberty Alliance (Brant-Zawadzki and Teo, 2009). The Tea Party Express was created in the summer of 2009 through the efforts of a political action committee and a Republican-leaning consulting and public relations firm. It went on to raise and donate more than 2.7 million dollars to election candidates during 2009 and 2010 (Skocpol and Williamson, 2012, pp. 106–7).

There are, however, dangers in overstating these ties. Accounts can, if only by implication, assign too much structural coherence to the movement and exaggerate the strength of its relationships with its allies. The relationships between SMOs and the movement at local or grassroots level have often been relatively weak, strained and subject to contestation. Lisa Disch identifies different layers or strata within it. She points first to grassroots activists using social networking sites so as to create 'protest actors', second, to 'elite established elements' such as lobbying and consulting firms or other pre-existing organizations within the Republican orbit, third, to 'populist established elements' within which she includes militia groups and those who share a 'John Bircher discourse' and fourth, media elements, most notably Fox News but also including blogs and other outlets (Disch, 2011, p. 127).[9]

A further caveat should be entered. Although many of the studies emphasize political relationships, particularly those there have been suggestions that some Tea Party SMOs are not so much policy entrepreneurs but are instead pursuing more traditional forms of entrepreneurialism. They are, it is said, securing revenue from grassroots activists. There was disquiet when the National Tea Party Convention was held in February 2010. There was a $550 ticket price and reports suggested that the billed speakers would each be paid $100 000 (NBC News, 2010). There were also claims that there was continual pressure on local activists to give money to national organizations and submit their contact lists so that national databases could be created and used for other, often commercial, purposes (Mencimer, 2011).

THE FRAMES AND DISCOURSES OF THE TEA PARTY MOVEMENT

Studies of the frames and forms of discourse used by Tea Party activists and groups are for the most part fragmentary. Often, the movement's thinking has been said to amount to little. Indeed, it has been described in brutal terms as a Twitter feed in search of an ideology (quoted in Miller and Walling, 2012, p. 5).[10] Nonetheless, the movement's ideas and, in particular, the frames that it crystallized around and deployed have a breadth and substance that are not immediately evident. They played a significant part in explaining the movement's emergence and later take-off into self-sustained growth.

David Snow and Robert Benford's threefold categorization of collective action frames can be employed. The diagnostic frame around which the Tea Party movement took shape pointed to bloated or 'big government', which, it was said, not only posed a threat to the liberty of the citizen but through 'crowding out' displaced private sector economic activity and thereby impeded recovery from the recession. The answer (the prognostic frame) lay in institutional and extra-institutional resistance to the measures being pursued by the Obama administration, most notably healthcare reform. The movement's motivational frame (structured around reasons to join processes of collective action) was built around the seeming weakness and vulnerability of the Obama administration and Congressional Democrats as well as the openness of Republican Party structures to change through, for example, primaries.

Such constructions gained credence and traction in January 2010 when Scott Brown won the special Senate election held in Massachusetts following Edward Kennedy's death. The Massachusetts election had a two-fold significance. First, the Republicans won through, it was said, the movement's campaigning efforts in a state that had traditionally been solid Democratic political territory. Second, Brown's victory denied the Democrats a filibuster-proof, 60-seat majority in the Senate, thereby making the passage of legislation very difficult indeed.

William Gamson's classification of collective action frames offers a basis for analysis. He has argued that if a frame is to motivate political action, it must incorporate a sense of injustice, agency and identity (Gamson, 1993, pp. 31–109). Most studies of the Tea Party movement do not consciously or explicitly address the construction and purpose of frames or categorizations such as these are implicitly related to them.

Injustice

The Tea Party movement's perceptions and discourses were structured around a sense of political, economic and cultural injustice and dispossession. They drew in the first instance upon the belief that there had been a process of political usurpation as government seemed to secure greater powers. At times, this edged towards conspiracy theories. In his accounts of Tea Party activities published in *Rolling Stone*, Matt Taibbi talked of the influence of Congressmen Ron Paul and his son, Rand Paul, who was elected to the Senate in November 2010, and the ways they popularized the belief (although such ideas were already common currency among sections of the radical right) that US sovereignty was under threat:

> [B]oth Paul and his father preached about the apocalyptic arrival of a '10-lane colossus' NAFTA superhighway between the U.S. and Mexico, which the elder Paul said would be the width of several football fields and come complete with fiber-optic cable, railroads, and oil and gas pipelines, all with the goal of forging a single American-Mexican state. (Taibbi, 2010)

Fears of 'big government' and a loss of sovereignty overlapped with hostility towards the 'new class' that appeared to have captured the machinery of government and the highly educated elites that constituted a significant fraction within that class. At times, there was a populist scepticism towards expertise itself (Skocpol and Williamson, 2012, pp. 52–4).[11] This taps a vein that has long characterized US political culture.[12] In his 1963 book *Anti-Intellectualism in American Life*, Richard Hofstadter suggests that suspicion of intellect that has informed many movements is rooted in evangelical faith. Although once tied to anti-urbanity it has to some extent been brought forward into urban settings. The Tea Party movement's understanding of the 'new class' was also allied, perhaps unconsciously, with the concepts associated with public choice theory insofar as the movement's critiques often incorporate the idea of government expansion and aggrandizement by self-serving bureaucrats. As David Brooks, the *New York Times* columnist, has noted:

> The tea party movement is a large, fractious confederation of Americans who are defined by what they are against. They are against the concentrated power of the educated class. They believe big government, big business, big media and the affluent professionals are merging to form self-serving oligarchy – with bloated government, unsustainable deficits, high taxes and intrusive regulation. (Brooks, 2010)

Hostility to the 'new class' intertwined with other themes. Like many earlier movements of the radical and populist right, the Tea Party movement marshalled 'producerist' notions (Formisano, 2012, p. 20). As Lauren Langman and George Lundskow note, 'this ideology has been a part of right populist culture for many decades' (Langman and Lundskow, 2012, p. 591). Chip Berlet has pointed to the ways in which Tea Party producerism is structured around particular representations of Otherness that portray producers under threat: 'The producerist storyline claims that heroic "productive" middle-class stalwarts are defending themselves against the squeezing vise grip of corrupt parasitic elites above and lazy, sinful and subversive parasites below' (Berlet, 2012, p. 568).[13]

Theda Skocpol and Vanessa Williamson talk in similar terms by referring to the movement's representations of 'workers versus freeloaders' (Skocpol and Williamson, 2012, pp. 64–8). Non-producers (or 'freeloaders') include elites (such as those who are highly educated and in some accounts finance capital) and those at the lowest end of the socioeconomic scale who are often seen as purposively unproductive. Such representations are tied to notions of an 'underclass' locked, despite radical welfare reform legislation in 1996, into dependency upon government largesse.

The structural distinction between producers and non-producers has informed the movement's perceptions of federal and state government programmes. Despite its defining commitment to 'small government', there is a significant degree of support for, or at least acquiescence towards, government programmes that appear to be directed towards those who are productive and therefore in some senses 'deserving'. In contrast, provision given to non-producers is regarded as illegitimate. As Williamson et al. (2011, p. 1) record: 'Tea Partiers are not monolithically hostile toward government; they distinguish between programs perceived as going to hard-working contributors to US society like themselves and "handouts" perceived as going to unworthy or freeloading people'.

Such sentiments intersect with racial discourses. As a group, the poor, particularly if understood as an 'underclass', includes disproportionate numbers drawn from the ethnic and racial minorities:

> Opposition is concentrated on resentment of perceived federal government 'handouts' to 'undeserving' groups, the definition of which seems heavily influenced by racial and ethnic stereotypes. More broadly, Tea Party concerns exist within the context of anxieties about racial, ethnic, and generational changes in American society. (Williamson et al., 2011, p. 26)

There are data to support this. In the 2010 *New York Times* and CBS News survey, 25 per cent of Tea Party respondents said that the Obama administration 'favored blacks over whites' (compared with 11 per cent of the general population) (*New York Times*/CBS News, 2010, p. 24). Significantly, rather higher numbers of Tea Party supporters (82 per cent) saw illegal immigration as a 'very serious' problem (compared to 60 per cent of the general population) (Skocpol and Williamson, 2012, p. 57). There is also evidence that disproportionate numbers in the movement think in terms of negative racially based stereotypes. Sixty-eight per cent of Tea Party whites agreed with the statement that 'if Blacks would just try harder they would be as well off as Whites' while only 35 per cent of non-Tea Party whites agreed (Zeskind, 2011, p. 502).

Furthermore, there appears to be a spillover effect between racialized representations of an unproductive underclass and reactions to President Obama himself. Indeed, some accounts of the movement are structured around claims that the Tea Party was, in large part, a racialized response to Obama's election victory in November 2008.[14]

In some instances, assertions such as these have not been based upon direct primary evidence but instead on the application of a particular logic to the claims made by the movement or efforts to discern 'underlying' motives. Nonetheless, polling data suggest that 'Birtherism' (the racially tinged belief that President Obama was not born in the USA and is therefore not constitutionally eligible to serve as president) has some resonance within the movement. An April 2011 poll found that 45 per cent of Tea Party supporters believed that Obama was born in another country. Only 34 per cent accepted that the president had been born in the USA (Condon, 2011). Some of the scholarly literature addresses the political significance of Obama himself although it is often understood in terms of its interaction with other variables. Alan Abramowitz notes:

> Obama's mixed racial heritage, his ambitious policy agenda, and the extraordinarily diverse coalition of liberals, you people, and racial minorities that

supported him in 2008 all contributed to a powerful negative reaction on the part of many economic and social conservatives aligned with the Republican Party and perhaps among whites who were simply upset about having a black man in the White House. (Abramowitz, 2012, p. 196)

Leonard Zeskind also stresses what he regards as the racial component to the movement's thinking and activities. He argues that 'the self-evident signs of racial animus have been omnipresent at Tea Party events' (Zeskind, 2011, p. 500). Furthermore, he argues, the movement's commitment to the original Constitution of 1787, the contents and character of which reflected the inegalitarian context within which it was written, is in itself an assertion of a racial hierarchy: 'By making an exclusionary claim on the nation's founding moments, they actually set themselves apart from other Americans' (ibid., p. 495).

Alongside race, the movement's discourses also have a generational edge. The movement's ranks were disproportionately drawn from the older age cohorts. In April 2010, a poll found that just 7 per cent of Tea Party supporters were in the 18–29 age bracket. Seventy-five per cent were aged between 45 and 64. Twenty-nine per cent were aged over 64 (*New York Times*/CBS News, 2010, p. 41). Theda Skocpol and Vanessa Williamson suggest that the movement rests in part on concerns that younger people are to some degree also workshy: 'young people feature prominently in the stories Tea Partiers tell about undeserving freeloaders, and anecdotes about people in their own families sometimes stand in for larger generational tensions' (Skocpol and Williamson, 2012, p. 72). Arguably, such sentiments are tied to the growing numbers of young people who live at home or remain financially dependent upon their parents (Shah, 2013).

Skocpol's comments can be situated within the analysis of American political development that stresses the uneven and partial character of government social provision and the political configurations that this has created in its wake. In contrast with many countries of Europe, US provision is structured around tax concessions (rather than direct forms of government expenditure) and the intersection between the public and private spheres. For example, many employers provide health coverage while senior citizens are supported through Medicare and some of those in low-income groupings are assisted by Medicaid. Within this context, different constituencies perceive their interests in very different and often competing ways. There were fears among seniors that Medicare would be 'diluted' if health provision was extended (through 'Obamacare') to other groupings (Saad, 2010).

Just as some see a racialized component and a generational edge in the

Tea Party movement's perceptions of injustice and dispossession, others point to the ways in which they were informed by particular notions of morality and faith. They emphasize the movement's 'borrowing' of frames and discourses from the Christian right. From the late 1970s onwards, the Republican right and much of the conservative movement had been heavily influenced by religious conservatism. Christian right organizations such as the Moral Majority, the Christian Coalition and the Family Research Council had put forward a political agenda structured around moral traditionalism, 'family values', as well as opposition to abortion. Such an agenda implied a substantial degree of government intervention and regulation within some social spheres.[15]

Tea Party supporters and the Christian right both shared a sense that traditional principles and that defined American identity were under siege. Furthermore, the Tea Party movement's embrace of 'constitutional government' was, perhaps paradoxically, allied with the belief that the state had a part to play in upholding the principles underpinning a 'Christian nation'. Sixty-three per cent of movement respondents in a 2010 Public Religion Research Institute (PRRI) study said that abortion should be illegal in all or most cases and just 18 per cent supported same-sex marriage (Jones and Cox, 2010, p. 4). In an article based upon participant observation, Angelia Wilson and Cynthia Burack take the argument a stage further and conclude that the Tea Party movement brought economic and moral issues together. It thereby unified the right in a single, but arguably loose and unstable, frame. Wilson and Burack assert that the Tea Party movement served as:

> the most conspicuous contemporary vehicle for reconciliation between Christian and economic conservatives...the Christian right elites are willing to accommodate strategically the precedence of economic issues but only if these are accompanied by a commitment to familiar Christian right positions on social issues. (Wilson and Burack, 2012, p. 172)[16]

These ideational associations between the Tea Party movement and the Christian right were bolstered by interlocking networks and significant overlaps of individual activists. The 2010 PRRI survey conducted found that 47 per cent of those who regarded themselves as 'part the Tea Party movement' also defined themselves as being 'part of the Christian conservative movement' (Jones and Cox, 2010, p. 3). In a nuanced account Chip Berlet suggests that religious conservatives (and other more radical rightist strands) came to the fore once the movement had become established: 'At first much of the energy for organizing the grassroots portion of the Tea Party movement came from libertarians and supporters of Ron Paul. Over time, participants in the pre-existing Christian Right and

Patriot Movements emerged as playing an increasingly significant role in local units and chapters of the Tea Party movement' (Berlet, 2012, p. 566).

Identity

The movement's self-representations and the inter-subjective meanings around which it was constructed rested on notions of a citizenry reclaiming its rights from oppressive and tyrannical government. Its use of the Gadsden flag (depicting a coiled but ready rattlesnake and the words 'Don't tread on me') on rallies, in leaflets and on websites, is significant. The images date from the revolutionary war but were tied to more contemporary populist themes. There were, in other words, processes of cultural *bricolage*, whereby old elements are recombined and mixed together with new elements.[17]

Citizenship, by definition, imposes boundaries. The notions of inclusion and exclusion introduced by producerist notions have already been noted. Those who seemingly fail to contribute, either because they belong to an underclass or the political and administrative elites, are non-producers. There are echoes of the possessive individualism that C.B. Macpherson depicted in his classic study of seventeenth-century liberalism whereby some are, or have seemed to place themselves, outside the ranks of citizenship (Macpherson, 2010).

Arguably, the movement's definitions of identity are also structured by gender. Although, as noted above, disproportionate numbers of Tea Party supporters endorsed positions, including an attachment to the traditional family and notions of wives as 'caretakers', associated with social conservatism and the Christian right, studies suggest that women were well represented amongst committed activists. Women were 'disproportionately active in running the Tea Party ground game' (Skocpol and Williamson, 2012, p. 43). In this, as Skocpol and Williamson note, the Tea Party movement is similar to many other forms of civic activism.

Women were not only visible in the 'ground game'. Former Alaska governor Sarah Palin, the Republicans' vice-presidential candidate in 2008, was a political lodestar for many. Indeed, she remained such until announcing in October 2011 that she would not contest the 2012 presidential election. Congresswoman Michele Bachmann, who represented Minnesota's sixth district mounted a bid for the Republican presidential nomination until withdrawing at the beginning of 2012.

The role of those women who were defined and sometimes defined themselves as 'Mama Grizzlies' has been given some attention. Data suggest that grassroots Republican voters are significantly less likely to support a woman candidate in the party's primaries. Indeed, a 2003 study found that there was a 13.6 per cent drop in support among male Republican voters if the candidate was female. Among Republican women, the drop was smaller but still 'quite powerful' (cited in Schreiber, 2012, p. 553). This may be because of straightforward prejudice, a belief (particularly amongst social conservatives) that mothers should be at home with young children, or an assumption that women will hold more liberal positions than men.[18] Against this background, it may be that Tea Party and Republican women, particularly those who are seeking public office, have to assert their conservatism and opposition to 'big government' more vigorously and in a more abrasive way than men. However, at the same time, they do not for the most part represent themselves as 'women candidates'. Often, in campaign advertising, they refer to their marital status but not motherhood (ibid., pp. 557–8). Those (such as Palin and Bachmann) who did emphasize their role as mothers sought to stress the ways in which the actions of the Obama administration had forced them, almost against their will, into the political arena.

The political and personal abrasiveness that Tea Party women were perhaps compelled to employ when projecting themselves made them movement favourites. However, at the same time, it limited their broader electoral appeal. In the November 2010 mid-term elections, Sharon Angle and Christine O'Donnell, the Republicans' Senate candidates in Nevada and Delaware respectively, secured enthusiastic backing within the movement but went down to defeat in the general election. Both had a long record of injudicious statements that were used to discredit them and cast significant doubts upon their political credibility.

Agency

Collective action also requires a frame structured around a recognition that conditions can be changed through such action and pointing the way towards the adoption of particular categories or types of action. Notions of agency (and thereby capacity) interact with representations of particular moments and events that are given a pivotal significance and celebrated in a movement's self-narrative.

Tea Party activists emphasize the place of the 'Santelli rant' in the movement's history. It vividly expressed and conveyed the claim that the movement had its origins in a spontaneous protest against the growth of the state. It compounded and magnified representations of grassroots rebellion. Rick Santelli, a CNBC correspondent made a televised outburst that quickly became a rallying point. Responding to a question on a live broadcast about the Homeowners Affordability and Stability Plan, which offered financial aid to homeowners seeking to avoid foreclosure, Santelli asked those around him:

> How many of you people want to pay for your neighbour's mortgage who has an extra bathroom and can't pay their bills?. . . President Obama, are you listening?. . . We're thinking about having a Chicago tea party in July. All of you of capitalists that want to show up to Lake Michigan, I'm going to start organizing it. (Quoted in McCain, 2009)

THE MOVEMENT'S IMPACTS

What has been the overall impact of the Tea Party movement? Social movement studies distinguish between the different forms of impact that a social movement can make.

First, the movement made 'procedural' impacts insofar it has hardened out many of the openings the US political process offers to organized interests and movements. Commentators have often noted the porosity of the American state. It has a sprawling character particularly when taken together with a party system that is structured by intense partisanship but that is still in many ways organizationally fragmented. The Tea Party movement ensured that the Republican 'establishment' (as the party's elites in Washington DC and the state capitals have been dubbed) is subject to greater accountability by grassroots activism. Put another way, the processes of 'party decline' over recent decades weakened precinct and other local-level forms of organization. Although it insisted upon its independence from the Republican Party, the Tea Party movement rebuilt conservative networks that not only campaigned and canvassed but also at the same time checked the party's elites.[19]

Second, the movement had 'structural' impacts. It changed the structure of political opportunity and the character of the coalitional blocs that formed or might otherwise have taken shape. Matt Guardino and Dean Snyder, who write from a class-based perspective, argue that the Tea Party movement sought to hold neoliberalism and the neoliberal bloc together in the face of calls for greater government interventionism and redistributive forms of politics. In other words, it sought to pull back those who might otherwise, under the weight of the prolonged economic crisis and calls for a bipartisan response, have turned to the interventionist or demand-led forms of policy canvassed by many Democrats:

> We argue that the Tea Party serves a specific political purpose: to hold together the New Right coalition, consisting of business elites allied with elements of the white middle and working classes, in the face of the financial crisis of 2008 and subsequent Great Recession. (Guardino and Snyder, 2012, pp. 527–8)

The movement, they argue, has sought to mobilize the white middle and lower-income groupings so as to drive the remaining Republican moderates out of the party, thereby preventing the formation of a cross-partisan coalitional bloc that might, particularly after the Democrats took control of Congress (2007) and the White House (2009), have coalesced around higher tax rates (so as to reduce the government budget deficit) and further regulatory burdens on industry. The goal of the Tea Party movement, and the authoritarian populist discourses with which it was associated, Guardino and Snyder suggest, was to prevent a retreat from the neoliberal policy regime that had become increasingly embedded from the 1970s onwards (ibid., p. 531).

Third, the movement had 'substantive' impacts. These can take two forms. First, there are what have been termed 'reactive' impacts. A movement can prevent or impede the emergence of 'new disadvantages'. The Tea Party movement, for example, ensured that Republican members of Congress stood more or less firm against the legislation pursued by the Obama administration and the Congressional Democrats. While it could not prevent the passage of health care reform ('Obamacare') in 2010 (which was only enacted using the arcane process of 'reconciliation') movement activities contributed to the dropping of some of its more radical components, most notably the 'public option'. This would have created government health insurance in competition with the private sector.

There were also 'proactive' impacts. In particular, the movement fuelled a shift in character of Congressional representation. Once those elected in November 2010 had taken their seats, 64 members of the Republican conference in the House of Representatives (which totalled 242 members) joined the Tea Party caucus that had been formed in July 2010 by Michele Bachmann (Miller et al., 2012, p. 365).[20] Furthermore, as Clarence Lo notes, the political impact of the movement will be evident in the years to come through the election of figures such as Senators Marco Rubio and Rand Paul (Lo, 2012, p. 118).[21]

Fourth, movements have 'sensitizing' impacts. In other words, their thinking and activities influence other political actors and public opinion more broadly. Through the efforts of Tea Party activists, as well as other conservative organizations and outlets, opinion on healthcare reform shifted markedly during 2009. In February 2009, according to a poll conducted by the Kaiser Family Foundation, just 11 per cent of respondents felt that they and their families would be 'worse off' if healthcare reform was enacted. By August the figure had risen to 31 per cent (PollingReport. com, 2013a, p. 5). Nonetheless, if more generalized and longer-run trends are considered, the movement's impact may have been more limited. Gallup asked 'Do you think the federal government today has too much power, has about the right amount of power, or has too little power?' Although not particularly marked, there was a fall in the proportion of respondents believing that the federal government had 'too much power' (from 59 per cent to 54 per cent) between September 2010 and May 2013 (PollingReport.com, 2013b). If anything, therefore, the movement lost impetus. This seems to have reflected the relative buoyancy of President Obama's approval ratings, a degree of movement exhaustion, and increasing tensions within the conservative right as national security issues came to the fore. Whereas some, most notably Senator Rand Paul, drew on the libertarian tradition to stress the threat that surveillance systems posed to individual freedoms others emphasized the continuing dangers posed by terrorism.

CONCLUSIONS AND SUGGESTIONS FOR FURTHER RESEARCH

Right-wing movements in the USA have a chequered history. Some have sustained and reproduced themselves. Despite ebbs and flows, the Christian right, which emerged in the 1970s around issues such as abortion and homosexuality, has maintained an existence over almost 40 years. Insofar as it constitutes a 'movement', the gun lobby is a more or less permanent fixture within the US political process. Others, however, such as the 'anti-tax revolt' or overt efforts to hold back minority rights have proved less durable or, as in the case of the former, were subsumed within broader movements. The militia movement, which secured widespread attention in the 1990s, lost much of its earlier élan.

In some respects, the Tea Party movement has always been rather fragile. As has been noted, many movement organizations depend upon established conservative networks. High levels of activism, which to a degree defined the movement's self-representations, are invariably difficult to sustain. Furthermore, the movement's strategy failed to yield the political dividends that many activists had sought. In 2012, a candidate who many regarded with suspicion was picked as Republican presidential candidate and then lost a race with President Obama that many on the right had expected him to win. Given this, there are reasons to think that the movement will share the traditional fate of minor parties. As Richard Hofstadter noted in 1955, they are 'like bees. . .once they have stung, they die'. Furthermore, towards the end of 2013, there were clear signs that the Republican 'establishment' was reasserting itself after the failure of efforts to defund the Affordable Care Act and prevent an increase in the federal government debt ceiling. It seemed that once a threshold had been passed in terms of their numbers, more mainstream Republicans were less fearful of primary challenges by Tea Party-aligned candidates.

Notwithstanding this, however, there were signs in 2013, once the dust from the presidential election had settled, that the movement had a more durable character than commentators had suggested. Media revelations that the Internal Revenue Service had targeted Tea Party and other conservative groups that had applied for tax-exempt status reinvigorated fears of oppressive government and donations to networks such as the Tea Party Patriots sharply increased (Langley, 2013). The movement also mobilized against the administration's determination to take military action in Syria. There were at the same time indications that leading Congressional Republicans were likely to face credible primary challenges by Tea Party-backed candidates (Steinhauer, 2013). The structural openness of the US parties and the policy tensions within the contemporary right, stretching across immigration, fiscal policy and the role of government more broadly, may sustain the movement for years to come. And, if Tea Partiers can come together around one candidate at an early stage in the 2016 presidential primaries, they could be well placed to shape the nominating process.

Further research could usefully draw upon some of the less familiar subfields within political science. There is, as this chapter has argued, a relationship between the movement's discourses and logics and the structural characteristics of the American state. Its historical development created particular patterns of group competition while its porousness constitutes an 'invitation to struggle'. At the same time, the movement's leverage over the Republican Party has important implications for the future of the party system and the patterns of electoral competition. Thus, future research may well go beyond social movement literature and instead be situated within American Political Development (APD) and theories of electoral behaviour.[22]

NOTES

1. John Green, James Guth and Clyde Wilcox are an exception. They treat the Christian right as a social movement (Green et al., 1998, p. 117). William Miller and Jeremy Walling refer to the Tea Party movement as a 'hybrid social movement' (Miller and Walling, 2012, p. 8).
2. Those who argue in this way can point to an April 2010 poll conducted for the *New York Times* and CBS News. It found that only 13 per cent of supporters had attended a meeting or rally while just 2 per cent had given money. A further 5 per cent said that they had done both. More than three-quarters (78 per cent) said that they had done neither (*New York Times*/CBS News, 2010, p. 33).
3. There are, however, tensions between Republican Party elites. Whereas some embraced

and funded the movement others feared that its tactics might have, if unchecked, damaging electoral consequences.
4. Buckley, who died in 2008, was the founder of the *National Review* and has been described as the conservative 'Pope'.
5. As an illustration Hofstadter cited the celebrated claim by Robert Welch, founder of the John Birch Society who asserted that President Dwight Eisenhower was 'a dedicated, conscious agent of the Communist conspiracy' (quoted in Hofstadter [1964] 1996, p. 28).
6. This account, which stands in contrast to those that represent the Tea Party movement as a reaction against those most severely hit by economic shifts, has to be squared with empirical surveys of the movement indicating that participants were drawn from more affluent groupings and older age cohorts (*The New York Times*/CBS News, 2010, p. 41).
7. Tea Party Patriots of Jessamine County mission statement, accessed 26 May 2014 at http://www.teapartypatriots.org/groups/tea-party-patriots-of-jessamine-county/.
8. FreedomWorks is led by former Republican House of Representatives Majority Leader Dick Armey.
9. A question mark can be put against claims that there was a 'Bircher' component within the movement. The point is more often asserted than supported.
10. To an extent, and Theda Skocpol and Vanessa Williamson note, the movement draws upon beliefs that have a resonance with the general population (Skocpol and Williamson, 2012, p. 47).
11. The term 'populism' should, however, be used with a degree of caution. Although populism can take left- and right-wing forms, it often incorporates hostility to financial as well as political elites. There has, however, been only limited evidence of opposition to Wall Street among Tea Party activists and supporters.
12. Charles Postel questions accounts that describe the Tea Party movement as 'populist'. The US populist tradition, he argues, has long been tied to progressivism and calls to 'spread the wealth' (Postel, 2012, p. 28).
13. Charles Postel rejects the application of the concept of 'producerism' to Tea Party thinking. It, he argues 'sends only occasional barbs toward the corporate executives, bankers, and lobbyists, who in the past were the systematic targets of "producerist" movements. Instead, today's Tea Party usually celebrates the corporate elites as heroes of the market' (Postel, 2012, p. 33). The contrast with past movements is, of course, valid but movements often redraw the boundaries (in this case between producers and non-producers) and redefine the character of the 'Other' that exist within particular ideational traditions.
14. Studies suggest that some voting patterns in the 2008 presidential elections had a racial edge. Gary Segura and Ali Valenzuela conclude in their analysis of the impact of racial resentment on the Obama campaign that '(m)ultivariate models of the two-party vote and evaluation of Obama reflect the consistent and substantial negative impact of racial animus, as captured by the racial resentment battery of questions' (Segura and Valenzuela, 2010, p. 511).
15. Successive Republican presidents and Congressional leaders sought to reconcile or at least accommodate these tensions.
16. Some scholars and commentators have a different perspective. They argue that the emergence of the Tea Party movement appeared to constitute a radical shift towards economic issues and the forms of 'small government' sought by libertarianism and a move away from moral and cultural issues. Gerald Russello notes that: 'The heat of the culture wars of the 1980s has lessened, and the conservative and libertarian members of the Tea Party share a desire to reduce the size and reach of government' (Russello, 2012, p. 42).
17. The concept of *bricolage* has been discussed (within the context of institutional change) by John Campbell (Campbell, 2004, pp. 69–74).
18. There is evidence that Republican voters were particularly reluctant to back childless women candidates (Schreiber, 2012, p. 553).

19. Up until the birth of the Tea Party movement, as Williamson et al. note, grassroots conservatism had been largely tied to the Christian right and faith-based organizations (Williamson et al., 2011, p. 27).
20. At the beginning of January 2013, the caucus had 49 members.
21. Few would contest the claim that the movement also had a negative impact on the Republicans' electoral fortunes. Christine O'Donnell's capture of the Republican Senate nomination in Delaware, and her subsequent defeat in the general election, has been widely noted. In a race that the Republicans might have expected to win, Sharon Angle failed to dislodge Senate Majority Leader Harry Reid in Nevada. In the 2012 presidential election, some attribute Mitt Romney's defeat to the rightward positions that he was compelled to adopt during the long primary season.
22. For an account of American Political Development (APD), see Orren and Skowronek (2002).

REFERENCES

Abramowitz, A.I. (2012), 'Grand old tea party: partisan polarization and the rise of the tea party movement', in L. Rosenthal and C. Trost (eds), *Steep: The Precipitous Rise of the Tea Party*, Berkeley and Los Angeles, CA: University of California Press, pp. 195–211.

Baker, K. (2012), 'Angry white men: can the G.O.P. genuinely change its attitude toward minorities and women?', *Harper's Magazine*, 8 November, accessed 18 May 2014 at http://harpers.org/blog/2012/11/angry-white-men/.

Bell, D. (1963), *The Radical Right: The New American Right Expanded and Updated*, New York: Doubleday and Company.

Berlet, C. (2010), 'Taking tea partiers seriously', *The Progressive*, February 2010, accessed 18 May 2014 at http://www.progressive.org/berlet0210c.html.

Berlet, C. (2012), 'Collectivists, communists, labor bosses, and treason: the Tea Parties as right-wing populist counter-subversion panic', *Critical Sociology*, **38**(4), 565–87.

Borchert, S. and A. DiMaggio (2011), 'Thoughts on the Tea Party: interview with Anthony DiMaggio', *Monthly Review Press*, accessed 18 May 2014 at http://monthlyreview.org/press/interviews/thoughts-on-the-tea-party/.

Brant-Zawadzki, A. and D. Teo (2009), 'Anatomy of the Tea Party movement: Tea Party Patriots', *Huffington Post – The Blog*, 11 December, accessed 18 May 2014 at http://www.huffingtonpost.com/alex-brantzawadzki/anatomy-of-the-tea-party_b_380567.html.

Brooks, D. (2010), 'The Tea Party teens', *The New York Times*, 4 January, accessed 18 May 2014 at http://www.nytimes.com/2010/01/05/opinion/05brooks.html?_r=0.

Campbell, J.L. (2004), *Institutional Change and Globalization*, Princeton, NJ: Princeton University Press.

Condon, S. (2011), 'Poll: one in four Americans think Obama was not born in US', CBS News, 21 April, accessed 18 April 2014 at http://archive.wtsp.com/rss/article/188192/81/Poll-1-in-4-think-Obama-was-not-born-in-US.

Disch, L. (2011), 'Tea Party movement: the American "precariat"', *Representation*, **47**(2), 123–35.

Edwards, B. and J.D. McCarthy (2003), 'Resources and social movement mobilization', in D.A. Snow, S.A. Soule and H. Kriesi, *The Blackwell Companion to Social Movements*, Oxford: Wiley-Blackwell, pp. 116–52.

Formisano, R.P. (2012), *The Tea Party*, Baltimore, MD: The Johns Hopkins Press.

Gamson, W.A. (1993), *Talking Politics*, Cambridge, UK: Cambridge University Press.

Green, J.C., J.L. Guth and C. Wilcox (1998), 'Less than conquerors: the Christian right in state Republican parties', in A.M. Costain and A.S. McFarland, *Social Movements and American Political Institutions*, Lanham, MD: Rowman & Littlefield, pp. 117–35.

Guardino, M. and D. Snyder (2012), 'The Tea Party and the crisis of neoliberalism:

mainstreaming new right populism in the corporate news media', *New Political Science*, **34**(4), 527–48.
Hacker, J.S. (2008), *The Great Risk Shift: The New Economic Insecurity and the Decline of the American Dream*, Oxford: Oxford University Press.
Hofstadter, R. (1963), *Anti-Intellectualism in American Life*, New York: Knopf.
Hofstadter, R. ([1964] 1996), *The Paranoid Style in American Politics and Other Essays*, Cambridge: Harvard University Press.
Jones, R.P. and D. Cox (2010), *Religion and the Tea Party in the 2010 Election: An Analysis of the Third Biennial American Values Survey*, Public Religion Research Institute, accessed 18 May 2014 at http://publicreligion.org/site/wp-content/uploads/2010/05/Religion-and-the-Tea-Party-in-the-2010-Election-American-Values-Survey.pdf.
Kroft, S. (2012), 'The pledge: Grover Norquist's hold on the GOP', CBS News, 26 August 2012, accessed 18 May 2014 at http://www.cbsnews.com/8301-18560_162-57497502/the-pledge-grover-norquists-hold-on-the-gop/.
Langley, M. (2013), 'Powered by outrage at the IRS, the Tea Party makes a comeback', *The Wall Street Journal*, 28 August, A1, A12.
Langman, L. and G. Lundskow (2012), 'Down the rabid hole to a tea party', *Critical Sociology*, **38**(4), 589–97.
Lerer, L. and A. Fitzgerald (2010), 'Tea Party wins house for Republicans, wants rewards in Congress', *Bloomberg*, 4 November, accessed 18 May 2014 at http://www.bloomberg.com/news/2010-11-04/tea-party-wins-house-for-republicans-wants-rewards-in-congress.html.
Lipset, S.M. (1960), *Political Man: The Social Bases of Politics*, New York: Doubleday and Company.
Lo, C.Y.H. (2012), 'Astroturf versus grass roots: scenes from early Tea Party mobilization', in L. Rosenthal and C. Trost (eds), *Steep: The Precipitous Rise of the Tea Party*, Berkeley and Los Angeles, CA: University of California Press, pp. 98–130.
Macpherson, C.B. (2010), *The Political Theory of Possessive Individualism: Hobbes to Locke*, Don Mills, ON: Oxford University Press Canada.
Mayer, J. (2010), 'Covert operations', *The New Yorker*, 30 August, accessed 18 May 2014 at http://www.newyorker.com/reporting/2010/08/30/100830fa_fact_mayer.
McCain, R.S. (2009), 'Tea Party nation', *The American Spectator*, 13 November, accessed 18 May 2014 at http://spectator.org/articles/40549/tea-party-nation.
McCarthy, J.D. and M. Zald (1977), 'Resource mobilization and social movements', *The American Journal of Sociology*, **82**(6), 1212–41.
Meagher, R. (2012), 'The "vast right-wing conspiracy": media and conservative networks', *New Political Science*, **34**(4), 469–84.
Mencimer, S. (2011), 'Tea Party Patriots investigated: "They use you and abuse you"', *Mother Jones*, 14 February, accessed 18 May 2014 at http://www.motherjones.com/politics/2011/02/tea-party-patriots-investigated?page=2.
Meyer, D.S. and S. Staggenborg (1996), 'Countermovements, and the structure of political opportunity', *American Journal of Sociology*, **101**(6), 1628–60.
Miller, W.J. and J.D. Walling (2012), 'Tea party redux: making sense of the midterm Senate election', in W.J. Miller and J.D. Walling, *Tea Party Effects on 2010 US Senate Elections*, Lanham, MD: Lexington Books, pp. 351–60.
Miller, W.J., J.D. Walling and B.P. Smentkowski (2012), 'Adding pieces to the chess set: new players for an old game', in W.J. Miller and J.D. Walling, *Tea Party Effects on 2010 US Senate Elections*, Lanham, MD: Lexington Books, pp. 361–74.
Moran, N. (2008), 'William F. Buckley, leading conservative, dies at 82', *Bloomberg*, 27 February, accessed 18 May 2014 at http://www.bloomberg.com/apps/news?pid=newsarchive&sid=aFkLZtr5m_ZQ.
NBC News (2010), 'Tea Party Convention loses speakers, steam', NBC News, 29 January, accessed 18 May 2014 at http://www.nbcnews.com/id/35126561/ns/politics-more_politics/t/tea-party-convention-loses-speakers-steam/.
New York Times/CBS News (2010), *National Survey of Tea Party Supporters*, 5–12

April, accessed 18 May 2014 at http://documents.nytimes.com/new-york-timescbs-news-poll-national-survey-of-tea-party-supporters?ref=politics.
Orren, K. and S. Skowronek (2002), 'The study of American Political Development', in I. Katznelson and H.V. Milner, *Political Science: The State of the Discipline*, New York: W.W. Norton, pp. 722–54.
PollingReport.com (2013a), *Health Policy*, accessed 18 May 2014 at http://www.pollingreport.com/health5.htm.
PollingReport.com (2013b), *Major Institutions – Government: Federal*, accessed 18 May 2014 at http://www.pollingreport.com/institut.htm#Federal.
Postel, C. (2012), 'The Tea Party in historical perspective', in L. Rosenthal and C. Trost (eds), *Steep: The Precipitous Rise of the Tea Party*, Berkeley and Los Angeles, CA: University of California Press, pp. 25–46.
Robinson, W.I. and M. Barrera (2012), 'Global capitalism and twenty-first century fascism: a US case study', *Race and Class*, **53**(3), **4**, 4–29.
Russello, G.J. (2012), 'The Tea Party and the future of the libertarian–conservative alliance', *Perspectives on Political Science*, 41(1), 41–4.
Saad, L. (2010), 'Verdict on healthcare reform bill still divided', *Gallup Politics*, 22 June, accessed 18 May 2014 at http://www.gallup.com/poll/140981/verdict-healthcare-reform-bill-divided.aspx.
Schreiber, R. (2012), 'Mama Grizzlies compete for office', *New Political Science*, **34**(4), 549–63.
Segura, G.M. and A.A. Valenzuela (2010), 'Hope, tropes and dopes: Hispanic and white racial animus in the 2008 election', *Presidential Studies Quarterly*, **40**(3), 497–514.
Shah, N. (2013), 'More young adults live with parents', *The Wall Street Journal*, 28 August, A2.
Skocpol, T.A. and V. Williamson (2012), *The Tea Party and the Remaking of Republican Conservatism*, Oxford: Oxford University Press.
Snow, D.A., S.A. Soule and H. Kriesi (2003), 'Mapping the terrain', in D.A. Snow, S.A. Soule and H. Kriesi, *The Blackwell Companion to Social Movements*, Oxford: Wiley-Blackwell, pp. 3–16.
Steinhauer, J. (2013), 'G.O.P. senators fail to head off primary challenges by Tea Party rivals', *New York Times*, 30 August, accessed 18 May 2014 at http://www.nytimes.com/2013/08/31/us/politics/gop-senators-fail-to-head-off-tea-party-rivals.html?pagewanted=all&_r=0.
Taibbi, M. (2010), 'The truth about the Tea Party', *Rolling Stone*, 28 September, accessed 18 May 2014 at http://www.rollingstone.com/politics/news/matt-taibbi-on-the-tea-party-20 100928.
Washington Post (2010), 'The top national players in the tea party', *The Washington Post*, accessed 18 May 2014 at http://www.washingtonpost.com/wp-dyn/content/graphic/2010/09/26/GR2010092600175.html?sid=ST2010092600314.
Williamson, V., T. Skocpol and J. Coggin (2011), 'The Tea Party and the remaking of republican conservatism', *Perspectives on Politics*, **9**(1), 25–43.
Wilson, A.R. and C. Burack (2012), '"Where liberty reigns and God is supreme": the Christian right and the Tea Party movement', *New Political Science*, **34**(2), 172–90.
Zernike, K. (2010), *Boiling Mad: Inside Tea Party America*, New York: Times Books.
Zeskind, L. (2011), 'A nation dispossessed: the Tea Party movement and race', *Critical Sociology*, **38**(4), 495–509.

22. The animal rights movement
Lyle Munro*

INTRODUCTION

Despite the long history of animal protection groups and their concern for non-human animals (hereafter simply 'animals'), it is only in the last half-century or so that one can speak of a stratified movement for animal protection consisting of welfarists, liberationists and rightists. Philosophical concerns about animal cruelty predate the contemporary animal rights movement (hereafter the 'animal movement') by several centuries. Compared to the contributions of philosophers from Plato in 400 BC to Singer in 1975, social scientists until very recently have had little interest in or impact on the animal cause. For example, in the emerging field of human-animal studies (HAS), animal issues have largely been confined to a few specialist journals and more recently to edited anthologies of previously published articles (e.g., Wilkie and Inglis, 2007; Flynn, 2008; Arluke and Sanders, 2009). In Wilkie and Inglis, a collection in five volumes of 90 previously published papers, the disciplines of anthropology, geography, sociology, psychology and feminist studies are the main ones represented. However, there are no articles on the politics, ethics and sociology of the animal rights movement and virtually no mention of animal cruelty. Only in the Arluke and Sanders collection is the sociology of the animal movement referred to and then only in four papers from a total of 35 while in Flynn's edited volume of 31 chapters only one paper focuses specifically on the animal movement. Furthermore, given the multitude of studies on racism, sexism and classism, the virtual invisibility in the scholarly literature of 'speciesism' and its consequences for animals is surprising, especially in the context of the massive scale of animal suffering and deaths in what Noske (1989) labels 'the animal industrial complex'.

For most people the concept of animal rights is so alien that the task of the animal movement's leadership is to normalize it: 'If there is a telos of social movement activity', writes Scott, 'then it is the normalization of previously exotic issues and groups' (1990, p. 10). While there are some notable exceptions, most social science writing on 'the animal issue' has focused on animals as inconveniently 'out of place' (e.g., Fine and Christoforides, 1991; Marvin, 2000; Irvine, 2003; Jerolmack, 2008) and dangerous animal rights extremists as 'out of control' (e.g., C. Bryant,

1991; Bryant and Snizek, 1993; Kerasote, 1993; Wolfe, 1993; Dizard, 1994). The present chapter will highlight animal cruelty as a social problem and as the primary grievance of the animal protection movement in its four manifestations (see Figure 22.1).

OVERVIEW OF THE MOST IMPORTANT RESEARCH ENDEAVOURS IN THE FIELD

Robert Agnew (1998) and Cass Sunstein (2000) have lamented social science's neglect of animal issues, describing animal abuse as one of the most seriously neglected moral and legal problems of our time. Few sociologists or political scientists have analysed the animal movement's broad agenda or its grievances. Notable exceptions include Garner (1993, 1998, 2006, 2010) in political science and in sociology Jasper (1997, 1999, 2004) and his colleagues (Jasper and Nelkin, 1992; Jasper and Poulsen, 1995); Benton (1993, 1995); Nibert (2002, 2003), Munro (2005a), Torres (2007) and Cherry (2010). Piers Beirne's innovative ideas as a criminologist along with those of Barbara Noske and Robert Agnew in anthropology and social psychology respectively are also featured briefly in this chapter along with one or two sociologists who are critical of the movement.

According to Barnes (1995) and Crook et al. (1992) the animal movement is a new social movement (NSM) that defends non-human animals as 'subjects of a life' (Regan, 1984) via specific strategies that depend on publicity in the print and electronic media. Together, these two versions indicate *why* the movement exists and *how* it presses its claims. There are, of course, other ways of describing the movement depending on the author's particular stance, whether favourable or unfavourable. The animal movement has been linked to the environmental movement (Eckersley, 1992) and eco-pax movements (Pakulski, 1991) while Sutherland and Nash (1994) see such groups as part of a new environmental cosmology. 'The ecopax movements in the West', write Crook et al., 'attract civil rights campaigners, feminist supporters, animal-liberationists and a host of other groups' (1992, p. 153).

Needless to say, these movements have attracted their share of criticism. Critics include Alan Wolfe (1993) who has attacked the idea of 'speciesm' [sic] and has nominated ecological and animal rights groups as the fastest growing political movements in the West and the most threatening to humanist values and the lifestyles of ordinary people. Meanwhile, Habermas trivializes the concern for animals as sentimentality and dismisses vegetarianism as an irrational taboo (in Vogel, 1996, p. 153) while Tester (1991) offers a profoundly unsociological critique of animal rights as a puritanical cult. More sympathetic analyses of the movement from a number of social scientists are discussed in the next section.

Political Science

According to Robert Garner (2006) the animal welfare ethic is flawed because it does not reject speciesism, the idea that humans are superior to non-human animals. Although he sees the welfarist position as philosophically weak, its political strategy, he argues, is not. It makes sense politically 'to focus on reforms improving the treatment of animals which do not compromise significant human interests, and to engage in campaigns to try and shift perceptions on what is regarded as unnecessary suffering' (Garner, 2006, p. 161).

Garner has recently debated Gary Francione over strategy (in Francione and Garner, 2010) where Garner's preference for improvements in animals' lives via regulation contrasts with Francione's demand for the abolition of all practices involving our use of animals. Garner's view is likely to appeal to most animal protectionists insofar as animal welfare's pursuit of incremental legislation delivers more improvements in our treatment of animals than moral egalitarianism: 'Getting something of what you want is better than nothing' (Garner, 2006, p. 161). This strategy also endorses 'the psychology of small wins' (Weick, 1984) whereby activists are inspired by the success of a political win, no matter how small.

Dutch animal protectionists have perhaps been the most successful campaigners within institutional politics as the Netherlands is the only country in the world with an animal rights party; founded in 2002, it now has over 10 000 members, an impressive number that dwarfs the membership of most political parties in other democratic states. The party is also represented in some state legislatures and local government authorities, a total of 20 elected members in 2009. Its website – www.partyfortheanimals.nl – offers a 13-step course that people can access to learn how to start up an animal party in their country. The idea of a party for animals is so novel, the course observes, that any publicity is good publicity because it raises people's awareness of the plight of animals. However, raising awareness of animal suffering is not enough to achieve lasting improvements in animal welfare as was demonstrated in the recent live animal export controversy in Australia (see Munro, 2014).

Sociology

As noted already, the animal movement as an NSM employs specific strategies that depend on publicity in the mass media. The use of drama and spectacle, often involving scandalizing images, has been a key tactic in achieving mass media exposure for the animal movement; hence Jasper's (1999) emphasis on the importance of morally challenging images, 'extreme rhetoric' and 'moral shocks' in recruiting supporters to the animal rights movement.

In their pioneering book on the animal rights movement, Jasper and Nelkin (1992) identified three movement strands – animal welfarists, pragmatists and fundamentalists – which broadly correspond to the distinctions between animal welfarists, liberationists and rightists adopted in this chapter. Jasper and Nelkin pointed out in a summary table (1992, p. 178) that animal welfarists favour protective legislation (cf. animals as a political issue); pragmatists follow Singer's utilitarianism and use negotiation and compromise (cf. animal abuse as a social problem to be resolved pragmatically and sometimes by confrontation); and fundamentalists employ 'moralistic rhetoric' (cf. animals as a moral or ethical issue). In the latter case, the term 'abolitionists' is a more accurate description of animal rights advocates who seek, by the non-violent means advocated by the rights philosopher Tom Regan (1984), to eliminate all animal exploitation. The term 'fundamentalist' serves better as a label for the uncompromising animal rights extremists in the Radical Animal Liberation Movement (RALM), who use violent tactics to achieve their goals (Fluekiger, 2008).

The Marxist sociologist Benton (1993, 1995) is optimistic that people can be persuaded to see that animals, like humans, have basic needs that any decent society would wish to satisfy. Benton argues that ordinary people will be willing to accept that animals have needs rather than rights. He notes how humans are bound to animals in a variety of social relationships such as in entertainment contexts, zoos and circuses, pet-keeping, as well as the presumed benefits of animal experimentation and intensive farming. Still, in most of these contexts animals are treated as property and not as sentient beings. Benton draws parallels between factory-farmed animals and the conditions of workers in abattoirs and in intensive animal factories. He looks forward to the emergence of 'affective ties of trust, loyalty, compassion and responsibility' (1995, p. 175) in our relations with animals but acknowledges that this is unlikely given that it is against the interests of workers to object to the exploitation of animals dependent as they are on animal-user industries for their employment.

David Nibert (2002, 2003) asserts that the animal movement represents a rejection of oppressive structures of domination including classism, racism, sexism, and especially speciesism; the latter, given its unfamiliarity to most people, has not attracted anything like the first three's vast network of scholarly commentators. In a recent book – *Animals and Sociology* – Kay Peggs (2012) draws on Nibert's stratification thesis to show how the 'otherness' of animals is used to exploit them in much the same way as vulnerable humans are oppressed by their stronger counterparts in terms of race, class and gender dynamics. Peggs devotes a chapter to each of the four main contexts in which animals are exploited: in rural and urban environments, in sport and entertainment, as food, and as research objects in animal experiments. However, only on the topic of animal experimentation does the author acknowledge the animal movement's importance in its long-running campaigns against vivisection.

Bob Torres (2007), like Kay Peggs, utilizes Nibert's work to argue the case for the oppressive hierarchies of domination in class relations, sexism, racism and speciesism. Nibert's 'entanglements of oppression', Torres argues, are underpinned by capitalism, which he believes is chiefly responsible for these injustices. Torres maintains the animal rights movement has failed to comprehend the perniciousness of capitalism and the way it turns living creatures into commodities for profit in factory farms, research laboratories and abattoirs. Torres's solution to undermining exploitative capitalism – the adoption of social anarchism's ideology and tactics along with a vegan lifestyle – is fanciful in the extreme. That said, there is increasing evidence for Elias's (1978) prediction that vegetarianism in the long term will become the dietary future of humanity.

Elizabeth Cherry's (2010) study of animal activists in France and the USA revealed how the concept of 'anti-speciesism' – a term that has failed to catch on outside the movement – was popular among her French informants because of its potential for making common cause with movements against racism and sexism. Cherry analysed the French activists' tactics as physical (e.g., a woman wearing a circus elephant's shackles), discursive (e.g., does a hen have a right to a beak?) and iconographic (foie gras evoked in a poster where ducks and geese force-feed humans). Such tactics, designed to recruit bystanders via moral shocks (Jasper and Poulsen, 1995), may also alienate potential supporters as Cherry acknowledges and as Mika (2006) discovered in a controversial student experiment. Jasper (1997, p. 180) maintains an effective moral shock must have explicit cognitive, emotional and moral dimensions if it is to mobilize supporters; whether or not these conditions are met in some of the more controversial campaigns by the People for the Ethical Treatment of Animals (PETA) is a question that for reasons of space limitations cannot be addressed here (see Mika, 2006 and Munro, 2005b on the efficacy of animal rights strategies and tactics).

Anthropology, Social Psychology, Criminology, Ecofeminism

An additional number of authors deserve mention, however briefly, for their insights about the animal movement from the perspectives of their disciplines. The anthropologist Barbara Noske's (1997) *Beyond Boundaries: Humans and Animals* is an exemplary analysis of animals' lives in factory farms and research laboratories. Cramped in narrow cages and stalls, animals are unable to bond with other animals and even with their offspring such is the total disregard for the misery of animals destined for the slaughterhouse or the research lab. Workers often have powerful unions to go into battle for them against their oppressors, whereas the animals must rely on the goodwill of those sympathetic to their plight.

Robert Agnew's (1998) paper on the causes of animal abuse is an insightful examination of the social psychology of both one-on-one and institutionalized animal cruelty where he discusses the dominant concerns of the animal movement, namely factory farming, animal research and blood sports affecting animals in the wild. Agnew's analysis is unique in its attempt to conceptualize the psychological dimensions of both an individual's and corporate involvement in animal abuse.

The criminologist Piers Beirne (1995, 1999, 2007) is one of the very few in his discipline to take animal abuse seriously. He has written extensively on the neglect of cruelty by his fellow criminologists and criminology's casting of animals as creatures of anthropocentrism and anthropomorphism (1995). While his analysis of animal abuse accords with Nibert's (2002) 'entanglements of oppression' thesis, Beirne goes further by drawing attention to the mass extermination of animals for the social problems of animal homelessness, overpopulation and aggression.

The women's movement, especially the strand known as ecofeminism, broadly sympathizes with animal rights sentiments; furthermore, its philosophical leaders tend to be more forthright than the social science establishment in their defence of animals and their habitat. There is now a large ecofeminist literature on animals and the environment (see Vance, 1993 for an outline and Cudworth, 2003, Chapter 2). The ecofeminist critique is particularly important as a corrective to the animal movement's most prominent philosophers whose preoccupation with rationality and reason, Ruddick (1980) points out, ignores the maternal ethic of care and humility and feelings such as pity and love. For many ecofeminists, the abuse of animals as a social problem is no less deserving of moral condemnation than other, more recognized abusive practices such as racism – and its offshoots ethnic cleansing, slavery, lynchings, hate crimes against people of colour and so on, and sexism with its related violations of bodily integrity including clitoridectomy, rape and wife bashing.

OVERVIEW OF THE MOST IMPORTANT THEORETICAL AND EMPIRICAL RESEARCH RESULTS

Felix Kolb's (2007) comprehensive review of the social movement literature identified the main variables or themes in the majority of studies, namely the strength of the movement, its goals and its tactics, with the latter constituting the movement's strategy. According to Kolb, strategy is one of the most under-theorized topics in social movement theory (p. 45). An attempt to address the deficiency as it applies to the animal movement follows.

Animal protection strategies can be categorized as consisting of two broad choices, each with additional approaches to activism: Publicity (Persuasion and Protest) and Interference (Non-cooperation and Intervention). Four animal protection entities have been selected to represent each of these four strategies: The Party for Animals (Persuasion); Animals Australia (Protest); Vegan Outreach (Non-cooperation) and the World Society for the Protection of Animals – WSPA (Intervention). These political, NGO and SMO entities are also broadly representative of animal advocacy in Holland, Australia, the USA and the UK where WSPA has its headquarters.

As illustrated in Figure 22.1, mainstream animal protectionists come in three main guises –welfarists (e.g., WSPA, RSPCA), liberationists (e.g., Animals Australia) and rightists (e.g., Vegan Outreach, PETA) – with each having its own preferred strategies and tactical repertoires; clearly, the available tactics are often utilized by these different groups while remaining united in their belief that animals are sentient beings rather than property or things to be commodified as food, research tools or sporting trophies.

In anthropocentric thinking, animals deserve kindness rather than rights and their interests are subordinated to the demands of human well-being. This corresponds to the moral orthodoxy of animal welfare that Clark (1997) calls 'the norm of *moderate* concern for animals' (original emphasis). In stark contrast, animal rights proponents demand the *abolition* of animal exploitation, while animal liberation as espoused by Peter Singer (1975, 1990) falls in between these two extremes. As indicated in Figure 22.1 member groups in the RALM are ideologically and programmatically divorced from the mainstream groups. The philosophies of the movement's four strands are described below.

Animal Protection Strategies and Tactics

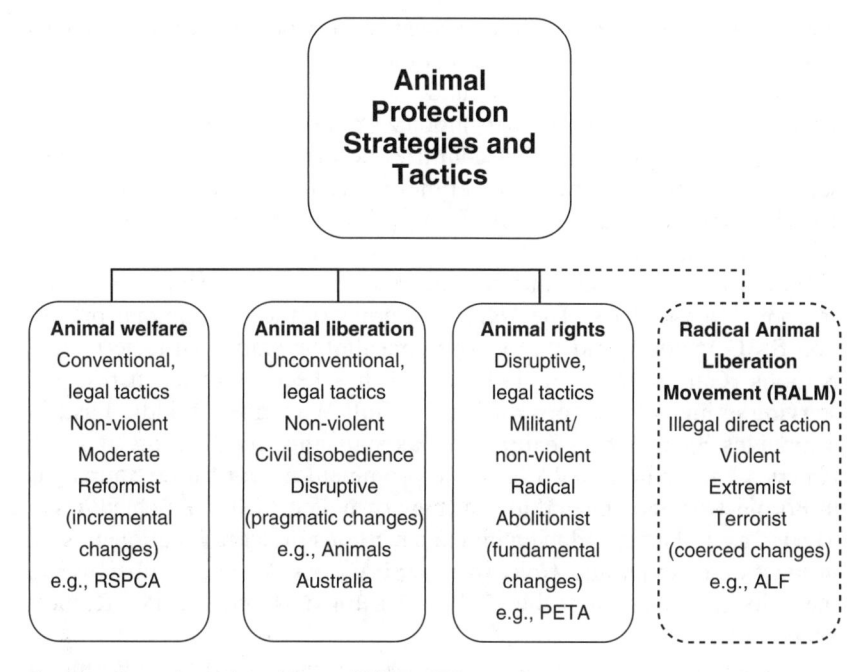

Animal welfare
Conventional, legal tactics
Non-violent
Moderate
Reformist
(incremental changes)
e.g., RSPCA

Animal liberation
Unconventional, legal tactics
Non-violent
Civil disobedience
Disruptive
(pragmatic changes)
e.g., Animals Australia

Animal rights
Disruptive, legal tactics
Militant/non-violent
Radical
Abolitionist
(fundamental changes)
e.g., PETA

Radical Animal Liberation Movement (RALM)
Illegal direct action
Violent
Extremist
Terrorist
(coerced changes)
e.g., ALF

Source: Reproduced from Munro (2011, p. 172).

Figure 22.1 Modes of animal protection

Animal Welfare: Promoting Kindness and Respect

For much of its history the Royal Society for the Prevention of Cruelty to Animals (RSPCA) was characterized by its respectability and a belief in 'kindness, mildness and self-restraint' (Turner, 1980, p. 69) and thus was unlikely to challenge elites, most notably in the hunting fraternity and the animal-user industries more generally. Change was forced upon the venerable organization in the 1960s when a number of animal rights activists managed to outnumber and outvote the conservative members of the RSPCA in England and compel the NGO to campaign against the popular, upper-class sport of hunting with hounds as well as other alleged cruelties.

The World Society for the Protection of Animals (WSPA) – an NGO affiliated with the RSPCA – willingly takes on some of the most challenging cases of animal cruelty in countries where there is little or no tradition of animal welfare. Three of its major campaigns are the overpopulation of dogs, live animal transportation and the destruction of wildlife habitats (Donald, 1998, p. 12). WSPA, like Animals Australia and other progressive animal groups, uses a strategy of reminding governments of its obligations to outlaw illegal or cruel practices towards animals and if this fails, documentation by means of undercover investigations, photographs, videos and the like are used to mobilize public opinion. This typically means people in more affluent countries become outraged by what they see as unusually cruel practices that they associate with the 'distant suffering' (Boltanski, 1999) of animals in countries where the welfare of animals is rarely considered.

WSPA's London headquarters oversees some 300 member societies in about 70 countries. The NGO is unique as the only animal protection SMO in the world that enjoys consultative status with the United Nations (Garner, 1993, p. 190). WSPA has been involved in rescuing starving animals from zoos during the Gulf War in the Middle East, in campaigns against bear-baiting in Pakistan and bull-fighting in Latin America and Spain. WSPA has been prominent in dog rescue campaigns in Bosnia-Herzegovina and in shutting down illegal cat killing facilities in Mexico as well as introducing humane methods of pet population control in places like India and Colombia. WSPA's best-known campaigns are the 'Libearty' (rescuing abused bears) campaign and the Pet Respect programme.

WSPA's 'Libearty' campaign aims to prevent bears from suffering in contexts that every fair-minded person would find unacceptable. Bears are dissected for their body parts, which are used for medicinal purposes; they are used for entertainment and sport in hunting, in bear-baiting contests and as 'dancing bears'; and finally bears are eaten in ways that would shock the average carnivore: 'The live cub is slowly lowered into a tank of hot water while the guests watch. They eat its paws and meat, then take the gall bladder home to dry' ('Libearty' promotional brochure). This latter practice is said to be enjoyed by tourists from Korea and Taiwan who travel to Thailand for the experience.

WSPA is adept in the politics of emotion as are other successful animal SMOs. Its glossy magazine *'Libearty' News* is replete with eye-catching pictures of impressive, healthy bears in the wild that the organization has rescued from 'the living hell of bear farms in China and Vietnam'. Other bears rescued from bear-baiting in Pakistan or the banquet tables of Thailand are given their own names – Eric, Paddington, Black Cloud – to bring home their individuality to readers. These bears are contrasted with the maltreated, pitiful creatures held captive in bear farms, paraded as dancing bears, exhibited in zoos or strung up as trophies.

The scale of pet overpopulation in India is one of WSPA's most daunting challenges. In 1994 WSPA began its global Pet Respect campaign to establish humane and effective pet population control in developing countries and to teach people respect for cats and dogs. It uses the three-pronged approach of education, sterilization and legislation, the latter focusing on breeding, anti-cruelty and registration measures. Conflicting religious beliefs and cultural practices mean there has been resistance to the introduction of the pre-stunning of animals since many vegetarians are opposed to the modernization of Indian slaughterhouses for fear that this will lead to an increase in meat eating (Townend, 1981, p. 12). Overcoming cultural barriers to achieve Western standards of animal welfare is no easy matter and yet with its Pet Respect campaign in India, WSPA has made significant progress.

In the 1960s and early 1970s there was a widespread feeling that social change was in the air. It was a period during which several social movements emerged to defend the rights of blacks, women, gays, the environment and animals. Tarrow (1994) described the phenomenon as a protest cycle when 'there is a heightened conflict throughout the society, a rapid diffusion of contention across different groups, a quickened pace of innovation, and new or transformed collective frames' (in Buechler, 2011, pp. 138–9). Animal liberation as espoused by Peter Singer was well suited to these times, which provided a receptive audience for his manifesto.

Peter Singer's *Animal Liberation*

Many observers believe *Animal Liberation* (1975) written by the Australian philosopher Peter Singer launched the modern animal rights movement. Singer chose the title of his manifesto as the term resonated with the liberation movements of gays, blacks and women in the 1960s and 1970s; more importantly, Singer is not an advocate of 'animal rights' although he acknowledges that the term is a useful political slogan. Animal liberationists who espouse Singer's utilitarian philosophy advocate a pragmatic approach to our treatment of animals. Thus factory farming is seen as morally repugnant, but traditional farming is not; recreational hunting is condemned as a bloodsport, but subsistence hunting is not; and on the controversial issue of animal experimentation, liberationists, rather than demanding the total abolition of animal research, call on experimentalists to adopt the 3Rs – reducing, refining and replacing the use of animals in research with alternatives.

Critics of animal rights activists are inclined to label them – in ascending order of deviance – as 'radicals', 'extremists' and 'terrorists'. While Singer's manifesto in 1975 may have spawned various extremist groups and individuals, Singer himself is a utilitarian whose aims are pragmatic. As an ethical rule, utilitarianism has several advantages over other arguments, including simplicity, empirical objectivity and its consequentialism

(Matheny, 2006). Matheny goes on to advocate utilitarianism as a theory that helps us decide on the rightness or wrongness of our use of animals as food, as laboratory specimens and as captive animals.

As depicted in Figure 22.1 the pragmatism of animal liberation offers animal protectionists a position *between* the proponents of regulation (cf. moral orthodoxy) or abolition (cf. moral egalitarianism) as well as the prospect of finding common ground with like-minded groups in other social movements. Animal liberationists frame speciesism as a social problem comparable to sexism and racism and other forms of intra-species exploitation and so are amenable to coalition building with progressive social movements such as social justice, consumer, public health and environmental groups. One particular issue that has the potential for coalition building in the social movement sector is the live animal export industry.

Animals Australia, which leads the movement in this campaign, is usually referred to in the mass media as an animal rights group although it is more accurately described as a pragmatic animal liberation organization because of its close association with Peter Singer, one of its co-founders. Founded in 1980, it is made up of numerous grassroots activist groups and ranks with the RSPCA as one of the largest animal protection bodies in Australia. Animals Australia uses persuasive communication via the mass media and education to promote its animal liberation agenda. It frequently works with the welfarist RSPCA on campaigns such as its opposition to the live animal export trade in Australia, its most recent high-profile campaign.

Lyn White, a former police officer, is currently Animal Australia's live export campaign director and investigator. White has gained media prominence for the cause of animals armed only with a digital camera and a commitment to expose the extent of animal suffering in the live export trade to the Middle East and parts of Europe and Asia. Her latest endeavour featured in the award-winning *Four Corners* expose 'A Bloody Business' that was aired in mid-2011 by the ABC (Australian Broadcasting Commission). The programme framed animal cruelty as the 'distant suffering' (Boltanski, 1999) of Australian cattle and dramatically exposed the widespread indifference of the live animal export industry to animal abuse and the failure of the responsible authorities to regulate the trade satisfactorily.

As a result of the nation-wide outrage that the story sparked, the Australian government was forced to place a temporary ban on the Indonesian trade. The professionalism of the investigative journalism for which *Four Corners* is renowned and the film footage shot by Lyn White and corroborated by the RSPCA's chief scientist Dr Bidda Jones produced shocking visual images of animal torture that caused an immediate and unprecedented public outcry against the trade. Yet, in less than a month, the meat industry succeeded in having the ban lifted and the campaign petered out when the government insisted there were now animal welfare improvements in the new guidelines for regulating the trade; the animal activists expressed deep disappointment that Australian animal welfare standards such as pre-stunning were not mandated. In this important sense, the campaign failed for reasons discussed elsewhere (see Munro, 2014).

Animal Rights: A Challenge to Liberal Democracy?

Animal rightists, in contrast to liberationists, perceive speciesism as a moral problem in the same way that they see vegetarianism (and veganism) as an ethical issue and as an essential prerequisite for animal rights membership. The animal welfare strategy favours working within the political process to achieve incremental welfare advances in the law; to a lesser extent, pragmatic animal liberation groups are also willing to pursue the reformist route. However, animal rights proponents favour more militant, disruptive (albeit non-violent) protests in pursuit of their abolitionist agenda. In eschewing incremental changes via moderate or pragmatic strategies, animal rights activists seek fundamental changes in the way individuals and industries treat animals. Following Regan (1984), animal rightists demand the abolition of all practices in which humans use other animals, including pet-keeping. Garner has recently suggested that animal rights would be taken more seriously if the argument for moral egalitarianism was jettisoned and replaced by 'a much more (morally and politically) acceptable version of animal rights based on the sentiency of animals and not their personhood' (2010, p. 128).

The issue of vegetarianism also raises an important question about what Perlo (2007) calls 'strategies for promoting animal rights'. In a recent study of five animal rights organizations in the USA, Freeman (2010) focused on national groups that advocated veganism and the rights of animals rather than welfare's acceptance of the consumption of meat derived from 'humane' farming. The organizations were in order from the largest to the smallest as follows: People for the Ethical Treatment of Animals (PETA), Farm Sanctuary, Farm Animal Rights Movement (FARM), Compassion Over Killing (COK) and Vegan Outreach. Freeman found that these organizations were driven by four 'problem frames': (1) the suffering of animals due to cruelty; (2) the commodification of animals as objects; (3) the harmfulness of animal agribusiness and animal products to humans and the environment; and (4) the needless killing and death of animals for food (p. 169). Interestingly, only Vegan Outreach failed to mention the health benefits of a vegetarian/vegan diet while PETA went further than other groups by highlighting health messages that included weight reduction and sex appeal enhancement for people who avoided meat in their diet. The negative impact of a meat-based diet on the environment were also emphasized in the websites of PETA, Farm Sanctuary and FARM; Vegan Outreach and COK evidently believe that what matters to the contemporary vegetarian movement is compassion for animal suffering.

Vegan Outreach has its headquarters in Tucson, Arizona and is a non-profit organization, the mission of which is to convert as many people as possible to a meat-free vegan or vegetarian lifestyle. According to their website www.veganoutreach.org accessed in mid-February 2013 some 27 000 people stated that they liked what the group stands for. At that time, the organizers reported that close to 9 million advocacy pamphlets had been distributed in the last decade. Pamphleteering appears to be the group's main recruiting strategy and includes a very successful 'Adopt a College' programme whereby supporters hand out leaflets to high school and university students in the USA. This is one of the social movement sector's oldest tactics and one that has been successfully used in many education campaigns. According to John Bryant of the League Against Cruel Sports in the UK, handing out leaflets as a form of persuasive communication is one of the best ways to convert people to the animal cause: 'The leaflet is our media. In nearly twenty years in animal welfare and rights I have rarely found a campaigner who did not join the movement after being handed a leaflet – usually in the street' (Bryant, 1982, p. 88).

Purists in the animal rights stream almost always insist on a commitment to vegetarianism (and ideally veganism) as a basic principle of membership in the movement. Yet a widespread conversion to ethical vegetarianism, not to mention veganism, is surely unrealistic in the foreseeable future. A more pragmatic strategy is suggested by Frank (2004) who emphasizes the role of radical animal activists via sometimes illegal, non-violent, undercover actions in raising consumer awareness about serious food regulation defects that are likely to change consumer eating habits. Animal welfarists, liberationists and rightists could unite in common cause on this issue by promoting a vegetarian lifestyle that includes not just animal welfare considerations but also environmental and health improvements for humans. (See Franklin, 1999 and Akhtar, 2012 below for details on the issue of animals and public health.)

According to Sorenson (2003), moderate reforms in Canada designed to protect animals from cruel treatment by individuals – and of no relevance to corporations – were met with strenuous opposition by the animal-user industry determined to ensure animal welfare did not pose 'a challenge to human uniqueness' (p. 397). Meanwhile, advocates of violence in defence of animals find their niche in the outsider groups that make up the membership of the Radical Animal Liberation Movement (RALM), the acronym used by Fluekiger (2008) to identify activists outside the mainstream movement.

The Radical Animal Liberation Movement (RALM)

Although RALM is dramatically different from the ideology and practice of Singer's style of animal liberation, the latter is frequently and often deliberately confused with the violent, extremist actions of RALM groups. It should also be noted that Fluekiger's understanding of what is 'radical' in the RALM covers 'direct actions, including sabotage and vandalism, the liberation of animals, arson, and home visits' (p. 111), actions that would alienate most mainstream animal advocates. RALM activists are not radicals or terrorists in the conventional meanings of these terms, as virtually all social activists who challenge the status quo could be viewed as radicals, while the more sinister designation of 'terrorist' should only apply to those who plan and carry out deadly, random attacks in the public domain. That said, it needs to be acknowledged that groups such as the Animal Liberation Front (ALF) and Stop Huntingdon Animal Cruelty (SHAC) do use violence against alleged animal abusers and sometimes even terror, if the spread of fear can be described as a terror tactic.

In acknowledging the diversity of groups in the animal protection movement, Humphrey and Stears (2006) identify two broad political strategies that distinguish these different groups: the politics of cost-levying and the strategy of moral disagreement; put simply, the difference is between the politics of coercion versus the politics of persuasion. Cost-levying via coercion includes actions that damage property such as animal laboratories, while the moral disagreement strategy seeks to persuade an audience to support the group's cause, sometimes via shocking imagery such as in the television programme 'A Bloody Business' on animal abuse in Indonesia.

Humphrey and Stears defend these non-deliberative tactics because of the animal activists' urgent need to put a stop to the scale of animal deaths perpetrated by the animal industrial complex. Furthermore, they argue that empowering activists to challenge these powerful and entrenched interests 'would appear to be a desirable rather than an undesirable form of democratic political action' (p. 108) and one that political theorists should be encouraged to respect. The authors insist, however, that this is not an endorsement of 'anything goes', but rather a theory of democracy that is 'less normatively prescriptive than existing theories of deliberation' (p. 417).

According to Tarrow (1998), social movements are tasked with choosing between conventional, disruptive and violent repertoires – terminology that accurately categorizes the strategies employed by animal welfarists (moderate and conventional), animal rightists (militant and disruptive), and liberationists in the RALM (extremist and violent) while Singer's style of animal liberation is closer to animal welfare in practice, and to animal rights politically. These four strands represent broad animal protectionism, which overwhelmingly is non-violent.

The abolitionist Gary Francione (1996) claims there are only two strands to the movement – animal rights and the 'new welfarism' – whose respective strategies offer a choice between abolition or regulation. However, for many animal protectionists these options are too restrictive, as indicated in the large numbers of groups that are neither abolitionist nor reformist. The range of animal protection ideologies, strategies and tactics – as represented in Figure 22.1 – is more complicated than Francione allows. In any event, activists have little interest in the philosophical differences among animal rights philosophers. Still, most animal SMOs and leaders would agree with Francione and Garner that 'the practical strategy of animal advocates must necessarily be informed by theory, and their political, legal, and social campaigns will be determined by [it]' (2010, pp. xi–xii). How this might be achieved is taken up in the next section.

ASSESSMENT OF THE MOST IMPORTANT MIDDLE-RANGE THEORIES AND CONCEPTS

A recent book by the sociologist Steven Buechler (2011) is utilized here to describe some of the most important middle-range theories and concepts pertaining to the animal movement. Buechler has comprehensively evaluated the theoretically and conceptually complicated field of social movement studies, a field that is riddled with jargon and numerous variations on different theories. In doing so, he provides an informative account of 'an attempted synthesis' (pp. 188–91) of the dominant perspectives in social movement theory in the 1990s, namely political opportunities, mobilizing structures and framing processes. He notes that the synthesizing attempt produced a hierarchy rather than an authentic synthesis, with resource mobilization and political process theory re-emerging as the dominant paradigms along with framing theory as a junior partner (p. 190). In the present chapter, these processes and related concepts are also given prominence as they are seen as useful analytical tools for understanding the animal protection movement. Some of the most promising approaches are depicted in Table 22.1.

In his discussion of the three dominant social movement paradigms,

Table 22.1 Correspondence between various perspectives on social movements

Author(s)	Perspectives and Terminology		
McAdam et al. (1996)	Political opportunity	Mobilizing structures	Framing
Snow and Benford (1988)	Diagnosis	Prognosis	Motivation
Hannigan (1995)	Assembling claims	Presenting claims	Contesting claims
Gamson (1992)	Injustice frame	Agency frame	Identity frame

Buechler points out that opportunity in the US context was used to explain the emergence of particular social movements; that mobilizing structures refer to the formal SMOs associated with resource mobilization *and* the informal networks recognized by political process theorists; and in the case of framing, that social constructionist ideas on identity, meaning and culture resonated with NSM scholars. The relevance to the animal movement of these paradigms, as well as the concepts summarized in Table 22.1, are outlined next.

Social Movement Framing

The concept of social movement framing pioneered by Wilson (1973) has since been comprehensively developed by Snow and Benford (1988) and more recently by Snow and Byrd (2007). These theorists argue that all social movements have three core framing tasks, namely diagnostic, prognostic and motivational framing, or in Wilson's (1973) original terminology, a movement's diagnosis, prognosis and motivation. In the case of the animal movement, issue entrepreneurs identify animal exploitation as a social problem in much the same way that environmental threats are increasingly constructed as anthropogenic social problems (Yearley, 1992; Hannigan, 1995). The animal movement's diagnostic frame is to target animal abuse as a social problem on a par with harming children, women, the elderly, and most pertinently in the culturally sanctioned contexts of animal experimentation, intensive farming and recreational hunting.

The role of animal rights activists is to uncover, name and frame as injustices the abuse of animals, particularly in the institutionalized contexts of factory farms, research laboratories, in circuses, theme parks and zoos and in the wild. This diagnostic work precedes the prognosis, that is, the choice of tactics the movement employs to prosecute its cause. As noted by Francione and Garner (2010) above, the practical strategy of animal activism and the campaign tactics employed by activists need to be philosophically sound and theoretically informed for a campaign to succeed; put simply, there must be a compelling argument for the movement's actions; the argument might be ethical, environmental, political or for reasons of public health. Mobilizing structures in the iconic form of social movement organizations (SMOs) – each with its distinctive strategies – have been developed to garner support for one kind of SMO or another; these effectively offer movement sympathizers the choices summed up in Figure 22.1.

John Hannigan on Claims-making

Hannigan's (1995) *Environmental Sociology* is subtitled 'A Social Constructionist Perspective', one he advocates because '(it) focuses on the social, political and cultural processes by which environmental conditions are defined as being unacceptably risky and therefore actionable' (p. 30). Environmental problems in this book are analysed within a social problems tradition of sociology where the process of claims-making is held to be as important as the objective reality of the problem. Hannigan conceptualizes the process as three dimensional: claims are assembled, presented and contested, a process that is strikingly similar to Snow and Benford's (1988) model and also to Gamson's (1992) three-fold analysis.

Hannigan's model is clearly applicable to the animal movement where animal advocates, primarily philosophers and SMOs, assemble ethical, environmental and scientific claims in defence of animals they believe are exploited by the animal-user industries. These claims are then presented in a variety of ways, especially via the print and electronic media, including SMO websites, pamphlets and in recent times, via social media networks. The claims range from visceral appeals featuring disturbing images of animal cruelty to proposed solutions such as 'Go Veg' campaigns; other examples of persuasive communication include academic books such as Akhtar's (2012) *Animals and Public Health*, which focuses on knowledge claims and Jonathan Safran Foer's (2009) best-selling *Eating Animals*, a book that has an experiential focus. Needless to say, pro-animal claims are vigorously contested by the animal-user industries either by counter-arguments or in some cases in courts of law such as in the McLibel trial in the mid-1990s in England (see Vidal, 1997).

William Gamson on Injustice, Agency and Identity

In his influential book, *Talking Politics*, Gamson (1992) highlights injustice, agency and identity as key collective action frames, all of which are relevant to the animal movement. As noted already, activists take up the cause of justice for animals by challenging the allegedly cruel practices of the animal-user industries. The injustice frame constructs cruelty as morally reprehensible because animal suffering, like the suffering of innocent humans, is an effective catalyst for arousing the moral indignation of ordinary people. If the agency frame is to be successful it needs to make people believe they have the wherewithal to effect social change. This feeling of empowerment provides a link to the third of Gamson's frames – the identity frame – whereby ordinary people are politicized by their participation in a movement. Piven and Cloward (1977) use the concept of 'cognitive liberation' to describe how (1) people lose faith in the system (e.g., to prevent animal cruelty); (2) otherwise indifferent individuals begin to speak up about their grievances (e.g., their opposition to the live animal export trade in the UK and Australia); and (3) how these individuals learn their protests are effective (e.g., when English activists stopped the live animal export trade to European ports in the mid-1990s). It is then that the activists experience 'cognitive liberation' and, we can add, a sense of collective identity. In addition, for cognitive liberation to occur the opportunity and climate for change need to be favourable.

Key Concept: Political Opportunity Structure

Van der Heijden (2006) suggests that the concept of political opportunity structure (POS) is useful in clarifying why movements often peter out after gaining an initial, sometimes surprising advantage over elites or authorities. He cites Tarrow's (1994) analysis, which synthesizes the main approaches to POS. The fate of a social movement in this formula depends on the following criteria: (1) how open or closed the political system is to challengers; (2) the stability or instability of the elites in the polity; (3) the presence or absence of influential allies; and (4) the state's ability or inclination to repress dissidents.

It seems obvious that the political context is a crucial factor in a movement's success or failure, since strategies and tactics that are effective in one particular period or political environment may not be effective in another. Thus the animal protection movement that emerged in the eighteenth century was part of a humanitarian tide of reform that sought to end cruel practices inflicted on both humans and animals (Halttunen, 1995). In the nineteenth century, according to Turner (1980), animal protection was established as an Anglo-American tradition when the RSPCA and the American equivalent formalized the virtues of the Victorian age by embracing 'kindness, mildness and self-restraint'. These early pioneers were conservative, respectable, middle-class folk unlikely to challenge upper-class pastimes such as hunting with hounds. The political and cultural climate of the 1970s was characterized by the emergence of liberation movements supporting the rights of blacks, people of colour, gays and women; the time and opportunity had come for Singer's arguments for animal liberation to be taken seriously. Since then, the contemporary movement's impact can be seen in the emergence of countervailing forces in the form of counter-movements against animal rights.

Key Concept: Counter-movements

Mottl (1980, p. 624) defines a counter-movement as 'a response to the social change advocated by an initial movement (which) mobilizes human, symbolic and material resources to block institutional social change or to revert to a previous status quo'. In its critique of instrumentalism and its challenge to anthropocentric thinking (Jasper and Nelkin, 1992), the animal movement has been condemned as undermining human welfare, particularly when it campaigns against animal experimentation or the rights of indigenous peoples to hunt for food and fur. In addition to individual critics of the animal movement such as Michael Leahy (1991) and Alan Wolfe (1993), there are now formidable organized groups or counter-movements that seek to subvert animal rights as a political and social movement.

'Counter-movements', according to Buechler, 'are more likely to emerge when a movement appears to be succeeding, when an appropriate ideology is available and when resources and opportunities are available for such mobilization' (2011, p. 121). Similarly, Meyer and Staggenborg (1996, p. 1635) concur but add two further conditions, namely when the movement's goals threaten vested interests and when political allies are available to the counter-movement. Under these conditions, the counter-mobilization may overwhelm the original protest movement in size and intensity. For example, Jasper and Poulsen (1995) note how the biomedical lobby reacted to animal rights protests against animal experimentation by making effective alliances and by framing their work as beneficial to sick children. Likewise, Arluke and Groves (1998) identified four categories of oppositional groups: (1) grassroots public relation organizations such as Put People First and Americans for Medical Progress; (2) patient-originated groups such as Incurably Ill for Animal Research (iiAR); (3) advocacy groups like the National Association for Biomedical Research; and (4) professional associations like the American Medical Association (AMA) and the National Institute of Mental Health (NIMH). In a detailed study of how medical scientists seek to enhance their professional credibility, Arluke and Groves (1998, p. 145) argue that they do so primarily by attempting to construct a 'moral identity that is superior to their opponents'.

SKETCH OF RELEVANT FUTURE DEVELOPMENTS AND RESEARCH

This final section will look at possible future developments in social movement theory generally, and more specifically at some likely directions for the animal movement. Steven Buechler's (2011) comprehensive overview of the literature on social movement theory is a good starting point for addressing the first of these two topics. According to Buechler, social movement theorists are divided between structuralists (represented in the work of McAdam et al., 2001) and culturalists (represented by Goodwin et al., 2011). The structuralists' account in McAdam et al.'s 2001 *Dynamics of Contention*, reports Buechler, emphasizes episodes of contention such as strikes, revolutions and spontaneous uprisings, while the culturalists in Goodwin et al.'s 2011 *Passionate Politics* reject this approach as one that privileges political activism at the expense of *cultural* contention in social movements (Buechler, 2011).

The advocates in these two schools of thought are unlikely to come to any agreement on how their positions might be reconciled, and Buechler sees little hope of any synthesis between these and other competing paradigms in social movement theory. For social movement activists, there is little interest in theoretical disputes of this kind. Two books at the opposite ends of a continuum that might interest animal movement leaders are reviewed next: *Zoopolis* takes an animal-centric position while *Animals and Public Health* caters to the interests of both human and non-human species.

Zoopolis

Zoopolis (Donaldson and Kymlicka, 2011) raises some interesting questions about the efficacy of animal rights theory (ART). To these political philosophers, ART has few followers outside a narrow academic circle, small numbers of vegan enthusiasts and direct action proponents in the animal movement. For the animal movement to build strong public support, they argue that human–animal relationships need to be based on a political theory of 'citizenship' within a polity they refer to as a zoopolis, which would put animals on a par with humans. Depending on the context in which they live, animals would be classed as akin to their human counterparts as follows: citizens (domesticated animals); denizens (invading non-indigenous animals in urban spaces who will enjoy the status of co-residents albeit as resident aliens with a right to stay but lacking full citizenship rights); and in the case of wild animals, citizens in their own sovereign territories much like sovereign nation-states free from the threat of invasion.

While many people would no doubt see such thinking as fanciful, Donaldson and Kymlicka believe their zoopolis is more animal-friendly (meaning human and non-human animals presumably) than the strict animal rights position of abolition, which would ultimately see the extinction of animals used by humans for food, research and entertainment and so on. Cochrane's (2012) review of *Zoopolis*, aptly titled 'Rex and the city', while not fully endorsing the idea, praises the book for its novel, groundbreaking application of the aforementioned concepts borrowed from liberal political philosophy. If a zoopolis was to emerge in a particular locale, it would only do so if the movement focused less on animal welfare and more on human welfare. The next section considers the importance of both for enhancing the life chances of all species.

Animals and Public Health

Ayshar Akhtar's (2012) *Animals and Public Health* offers a convincing argument for the eradication of the worst forms of animal exploitation, and seeks to appeal to both sides of the animal-consumption debate. Akhtar proposes an alternative approach to what she sees as a false choice between human and non-human interests in the controversial issues of factory farming and animal experimentation. Advocates for human welfare, she suggests, can also be advocates for animal welfare without sacrificing human health and well-being: 'Our mental and physical health, the state of our environment, the safety of our food, and the efficacy and safety of our medical treatments are inextricably tied to how we choose to treat other animals' (p. 18). She believes eliminating or at least reducing the consumption of animal products is the easiest and most comprehensive solution to health, environmental, humanitarian and animal welfare problems.

Akhtar calls for human-based tests to replace animal experiments and a meat-free dietary regime, which she suggests will 'single-handedly help thwart epidemics, curtail global warming and lengthen our lives – and reduce the number of animals in factory farms' (p. 173). All of this might be dismissed as wishful thinking, but the factual basis for these arguments is difficult to deny. *Animals and Public Health* describes a multitude of problems linked to the mistreatment of animals and how these impact adversely on the life chances of all species. Some random examples from the book: the wildlife trade threatens biodiversity loss; deadly infectious diseases, both known and unknown have emerged; factory farms contribute to global warming; instances of tainted food production; spoiled environments; bird flu and other pathogens. The costs of animal experiments, according to the results of Akhtar's research, outweigh the benefits; her research includes close to 200 footnotes on findings concerning the relevance of animal models used for clinical trials, which essentially conclude that they are bad science and bad policy. As many others opposed to animal research have suggested, the life chances of both human and non-human species would be enhanced if the 3Rs of replacement, reduction, refinement were implemented instead of continuing with costly and risky animal experiments. However, many if not most animal researchers insist that not using laboratory animals in certain cases will endanger human health and well-being (see Munro, 1999 on the prospects of a common cause movement that includes animal experimentalists and anti-vivisectionists).

Finally, as this chapter has shown, the animal movement lends itself to interdisciplinary work, a field that Buechler (2011) predicts will become a growth area especially in the 'harder' disciplines (political science and economics) and in sociology's kindred fields of psychology and anthropology (p. 211). He believes, however, that research should only be encouraged if it yields genuine insights about social movements and does not simply add to the confusing proliferation of concepts already plaguing the literature; the production of useful knowledge for social movement scholars and activists alike should be the goal. Traditionally, sociologists such as those featured in this chapter have had little difficulty working with each other's ideas to produce new knowledge. One way for social scientists to produce really useful knowledge is to build relationships with social movement activists via scholar–activist collaboration, an idea that cannot be explored here but is discussed in Munro (2012, pp. 174–7). Suffice it to say that the results of scholar–activist projects should yield genuine interdisciplinary insights and 'practical wisdom' that is so often missing in standard academic articles.

CONCLUSION

As the animal movement is one of the most controversial social movements of our era, there are many interesting issues and questions that need to be explored before the movement can safely be labelled mainstream. A number of research questions are suggested next that might serve as topics for journal papers on issues such as the politics and sociology of the animal movement, the social significance of animal abuse, the strategic choices available to activists and the prospect of scholar–activist collaboration on animal movement issues.

First, is the Dutch experience in establishing a Party for the Animals worth replicating in comparable democracies? Second, is it desirable for sociologists to replace philosophers as the new 'midwives of the animal rights movement' (Jasper and Nelkin, 1992)? Third, what is the empirical evidence for the claim that animal abuse is on a par with spouse abuse, elder abuse and child abuse? Fourth, what is the most effective strategy animal protectionists can choose from in the different strands such as welfare, liberation, rights and the RALM? Fifth, are violent or non-violent strategies and tactics more effective in achieving improvements in animal welfare and is violence justified in certain cases for preventing animal cruelty? Last, what are some of the benefits and risks of scholar–activist collaboration in studying the animal rights movement?

NOTE

* I would like to acknowledge the online journal *Sociology Compass* as a resource for literature reviews and specifically for the use of my own article (Munro, 2012), part of which is reproduced in the first section of this chapter.

REFERENCES

Agnew, R. (1998), 'The causes of animal abuse: a social-psychological analysis', *Theoretical Criminology*, **2**(2), 177–209.

Akhtar, A. (2012), *Animals and Public Health: Why Treating Animals Better is Critical to Human Welfare*, Houndmills, UK/New York: Palgrave Macmillan.

Arluke, A. and J. Groves (1998), 'Pushing the boundaries: scientists in the public arena', in L. Hart (ed.), *Responsible Conduct with Animals in Research*, New York: Oxford University Press, pp. 145–64.

Arluke, A. and C. Sanders (2009), *Between the Species: Readings in Human–Animal Relations*, Boston, MA: Pearson Education.

Barnes, B. (1995), *The Elements of Social Theory*, London: University College London Press.

Beirne, P. (1995), 'The use and abuse of animals in criminology: a brief history and current review', *Social Justice*, **22**(1), 5–31.

Beirne, P. (1999), 'For a non-speciesist criminology: animal abuse as an object of study', *Criminology*, **37**(1), 117–47.

Beirne, P. (2007), 'Animal rights, animal abuse and green criminology', in P. Beirne and N. South (eds), *Issues in Green Criminology*, Cullompton, UK/Portland, OR: Willan Publishing.

Benton, T. (1993), *Natural Relations: Ecology, Animal Rights and Social Justice*, London: Verso.

Benton, T. (1995), 'Animal rights and social relations', in A. Dobson and P. Lucardie (eds), *The Politics of Nature: Explorations in Green Political Theory*, London: Routledge.

Boltanski, L. (1999), *Distant Suffering: Morality, Media and Politics*, Cambridge, UK: Cambridge University Press.
Bryant, C. (1991), 'Deviant leisure and clandestine lifestyle: cockfighting as a socially devalued sport', *World Leisure and Recreation*, **133**, 17–21.
Bryant, C. and W. Snizek (1993), 'On the trail of the centaur', *Society*, **30**(3), 25–35.
Bryant, J. (1982), *Fettered Kingdoms*, Manchester: Fox Press.
Buechler, S. (2011), *Understanding Social Movements: Theories from the Classical Era to the Present*, Boulder, CO/London: Paradigm Publishers.
Cherry, E. (2010), 'Shifting symbolic boundaries: cultural strategies of the animal rights movement', *Sociological Forum*, **25**(3), 450–75.
Clark, S.R.L. (1997), *Animals and Their Moral Standing*, London: Routledge.
Cochrane, A. (2012), ' "Rex and the city" a review of *Zoopolis: A Political Theory of Animal Rights* by Sue Donaldson and Will Kymlicka', *The Philosopher's Magazine*, **58**(3), 115–16.
Crook, S., J. Pakulski and M. Waters (1992), *Postmodernization: Change in Advanced Society*, London: Sage Publications.
Cudworth, E. (2003), *Environment and Society*, London and New York: Routledge.
Dizard, J. (1994), *Going Wild: Hunting, Animal Rights, and the Contested Meaning of Nature*, Amherst, MA: University of Massachusetts Press.
Donald, R. (1998), 'Welcome to WSPA', *Animals Today*, **6**(3), 1–13.
Donaldson, S. and W. Kymlicka (2011), *Zoopolis: A Political Theory of Animal Rights*, New York: Oxford University Press.
Eckersley, R. (1992), *Environmentalism and Political Theory: Toward an Ecocentric Approach*, London: UCL Press.
Elias, N. (1978), *The Civilising Process, Vol. 1, The History of Manners*, Oxford: Blackwell.
Fine, G. and L. Christoforides (1991), 'Dirty birds, filthy immigrants, and the English sparrow war: metaphorical linkages in constructing social problems', *Symbolic Interaction*, **14**(4), 375–93.
Fluekiger, J.-M. (2008), 'The Radical Animal Liberation Movement: some reflections on its future', *Journal for the Study of Radicalism*, **2**(2), 111–32.
Flynn, C. (ed.) (2008), *Social Creatures: A Human and Animal Studies Reader*, New York: Lantern Books.
Francione, G. (1996), *Rain Without Thunder: The Ideology of the Animal Rights Movement*, Philadelphia, PA: Temple University Press.
Francione, G. and R. Garner (2010), *The Animal Rights Debate: Abolition or Regulation?*, New York: Columbia University Press.
Frank, J. (2004), 'The role of radical animal activists as information providers to consumers', *Animal Liberation Philosophy and Policy Journal*, **2**(1), 1–13.
Franklin, A. (1999), *Animals and Modern Cultures: A Sociology of Human–Animal Relations in Modernity*, London: Sage.
Freeman, P.C. (2010), 'Framing animal rights in the "Go Veg" campaigns of U.S. animal rights organizations', *Society & Animals*, **18**(2), 163–82.
Gamson, W. (1992), *Talking Politics*, Cambridge, UK: Cambridge University Press.
Garner, R. (1993), *Animals, Politics and Morality*, Manchester: Manchester University Press.
Garner, R. (1998), 'Defending animal rights', *Parliamentary Affairs*, **51**(3), 458–69.
Garner, R. (2006), 'Animal welfare: a political defense', *Journal of Animal Liberation and Ethics*, **1**, 161–74.
Garner, R. (2010), 'Animals, ethics and public policy', *The Political Quarterly*, **81**(1), 123–30.
Goodwin, J., J. Jasper and F. Polletta (2011), *Passionate Politics: Emotions and Social Movements*, Chicago, IL: University of Chicago Press.
Halttunen, K. (1995), 'Humanitarianism and the pornography of pain in Anglo-American culture', *The American Historical Review*, **100**(2), 304–34.
Hannigan, J. (1995), *Environmental Sociology: A Social Constructionist Perspective*, London: Routledge.
Humphrey, M. and M. Stears (2006), 'Animal rights protest and the challenge of deliberative democracy', *Economy and Society*, **35**(3), 400–22.

Irvine, L. (2003), 'The problem of unwanted pets: a case study in how institutions "think" about clients' needs', *Social Problems*, **50**(4), 550–66.
Jasper, J. (1997), *The Art of Moral Protest: Culture, Biography and Creativity in Social Movements*, Chicago, IL: University of Chicago Press.
Jasper, J. (1999), 'Recruiting intimates, recruiting strangers: building the contemporary animal rights movement', in J. Freeman and V. Johnson (eds), *Waves of Protest: Social Movements Since the Sixties*, Lanham, MD: Rowman & Littlefield.
Jasper, J. (2004), 'A strategic approach to collective action: looking for agency in social movement choices', *Mobilization*, **9**(1), 1–16.
Jasper, J. and D. Nelkin (1992), *The Animal Rights Crusade: The Growth of a Moral Protest*, New York: The Free Press.
Jasper, J. and J. Poulsen (1995), 'Recruiting strangers and friends: moral shocks and social networks in animal rights and anti-nuclear protests', *Social Problems*, **42**(4), 493–512.
Jerolmack, C. (2008), 'How pigeons became rats: the cultural-spatial logic of problem animals', *Social Problems*, **55**(1), 72–94.
Kerasote, T. (1993), *Bloodties: Nature, Culture and the Hunt*, New York: Random House.
Kolb, F. (2007), *Protest and Opportunities: The Political Outcomes of Social Movements*, Frankfurt/New York: Campus Verlag.
Leahy, M. (1991), *Against Liberation: Putting Animals in Perspective*, London: Routledge.
Marvin, G. (2000), 'The problem of foxes: legitimate and illegitimate killing in the English countryside', in J. Knight (ed.), *Natural Enemies: People–Wildlife Conflicts in Anthropological Perspective*, London/New York: Routledge.
Matheny, G. (2006), 'Utilitarianism and animals', in P. Singer (ed.), *In Defense of Animals: The Second Wave*, Malden, MA: Blackwell Publishing, pp. 13–25.
McAdam, D., J. McCarthy and M. Zald (eds) (1996), *Comparative Perspectives on Social Movements: Political Opportunities, Mobilizing Structures and Cultural Framings*, Cambridge, UK: Cambridge University Press.
McAdam, D., S. Tarrow and C. Tilly (2001), *Dynamics of Contention*, New York: Cambridge University Press.
Meyer, D. and S. Staggenborg (1996), 'Movements, counter-movements, and the structure of political opportunity', *American Journal of Sociology*, **101**(6), 1628–60.
Mika, M. (2006), 'Framing the issue: religion, secular ethics and the case of animal rights mobilization', *Social Forces*, **85**(2), 915–41.
Mottl, T. (1980), 'The analysis of counter-movements', *Social Problems*, **27**(5), 620–34.
Munro, L. (1999), 'From vilification to accommodation: making a common cause movement', *Cambridge Quarterly of Healthcare Ethics*, **8**(1), 46–57.
Munro, L. (2005a), *Confronting Cruelty: Moral Orthodoxy and the Challenge of the Animal Rights Movement*, Leiden/Boston, MA: Brill Academic Publishers.
Munro, L. (2005b), 'Strategies, action repertoires and DIY activism in the animal rights movement', *Social Movement Studies*, **4**(1), 75–94.
Munro, L. (2012), 'The animal rights movement in theory and practice: a review of the sociological literature', *Sociology Compass*, **6**(2), 166–81.
Munro, L. (2014), 'The live animal export controversy in Australia: a moral crusade made for the mass media', *Social Movement Studies: Journal of Social, Cultural and Political Protest* [published online 27 January 2014], DOI: 10.1080/14742837.2013.874524.
Nibert, D. (2002), *Animal Rights/Human Rights: Entanglements of Oppression and Liberation*, Lanham, MD: Rowman & Littlefield.
Nibert, D. (2003), 'Humans and other animals: sociology's moral and intellectual challenge', *The International Journal of Sociology and Social Policy*, **23**(3), 5–25.
Noske, B. (1989), *Humans and Other Animals: Beyond the Boundaries of Anthropology*, London: Pluto Press.
Noske, B. (1997), *Beyond Boundaries: Humans and Other Animals*, Montreal, ON: Black Rose Books.
Pakulski, J. (1991), *Social Movements: The Politics of Moral Protest*, Melbourne, VIC: Longman Cheshire.

Peggs, K. (2012), *Animals and Sociology*, New York/Houndmills, UK: Palgrave Macmillan.
Perlo, K. (2007), 'Extrinsic and intrinsic arguments: strategies for promoting animal rights', *Journal of Critical Animal Studies*, **V**(1), 1–14.
Piven, F. and R. Cloward (1977), *Poor People's Movements: Why They Succeed, How They Fail*, New York: Pantheon Books.
Regan, T. (1984), *The Case for Animal Rights*, London: Routledge.
Ruddick, S. (1980), 'Maternal thinking', *Feminist Studies*, **6**(2), 350–51.
Safran Foer, J. (2009), *Eating Animals*, New York: Little, Brown and Co.
Scott, A. (1990), *Ideology and New Social Movements*, Boston/London: Unwin Hyman.
Singer, P. (1975), *Animal Liberation: A New Ethics for Our Treatment of Animals*, New York: New York Review and Random House.
Singer, P. (1990), *Animal Liberation*, 2nd edition, London: Jonathon Cape.
Snow, D. and R. Benford (1988), 'Ideology, frame resonance and participant mobilization', in B. Klandermans, H. Kriesi and S. Tarrow (eds), *From Structure to Action: Comparing Social Movement Research Across Cultures, International Social Movement Research, A Research Annual*, Greenwich, CT: JAI Press, pp. 197–217.
Snow, D. and S. Byrd (2007), 'Ideology, framing processes, and Islamic terrorist movements', *Mobilization*, **12**(1), 119–36.
Sorenson, J. (2003), 'Some strange things happening in our country: opposing proposed changes in anti-cruelty laws in Canada', *Social and Legal Studies*, **12**(3), 377–402.
Sunstein, C. (2000), 'Standing for animals', *UCLA Law Review*, **47**, 1333–68.
Sutherland, A. and J. Nash (1994), 'Animal rights as a new environmental cosmology', *Qualitative Sociology*, **17**(2), 171–86.
Tarrow, S. (1994), *Power in Movement: Social Movements and Collective Action and Politics*, Cambridge, UK: Cambridge University Press.
Tarrow, S. (1998), *Power in Movement: Social Movements and Contentious Politics*, 2nd edition, Cambridge, UK: Cambridge University Press.
Tester, K. (1991), *Animals and Society: The Humanity of Animal Rights*, London: Routledge.
Torres, B. (2007), *Making a Killing: The Political Economy of Animal Rights*, Oakland, CA: AK Press.
Townend, C. (1981), *A Voice for the Animals: How Animal Liberation Grew*, Sydney: Kangaroo Press.
Turner, J. (1980), *Reckoning with the Beast: Animals, Pain and Humanity in the Victorian Mind*, Baltimore, MD: The Johns Hopkins University Press.
Vance, L. (1993), 'Remapping the terrain: books on ecofeminism', *Choice*, **30**, 1585–93.
Van der Heijden, H.-A. (2006), 'Globalization, environmental movements, and international political opportunity structures', *Organization and Environment*, **19**(1), 28–45.
Vidal, J. (1997), *McLibel: Burger Culture on Trial*, London: Macmillan.
Vogel, S. (1996), *Against Nature: The Concept of Nature in Critical Theory*, New York: State University of New York Press.
Weick, K. (1984), 'Small wins: redefining the scale of social problems', *American Psychologist*, **39**(1), 40–49.
Wilkie, R. and D. Inglis (eds) (2007), *Animals and Society: Critical Concepts in the Social Sciences, Vols 1–5*, London: Routledge.
Wilson, J. (1973), *Introduction to Social Movements*, New York: Basic Books Inc.
Wolfe, A. (1993), *The Human Difference: Animals, Computers and the Necessity of Social Science*, Berkeley, CA: University of California Press.
Yearley, S. (1992), *The Green Case: A Sociology of Environmental Issues, Arguments and Politics*, London: Routledge.

PART IV

SOCIAL MOVEMENTS AND POLITICAL CITIZENSHIP IN THE GLOBAL SOUTH

23. Social movements and political citizenship in China
Lei Xie

INTRODUCTION

On Environment Day, 5 June 2007, about 1000 residents of Liulitun in the Haidian District of Beijing made an organized petition to the National and Beijing government units against plans to construct a waste incineration plant near their homes. They wore T-shirts printed with the slogan, 'No waste incineration plants at Liulitun', and also displayed posters that read 'We refuse cancer', 'Oppose incinerating garbage' and 'We want good health'. The opposing residents were mostly middle-class homeowners living in well-built estates. They began organizing their campaign and peaceful protests in early 2006 through internet forums. Moreover, to place additional pressure on the government to respond, they took legal measures including filing an environmental administrative litigation law suit, which was accompanied by a collective petition letter signed by 137 residents. The homeowners also successfully put the issue on the political agenda of the Beijing People's Congress and Haidian People's Political Consultative Conference, and developed a media strategy to defend their environmental interests. Within several weeks, prestigious national newspapers published articles supporting the residents' concerns, focusing on three issues in particular: the necessity of establishing public consultation; how far the Beijing administration is accountable for the Haidian government's environmental governance; and the extent to which decisions should be based on scientific grounds and the involvement of public participation. The strength of the public consensus in this case affected specific policy decisions, such that, by mid-June, the Ministry of Environmental Protection (MEP) had halted the project, acknowledging both the residents' opposition to its proposed location and the lack of public participation in the environmental impact assessment process.

The case of Liulitun was not the first where the Chinese public were successful, at least temporarily, in stopping a major infrastructure project endorsed by the Municipal government. Similar to earlier collective actions, it saw the emergence of an effective network among local residents, environmentalists, scholars and the media. The Liulitun protest is typical of similar environmental movements in China in that it did not lead to demands for democratization and political reforms, hence it has been referred to as 'depolicized politics' or 'self-imposed censorship' (Ho and Edmonds, 2008). In this respect, social movements in China can be distinguished from those in liberal democratic societies in three ways:

1. *Scale of actions.* China's restrictive political system limits the options open to people for forming movements or to systematically organize large-scale collective actions. Social movements are rarely directed against the national government (O'Brien and Li, 2006), and even fewer focus on the transnational level (Lee, 2007). Organizations, which are crucial actors in social movements in Western liberal contexts, are also largely limited in China. Although it has been argued that NGOs have achieved a high level of associational autonomy in the expanding organizational space between state organs and enterprise in China (Zhang et al., 2009), they still exhibit a supplementary relationship with the state as opposed to being fully independent from the state. Therefore, using organizations as a unit of study is unlikely to be fruitful in social movement studies (Wei, 2003).
2. *The choice of strategies.* China's political system precludes the adoption of radical forms of social action. As can be seen from the movement described above, participants are usually highly cautious in choosing which forms of action to take and are likely to adopt combined legal and 'semi-legal' strategies (Ying and Jin, 2000). Social movements in China are hardly distinguishable from political participation, and tend to adopt mixed strategies involving both institutionalized and non-institutionalized forms of action (Li, 2008). However, the latter is usually not a focus in the study of collective actions and is often excluded as part of movement dynamics.
3. *Outcomes.* Social movements in China are often observed to focus on single issues, and to be motivated by concerns for rule compliance that stop short of challenging state authority (Cai, 2006). It is true that the political implications of Chinese social movements are difficult to measure because their activities have had relatively little in the way of direct substantial impact on the formal structure of the political system. Even when movements have achieved reactive government responses, their opposition has been too weak to make major impacts on China's resilient political system (Friedman, 2009). Thus, given the limited scope of current studies of the outcomes of these movements (Xiao and Kong, 2011), our understanding of the characteristics of Chinese social movements remains limited.

Various terms have been used to capture the dynamics of the rising social movements in China, including *kangzheng*, meaning 'protest', 'resistance' or 'collective incidence' (Xiao and Kong, 2011). Unlike some who view collective actions as forms of resistance of contentious politics (O'Brien and Li, 2006), in this chapter it is argued that they represent movement actions that develop and are sustained over time. Four features of social movements are emphasized below (Diani, 1992, p. 7): (1) networks of informal interactions between pluralities of individuals, groups and/or organizations; (2) shared beliefs and solidarity; (3) collective actions directed at contentious issues; (4) participants within movements displaying actions that fall both within non-institutional and institutional spheres.

The chapter is structured as followed. The first part will provide a succinct overview of the major social movements in contemporary China. The second part will provide a review of scholarship on social movements in China. This is followed by a discussion on the development of the concept of political citizenship and its application in present-day China. The chapter will conclude with remarks about the relationship between social movements and political citizenship in future research endeavours.

SOCIAL MOVEMENTS IN CONTEMPORARY CHINA

This section provides a general review of the most important movements of the last quarter-century. The aim here is not to provide an exhaustive overview of every distinct type of contemporary social movement in China. Instead, this section will focus on a few major ones that have been subject to a significant amount of scholarship, concentrating in particular on their goals, characteristics and action repertoires.

Before the Open Door reform of 1978, collective actions in China were mostly organized through political campaigns led by the Chinese Communist Party (CCP). The success of such political campaigns was based on the Party's close control over individuals through its umbrella organizations. As early as 1930, not long after the establishment of the CCP itself, a political campaign was developed as a result of factional divisions within the Party in Jiangxi, where it was based. More radical campaigns emerged during the late 1950s and early 1960s, which peaked during the 1970s, recalling earlier Cultural Revolutions. Public opinion was shaped during this time along Party-dominated lines. In this regard, it has been suggested that Chinese individuals were successfully mobilized in support of political causes not by any 'particularistic and private interests', but rather collective interests such as 'family, lineage or nation' (Pye, 1995, p. 42). Government-organized NGOs (GONGOs) were established to unite eight types of social groups representing non-Party members.[1] To a large extent, these bodies worked to represent the public's interests while keeping tight control over them.

A distinct outburst of political protest can be seen in the 1989 Student Social Movement, one of the few movements to demand democratization and political reforms. It took place in the context of growing rights consciousness at the beginning of market reforms, which were met with political hurdles. Despite the fact that students were the main participants in the movement, support was also received from workers and intellectuals. Thus, in addition to the main thrust of the movement in Beijing, workers and other social groups became involved in other large cities across China. This movement has mainly been studied in terms of its emergence, which, some have argued, was rooted in emotions embedded deeply in Chinese culture. From a political-sociological perspective, Zhao argues that there was a shift in the public's perception of the legitimacy of the state, orienting toward demanding moral and economic performance. This was in contrast to in the past when nationalism and leftist ideology was dwelt on. Such a gap directly animated the emergence of the movement (Zhao, 2000). When the authorities did not respond to peaceful demonstrations, more radical forms of action were adopted including large-scale hunger strikes.[2] Adopting the concept of emotional achievement, Yang identified an active pursuit of emotional experiences and suggested that feelings of self-realization were gained through the movement, which in turn facilitated identity formation within it (Yang, 2000).

Peasants' Movements

Since political activism reached a peak in 1989, the last two decades have seen workers and peasants emerge as the major social groups involved in movements (Liu, 2008). In rural areas, growing de-collectivization of the rural economy, and increasing unemployment (reaching 20 per cent), taxation and other fees have generated discontent among peasants. Spurred on by various political causes, some peasants have begun to channel their discontent into movements, particularly where cadres violate popular notions of equity, fairness or justice (Biano, 2001; Bernstein and Lü, 2003). Issues linked to land and the environment have been the greatest drivers of social movements in rural areas.

Although heated scholarly debates have developed around the peasants' movement, no consensus has been reached regarding its causes, characteristics and significance. Many have recognized that rural residents are becoming increasingly active in adopting institutional channels to defend their rights, including to complaint,[3] judicial relief and legal measures of public administrative litigations (O'Brien and Li, 2006; Van Rooij, 2006). Chinese scholars, represented by Jianrong Yu, have argued that this trend represents a visible political movement that is often oriented towards local government, usually county authorities. Empirical data on land disputes indicates that in recent years, movement networks have developed across higher administrative level at county level. Self-organized village associations have formed that collectively represent their members' interests (Yu, 2003), and public support from peer villagers as well as legal professionals, public intellectuals and NGOs (Yu, 2007; Woodman, 2011). Rights-based identities among participants are being formed along with a sense of being part of a broader social movement, or of self-esteem and solidarity, which plays an important role among participants in enhancing their sustained participation in collective actions (O'Brien and Li, 2005; Woodman, 2011).

In comparison, some view peasants' movements as sporadic and disorganized, or at least loosely organized, and oriented towards seeking materialistic interests. These collective actions are a sign of participants being reactive to particular issues, but lacking in proactive initiatives (Ying, 2007; Gao, 2011). Lawful claims have been made about rights that have been granted to them. For instance, the claim of 'environmental injustice' was only used as a token to support demands for economic benefits (Xiong, 2007).

Labour Movements

Over the past few decades, there has been a rapid growth in the number and geographical spread of labour movements in China. Across the country, coordinated actions have been organized with several hundred thousand participants (CLB, 2012). The goals of these movements have diversified, resulting in 'an increasingly fluid and dynamic relation between state and labour' in China (Lee, 1998, p. 28). Earlier movements took place in areas where industrial sectors concentrated and saw collective actions organized by laid-off workers from state-owned enterprises (SOEs). Unsatisfactory arrangements put in place for laid-off workers, including pension deals, are believed to have contributed to the emergence of such movements (Cai, 2006; Lee, 2007). Workers were found to be more likely to organize collective actions when their subsistence was threatened (F. Chen, 2000). In comparison, recent labour movements have developed along the coast in Special Economic Zones where China's light and labour-intensive industrial sector is located. Industry in these areas mostly relies on migrant workers, who dispute with factory owners in Hong Kong, Taiwan and South Korea as well as multinational corporations. They represent a distinct peasant group working in urban industries. Their *hukou* (administrative residential) status remains 'peasant', significantly distinguishing them from urban workers. It has been argued that those workers laid off from state-owned industries who shared a memory of the socialist period react differently from those who oppose the privatization of state-owned properties (Lee, 1998). New labour movements that have developed in affluent regions of the country are more focused on labour processes and rights abuses such as living conditions, managerial abuse and workplace (F. Chen, 2003; Friedman and Lee, 2010). They are observed to be adopting legal measures to defend their interests, particularly after the passage of the Labour Contract Law in 2008 (Wong, 2011).

It is argued that these movements are constrained by the limits of the law (ibid.), particularly when lax enforcement of the law is prevalently observed (Friedman and Lee, 2010). Support for the adoption of legal measures also comes from other organized groups, including unions, grassroots groups, NGOs and other international groups (e.g., China Labour Bulletin, Students and Scholars Against Corporate Misbehaviour). However, these organized bodies are not always found to be successful in representing workers' interests or promoting an agenda in their favour (Ding et al., 2002; F. Chen, 2009). Empirical research indicates that space is allowed for grassroots NGOs to develop, particularly when they help to mitigate tensions between workers and their employers (Friedman, 2009). However, migrant workers' associations have been found to lack autonomy under the restrictive political regime in China (Froissart, 2006), and often act as means for political stabilization under the rule of the Party state (Friedman and Lee, 2010).

Urban Movements

New waves of collective action have further developed in relation to the demographic complexity of urban areas, where homeowners, private entrepreneurs, retired soldiers, students and intellectuals have been identified as drivers of social movements (Yu and Zhao, 2006; Xiao and Kong, 2011). The repertoire of actions taken by these movements differs from those of the previous two discussed above.

The foci of scholarly work on homeowners' movements vary. Some focus on movement dynamics such as power struggles between homeowners, property developers and the state (Guo and Shen, 2012). Homeowners or urban dwellers are aware of the power of organizations and thus attempted to organize their own, preferably independent, associations. For example, in urban homeowners' movements, committees of property owners play significant roles in mobilizing participants (Read, 2003, 2008; Zhang and Liu, 2005).[4] They are found to represent and act on behalf of individual citizens' interests (Cai, 2005; Heberer, 2009), and help citizens to pursue movement targets, activities and pressure against powerful actors, including the state and property developers (Read, 2008). This is particularly the case when disputes arise between residents and developers; and government protects the latter. There is a 'minimum of self-determination and autonomy' in the sense that 'members of a community make decisions regarding their community and its scope', including the involvement in making decisions and the administration of policies concerning community affairs (Heberer, 2009, p. 501). In other instances, these movements indicate a trend of 'de-organization'. NGOs are found to struggle to survive, faced with an uncertain relationship with the state, financial restraints and a lack of publicity (Martens, 2006; Xie, 2009). Loosely organized networks are developed as alternative sources of mobilization. The internet is stressed as a favoured platform, which is found to promote information exchange and the organization of collective actions (G. Yang, 2005; Yip and Jiang, 2011; Li and Li, 2013).

Various views exist on the political implications of homeowners' movements. Some believe these groups passively defend themselves as subjects obeying or accepting the contracts approved by government authority (Zhuang, 2011; P. Chen, 2009; Perry, 2009). Others suggest that these distinctive groups have formed their own interests. Along with the reduction of political control over individuals, a growing sense of privacy and the recognition of urban lifestyle are visible among homeowners. This sense of collective identity is spatially embedded within the arena of privately owned spaces and, it is argued, encourages individuals to defend their rights (Tomba, 2005). Therefore, a growing sense of ownership rights and related property-based interests are leading to the establishment of a civil society whereby citizens may advance their interests (Gold, 1998; Guo and Shen, 2012).

Environmental Movements

Aside from major concerns that are mostly related to individual citizens' material interests, environmentalism has become another focus in urban movements. This is one of the few movements that has seen the mobilization of diverse social groups. Another distinctive feature of urban environmental activism is citizens' willingness to defend their environmental welfare, particularly by exposing the misconducts of local officials (see Zhu and Ho, 2008), demanding access to sunshine and articulating discontent against pollution and health-related concerns. This differs greatly from rural residents, for whom environmental concerns are hardly sufficient to mobilize them into collective actions. Another major type of environmentalism bears some similarities to early environmental movements found in developed societies, where the main concerns lie in nature conservation and environmental education. The increasing level of environmental awareness among Chinese citizens is symbolized by the organization of environment non-governmental organizations (ENGOs) and voluntary groups, which have been active in raising the public's environmental awareness, supervising polluting enterprises and participating in environmental decision-making (Yang, 2005; L. Xie, 2009).

Women's Movements

The women's movement in China advocates the promotion of gender equality. It has been strongly controlled by the government, for instance through the dominance of government-organized NGOs (Howell, 1996; Jacka, 2010), the prioritized policy focus on economic growth (Howell, 1997), and the adoption of official political discourses (D. Liu, 2006). Since the 1990s, close relationships have been built with international women's NGOs and transnational activism networks. It has been found that the Chinese women's movement has developed its own agenda, which is based on the limited autonomy of movement activists and the political opportunities it possesses in China's restrictive political system (D. Liu, 2006; Friedman, 2009). Although significant progress has been made in promoting women's rights in China (Kaufman, 2012), the implementation of an international participatory agenda is not sufficient to achieve the goal of changing gender relations if institutional factors in local government are not tackled (Jacka, 2010). At the same time, it is also argued that cultural factors prevent the Chinese from being actively involved in transnational activism networks, including distrust toward international actors and uneven development within the NGO community (Hilderbrandt, 2012).

SOCIAL MOVEMENTS AND SOCIAL MOVEMENT SCHOLARSHIP

In recent years, an increasing body of scholarship has developed around the subject of social movements in contemporary China, representing growing academic interest in the subject as well as practical concerns shown by political authorities. This scholarship also reflects the growing attention being paid to NGOs, self-organized groups and volunteering, referring in turn to work and activities conducted in domains not run by government or for-profit organizations. Chinese academics' research on the issue is mostly funded through government programmes based in higher-education institutions. Very few independent research institutes have been established. Nor do we see specialized research groups on this topic abroad. One distinctive discourse refers to social movements as 'mass incidents' or a growing 'public crisis'. Not surprisingly, limited independence has been enjoyed by the majority of the Chinese scholars, who avoid investigating the nature of the political regime as a potential trigger for social movements.[5] The majority of the Chinese scholarship aims to provide policy recommendations on maintaining stability (*weichi wending*, often shortened to *weiwen*),[6] thus focusing its research on collective actions that seem to pose a potential threat to social and political stability.

In the study of social movements, three major theoretical approaches are influential: grievance theory, resource mobilization and political opportunity structure. From varying angles, each of these perspectives has provided understanding of certain aspects of social movements in China.

Grievance

The past decade has seen an increase in the adoption of grievance as a theoretical approach to explain the emergence and targets of social movements. The literature in this regard has identified a growing source of grievances, covering issues ranging from frustration toward unsatisfactory income level and living conditions (Z. Yang, 2012) to those resulting from the adoption of legal approaches in the resolution of disputes (Y. Xie, 2010). Scholarly work indicates that although certain social groups are likely to develop dissatisfaction to greater or lesser degrees, the formation of collective actions is more likely to occur among the general public.

Earlier studies on grievances stress that dissatisfaction tends to be rooted in economic reforms that lead to substantial changes in the establishment of market mechanisms, thus resulting in instability and insecurity (see also White, 1992). Workers and peasants are among the most frequently studied groups. Collective actions tend to form in response to various issues causing resentment, including housing, medical welfare, unemployment and level of income. With objective material interests being at the heart of these grievances, the deprived classes tend to vent their dissatisfaction through the organization of social actions (Zheng, 2004). Recently, collective actions are also found to be combined with discontent toward political institutions due to weakened trust toward political authorities. Protesters become frustrated when legal approaches are sought without a clear solution. These movements have been found to direct their discontent towards various targets, including national government, local government and non-political bodies, such as media or private corporations (D. Liu, 2004), with the latter two frequently being highlighted in the literature. Local government in particular has been a focal point of discontent when self-interested local authorities have protected corporate interests, engaged in corruption (Zheng, 2004), breached laws (Pan et al., 2010; Y. Xie, 2010), and/or made inappropriate political decisions (Pei, 1997). For urban homeowners' movements, the sources of grievances hold no immediate solutions as far as the resolution of issues pertaining their properties may be concerned (Read, 2003). Indeed, problems with property may stem from unreasonable or low-quality services provided by developers, as well as corruption within government.

These scholarly works also suggest that patterns of grievances have changed; the number of grievances has increased in terms of speed and volume (D. Liu, 2004; Michelson, 2007). The trigger of discontent may be non-material issues or personal reasons. Recent studies indicate that emotions are another major source of grievance. Investigations of nationalist movements indicate that a significant proportion of participants are well-educated university students, intellectuals and graduates from overseas, who have developed rising sentiments of political identity or loyalty toward the nation. These feelings are often invoked when disagreements arise in China in relation to territorial and resource disputes, as well as in international forums (Yang and Zheng, 2013). Additionally, the pressures of modern society can result in the accumulation of forms of distress or frustrations linked to life expectations not being met. Such emotions have been seen in a number of social groups, including nationalist and peasant movements, which often vent their discontent through collective actions in certain contexts (Guo, 2009). A spillover effect has been identified as animating collective actions involving feelings of deprivation among these social groups (Ru et al., 2009).

This perspective provides understanding of the motivations underpinning collective actions taken by movements (D. Liu, 2004). No systematic theses have been developed on the types of grievances and the characteristics of their changing patterns. How will the above-identified major sources of grievances evolve over time? Which types account for the most significant source, the objective conditions or subjective ones, particularly when they are formed from social cognition or other psychological conditions? If and how will the volume of grievances affect movement repertoire? How to understand the changing patterns of grievances? Are grievances group based; is there a correlation between certain social groups and the sources of grievances they are likely to experience? It has been noticed that grievances alone are barely enough to mobilize collective actions (Michelson, 2007). Will certain sources of grievances tend to be more powerful to mobilize collective actions than others? This approach informs us little on the choice of actions made by aggrieved social groups and the likely movement repertoires developed. According to numerous theorists, grievances alone are not sufficient for social movements to take place. In order to transform grievances into collective actions, the mobilization of resources is of significance.

Resource Mobilization

Resource mobilization theory is often adopted to explain the emergence and outcomes of social movements in China. By examining the types of resources useful to movement mobilization, one of the main theses of this theory is that acquiring resources (particularly those previously controlled by government) promotes movement development (Y. Xie, 2008). The more movement participants can access key resources, the more likely they are to succeed in achieving their goals.

Various types of resources are identified as useful in movement mobilization, for instance those attached to individuals such as time, knowledge, contacts and so on. Sympathy or recognition from the media or government are also considered key resources. In peasants' movements, political connections have been highlighted as important resources for gaining access to state institutions and possibly generating influence (Michelson, 2007). Similar findings are noted in studies of urban homeowners' movements (Zhang, 2005), for which alliances formed between protesters and the mass media form a distinct strategy. Given the limited autonomy permitted by the restrictive regime, the mass media has tended to act sympathetically toward social movements (G. Yang, 2005; Zhu and Ho, 2008), particularly those in urban contexts.

The capacity of movement participants to mobilize available resources is also found to be an important type of resource. Descriptive case studies have been used to illustrate that the organizers or initiators of collective actions play an important role in achieving their movements' goals. This consensus has been reached with respect to most of the social movements in China, including peasants' movements (Yu, 2004; Li and O'Brien, 2008), workers' movements (Cai, 2006), urban homeowners' movements (Ying, 2007), and environmental movements (Zhu and Ho, 2008). These individuals are usually charismatic members of local elites or stakeholders, who are able to use their personal networks to mobilize, plan and direct acts of dissent.

This perspective finds that along with declining state control over society, access to key resources contributes to understanding of the emergence, dynamics and outcomes of social movements, which represent changing relations between the state and society. However, the use of this approach has shown it to have limited explanatory powers regarding social movement dynamics. The usefulness of resources to the mobilization of social movements in China remains ambiguous. In addition to material and political resources, rights consciousness and legal knowledge may be counted as useful ways for movements to reach their goals (Y. Chen, 2006). Furthermore, the significance of movement resources is dubious. In urban homeowners' movements, it is recognized that in some cases movements rich in resources, including those considered key ones, are not guaranteed success or leverage. This outcome implies that contextual factors, very often embedded in local political processes (Zhang, 2005), may affect the successfulness of movements (Ying, 2007). Therefore, movement resources do not constitute the sole factors determining movement outcomes.

Political Process and Political Opportunity Structure

The Chinese Communist Party (CCP) is designed to maintain a monopoly over the state. In China's political structure, certain institutional arrangements have been made in order to balance power between the legislative, the executive and the judiciary. China's primary legislative body – the National People's Congress (NPC, almost 3000 members) and its many different local and regional branches – represents one institutional arrangement for public participation. The Chinese People's Political Consultative Conference (CPPCC) is another important organ in the formal institutional structure, which provides the masses with opportunities to participate in political consultation. The Party state maintains strong control over these two institutions, although it is argued that this relationship is changing and that the two institutions are gaining greater organizational capacities to interact with the CCP (Cho, 2002, 2008; O'Brien, 2009). China lacks an independent judiciary. The CCP holds a decisive influence through its power to nominate candidates for all major positions in the people's courts. Another feature of China's bureaucracy is its institutional structure, which is often found to have fragmented and uncoordinated interests (Lieberthal, 2004).

In comparison to the above two scholarly perspectives, strong attention has been focused on features of the political system and its impact on social movements in China. This theoretical perspective is particularly favoured by Chinese scholars. The major dimensions of political systems developed in relation to social movements include formal political institutions, the configuration of power, the informal strategies of political elites and the political output system (Tarrow, 1998). These dimensions have all been seen as highly relevant to understanding the characteristics of China's political system regarding the development of movements.

By reviewing the core variables developed in capitalist and (post-) socialist countries, from a comparative perspective the features of the Chinese political system are understood in a few dimensions (Xie and Van der Heijden, 2010). The formal institutional structure has been found to be a flexible means of containing social movements and assimilating their actors. Three important institutional variables are identified: territorial decentralization; the division of functional power between the legislature, the executive and the judiciary; and the electoral system. Given the flexible characteristics of the Chinese authoritarian regime, the first two variables see constant changes taking place. The features of the Chinese political institutions have also been suggested as determinants of the nature of social movements, while also being shaped in response to the demands of the latter.

The configuration of power seems to be another important dimension in China's POS, primarily with respect to its public administration system. One feature of this usually poorly coordinated political system is the blurred boundary within it between established values and informal or immature ones. It is argued that this feature leads social movements to resort to adopting institutionalized forms of action, including making complaints and using administrative litigation (Pei, 1997, 2010; O'Brien and Li, 2004; Gallagher, 2006; Michelson, 2007) and other formal channels (O'Brien and Li, 1995; Ying, 2001). In particular, this feature of the political system is thought to have resulted in peasant movements being referred to as 'boundary-spanning contention', that is, stressing that movement actions are characterized as occurring within officialdom (O'Brien, 2003). Collective actions of this type, it is suggested, are capable of realizing their goals and possibly achieving better movement outcomes.

The informal strategies adopted by political elites, or the politic leadership, is of great importance to the generation and mobilization of movements. As argued by Zhao (2000), one of the crucial factors affecting which strategies movements select is the attitude of unitary governing elites, who prefer tight control over society. For this reason, participants deliberately adopt cultural frames to gain sympathy from the public and avoid immediate repression by the political authorities. Another way of viewing the significance of political elites is in terms of the influence of cultural heritage; in this regard, the Chinese public rely on informal mechanisms to produce impacts in their political participation behaviour (Shi, 1997). Studies of environmental movements indicate that through informal connections or *guanxi* with government officials, environmental NGOs and civil society groups are active in seeking policy information and generating influence (L. Xie, 2009). Hence this dimension helps us to understanding the role that political elites play in social movements as potential individual activists.

The political output structure seems to be one of the most relevant dimensions in explaining the actions and repertoires of movements. This dimension focuses on the capacity of a political system to effectively implement policies that maintain its rule. It has been argued that state capacity began to decline during the period of economic transition (Wang and Hu, 1993). An indicator of weakened political output structure is the changing role that the state has played in driving economic transition. Social movements rose when the government did not meet the public's expectations (Y. Xie, 2008). Another key capacity representing state power is the degree to which coercion is used. The weakening state control found in state-owned enterprises and *danwei*, the basic unit of political control in China, provided opportunities for laid-off workers to mobilize towards collective actions (Cai, 2002). Ineffective policing has also been found to cause continuous public opposition. Various methods were adopted including repression (Y. Chen, 2006) and placating protesters with material incentives (Zhang and Li, 2012). All of these factors have helped collective actions to take place (Cai, 2004).

This theoretical perspective is useful for the understanding it provides of the causes and characteristics of movements, and the impacts they have on the state. With the exception of formal institutional structure, most of the dimensions identified by political opportunity structure theory have been adopted in movement studies, and have proven to be powerful tools for understanding the characteristics of social movements in China, in particular from a diachronic point of view. However, this also represents a weakness of this approach, since it tends to focus on certain features of political systems while neglecting changes in other aspects of those same systems that are conducive to providing opportunities for social movements.

RIGHTS CONSCIOUSNESS AND CITIZENSHIP NOTIONS IN CHINA

In recent scholarly discussions, especially between scholars of China studies in the USA, a perspective has been developed focusing on the growing rights consciousness of the Chinese population. It is suggested that in the interactions between the society and the state, various forms of rights claims have been made, ranging from social, economic and property rights (Zhang, 2005) to welfare provision by government and legal protection against state misdeeds (Van Rooij, 2006). Rights claims therefore constitute a key cause in the emergence of social movements. However, the concept of citizenship has not been systematically developed to apply to the Chinese context. Instead, it has generally been referred to as 'lawful rights' (O'Brien and Li, 2006), economic rights, or political rights.[7] The following section aims to answer the question of whether this trend indicates an awareness of political citizenship among citizens and what this concept means in China.

The Chinese have developed their own conceptions of rights, which differ from those familiar in Western contexts (Keane, 2001; Perry, 2008). Confucianism, one of the dominant traditional schools of thought, has been found to have a tendency to deny individual rights and self-interest (Pye, 1995). This attitude was maintained and reinforced by communism (ibid.). Citizenship is a foreign concept to the Chinese, although the term 'citizen' has been known since the late nineteenth century (Harris, 2002). The evolution of the Chinese understanding of 'citizenship' points to changes in how the relationship between individuals and 'their communities, their nationalities or state' has been understood in China (ibid., p. 198). Discourse on citizenship is weakly developed in China, both in practice and in political thought (Harris, 2002; Perry, 2008). Reviewing the historical interpretations of citizenship in China, Harris argues that various sets of terms were developed in response to changing political and economic conditions (Zarrow, 1997; Harris, 2002). There are two main foci underlying the idea of citizenship. 'Citizen' in Chinese refers to *gongmin* (loosely translated as 'public people'). The relationship between the individual and his or her community or state is strongly emphasized within this concept as meaning ethical responsibility toward the collective good. Collectiveness is valued more than the political rights and liberties of individuals (Keane, 2001). In the development of modern political thought, the making of the state and its modernization has been emphasized (Harris, 2002). T.H. Marshall's work (1950) on modern citizenship has an authoritative status. His account of modern political rights is only mid-way from a primary development of civil rights toward the achievement of social rights. Citizenship duties and responsibilities are understated than an emphasis on provisions and entitlements (in the form of goods and access) (Dahrendorf, 1994; Dobson, 2003). By contrast, in China citizen rights refer only to the entitled rights that allow them to contribute to the needs of the nation (Nathan, 1986; Pei, 2010). Thus, in comparison to modern Western thought,[8] the notion of obligations is emphasized over civil liberties that demand inalienable rights against the state. Such a tendency is deeply rooted in the concept of positive liberty, which emphasizes the role that community or state plays in influencing individual conduct and their achieving self-realization and other social goods (Howland, 2005). Referring to a liberal individual or inalienable rights against the state reflect developments in China's political discourse since the 1990s, when economic reforms led to changes in the relationship between the state and society (Keane, 2001).

POLITICAL CITIZENSHIP AND ITS APPLICATION TO SOCIAL MOVEMENTS

Aside from the literature focusing on the development of political freedom in social movements, little has been done to investigate the analytical content of the notion of citizenship. This section further reviews the relevant literature on social movements that discusses the underlying meanings of citizenship in the Chinese context. In this way, political citizenship is conceptualized in terms of two dimensions that both show an increase in volume: civility and membership.

Citizenship as Civility

The development of political citizenship is not only a reflection of how society responds to economic and political changes; its meanings have also been explored in terms of civility, which refers to certain traits embodied by individual citizens (Y. Xiao, 2009; B. Gao, 2012). According to the interest-based account of liberalism, civility describes 'a standard of conduct that citizens can rightfully expect from strangers', seen both as tolerance and affirmation to others' pursuits (Sinopoli, 1995, abstract). These norms are not limited to particular political systems. In China, civic virtue is recognized in the organization of formal and informal social groups that have strong implications for the mobilization of social movements. Such movements are in turn based on recognition, trust and shared identity among citizens, and as such contribute to the development of civil society (J. Zhang, 2000; Xia, 2003), particularly in middle-class urban communities (Tao, 2007). The emergence of civility has been remarked upon in urban homeowners' movements in China. Similar to the findings of studies of democratic societies, Chinese homeowners tend to be more politically active than their non-homeowning peers. As a result of their having acquired substantial assets, homeowners tend to show greater enthusiasm for political participation and have helped to drive the growth in social movements (Wei, 2003; Read, 2003). It has been suggested that local community groups help to foster rights consciousness, thus indicating that the growth of political citizenship is rooted in trust and social interaction (Min, 2011). The involvement of volunteers in community activities is also regarded as facilitating a sense of civility. Networking activities based on shared social capital have been increasingly identified among grassroots groups as well as those originally facilitated by government authorities (Xu and Chow, 2006).

In China, the formation of civility is strongly influenced by the country's cultural heritage. In traditional Chinese society, personal ties and social connections, or '*guanxi*', play significant roles in building and maintaining trust (Bian, 2002). As illustrated by the vivid development of environmental movements, environmental activists tend to be more inclined to make use of personal networks to mobilize movements, whose participants differ in terms of age, occupation and income levels. This practice is particularly prevalent in places where the conventional Chinese culture of personal networking still prevails, and used less frequently where the local culture has diverged from those traditional norms (Xie, 2009).

The literature has shown that there is a growing number of international NGOs working in China on the issues of poverty relief, healthcare, education, the environment and other local and global issues. By being recruited to international groups such as *Médicins Sans Frontières*, Chinese individuals are given greater opportunities to become volunteers. Civility is indicated through attitudes such as mutual respect and cosmopolitanism.

Citizenship as Membership

Civility represents individuals' becoming aware of their political rights. Shils has argued that this often reflects a shift away from parochial concerns towards a broader sense of collectiveness; hence substantive civility is reached once individuals 'give precedence to the common goods' over their personal or parochial interests (Shils, 1997, pp. 12–13). In the Chinese context, liberation is defined as citizenship that involves both the right to be treated by fellow human beings as equal with respect to the making of collective choices; and the obligation of those implementing such choices to be equally accountable and accessible to all members of the polity (O'Donnell et al., 1986; Shi and Lou, 2010). In Western contexts, political entitlements or liberties result from exchanges between the public and the state that end up in laws and established institutions. In China, political citizenship refers to demands for rights, both within the boundaries of the existing law and as having the potential to extend beyond current legislature to incorporate civic and/or political liberties. Therefore, demands for legal rights may be regarded as catalysts of a process whereby things not legal at the outset are eventually incorporated into the law.

Citizenship of this nature can be distinguished in terms of thin and thick citizenship (Tilly, 1996, p. 8). Thick citizenship refers in almost all respects to transactions of rights and obligations, including economic and political rights. In this way, political participation is key to the realization of citizenship. Thick citizenship is often found in Western literature focusing on membership in the state and government. In comparison, thin political citizenship places emphasis on actual participatory behaviour.

The development of citizenship oriented towards improving political liberty has been seen in rural areas, and has led to the adoption of village elections for the past decades. The nature of communities in China can be divided along urban and rural lines. Rights consciousness has been boosted by democratic practices in rural grassroots elections. Moreover, village citizenship is formed in the context of individual villagers being physically attached to their communities, as universally granted by the state (He, 2005). Studies of recent peasant movements have led one group of scholars to suggest that thick citizenship has emerged in different social groups through the assertion of political rights against the state (Heimer and Thogersen, 2006; Goldman, 2007). Peasants' movements reflect rising tensions between individuals and the state, especially when individuals show growing rights awareness and assertiveness in articulating their interests (Shi, 2000; O'Brien, 2001). Scholars of peasants' movements have also been cautious when investigating the nature of rights development in rural areas, highlighting thin citizenship as the driver of changes in such contexts. This is because rights consciousness is rooted deeply within the boundaries of existing rules and institutions, and so neither challenges nor threatens the authorities determining the rules (Perry, 2008; Perry and Selden, 2010). Migrant workers, who are different from other peasant groups (Yu and Wei, 2009), have formed their own distinctive identity. The nature of the political demands made by migrant workers and the impact of citizenship on the movement they embody differ. Migrant workers' political actions are characterized by greater reliance on legal institutions than ordinary peasant groups, which are more subdued due to their trust in the government and thus less likely to make direct demands linked to their individual rights (Cheng, 2012).

The dynamics of social movements indicate that their participants do not passively accept official interpretations of laws and the execution of power. These bottom-up initiatives, it is argued, have extended the boundaries of existing rules and institutions to encompass subscriptions of rights that have not been clearly prescribed (Yu, 2004; L. Li, 2010). Democratic political participation has been realized in both policy- and law-making, albeit at a low institutional level (L. Li, 2010).

To sum up, the above analysis has shown that citizenship, either in the forms of civility or membership, is, to some extent, evident in the development of most of the major social movements in China. Linking back to those characteristics of the movements discussed in the first section, we can conclude that the Chinese social movements involve collective actions rooted in the emergence of political citizenship.

FUTURE RESEARCH

Past studies of social movements have proven to be successful in explaining some of their aspects. In order to holistically understand the characteristics of Chinese social movements as identified above, a shift in perspective is suggested, involving the adoption of the concept of political citizenship.

The concept of political citizenship offers a powerful means of understanding Chinese social movements that are characterized as being both constrained and mobilized within the boundaries of established political institutions. As analysed above, two dimensions of political citizenship can be identified in the literature: civility (i.e., tolerance, cooperation, recognition and bonding between individual members); and membership (i.e., towards the community or collective good). By investigating and distinguishing between these dimensions, the concept of political citizenship may shed fresh light on the characteristics of social movements in China. Future studies may discuss the development and interactions between the two dimensions in relation to the evolution and dynamics of social movements. In turn, several questions may arise from this approach. Does thin citizenship correlate to an immature phase in social movements while thick citizenship represents their evolution, and in what ways? How has the notion of political citizenship been shaped in the Chinese context, particularly with regard to its social and political culture? Can evolution in social movements be identified by investigating developments in the notion of political citizenship over time, and if so, then in what ways? By examining the narratives and discourses of citizenship at different times, the relationship between citizenship and the development of social movements can be further explored. This concept will contribute to studies of social movements that are neither oriented towards regime change nor developed in opposition to political elites. In particular, it may be asked: how will the development of citizenship promote the development of post-materialist values among the urban middle class, which is one of the most successful groups involved in movements? This approach can provide fresh insights without limiting research to focusing on conflicts between society and the state; a perspective often adopted in liberal democratic contexts.

Methodologically, the concept of citizenship brings insights to our understanding of individual citizens, at the microcosmic level of analysis, in terms of their mobilization and participation in social movements.

Meanwhile, at the meso-level of analysis, it also helps us to investigate how individual citizens interact with organizational entities, NGOs and community groups, all of which may affect the outcomes of collective actions.

The adoption of the concept of citizenship can also contribute to analysis of the political impact of social movements, specifically regarding democratization and political participation. By distinguishing between the different dimensions of citizenship, insights can be provided into the significance of social movements in the Chinese context, where the space between political participation and formal daily politics is blurred. A question to be asked in future research is: what kinds of political reforms have been undertaken as a consequence of the actions of social movements?

In a time of globalization, another research direction will be to examine the impact of transnational movements on the development of citizenship in China. To what extent are the Chinese social movements affected by the development of transnational social movements, such as those concerned with environmental issues, human rights and anti-globalization? Is Chinese citizenship orienting towards global governance? And to what extent is such a process affected by social, political and cultural factors within China?

NOTES

1. These groups are workers, the youth, women, scientists and engineers, business people, the Chinese abroad (diaspora) and artists. Some were developed in the Chinese Communist Party's seizing of power during revolutionary time.
2. A collective hunger strike among students started with about 300 and the number went up to 3000 in mid-May.
3. The complaint (*xinfang*) system serves as an institutional channel through which the public's grievances can be addressed, and court judgements can be challenged. They pass their files to government administrative agencies of the same rank or inferior to them for a response.
4. Committees of property owners are also referred to as Residents' Committees.
5. Jianrong Yu is one of the few exceptions; see one of his recent publications, 'China's rigid stability', accessed 22 May 2014 at http://www.thechinastory.org/2013/01/chinas-rigid-stability-an-analysis-of-a-predicament-by-yu-jianrong-%E4%BA%8E%E5%BB%BA%E5%B5%98/.
6. The maintenance of stability has been discussed and issued in policy papers at the Sixth Plenary Session of its Sixteenth Central Committee of Chinese Communist Party.
7. Civil liberties includes rights that are prescribed by constitution. They are operationalized by freedom of expression, residence, religion and association. Political rights refer to personal political rights, independence of the legal system, equal treatment by the government and influence on government policy.
8. Obligations to the tribe, state, clan, feudal lord, community, God, and so on, can be found very clearly in pre-modern European societies.

REFERENCES

Bernstein, T. and X. Lü (2003), *Taxation Without Representation in Contemporary Rural China*, Cambridge, UK: Cambridge University Press.

Bian, Y. (2002), 'Institutional holes and job mobility processes: *guanxi* mechanism in China's emergent labor markets', in T. Gold, D. Guthrie and D. Wank (eds), *Social Connections in China: Institutions, Culture, and the Changing Nature of Guanxi*, Cambridge, UK: Cambridge University Press.

Biano, L. (2001), *Peasants Without the Party: Grass-roots Movements in Twentieth-century China*, Armonk, NY: M.E. Sharpe.

Cai, Y. (2002), 'The resistance of Chinese laid-off workers in the reform period', *The China Quarterly*, **170**, 45–62.

Cai, Y. (2004), 'Managed participation in China', *Political Science Quarterly*, **119**(3), 425–51.

Cai, Y. (2005), 'China's moderate middle class: the case of homeowners' resistance', *Asian Survey*, **42**(5), 777–99.

Cai, Y. (2006), *State and Laid-off Workers in Reform China: The Silence and Collective Action of the Retrenched*, London: Routledge.

Chen, F. (2000), 'Subsistence crises, managerial corruption and labour protest in China', *The China Journal*, **44**, 41–63.

Chen, F. (2003), 'Industrial restructuring and workers' resistance in China', *Modern China*, **29**(2), 237–62.

Chen, F. (2009), 'Union power in China: source, operation, and constraints', *Modern China*, **35**(6), 662–89.

Chen, P. (2009), 'From "property rights" to "citizenship rights": a review of researches on homeowners' rights protection in China today', *Open Times*, **4** (in Chinese).

Chen, Y. (2006), 'Ability of action and system restriction: middle class in the urban movement', *Sociological Studies*, **4** (in Chinese).

Cheng, P. (2012), 'Superior justice, village despot, go-getter: three key words in peasants' petition and resistance', accessed 23 May 2014 at http://www.usc.cuhk.edu.hk/PaperCollection/webmanager/wkfiles/2012/8772_1_paper.pdf (in Chinese).

Cho, Y. (2002), 'From "rubber stamp" to "iron stamps": the emergence of Chinese local People's Congresses as supervisory powerhouses', *The China Quarterly*, **171**, 724–40.

Cho, Y. (2008), *Local People's Congresses in China*, New York: Cambridge University Press.

CLB (2012), *A Decade of Change: The Workers' Movement in China 2000–2010*, Chinese Labour Bulletin Research Report, March, accessed 19 May 2014 at http://www.clb.org.hk/en/sites/default/files/File/research_reports/Decade%20of%20the%20Workers%20Movement%20final.pdf.

Dahrendorf, R. (1994), 'The changing quality of citizenship', in B. van Steenbergen (ed.), *The Condition of Citizenship*, London: Sage.

Diani, M. (1992), 'The concept of social movement', *The Sociological Review*, **40**(1), 1–25.

Ding, D., K. Goodall and M. Warner (2002), 'The impact of economic reform on the role of trade unions in Chinese enterprises', *International Journal of Human Resource Management*, **13**(3), 431–49.

Dobson, A. (2003), *Citizenship and the Environment*, Oxford: Oxford University Press.

Friedman, E. (2009), 'External pressure and local mobilization: transnational activism and the emergence of the Chinese labor movement', *Mobilization*, **14**(2), 199–218.

Friedman, E. and C. Lee (2010), 'Remaking the world of Chinese labour: a 30-year retrospective', *British Journal of Industrial Relations*, **48**(3), 507–33.

Froissart, C. (2006), 'Escaping from under the Party's thumb: a few examples of migrant workers' strivings for autonomy', *Social Research*, **73**(1), 197–218.

Gallagher, M. (2006), 'Mobilizing the law in China: "informed disenchantment" and the development of legal consciousness', *Law and Society Review*, **40**(4), 783–816.

Gao, B. (2012), 'The concept of civil society and China's reality', *Thinking*, **1**.

Gao, W. (2011), 'Collective incidents', *Twenty-First Century*, **6**, 115–23 (in Chinese).

Gold, T. (1998), 'Bases for civil society in China', in K.-E. Brodsgaard and D. Strand (eds), *Reconstructing Twentieth-century China: State Control, Civil Society, and National Identity*, Oxford: Clarendon Press, pp. 163–88.

Goldman, M. (2007), *Political Rights in Post-Mao China*, Ann Arbor, MI: Association for Asian Studies.

Guo, S. and Y. Shen (2012), 'The politics of living: an empirical study of right protection and community construction in B City', *Open Times*, **2**.

Guo, X. (2009), 'An analysis of group incidents from the perspective of social psychology', *Journal of Shaoxing College of Arts and Sciences*, **2** (in Chinese).

Harris, P. (2002), 'The origins of modern citizenship in China', *Asia Pacific Viewpoint*, **43**(2), 181–203.

He, B. (2005), 'Village citizenship in China: a case study of Zhejiang', *Citizenship Studies*, **9**(2), 205–19.

Heberer, T. (2009), 'Evolvement of citizenship in urban China or authoritarian communitarianism? Neighborhood development, community participation and autonomy', *Journal of Contemporary China*, **18**(61), 491–515.

Heimer, M. and S. Thogersen (2006), *Doing Fieldwork in China*, Honolulu: University of Hawaii Press.

Hilderbrandt, T. (2012), 'Development and division: the effect of transnational linkages and local politics on LGBT activism in China', *Journal of Contemporary China*, **21**(77), 845–62.

Ho, P. and R.L. Edmonds (eds) (2008), *China's Embedded Activism: Opportunities and Constraints of a Social Movement*, Milton Park, UK: Routledge.

Howell, J. (1996), 'The struggle for survival: prospects for The Women's Federation in post-Mao China', *World Development*, **24**(1), 129–43.

Howell, J. (1997), 'Post-Beijing reflections: creating ripples, but not waves in China', *Women's Studies International Forum*, **20**(2), 235–52.

Howland, D. (2005), *Personal Liberty and Public Good: The Introduction of John Stuart Mill to Japan and China*, Toronto, ON: University of Toronto Press.

Jacka, T. (2010), 'Women's activism, overseas funded participatory development, and governance: a case study from China', *Women's Studies International Forum*, **33**(2), 99–112.

Kaufman, J. (2012), 'The global women's movement and Chinese women's rights', *Journal of Contemporary China*, **21**(76), 585–602.

Keane, M. (2001), 'Redefining Chinese citizenship', *Economy and Society*, **30**(1), 1–17.

Lee, C.K. (1998), 'The labor politics of market socialism: collective inaction and class experiences among state workers in Guangzhou', *Modern China*, **24**(1), 3–33.

Lee, C. (2007), *Against the Law:Labour Protests in China's Rustbelt and Sunbelt*, Berkeley, CA: University of California Press.

Li, L. (2008), 'Political trust and petitioning in the Chinese countryside', *Comparative Politics*, **40**(2), 209–26.

Li, L. (2010), 'Rights consciousness and rules consciousness in contemporary China', *The China Journal*, **64**, 47–68.

Li, L. and S. Li (2013), 'Becoming homeowners: the emergence and use of online neighbourhood forums in transnational urban China', *Habitat International*, **38**, 232–9.

Li, L. and K. O'Brien (2008), 'Protest leadership in rural China', *The China Quarterly*, **193**, 1–23.

Lieberthal, K. (2004), *Governing China: From Revolution Through Reform*, 2nd edition, New York: W.W. Norton.

Liu, D. (2004), 'Interpretation of resentment, mobilization structure and rational choice: an analysis of the possibility of collective behaviour in China's urban areas', *Open Times*, **4** (in Chinese).

Liu, D. (2006), 'When do national movements adopt or reject international agendas? A comparative analysis of the Chinese and Indian women's movements', *American Sociological Review*, **71**(6), 921–42.

Liu, N. (2008), 'Thoughts about collective actions in contemporary China', *Open Times*, **3** (in Chinese).

Marshall, T.H. (1950), *Citizenship and Social Class*, London: Pluto Press.

Martens, S. (2006), 'Public participation with Chinese characteristics: citizen consumers in China's environmental management', *Environmental Politics*, **15**(2), 211–30.
Michelson, E. (2007), 'Dear lawyers, political embeddedness, and institutional continuity in China's transition from socialism', *American Journal of Sociology*, **113**(2), 352–414.
Min, X. (2011), 'Community conflict: the path dependence of civility construction – a case study of five cities', *Journal of Social Sciences*, **11**.
Nathan, A. (1986), 'Sources of Chinese rights thinking', in R. Edwards, L. Henkin and A. Nathan (eds), *Human Rights in Contemporary China*, New York: Columbia University Press.
O'Brien, K. (2001), 'Villagers, elections and citizenship in contemporary China', *Modern China*, **27**(4), 407–35.
O'Brien, K. (2003), 'Neither transgressive nor contained: boundary-spanning contention in China', *Mobilization*, **8**(1), 51–64.
O'Brien, K. (2009), 'Local People's Congresses and governing China', *China Journal*, **61**, 131–41.
O'Brien, K. and L. Li (1995), 'The politics of lodging complaints in rural China', *The China Quarterly*, **143**, 756–83.
O'Brien, K. and L. Li (2005), 'Popular contention and its impact in rural China', *Comparative Political Studies*, **38**(3), 235–59.
O'Brien, K. and L. Li (2006), *Rightful Resistance in Rural China*, New York: Cambridge University Press.
O'Donnell, G., P. Schmitter and L. Whitehead (1986), *Transitions from Authoritarian Rule*, Baltimore, MD: Johns Hopkins University Press.
Pan, Y., H. Lu and H. Zhang (2010), 'The formation of class: labor control on construction sites and the collective resistance of construction workers', *Open Times*, **5** (in Chinese).
Pei, M. (1997), 'Citizens v. mandarins: administrative litigation in China', *The China Quarterly*, **152**, 832–62.
Pei, M. (2010), 'Rights and resistance: the changing contexts of the dissident movement', in E. Perry and M. Selden (eds), *Chinese Society: Change, Conflict and Resistance*, 3rd edition, New York: Routledge.
Perry, E. (2008), 'Chinese conceptions of "rights": from Mencius to Mao – and now', *Perspectives on Politics*, **6**(1), 37–50.
Perry, E. (2009), 'A new rights consciousness?', *Journal of Democracy*, **20**(3), 17–24.
Perry, E. and M. Selden (2010), *Chinese Society: Change, Conflict and Resistance*, 3rd edition, London: Routledge.
Pye, L. (1995), 'Factions and the politics of *guanxi*: paradoxes in Chinese administrative and political behaviour', *The China Journal*, **34**, 35–53.
Read, B. (2003), 'Democratizing the neighbourhood? New private housing and home-owner self-organization in urban China', *The China Journal*, **49**, 31–59.
Read, B. (2008), 'Assessing variation in civil society organizations – China's home-owner associations in comparative perspective', *Comparative Political Studies*, **41**(9), 1240–65.
Ru, X., X. Lu and P. Li (2009), *Society of China: Analysis and Forecast*, Beijing: Social Sciences Academic Press.
Shi, T. (1997), *Political Participation in Beijing*, Cambridge, MA: Harvard University Press.
Shi, T. (2000), 'Cultural values and democracy in Mainland China', *The China Quarterly*, **162**, 540–59.
Shi, T. and D. Lou (2010), 'Subjective evaluation of changes in civil liberties and political rights in China', *Journal of Contemporary China*, **19**(93), 175–99.
Shils, E. (1997), *The Virtue of Civility: Selected Essays on Liberalism, Tradition, and Civil Society*, Indianapolis, IN: Liberty Fund.
Sinopoli, R. (1995), 'Thick-skinned liberalism: redefining civility', *American Political Science Review*, **89**(3), 612–20.
Tao, Q. (2007), *Modern 'Businessman Tribe' in Fujie*, Beijing: Social Sciences Academic Press (in Chinese).

Tarrow, S. (1998), *Power in Movement: Social Movements and Contentious Politics*, 2nd edition, New York: Cambridge University Press.
Tilly, C. (1996), 'Citizenship, identity and social history', in C. Tilly (ed.), *Citizenship, Identity, and Social History, International Review of Social History*, Supplement 3, Cambridge, UK: Cambridge University Press.
Tomba, L. (2005), 'Residential space and collective interest formation in Beijing's housing disputes', *The China Quarterly*, **184**, 934–51.
Van Rooij, B. (2006), *Regulating Land and Pollution in China, Lawmaking, Compliance, and Enforcement: Theory and Cases*, Leiden: Leiden University Press.
Wang, S. and A. Hu (1993), *Zhongguo guojia nengli baogao. Liaoning renmin chubanshe* [A Study of China State Capacity] (in Chinese).
Wei, F. (2003), *The Civil Society and Public Sphere Debate: Western Reflections on Chinese Political Culture*, Beijing: Social Sciences Academic Press.
White, G. (1992), 'Xiaoshan: prospects for civil society in China: a case study of Xiaoshan city', *The Australian Journal of Chinese Affairs*, **29**, 63–87.
Wong, L. (2011), 'Chinese migrant workers: rights attainment deficits, rights consciousness and personal strategies', *The China Quarterly*, **208**, 870–92.
Woodman, S. (2011), 'Law, translation and voice: transformation of a struggle for social justice in a Chinese village', *Critical Asian Studies*, **43**(2), 185–210.
Xia, J. (2003), 'The first signs of the civil society of China: the committee of owners as an example', *Journal of Literature, History and Philosophy*, **3** (in Chinese).
Xiao, T. and W. Kong (2011), 'Consequences of collective actions in contemporary China: a review of domestic scholarship', *Journal of Comparative Economic and Social Systems*, **2** (in Chinese).
Xiao, Y. (2009), 'Civility: what is seen and what is not', *People's Forum (Renmin Luntan)*, **9** (in Chinese).
Xie, L. (2009), *Environmental Activism in China*, London/New York: Routledge.
Xie, L. and H.-A. van der Heijden (2010), 'Environmental movements and political opportunities: the case of China', *Social Movement Studies*, **9**(1), 51–68.
Xie, Y. (2008), 'Political protests in social communities', *Modern China Studies*, **2** (in Chinese).
Xie, Y. (2010), 'From legal opposition to street actions', *Open Times*, **9** (in Chinese).
Xiong, Y. (2007), 'Market and environmental protests', *Dushu*, **9**, 17–22.
Xu, Q. and J. Chow (2006), 'Urban community in China: participation and development', *International Journal of Social Welfare*, **15**(3), 199–208.
Yang, G. (2000), 'Achieving emotions in collective action: emotional processes and movement mobilization in the 1989 Chinese student movement', *The Sociological Quarterly*, **41**(4), 593–614.
Yang, G. (2005), 'Environmental NGOs and institutional dynamics in China', *The China Quarterly*, **181**, 46–66.
Yang, L. and Y. Zheng (2013), '*Fen qings* (angry youth) in contemporary China', *Journal of Contemporary China*, **21**(76), 637–53.
Yang, Z. (2012), 'Social structure transition, resentment gathering, common destiny and the workers' collective action in South China', *Journal of Social Sciences*, **7** (in Chinese).
Ying, X. (2001), *From Asking for a Statement to Balancing Relations (Baiping Lishui), a Story of a Hydroelectric Station Area in Southwest China*, Beijing: Sanlian Press, accessed 22 May 2014 at http://www.threegorgesprobe.org/gb/documents/MigrantStory.pdf (in Chinese).
Ying, X. (2007), 'Grassroots mobilization and the mechanism of interest expression of the peasants group: a comparative study of four cases', *Sociological Studies*, **2** (in Chinese).
Ying, X and Jin, J. (2000), 'Problematizing process in collective appeal', *Tsinghua Sociological Review* (Special Collection), Xiamen: Lujiang Publishing House (in Chinese).
Yip, N. and Y. Jiang (2011), 'Homeowners united: the attempt to create lateral networks of homeowners' associations in urban China', *Journal of Contemporary China*, **20**(72), 735–50.

Yu, J. (2003), 'Farmers' organized protests and its political risk', *Strategy and Management*, **3** (in Chinese).
Yu, J. (2004), 'Struggle by law of the Chinese contemporary peasants: an interpretive frame for farmers' defending rights', *Sociological Studies*, **2** (in Chinese).
Yu, J. (2007), 'Social conflict in rural China', *China Security*, **3**(2), 2–17.
Yu, J. and F. Wei (2009), 'Politics vary with different migrant workers', *Nanfang luncong*, **1**.
Yu, Z. and D. Zhao (2006), 'Differential participation and the nature of a movement: a study of the 1999 anti-U.S. Beijing student demonstrations', *Social Forces*, **84**(3), 1755–77.
Zarrow, P. (1997), 'Citizenship in China and the West', in J. Fogel and P. Zarrow (eds), *Imagining the People: Chinese Intellectuals and the Concept of Citizenship, 1890–1920*, Armonk, NY: M.E. Sharpe.
Zhang, J. (2000), *Problems of Rural Level Governance in China* [Jiceng zhengquan: xiangcun zhidu zhuwenti], Hangzhou: Zhejiang People's Press.
Zhang, L. (2005), 'Beijing house owners' rights protection movement: reason for breakout and mobilization mechanism', *Sociological Studies*, **20**(6), 1–39 (in Chinese).
Zhang, L. and L. Liu (2005), 'Property management as a new public space: the tension between an over-powered state and an underprivileged society in China', *Society*, **1** (in Chinese).
Zhang, Y. and J. Li (2012), 'Creating consent', *Open Times*, **7**.
Zhang, Z., M. Fan and T. Wang (2009), 'A study on the interaction between governmental and non-governmental organizations under the state corporatism', *Society*, **29**(4), 167–94.
Zhao, D. (2000), 'State–society relations and the discourses and activities of the 1989 Beijing student movement', *American Journal of Sociology*, **105**(6), 1592–632.
Zheng, Y. (2004), *Globalization and State Transformation in China*, Cambridge, UK: Cambridge University Press.
Zhu, J. and P. Ho (2008), 'Not against the state', in P. Ho and R.L. Edmonds (eds), *China's Embedded Activism: Opportunities and Constraints of a Social Movement*, Milton Park, UK: Routledge.
Zhuang, W. (2011), 'Beyond state-conferred rights? A case study on homeowners' confrontation in Guangzhou', *Society*, **31**(3), 88–113 (in Chinese).

24. Social movements in India
Dip Kapoor

INTRODUCTION

India has a rich history of organized and spontaneous social activism from across the political-ideological spectrum. Social movement scholarship, however, has been relatively slow to acknowledge these political and social formations and to develop knowledge *of* and *for* social movements. The dominant scholarship on the subject has been the province of historians, sociologists, and, until more recently, political scientists. Of late it has also become the province of the relatively nascent fields of political sociology/ anthropology/ecology; development studies; environmental studies; Dalit[1] (caste) and women's/gender studies; and critical adult/popular education, with the latter more evident in materials produced by people's movements and NGOs. Academic, as in the case of the widely acknowledged *Economic and Political Weekly*, and popular journalism have been more diligent about consistent reporting and analysis on the social movement front. Websites dedicated to specific movements or movement sectors, such as the National Alliance of People's Movements India; Mines, Minerals and People India; Mining Zone Peoples' Solidarity Group and Sanhati; and the *Lokayan Bulletin* are rich sources of information and political analysis pertaining to contemporary social movements in India.

A cartography of the scholarship to date suggests a cacophony of case and empirical studies littering the social movement academic landscape, along with rich discussion and clarification around movement typologies and taxonomies and intra-movement micro-characteristics of one variety or another (M.S.A. Rao [1979] 2006; G. Shah [1990] 2004; Oommen [1990] 2010). Structural-functionalist and dialectical-Marxist (including later versions of a post-Marxist ilk and/or class analysis and its variations with caste and gender – see Omvedt, 1993) theoretical and methodological perspectives dominate the theoretical-analytical milieu. Building on the classical traditions are re-contextualized Euro-American perspectives and debates pertaining to old and new movements (Omvedt, 1993; R. Singh, 2001) or the imbrications of a Red and Green politics noted in political/cultural ecology (Guha, 1997a; Baviskar, 2008) or versions of popular democracy/micro-movements (R. Kothari, 1984; Sheth, 1993) and development-displacement–related movements (Baviskar, 1995;

Mehta, 2009; Oliver-Smith, 2010; Padel and Das, 2010) addressing accumulation by dispossession in the post-1991 era of the neoliberalization (globalization) of the Indian economy (Oommen, 2010b). Caste politics adds a unique Indian dimension if not socio-political complexity to movement analysis in India (Omvedt, 1993, 1994, 1995; Guru and Chakravarty, 2005; Chatterji, 2009; A. Rao, 2009) – a dimension that has also made a contribution towards the broader discussion around race/class politics internationally, as was the case at the first UN World Conference Against Racism, Racial Discrimination, Xenophobia and Related Intolerance in Durban, South Africa in 2001.

This chapter sketches a map of Indian social movements by adhering to the contours of the dominant scholarship, while taking detours to integrate relatively unacknowledged areas of scholarship pertinent to the contemporary social movement landscape of the country. The emphasis is on the post-independence period and on foregrounding contemporary movements that continue to provide opportunities for movement scholars and activists to make knowledge contributions towards movement politics and to academic inter- and non-discipline–specific (G. Shah [1990] 2004) knowledge production. After introducing some of the prominent and different theoretical approaches to the study of various movements in India, the chapter considers the literature and some key contemporary observations pertaining to social movements concerning peasants and new farmers, informal economy and industrial workers, women, and human rights. Brief paragraphs concerning Dalit and environmental movements are included in relation to particular theoretical orientations considered in the first part of the chapter. Finally, a few key projections and pointers regarding the future of social movements and research in India are proposed.

Movements not considered due to these delimitations include sub-national/autonomy and separatist/independence movements (e.g., Kashmir, Assam, and eastern states/regions) and conservative/right-wing movements (linguistic and religious chauvinism, including the Saffron/Hindutva[2] movements) (see Oommen, 2010a on this, for example); and a fading literature on student movements given Ghanshyam Shah's ([1990] 2004, p. 217) observation that these movements have been few and far between on university campuses since the 1980s.

THEORETICAL APPROACHES TO THE STUDY OF SOCIAL MOVEMENTS IN INDIA

Key compilations of movement studies and literature across movements, whether defined by constituencies (e.g., Dalit or peasants) or issues (e.g., environment or human rights) have been undertaken since the late 1970s with repeat or new editions (partially updated) published in the early 2000s (e.g., Rao [1979] 2006; Shah [1990] 2004; Oommen [1990] 2010; Omvedt, 1993; R. Singh, 2001; Ray and Katzenstein, 2005). The contributions by Gail Omvedt (1993) and Raka Ray and Mary Katzenstein (2005) discuss a cross-section of movements in historical and macro-contextual terms. Collections by Ghanshyam Shah ([1990] 2004) and two volumes (2010a, *Issues of Identity* and 2010b, *Concerns of Equity and Security*) edited by T. Oommen address several movements delineated in terms of issues and/ or constituencies, while providing some insights and findings potentially relevant to all or some of these movements, with Shah ([1990] 2004, p. 12) unequivocally stating that he 'does not feel confident enough to arrive at generalization on social movements' in India. There is an apparent scholarly consensus that Indian authorship has tended to focus on case studies of particular movements with little attempt at extrapolations to formulate theories or a general theory of social movements (R. Singh, 2001; Oommen, 2010a).

Theoretical and methodological approaches in social movement studies have distinctly tended to rely on structural-functionalist and dialectical-Marxist approaches, while the focus on studying social movements has simultaneously introduced innovations in sociological paradigms and methods of observation (e.g., social historiography and theories of collective behaviour) that have encouraged innovation and enormous variations as well. Furthermore, the study of movements particular to Indian society and polity, such as tribal (Adivasi), anti-caste (e.g., Dalit), peasant and religious movements, has innovated and added to processual studies of *becoming* (rather than formal treatment of social structures or studies of *being*), which in turn have encouraged inter-disciplinarity and multi-disciplinarity (particularly between history, political science, and psychology, if not sociology), while encouraging paradigm mixes as well, such as Marxism with structuralism and functionalism, with phenomenology or ethno-sociology (R. Singh, 1986, p. 102).

Structural-functionalist Approaches

The functionalist paradigm (framework) is variously deployed in the work of several scholars (K.S. Singh, 1982; Surana, 1983; Oommen, 1984, [1990] 2010; K. Shah, 1984; P. Mukherji, 1987; Gore, 1989, 1993; G. Shah [1990] 2004; Chaudhuri, 1992; Y. Singh, 1993). Society is defined as an organized whole based on values consensus, norms, ideologies, relational structures, and the social structuring of symbolic and cultural heritages, which taken together glue interconnected parts while demonstrating an ability to resolve conflict and deviance by producing adaptive/adjustive possibilities, enabling reforms. These studies also demonstrate wide variations in application including: the ethno-symbolic (Bagahi and Danda, 1982; Hussain, 1987; V. Das, 1990); critical (Gore, 1989, 1993); interactionist (Oommen, 1972, [1990] 2010); civilizational (Y. Singh, 1993); and structural-historical (K.S. Singh, 1982; Sinha, 1984; Sachchidananda, 1985; Chaudhuri, 1992) traditions, along with the frequent use of mixed methodologies. For instance, the work of sociologist M.S. Gore, which addresses leadership, identity, and movements in relation to Jyotiba Phule and the non-Brahman movement (1989) and Ambedkar's protest ideology (1993), epitomizes a critical functionalist orientation in Indian movement studies, while demonstrating the related utility of ethno-methodological socio-analysis and phenomenology. His conception of society is values based and norm/principle centered while also being in a constant state of socio-political praxis (an emphasis on the interplay of values, ideologies, and social action) given the imperfections of social stratifications and hence the related germination of movements for liberty, justice, equality, and freedom. The role for sociology and movement studies, according to Gore (1983) then, is to inform social policy for social welfare. In a similar vein, T.K. Oommen's Weberian construction of charismatic movements (1972) and his prognosis for Indian social movement studies defines a rather eclectic approach to functionalist applications where he combines a 'dialectics between historicity (past experiences), social structure (present existential conditions) and the urge for a better future (human creativity)' as 'the focal points to the study of social movements' ([1990] 2010, p. 30).

In methodological terms, structural-functionalist studies have relied on a variety of possibilities as well, including phenomenological (Sengupta, 1982) and ethno-symbolic (K.S. Singh, 1982) approaches to the study of meanings that social collectivities such as tribes, castes, and communities have attached to indigenous social and cultural institutions and practices and symbolic heritages. The ethno-symbolic approach has sought to demonstrate the millenarian core in tribal movements and assertions and/ or the role of precipitating factors in social movements in the setting of conflict and contestation (R. Singh, 2001, p. 170).

Dialectical-Marxist and Related Critical-structural Approaches

The dialectical-Marxist paradigm (framework) of movement studies (Banerjee, 1980, 1984; Byres, 1980; Gough, 1980; Omvedt, 1980a, 1981, 1993, 1994; Upadhyaya, 1980; Dhanagare, 1982, 1983; Gupta, 1982; Desai, 1986a; Patnaik, 1987; Singh, 1987; Dhanagare and John, 1988; Patil, 1988; Sharma, 1988) deploys material class dialectics as a philosophy and methodology understood in terms of modes of production, class formations, and social structure and a materialist conception of social transformation and history, including material determinations of class consciousness and the related notions of ideology and alienation. This paradigm has made a prolific contribution towards Indian social movement studies, especially in relation to peasant (rural) movements/studies if not industrial working class movements.

Subaltern studies (Ludden, 2005), influenced by the political theory of the Italian Marxist Antonio Gramsci (Guha, 1983), critiques notwithstanding (Alam, 1983; Bannerji, 2000; Brass, 2001; H. Singh, 2003; S. Sarkar, 2005), represents attempts to write histories of peasant and tribal insurgency and rebellion *from below* while emphasizing the politics of an *autonomous domain* of subaltern political consciousness (as opposed to the standard pejorative reference to a pre-political or elite-determined consciousness) and a colonial elite/class dominance without hegemony (Guha, 1997b). Contrary to colonial/elite historiography, peasant and tribal counter-insurgency 'was a motivated and conscious undertaking' (numerous planned revolts of peasants/tribals are cited including the Santhal *hool*, the Kol, Rangpur *dhing*, Munda, Chuar Rebellion etc.), a point that has either been glossed over or pejoratively described as a 'natural phenomenon', 'spontaneous' and wherein 'insurgency is regarded as external to the peasant's consciousness' (see Chatterjee, 2009, pp. 195–6 on the works of Ranajit Guha).

Contemporary discussions in subaltern studies have introduced the concept of 'political society' (Chatterjee, 2004, 2011) and allude to the prospect of understanding subaltern activism and movements (e.g., by Adivasi/tribal, Dalit/untouchable castes, peasants, agricultural/unfree labour) in terms other than that of old-new civil society movement approaches. In fact, in a Weberian analysis that is contrary to the Gramscian origins of the subalternist project pioneered by Ranajit Guha (see S. Sarkar, 2005 on the same topic) pertaining to the prospects and requirements of 'democracy and economic transformation in India' in the contemporary period, Partha Chatterjee (2008) suggests that civil society will need to address (in what amounts to an act of containment of the dangerous classes) 'the bulk of the population in India that lives outside the orderly zones of civil society', that is, a *'political society* where people have to be fed, clothed and given work, if only to ensure the long term and relatively peaceful well-being of civil society' (p. 62; my emphasis). He suggests that the widening and deepening of the state (apparatuses of government and governmentality) has transformed the quality of mass politics in India over the last two decades, enabling a shift from rebel consciousness characteristic of the colonial subject and period (peasant insurgency politics characterizing Ranajit Guha's earlier analysis) when the state and ruling authority was outside the bounds of the peasant community, to citizens demanding inclusive justice and fairness pertaining to governmental services today given that the state has 'penetrated deep in to the everyday lives of rural people' (Chatterjee, 2012, p. 46). Echoing Kalyan Sanyal's (2010) analysis on how primitive accumulation of capital today is being accompanied by a reversal of its effects through various social expenditure schemes (e.g., National Rural Employment Guarantee Scheme, NREGS) akin to a *passive revolution* wherein left and right politics do not question the dominance of capital but merely contest social expenditures, Chatterjee suggests that the mass agitation tactics of today (road blocks, disruption of train services, street violence etc.) are more likely within the theoretical ambit of a politics of *governmentality* (tussles over distribution of governmental services) rather than a politics of *sovereignty*, which characterized peasant colonial subject insurgency captured in an earlier period of subaltern studies. Referring to an 'overlap of the politics of sovereignty with the politics of governmentality' (2012, p. 47), he does acknowledge that if the former predominates (as may be the case with Adivasi and Dalit politics at the margins of or outside political society (Chatterjee, 2008, p. 61)), then it is Ranajit Guha's colonial subject peasant analytic/framework that is still relevant in terms of understanding today's mass politics in the country.

Ranajit Guha (2001, pp. 41–2), however, acknowledges that the 'colonial experience has outlived decolonization and continues to be related significantly to the concerns of our time' in relation to subaltern political projects, echoing the 'double articulation' (p. 11) of governance thesis by the British and by Indian elites, currently referencing the agents/institutions of a globalizing (colonial and imperial) capital and local/national comprador[3] classes. In keeping with Guha's conflict perspective, Partha Chatterjee's Weberian conception of 'political society' can be potentially reinterpreted as a space of contestation, distinguishing a political (uncivil) society subaltern social movement politics, addressing, for example, Special Economic Zones (SEZs) and pre-/post-independence 'accumulation by dispossession' (Harvey, 2003) and development-displacement (Baviskar, 1995; Rajagopal, 2003; Patel and McMichael, 2004; Menon and Nigam, 2007; Neeraj, 2007; Mehta, 2009; Sundar, 2009; McMichael, 2010; Oliver-Smith, 2010; Oommen, 2010b; Padel and Das, 2010; Sahoo, 2010; A. Shah, 2010; Kapoor, 2011, 2013; Levien, 2012; Munshi, 2012) from a civil-societarian new social movement (NSM) or a labour OSM politics in a post-1990 globalizing phase/era of economic liberalization, 'triggering off a new set of mobilizations' wherein 'economic re-colonization and cultural invasion are inducing sporadic collective mobilizations in India, although not yet crystallized into sustained movements' (Oommen, 2010b, p. 37).

Considerations of the wider political economy and societal conditions and social movement germination/prospects, maturity and/or suffocation, dissolution, and longevity discussed in terms of political opportunity structures or master frames or Pierre Bourdieu's notion of fields are relatively recent theoretical-analytical deployments pertaining to social movement analysis in India. For examples, see Khagram (2004) in relation to big dam politics and political opportunity structures, or Raka Ray (1999) with respect to women's movements and 'fields of protest', or Raka Ray and Mary Katzenstein's (2005) edited collection and analysis of several movements in relation to a shifting or replaced Nehruvian social-democratic master frame.

Studies rarely begin with any explicit clarifications about Indian society and there is generally a lack of conscious effort to relate the transforming structure of Indian society to the changing forms and strategies of social movements (R. Singh, 2001). Dipankar Gupta's (1982) study of the Shiv Sena (Hindu right) mobilizations in Bombay between 1966 and 1974 or Gail Omvedt's study of Dalit movements (1994) are exceptions in this regard, illustrating social-movement–society imbrications while providing examples of post-/neo-Marxist versions for understanding movements.

In sum, few studies actually deal with the problems of definition and meaning of a social movement and these attempts are often indicative of a neoclassical (functionalist and Marxist-structuralist variations) theoretical orientation of Western scholarship (R. Singh, 2001), which has moved towards new paradigms for social movement studies and is applying new methods of explanation as in the case of the predominantly non-class–centric models entertained in discussions about new movements – a discussion/application that is in an embryonic stage in Indian scholarship (Guha, 1982, 1989; Sheth, 1983; R. Kothari, 1984; Sethi, 1984; Frank and Fuentes, 1987; Omvedt, 1988; Gadgil and Guha, 1992).

New Social Movement Approaches

According to Rajendra Singh (2001, p. 154), 'the emergence of NSMs can, in many ways, be seen as the positive consequence of the paradigmatic collapse and crisis in the structure of the [dominant – my addition] theoretical models of movement studies'. Gail Omvedt (1993, p. 302) suggests that the concept of NSM does delimit a genuine empirical phenomenon. According to Omvedt, these movements are defined by the following characteristics (ibid., pp. xv–xvi):

- They have a broad overall organization, structure, and ideology aimed at social change.
- They are 'new' in that their ideologies define, explain, and address exploitation in a manner related to traditional Marxism but with clear differences as well (e.g., they are not popular movements willing to follow under the vanguardship of the working class and its parties or accept their working class ideology).
- They are movements of groups that were either ignored as exploited by traditional Marxism (women, Dalits and Shudras[4]) or who were exploited in ways related to the new processes of contemporary capitalism (e.g., peasants forced to produce for capital through market exploitation managed by the state, or peasants or forest dwellers victimized by environmental degradation) but left unconceptualized by a Marxist preoccupation with private property and wage labour.
- An analysis of their position requires a modified Marxist analysis of contemporary capitalism, that is, 'while Marxism has been called the historical materialism of the proletariat, what is needed today is a historical materialism of not only industrial factory workers, but also of the peasants, women, tribals, dalits and low castes and oppressed nationalities' (p. xvi). Omvedt presents a novel approach to defining movements by adhering to Marxist class analysis while simultaneously incorporating the discourse of non-class new movements (Omvedt, 1993) and referring to the anti-caste movement as the central democratic movement of Indian society (1994, p. 10), an approach that has been described as being 'contradictory' if not 'theoretically inconsistent' (R. Singh, 2001, p. 145).

Studies on *Dalit movement politics* have identified the following historical and contemporary actions (Guru and Chakravarty, 2005; Kumar, 2010) by Dalits against caste/ism and untouchability and to forge a new social location in India with varied success and always faced with the paradox of naming and subsequently inscribing caste in order to disinter its strictures from Hindu society:

- socio-religious movements to escape and/or modify the Hindu social order (e.g., Dr. Ambedkar's conversion to Buddhism in 1956);
- Dalit political mobilization and the formation of the Independent Labour Party (ILP) formed by Ambedkar in 1936, which was the foundation for the Republican Party of India (RPI) – and the recent arrival of the Dalit-based Bahujan Samaj Party (BSP) in Uttar Pradesh (UP);

- a Dalit intellectual movement spearheaded by Dalit writers like Jyotiba Phule and E.V. Ramaswamy;
- radical struggle and the formation of the Dalit Panthers by rural Dalit youth in 1972;
- the movement of Dalit employees under Kanshi Ram and the establishment of the Scheduled Castes, Scheduled Tribes, Other Backward Classes and Minorities Welfare Association in 1971;
- the Dalit women's movement that established the National Federation for Dalit Women (NFDW) in 1994 in Delhi; and
- mobilization through Dalit NGOs and the National Campaign for Dalit Human Rights (NCDHR).
- (Gokhale, 1979; Jogdand, 1991; Omvedt, 1994, 1995; Ilaiah, 1996; Mendelsohn and Vicziany, 1998; Ghosh, 1999; Zelliot, 2001; Pai, 2002; Rodrigues, 2002; Rao, 2003)

Dalit scholars have intimated that the historic moment open to a consideration of mass poverty and social justice for Dalits has lapsed. The fundamental economic and social questions relevant to Dalits are being side-tracked by the soft resistance of social movements, political parties and NGOs (Guru and Chakravarty, 2005, p. 154).

Red–Green and In-between Approaches: Political Ecology, Cultural Politics, and Popular Democracy (Micro-movements)

In relation to Indian environmentalism, Amita Baviskar (1995, 2005, 2008) suggests another approach to movement studies, one that explores Indian 'environmentalisms of the poor' as combining a 'Red' politics preoccupied with material and distributive justice and a 'Green' politics pertaining to ecological concerns in contrast to a post-materialist wilderness and/or aesthetic environmentalism in the 'First World'. In other words, environmental degradation and social injustice are seen as two sides of the same coin, an insight she suggests is endorsed by the environmentalist Anil Agarwal of the NGO Center for Science and Environment, Medha Patkar of the Narmada Bachao Andolan (NBA) (Movement to Save the River Narmada), and Father Thomas Kocherry of the Kerala Fishworkers' Forum alike. This ideology has been translated into scholarly terms through the work of Madhav Gadgil and Ramachandra Guha (1992) on the non-violent Chipko movement against tree-felling in the Garhwal Himalayas in the 1970s, and shared by several leading environmentalists in India who point to the lopsided, iniquitous, and environmentally destructive development in India, pitting 'omnivores' (iron triangle of political-economic class elites) against ecosystem people submerged in a sea of poverty as development-displacement forces subalterns to migrate to urban slums, augmenting the swollen ranks of the impoverished (Baviskar, 2005, p. 163). In addition to Chipko, similar movement analysis pertaining to Red–Green varieties and environmentalisms of the poor (Guha and Martinez-Alier, 1998) have been made with reference to Narmada (NBA), the Chilika Bachao Andolan (Movement to Save Chilika Lake) against aquaculture in Orissa, the Kerala Fishworkers' Forum campaign against mechanized trawlers and movements against eucalyptus plantations on common lands in Karnataka, among several other displacement-related mobilizations in the country.

As a *political ecology approach* to Indian environmental movements that 'assumes that cultural identities are pre-formed, derived directly from an objective set of interests based on shared locations in terms of class, gender or ethnicity that challenge nationalism and/or capitalism' (Baviskar, 2008, p. 6), which subsequently forms the basis of contention over forests and other environmental resources, material use value is seen as the primary significance of natural resources, setting up the binaries of 'virtuous peasant' versus 'vicious state' (Sivaramakrishnan and Agrawal, 2003, p. 391). A *cultural politics approach* to environment/movements, on the other hand, treats culture itself as a site of struggle wherein identities, interests, and resources are not predetermined givens but *emergent*, that is, the practices of subjects are not understood through structurally determined categories but through the specificity of contradictory lived experience as the environment has value within a larger economy of meaning or the social life of things (Sivaramakrishnan and Agrawal, 2003; Cederlof and Sivaramakrishnan, 2006; Baviskar, 2008; Subramanian, 2009; A. Shah, 2010). According to Baviskar (1995), political ecology approaches, while intended as a gesture of solidarity, resort to an uncritical reproduction of claims by marginalized groups (singular narratives to explain natural resource struggles) thereby failing to offer much analytical purchase. In other words, 'we need to locate environmental movements within a discursive framework constituted by unequal structures of the global political-economy, while also examining the negotiation of meanings between different (unequal) groups that constitute social movements' (e.g., environmentalism of the poor emerging as collaboration with middle-class actors and audiences) (Baviskar, 2005, p. 161). Critical ethnography is proposed as the methodology with the best tools to represent such contingent processes under which people make history (Baviskar, 2008; A. Shah, 2010).

Seminal contributions towards the study of *environmental movements* include contributions by Guha and Gadgil (1989) on the resistance of hunter gatherers and shifting (*jhum*) cultivators and an overview of resource conflicts in colonial India; Guha on the Chipko movement (1989); Shiva and Bandopadhyaya (1986) and Shiva (1988) on passive resistance (people's ecology movements) to save trees and wildlife (e.g., the Bishnois of Khejri in Rajasthan) from three centuries ago to today; and Baviskar's research on the Narmada Bachao Andolan (1995). Gadgil and Guha (1998, p. 469) provide a useful classification of various strands of Indian environmental movements, including crusading Gandhians, ecological Marxists, appropriate technologists, scientific conservationists, and wilderness enthusiasts, while Harsh Sethi (1993) provides another five-category scheme based on resources and their exploitation/exploiters and resistances. Andharia and Sengupta (1998, pp. 429–31) provide a very useful classification scheme identifying ecological categories (e.g., forests), issues (e.g., right to forest access) and resistances (e.g., Chipko and Appiko). Similar schemes for identifying and studying urban environmental movements are yet to be attempted.

Social movements in India have also been understood in relation to the reinvention of *participatory democracy by micro-movements* (Sheth, 1984) in the mid-1970s in opposition to the hegemonic forces of globalization, while expanding the arena of politics beyond representational institutions of elections and political parties. Variously referred to as grassroots movements, non-party political formations, social action groups, and movement groups, these micro-movements differentiated themselves from welfare, philanthropic, and non-political NGOs and numbered some 30 000 movement groups by the turn of the century. The goal of these micro-movements was to democratize development and transform society through the empowerment of the people (people power or *lokshakti*) (R. Kothari, 1984; Sethi, 1984; Sheth, 1984, 2005). According to Rajni Kothari (1984), the decline of mainstream institutions of representative democracy including the legislatures, elections, political parties, and trade unions that had begun in the late 1960s, became apparent when the 'Emergency'[5] was imposed (1975–77) by Prime Minister Indira Gandhi, the highest-intensity and the politically largest example being the Jayaprakash Narayan or J.P. Movement led by the popular socialist leader of the independence movement who dedicated his whole life to the 'Gandhian way'. Such movements took up issues and constituencies abandoned by political parties and trade unions and those poorly served by the bureaucracy, developing as civil-associational groups (often led by men and women who had left their professional careers to join) leading political struggles on issues articulated to them by the people themselves (Sethi, 1984; Sheth, 2005). The influence of these micro-movements waned in the late 1980s/early 1990s as many were transformed into bureaucratic NGOs with funding, losing the motivation for social transformation, while others splintered for lack of a coalescing political purpose. The specter of globalization and the neoliberalization of the Indian economy by the mid-1990s revived protests and coalition politics and NGOs were reversed into movements countering the forces of hegemonic globalization, including the emergence of the National Alliance of People's Movements, the Living Democracy Movement, the Coalition for Nuclear Disarmament and Peace, and the National Campaign for People's Rights (Sheth, 1999; S. Kothari, 2001). The main effort of these micro-movements today is to make development into a bottom-up process, seeking to change the power relations on which the conventional models of development and globalization are premised. In other words, their objective remains the same as before, which is to ensure that those at the lowest rungs find their rightful place as producers in the economy and citizens in the polity, but they are formulating these old issues of development in new political terms (A. Roy, 1996; B. Roy, 1999; Tarkunde, 2003; Sheth, 2005). Drawing liberally on Gandhian economic and political thinking including conceptions of *swaraj* (self-governance), *swadeshi* (community control over resources) and *gram swaraj* (village republic) to reinvent a politics of participatory democracy and non-violent activism (e.g., organizing walkathons of *pad yatras*), a badge that not all of them would care to claim, these movements and non-party political formations have also (contrary to any such claims by their main intellectual protagonists) been likened to NSMs and described as displaying a 'conscience perspective' (R. Singh, 2001, p. 207). The latest expression of an urban middle-class populist Gandhian-inspired 'conscience perspective' is the Anna Hazare-led anti-corruption movement, culminating in the passage of the Lokpal Bill (passed in the Lok Sabha in December 2013) sanctioning a corruption watchdog body, which would include the PM's office under its purview.

SOCIAL MOVEMENTS

Peasant and New Farmer Movements

Peasant movements have been active in British colonial and post-colonial periods despite the caste fatalisms of Hinduism, according to Kathleen Gough (1974) who counted 77 revolts during the British colonial period (classified as restorative, religious, social banditry, vengeance, and mass insurrection) over the last two centuries (ibid., p. 1319). Ranajit Guha (1983) counts 110 known instances over 117 years during British rule, and similar conclusions are drawn by A.R. Desai (1978, p. xii; 1986a) who points to militant struggles lasting over many years involving hundreds of villages. This is contrary to Barrington Moore's (1967) conception of the Indian peasant as passive and docile and Eric Stokes's (1978) observation that peasant rebellions were strangely absent in Indian history.

There is a strong (200-year) tradition of armed uprisings reaching back to Moghul times in all regions against landlords, revenue agents/bureaucrats, money-lenders, police, and military forces. Peasant revolts since the 1920s have been coordinated with oppositional political parties and have either been struggles for regional autonomy by tribals/Adivasis (e.g., Santhals, Oraons and others in Jharkhand or Kashmiri and Naga/Mizo tribal nationalisms in the eastern states) or class struggles under the tutelage of India's communist parties, seven of which began in the 1960s. The most successful communist-led uprisings, all involving a large component of tribal/Adivasi people, were those of Tebhaga in 1946 (demand for a greater share of crop for share-croppers [*adhiars*] from occupying tenants [*jotedars*]), Telangana in 1946–48 (cancellation of peasant debts and abolition of illegal exactions by landlords [*desmukhs*]) and Naxalbari in Bengal in 1967 and Andhra Pradesh in 1969–71 (land occupation and hand-overs to peasants/tribals from landlords and *zamindars* [aristocrats]/*jotedars* under the Land Act) (M. Rao, 1971; Alavi, 1973; Gough and Sharma, 1973; Mukherji, 1987).

The sheer volume of peasant movement studies (see related listings in Dhanagare, 1983; G. Shah [1990] 2004; Omvedt, 1993; R. Singh, 2001; SinghaRoy, 2004; Oommen, 2010b), suggests that the peasantry is a viable concept (in relation to other categories of locating subalternity like tribe/Adivasi) in India and does refer to a contemporary category of people in the Indian countryside accounting for 70 percent of the population who are rural labour/smallholders (Oommen, 2010b, p. 45).

A considerable amount of ink has been spilt by the left intelligentsia (for Gandhian-inspired Sarvodaya and non-violent movements like Bhoodan-Gramdan initiated in 1951 by his disciple Acharya Vinoba Bhave, see Oommen, 1972 – a movement that inspires the current Ekta Parishad land initiative led by P.V. Rajagopal in Bihar/Eastern India) over how to divide and classify peasants and related claims pertaining to the political goals/unity, degree and methods of social movement activism entertained by the various categories. Hamza Alavi notes that several modes of production coexist and are structurally differentiated, thereby making it unfeasible to suggest one hierarchical class structure (1973, p. 293). His three-sector classification scheme includes:

- landlords and land owners and poor peasant classes who cultivate their land as landless/share-croppers;
- independent subsistence smallholder cultivators who do not exploit the labour of others (middle peasants); and

- capitalist farmers who employ capital and turn farming into a business by exploiting poor peasants.

The middle peasant category is an ongoing source of debate, with some even suggesting there are no middle peasants. Others have even classified contemporary farmers' movements as 'new' and 'non-class movements', which coincide with an environmental thrust/movements (Omvedt, 1993, p. 125), an assertion that is contested as being purely rhetorical while enabling rich peasants to reinforce their hegemony over the movement (Dhanagare, 1995), if not helping an agenda where new farmers, ecofeminists, and sections of the left (new movements?) become complicit in reproducing an ideological space permitting right-wing political organizations to reappropriate the Indian past (Brass, 1994, p. 48).

Alavi's (1973, pp. 333–4) analysis in relation to the political role of the various peasant classes of Tebhaga and Telangana movements in India led by the Communist Party, when compared to the Chinese and Russian revolutions, led him to conclude that middle peasants, by virtue of their relative economic independence, had greater revolutionary potential than dependent poor peasants who are initially the least militant class. Referring to this as the replacement of one myth by another, Dhanagare (1983) and others (Gough, 1968; Alexander, 1975; Sarkar, 1979; Pavier, 1981; A. Das, 1983, 1987; Duyker, 1987) assert otherwise, based on their respective studies of Tebhaga, Telangana, Naxalite, Bhoomi Sena and other movements. Some of these studies and experiences demonstrate how rich and middle-class peasants used the movement (poor peasants) to secure their own class/landed interests only to abandon the struggle thereafter. Similar studies in relation to the Naxalite and Telangana movements point to the limited longevity of industrial-worker/agricultural-labour movement solidarity under the auspices of Communist Party-led efforts, if not the inability of the Naxalite movement to organize and mobilize poor and landless peasants (Banerjee, 1980). Dhanagare's (1983) extensive review of Marxist literature on peasant movement studies (socio-historical treatments of movements), including the Moplah Rebellion in Malabar, Tebhaga in Bengal, Bardoli Satyagraha in Gujarat, and the peasant uprisings/struggles in Telangana in Andhra and Oudh in UP, leads him to conclude that the poor peasant class movements were generally millennial and insurrectionary while rich/middle-class peasantry resorted to non-violent resistance that was of a nationalist political tenor. Other scholars have suggested that it is difficult to arrive at a theory regarding the revolutionary potential of different classes because of the complexity of such struggles in relation to the colonial experience (Chatterjee, 1986).

New farmers' movements (unlike peasant movements, these movement constituencies produce for the market to a greater extent and are influenced by capital in agriculture) that emerged in the 1970s and the 1980s in the form of the Bharatiya Kisan Sangh (BKS; Punjab and then UP), Vivasayigal Sangam (Tamilnadu), Shetkari Sanghatana (Maharashtra), Khedut Samaj (Gujarat) and the Rajya Rayatu Sangha (Karnataka/ KRRS[6]) (Omvedt 1993, 2005; Dhanagare, 1999; Herring, 2005) took up concrete issues affecting all rural classes. These pertained to terms of trade, prices, technology, GM seeds, water/irrigation, Bt cotton, and the Dunkel-GATT prescriptions and capital accumulation in agriculture in the post-Green Revolution (HYV[7]) era unevenly, forming a tenuous coalition plagued by differences in vision and politics (e.g., embracing globalization/liberalization and genetic technologies) between its outspoken leaders (e.g., Sharad Joshi/Shetkari Sanghatana, which claimed to have 70 percent of farmer/peasant support for liberalization/technology versus Nanjundaswamy/KRRS), political party affiliations and internal schisms. Still able to mobilize large constituencies, the new farmers' movements gradually lost momentum in the mid- to late 1990s (Omvedt, 2005). Today, cotton farmer suicides (17 638 in 2009 alone) linked to agricultural liberalization and GM technologies plague the current rural landscape (Center for Human Rights and Global Justice, 2010).

Recent debates about the 'agrarian question' in India and left politics (Lerche et al., 2013), while preoccupied with the semi-feudal versus capitalist agriculture thesis and its implications for Communist Party of India (Maoist/Marxist) political strategy, also provide insight into the current impetus/direction for peasant/rural politics in the countryside. The classical theory of agrarian transition based on the semi-feudal thesis (landlord classes and peasant differentiation in the country) points to the need for peasant/rural organizing to focus on semi-feudal relations *within* and to enable state-led national (agrarian and industrial) development strategy (radical land reforms agenda) by breaking with the neoliberal world order that is the current trajectory of the communist parties and of the Maoist movement (D'Souza, 2009; Mukherji, 2012). The Maoist movement was recently dubbed by Prime Minister Manmohan Singh as the greatest threat to India's internal security, which warranted the launching of Operation Green Hunt (2009), arguably the single largest deployment of state paramilitaries and armed police. Alternatively, another proposition emphasizes the need for a 'people's' (popular as opposed to class-specific) struggle including landless peasants, Adivasis, Dalits and Other Backward Castes against state/corporate/civil-society–led global capitalist development-displacement, which is increasingly fusing local and global markets, domestic and multinational capital, and has involved a growing dispossession of the peasantry and usurpation of national resources (McMichael, 2008;

Patnaik, 2010; Basu and Das, 2013; Via Campesina – www.viacampesina. org). Examples include SEZ-based and other industrial acquisitions – land acquisition protests in Singur, West Bengal against Tata Motors with Tata withdrawing in 2008; the Plachimada, Kerala water protests leading to Coca Cola's withdrawal in 2003; Adivasi NBA protests against UK-based Vedanta-Sterlite bauxite mining in Niyamgiri, Lanjigarh, in Orissa (now Odisha). Such development-displacement–related movements (variously analysed in terms of their movement teleology) dot the rural landscape in the post-liberalization era (Routledge, 1993; Baviskar, 1995; Kamat, 2001; Rajagopal, 2003; Whitehead, 2003; Patel and McMichael, 2004; Menon and Nigam, 2007; Sundar, 2009; Da Costa, 2010; McMichael, 2010; Nilsen, 2010; Oliver-Smith, 2010; Oommen, 2010b; Sahoo, 2010; A. Shah, 2010; Kapoor, 2011, 2013; Mookerjea, 2011; Levien, 2012; Munshi, 2012; Choudry and Kapoor, 2013).

Informal Economy and Industrial Working Class Movements

The Self-employed Women's Association of India (SEWA) is a flagship organizing and social action effort addressing women workers in the informal economy, which includes 92 percent of the work force (Chakrabarti, 2011, p. 39). The formative conflict addressed by the emerging organization in 1972 was over the right to form a trade union (TU) normally focused on wage labour in the urban economy with self-employed casual labour associated with the textile industry. The TUs argued that the self-employed had no employers by definition. Establishing a precedent, SEWA's approach and success at organizing casual labour (subordinate/marginalized caste women) helped spur on the development of similar organizing and activism (with varied organizational forms in rural contexts) by women in the informal economy across the country. These included the waste pickers in Pune (KKPKP); the Karnataka Domestic Workers' Union in Bangalore; a sex workers' collective in two states (VAMP); Uttarakhand Mahila Parishad (UMP) and the associated Environmental Education Center; and SNEHA, a fishing women's organization in Tamilnadu (see chapters by Pande, Rethinam, Menon, Narayan and Chikarmane, Seshu, and Bhatt in Kabeer et al., 2013). They also included women garment worker organizing under Center for Development Initiatives (CIVIDEP, Bangalore) (RoyChowdhury, 2005); the Karnataka Koligari Nivasa Sangathana (KKNS) addressing marble and construction workers (RoyChowdhury, 2003); and the Working Women's Forum (WWF, Madras) (Kalpagam, 1994). These contributions, while foregrounding the relative socio-economic success of these initiatives, despite socio-political tensions created by public/private-sector micro-credit and self-help group interventions (de-politicization impacts), continue to point to informal economy gender-/caste-based organizing efforts and movement tensions around gender, caste, and dealings with the TU sector, if not state/corporate actors. Disempowered by class and gender, such credit-based service-focused developmental approaches (micro-battles), which have moved from a politics of class to one of community, do not necessarily address exploitation by capital through extraction of surplus value from a relatively disempowered population as capital–labour relationships become fluid, temporary, and in search of lower wage/working condition environments in the 'Third World'. However, SEWA has become a national union with a membership of over 500 000 across eight SEWA organizations in the country in a federated structure, becoming a founding member of the new International Trade Union Confederation (INTUC) in 2006. SEWA has also been a major actor in the global movement of workers in the informal economy, organizing street vendors into an international organizing and advocacy network called StreetNet in Durban in 2000, with organizations from over 27 countries involved (Chen, 2010).

Recent analyses of SEWA and informal labour organizing and activism in India (Breman, 2004; Bhatt, 2010; Gillan, 2010; Harriss-White, 2010; Hensman, 2010; Webster, 2011) suggest the following: (1) the growing willingness of TUs to organize informal workers in India may be the beginnings of a new counter-movement, despite suspicions both ways; (2) Barbara Harriss-White (2010) in particular also speaks to a counter-movement from above as the Indian state has opened up new possibilities for organizing in the informal economy (since 2004), echoing similar analyses suggesting a 'passive revolution' advanced by Kalyan Sanyal (2010) and Partha Chatterjee (2012); and (3) there is an emergence of a new form of unionism that protects workers within their informal employment status, rather than trying to transform them into formal sector workers, recruiting members through slums rather than worksites, that is, demands are not just aimed at employers but also on the state for benefits (Agarwala, 2006). There is a paucity of studies on unorganized workers in the non-industrial sector and the use of strikes, with a few exceptions including women workers' struggles in the coir industry in Kerala (Velayudhan, 1985) and Kannan's (1988) study on cashew workers, toddy tappers[8] and bidi workers'[9] demands for more wages. Relatedly, as rural development-dispossession forces urban migration, creating a planet of slums (Davis, 2004), shack/street/platform-dweller movements (see Patel et al., 2001; McMichael, 2010) will continue and also raise the decibel level of urban movement activism in the unorganized sector.

Karnik (1966) considers the Bombay textile workers' strike in 1877 as marking the beginning of the labour movement in India, with the end of the nineteenth century witnessing numerous strikes in textiles, jute, plantations, mines, and railways in Bombay, Calcutta, Ahmedabad, and Madras. Trade unions along modern lines developed after World War I with the Madras Labour Union textile workers' strike in 1918 (leading to the subsequent establishment of the Textile Labour Association in 1920) followed by the TISCO iron and steel workers union/strike in 1920, with strikes in this period taking place without effective trade union initiatives (Chandavarkar, 1998). Statistical reviews of strike action suggest 396 strikes in 1921 with a peak of 1811 strikes at the time of independence in 1947 (Vaid, 1972; Ramaswamy and Ramaswamy, 1981; Pattnaik, 1993). Most studies examine methods for securing worker demands including strikes (and causes for strikes), the use of Gandhian *satyagrahas* (hunger strikes), *gheraos* or encirclements, bandhs and *hartals* (general strikes), demonstrations, mass casual leave, work to rule, cutting of the electricity supply and so on (Kannappan and Saran, 1967; Aggarwal, 1968).

Numerous studies also examine strikes and working class struggles historically and in relation to the socio-economic structure and political system influencing these processes from a social and political perspective (Newman, 1981; Lieten, 1982, 1983; Patel, 1987; Chakrabarty, 1989; Chandavarkar, 1998; Gooptu, 2001). The studies include descriptive accounts of various strikes by jute, railway, tramway, and Bata shoe workers in the 1920s–30s (Saha, 1978) and in four South Indian centers around social origins, recruitment patterns and leadership (Murphy, 1981; Newman, 1981); of working class (consciousness) movements in Bombay (Lieten, 1983); and of the unparalleled textile workers' strike in Bombay (1982–83) given the numbers organized, including unorganized labour and in/outside leadership (Bakshi, 1986; Lakha, 2002).

Recent historical and contextual analyses of the trade union movement in India (Sodhi, 1994; Bhowmik, 1997; Bhattacharjee, 2000; Chibber, 2005) suggests that the class compromise has been replaced by a politics of accommodation as trade unions have substituted inclusion in policy agencies for mobilization. Vivek Chibber's (2005) analysis suggests that this occurrence was predetermined and settled in the post-independence period by the Indian National Congress and the demobilization of labour (including the largest militant unions like the All India Trade Union Congress formed in 1920 and the Indian Federation of Labour, which were part of a labour upsurge in the colonial era) via the Industrial Truce Conference in 1947, and preceding steps to legislate a bigger role for the state (The Industrial Disputes Act, 1947). This Act reduced the scope for collective bargaining and the establishment of a mega-federation called the Indian National Trade Union Congress (INTUC) committed to arbitration, labour peace and Congress resolutions, which disavowed militancy and cleared the way for a compact with capital. Contrary to this national model, Chibber (2005) points to the case of the Kerala Confederation of Trade Unions that mobilized under-class interests to empower union bargaining with employers, given that they could rely on a sympathetic state government in the Communist Party of India (Marxist) (CPM). This compelled employers to upgrade plants and equipment. According to Bhattacharjee (2000), the demise of the post-independence tripartite industrial relations system of state–union–employer at the national level by the forces of neoliberal globalization and regional competition in the post-1991 economic environment has led to the decentralization of bargaining across regions, sectors and unions, weakening labour's prospects in a competitive system.

Women's Movements

Colonial rule, the independence movement and international/Western women's activisms have together contributed towards the development and maturation of women's movements in India, which go back a century in the making (Sangari and Vaid, 1989; Agnihotri and Mazumdar, 1995). Responses to male dominance have also been addressed with an eye to the specificity of national history and culture as the nature of such dominance is different/specific in ways peculiar to India, calling for locally tailored resistances/responses (Liddle and Joshi, 1986; Niranjana, 2000). Others, like Madhu Kishwar (editor of the journal *Manushi*), have argued for the need to look into Indian cultural resources to transform these relationships (Kishwar and Ruth, 1984; B. Ray, 2002).

Participation of women in various movements (freedom movement, peasant, tribal, student movements etc.) have been described as 'pre-movements' as they raise social and class issues but not issues affecting women per se, while nonetheless politicizing women (Omvedt, 1978, p. 373). The role of women in these movements has not been researched adequately and where it has (as in the case of the freedom movement) they often played the role of helpers based on community and home involvements (Alexander, 1984; Kelkar, 1984). Ilina Sen's (1990) anthology on women's participation in post-independence movements confirms this tendency. Social reformist movements including the establishment of the Women's Indian Association and the All India Women's Congress (AIWC) in 1920 (Everett, 1979) worked to spread education among women, enact laws against *sati*,[10] permit widow remarriage and abolish child marriage. These movements, however, continued to strengthen the role of women as wife, housekeeper, and mother within the inferior role confines of the Hindu/Vedic concept of *pativrata* (devoted, chaste, and tolerant wives) (K. Shah, 1984, pp. 135–45), an approach similar to

Gandhian (-inspired women's movements) essentialism around the same time (Patel, 1988). Similar analyses of women's activism along communal lines (communal riots) suggests that Hindu women's organizations championing Hindutva (Saffron politics) reinforce patriarchal values while mobilizing along communal affiliations (Sarkar, 1991; Omvedt, 1993; Agnes, 1994). Women's roles in agrarian movements (peasant and tribal and Communist Party-led activisms including armed struggles in the 1940s or trade union activism) have also been studied, coming to similar conclusions – women struggle to articulate issues specific to women within these movements and these movements fail to address (and ignore) patriarchy (Custers, 1986; Kannan, 1988; Sen, 1989; Agarwal, 1994).

A number of micro/macro-studies (Omvedt, 1980b; Kishwar and Ruth, 1984; Desai and Patel, 1985; Agnes, 1992; Datar, 1993; Purushothaman, 1998; R. Ray, 1999) have begun to document women's movements on 'women's issues' including addressing rape, sexual harassment in the work place, violence against women in private/public spaces, dowry, amniocentesis and sex selection, population policy, political violence, the rise of fundamentalism and communalism and gender inequality, and women as economic beings (e.g., 94 percent of women workers are part of the informal sector; Agnihotri and Mazumdar, 1995). Rajni Palriwala's case study (2010, p. 210) of the anti-dowry (and bride-burning) movement and the development of the women's coalition, the Forum for Consciousness Against Dowry (DVCM) discusses action strategies employed by women's movements including:

- struggle within parliament/lobbying;
- legal aid, counselling, consciousness raising;
- collective educational and research actions (including street theater, poetry, and public seminars);
- signature and postcard campaigns; and
- *dharnas* (sit-ins), rallies, and marches including neighbourhood actions (leafleting and shaming of bride-burners).

Women's organizations and approaches across the board have been classified into the following (Desai and Patel, 1985):

- agitational and consciousness raising;
- grassroots mass-based organizations (e.g., labour organizations);
- groups concentrating on service provision (e.g., shelter, medical);
- professional women's organizations (e.g., lawyers and doctors);
- women's wings in political parties; and
- groups involved in research and documentation of women's issues.

The historical evolution of the women's movement tracing key conferences and forums has been addressed in different studies as well (Everett, 1979; Gandhi and Shah, 1991; Kumar, 1993; Omvedt, 1993). The literature suggests that the women's movements in India today need to form broad-based alliances (e.g., neoliberalism today provides such an opportunity); try to get past an essentially middle-class/Western-centric feminism; and consider 'focus', as women's politicization often gets blurred in movements addressing numerous issues/concerns.

Human Rights Movements

Human rights movements (HRMs), like environmental movements are assumed to be the concerns of all segments of society given their alleged universal import by HRM activists in India. Whether HR is or should be primarily state-centric or determined or leveraged by radical movements and civil society watchdog groups to hold the state accountable to various inter-/national HR commitments; whether it is or should be primarily about individual civil and political rights and/or collective economic, social and cultural rights; whether there is a single HRM in India today or many running parallel to each other or on mutually exclusive sets of assumptions; and whether the movement(s) can actually mobilize a mass base (who is its constituency?) beyond certain segments of the middle are some of the perennial questions for human rights movements and researchers today (Baxi, 1998; G. Shah [1990] 2004; Gudavarthy, 2008; Chakrabarti, 2011).

Although the movement did not acquire an organizational form before 1936, when the Indian Civil Liberties Union (ICLU) was established with Tagore as president, the seeds of germination were planted during the Indian Civil Rights Movement through direct actions and critical incidents, especially during the 1920s and 1930s (e.g., the 1931 protest against police firing on political prisoners in Hijli Jail, Calcutta). The ICLU played a key role in developing a civil liberties consciousness among a significant section of the population in colonial times. HRM scholarship traces the history of the HRM in India in terms of four phases including:

1. the civil liberties phase working within state–civil-society complementarity and the struggle to establish a rights-based civil society (1970s);
2. the democratic rights phase with a state versus civil society frame (1980s), post Indira Gandhi's imposed Emergency consisting of radical/militant movements squarely 'outside' the state;
3. the human rights phase (end of the 1990s) or political/civil-society split wherein radical movements were scrutinized for HR violations as well; and

4. the contemporary phase where the HRM is increasingly basing itself on an abstract moral/ethico-political dimension (beyond politics), while some are imploring for a return to collective rights orientations and a social movement politics given the rise of neoliberalism and religious fundamentalisms (Gudavarthy, 2008; Chakrabarti, 2011).

The Indira Gandhi Congress-imposed Emergency, suspending fundamental rights, led to the civil and democratic rights movement in its current shape, leading to the establishment of the People's Union for Civil Liberties (PUCL; taking up civil rights) and the People's Union for Democratic Rights (PUDR; taking up democratic rights) networked through various states and extended through the establishment of Committees of Concerned Citizens. The two unions differ on roles and political ideology (Haksar, 1991; Haragopal and Balagopal, 1998). Human rights groups have taken up different issues including: HR violations of rights of the poor (Desai, 1986b) and land, labour, police lawlessness, suppression of free expression, urban housing, academic freedom, communal conflict, treatment of women and so on (Rubin, 1987; Haksar, 1991). Haksar (1991) divides these issues into: (1) rights of prisoners; (2) police violence (e.g., torture); (3) anti-people laws (e.g., TADA/MISA/POTO); and (4) state oppression of bonded labourers, tribals, slum dwellers, landless peoples, and religious minorities. Common movement activities in HRMs include documentation of violations; fact-finding teams; dissemination/media; signature campaigns (including email campaigns); petitions; *dharnas*; public meetings and marches; and public interest litigation (Rubin, 1987; G. Shah [1990] 2004). The National Human Rights Commission (NHRC) was established shortly after passage of the Protection of Human Rights Bill (1993).

SOCIAL MOVEMENT RESEARCH IN INDIA: LOOKING BACK TO LOOK AHEAD

The following are a few key projections and pointers regarding the future of social movements and research in India:

1. Social movements will likely be triggered and shaped by the twin contemporary macro-forces of a conservative Saffron politics (the resurgence of Hindutva in the electoral realm post-2004 expressed through the current emergence of Narendra Modi as Prime Minister) or Hindu religious fundamentalism and the deepening and expansion

of neoliberalization of the economy (market fundamentalism). This will fuel, for example, religious/communal movements (and women's movements in response to and as part of same) and anti-displacement subaltern-class/social-group movements in rural/semi-urban areas, as SEZs are encouraged (particularly around mines and minerals), slum/informal-economy labouring class movements (with increased forced or voluntary rural–urban migrations) along with middle-class-consumer/anti-corruption/eco-aesthetic movements (see Baviskar and Ray, 2011). Many of these movements will likely resort to eco/human-rights–based strategic/real politics in order to achieve the global boomerang amplification effects ('marketing of rebellion'; Bob, 2005) as movements compete for attention and mass base.
2. There will be calls for a contextualized-theoretical eclecticism that reflects the multifaceted complex nature of Indian material and cultural politics today, as the question of one central conflict uniting disparate movements and cultural/material histories is increasingly more unlikely.
3. The study of movements to date has primarily been focused on academic knowledge production (scholarship *about* movements) as opposed to movement-relevant knowledge *for* social movements (Bevington and Dixon, 2005; Choudry and Kapoor, 2010). The line between the academic study of movements and participation in movements (as scholar activists and not just public sociology) will continue to blur (for academic and movement-political reasons) along with the development of research methodologies that are increasingly more action oriented and movement embedded (e.g., collective ethnographies; participatory action research).
4. There is a need for more studies on: (a) neglected regions and social groups (e.g., peasants/Dalits/Adivasi in Orissa, Madhya Pradesh, Rajasthan), (b) issues (e.g., anti-displacement and slum-dweller movements), (c) movement dimensions (e.g., the role of learning and knowledge production in and by movements – Indian adult education remains aloof and state/industry-centric), and (d) spatio-temporal connections in movements and scholarship (local–regional–national–global linkages and movements).

NOTES

1. Dalit is the term for a group of people who are traditionally regarded as 'untouchable' in the caste system.

2. Right-wing Hindu nationalist movement.
3. Formerly in China and some other Asian countries, a native agent of a foreign enterprise.
4. Fourth and lowest of the traditional *varnas*, or social classes of India.
5. Controversial 21-month period of state of emergency across the country. Elections were suspended, civil liberties curbed, political opponents were imprisoned, and the press censored.
6. Karnataka State Farmers' Association.
7. High-yielding varieties.
8. Professional tree climbers who specialize in collecting the sap from the bark of the coconut tree.
9. Workers who painstakingly place tobacco inside a small tendu leaf, roll the leaf, and secure the product with a thread.
10. Funeral practice where recently widowed women immolate themselves, typically on their husband's funeral pyre.

REFERENCES

Agarwal, B. (1994), 'Gender, resistance and land: interlinked struggles over resources and meanings in South Asia', *Journal of Peasant Studies*, **22**(1), 81–125.
Agarwala, R. (2006), 'From work to welfare: a new class movement in India', *Contemporary Asian Studies*, **38**(4), 419–41.
Aggarwal, A. (1968), *Gheraos and Industrial Relations*, Bombay: Tripathi.
Agnes, E. (1992), 'Protecting women against violence: review of a decade of legislation, 1980–89', *Economic and Political Weekly*, **27**(17), 19–33.
Agnes, E. (1994), 'Women's movement within a secular framework – redefining the agenda', *Economic and Political Weekly*, **29**(19), 1123–7.
Agnihotri, I. and V. Mazumdar (1995), 'Changing terms of political discourse: women's movement in India', *Economic and Political Weekly*, **30**(29), 1869–78.
Alam, J. (1983), 'Peasantry, politics and historiography: critique of new trend in relation to Marxism', *Social Scientist*, **11**(2), 43–54.
Alavi, H. (1973), 'Peasants and revolution', in K. Gough and H. Sharma (eds), *Imperialism and Revolution in South Asia*, New York: Monthly Review Press.
Alexander, K. (1975), 'Genesis of agrarian tension in Thanjavur', *Economic and Political Weekly*, **10**(49), 1881–6.
Alexander, R. (1984), 'Participant's perceptions: women and the Indian independence movement', *Samya Shakti – A Journal of Women's Studies*, **1**(2), 1–5.
Andharia, J. and C. Sengupta (1998), 'The environmental movement: global issues and Indian reality', *The Indian Journal of Social Work*, **59**(1), 422–49.
Bagahi, S. and A. Danda (1982), 'NE-BU-LA: a movement for regional solidarity', in K.S. Singh (ed.), *Tribal Movements in India, Vol. 1*, New Delhi: Manohar.
Bakshi, R. (1986), *The Long Haul, the Bombay Textile Worker's Strike*, Bombay: BUILD Documentation Centre.
Banerjee, S. (1980), *In the Wake of Naxalbari: A History of the Naxalite Movement in India*, New Delhi: Selected Books Publishing.
Banerjee, S. (1984), *India's Simmering Revolution: The Naxalite Uprising*, New Delhi: Selected Books Publishing.
Bannerji, H. (2000), 'Projects of hegemony: towards a critique of subaltern studies' resolution of the women's question', *Economic and Political Weekly*, **35**(11), 902–20.
Basu, D. and D. Das (2013), 'The Maoist movement in India: some political-economy considerations', *Journal of Agrarian Change*, **13**(3), 365–81.
Baviskar, A. (1995), *In the Belly of the River: Tribal Conflicts Over Development in the Narmada Valley*, Delhi: Oxford University Press.

Baviskar, A. (2005), 'Red in tooth and claw? Looking for class in struggles over nature', in R. Ray and M. Katzenstein (eds), *Social Movements in India: Poverty, Power and Politics*, Lanham, MD: Rowman & Littlefield.

Baviskar, A. (ed.) (2008), *Contested Grounds: Essays on Nature, Culture and Power*, New Delhi: Oxford University Press.

Baviskar, A. and R. Ray (eds) (2011), *Elite and Everyman: The Cultural Politics of the Indian Middle Classes*, New York: Routledge.

Baxi, U. (1998), 'The state and the human rights movements in India', in M. Mohanty and P. Mukherji (eds), *People's Rights: Social Movements and the State in the Third World*, New Delhi: Sage.

Bevington, D. and C. Dixon (2005), 'Movement-relevant theory: rethinking movement scholarship and activism', *Social Movement Studies*, **4**(3), 185–208.

Bhatt, E. (2010), *We Are Poor But So Many: The Story of Self-employed Women in India*, New Delhi: Oxford University Press.

Bhattacharjee, D. (2000), 'Globalising economy, localising labour', *Economic and Political Weekly*, **35**(42), 3758–64.

Bhowmik, S. (1997), 'On worker takeovers', *Seminar*, **452**, 45–50.

Bob, C. (2005), *The Marketing of Rebellion: Insurgents, Media and International Activism*, Cambridge, UK: Cambridge University Press.

Brass, T. (1994), 'Introduction: the new farmers movements in India', *Journal of Peasant Studies*, **21**(2), 3–26.

Brass, T. (2001), 'Moral economists, subalterns, new social movements and the (re) emergence of a (post) modernized (middle) peasant', in V. Chaturvedi (ed.), *Mapping Subaltern Studies and the Postcolonial*, New York: Verso.

Breman, J. (2004), *The Making and Unmaking of an Industrial Working Class: Sliding Down the Labour Hierarchy in Ahmedabad, India*, New Delhi: Oxford University Press.

Byres, T. (1980), 'Peasants as unfinished history', *Economic and Political Weekly*, **15**(31), 1308–13.

Cederlof, G. and K. Sivaramakrishnan (eds) (2006), *Ecological Nationalisms: Nature, Livelihoods, and Identities in South Asia*, Seattle, WA: University of Washington Press.

Center for Human Rights and Global Justice (2010), 'Every thirty minutes: farmer suicides, human rights and the agrarian crisis', New York: NYU School of Law, accessed 21 May 2014 at http://chrgj.org/documents/every-thirty-minutes-farmer-suicides-human-rights-and-the-agrarian-crisis-in-india/.

Chakrabarti, D. (2011), 'The human rights movement: in search of a realistic approach', *Economic and Political Weekly*, **46**(47), 33–40.

Chakrabarty, D. (1989), *Rethinking Working Class History: Bengal, 1890–1940*, Delhi: Oxford University Press.

Chandavarkar, R. (1998), *Imperial Power and Popular Politics: Class, Resistance and the State in India, 1850–1950*, Cambridge, UK: Cambridge University Press.

Chatterjee, P. (1986), 'The colonial state and peasant resistance in Bengal 1920–1947', *Past and Present*, **11**, February, 169.

Chatterjee, P. (2004), *The Politics of the Governed: Reflections on Popular Politics in Most of the World*, New York: Columbia University Press.

Chatterjee, P. (2008), 'Democracy and economic transformation in India', *Economic and Political Weekly*, **43**(16), 53–62.

Chatterjee, P. (ed.) (2009), *The Small Voice of History: Ranajit Guha*, Ranikhet, India: Permanent Black.

Chatterjee, P. (2011), *Lineages of Political Society: Studies in Postcolonial Democracy*, Ranikhet, India: Permanent Black.

Chatterjee, P. (2012), 'After subaltern studies', *Economic and Political Weekly*, **47**(35), 44–9.

Chatterji, A. (2009), *Violent Gods: Hindu Nationalism in India's Present – Narratives from Orissa*, New Delhi: Three Essays Collective.

Chaudhuri, B. (ed.) (1992), *Ethnopolitics and Identity Crisis: Tribal Transformations in India*, New Delhi: Inter-India Publications.

Chen, M. (2010), 'The Self Employed Women's Association', in T.K. Oommen (ed.), *Social Movements II: Concerns of Equity and Security*, New Delhi: Oxford University Press.
Chibber, V. (2005), 'From class compromise to class accommodation: labor's accommodation in to the Indian political economy', in R. Ray and M. Katzenstein (eds), *Social Movements in India: Poverty, Power and Politics*, Lanham, MD: Rowman & Littlefield.
Choudry, A. and D. Kapoor (eds) (2010), *Learning from the Ground Up: Global Perspective on Social Movements and Knowledge Production*, London/New York: Palgrave Macmillan.
Choudry, A. and D. Kapoor (eds) (2013), *NGOization: Complicity, Contradiction and Prospects*, London: Zed.
Custers, P. (1986), 'Women's role in Tebhaga movement', *Economic and Political Weekly*, **21**(43), 97–101.
Da Costa, D. (2010), *Development Drama: Reimagining Rural Political Action in Eastern India*, New Delhi: Routledge.
Das, A. (1983), *Agrarian Unrest and Socio-economic Change in Bihar, 1900–1980*, Delhi: Manohar.
Das, A. (1987), 'Revolutionary movement in Bihar', *Economic and Political Weekly*, **22**(22).
Das, V. (1990), 'Jharkhand movement: from realism to mystification', *Economic and Political Weekly*, **25**(30), 385–400.
Datar, C. (1993), *The Struggle Against Violence*, Calcutta: Stree Publications.
Davis, M. (2004), *Planet of Slums*, London: Verso.
Desai, A. (1978), *Peasant Struggles in India*, Bombay: Oxford University Press.
Desai, A. (ed.) (1986a), *Agrarian Struggle in India After Independence*, New Delhi: Oxford.
Desai, A. (ed.) (1986b), *Violation of Democratic Rights in India*, Bombay: Popular Prakashan.
Desai, N. and V. Patel (1985), *Indian Women: Change and Challenge*, Bombay: Popular Prakashan.
Dhanagare, D. (1982), 'Telangana: a movement revisited', *Economic and Political Weekly*, **17**(51), 2045–6.
Dhanagare, D. (1983), *Peasant Movements in India, 1920–1950*, Delhi: Oxford University Press.
Dhanagare, D. (1995), 'The class character and politics of the farmers' movements in Maharashtra during the 1980s', in T. Brass (ed.), *New Farmer's Movements in India*, Ilford, UK: Frank Cass.
Dhanagare, D. (1999), 'The new farmers' movement in Maharashtra', in F. Ishikawa (ed.), *South Asia Under the Economic Reforms*, Osaka: Japan Center for Asia Studies.
Dhanagare, D. and J. John (1988), 'Cyclical movement towards the "eternal" – nine theses on social movements: a critique', *Economic and Political Weekly*, **33**(21).
D'Souza, R. (2009), 'Sandwich theory and Operation Green Hunt', *Sanhati*, December 2009.
Duyker, E. (1987), *Tribal Guerrillas: The Santhals of West Bengal and the Naxalite Movement*, Delhi: Oxford.
Everett, J. (1979), *Women and Social Change in India*, Delhi: Heritage.
Frank, A. and M. Fuentes (1987), 'Nine theses on social movements', *Economic and Political Weekly*, **32**(35), L45–L52.
Gadgil, M. and R. Guha (1992), *This Fissured Land: An Ecological History of India*, Delhi: Oxford University Press.
Gadgil, M. and R. Guha (1998), 'Towards a perspective on environmental movements in India', *The Indian Journal of Social Work*, **59**(1), 450–72.
Gandhi, N. and N. Shah (1991), *The Issues at Stake: Theory and Practice in the Contemporary Women's Movement in India*, New Delhi: Kali for Women.
Ghosh, A. (ed.) (1999), *Dalits and Peasants: The Emerging Caste–Class Dynamics*, Delhi: Gyan Sagar Publications.
Gillan, M. (2010), 'Trade unions and the political representation of unorganized workers in India', draft paper presented to the Labour Movements Research Committee (RC44), International Sociological Association (ISA) 17th World Congress of Sociology, Gothenburg, Sweden, 11–17 July.

Gokhale, J. (1979), 'The Dalit Panthers and the radicalization of untouchables', *Journal of Commonwealth and Comparative Politics*, **17**(19), 77–93.

Gooptu, N. (2001), *The Politics of the Urban Poor in the Early Twentieth Century India*, Cambridge, UK: Cambridge University Press.

Gore, M.S. (1989), *The Non-Brahman Movement in Maharashtra*, New Delhi: Segment Book Distributor.

Gore, M.S. (1993), *Social Context of an Ideology: Ambedkar's Political and Social Thought*, New Delhi: Sage.

Gough, K. (1968), 'Peasant resistance and revolt in South India', *Pacific Affairs*, **16**(4), 526–44.

Gough, K. (1974), 'Indian peasant uprising', *Economic and Political Weekly*, **9**(32–34), 1391–412.

Gough, K. (1980), 'Modes of production in Southern India', *Economic and Political Weekly*, **15**(5/6/7), 337–64.

Gough, K. and H. Sharma (eds) (1973), *Imperialism and Revolution in South Asia*, New York: Monthly Review Press.

Gudavarthy, A. (2008), 'Human rights movements in India: state, civil society and beyond', *Contributions to Indian Sociology*, **42**(1), 29–57.

Guha, R. (1982), 'Ecological crisis and ecological movements: a bourgeois deviation?', *Economic and Political Weekly*, **17**(52), 2093–5.

Guha, R. (1983), *Elementary Aspects of Peasant Insurgency in India*, Delhi: Oxford University Press.

Guha, R. (1989), *The Unquiet Wood: Ecological Change and Peasant Resistance in the Himalaya*, Delhi: Oxford University Press.

Guha, R. (1997a), 'The environmentalism of the poor', in R. Fox and O. Starn (eds), *Between Resistance and Revolution: Cultural Politics and Social Protest*, New Brunswick, NJ: Rutgers University Press.

Guha, R. (1997b), *Dominance Without Hegemony: History and Power in Colonial India*, Cambridge, MA: Harvard University Press.

Guha, R. (2001), 'Subaltern studies: projects for our time and their convergence', in I. Rodriguez (ed.), *The Latin American Subaltern Studies Reader*, Durham, NC: Duke University Press.

Guha, R. and M. Gadgil (1989), 'State forestry and social conflict in British India', *Past and Present*, **123**(1), 141–77.

Guha, R. and Martinez-Alier, J. (1998), *Varieties of Environmentalism: Essays North and South*, New Delhi: Oxford University Press.

Gupta, D. (1982), *Nativism in a Metropolis: The Shiv Sena in Bombay*, New Delhi: Manohar.

Guru, G. and A. Chakravarty (2005), 'Who are the country's poor? Social movement politics and Dalit poverty', in R. Ray and F. Katzenstein (eds), *Social Movements in India: Poverty, Power and Politics*, Lanham, MD: Rowman & Littlefield.

Haksar, N. (1991), 'Civil liberties movement in India', *The Lawyers*, June.

Haragopal, G. and K. Balagopal (1998), 'Civil liberties movement and the state in India', in M. Mohanty and P. Mukherji (eds), *People's Rights: Social Movements and the State in the Third World*, New Delhi: Sage.

Harriss-White, B. (2010), 'Globalization, the financial crisis and petty production in India's socially regulated informal economy', *Global Labour Journal*, **1**(1), 155–77.

Harvey, D. (2003), *The New Imperialism*, London: Oxford University Press.

Hensman, R. (2010), 'Labour and globalization: union responses India', *Global Labour Journal*, **1**(1), 112–31.

Herring, R. (2005), 'Miracle seeds, suicide seeds, and the poor: GMOs, NGOs, farmers and the state', in R. Ray and M. Katzenstein (eds), *Social Movements in India: Poverty, Power and Politics*, Lanham, MD: Rowman & Littlefield.

Hussain, M. (1987), 'Tribal movement for autonomous state in Assam', *Economic and Political Weekly*, **22**(32), 1329–32.

Ilaiah, K. (1996), *Why I Am Not a Hindu: A Shudra Critique of Hindu Culture, Ideology and Political Economy*, Calcutta: Samya.

Jogdand, P. (1991), *Dalit Movement in Maharashtra*, New Delhi: Kanak.

Kabeer, N., R. Sudarshan and K. Milward (eds) (2013), *Organizing Women Workers in the Informal Economy: Beyond the Weapons of the Weak*, London: Zed.

Kalpagam, U. (1994), 'The discourse and practice of informal sector politics', in U. Kalpagam (ed.), *Labour and Gender: Survival in Urban India*, New Delhi: Vikas Publishing.

Kamat, S. (2001), *Development Hegemony: NGOs and the State in India*, New Delhi: Oxford University Press.

Kannan, K. (1988), *Of Rural Proletarian Struggles: Mobilization and Organization of Rural Workers in South-West India*, New Delhi: Oxford University Press.

Kannappan, S. and D. Saran (1967), 'Political strikes and violence in labour disputes', *Indian Journal of Industrial Relations*, 3(3), 123–7.

Kapoor, D. (2011), 'Subaltern social movement (SSM) post-mortems of development in India: locating trans-local activism and radicalism', *Journal of Asian and African Studies*, **46**(2), 130–48.

Kapoor, D. (2013), 'Trans-local rural solidarity and an anti-colonial politics of place: contesting colonial capital and the neoliberal state in India', *Interface: A Journal For and About Social Movements*, **5**(1), 14–39.

Karnik, V. (1966), *Indian Trade Unions: A Survey*, Bombay: Manaktalis.

Kelkar, G. (1984), 'Women's movement studies: a critique of the historiography', *Samya Shakti – A Journal of Women's Studies*, **1**(2).

Khagram, S. (2004), *Dams and Development: Transnational Struggles for Water and Power*, Ithaca, NY: Cornell University Press.

Kishwar, M. and M. Ruth (eds) (1984), *Search for Answers*, London: Zed.

Kothari, R. (1984), 'The non-party political process', *Economic and Political Weekly*, **19**(5), 216–24.

Kothari, S. (2001), 'Globalization, global alliances and the Narmada movement', in K. Kumar (1984), *Peasants in Revolt: Tenants, Landless, Congress and the Raj in Oudh*, Delhi: Manohar.

Kumar, K. (1993), *A History of Doing: An Illustrated Account of Movement for Women's Rights and Feminism in India 1800–1900*, New Delhi: Kali for Women.

Kumar, V. (2010), 'Different shades of Dalit mobilization', in T. Oommen (ed.), *Social Movements I: Issues of Identity*, New Delhi: Oxford University Press.

Lakha, S. (2002), 'Organized labour and militant unionism: the Bombay textile workers' strike of 1982', in G. Shah (ed.), *Social Movements and the State*, New Delhi: Sage.

Lerche, J., A. Shah and B. Harriss-White (2013), 'Introduction: agrarian questions and left politics in India', *Journal of Agrarian Change*, **13**(3), 337–50.

Levien, M. (2012), 'The land question: special economic zones and the political economy of dispossession in India', *Journal of Peasant Studies*, **39**(3–4), 933–69.

Liddle, J. and R. Joshi, (1986), *Daughters of Independence: Gender, Caste and Class in India*, New Delhi: Kali for Women.

Lieten, G. (1982), 'Strikes and strike-breakers: a Bombay textile mills strike, 1929', *Economic and Political Weekly*, **27**(14–16), April.

Lieten, G. (1983), *Colonialism, Class and Nation*, Calcutta: K.P. Bagchi.

Ludden, D. (ed.) (2005), *Reading Subaltern Studies: Critical History, Contested Meaning and the Globalization of South Asia*, New Delhi: Pauls Press.

McMichael, P. (2008), 'Peasants make their own history, but not just as they please...', *Journal of Agrarian Change*, **8**(2–3), 205–28.

McMichael, P. (ed.) (2010), *Contesting Development: Critical Struggles for Social Change*, New York: Routledge.

Mehta, L. (ed.) (2009), *Displaced by Development: Confronting Marginalization and Gender Injustice*, New Delhi: Sage.

Mendelsohn, O. and M. Vicziany (1998), *The Untouchables: Subordination, Poverty and the State in Modern India*, Cambridge, UK: Cambridge University Press.

Menon, N. and A. Nigam (2007), *Power and Contestation: India Since 1989*, London: Zed.
Mookerjea, S. (2011), 'On learning how to liberate the common: subaltern biopolitics and the end-game of neoliberalism', in D. Kapoor (ed.), *Critical Perspectives on Neoliberal Globalization, Development and Education in Africa and Asia*, Rotterdam: Sense Publishers.
Moore, B. (1967), *Social Origins of Dictatorship and Democracy*, London: Allen Lane.
Mukherji, N. (2012), *The Maoists in India: Tribals under Siege*, London: Pluto.
Mukherji, P. (1977), 'Social movement and social change: to a conceptual clarification and theoretical framework', *Sociological Bulletin*, **26**(1), 38–59.
Mukherji, P. (1987), 'Study of social conflicts: case of Naxalbari peasant movement', *Economic and Political Weekly*, **22**(8), 1607–17.
Munshi, I. (ed.) (2012), *The Adivasi Question: Issues of Land, Forest and Livelihood*, New Delhi: Orient Blackswan.
Murphy, E. (1981), *Unions in Conflict: A Comparative Study of Four South Indian Textile Centers, 1818–1939*, Delhi: Manohar.
Neeraj, J. (2007), *Globalization or Re-colonization*, Pune: Lokayat Press.
Newman, R. (1981), *Workers and Unions in Bombay, 1918–29*, Canberra: Australian National University.
Nilsen, A. (2010), *Dispossession and Resistance in India: The River and the Rage*, New York: Routledge.
Niranjana, S. (2000), 'Transitions and reorientations: on the women's movement in India', in P. d'Souza (ed.), *Contemporary India: Transitions*, New Delhi: Sage.
Oliver-Smith, A. (2010), *Defying Displacement: Grassroots Resistance and the Critique of Development*, Austin, TX: University of Texas Press.
Omvedt, G. (1978), 'Women and the rural revolt in India', *Journal of Peasant Studies*, **5**(3), 370–403.
Omvedt, G. (1980a), 'Caste and agrarian relations and agrarian conflict', *Sociological Bulletin*, **29**(2), 147–67.
Omvedt, G. (1980b), *We Will Smash This Prison*, New Delhi: Orient Longman.
Omvedt, G. (1981), 'Capitalist agriculture and rural classes in India', *Economic and Political Weekly*, **16**(52), 140–59.
Omvedt, G. (1988), 'New movements', *Seminar*, **352**, 39–44.
Omvedt, G. (1993), *Reinventing Revolution: New Social Movements and the Socialist Tradition in India*, Armonk, NY: M.E. Sharpe.
Omvedt, G. (1994), *Dalits and the Democratic Revolution*, New Delhi: Sage.
Omvedt, G. (1995), *Dalit Visions: The Anti-caste Movement and the Construction of the Indian Identity*, New Delhi: Orient Longman.
Omvedt, G. (2005), 'Farmer's movements and the debate on poverty and reform in India', in R. Ray and M. Katzenstein (eds), *Social Movements in India: Poverty, Power and Politics*, Lanham, MD: Rowman & Littlefield.
Oommen, T. (1972), *Charisma, Stability and Change: An Analysis of Bhoodan-Gramdan Movement in India*, New Delhi: Thomson Press.
Oommen, T. (1984), *Social Structure and Politics: Studies in Independent India*, Delhi: Hindustan Publishing.
Oommen, T. ([1990] 2010), *Protest and Change: Studies in Social Movements*, New Delhi: Sage.
Oommen, T. (ed.) (2010a), *Social Movements I: Issues of Identity*, New Delhi: Oxford University Press.
Oommen, T. (ed.) (2010b), *Social Movements II: Concerns of Equity and Security*, New Delhi: Oxford University Press.
Padel, F. and A. Das (2010), *Out of this Earth: East India Adivasis and the Aluminum Cartel*, New Delhi: Orient Blackswan.
Pai, S. (2002), *Dalit Assertion and the Unfinished Democratic Revolution: The BSP in UP*, New Delhi: Sage.
Palriwala, R. (2010), 'The anti-dowry movement in Delhi', in T. Oommen (ed.), *Social Movements II: Concerns of Equity and Security*, New Delhi: Oxford University Press.

Patel, R. and P. McMichael (2004), 'Third Worldism and the lineages of global fascism: the regrouping of the Global South in the neoliberal era', *Third World Quarterly*, **25**(1), 231–54.
Patel, S. (1987), *Making of Industrial Relations in the Ahmedabad Textile Industry, 1918–19*, Bombay: Oxford University Press.
Patel, S. (1988), 'Construction and reconstruction of women in Gandhi', *Economic and Political Weekly*, **23**(8), 377–87.
Patel, S., S. Burra and C. d'Cruz (2001), 'Slum/shack dwellers international: foundations to tree tops', *Environment and Urbanization*, **13**(2), 45–59.
Patil, C. (ed.) (1988), *Revolt Studies: One*, Calcutta: Asiatic Book Agency.
Patnaik, U. (1987), *Peasant Class Differentiation: A Study in Method with Reference to Haryana*, New Delhi: Oxford University Press.
Patnaik, U. (2010), 'The new primitive accumulation and the peasantry', abstract of P. Sundarayya Memorial Lecture, 19 May, Hyderabad, accessed 30 April 2013 at http://indiacurrentaffairs.org/the-new-primitive-accumulation-and-the-peasantry-utsa-patnaik/.
Pattnaik, S. (1993), *Strike: A Study of Conflict*, New Delhi: Gyan Publishing House.
Pavier, B. (1981), *The Telangana Movement, 1944–51*, Delhi: Vikas.
Purushothaman, S. (1998), *The Empowerment of Women: Grassroots Women's Networks and the State*, New Delhi: Sage.
Rajagopal, B. (2003), *International Law from Below: Development, Social Movements and Third World Resistance*, Cambridge, UK: Cambridge University Press.
Ramaswamy, E. and U. Ramaswamy (1981), *Industry and Labour: An Introduction*, New Delhi: Oxford University Press.
Rao, A. (ed.) (2003), *Gender and Caste*, New Delhi: Kali for Women.
Rao, A. (2009), *The Caste Question: Dalits and the Politics of Modern India*, Berkeley, CA: University of California Press.
Rao, M. (1971), *Maoism in India*, New Delhi: Vikas.
Rao, M.S.A. ([1979] 2006), 'Conceptual problems in the study of social movements in India', in M.S.A. Rao (ed.), *Social Movements in India: Studies in Peasant, Backward Classes, Sectarian, Tribal and Women's Movements*, New Delhi: Manohar.
Ray, B. (2002), *Early Feminists of Colonial India: Sarala Devi Chaudhurani and Rokeya Sakhawat Hossain*, New Delhi: Oxford University Press.
Ray, R. (1999), *Fields of Protest: Women's Movements in India*, Minneapolis, MN: University of Minnesota Press.
Ray, R. and F. Katzenstein (eds) (2005), *Social Movements in India: Poverty, Power and Politics*, Lanham, MD: Rowman & Littlefield.
Rodrigues, V. (2002), *Essential Writings of B.R. Ambedkar*, Delhi: Oxford University Press.
Routledge, P. (1993), *Terrains of Resistance: Nonviolent Social Movements and the Contestation of Place in India*, New York: Praeger.
Roy, A. (1996), 'From bureaucracy to people's movement', *Lokayan Bulletin*, **13**(1), 51.
Roy, B. (1999), 'The politics of waste and corruption', *Lokayan Bulletin*, **16**(1), 19–40.
RoyChowdhury, S. (2003), 'Old classes and new spaces: urban poverty and new trade unions', *Economic and Political Weekly*, **38**(50), 5277–84.
RoyChowdhury, S. (2005), 'Labor activism and women in the unorganized sector', *Economic and Political Weekly*, **40**(22–23), 2250–55.
Rubin, B. (1987), 'The civil liberties movement in India', *Asian Survey*, **27**(3), 371–92.
Sachchidananda, S. (1985), 'Tribal studies', *Survey of Research in Sociology and Social Anthropology, 1969–79 (ICSSR), Vol. 1*, New Delhi: Satvahana Publications.
Saha, P. (1978), *History of the Working Class Movement in Bengal*, New Delhi: People's Publishing House.
Sahoo, S. (2010), 'Political mobilization, the poor and democratization in neo-liberal India', *Journal of Contemporary Asia*, **40**(3), 487–508.
Sangari, K. and S. Vaid (1989), *Recasting Women: Essays in Colonial History*, New Delhi: Kali for Women.

Sanyal, K. (2010), *Rethinking Capitalist Development: Primitive Accumulation, Governmentality and Post-colonial Capitalism*, New Delhi: Routledge.
Sarkar, K. (1979), 'Kakdwip Tebhaga movement', in A.R. Desai (ed.), *Peasant Struggles in India*, Delhi: Oxford University Press.
Sarkar, S. (2005), 'The decline of the subaltern in subaltern studies', in D. Ludden (ed.), *Reading Subaltern Studies: Critical History, Contested Meaning and the Globalization of South Asia*, New Delhi: Pauls Press.
Sarkar, T. (1991), 'Woman as a communal subject: Rashtrasevika Samiti and Ram Janmabhoomi movement', *Economic and Political Weekly*, **26**(35), 2057–65.
Sen, I. (1989), 'Feminist, women's movements and the working class', *Economic and Political Weekly*, **24**(29), 1639–41.
Sen, I. (1990), *A Space Within the Struggle: Women's Participation in People's Movements*, New Delhi: Kali for Women.
Sengupta, N. (ed.) (1982), *The Fourth World Dynamics: Jharkhand*, Delhi: Authors Guild Publication.
Sethi, H. (1984), 'Groups in a new politics of transformation', *Economic and Political Weekly*, **19**(7), 305–16.
Sethi, H. (1993), 'Survival and democracy: ecological struggles in India', in P. Wignaraja (ed.), *New Social Movements in the South: Empowering the People*, New Delhi: Vistaar Publications.
Shah, A. (2010), *In the Shadows of the State: Indigenous Politics, Environmentalism, and Insurgency in Jharkhand, India*, Durham, NC: Duke University Press.
Shah, G. ([1990] 2004), *Social Movements in India: A Review of the Literature*, New Delhi: Sage.
Shah, K. (1984), *Women's Liberation and Voluntary Action*, Delhi: Ajanta Publishers.
Sharma, J. (1988), *Total Revolution*, Delhi: Jan Hit Prakashan.
Sheth, D. (1983), 'Grass-roots stirrings and the future of politics', *Alternatives*, **9**(1), 1–24.
Sheth, D. (1984), 'Grass-roots initiatives in India', *Economic and Political Weekly*, **19**(6), 259–62.
Sheth, D. (1993), 'Politics of social transformation: grassroots movements in India', in R. Falk, R. Johannen and S. Kim (eds), *The Constitutional Foundation of World Peace*, New York: State University Press.
Sheth, D. (1999), 'Globalization and the grassroots movements', *Seminar*, **473**, 77–82.
Sheth, D. (2005), 'Micro-movements in India: towards a new politics of participatory democracy', in B. Sousa Santos (ed.), *Democratizing Democracy: Beyond the Liberal Democratic Canon*, London: Verso.
Shiva, V. (1988), *Staying Alive: Women, Ecology and Survival in India*, Delhi: Kali for Women.
Shiva, V. and J. Bandopadhyaya (1986), 'Environmental conflicts and public interest science', *Economic and Political Weekly*, **21**(2), 84–90.
Singh, H. (2003), 'Princely states, peasant protests and nation building in India: the colonial mode of historiography and subaltern studies', *Social Movement Studies*, **2**(2), 213–28.
Singh, K.S. (1982), *Tribal Movements in India, Vol. I*, Delhi: Manohar.
Singh, R. (1986), 'Agrarian social structure and peasant unrest: a study of land-grab movement in district Basti', in A. Desai (ed.), *Agrarian Struggle in India After Independence*, Delhi: Oxford University Press.
Singh, R. (2001), *Social Movements, Old and New: A Post-modernist Critique*, New Delhi: Sage.
Singh, Y. (1993), *Social Change in India*, New Delhi: Haranand Publications.
SinghaRoy, D. (2004), *Peasant Movements in Post-colonial India: Dynamics of Mobilization and Identity*, New Delhi: Sage.
Sinha, S. (1984), *Life and Times of Birsa Bhagwan*, Patna: Secretariat Press.
Sivaramakrishnan, K. and A. Agrawal (eds) (2003), *Regional Modernities: The Cultural Politics of Development in India*, Stanford, CA: Stanford University Press.

Sodhi, J. (1994), 'Emerging trends in industrial relations and human resources in India', *Indian Journal of Industrial Relations*, **30**(1), 19–37.

Stokes, E. (1978), *The Peasants and the Raj: Studies in Agrarian Society and Peasant Rebellion in Colonial India*, Delhi: Vikas.

Subramanian, A. (2009), *Shorelines: Space and Rights in South India*, Stanford, CA: Stanford University Press.

Sundar, N. (2009), *Subalterns and Sovereigns: An Anthropological History of Bastar (1854–2006)*, New Delhi: Oxford University Press.

Surana, P. (1983), *Social Movements and Social Structure*, New Delhi: Manohar.

Tarkunde, V. (2003), 'Partyless politics and people's (humanist) state: a picture for public discussion', *The Radical Humanist*, **66**(10), 1–4.

Upadhyaya, A. (1980), 'Peasantization of Adivasis in Thane district', *Economic and Political Weekly*, **15**(52), 134–46.

Vaid, K. (1972), *Gheraos and Labour Unrest in West Bengal*, New Delhi: Shri Ram Centre.

Velayudhan, M. (1985), 'The crisis and women's struggle in India (1970–77)', *Social Scientist*, **13**(6), 145–57.

Webster, E. (2011), 'Organizing in the informal economy: Ela Bhatt and the Self Employed Women's Association of India', *Labour, Capital and Society*, **44**(1), 98–125.

Whitehead, J. (2003), 'Space, place and primitive accumulation in Narmada Valley and beyond', *Economic and Political Weekly*, **38**(40), 4224–30.

Zelliot, E. (2001), *From Untouchables to Dalits and Other Essays*, New Delhi: Manohar.

25. Social movements and political citizenship in Africa
Patrick Bond

INTRODUCTION

Is Africa 'rising' as a great new economic power, or is the continent better seen as witnessing early – and potentially widespread – 'uprisings', in a context of *worsening* economic conditions (understood in the broadest sense), as climate catastrophe also bears down on a billion Africans? Reading the business press, one would not know that Africa is losing an estimated 6 per cent of its wealth each year, thanks to the 'resource curse'.[1] You would be forgiven for having the opposite impression when reading most reports from elite Afro-optimists, namely those with pro-globalization, export-oriented, petro-minerals–centric economic ideologies, especially because these reports invariably ignore the dangers to most African countries from climate change, and because they discount social unrest. For example, most multilateral financial institutions celebrate Africa's national economies as among the world's leading cases of 'recovery' after the 2008–09 meltdown, and most (though not all) ignore signs of growing discontent.

The neoliberal position neglects several dangers that have made Africa's supposedly resilient economies far more vulnerable to both global and local economic and environmental crises, and hence neoliberals cannot comprehend social movement resistances now developing in response. These dangers include excessive financial and trade integration into a volatile world economy, resource extraction costs, the 'ecological debt' (as well as other non-remunerated value transfers) and climate change 'loss and damage' (as the United Nations now terms it), as well as internal features of economies suffering from resource curse and processes of extreme uneven and combined development. These features are all generating not only pressures on societies from above, but also upsurges of protest from below. This chapter reviews, briefly, the pressures and some of the resistances.

It is telling that a Polanyian double movement emerged in civil (and often uncivil) society especially beginning in 2011. This was true not only in North Africa where socio-economic grievances are central to the revolts in even the (neoliberally) best performing of African countries, Tunisia, but also in Sub-Saharan Africa, where after years of ineffectual 'IMF riots', growing unrest is having a surprisingly powerful effect in crucial sectors and geographical spaces from Senegal in the west, to Uganda in the centre and to Swaziland in the south. South Africa's 2012 revolts, including the labour unrest that precipitated the premeditated massacre of 32 striking mineworkers at the Marikana platinum complex, deserve special attention in this respect, for nearly 1900 'violent protests' were recorded by police in 2012–13 (Mthethwa, 2013). The uprising continued into 2014 with more mass strikes – including 80 000 mineworkers in January 2014 who, for many weeks shut down the source of 80 per cent of the world's platinum supply – and community 'service delivery protests', resulting in more high-profile police shootings of protesters, and a growing split of civil society organizations from the ruling party's historic alliance of nationalists, workers and poor people. Before reviewing such details, we consider the core problems within a crisis-ridden world economy, one in which African vulnerability has become a crucial feature, in spite of advertised gross domestic product (GDP) increases that would be expected to provide much more immunity from global volatility.

'AFRICA RISING' WITHIN A WORLD CAPITALIST CRISIS

Africa's exploitative trade, finance, investment and labour migration relations within crisis-ridden world capitalism have evolved somewhat in recent years. From the early 2000s, ongoing resource extraction by Western firms was joined, and in some cases overtaken, by China. The phenomenon of 'land grabbing' combined with larger-scale development of biofuels and genetic modification, while domestic financial liberalization generated not only rising credit access, but also over-indebtedness. Still, Africa's subordinate position in the international economic order did not change.

In *Looting Africa* (Bond, 2006), I set out a full argument about how a deep-seated world crisis has unfolded over the past four decades, and how Africa's vulnerability worsened in the process, as neoliberal policies wrecked self-protection mechanisms across the continent. To summarize and update these concerns, it is first useful to go back to 1971 when the post-World War II Bretton Woods system broke down. This was the beginning of a general rise in economic and especially monetary instability, with speculative bubbles and panics reflecting uncontrolled financial turbulence. To some extent, these were offset or displaced by bailouts, but they generally destroyed more than 15 per cent of the value of financial assets at stake within a short period of time. The bailouts required to stabilize matters had to be ever larger, and to illustrate, in 2012 more rounds of 'quantitative easing' (money printing) and commitments to bailing out the lenders to Southern Europe were announced by the US Federal Reserve, European Central Bank and Bank of England. Then in mid-2013, an announcement of future 'tapering' of US quantitative easing in turn crashed most of the major emerging markets' currencies, leaving Brazil, India and South Africa not merely members of the BRICS group (with China and Russia), but now also members of the so-called 'Fragile Five' economies battered by currency speculators on account of their large current account and budget deficits.

Powerful underlying forces associated with world capitalist crisis tendencies are the main reason for such extreme turbulence. Stagnation characterized the real sector, and the world's per capita annual GDP increase fell from 3.6 per cent during the 1960s, to 2.1 per cent during the 1970s, to 1.3 per cent during the 1980s, to 1.1 per cent during the 1990s, followed by a rise to 2.5 per cent for the first half of the 2000s, but then a crash in absolute terms at the end of the 2000s, and a very weak recovery after 2010. To be sure, the character of goods measured over time has changed (high-technology products enjoyed by so many people today were not available in the last century). But the overall story of 'overaccumulated capital' generating stagnation, uneven development, financialization and ultimately unprecedented crises remains critical (Harvey, 2003).

In this global context, it is even more critical to be sceptical about the 'Africa Rising' argument that has been so dominant in the mainstream media in recent years. To illustrate, here is *Time* magazine's Africa correspondent Alex Perry (2012), writing the cover story for the first week of December 2012:

> Africa owes its takeoff to a variety of accelerators, nearly all of them external and occurring in the past 10 years:
> - billions of dollars in aid, especially to fight HIV/AIDS and malaria;
> - tens of billions of dollars in foreign-debt cancellations;
> - a concurrent interest in Africa's natural resources, led by China; and
> - the rapid spread of mobile phones, from a few million in 2000 to more than 750 million today.
>
> Business increasingly dominates foreign interest in Africa. Investment first outpaced aid in 2006 and now doubles it.

It would be more accurate to rewrite these lines as follows:

> Africa owes its economic decline (running at more than 6 per cent of gross income per year once non-renewable resource depletion is considered) to a

variety of accelerators, nearly all of them external and occurring in the past centuries during which slavery, colonialism and neo-colonialism locked in the continent's underdevelopment, but several of which – along with climate change – were amplified in recent years:

- stagnant overseas development aid (Elliott, 2012) – around 60 per cent 'phantom' (Action Aid, 2006) anyhow – to most African countries (except to 14 'fragile states' [IMF, 2009]), with Washington leading further cuts in funding to fight HIV/AIDS and malaria (Shaw, 2012);
- tens of billions of dollars in foreign debt cancellation (of what was mainly unrepayable 'odious' loans to dictators [CADTM, 2008]) in 2005 yet at the same time a squeeze on low-income African finance ministries that immediately afterwards caused a dramatic rise in debt repayments (from 5 to 8 per cent of export earnings [IMF, 2009]);
- a concurrent looting of Africa's natural resources, led by China and the West, resulting in dramatic recent falls in mineral and petroleum wealth (when calculated as 'adjusted net saving' to incorporate resource-stripping); and
- the rapid spread of mobile phones, which because of high costs and low internet connectivity, has done very little to solve the digital divide (Calandro et al., 2010).

Banking increasingly dominates foreign interest in Africa, as elite disinvestment into Western and Eastern financial markets continues to outpace aid and investment, amounting to an estimated $1.4 trillion in capital flight from the continent – both Sub-Saharan and North ends – from 1970–2010 (Ndikumana and Boyce, 2012a, 2012b).

The Africa Rising narrative became ubiquitous in the mainstream press from late 2010, with a peak in early 2013 in the wake of the *Time* coverage. Highlights included a report by the Washington-based International Institute of Finance; the *African Economic Outlook 2011* from the Organisation for Economic Co-operation and Development, United Nations Economic Commission for Africa, United Nations Development Programme and African Development Bank; the World Economic Forum's 2011 *Global Competitiveness Report*; the African Development Bank's discovery of a vast new middle class in 2011; the International Monetary Fund's African *Regional Economic Outlook*; the World Bank's 2011 Africa strategy; and IMF research on African growth (see Bond, 2011 for critiques).

Although there is a case that on a per-capita GDP basis, there has been an upward trend, none of these Afro-optimist statements reveal that the continent is actually *losing* a net 6 per cent of gross national income each year thanks to the resource curse writ large (measured as 'adjusted net savings'). Recent recalibrations of GDP measure raw materials stripped from Africa's soil not just as one-off credits to GDP, but also as debits:

the decline in 'natural capital' that occurs because the minerals and petroleum are *non-renewable*. Once drilled out, they are lost forever. As a result, it is obvious to even the World Bank (2011, p.11) that Africa's wealth is *shrinking rapidly*, measured as 'adjusted net savings' to incorporate non-renewable resource loss and the failure of multinational mining corporations to reinvest.[2]

The World Bank's book *The Changing Wealth of Nations* – from where the negative 6 per cent figure comes – is rather conservative in calculating non-renewable resource depletion, leaving out several important minerals, and also neglecting the tax fraud and transfer pricing associated with transnational capital, as well as pressure on the current account that follows from persistent export of profits and dividends. In Africa, these problems are documented by Khadija Sharife (2011) in *Tax Us If You Can* and by Leonce Ndikumana and James Boyce (2011, 2012a, 2012b) in various studies that deserve much more attention, for example, their recent book on *Africa's Odious Debts* and updated 1970–2010 estimates of flight capital from Africa.

AFRICA'S *UP*RISING

As we will see in more detail towards the end of the chapter, the conditions created by the combination of austerity, dictatorial regimes, socio-political injustice and ecological stresses have generated a new wave of protests across the continent since 2010. In a 2013 measurement by the African Development Bank (AfDB) based upon Agence France-Presse journalistic data, major public protests rose from an index of 100 in 1996 to nearly 250 in 2012, including Algeria, Angola, Burkina Faso, Chad, Egypt, Gabon, Morocco, Nigeria, South Africa, Tunisia and Uganda (AfDB et al., 2013).

As a result, the beginnings of a Polanyian 'double movement' – that is, excessive market penetration of society countered by social activism, as identified by Karl Polanyi (1944) in *The Great Transformation* – stirred in Africa around 2010. The upswing in uprisings began in the three North African countries where regime changes resulted within a year, but there is also evidence of increasing protest south of the Sahara, including in South Africa's platinum mines where the Marikana massacre of August 2012 was one result, and in December 2013 the cleavage of the largest trade union (the National Union of Metalworkers of South Africa) from the ruling party was another.

But a central challenge remains in most African countries: can nascent economic justice movements follow the Latin American road in which IMF riots during the 1980s paved the way for more sustained construction of social movements to channel activism more effectively, and even changes in government? Aside from ongoing progressive mobilizations in Egypt and Tunisia in reaction to IMF and fundamentalist Islamic repression, only in South Africa is that process apparently ascendant. But the potential remains great. According to AfDB et al. (2013, p. 16):

> Public protests in North Africa in 2012 had a political undertone that reflected an extension of the Arab Spring revolts. The protests were primarily motivated by calls for further and deeper political reforms... Protests in Sub-Saharan Africa were mostly over economic concerns. More than half of public protests were to demand salary increases or to complain against the increasing cost of living.

The AfDB added, in 2011 'nearly all African countries faced increased protests' while the 2012 experiences were concentrated in fewer, larger countries (ibid.).

Of concern, however, is that these Agence France-Presse protest figures – only 250 in 2011, for example – are vast underestimates, given that in South Africa alone, the number of *violent* protests in the year 2012–13 was recorded by police as 1882, with nearly 10 500 additional non-violent 'Gatherings Act' incidents. There, police minister Nathi Mthethwa (2013) observed that 'Over the past four years, a total of 46 180 incidents were attended to and all were successfully stabilized, with 14 843 arrests effected' – although debate continues on how successful the police were in Marikana, as a result of incontrovertible evidence (most supplied from their own computers after clumsy cover-ups) that their massacre of mineworkers was premeditated, and entailed planting of weapons on mineworker corpses (*The Globe and Mail*, 2013). Nationally, it is difficult to identify decisive trends and correlate these to particular political causalities, but it is evident that a higher level of violent incidents occurred after 2008, perhaps due to the combination of the global economic crisis (leaving more than 1 million South Africans newly unemployed) and the rise in electricity prices of 128 per cent that occurred over the subsequent four years.

The varied nature of these local gatherings makes them difficult to quantify, but according to official police 'crowd management' statistics, in the period 2009–10 there were 8905 incidents, 1008 of them classified 'unrest' incidents. In the period 2010–11 there were 12 654 incidents, 973 of them classified 'unrest' incidents. In the 2011–12 period (as of April 2012) there were 11 033 incidents and 1091 of these are classified 'unrest' as opposed to 'peaceful'. In the case of 'unrest' incidents the police intervene (often using force) where they perceive threats to security or damage to property. 'Peaceful' incidents are defined as those where there is cooperation between the police and the convener and where no police intervention is necessary. The many more incidents of protest where there are fewer than 15 people are not recorded by the police, as such events are not considered applicable under the Gatherings Act (yet in many cases, larger protests occur with participants placing themselves in groups of 14 or more at a 50-metre distance in the event that they did not obtain police permission) (Bond and Mottiar, 2013).

Data of this sort should be considered valid only insofar as reliable trends can be discerned, and this is a matter of subjectivity when it comes to protest, given that definitions vary dramatically and that those recording the events – especially Agence France-Presse journalists – do so in a manner that fluctuates over time. Protests become regular and hence no longer of news value. In 2013, more sophisticated cartographic representations and correlations to media databases became available, even if the Africa protest records found in Northern press reports are a small fraction of what was happening on the ground (Beieler, 2013).

There are no scientific studies to date, and the rest of this chapter relies mainly on qualitative analysis, but it is worth considering at least one of the causal vectors, namely rising food prices, where direct correlations between prices and food riots have been observed. There are a great many other areas in which such correlations could be made, including climate – the subject of the work of the Pentagon-funded Robert Strauss Institute at the University of Texas-Austin – as we see in the next section.

Another causal vector that will continue is the traditional class struggle. The ability of labour to move from micro-shopfloor and industry-level demands to national policy will be crucial to Africa's future uprisings. For optimists, the World Economic Forum's September 2013 *Global Competitiveness Report* demonstrated that Africa's labour protesters are by far the world's most militant, even if not yet most effective. In one questionnaire given to representative samples of corporate managers, the topic of 'Cooperation in labour–employer relations' is quantified on a scale of 1 to 7, from 'generally confrontational' to 'generally cooperative'. The mean for the world's working classes was 4.3, that is, with a bias towards quiescence. Table 25.1 shows a sample of 49 countries drawn from all 148 countries surveyed, of which 39 are African: Northern Hemisphere and Asian workers are most pliable, and African (especially South African) are most militant. Of the 39 African countries surveyed, 30 were higher than (or at) the world mean level of militancy. South Africa was by far the most militant working class, for the second year in a row.

In addition to movements to democratize societies, which are invariably drawn from and compel further struggles for socio-economic justice, innumerable micro-struggles continue. These include community campaigns to

Table 25.1 *Africa's relative labour militancy, 2013, sample of 49 countries (ten most pliable working classes, along with 39 African countries, ranked least to most militant)*

Least to Most Labour Militancy

1 Switzerland 6.0	93 Uganda 4.1
2 Singapore 6.0	95 Malawi 4.1
3 Denmark 5.8	100 Nigeria 4.1
4 Norway 5.8	102 Guinea 4.0
5 Netherlands 5.7	104 Namibia 4.0
6 Sweden 5.7	108 Botswana 4.0
7 Qatar 5.6	110 Burkina Faso 4.0
8 Hong Kong 5.6	114 Gabon 3.9
9 Japan 5.6	116 Tanzania 3.9
10 Austria 5.5	117 Egypt 3.8
28 The Gambia 5.0	118 Cape Verde 3.8
32 Rwanda 4.9	119 Tunisia 3.8
36 Côte d'Ivoire 4.8	121 Ethiopia 3.8
38 Mauritius 4.8	122 Lesotho 3.8
45 Seychelles 4.6	123 Zimbabwe 3.7
54 Mali 4.5	126 Cameroon 3.7
57 Senegal 4.5	127 Benin 3.7
63 Sierra Leone 4.4	130 Mozambique 3.6
66 Madagascar 4.4	137 Algeria 3.4
67 Zambia 4.3	141 Chad 3.3
69 Ghana 4.3	142 Mauritania 3.3
73 Kenya 4.2	143 Burundi 3.2
78 Liberia 4.2	145 Angola 3.1
85 Libya 4.2	148 South Africa 2.6
91 Morocco 4.1	

Source: World Economic Forum (2013).

preserve natural resources and rethink the merits of extractive industries (especially minerals, fossil fuels and river sources), in places like the Niger Delta, Zimbabwe's diamond fields and South Africa's platinum and titanium belts (many of which have been mapped at EJOLT, 2014). Others are national initiatives of labour and its allies to meet basic needs and balance local economies through domestic ('import-substitution') production, with South Africans the most active, as we will conclude. Finally, there are numerous struggles associated with extremely serious Islamic or other religious-based insurgencies, in not only Egypt but Somalia, South Sudan, Uganda, Kenya, Mali, Nigeria and Tunisia (AfDB, 2013). Aside from occasional condemnations of US imperialism in Africa, usually these faith-based civil conflicts do not feature in the broader discourses of African citizenries rising up against injustice. But while chaos characterizes large swathes of Africa, groups like The Lord's Resistance Army, Boko Haram and Al-Shabaab will continue to prosper.

Under these circumstances, are we entering an 'African century'? How can we be, if Africa is the continent that will suffer most from climate change? Before addressing more specific instances of African civil society uprisings against what appear to be structured systems of global injustice, consider the most critical one, so as to understand how ordinary activists generated a critique of climate *in*justice.

AFRICAN CLIMATE JUSTICE

Even World Bank (2012) president Jim Yong Kim has recently expressed concern about a 4 degree (minimum) temperature rise, 'which is what scientists are nearly unanimously predicting by the end of the century, without serious policy changes'. Already 400 000 die from climate change each year (*Daily Beast*, 2012). Christian Aid (2006) estimates that 185 million Africans will perish from climate-change related causes this century. The United Nations Framework Convention on Climate Change holds regular Conferences of the Parties (COPs) but as the Warsaw COP19, Doha COP18, Durban COP17 and every other climate gathering has shown, those with power, from Washington and Brussels to Beijing and Pretoria, are increasingly aware but judging by their negotiations strategies in the COPs, don't care about widespread climate destruction – even when in November 2012 it came home to Manhattan when $60 billion in hurricane-related damage was done in a short period.

The African component of the international 'Climate Justice' movement is critical, given the continent's extreme vulnerability to climate change, and the 'climate debt' it is owed, given that Africa (South African and Nigerian-based corporations aside) has not contributed even a small fraction to the world's greatest man-made crisis. The broader Climate Justice movement emerged in part from Africa during the early 2000s, fusing a variety of progressive political-economic and political-ecological currents. Africa soon became the source of some outstanding examples of social mobilization against climate change, its sources and its impacts. One network, the Pan African Climate Justice Alliance (PACJA), built a coalition of 500 groups between 2008 and 2013 (Bond, 2014).

The stakes could not be higher. Aside from drowning small island states and drying out the glacier, snow and water supplies of the Andes,

Himalayas and other mountains, it is widely understood that the most harmful climate change process is 'cooking the continent' of Africa, to cite the book by Nigerian activist Nnimmo Bassey (2011). Climate damage to Africa will include rapid desertification, more floods and droughts, worse water shortages, increased starvation, climate refugees jamming shanty-packed megalopolises and the spread of malarial and other diseases. The danger is imminent, for 8 of the 20 countries that the Center for Global Development expects to be most adversely affected by extreme weather events by 2015 are African: Djibouti, Kenya, Somalia, Mozambique, Ethiopia, Madagascar, Zambia and Zimbabwe. In the Horn of Africa, those affected are anticipated to include 14 per cent of Djiboutis, 8 per cent of Kenyans, 5 per cent of Ethiopians and 4 per cent of Somalis (Wheeler, 2011, p. 15).

The climate-justice political tradition typically names the for-profit Northern economy as the underlying cause of the climate crisis, resulting in an uncompromising opposition to market-based strategies such as carbon trading. There is also an ambitious emphasis on emissions cuts (far greater than those proposed by UN negotiators), and a marked disdain for the inadequacy of official global-scale and most national climate mitigation efforts. In a rejection of technocratic and tinkering responses to climate change, climate justice offers a hostility to technological fixes and geo-engineering, and instead advocates a search for prefigurative post-carbon lifestyles and production systems. Climate justice activists seek explicit alliances with activists specializing in food sovereignty and land access (Via Campesina is typically central within climate justice mobilizations), decommodified water, renewable energy, economic justice and other overlapping struggles – given how many issues have climate implications. This is a feature of a broader orientation to the politics of the 'Global South' (not just North–South power adjustments), and an openness to fusing traditional Left and radical environmental politics with new 'Rights of Nature' strategies, ecofeminist and ecosocialist philosophies, and horizontalist political strategies and tactics, especially in concrete sites of struggle.

The inadequacy of global climate negotiations, and the turn by the United Nations towards 'Type II Partnerships' involving corporations together generated enormous frustration in civil society. Indeed, by the time of the 2002 World Summit on Sustainable Development in Johannesburg, many activists had come to the conclusion that the UN was part of the problem, not the solution. This frustration was dramatized by a march of 30 000 against that UN summit in Johannesburg, from a poor neighbourhood in Alexandra across to Sandton (the wealthiest suburb in Africa) where the convention was held.

614   *Handbook of political citizenship and social movements*

In short, it was in part because of experiences in Africa that climate justice arrived on the international scene as a coherent political approach in the wake of the failure of a more collaborative strategy between major environmental NGOs and the global managerial class. The first effort to generate a global climate advocacy movement in civil society was the Climate Action Network (CAN), which still has a small presence in Africa. But from 1997 in Kyoto, CAN adopted as its core strategy an emphasis on regular UN interstate negotiations aiming at minor, incremental emissions reductions augmented by carbon trading and related offsets. The cul-de-sac of CAN's commitment to carbon trading was confirmed when Friends of the Earth International broke away in 2010, with strong inputs by its African affiliates, especially Nigerian and South African. But even before this, at the time of the December 2009 COP15, CAN's critics from the climate justice movement made the case for an alternative strategy with such force that they gained half the space reserved for non-governmental delegations in Copenhagen's Bella Center.

Core concerns of climate justice activists expressed at Copenhagen and since have included the decommissioning of the carbon markets so favoured by elites, massive investments in renewable energy, a thoroughly reformed agricultural system, public transport and other transformative infrastructure, production and disposal technologies. Strategically, however, it soon became evident that the next stage of the climate justice struggle was necessarily to retreat from a naively over-ambitious reform agenda at the global scale, given the adverse power balance. Instead of politely asking United Nations Framework Convention on Climate Change (UNFCCC) delegates to save the planet, the challenge for climate justice activists from Copenhagen in 2009 into the future would be to whistle-blow and prevent further deterioration in global environmental governance at the annual COPs, but in the meantime to intensify both local and national activism.

Earlier, frustration with the Kyoto Protocol – especially the so-called Clean Development Mechanism (CDM) projects that entail carbon trading applied to the Third World – reached a critical mass in 2004 when the Durban Group for Climate Justice gathered for an historic meeting. A global civil society network, the Durban Group was formed to oppose carbon trading's 'privatization of the air'. Participants worried that the main test case, the EU's Emissions Trading Scheme, not only failed to reduce net greenhouse gases there, but suffered extreme volatility, an inadequate price, the potential for fraud and corruption, and the likelihood of the market crowding out other, more appropriate strategies for addressing the climate crisis (Bond, 2012). Similar controversy surrounds REDD (Reducing Emissions from Deforestation and Forest Degradation), which, in theory, sells investors forest protection. But notwithstanding disagreements in civil society, it was increasingly seen by African advocacy networks such as Durban's TimberWatch as a boon to voracious commercial forestry and a danger to indigenous peoples, given that proper safeguards were not adopted. In March 2013 at the World Social Forum in Tunis, such pressure led to a 'No REDD in Africa' network accusing proponents of contributing to a potential 'genocide', followed up by a Maputo conference to advance the network's agenda in September 2013.

In sum, the emissions markets were the wrong idea (a neoliberal strategy) in the wrong place (financial markets) at the wrong time (the 2000s era of repeated bubbles and bursts). In addition to opposing cap-and-trade schemes, there are numerous other concrete African climate justice campaigns. Some defend against land grabs that promote energy-negative and disruptive land grabs. Others contest mega-dams (such as the Gibe in Ethiopia, the Mphande Nkuwa in Mozambique, the Bujagali in Uganda and the Inga in the Democratic Republic of the Congo) in part because methane emissions from rotting vegetation is so climate destructive. Others address land and agricultural adaptation from the standpoint of rural peasant women producers. Others attack the underlying causes of Africa's emissions in mineral-extraction sectors that consume the most coal-fired and oil-related electricity.

Some campaigns aim to 'leave the oil in the soil, coal in the hole, tar sands in the land and shale gas under the grass', exemplified in South Africa's Karoo region where Shell fracking has been fought, and in Nigeria where Niger Delta activists have intimidated oil companies through both non-violent and armed struggle. In the former category, Environmental Rights Action in Port Harcourt insists on an end to extraction and exploration on grounds of the climate threat, and the descendants of Nigerian writer and activist Ken Saro-Wiwa and eight of his Ogoni movement comrades won a precedent-setting out-of-court-settlement with Shell in June 2009 that may scare off other oil firms. In the latter category, even after an amnesty in 2009 had a divide-and-conquer effect, the Movement for the Emancipation of the Niger Delta (MEND) continued to kidnap foreign oil workers, demanding they vacate the Delta for good.

After a combined struggle of this type, Shell was evicted from Ogoniland in June 2008, 13 years after the company was accused of collaborating with Saro-Wiwa's execution, and a year later, Saro-Wiwa's family (and those of eight others executed at the same time) won $15.5 million from Shell in an Alien Tort Claims Act case settled out of court, a large amount of which was recommitted to movement building (*The Guardian*, 2009). An estimated 1.5 million tonnes of oil have spilled since Delta drilling began in the late 1950s, the equivalent of an *Exxon Valdez* spill each year, costing more than $5 billion in annual environmental damage. In his closing statement at the trial prior to his execution, Saro-Wiwa demanded that Shell vacate the area: 'The military dictatorship holds down oil-producing areas such as Ogoni by military decrees and the threat or actual use of physical violence so that Shell can wage its ecological war without hindrance' (cited in *Wiwa* v. *Shell 2009*, in Bassey, 2011).

At the time, Shell executives met with the Nigerian High Commission in London, stating that if the 'Ogoni virus spreads to other areas in the Delta it would be the end of the oil business' (cited in *Wiwa* v. *Shell 2009*). In court, the plaintiffs had alleged that Shell hired Nigerian police for internal security; that Shell purchased vehicles and arms for the military; that Shell requested military support to build a pipeline through Ogoniland; that Shell assisted and financed the Nigerian military to repress the resistance of the Ogoni people; and that the firm participated in the arrest of Saro-Wiwa and others on fake murder charges and bribed witnesses to produce false testimony. The exposure by WikiLeaks of Shell's ongoing influence in Lagos politics suggests that the Ogoni virus must spread far faster if Nigeria is to be free, and if both the Niger Delta's ecology and the climate are to be spared (Bassey, 2011).

Indeed, most remarkably, rather than letting such destruction rest at the scale of the local, Environmental Rights Action led the climate justice movement in Nigeria, West Africa, and globally in Copenhagen to a much deeper critique of ecological responsibility. In opposition to the shifting, stalling and stealing that characterizes economic and environmental commodification in their own region, and in relation to world financial and oil markets, Environmental Rights Action and its visionary leader Nnimmo Bassey – who was also Friends of the Earth International chairperson for several years – jumped scale to demand that the oil be left in the soil and under the Gulf of Guinea water, given the threat to the planet. In contrast, MEND is a variegated force, including some who are apparently opportunistically self-seeking in mere financial terms, with merely criminal backgrounds (Oriole, 2013). But whatever their motives, they are effective, for in 2007, *Nigeria Business* estimated that 20 per cent of the Niger Delta's oil extraction was disrupted the year before (Umezuruike, 2007). According to a US specialist in guerrilla war, John Robb (2006), at that point MEND was a formidable insurgency:

- Since it first emerged in early 2006 MEND, which says it is fighting for a larger share of southern Nigeria's oil revenue to go to local people, has cut Nigeria's oil production by more than one-quarter.
- *Swarm-based manoeuvres*: guerrillas are using speed boats in the Niger Delta's swamps to quickly attack targets in succession.

Multiple, highly manoeuvrable units have kept the government and Shell's defensive systems off-balance defending the sprawling network. Radically improved firepower and combat training: allowing guerrillas to overpower a combination of Shell's Western-trained private military guards and elite Nigerian units in several engagements.
- *Effective use of system disruption*: targets have been systematically and accurately selected to completely shut down production and delay and/or halt repairs, and the guerrillas are making effective use of Shell's hostages to coerce both the government and the company.

In another innovative example of resistance to climate change, the Cape Town-based Alternative Information and Development Centre hosts a 'Million Climate Jobs' campaign involving leading progressive labour officials from the metalworkers, transport workers and municipal workers unions, fusing with community activists and environmentalists. As their website (Million Climate Jobs, 2014) explained: 'Climate jobs are decent, primarily publicly driven jobs that directly reduce the causes and impacts of climate change'. Climate jobs involve:

- the building of renewable energy power stations such as wind, solar, wave and tidal;
- the building of public transport networks that would reduce the need for private cars and fossil fuel intensive trucks;
- energy efficiency in construction and housing, including retrofitting;
- transforming industrial agriculture;
- reforming production and consumption; and
- addressing the energy intensification of the economy.

Significant jobs would be created in the related areas of research, education and training, to ensure the country has the skills to undertake the transition to a low-carbon, labour-absorbing and socially developed sustainable future economy. By linking climate change to the transition to a sustainable, low-carbon economy that provides meaningful mitigation opportunities, the campaign will stimulate the interest of many sectors of South African society who do not realize the immediate relevance of climate change.

Another case of civil society resistance to climate change involves a growing critique of the 'Green Economy', in which the Gabarone Declaration of May 2012 and Rio+20 of June 2012 featured prominently, as some African governments sought to commodify nature in order to save it. In contrast, PACJA signed a declaration against the Green Economy as 'the privatization of nature'. PACJA and indigenous people's allies committed to 'recognize our responsibilities to protect Mother Earth and work towards a new paradigm that rejects the property right regimes with a new set of laws that recognizes the Rights of Nature – the Rights of Mother Earth' (PACJA, 2012).

A partial ecological debt accounting was published by environmental scientists in early 2008, and counted $1.8 trillion in concrete damages over several decades (Srinivasan et al., 2008). Richard Norgaard, ecological economist at the University of California, Berkeley, generated a crucial finding: 'At least to some extent, the rich nations have developed at the expense of the poor, and, in effect, there is a debt to the poor' (*The Guardian*, 2008). The study included factors such as greenhouse gas emissions, ozone layer depletion, agriculture, deforestation, over-fishing, and the conversion of mangrove swamps into shrimp farms, but did not (so far) succeed in calculating other damages, for example, excessive freshwater withdrawals, destruction of coral reefs, biodiversity loss, invasive species and war.

Yet African ecological debt advocates must be very careful to not adopt the Green Economy's approach to valuing nature so as to generate new markets. The idea of ecological debt – especially related to climate damage – entails collective reparations and an accountability system that generates structural change, as opposed to merely a 'fine' for wrongdoing. In other words, the 'fine' (polluter pays) must be followed by a *ban* on further pollution, for there to be restorative justice. At all costs, the approach termed 'Payment for Ecosystem Services' should be avoided, so as to halt the growth of markets in nature, offsets and carbon trading.

How, then, to pay the climate debt? It became clear to many civil society groups in recent decades that post-colonial African governments were too easily corrupted, just as were UN agencies and aid (and even international NGO) bureaucracies.

The solution to the payment distribution problem appeared in 2009: the idea of simply passing along a monthly grant – universal in amount and access, with no means-testing or other qualifications – to each African citizen via an individual Basic Income Grant (BIG) payment. By all accounts, the village of Otjivero, Namibia, was an exceptionally successful pilot for this form of redistribution. There was an enormous impact from BIG on social indicators, including food, education and health security, and domestic violence, begging and sex work (and with it, transfer of HIV and STDs) declined considerably (Sharife and Bond, 2013). The first priority would be to supply a Basic Income Grant to Africans who live in areas most adversely affected by droughts, floods or other extreme weather events. Logistically, the use of Post Office Savings Banks or rapidly introduced Automated Teller Machines would be sensible, although currency distortions, security and other such challenges would differ from place to place. The Namibian case has much to recommend it, in part because it is amongst the driest sites in Africa.

Such a strategy would be just an emergency salve on a burning problem: how to ensure that the greenhouse gas 'polluters pay' in a manner that first, compensates their climate change victims; that second, permits transformation of African energy, transport, extraction, production, distribution, consumption and disposal systems; and that third, in the process assures the 'right to development' for Africa in a future world economy constrained by emissions caps. Extremely radical changes will be required in all these activities in order not only to ensure the safety of the species and planet, but also that Africans are at the front of the queue for long-overdue ecological and economic compensation, given the North's direct role in Africa's environmental damage.

The contemporary argument for climate debt to be paid is simply the first step in a long process, akin to decolonization, in which the master – the polluting Global North (South Africa included) – must know that the tools with which his house were built, including the profit motive and markets, are not and cannot be effective in remodelling for a new society. And he must also know that not only is it time to halt the reliance on fossil fuels, but having 'broken' the climate, it is his responsibility to foot the clean-up bill. And that, finally, must be done without creating new market strategies to privatize nature and contribute to world financial chaos and corruption; it must be done to achieve justice, via direct payments to the victims of the crisis the master has created. These are some of the lessons of climate justice in, by and for Africa, and it is very likely that the growing climate crisis will compel many more civil society groups in Africa to draw these lessons into their work.

SPECIFIC AFRICAN UPRISINGS

In addition to climate, the reproduction of Africa's exploitative trade, finance, investment and labour-migration relations within crisis-ridden world capitalism has met with sustained – albeit still uncoordinated and largely ineffectual – resistance, as the data reviewed earlier suggest. This is especially true in North Africa, where counter-revolution has prevailed in most countries. Since the Washington Consensus narrative was unchanged in all-important respects, contradictions grew more extreme. Initially, for example, there was even awareness in Egypt's military that neoliberal reforms carried out by Mubarak were responsible for the revolts insofar as they compelled a core working-class constituency – independent trade unions – to view their struggles in political terms. This was conceded in May 2011 by no less a figure than Major General Mohamed al-Assar of the Supreme Council of the Armed Forces:

> The military brass were deeply opposed to the privatization programme. That in turn eased their decision to side with the Egyptian public against the 30-year autocratic rule of Mubarak. Al-Assar told state television on Wednesday that the army has been against the 'plans to sell Egypt' and viewed them as a threat to social peace. He said that Field Marshal Mohammed Tantawi, the council's president and minister of defence, had repeatedly raised objections to the privatization programme, as shown in the minutes of several cabinet meetings he attended. His opinion was often overruled by Mubarak and other top officials who had favoured following economic prescriptions from Western countries. (Mekay, 2011)

However, it is equally certain that the counter-revolutionary forces in Egypt, including the army leadership that retook power in 2013, would not be able to deliver the socio-economic progress demanded in Tahrir Square. They soon banned strikes and protests. With class struggles constantly breaking out as part of the process, Samir Amin (2011) celebrated the earlier groundedness of the movements:

> The workers' strikes in 2007 (the strongest strikes on the African continent in the past fifty years), the stubborn resistance of small farmers threatened with expropriation by agrarian capital, and the formation of democratic protest groups among the middle classes (like the 'Kefaya' and 'April 6' movements) foretold the inevitable explosion – expected by Egyptians but startling to 'foreign observers'. . . Although the youth movement is diversified in its social composition and in its political and ideological expressions, it places itself as a whole 'on the left'. Its strong and spontaneous expressions of sympathy with the radical left testify to that.

Under IMF dictates to repay Mubarak's $33 billion debt, the army leadership (even with an electoral mandate expected in 2014) will not be able to deliver the socio-economic progress demanded in Tahrir Square, thus ensuring protest for many years to come once the dust settles on the fully-militarized new government.

What lessons would be drawn for other country-specific protesters, including the ways to spark such rapid and deep revolts that a dictator can be removed from power with at least temporary support from the military? Perhaps the most acute observer of the potential for emancipation in Africa is Sokari Ekine (2011), who follows the continent's blogs at the weekly *Pambazuka News*. Her mid-2011 review of developments in several countries is revealing:

Uganda, Swaziland, Kenya, and Botswana actions are in response to concerns over food security, rising unemployment particularly amongst youth, political marginalization, corruption of government officials and a pushback against the entrenched leadership of the circle of 'rulers for life'. Military dictators have been replaced by democracy dictatorships under militarised states.

Eastern Africa was typical of the resulting fusion of neoliberalism and repression. In Kampala, wrote Ekine (2011):

> The government has blamed inflation on external factors out of their control, obviously believing Ugandans are so ill-informed as to not make the connection between the $740 million spent on fighter jets and tanks... Museveni who, in a show of militarism, chose to wear military fatigues during the recent swearing in of MPs, complained that his guests, President Kabila of the DRC and Goodluck Jonathan of Nigeria, were pelted with stones by people.

In Nairobi, Ekine (2011) reported, 'Grassroots movements such as Bunge La Mwananchi [The People's Parliament] and the "Unga Revolution" [a collection of civil society groups including Bunge La Mwananchi] campaigning for economic and social rights have been formed in response to the rising cost of living and loss of social benefits'.

The same dynamic was observed in Southern Africa. In Manzini:

> [t]he Swazi pro-democracy uprisings which began on 12 April were met with beatings, teargas and hundreds of arrests. Many of the protesters were driven 100 miles into the country where they were dumped by the police. Student leader Maxwell Dlamini and Musa Ngubeni of the Swaziland Youth Congress were arrested, tortured and remain in detention. (Ekine, 2011)

In Gaborone:

> Botswana, much revered in the west as 'Africa's success story', public sector workers – transport, schools, clinics and government staff – began striking on 18 April. The ruling party has been in power for 45 years and people are calling for a change. The leader of the opposition, Duma Boko has called for an Egypt-style uprising. (Ekine, 2011)

In Harare in February 2011, Robert Mugabe's forces arrested 45 attendees of an International Socialist Organisation Zimbabwe meeting who were reviewing footage from Tahrir Square and Tunisia.

West Africa had similar issues but more success with country-specific and demand-specific protesting. In Dakar, Senegal's well-respected mass movements rose up in June 2011, burning down the country's national electricity building and tax authority. They protested at cabinet ministers' houses to force both a resolution of an energy crisis and a withdrawal of

President Abdoulaye Wade's proposed legislation that would have seen him extend his neoliberal political rule. That protest was successful, as was the January 2012 'Occupy Nigeria' national demonstrations against the doubling of the fuel price mandated by IMF Managing Director Christine Lagarde, who had visited a few days earlier. Millions of Nigerians took to the streets as an eight-day strike cost $1.3 billion in output. It quickly became evident to President Goodluck Jonathan that he would have to concede on the socio-economic front, or be ousted from power.

This degree of anger must, at some stage, result in a more effective Polanyian double movement than has happened to date. The earlier era of protests – in the form of IMF riots – did not derail neoliberalism in Africa, even though after the debt crisis got underway in the early 1980s, World Bank president A.W. Clausen (1983) was worried enough to tell a board meeting:

> We must ask ourselves: How much pressure can these nations be expected to bear? How far can the poorest peoples be pushed into further reducing their meagre standards of living? How resilient are the political systems and institutions in these countries in the face of steadily worsening conditions? I don't have the answers to these important questions.

More recently, the world's elites have been aware of the potential for more sustained critique, for in 2011 the IMF's then managing director, Dominique Strauss-Kahn, was asked by a journalist, 'Do you have any fears that there is perhaps a far left movement coming through these revolutions that want more, perhaps, closed economies? I mean, there have been a lot of pictures of Guevara there'. His answer:

> Good question. Good question. There's always this risk, but I'm not sure it will materialize. Look, during the global financial crisis we went just through, at the beginning many were afraid of the possibility of an increase in protectionism. It didn't happen. Why? Because, I think, that most governments, maybe not all of them, but most governments and most people, man on the street, have understood that there was no good solution in this direction. I'm not saying that everybody agrees with this, but most had understood that the closed economy was not the way to benefit from global growth and certainly from investment. And we're in a globalized world, so there is no domestic solution. (International Monetary Fund, 2011)

To make the case that we need not worry about Africans inspired by Che – whose mid-1960s' fight against Mobutu alongside (briefly) the father of current Democratic Republic of Congo president Joseph Kabila, was utterly miserable – Strauss-Kahn used as a proxy 'protectionism'. In the case of South Africa, normally amongst Africa's most aggressively neoliberal regimes, Strauss-Kahn should have been worried, for in 2009, a

Communist Party member, Rob Davies, was made trade minister, and by 2013 he had begun widespread cancellation of free trade deals, and even imposed an 82 per cent tariff on import of Brazilian chickens. The 'domestic solution' Strauss-Kahn despises is also to be found in the re-imposition of capital controls, defaults on 'odious debt', state-directed investment and favourable interest rates (Asian 'developmental state'-style), Keynesian reflation and more social spending. These strategies are all gaining steam, leading *The Economist* to worriedly headline its 12 October 2013 special issue on the world economy, 'The Gated Globe'.

What the IMF leader should also have considered was a deeper set of critical reactions to the era of African neoliberalism in which financialization has fused with extractivist accumulation, and in which the 'Africa Rising' argument is increasingly revealed as far from the truth. If so, then the 'far left movement' seeking 'closed economies' – that is, those protected from especially the ravages of deregulated global finance – would find a much more compelling Polanyian double movement that has emerged in civil (and often uncivil) society. As we have seen, the resistance stiffened especially beginning in 2011. This is true not only in North Africa where socio-economic grievances were central to understanding revolts in even the (neoliberally) best-performing of African countries, Tunisia, but also in Sub-Saharan Africa, where after years of ineffectual IMF riots, growing unrest was observed in crucial sectors and geographical spaces from Senegal in the west, to Uganda in the centre and to Swaziland in the south. Most crucially, the South African bottom-up rupture with the African neoliberal-nationalist script is worth following; indications in late 2013 are that connectivities can be found in sites of grassroots and labour struggle, offering hope for stronger alliances of poor and working people than we have ever known here, perhaps also beyond South Africa's borders. A February 2014 General Strike call against the South African finance ministry – on Budget Day speech in parliament – would be one indication of the ability of the National Union of Metalworkers of South Africa (NUMSA) to reach downwards into the unemployed and especially youth, for support and linkage to the communities' service delivery protests.

If such protests can coagulate and move from local to national to continental to global scales in coming years, what would they be potentially articulating, as an antidote to 'Africa Rising' rhetoric? According to Jumoke Balogun (2013):

> African governments hold the solution to a more equitable society. By closing the skills gap, initiating a more progressive corporate tax system, and providing subsidies for public services that protect the bottom percentile, many countries can begin to turn the tide. However, we must all first admit that most Africans

are not rising with Africa, and that wealth disparity is a major obstacle to overall development.

Once that admission is accepted, further words of counsel are provided by Ama Biney, *Pambazuka News* editor:

> Ultimately, fundamental to Africa genuinely 'rising' must be a critical examination of what this 'rising' will entail. What kind of development do we envisage for Africa? Does it only lie in economic development and progress? What about social and cultural development? What about the psyche and aesthetics that a people adhere and aspire to? What kind of economic development will ensure that the economy is controlled by the greatest number of ordinary people rather than the minority? If Africa is to rise, surely it must rise for the greatest majority of its people – particularly the unemployed youth in many African countries; those living with disabilities ostracised and stigmatised by cultural taboos and attitudes; albino individuals who also face similar stigmatisation; women; the poor; those in need of ARV drugs to prolong the quality of their lives as they live with HIV/AIDS as well as LBGTI individuals persecuted in many African countries?
>
> However, at the moment it seems the type of development the 'Africa is rising' evangelists envisage is that which Fanon warned us against: an imitation of Europe and a desire to catch up with Europe. There appears little desire or will to seek an alternative to capitalism, one that is centred on the ideas and interests of ordinary people. There was no blueprint for capitalism yet it was constructed on the backs of African slaves and wage labourers around the world. Similarly, there is no model nor blueprint for socialism yet many are seduced by TINA (There is No Alternative to Capitalism) which maintains the neoliberal status quo. If Africa is to rise, it must heed Thomas Sankara and 'dare to invent the future' based on a new egalitarian economic system that centres people before profits and in which ordinary people critically control the production of what they produce and how they produce it.

NOTES

1. 'A paradoxical situation in which countries with an abundance of non-renewable resources experience stagnant growth or even economic contraction. The resource curse occurs as a country begins to focus all of its energies on a single industry, such as mining, and neglects other major sectors. As a result, the nation becomes overly dependent on the price of commodities, and overall gross domestic product becomes extremely volatile. Additionally, government corruption often results when proper resource rights and an income distribution framework is not established in the society, resulting in unfair regulation of the industry. The resource curse is most often witnessed in emerging markets following a major natural resource discovery. Also known as the 'paradox of plenty' (Investopedia, accessed 25 May 2014 at http://www.investopedia.com/terms/r/resource-curse.asp).
2. According to the *Changing Wealth of Nations*, the wealth of resource-based countries Norway, Canada and Australia soared during this period (World Bank, 2011),

because their extraction is done largely by home-grown companies that reinvest and return profits to local shareholders. Most of the extractive corporations operating in Africa send profits to London, New York, Melbourne, Paris, Toronto, Rio de Janeiro, Shanghai or Beijing, with Johannesburg representing a 'branch plant' halfway house (no longer the site of accumulation for the South African mining capital). The world's largest mining and metals house, BHP Billiton, is actively disinvesting, and Africa's largest company, Anglo American, is continuing its shift of investment outside South Africa. In sum, a much different kind of resource curse than typically argued by mainstream economists is at work.

REFERENCES

Action Aid (2006), *Real Aid: An Agenda for Making Aid Work*, accessed 22 May 2014 at http://www.actionaid.org/sites/files/actionaid/real_aid.pdf.
African Development Bank (AfDB), OECD Development Centre, UN Development Programme and Economic Commission for Africa (2013), *African Economic Outlook*, accessed 22 May 2014 at http://www.africaneconomicoutlook.org/fileadmin/uploads/aeo/PDF/Pocket%20Edition%20AEO2013-EN.web.pdf.
Amin, S. (2011), 'An Arab springtime?', *Monthly Review*, 2 June, accessed 22 May 2014 at http://monthlyreview.org/commentary/2011-an-arab-springtime.
Balogun, J. (2013), 'Africa is rising. Most Africans are not', Compare Afrique online, 15 February, accessed 22 May 2014 at http://www.compareafrique.com/africa-is-rising-most-africans-are-not/.
Bassey, N. (2011), *To Cook a Continent: Destructive Extraction and the Climate Crisis in Africa*, Oxford: Fahamu Books.
Beieler, J. (2013), 'Protest mapping', State College, Penn State University, accessed 22 May 2014 at http://johnbeieler.org/protest_mapping/.
Biney, A. (2013), 'Is Africa really rising?', *Pambazuka News*, 31 July and 4 September, accessed 22 May 2014 at http://pambazuka.org/en/category/books/88474 and http://pambazuka.org/en/category/features/88748.
Bond, P. (2006), *Looting Africa*, London: Zed Books.
Bond, P. (2011), 'Africa's 'Recovery', *Africa Insight*, **41**(3), 30–45.
Bond, P. (2012), *Politics of Climate Justice*, Pietermaritzburg, ZA: University of KwaZulu-Natal Press.
Bond, P. (2014), 'Climate justice in, by and for Africa', in M. Dietz and H. Garrelts (eds), *Routledge Handbook of the Climate Change Movement*, London: Routledge.
Bond, P. and S. Mottiar (2013), 'Social protest in South Africa', *Journal of Contemporary African Studies*, **31**(2), 283–302.
CADTM Commission to Annul Third World Debt (2008), 'Topicality of odious debt doctrine', Brussels, 8 August, accessed 22 May 2014 at http://cadtm.org/Topicality-of-the-odious-debt.
Calandro, E., A. Gillwald, M. Moyo and C. Stork (2010), *Comparative Sector Performance Review 2009/2010: Towards Evidence-based ICT Policy and Regulation, Volume Two, Policy Paper 2*, accessed 22 May 2014 at http://www.researchictafrica.net/publications/Policy_Paper_Series_Towards_Evidence-based_ICT_Policy_and_Regulation_-_Volume_2/Vol_2_Paper_5_-_Comparative_ICT_Sector_Performance_Review_2009_2010.pdf.
Christian Aid (2006), *The Climate of Poverty: Facts, Fears and Hope*, report, accessed 25 May 2014 at www.christianaid.org.uk/Images/climate-of-poverty.pdf.
Clausen, A.W. (1983), 'Speech by the World Bank President to Board of Directors', Washington, DC: World Bank.
Daily Beast (2012), 'Climate change kills 400,000 a year, new report reveals', 27 September, accessed 25 May 2014 at http://www.thedailybeast.com/articles/2012/09/27/climate-change-kills-400-000-a-year-new-report-reveals.html.

EJOLT (2014), 'Environmental Justice Organisations, Liabilities and Trade Atlas', accessed 22 May 2014 at http://ejatlas.org.
Ekine, S. (2011), 'Defiant in the face of brutality: uprisings in East and Southern Africa', *Pambazuka News*, 2 June, accessed 22 May 2014 at http://pambazuka.org/en/category/features/73738.
Elliott, L. (2012), 'Aid to Africa dwindles as Euro crisis rages on', *Mail&Guardian*, 29 June, accessed 22 May 2014 at http://mg.co.za/article/2012-06-29-aid-to-africa-dwindles-as-euro-crisis-rages-on.
Harvey, D. (2003), *The New Imperialism*, Oxford: Oxford University Press.
International Monetary Fund (2009), *Africa: Regional Economic Outlook*, Washington, DC: IMF.
International Monetary Fund (2011), 'Transcript of a group interview with Managing Director Dominique Strauss-Kahn and Middle East journalists', Washington, 6 April, accessed 25 May 2014 at http://www.imf.org/external/np/tr/2011/tr040611.htm.
Mekay, E. (2011), 'Privatisation aided Egypt revolt, army says', InterPress Service, 8 April, accessed 22 May 2014 at http://www.ipsnews.net/2011/04/privatisation-aided-egypt-revolt-army-says/.
Million Climate Jobs (2014), accessed 25 May 2014 at http://www.climatejobs.org.za/.
Mthethwa, N. (2013), 'Remarks by the Minister of Police, E.N. Mthethwa, MP, on the occasion of the release of the 2012/13 South African Police Service National Crime Statistics, SAPS Tshwane Training Academy', Pretoria, accessed 25 May 2014 at http://govza.gcis.gov.za/node/487649.
Ndikumana, L. and J. Boyce (2011), *Africa's Odious Debts*, London: Zed Books.
Ndikumana, L. and J. Boyce (2012a), *Capital Flight from North African Countries*, University of Massachusetts/Amherst Political Economy Research Institute, accessed 22 May 2014 at http://www.peri.umass.edu/fileadmin/pdf/ADP/NAfrica_capitalflight_Oct15_2012.pdf.
Ndikumana, L. and J. Boyce (2012b), *Capital Flight from Sub-Saharan African Countries: Updated Estimates, 1970–2010*, University of Massachusetts/Amherst Political Economy Research Institute, accessed 22 May 2014 at http://www.peri.umass.edu/fileadmin/pdf/ADP/SSAfrica_capitalflight_Oct23_2012.pdf.
Oriole, T. (2013), *Criminal Resistance: The Politics of Kidnapping Oil Workers*, Farnham, UK: Ashgate.
Pan African Climate Justice Alliance (PACJA) (2012), 'World urged to reject false solutions for green economy', Rio de Janeiro, 6 July, accessed 25 May 2014? at http://pacja.org/?option=com_content&view=article&id=302%3Aworld-urged-to-reject-false-solutions-for-green-economy&Itemid=130.
Perry, A. (2012), 'Africa rising', *Time*, 3 December, accessed 22 May 2014 at http://content.time.com/time/magazine/article/0,9171,2129831,00.html.
Robb, J. (2006), 'Nigerian evolution', *GlobalGuerrillas blog*, accessed 25 May 2014 at http://globalguerrillas.typepad.com/globalguerrillas/2006/01/nigerian_evolut.html.
Sharife, K. (2011), *Tax Us If You Can: Why Africa Should Stand up for Tax Justice*, Oxford: Fahamu Books, accessed 22 May 2014 at http://www.taxjustice.net/cms/upload/pdf/tuiyc_africa_final.pdf.
Sharife, K. and P. Bond (2013), 'Ecological reparations: can the "Green Economy" incorporate litigative justice and eco-debt payments, or does global climate governance require environmental justice and a redistributive Basic Income Grant?', *South African Journal of Human Rights*, **29**(1), 144–69.
Shaw, A. (2012), 'Experts: Africa countries lose AIDS funding', Associated Press, 19 July, accessed 22 May 2014 at http://news.yahoo.com/experts-africa-countries-lose-aids-funding-120711764.html.
Srinivasan, U., S. Carey, E. Hallstein, P. Higgins, A. Ker, L. Koteen, A. Smith, R. Watson, J. Harte and R. Norgaard (2008), 'The debt of nations and the distribution of ecological impacts from human activities', *Proceedings of the National Academy of Sciences of the United States of America*, **105**(5), accessed 22 May 2014 at http://www.pnas.org/content/105/5/1768.

The Globe and Mail (2013), 'Police lied, covering up killings in South African mine massacre, inquiry finds', 19 September, accessed 25 May 2014 at http://www.theglobeandmail.com/news/world/inquiry-unearths-police-cover-up-in-south-african-marinkana-massacre/article14414358/.

The Guardian (2008), 'Rich countries owe poor a huge environmental debt', 21 January, accessed 22 May 2014 at http://www.guardian.co.uk/science/2008/jan/21/environmental.debt1.

The Guardian (2009), 'Shell pays out $15.5m over Waro-Wiwa killing', accessed 25 May 2014 at http://www.theguardian.com/world/2009/jun/08/nigeria-usa.

Umezuruike, E. (2007), 'The Niger Delta challenge', *NigeriaBusiness*, 23 January, accessed 25 May 2014 at http://www.thenigeriabusiness.com/column6.html.

Wheeler, D. (2011), 'Quantifying vulnerability to climate change: implications for adaptation assistance', Center for Global Development Working Paper No. 240, Washington, DC: Center for Global Development, accessed 1 June 2013 at http://www.cgdev.org/content/publications/detail/1424759.

World Bank (2011), *The Changing Wealth of Nations*, Washington, DC: World Bank.

World Bank (2012), 'New report examines risks of 4 degree hotter world by end of century', press release, 18 November, Washington, DC, accessed 25 May 2014 at http://www.worldbank.org/en/news/press-release/2012/11/18/
new- report-examines-risks-of-degree-hotter-world-by-end-of-century.

World Economic Forum (2013), *Global Competitiveness Report, 2013–2014*, Davos, accessed 22 May 2014 at http://www.weforum.org/issues/global-competitiveness.

26. Political citizenship and social movements in the Arab world
Roel Meijer

INTRODUCTION

In 2010 and 2011 the Middle East and North Africa (MENA region) captured world attention as people rose up en masse to end the regimes that had suppressed and humiliated them for so long. This was expressed in the slogan 'The people demand the fall of the system'. The people (*al-sha'b*) as agency were back. Their aspirations were expressed in the demand for dignity (*karama*), ending corruption, implementing justice and creating jobs. The remarkable aspect of the uprisings was that the demands were made by people who regarded themselves as citizens (*muwatinun*).

I will argue that the Middle East has indeed changed and that these changes have been on the cards for a long time. But not only are the Arab uprisings a turning point for the Middle East, they have also been so for Middle East studies. Two long-neglected fields of research, citizenship studies and social movement theory, can help to re-analyze Middle Eastern history over the past two centuries. Applying citizenship studies and social movement theory has several advantages over other orientations that have dominated the academic field during the past decades. Citizenship studies has the advantage that it focuses research on the core object of politics: how does politics impinge on the civil, political, social and cultural rights of the citizen? Besides including legal studies, political philosophy, sociology and political science, citizenship studies also takes a long-term view: how has the position of the subject/citizen changed over time? Social movements theory gives agency to the citizen: how has contestation influenced the position of the citizen? Both studies can correct the tendency to portray the Arab as passive and indolent, or the exact opposite, fanatical and religious, so reminiscent of the orientalist tradition (Said, 1978).

In this chapter I will first deal with dominant interpretations of Middle Eastern politics and their limitations. Then I will deal with citizenship studies and subsequently with social movements theory, followed by an outline of how citizenship studies and social movement theory can be applied to the Middle East history. Finally I will analyze the Arab uprisings with the help of these two disciplines.

THEORIZING THE MIDDLE EAST

Both citizenship studies as well as social movements theory are latecomers to Middle East studies. Citizenship studies has hardly been applied at all to the Middle East, while social movement theory has only been around for two decades. Middle East studies has been overwhelmingly dominated by other disciplines. For a long time Oriental studies, with the focus on Islam, languages and texts, reigned supreme. Ethnography did exist in the colonial era, but it was often used for the political purposes of the colonial powers. It emphasized the cultural and religious diversity, based on the mosaic model. Not until the 1950s did anthropology (Varisco, 2005) and political science become mature studies. While the first mostly concentrated on the micro-level, the second was heavily influenced by modernization theory, as represented by Lerner (1958) and Halpern (1964). It focused on the new elites as modernizers of the region. Ordinary citizens were regarded as passive entities. They would acquire full rights and capabilities once society had reached a certain level of social differentiation and economic development.

These optimistic visions were discredited when most Arabic countries had developed into repressive regimes in the 1960s. Modernization theory as the main discipline was succeeded by political economy (Abdel-Fadil, 1980; Amin, 1980; Richards and Waterbury [1990] 1996). Its adherents analyzed how the interplay of politics and economics produced the authoritarian state that had come to dominate the Middle East, especially emphasizing the economic dimension and regarding the citizen as a passive tool worked upon by the state. Citizens were indicators of human development rather than active subjects. The focus on the Arab authoritarian and corporatist state, analyzed in structuralist terms by Ayubi (1995), likewise left little room for agency. Typically, the uprisings of the 1980s were often regarded as 'bread riots'. The passivity of citizens was further enhanced in the rentier-state theory applied to Gulf States, originally expounded by Luciani (1990). Later on the theory was extended to neighboring non-oil states, which were regarded as 'semi-rentier states'.

In the meantime, anthropology had increasingly started to work on the national level, but in terms of people's own definition, neglecting the legal and political dimension. Intellectual history, insofar as it was pursued, built on Albert Hourani's *Arab Thought in a Liberal Age, 1798–1939* (Hourani, 1962), focusing on Arab nationalism, Islamic reformism and identity politics. Conceptualization of politics among intellectuals and politicians, so crucial for determining the status and capacities of citizens, was largely neglected by the next generation, such as William Cleveland (1971), Israel Gershoni (1981; Gershoni and Jankowski, 1986, 1995) and

Paul Salem (1994). It is true that social history gained adherents in this period. Left-wing and Marxist historians focused on workers' movements, emerging trade unions (Beinin and Lockman, 1988), and communist parties (Botman, 1988; Ismael, 1990, 2004, 2008), with the aim of analyzing why a social revolution had failed. Their drawback was that they gave workers too much weight. At the same time, the greater interest in sociology and society also led to in-depth studies of the 'failure of modernization', especially patronage systems and the persistence of clientelism and political cliques (Springborg, 1982; Bill and Springborg, 1999). Though extremely helpful in defining the specificities of Arab political culture, only later on were they incorporated into overarching theories of blocking equal rights of citizens.

After the fall of the Berlin Wall in 1989 and the third wave of democratization, the focus shifted towards the role of civil society (Norton, 1995, 1996). The main question was to what extent did civil society exist in the Middle East and how could it promote the regional transition towards greater democratization? When at the end of the 1990s this transition did not materialize, the pendulum swung back to focus on the state and its resilience to democratization. Co-opted by the state, dependent on foreign funds and lacking democratic potential, Islamic NGOs were often highly conservative and civil society was no longer seen as an agent of change (Abdelrahman, 2004; J.A. Clark, 2004).

Authoritarian resilience theories constituted the main trend in political science in the first decade of the 2000s but were severely handicapped by an ingrained functionalist analysis of the authoritarian states, which were always capable of meeting all challenges to their power, most famously epitomized by Steven Heydemann's report *Upgrading Authoritarianism in the Arab World* for Brookings (2007). The deepening gloom over the Middle East was enhanced by numerous analyses of the Islamist movement as the main resistance to the authoritarian state. The debate on Islamic movements was marred by the question of whether they were democratic or not (J.A. Clark, 2012), most researchers coming down on the negative side, and those that did not often exaggerating the positive, democratic inclinations of these movements (Abed-Kotob, 1995; Tamimi, 2001; El-Ghobashy, 2005).

The introduction of new disciplines, such as Foucaultian analysis of Egypt or Tunisia by Timothy Mitchell (1991, 2002) and Hibou (2011), further deepened the depressive portrayal of Middle Eastern societies as fully controlled by mechanisms of power, denying the citizen any form of agency. It is only with the introduction of social movement theory in the 2000s (Mishal and Sela, 2000) that agency was incorporated into Middle East studies on a more theoretical level. Wiktorowicz's (2004) seminal anthology on the application of social movement theory to Islamic movements and Mohammed Hafez's work (2004) was a breakthrough, although the latter in particular suffered from a mechanical application of Western concepts.

Connecting social movement theory with Islamic movements became a trend in this decade (Wickham, 2002; Hafez, 2004; Gunning, 2007). With few exceptions (Denoeux, 1993), applying social movement theory to broader sections of the population took longer (Thompson, 2013; Tripp, 2013a). Beinin and Vairel (2011) and Bennani-Chraïbi and Fillieule (2003) strive in their anthologies to adapt social movement theory to a different political environment and address the more theoretical problems associated with applying Western concepts to an entirely different environment. Earlier, others like Asef Bayat (2000, 2005, 2007, 2010) had developed their own specific angles of approach, coining the term 'non-movement' for the subterranean informal networks that pass for movements in the authoritarian setting in the Middle East. Just after the Arab uprisings, a vehement debate erupted that criticized the dominance of authoritarian resilience theory, the lack of analysis of social movements, and in general the lack of tools to analyze any of the recent developments (Gause, 2011; Pace and Cavatorta, 2012). In feminist studies rights were prominent and from its legal orientation often geared to women as citizens (Ahmed, 1992; Moghadam, 1993).

CITIZENSHIP STUDIES, SOCIAL MOVEMENT THEORY, AND THE MIDDLE EAST

Which elements constitute citizenship and how can they be applied and adjusted to the Middle East and in what way can they provide a better insight into historical and current developments in the region?

First, the basis of citizenship is the idea of 'rights'. T.H. Marshall, in his famous essay 'Citizenship and Social Class' ([1950] 1965) makes a distinction between three separate types of rights that emerged in Great Britain: (1) civil rights (equal right to property and safety, equality before law, and access to trial, freedom of speech and faith), which emerged in the eighteenth century; (2) political rights (passive and active right to vote, freedom of organization and the right to establish political parties), introduced in the nineteenth century and extended further in the twentieth century; (3) social rights (right to social welfare in the form of health care, education, pension, unemployment fees) emerging during the welfare state in the second half of the twentieth century.

Second, since Marshall the model has become more *refined* as economic, cultural (for ethnic minorities) and sexual rights (LGBTI rights) were included (Isin and Turner, 2002). All of these are highly relevant for the Middle East in the sense that tracing rights over time provides a specific focus on citizenship as one of the main themes in history.

Third, citizenship can be analyzed by means of a 'comparative model'. Michael Mann has extended the scope of analysis to include other European countries, defining five different citizenship trajectories: liberal (Great Britain and the United States as separate categories), reformist, authoritarian monarchist (Germany, Japan), fascist (Germany and Italy in the twentieth century) and authoritarian socialist (USSR) (Mann, 1987). He argues that these different trajectories are determined by ruling class strategies. Besides introducing a comparative model that is useful for the Middle East, Mann's emphasis on 'politics of citizenship' of the elite can be regarded as a forerunner of the Middle Eastern 'authoritarian resilience' theories, which also concentrate on top-down 'citizenship policy', directed 'from above'.

Fourth, the citizenship model is not only comparative, but it is also made more complex by identifying different 'combinations of rights' in the countries, which determine their history. For instance, at the beginning of the twentieth century, the capitalist, liberal United States had strong civil rights (although not for African Americans) but weak social rights, while the nineteenth-century authoritarian monarchies, such as Germany, Japan and Austria, had weak political rights but relatively strong social rights.

Fifth, Bryan Turner has added the notion of 'active and passive citizenry' and the importance of 'struggle'. Unlike Mann, he argues that 'it is important to put a particular emphasis on the notion of social struggles as the central motor of the drive of citizenship' (Turner, 1989, p. 193). This he calls 'citizenship from below'. In this way social movement theory and citizenship rights are linked and the fluctuations between 'passive' and 'active', 'demobilization' and 'mobilization' and 'depoliticization' and 'politicization' makes the model dynamic.

Sixth, closely related to the previous point is the importance of political 'participation'. Bellamy and Palumbo argue that full citizenship rights can only be achieved if citizens actively participate in the political process. Once in place, rights can only be sustained by paying taxes, voting and actively taking part in political deliberations. Rights therefore also imply 'duties' and 'obligations' (Bellamy and Palumbo, 2010). They point out that citizenship assumes civic virtues, civility and civic responsibility. Hence, the depth and commitment of citizenship differs from one country to another. For the Middle East, where social movements can be 'silent movements' (Tuğal, 2009) civic virtues can also be concentrated in religious communities rather than the nation, or civil society.

The seventh factor is the 'inclusion–exclusion' dichotomy, or the *extent* of the concept. The question of who is a member of the political community and on what grounds, especially in the Middle East, with its numerous minorities, is extremely important.

Eighth is the issue of 'identity' and 'loyalty'. The citizen is required to be loyal to the nation and derives his or her loyalty from membership to that political and cultural community.

Finally, the dichotomy between the 'individual' and the 'community' is crucial for the Middle East. Many believe that a society can only become liberal when the primordial relations are broken. The formations of tribes, clans, patronage systems, which belong to the *Gemeinschaft*, must be replaced by individuals that belong to a *Gesellschaft* (Turner, 2000). Taking this too literally, however, would undermine any attempt at applying citizenship theories as outlined above to the Middle East, as the individual is only just emerging and family is still the dominant factor in society (Singerman, 1995). What is needed is an analysis of the ways in which the state penetrates these communities and creates citizens from above, while citizens in many diverse ways contest these attempts to control their lives. A definition of citizenship can be drawn up that consists of three elements: extent (who belongs to the body politic?), content (how is citizenship defined?), and depth (what contribution can the citizen make to the common good, how deep is his or her commitment?) (Faulks, 2000, p. 7).

From the brief survey of Middle Eastern studies above, however, it is clear that citizenship studies have hardly been applied in the Middle East, except for some very specific topics. For a long time it has been the focus of minority studies (Berbers in North Africa and Kurds in Iraq, Syria, and Turkey, Jews in the whole Middle East) (Van Bruinessen, 1991; White, 2011; Castellino and Cavanaugh, 2013), the fate of the Palestinians in the Israeli–Palestinian conflict, and more recently for migrants in the Persian Gulf (Longva and Roald, 2011; Davidson, 2012). The issue of equal rights has also been prominent in women's studies (Ahmed, 1992; Moghadam, 1993; Joseph, 2000, 2013; Keddie, 1993).[1] With the exception of Butenschøn and his school of researchers (Butenschøn et al., 2000; Longva and Roald, 2011; Maktabi, 2012), Rachel Scott (2010), and historians who studied French colonial history in particular, such as Thompson (2000), Lewis (2014), White (2011) and a few others (Parolin, 2009), citizenship rights and the concept of citizenship has not been a topic as such. In renowned journals such as the *Journal of Citizenship Studies* very little has been published on the Middle East, although one of its founders Bryan Turner has himself written extensively on the region (1978, 2000), while the other founder Engin Isin addresses topics such as citizenship after

634   *Handbook of political citizenship and social movements*

orientalism (Isin, 2002). One of the explanations is that sociology has been underdeveloped in the Middle East and, surprisingly, very few attempts have been made to build overarching theories of society and its transition over the past 200 years.

Despite the little specific research on citizenship rights and the position of citizens, it is possible to trace the history of citizenship in the Middle East. In fact, many historians, often unconsciously, integrate the history of citizenship into studies of the different countries of the Middle East. This is especially the case with Ruedy (1992) for Algeria, Perkins (2004) for Tunisia, Tripp (2007) and Dawisha (2009) for Iraq, and White (2011) and Thompson (2000) for Syria. It is in the thick narratives of the past, describing the application of discriminatory colonial practices, different forms of exclusion, the institutionalization of privilege, and the introduction of Western legal notions such as property laws, constitutions, and the rise of different, conflicting nationalisms, or the social contract of the 1960s that one can trace citizenship rights. In these narratives one can trace citizenship rights and forms of communities, either imposed from above by the state or formed by individuals and groups as alternative forms of solidarity from below.

Because they are foreign to the region both citizenship studies and social movements theory must be adjusted to the new political, social and cultural environment. For a long time researchers believed that social movements did not exist in the Middle East because resistance only emerged as violent outbreaks and revolts (Badie, 1987). A greater impediment is that social movement theory has been developed in a Western democratic context (Tarrow, 1998; Della Porta and Diani, 1999; McAdam et al., 2001; Tilly, 2006, 2007; Tilly and Wood, 2009) where resource mobilization, political opportunity structures (POS), repertoires and framing have been much more obvious. Applying social movement theory to the Middle East was hampered by the fact that most social movements are Islamic movements and have for a long time been claimed by Islamic studies rather than sociology. Moreover, in the long tradition of repressive states social movements were not always easy to discern because they did not fit the Western definition of social movements as 'collective challenges based on common purposes and social solidarities, in sustained interaction with elites, opponents, and authorities' (Tarrow, 1998, p. 4). Middle Eastern social movements have not been open. Rather, they adopted more circumscribed and covert tactics based on informal networks than formal organizations, which are often not directed to promote individual rights but communitarian ones, and often are not directed at the state, but, as new social movements, focus on changing conduct and the lifestyle of people, such as is the case with the Salafis (Meijer, 2009b; Pall, 2014). As Beinin and Vairel (2011) and Bennani-Chraïbi and Fillieule (2003) explain, social movements are less easily traceable in the Middle East where contestation is often reflected in everyday practices. Moreover, they differ ideologically from the West. Whereas in the Western world social movements are associated with liberalism, republicanism and socialism, and associated with virtues and ethos associated with these currents, in the Middle East they are often related to Islamic reformism, modern Islamic currents, and even apolitical Salafism (Wiktorowicz, 2004; Meijer, 2009b) and Christian sectarianism. Concepts of 'the good' are often determined by family ethos (Singerman, 1995, p. 43). This means that citizenship studies and social movement theory must be constantly adjusted, contextualized and refined (Beinin and Vairel, 2011). As much as we are forced to talk about non-movements, silent movements, and informal networks of the marginalized in the Middle East, we have to talk about the non-citizen, the marginalized citizen (Ismail, 2011b), or the 'child citizen' (Wedeen, 1999). In contrast to citizenship studies, the Arab uprisings have given a new impulse to social movement theory and the number of articles on social movements has increased (Ayeb, 2011; Leenders, 2012, 2013; Leenders and Heydemann, 2012; Hoffman and König, 2013). Even specialized journals such as *Mobilization* and the French *Mouvements* have paid attention to the regional phenomenon (Clarke, 2011; Dorsey, 2011) with a special issue of *Mobilization* in 2012 and *Mouvements* in 2011. A real breakthrough and an historical overview still lie in the future. This chapter is a beginning.

Finally, I propose to include the notion of the political as the lynchpin of the citizenship/social-movement theory model. As Peter Nyers puts it in the tenth anniversary issue of the *Journal of Citizenship Studies*: 'Ultimately, citizenship should be studied because it is the prism through which to address the political' (2007, p. 3). I have adopted the notion of the political from Mouffe (1993), Hannah Arendt (1992), and Rosanvallon (2013). They argue that politics cannot exist without antagonism and pluralism, and the recognition of clash of interests, antagonism, difference, distinction, and contestation (Rosanvallon, 2013, pp. 119–23). Furthermore, consensus, universalism, and unanimity as 'antipolitics' are detrimental to politics in general and more specifically for democracy (Mouffe, 1993, p. 5). My argument is that in the Middle East a massive swing towards a rights-based political discourse has taken place during the three decades preceding the Arab uprisings and that mass mobilization has forced political space to expand to an unprecedented extent in the region. For the first time topics have moved out of the shadows of the non-political, the familial, the tribal, and the religious or technocracy into the public arena, forcing segments of society, otherwise reticent, to become involved in politics, to openly debate and support political demands through action, creating common goals. In this process, non-citizens have transmorphed into citizens and covert non-movements have metamorphosed into overt movements, expressing their opinions openly on civil, political, and economic rights, even if in some countries such as Syria, only for a brief period. Violence, jihadism, the rule of the military and technocracy with their rejection of deliberation and emphasis on unity and indivisibility all conspire to end the political, the emergence of social movements and demands for citizenship rights. Once the political has collapsed mobilization can continue but not for the common good. It will then support sectarian divisions, the clan, the tribe, and personal goals. Instead of inclusion it is based on exclusion, instead of trust – distrust.

A HISTORY OF CITIZENSHIP IN THE MIDDLE EAST

The trajectory of citizenship in the Middle East can be represented in seven historical phases (Table 26.1) with different combinations of rights. This model applies especially to the republics of Egypt, Iraq, Syria, Tunisia, and Algeria and to a lesser extent to the monarchies of Jordan and Morocco (the Gulf monarchies I have left aside).

In the classic Islamic empires of the Middle East no equivalent of the concept of the individual citizen (*citoyen*, *Bürger*) with specific rights existed as in Europe. The term *ra'aya* (the flock) or public (*al-'amma*) connotes subjects who do not belong to the privileged classes (*al-khassa*). The *shari'a*, however, did protect people's livelihood, property and adherence to contracts (Zubaida, 2003; Vikør, 2006; Hallaq, 2009). The strong sense of collective is reflected in the positive connotation of the word society or community (*jama'a* or the *umma*). The *bay'a*, often regarded as a pledge of allegiance of the subjects to the ruler, did, however, take the form of a contract (Lewis, 1988). In these empires, the state stood above a segmented society and its different social and religious formations (tribes, *millets*, guilds, neighborhood organizations) organized as separate communities with a large degree of autonomy. Politics was limited to the rulers, because the *ulama* (religious scholars) shunned politics as contaminating the purity of religion.

The next phase (1830–1930) saw the crumbling of the Ottoman Empire, the establishment of the colonial state and protectorates in most parts of the Middle East, followed after World War I by the mandate system in Lebanon, Syria, Iraq, Jordan, and Palestine. This phase covers the transition from the multi-religious, multi-ethnic, and multi-lingual Ottoman Empire to a series of more or less homogeneous nation-states and based on the ideal of equal citizen.

Table 26.1 Rights in the Middle East, 1500–2013

	Phase 1 1500–1830	Phase 2 1830–1930	Phase 3 1930–56	Phase 4 1956–70	Phase 5 1970–90	Phase 6 1990–2010	Phase 7 2011–present
Civil rights		*	*	*	**	*	*
Political rights		*	**	*	*	**	
Social rights			*	***	**		
Cultural/minority rights	**	*			*	*	*
Economic rights		*	***	*	**	***	*
Inclusion	*	***	*	**		**	*
Exclusion	**	–	**	**	*	*	**
Mobilization/active	*	**	***	*	**	*	***
Passive/ depoliticization	**	–		***	*		
Specifics	Millet[a] system, traditional leaders	'Liberal age', patronage (za'im)	Authoritarian movements	Etatism, 'social contract', corporatism/ collectivism	'Liberalization', neoliberalism/ political parties	Increased corruption, gap between rich and poor, repression	Popular uprising, elections, constitutional reforms

Notes:
a. The millet system is based on a division of society in recognized religious communities who had a certain degree of autonomy and enjoyed protection by law.
* weak; ** moderately strong; *** strong.

For numerous reasons reforms in this period failed. First, the colonial state was based on asserting Western political, economic, and social dominance and legal privileges. Second, the process of integration was often brutal and incomplete, Western armies often waging bloody wars of subjugation (Algeria 1830–70, Morocco 1912–36, Iraq 1920, Syria 1925). In the orientalist mind of the colonizer the local population (*les indigènes*) were not considered to be ripe for full citizenship (Ruedy, 1992). Citizenship in Algeria was mainly limited to the *colons* (French colonizers). Third, in the nineteenth century, Western citizenship was more highly prized than the Ottoman Empire for its privileges: it gave minorities protection by foreign consulates.

Local resistance in the nineteenth century was mostly in terms of defensive *jihad*, or war against the infidel. Though it was based on notions of social justice it was not based on citizenship rights. Only when the traditional resistance to this process of unification was broken and it moved from the countryside to the growing urban areas and a new (Westernized) elite appeared in the twentieth century – speaking the Western legal and political languages of sovereignty and rights – did a new form of resistance appear based on social movements and citizenship rights (Ruedy, 1992, p. 132; Pennel, 2000, pp. 211–16; Vermeren, 2011, p. 104).

Characteristic of this period is also the growing aversion to political pluralism and the diversity of the Ottoman Empire, precisely because it had led to privileges and distinctions, which increasingly became associated with weakness. When nationalism (*wataniyya*) gained momentum, the political remained limited to the struggle for independence and unity of the nation (*watan*). The earliest nationalist parties, such as the Wafd (1919) in Egypt, the Destour (1920) in Tunisia, and the Parti du Peuple Algérien (1937) in Algeria, spoke in name of the people and tried to monopolize power, condemning the term 'party system' (*hizbiyya*) as leading to division of resistance (Deeb, 1979; Stora, 2004). The first major reformist Islamist party, the Muslim Brotherhood, founded in 1928, similarly proclaimed that Islam was a 'complete system' (*al-nizam al-kamil*) to which the individual was subordinated (R.P. Mitchell, 1969, p. 33). The content of the term citizenship (*muwatana*) in the 1920s reflects this totalizing trend. The citizen (*muwatin*) was not an individual but first and foremost a member of the nation (*al-watan*), the collective and the community (*al-jama'a*), to which he or she was subordinated.

When during the third phase (1930–56) the 'masses' and lower middle classes were included in the nationalist struggle and social rights emerged as an important ingredient of nationalism, liberalism was further brought under pressure. The rise of social rights was closely related to the rise of trade unions in Egypt, Iraq, and Morocco in the 1930s. In fact, the new nationalist parties such as the Neo-Destour (1934) in Tunisia, the communist movement in Egypt and Iraq (1940s), the Istiqlal (1944) in Morocco became strong because they were able to mobilize a coalition of classes, consisting of the workers, students and middle classes. Major moments of mobilization were the 'Wathba' (the leap) (1948) and the 'Intifada' (1952) in Iraq, the Workers' and Students' Committees in Egypt (February–March 1946), mass demonstrations in Tunisia (1938, 1954) and protests in Morocco (1952–56) (Beinin and Lockman, 1988; Tripp, 2007; Dawisha, 2009).

This does not mean that there were no liberals in this period. In fact, they appeared for the first time in the third phase, but again in combination with other ideologies. They called for freedom of speech, pluralism, social reform, and deepening of parliamentary democracy. These intellectuals realized that a viable independent nation-state could only exist if all citizens were included and obtained equal civil, political, and social rights (Gordon, 1992; Meijer, 2002). The press was often more liberal and pluralistic than political parties.

Another setback for liberalism in the sense of cultural pluralism was the end of the cosmopolitan cities in the Middle East. As a result, the extent of citizenship became more exclusive. Alexandria, Beirut, Algiers, and Smyrna (Izmir) changed radically in character with the end of colonial protection (Zubaida, 1999). The toll was staggering: 1.2 million Greeks were evicted from Anatolia after the defeat of the Greek invasion in 1923 (B. Clark, 2007); Assyrians were massacred in Iraq in 1933 (Luktiz, 1995); between 1956 and 1960, 200000 of the 500000 foreigners left Morocco (Pennell, 2000); 1 million *colons* left Algeria in the year after independence in 1962 (Stora, 2008); 200000 foreigners left Tunisia in the same period; 500000 Palestinians were evicted from Palestine in 1948 (Morris, 2007; Pappé, 2007).

THE AUTHORITARIAN BARGAIN

The fourth period (1956–1970; see also Figure 26.1) of authoritarian regimes and corporatism was as momentous for the history of the Middle East as the colonial division and the drawing of the borders of Iraq, Syria, Jordan and Lebanon. Although hailed as the emancipation from colonialism and imperialism, the subsequent period was disastrous in civil, political, and what later would be called cultural rights.

First, all the new nationalist movements that took power claimed to speak in the name of the nation and the people, which showed how little the totalizing terminology had changed since the 1920s. Second, after

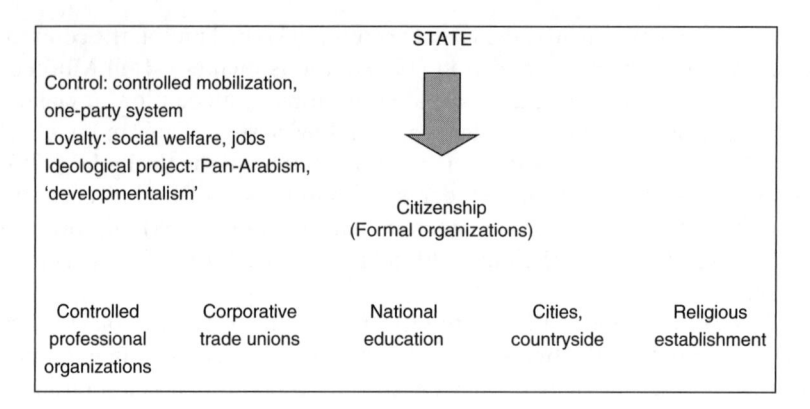

```
┌─────────────────────────────────────────────────────────────┐
│                          STATE                              │
│                                                             │
│  Control: controlled mobilization,                          │
│  one-party system              ⬇                            │
│  Loyalty: social welfare, jobs                              │
│  Ideological project: Pan-Arabism,                          │
│  'developmentalism'          Citizenship                    │
│                          (Formal organizations)             │
│                                                             │
│                                                             │
│   Controlled    Corporative    National    Cities,   Religious    │
│   professional  trade unions   education   countryside establishment │
│   organizations                                             │
└─────────────────────────────────────────────────────────────┘
```

Figure 26.1   The modern state at the height of its power, 1960s–1970s

independence, power became highly concentrated. For instance, the first president of Algeria Ahmed Ben Bella was leader of the Front de Liberation Nationale (FLN), as well as prime minister. Third, leadership was highly personalized. A personality cult was established around leaders such as Bourguiba of Tunisia, King Hassan II of Morocco, Abd al-Karim Qasim (in power 1958–63), Nasser, and later Hafez al-Assad of Syria and Saddam Hussein of Iraq. In all these cases leaders were portrayed as father figures, substituting politics with patriarchy and hierarchy (Sharabi, 1988; Wedeen, 1999). Fourth, in almost all Arab countries the parliamentary system was disbanded, limiting the room for politics to take place. A one-party system replaced the multi-party system in Iraq (1960), Syria (1958), Egypt (1953), Tunisia (1956), and Libya (1969). Typically, constitutions became a formality and functioned more as a declaration of intentions than as a set of fundamental citizenship rights. They were often drawn up in backrooms and accepted by a 99 per cent referendum. Fifth, the military came to dominate politics. The military came to power in 1952 in Egypt, temporarily in 1949 in Syria, and finally in 1963, and in 1956 in Algeria when Ben Bella was evicted and Boumedienne took power. In Morocco, Hassan II increasingly relied on the Mohamed Oufkir and the military (Willis, 2012). Sixth, the security services increased to an unprecedented scale (Kandil, 2012a). Seventh, in the newly created corporatist state, all civil institutions came under the control of the state and lost their autonomy. People's rights in Egypt were tied to being a member of the National Union and later Arab Socialist Union and the Neo-Destour in Tunisia, the Ba'th in Syria and Iraq. Eighth, the new states adopted the totalizing nationalist ideologies developed in the 1930s, suppressing all alternative forms of ethnic and religious identity (Tripp, 2007; Le Sueur, 2010, p. 16).

Political citizenship and social movements in the Arab world 641

For the first time violence was used by the state against its own people. Morocco became notorious for its 'years of lead' (1971–92), the Ba'th in Iraq for its reign of terror and the genocide of Kurds (al-Khalil, 1989); in Algeria as many as 100 000 Algerians perished in the killing of the Harkis (Algerian loyalists accused of collaborating with the French) after the war of independence, in Syria 50 000 died in Hama in 1982. Violence was based on the idea that the nationalist movement could claim total loyalty for achieving independence.

The result was that political space for debate and solving political issues and exchange of ideas shrunk dramatically. The political became limited to social engineering and technocracy. Leaders were notoriously suspicious of the people although they spoke in their name. The technocratic techniques that accompanied the top-down approach further deepened the process of depoliticization (Ayubi, 1995; Maghraoui, 2002; T. Mitchell, 2002).

The closure in the political field of civil and political rights was, however, compensated by a vast array of 'rights' obtained in the social field. The exchange of political and civil rights for social rights for broad sections of the population by populist authoritarian regimes has been called the 'authoritarian bargain'. These covered the reforms the colonial regimes had neglected like the expansion of primary and secondary education, the establishment of national universities, the creation of jobs in the public sector (especially after Europeans left and their property had been sequestered and nationalized), the huge expansion of the public sector, implementation of land reform, and the introduction of cooperatives, massive public housing projects, free health care, in addition to the rapid expansion of the transport system, extension of roads, electrification of the countryside, and bringing piped water to poor rural areas. Sometimes the social contract was a real bargain as in the case of the Egyptian trade unions, which were allowed to establish a federation (General Federation of Egyptian Trade Unions, GFETU) in exchange for the right to strike and collective bargaining. As part of the 'socialist' measures in 1961 the Egyptian state guaranteed jobs for university graduates. For the first time food subsidies were provided, becoming a drain on the national budget in the next decades.[2]

But not only did this period witness the inclusion of the middle and lower classes, neglected regions were also included, such as Upper Egypt (Fandy, 1994), the interior of Tunisia (Ayeb, 2011; Dot-Pouillard, 2013), the Rif in Morocco (Pennell, 2000), Kabylia in Algeria (Le Sueur, 2010), and rural areas in Syria (Hinnebusch, 2001; ICG, 2011). In this process, however, the new citizens became completely dependent on the state and its 'policy of citizenship from above'. State subsidies, the bureaucracy, and the public sector 'allowed the government to control a citizen's employment opportunities, the salary he would earn, the consumer goods he could purchase, the price he paid for these goods, and most of the activities that he could engage in' (Rutherford, 2008, p. 134). Information and travel was highly restricted and regulated. Not being employed by the state, as was the case with 'feudalists' and 'exploitive capitalists', was a form of ostracism. On the other hand, many upwardly mobile graduates would derive their 'dignity' and self-esteem, that is, their concept of citizenship, from becoming government employees and the amenities that went with it (Wickham, 2002, pp. 55–9).

The authoritarian bargain as a social contract was perhaps – next to establishment of borders in the 1920s for Lebanon, Syria, Iraq, and Jordan, and achieving independence after World War II – the most decisive political event in the Middle East in the twentieth century. It determined the extent, content, and depth of citizenship in most countries from the 1950s to the 1980s. The major drawback, as Mann described it for Europe, was that rights were handed down from above, by presidents as father figures, giving rise to the 'child citizen' in Syria (Wedeen, 1999), or the 'citizen as spectator' in Libya (Pargeter, 2012), creating passive citizens who lost what they had fought and died for during the independence struggle. It also denied the room for the political as a field of overt contestation. Not surprisingly, the counter-ideologies to Arab socialism were as brutal in self-denial of the individual citizen. The Islamist political thinker Sayyid Qutb reduced the citizen in his radical phase to a believer who basically had no other right than to obey the *shari'a* and submit to the sovereignty of God at the expense of human agency (Meijer, 2012b). The only political decision the believer could make was to renege on citizenship altogether and condemn the Nasserist society as a whole or its leader. Hasan al-Hudaybi's (General Guide of the Muslim Brotherhood to 1973) major achievement was to open up space for the believer to bring about change as a critical self-thinking citizen (Kepel, 1985). But his regained agency was mostly limited to preaching, *da'wa* (Zollner, 2009). Not until the 1980s, under the General Guide Umar al-Tilmisani, did the Brotherhood begin thinking about the political (Meijer, 2012a).

POLITICIZATION: DEMANDING CITIZENSHIP RIGHTS

The introduction of the *infitah* (economic opening) policy in Egypt in 1974 inaugurated the fifth period (1970–90) and marked a shift in state policy throughout the whole region. It led if not to the dismantlement of the public sector, which continued to grow until the oil crisis of the 1980s, at least to a retreat from many of the state's educational, social and health care obligations towards its citizens. Over the next decades this meant the dismantling of housing laws, rent protection, restrictions on property ownership, cheap health care, and equal education opportunities. The fifth period in the Middle Eastern history of rights lasted until the 1990s, when the last part of the introduction of neoliberalism was made: the privatization of the public sector. Compared to Europe the assault on the welfare state in the Middle East led to far greater economic exclusion, impoverishment, and the marginalization of the lower middle classes. It deepened the discrimination of minorities and furthered the deprivation of economically backward regions in Morocco, Tunisia, Egypt, Libya, and Syria (Achcar, 2013). As economic power became gradually concentrated in the hands of the very rich, over whom no political control was exerted, corruption grew to unprecedented levels and the difference between poor and rich increased, pushing in some countries 40 per cent of the population under the poverty line.

The Middle East after the collapse of the social contract witnessed the rise of new forms of contestation. The region was shaken by so-called 'bread riots' in the 1970s and 1980s (1977 and 1986 in Egypt, 1988 in Jordan, 1989 in Algeria, 1978 in Tunisia). Austerity measures led to a political opening up that allowed for periods of political liberalization (1989–92 in Algeria, 1987–92 in Tunisia, 1981–87 in Egypt, 1989–92 in Jordan, after 1992 in Morocco, and 2000–01 in Syria). Despite new ways of suppressing, pre-empting, co-opting, and controlling dissent, as explained in the authoritarian resilience theories (Heydemann, 2007; Schlumberger, 2007), the breathing space led to a period of politicization that is reflected in the emergence of a diversity of initiatives, developments, and demonstrations, which gradually led to a build-up of silent movements and non-movements, informal networks outside official channels, and finally during the last decade open movements. These were primarily in the labor movement (Allal, 2008; Beinin, 2012; Zemni, 2013b; Bogaert, forthcoming), in student demonstrations, the Egyptian Kifaya movement, human rights movements, judges' movements, and so on. The real background and build up is even after three years still not clear and needs to be studied in depth. Eventually they led to the Tunisian uprising (Allal, 2011; Ayeb, 2011), the February 20 Movement in Morocco (Bennani-Chraïbi and Jeghllaly, 2012; Salima, 2012; Hoffmann and König, 2013), the uprisings in Syria (ICG, 2011; Leenders, 2012, 2013) and in Egypt (Beinin, 2012; Kandil, 2012b; Sowers and Toensing, 2012).

In the following I will not delve too deeply into the social movements themselves but will show how social movements included citizenship rights to a much greater degree than during the mass uprisings of the independence struggle (Table 26.2; also see Figure 26.2).

Table 26.2 Comparison between rights in the struggle for independence with the rise of citizenship rights over the last 20 years

	Previous Period of Mobilization, 1930–56	Mobilization, 1990–2013	Contested	Main unresolved problems
Civil rights	Civil rights in the service of the struggle for independence and communal rights: Indivisibility of the nation Unity of the people Sovereignty of the nation (not the people)	Splintering of civil rights: Human rights Rule of law Equality before the law Rights for women Freedom of speech Freedom of organization	Main divisive questions: In what form? Based on which law? Which rights? To what extent? For which organizations (NGOs, trade unions, the press, religious organizations)?	Community vs the individual Stability vs rights Patronage vs independence
Political rights	In the service of independence and unity: National struggle for independence Often opposed to pluralism Opposed to parliamentary system	Pluralism: Competitive elections The right to establish political parties	Main questions: Which system (majority rule/ recognition of minorities, pluralism)? Division of powers? What kind of electoral system?	Broad notion of the political vs religious restrictions
Social rights	Development of the nation: 'Social justice' Jobs Education Social welfare, health State-led economic development	Individual demands: Employment Health care Education Communal demands: Sectarian	Diversity: For whom? Organized on what basis (religious, private, public)?	Organized by the state vs private (religious) initiative Collective vs individual
Cultural rights	Unity: Non-recognition of minority rights Assimilation of minorities into the unified nation	Ethnic community rights: Berbers (Algeria, Morocco), Kurds (Syria, Iraq) Religious community rights: Christian minorities (Iraq, Syria, Egypt)	Main questions: Communitarian rights, protection, or individual rights as citizen?	*Millet* vs nation-state Modern minority rights Federalism vs nation-state?

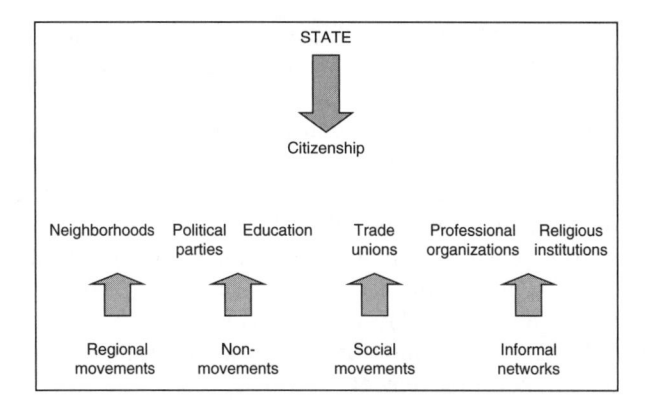

```
                              STATE
                                │
                                ▼
                           Citizenship


Neighborhoods   Political   Education   Trade      Professional    Religious
                parties                 unions     organizations   institutions
       ▲           ▲           ▲          ▲              ▲              ▲
       │           │           │          │              │              │

   Regional       Non-                  Social                    Informal
   movements    movements             movements                   networks
```

Figure 26.2   Rising resistance to the authoritarian state

Citizenship

The main difference with the mobilization of the 1950s is the new content the terms citizen (*muwatin*) and citizenship (*muwatina/mawatana*) have acquired during the past three decades. This has been part of global resistance against neoliberalism and the politics of exclusion (Hatem, 2012). Although in-depth research still must be done, it is clear that the term citizenship during the present wave of rights has been used in a fundamentally different manner than before, connoting personal rights versus an indigenous government rather than collective rights (of the nation) against foreign domination. This was, for instance, the case with the Muslim Brotherhood, when it announced in its party programs of 1984 reforms 'to provide citizens with services and work to ensure freedom and security, and make available to its citizens all necessary needs' (Al-Awadi, 2004, p. 84). In Bahrain and Saudi Arabia since the 1990s, social movements have abandoned Khomeini's rhetoric of the rule of the jurisconsults in favor of equal citizenship rights (Meijer and Wagemakers, 2013; Meijer, forthcoming). During the uprisings of 2011 even Salafis in Egypt made claims to citizenship rights, having to adopt a political language they normally eschew. The idea of a new social contract between citizens and the state, recognizing all citizenship rights, has become common (Wickham, 2002; Akhavi, 2003).

Human rights

Human rights organizations have mushroomed during the past 30 years, starting in 1977 when the Tunisian Human Rights Organization was established. They were run by liberals but also by the former left wing in the Middle East, which had become more aware of the necessity of preserving basic rights instead of promoting the socialist revolution (Stork, 2011). These organizations protested against the extension of emergency laws (which kept the constitution suspended), torture, military tribunals, unlawful detentions, limitations on the independence of civil society and restriction of democracy. Although the Islamist movement has not embraced universal human rights wholeheartedly (Mayer, 2013), the notion of basic rights and the rule of law to protect freedom of speech and organization (civil rights) has become recognized by mainstream movements in Egypt (Al-Awadi, 2004; El-Ghobashy, 2005), Tunisia (El Hachmi, 2000; Tamimi, 2001), Morocco (Zeghal, 2008; Wegner, 2011) and Jordan. Equal rights of minorities are also increasingly recognized by Islamist and nationalist movements.

Ending corruption and demands for accountability and transparency
Perhaps one of the strongest demands of the uprisings has been the end of the corruption that has taken a tremendous flight since the introduction of the free market economy in the 1970s. Economic corruption at the higher level has concentrated around the ruling families of Mubarak (Amin, 2011), Ben Ali (Beau and Graciet, 2009), Mohammed VI (Graciet and Laurent, 2012), Bashar al-Assad (ICG, 2011), but it has especially led to widespread outrage because it has also permeated the lowest levels of the bureaucracy and daily life of citizens. It has become especially widespread with the privatization drive of public companies during the past two decades. Heightened attention to corruption indicates a new awareness of equality, justice and awareness of civil and political rights.

Rule of law
Although all of the regimes increased their security services to an unprecedented scale, sometimes becoming larger than the army, over the past 30 years the rule of law has been increasingly valued. Realizing that they could only attract foreign investments if they installed an independent judiciary, sometimes the authoritarian regimes themselves were behind measures to promote the rule of law especially in regard to the protection of property rights (Moustafa, 2007). The rule of law has become accepted by the opposition as one of the main instruments in curbing the power of the state. The Muslim Brotherhood (Rutherford, 2008), the Moroccan Islamist party, the PJD (Zeghal, 2008) and most other Islamic parties have accepted the rule of law as a means to dismantle the authoritarian state. Demands to purge the judiciary during the Arab uprisings indicates the increasing value attached to the rule of law and civil rights.

Political rights and parties

Political parties have been re-established in the 1970s, but usually lost their appeal after they became co-opted by the authoritarian regimes. By the 1990s they had alienated the public in Egypt, Tunisia and Jordan. Recent research, however, has shown them to be much more independent and serious than most people have thought (Lust-Okar and Zerhouni, 2008). Elections and parliaments have functioned as a training ground not in preparation to take over power, but to learn techniques of negotiation and compromise – in short, to learn politics. For instance, the rights of the electorate were significantly improved with the control over elections by judges in Egypt in 2004. They, for instance, ensured more accurate registration of voters' registration rolls (Rutherford, 2008, p. 153). The uprisings have seen an expansion of the acceptance of political rights and parties, although they were often not in the forefront of the demonstrations. *Hizbiyya* (partyism) is only rejected by the purist Salafi trend (Lacroix, 2012).

Constitutions

The issue of constitutions (constitutionalism) was typical for the nineteenth century and the early twentieth century and was part of the process to increase civil and political rights. It was neglected in the subsequent period of the authoritarian social bargain. Only during the period of economic opening did constitutions regain some importance for attracting foreign investment. For instance, the Egyptian Supreme Constitutional Court was established in 1979, four years after *infitah*. Since then the interest in constitutions has grown, and activists used, for instance, the ambiguities in the Egyptian 1971 constitution to expand civil rights. Since 1991 Egyptian legal experts have called for the appointment of a committee of experts to draw up a new constitution that would limit the powers of the president and create a parliamentary system. In other Arab countries as well, constitutions have increased in importance (Brown, 2001; Khalaf and Luciani, 2006). The interest in the drawing up of new constitutions or adjusting old ones in Egypt, Tunisia, Libya, and Morocco (Maghraoui, 2011) after the uprisings demonstrates the world of difference with the period after independence and the importance of citizenship rights. The February 20 Movement in Morocco, the united opposition in Tunisia (Dalmasso and Cavatorta, 2013) and especially liberals in Egypt mobilized people in support of constitutional reforms that expand citizenship rights.

Pluralism

The expansion of the political during the past three decades has also enhanced pluralism. During the past three decades political pluralism has increasingly replaced the monolithic one-party state, except in Syria and Iraq. Within the Egyptian trade union movement, voices have been raised to dissolve the corporatist structures and found independent trade unions (Beinin, 2012). Egyptian professional syndicates became centers of experience of cooperation between different political currents and tried to become independent. The Islamist movement has opened up to liberal trends, moving significantly away from the totalizing ideology of the interbellum and authoritarian regimes (Meijer, 2012b). In the 2000s, coalitions between the left, liberals and the Islamist movement occurred in Tunisia (Haugbølle and Cavatorta, 2011) and in Egypt (Clarke, 2011), a development that a decade ago would have been unthinkable. Terms such as equal rights for women and minorities (Copts) have been introduced by liberals within the Islamist movement (Scott, 2010). The struggle against authoritarian rule has enhanced the value of civil and political rights. The focus has been on the independence of the judiciary, the expansion of the multiparty system. Participation in the electoral process, however limited it may have been, has further moderated the movements in Jordan, Morocco, and Egypt (Schwedler, 2007; Wegner, 2011). Although the end result is ambiguous (Brown, 2012; Meijer, 2012a), it is clear that the trend has been powerful and completely new and confirms the shift to a discourse of citizen rights and the recognition of difference.

Ideological changes
Islamic intellectuals in Egypt, such as Tariq al-Bishri, Kamal Abu al-Majd, Muhammad Salim al-'Awwa, but also leaders of the PJD (Justice and Development Party) in Morocco (Zeghal, 2008, pp. 187–207; Brower, 2009), and the leader of the Ennahda Party in Tunisia, Rachid Ghannouchi (Tamimi, 2001), have been influential in promoting a more liberal form of Islam. In many ways the shift in the Islamist movement is one towards rights and a modern concept of citizenship. The move was from concrete, individual or communal rights to abstract and universal rights (Wickham, 2004). The Wasatiyyah, or middle trend, has been active in broadening political space for human agency by means of individual interpretation (*ijtihad*) of terms such as the 'interests of the community' (*al-maslaha*), which can also be seen as the 'common good', necessity (*darura*), a willingness to accept Western law as long as it does not contradict the *shari'a*. As a result of the increased suspicions of the state a major shift has occurred towards politics as a 'contract' (*'aqd*) between citizens and the state. In this relationship the state must work in the 'interests' (*masalih*) of the people who should hold the state accountable (Rutherford, 2008, pp. 103–18). The trend has been reflected in the political reports and platform of the Muslim Brotherhood since 1992 (El-Ghobashy, 2005; Harnisch

and Mecham, 2009; Wickham, 2011, 2013). The Muslim Brotherhood accepted in 1995 that the *umma* (nation) is the source of all power and that the people should elect their leaders. First Copts and then women were declared equal citizens.

Autonomy and resistance against state intervention and patronage
Increasingly, autonomy and respect for one's independence have also been valorized as essential for upholding one's dignity. This applies not just to individuals but also to institutions. Already in the 1970s and 1980s administrative courts in Egypt had gained independence in appointments, promotions, and internal affairs. The Supreme Constitutional Court in Egypt and other courts have valued their independence from interference in appointments by the state. In 2000 the Judges Club became activist and committed to 'restoring the dignity of the judges' after the state had shown wide disrespect for the courts. Despite the corporative nature of the trade unions in Egypt, wildcat strikes started to gain in strength in the 1980s. Increasingly trade unions in Egypt and Tunisia adopted a critical stance toward state control and patronage over labor leadership.[3] In particular, the lower strata of the Tunisian trade union movement, the UGTT, played an active role during the uprisings against Ben Ali in Winter 2010–11. The first independent trade union in Egypt appeared in 2008.

Freedom of speech and media
The release of the media and the emergence of broadcaster Al-Jazeera played an important role breaking the monopoly of state media over public opinion in the 1990s (Lynch, 2006). Later, the internet took over this role. Though by no means liberal, the media became increasingly independent from state control, leading to greater information, but also initiating new debates, ending taboos, and opening the political field. In the 2000s Egypt's local written press had become independent. In Tunisia it became independent after the fall of Ben Ali.

Professional organizations and civil society
Professional organizations have become increasingly politicized over the past 30 years. Although in Egypt they have often been taken over by the Islamist movement they have become more aware of the interests of their members but also of larger issues such as human rights, or the issue of the Palestinians. Some organizations, like the Judges Club in Egypt, have advocated control over elections. The Lawyers' Organization in Tunisia actively participated in demonstrations during the uprisings in January 2011. The Doctors' Union in Egypt has actively tried to relinquish the hold of the Muslim Brotherhood over the movement. Anyone studying

the uprisings will have noticed that many institutions have demanded greater autonomy from the state and the right of self-rule, such as universities, trade unions, and the media. In Tunisia the Lawyers' syndicate played an important role in support of the revolution by joining the demonstrations when they reached the coast.

Civic responsibilities and civic/religious virtue

Radical Islamism is always associated with violence and self-sacrifice, or else it is associated with identity politics that is assumed to have little political content. This is only partly true. One of the challenges is to discern the instruments of community formation and the role of the individual in it and the claims and rights its members can make, but also the duties and civic responsibilities members impose on what have been called communities that can be regarded as 'parallel societies' (Wickham, 2002, pp. 93–118). In this sense more pietistic and radical groups/movements have created new forms of citizenship. The Jamaat al-Islamiyya in Egypt used the Islamic injunction of 'commanding good and preventing evil' to instill greater communal awareness and civic responsibility among the poor in neighborhoods in Cairo such as Imbaba (Meijer, 2009b). The 'religious virtues' they tried to spread also touched upon civic virtues, which with a stretch of the imagination can be associated with civic republicanism. These Islamist trends regarded public activism as a personal obligation (*fard al-'ayn*). They were concentrated in the newer areas in the large cities because of the lack of community services and 'institutional void'. They transformed the passive, demobilized citizen into an active, mobilized, 'committed Muslim' (*al-muslim al-multazim*) who became involved in communal work (Wickham, 2002, p. 122). Salafism and other piety movements created comparable group dynamics based on religious virtue. Though these movements were not directly political, and none of them were in the forefront of the Arab uprisings, they became politicized when political space opened up. Some members of the Nour Party became adept at playing the political game and used terms such as citizenship (Lacroix, 2012); others, like the Tunisian Salafi movement (Torelli et al., 2012), explicitly rejected these terms. But civility is not limited to Islamist movements. Increasingly it is also regarded as an important topic in other groups (Volpi, 2011).

Youth movements

Youth has played a crucial role during the uprisings. To what extent they really support citizenship rights consciously and directly is difficult to say, but it is clear that many of their informal networks formulated the demands for dignity and the removal of the dictators. The very fact that they are diverse and organized in informal networks has helped to promote the political. Almost every established political party has a youth movement that challenges the existing hierarchical relations. Long-term demographic developments have led to sociological transformations that enhance individualism, greater self-awareness, and political consciousness (Desrues, 2012). The April 6 Movement in Egypt is an example of such a movement, just like the February 20 Movement in Morocco. But Egyptian football hooligans have also become politicized during the past years, playing a major role in the uprisings as social movements (Dorsey, 2011). The weakening of patriarchal relations within families allows for greater individualization and self-awareness, emancipation of girls and women, which in turn have led to claims for rights and greater autonomy. This has also occurred within the Islamist movements (Wickham, 2002, p. 169). Established feminist NGOs have been challenged by new informal feminist movements led by younger women (Salima, 2012).

Regional autonomy movements
The collapse of the social contract and regional economic stimulation plans have led to the emergence of regional movements to claim their economic rights. This applies to the interior in Tunisia (Ayeb, 2011; Dot-Pouillard, 2013), the rural areas in Syria (ICG, 2011), Upper Egypt, as well as Cyrenaica in Libya (Pargeter, 2012). These are major movements, ranging from 50 to 10 per cent of the population, and have to be accommodated to reach a new consensus.

Ethnic and religious minorities (or oppressed majorities)
In all these countries minorities have reasserted themselves after it became apparent that the nation-state had failed to unify the country. This was the case with the Shiites in Iraq (60 per cent of the population) and Lebanon 35 per cent), the Kurds in Syria (10 per cent), the Berbers in Algeria (20 per cent) and Morocco. Many of them have demanded recognition of their cultural and linguistic rights. This is also the case with the Berbers during the Berber Spring in 1980 in Algeria. In Saudi Arabia and Bahrain, Shiites demanded equal rights as civil rights movements from the 1990s onwards (Meijer and Wagemakers, 2013). It is clear that equal rights have become one of the main issues with minorities. Equality has also become a major issue for Sunni political movements (Longva and Roald, 2011).

Informal networks and 'non-movements'
This is a huge subject that covers many different groups and millions of people living in the poorer neighborhoods and informal popular housing

quarters in huge Arab cities such as Baghdad, Beirut, Cairo, Alexandria, Tunis, Casablanca, and Algiers. Most of those people work in the informal economic sector. They live on the margin, the periphery of society, and can be regarded as non-citizens, semi-citizens or 'subject-citizens' whose contact with the state and conceptualization of citizenship is determined through contact with the police, practices of surveillance, or intermediation of local co-opted authorities, the so-called 'power men' (Ismail, 2006, 2011a). Many of the actions of these groups are not visible, open and principled but subterranean and diffuse. As Diane Singerman has shown, the informal politics of everyday life of the 'people' (*al-sha'b*) takes many forms. Their networks are often based on the family and communal relations and turn existing patronage and clientelist networks to their own advantage (Singerman, 1995). Though their ideas do not correspond with the more formal concepts of citizenship, their norms and values and concept of 'the good', dignity, social justice, and rights is expressed in an ideology of the weak. They often uphold a concept of a social contract and force the state to live up to its obligations towards the people. This applies both to republics such as Egypt as well as to monarchies such as Morocco (Vermeren, 2009; Bogaert, forthcoming). Even if services have been brought to a minimum and 'the realm of politics', in the words of Diane Singerman, has been reduced to 'distribution', the slightest change in these provisions can lead to vehement reactions (Singerman, 1995, p. 39). It was exactly these networks that supported the uprisings.

CONCLUSION

Research into the combination between citizenship studies, social movements, and the political is just beginning. All three disciplines pose great challenges for future research as we are just beginning to adjust citizenship studies and social movement theory to the region, to say nothing of political philosophy, one of the most underdeveloped disciplines for the region. Their combination can lead to a more complete picture of the Middle East. Tracing the extent, content, and depth of citizenship in the region in combination with social movement theory provides an ideal instrument to compare the position of citizens in the different countries with regard to the dynamics of inclusion/exclusion, active/passive citizenship, mobilization/demobilization, and tensions between individual/communitarian rights. They determine processes of politicization and depoliticization and the specific content of the political. At the same time they provide a greater degree of agency to citizens in a region where the tradition is to disregard citizenship as a category of analysis and citizens as an agency of change.

NOTES

1. These are just some of the titles referring to these cases. In the case of the Palestinians the bibliography is huge and that goes for the three other topics.
2. The authoritarian bargain has been called different things. For more see Rutherford (2008, pp. 133–4); Bianchi (1990, p. 81); Joel Beinin calls the agreement between Nasser and the workers before the March Crisis of 1954 an 'unspoken bargain' of 'no strikes in exchange for no-dismissals without cause' (1989, p. 74); Carrie Rosefsky Wickham also speaks of a 'social contract' (2002, pp. 23–4); so does Diane Singerman (1995, pp. 244–5); Nicola Pratt (2007, p. 44), calls it a 'bargain'. One of the reasons why Morocco did not follow suit was because the Istiqlal Party was unable to acquire a monopoly of power and implement the reforms the trade union UMC had demanded. For that reason the Istiqlal lost much of its appeal and Mehdi Ben Barka established the Union Nationale des Forces Populaires (UNFP) in 1959 (Pennell, 2000, pp. 307–8); Samir al-Khalil (pseudonym of Kanan Makiya), following Michael Mann and Bryan Turner, compares Iraq to the USSR in this respect (1989, pp. 93–9).
3. Kassem (2007, pp. 106–9); Cavallo (2008, pp. 239–55); Sami Zemni (2013b).

REFERENCES

Abdel-Fadil, M. (1980), *The Political Economy of Nasserism*, Cambridge, UK: Cambridge University Press.
Abdelrahman, M. (2004), *Civil Society Exposed: The Politics of NGOs in Egypt*, London: Tauris Academic Studies.
Abed-Kotob, S. (1995), 'The accomodationists speak: goals and strategies of the Muslim Brotherhood in Egypt', *International Journal of Middle East Studies*, **27**(3), 321–39.
Achcar, G. (2013), *The People Want: A Radical Exploration of the Arab Uprising*, Berkeley, CA: University of California Press.
Ahmed, L. (1992), *Women and Gender in Islam*, New Haven, CT: Yale University Press.
Akhavi, S. (2003), 'Sunni modernist theories of social contract in contemporary Egypt', *International Journal of Middle East Studies*, **35**(1), 23–49.
Al-Awadi, H. (2004), *In Pursuit of Legitimacy: The Muslim Brothers and Mubarak, 1982–2000*, London: Tauris Academic Studies.
al-Khalil, S. (1989), *Republic of Fear: The Inside Story of Saddam's Iraq*, New York: Pantheon Books.
Allal, A. (2008), 'Réformes et Néoliberales, Clientélisme et Protestations en Situation Autoritaire: Les Mouvements Contestataire dans le Bassin Minier de Gafsa en Tunisie' [Neoliberal reforms, clientelism and protests in authoritarian situations. Protest movements in the mining area of Gafsa in Tunisia], *Politique Africaine*, **117**(1), 107–25.
Allal, A. (2011), ''Avant on Tenait le Mur, Maintenant on Tenait le Quartier': Germes du Passage au Politique de Jeunes Hommes de Quartiers Populaires Lors du Moment Révolutionnaire à Tunis' ['Before people leaned against the wall now they occupy the quarter': background of the transition of the young men of the popular quarters during the revolutionary movement in Tunis], *Politique Africaine*, **121**(1), 53–67.
Amin, G. (1980), *The Modernization of Poverty: A Study of the Political Economy of Growth in Nine Arab Countries, 1945–70*, Leiden: Brill.
Amin, G. (2011), *Egypt in the Era of Hosni Mubarak, 1981–2011*, Cairo: The American University in Cairo Press.
Arendt, H. (1992), in U. Ludz (ed.), *Was ist Politik? Fragmente aus dem Nachlass* [What is Politics? Fragments from the Inheritance], Munich: Piper.
Ayeb, H. (2011), 'Social and political geography of the Tunisian revolution: the Alfa Grass Revolution', *Review of African Political Economy*, **38**(129), 467–79.

Ayubi, N.N. (1995), *Over-stating the Arab State: Politics and Society in the Middle East*, London: I.B. Tauris.
Badie, B. (1987), *Les Deux Etats: Pouvoir et Société en Occident et en Terre d'Islam* [The Two States: Power and Society in the West and in the Islamic World], Paris: Fayard.
Bayat, A. (2000), 'Social movements, activism and social development in the Middle East', Civil Society and Social Movements, Programme Paper No. 3.
Bayat, A. (2005), 'Islamism and social movement theory', *Third World Quarterly*, **26**(6), 891–908.
Bayat, A. (2007), *Making Islam Democratic: Social Movements and the Post-Islamist Turn*, Stanford, CA: Stanford University Press.
Bayat, A. (2010), *Life as Politics: How Ordinary People Change the Middle East*, Stanford, CA: Stanford University Press.
Beau, N. and C. Graciet (2009), *La régente de Carthage: Main basse sur la Tunisie* [The Regent of Carthage. Hands on Tunisia], Paris: La Découverte.
Beinin, J. (1989), 'Labor capital and the state in Nasserist Egypt', *International Journal of Middle Eastern Studies*, **20**(1), 71–90.
Beinin, J. (2012), 'The rise of Egypt's workers', *The Carnegie Papers*, June, accessed 23 May 2014 at http://carnegieendowment.org/files/egypt_labor.pdf.
Beinin, J. and Z. Lockman (1988), *Workers on the Nile: Nationalism, Communism, Islam and the Egyptian Working Class, 1882–1954*, Princeton, NJ: Princeton University Press.
Beinin, J. and F. Vairel (eds) (2011), *Social Movements, Mobilization, and Contestation in the Middle East and North Africa*, Stanford, CA: Stanford University Press.
Bellamy, R. and A. Palumbo (eds) (2010), *Citizenship*, Farnham, UK: Ashgate.
Bennani-Chraïbi, M. and O. Fillieule (eds) (2003), *Résistance et Protestations dans les Sociétés Musulmanes* [Resistance and Protests in Muslim Societies], Paris: Presses de Sciences Po.
Bennani-Chraïbi, M. and M Jeghllaly (2012), 'The protest dynamics of Casablanca's February 20th Movement', *Revue Française de Science Politique*, **62**(5), 103–30.
Bianchi, R. (1990), *Unruly Corporatism: Associational Life in Twentieth Century Egypt*, Oxford: Oxford University Press.
Bill, J. and R. Springborg (1999), *Politics in the Middle East*, London: Longman.
Bogaert, K. (forthcoming), 'The revolt of small towns: the Meaning of Morocco's history and geography of social protest' (unpublished paper).
Botman, S. (1988), *The Rise of Communism, 1939–1970*, New York: Syracuse University Press.
Brower, M.L. (2009), *Political Ideology in the Arab World: Accommodation and Transformation*, Cambridge, UK: Cambridge University Press.
Brown, N.J. (2001), *Constitutions in a Nonconstitutional World: Arab Basic Laws and the Prospects for Accountable Government*, New York: Suny Press.
Brown, N.J. (2012), *When Victory is not an Option: Islamist Movements in Arab Politics*, Ithaca, NY: Cornell University Press.
Butenschøn, N., U. Davis and M. Hassassian (eds) (2000), *Citizenship and the State in the Middle East: Approaches and Applications*, New York: Syracuse University Press.
Castellino, J. and K.A. Cavanaugh (2013), *Minorities in the Middle East*, Oxford: Oxford University Press.
Cavallo, D. (2008), 'Trade unions in Tunisia', in E. Lust-Okar and S. Zerhouni (eds), *Political Participation in the Middle East*, Boulder, CO: Lynne Rienner, pp. 239–55.
Clark, B. (2007), *Twice a Stranger: How Mass Expulsion Forged Modern Greece and Turkey*, London: Granta Publications.
Clark, J.A. (2004), *Islam, Charity and Activism: Middle Class Networks and Social Welfare in Egypt, Jordan, and Yemen*, Bloomington, IN: Indiana University Press.
Clark, J.A. (2012), 'Islamist movements and democratic politics', in Rex Brynen et al. (eds), *Beyond the Arab Spring: Authoritarianism and Democracy in the Arab World*, Boulder, CO: Lynne Rienner, pp. 119–46.
Clarke, K. (2011), 'Saying enough': authoritarianism and Egypt's Kefaya movement', *Mobilization*, **16**(4), 397–416.

Cleveland, W.L. (1971), *The Making of an Arab Nationalist: Ottomanism and Arabism in the Life and Thought of Sati'al-Husri*, Princeton, NJ: Princeton University Press.
Dalmasso, E. and F. Cavatorta (2013), 'Democracy, civil liberties and the role of religion after the Arab awakening: constitutional reforms in Tunisia and Morocco', *Mediterranean Politics*, **18**(2), 225–41.
Davidson, C.M. (2012), *After the Sheikhs: The Coming Collapse of the Gulf Monarchies*, London: Hurst & Co.
Dawisha, A. (2009), *Iraq: A Political History*, Princeton, NJ: Princeton University Press.
Deeb, M. (1979), *Party Politics in Egypt: The Wafd and its Rivals, 1919–1939*, London: Ithaca Press.
Della Porta, D. and M. Diani (1999), *Social Movements: An Introduction*, Oxford: Blackwell Publishers.
Denoeux, G. (1993), *Urban Unrest in the Middle East: A Comparative Study of Informal Networks in Egypt, Iran and Lebanon*, New York: State University of New York Press.
Desrues, T. (2012), 'Moroccan youth and the forming of a new generation: social change, collective action and political activism', *Mediterranean Politics*, **17**(1), 23–40.
Dorsey, J.M. (2011), 'Pitched battles: the role of ultra soccer fans in the Arab Spring', *Mobilization*, **16**(4), 411–8.
Dot-Pouillard, N. (2013), *Tunisie: La Révolution et ses Passés* [Tunisia: The Revolution and its Past], Paris: L'Harmattan.
El-Ghobashy, M. (2005), 'The metamorphosis of the Egyptian Muslim Brothers', *International Journal of Middle East Studies*, **37**(3), 373–95.
El-Ghobashy, M. (2012), 'The praxis of the Egyptian revolution', *MERIP Report*, **258**, 2–13.
El Hachmi, H.M. (2000), *The Politicization of Islam: A Case study of Tunisia*, Boulder, CO: Westview Press.
Fandy, M. (1994), 'Egypt's Islamic group: regional revenge?', *Middle East Journal*, **48**(4), 607–25.
Faulks, K. (2000), *Citizenship*, London: Routledge.
Gause, G. (2011), 'Why Middle East studies missed the Arab Spring: the myth of authoritarian stability', *Foreign Affairs*, **90**(4), 130–40.
Gershoni, I. (1981), *The Emergence of Pan-Arabism in Egypt*, Tel Aviv: Shiloah Center for Middle Eastern and African Studies.
Gershoni, I. and J.P. Jankowski (1986), *Egypt, Islam and the Arabs: The Search for Egyptian Nationhood, 1900–1930*, Oxford: Oxford University Press.
Gershoni, I. and J. Jankowski (1995), *Redefining the Egyptian Nation, 1930–1945*, Cambridge, UK: Cambridge University Press.
Gordon, J. (1992), *Nasser's Blessed Movement: Egypt's Free Officers and the July Revolution*, New York: Oxford University Press.
Graciet, C. and E. Laurent (2012), *Le Roi Prédateur: Main Basse sur le Maroc* [Predator King: Takeover of Morocco], Paris: Editions du Seuil.
Gunning, J. (2007), *Hamas in Politics: Democracy, Religion, Violence*, London: Hurst & Co.
Hafez, M.M. (2004), *Why Muslims Rebel: Repression and Resistance in the Islamic World*, Boulder, CO: Lynne Rienner.
Hallaq, W. (2009), *Shari'a: Theory, Practice, Transformations*, Cambridge, UK: Cambridge University Press.
Halpern, M. (1964), *The Politics of Social Change in the Middle East and North Africa*, Princeton, NJ: Princeton University Press.
Harnisch, C. and Q. Mecham (2009), 'Democratic ideology in Islamist opposition? The Muslim Brotherhood's "civil state"', *Middle Eastern Studies*, **45**(2), 189–205.
Hatem, M. (2012), 'The Arab Spring meets the Wall Street Occupy Movement: examples of changing definitions of citizenship in a global world', *Journal of Civil Society*, **8**(4), 401–15.
Haugbølle, R. and F. Cavatorta (2011), 'Will the real Tunisian opposition please stand up?', *British Journal of Middle Eastern Studies*, **38**(3), 323–41.
Heydemann, S. (2007), *Upgrading Authoritarianism in the Arab World*, Analysis Paper No. 13, The Saban Center for Middle East Policy, Washington, DC: Brookings Institution.

Hibou, B. (2011), *The Force of Obedience: The Political Economy of Repression in Tunisia*, Cambridge, UK: Polity Press.
Hinnebusch, R.A. (2001), *Syria: Revolution From Above*, London: Routledge.
Hoffmann, A. and C. König (2013), 'Scratching the democratic façade: framing strategies of the 20 February Movement', *Mediterranean Politics*, **18**(1), 1–22.
Hourani, A. (1962), *Arabic Thought in a Liberal Age, 1798–1939*, Cambridge, UK: Cambridge University Press.
International Crisis Group (ICG) (2011), *Popular Protest in North Africa and the Middle East (VI): The Syrian People's Slow-Motion Revolution*, Middle East and North Africa Report No. 108.
International Crisis Group (ICG) (2013), *Tunisie: Violences et Défi Salafiste* [Tunisia: Salafist Violence and Challenge], Middle East/North Africa Report No. 137.
Isin, E. (2002), *Being Political: Genealogies of Citizenship*, Minneapolis, MN: University of Minnesota Press.
Isin, E.F. and B.S. Turner (eds) (2002), *Handbook of Citizenship Studies*, London: Sage Publications.
Ismael, T.Y. (1990) (with R. 'at El-Said), *The Communist Movement in Egypt, 1920–1988*, New York: Syracuse University Press.
Ismael, T.Y. (2004), *The Communist Movement in the Arab World*, London: Routledge/ Curzon.
Ismael, T.Y. (2008), *The Rise and Fall of the Communist Party of Iraq*, Cambridge, UK: Cambridge University Press.
Ismail, S. (2006), *Political Life in Cairo's New Quarters: Encountering the Everyday State*, Minneapolis, MN: University of Minnesota Press.
Ismail, S. (2011a), 'Authoritarian government, neoliberalism and everyday civilities in Egypt', *Third World Quarterly*, **32**(5), 845–62.
Ismail, S. (2011b), 'Civilities, subjectivities and collective action: preliminary reflections in light of the Egyptian revolution', *Third World Quarterly*, **32**(5), 989–95.
Joseph, S. (ed.) (2000), *Gender and Citizenship in the Middle East*, New York: Syracuse University Press.
Joseph, S. (2013), 'Gender and citizenship in Middle Eastern states', *MERIP*, **198**, accessed 22 May 2014 at http://www.merip.org/mer/mer198/gender-citizenship-middle-eastern-states.
Kandil, H. (2012a), *Soldiers, Spies, and Statesmen*, London: Verso.
Kandil, H. (2012b), 'Why did the Egyptian middle class march to Tahrir?', *Mediterranean Politics*, **17**(2), 197–215.
Keddie, N. (1993), *Women in the Middle East: Shifting Boundaries in Sex and Gender*, New Haven, CT: Yale University Press.
Kepel, G. (1985), *The Prophet and the Pharaoh: Muslim Extremism in Egypt*, London: Al Saqi Books.
Khalaf, A. and G. Luciani (eds) (2006), *Constitutional Reform and Political Participation in the Gulf*, UAE: Gulf Research Center.
Lacroix, S. (2012), *Sheikhs and Politicians: Inside the New Egyptian Salafism*, Washington, DC: Brookings Doha Center.
Leenders, R. (2012), 'Collective action and mobilization in Dar'a: an anatomy of the onset of Syria's popular uprising', *Mobilization*, **17**(4), 419–34.
Leenders, R. (2013), 'Social movement theory and the onset of popular uprisings in Syria', *Arab Studies Quarterly*, **35**(3), 273–89.
Leenders, R. and S. Heydemann (2012), 'Popular mobilization in Syria: opportunity and threat and social networks of the early risers', *Mediterranean Politics*, **17**(2), 139–59.
Lerner, D. (1958), *The Passing of Traditional Society: Modernizing the Middle East*, Glencoe, IL: Free Press.
Le Sueur, J.D. (2010), *Between Terror and Democracy: Algeria Since 1989*, London: Zed Books.
Lewis, B. (1988), *The Political Language of Islam*, Chicago, IL: The University of Chicago Press.

Lewis, M.D. (2014), *Divided Rule: Sovereignty and Empire in French Tunisia, 1881–1938*, Berkeley, CA: University of California Press.
Longva, A.N. and A.S. Roald (2011), *Religious Minorities in the Middle East*, Leiden: Brill.
Luciani, G. (ed.) (1990), *The Arab State*, London: Routledge.
Luktiz, L. (1995), *Iraq: The Search for National Identity*, London: Frank Cass.
Lust-Okar, E. and S. Zerhouni (eds) (2008), *Political Participation in the Middle East*, Boulder, CO: Lynne Rienner.
Lynch, M. (2006), *Voices of the New Arab Public: Iraq, Al-Jazeera, and Middle East Politics Today*, New York: Columbia University Press.
Maghraoui, A.M. (2002),'Depoliticization in Morocco', *Journal of Democracy*, **1**(4), 24–32.
Maghraoui, D. (2011), 'Constitutional reforms in Morocco: between consensus and subaltern politics', *The Journal of North African Studies*, **16**(4), 679–99.
Maktabi, R. (2012), 'The politicization of the demos in the Middle East: citizenship between membership and participation in the state', doctoral thesis, Department of Science, University of Oslo.
Mann, M. (1987), 'Ruling class strategies and citizenship', *Sociology*, **21**(3), 339–54.
Marshall, T.H. ([1950] 1965), 'Citizenship and social class', in *Class, Citizenship and Social Development*, New York: Anchor.
Mayer, A.E. (2013), *Islam and Human Rights*, Boulder, CO: Westview Press.
McAdam, D., S. Tarrow and C. Tilly (2001), *Dynamics of Contention*, Cambridge, UK: Cambridge University Press.
Meijer, R. (2002), *The Quest for Modernity: Secular Liberal and Left-wing Political Thought in Egypt, 1945–1958*, London: Curzon/Routledge.
Meijer, R. (2009a), 'Introduction', in R. Meijer (ed.), *Global Salafism: Islam's New Religious Movement*, London/New York: Hurst & Co/Columbia University Press, pp. 1–32.
Meijer, R. (2009b), 'Commanding right and forbidding wrong as a principle of social action: the case of the Egyptian Jama'a al-Islamiyya', in R. Meijer (ed.), *Global Salafism: Islam's New Religious Movement*, London/New York: Hurst & Co/Columbia University Press, pp. 189–220.
Meijer, R. (2012a),'The Muslim Brotherhood and the political: an exercise in ambiguity?' in R. Meijer and E. Bakker (eds), *The Muslim Brotherhood in Europe*, London/New York: Hurst & Co/Columbia University Press, pp. 291–316.
Meijer, R. (2012b), 'The problem of the political in Islamist movements', in A. Boubekeur and O. Roy (eds), *Whatever Happened to the Islamists? Salafis, Heavy Metal Muslims, and the Lure of Consumerist Islam*, London/New York: Hurst & Co/Columbia University Press, pp. 27–60.
Meijer, R. (forthcoming), 'Bahrain: dynamics of a conflict', in W. Zartman (ed.), *Intifada: Negotiating a Social Movement*, Athens, GA: University of Georgia Press.
Meijer, R. and J. Wagemakers (2013), 'The struggle for citizenship of the Shiites in Saudi Arabia', in S. Zemni and B. Maréchal (eds), *The Dynamics of Sunni–Shia Relationships: Doctrine, Transnationalism, Intellectuals and the Media*, London/New York: Hurst & Co/Columbia University Press, pp. 119–40.
Mishal, S. and A. Sela (2000), *The Palestinian Hamas: Vision, Violence, and Coexistence*, New York: Columbia.
Mitchell, R.P. (1969), *The Society of the Muslim Brothers*, Oxford: Oxford University Press.
Mitchell, T. (1991), *Colonising Egypt*, Berkeley, CA: University of California Press.
Mitchell, T. (2002), *Rule of Experts: Egypt, Techno-politics, Modernity*, Berkeley, CA: University of California Press.
Moghadam, V.M. (1993), *Modernizing Women: Gender and Social Change in the Middle East*, Boulder, CO: Lynne Rienner.
Morris, B. (2007), *The Birth of the Palestinian Refugee Problem Revisited*, Cambridge, UK: Cambridge University Press.
Mouffe, C. (1993), *The Return of the Political*, London: Verso.
Moustafa, T. (2007), *The Struggle for Constitutional Power: Law, Politics, and Economic Development in Egypt*, Cambridge, UK: Cambridge University Press.

Norton, A.R. (1995) (ed.), *Civil Society in the Middle East, Vol. I*, Leiden: Brill.
Norton, A.R. (1996) (ed.), *Civil Society in the Middle East, Vol. II*, Leiden: Brill.
Nyers, P. (2007), 'Introduction: why citizenship studies', *Citizenship Studies*, **11**(1), 1–4.
Pace, M. and F. Cavatorta (2012), 'The Arab uprisings in theoretical perspective. An introduction', *Mediterranean Politics*, **9**(2), 125–38.
Pall, Z. (2014), 'Salafism in Lebanon: local and transnational resources', dissertation, Utrecht University.
Pappé, I. (2007), *The Ethnic Cleansing of Palestine*, Oxford: Oneworld Publications.
Pargeter, A. (2012), *Libya: The Rise and Fall of Qaddafi*, New Haven, CT: Yale University Press.
Parolin, G.P. (2009), *Citizenship in the Arab World: Kin, Religion and Nation-State*, Amsterdam: Amsterdam University Press.
Pennell, C.R. (2000), *Morocco Since 1830: A History*, New York: New York University Press.
Perkins, K.J. (2004), *A History of Modern Tunisia*, Cambridge, UK: Cambridge University Press.
Pratt, N. (2007), *Democracy & Authoritarianism in the Arab World*, Boulder, CO: Lynne Rienner.
Richards, A. and J. Waterbury ([1990] 1996), *A Political Economy of the Middle East*, 2nd edition, Boulder, CO: Westview Press.
Rosanvallon, P. (2013), *The Society of Equals*, Cambridge, MA: Harvard University Press.
Ruedy, J. (1992), *Modern Algeria: The Origins and Development of a Nation*, Bloomington, IN: Indiana State University.
Rutherford, B.K. (2008), *Egypt after Mubarak: Liberalism, Islam, and Democracy in the Arab World*, Princeton, NJ: Princeton University Press.
Said, E. (1978), *Orientalism*, London: Routledge Kegan & Paul.
Salem, P. (1994), *Bitter Legacy: Ideology and Politics in the Arab World*, New York: Syracuse University Press.
Salima, Z. (2012), 'A new feminism? Gender dynamics in Morocco's 20 February Movement', *Journal of International Women's Studies*, **13**(5), 101–14.
Schlumberger, O. (ed.) (2007), *Debating Arab Authoritarianism: Dynamics and Durability in Non-democratic Regimes*, Stanford, CA: Stanford University Press.
Schwedler, J. (2007), *Faith in Moderation: Islamist Parties in Jordan and Yemen*, Cambridge, UK: Cambridge University Press.
Scott, R. (2010), *The Challenge of Political Islam: Non-Muslims and the Egyptian State*, Stanford, CA: Stanford University Press.
Sharabi, H. (1988), *Neopatriarchy: A Theory of Distorted Change in Arab Society*, Oxford: Oxford University Press.
Singerman, D. (1995), *Avenues of Participation*, Princeton, NJ: Princeton University Press.
Sowers, J. and C. Toensing (eds) (2012), *The Journey to Tahrir: Revolution, Protest, and Social Change in Egypt*, London: Verso.
Springborg, R. (1982), *Family, Power and Politics in Egypt: Sayed Bey Marei – His Clan, Clients and Cohort*, Philadelphia, PA: Pennsylvania University Press.
Stora, B. (2004), *Messali Hadj, 1898–1974*, Paris: Hachette.
Stora, B. (2008), *Les guerres sans fins: Un historien, la France et l'Algérie* [Wars Without End: A Historian, France, and Algeria], Paris: Editions Stock.
Stork, J. (2011), 'Three decades of human rights activism in the Middle East and North Africa: an ambiguous balance sheet', in J. Beinin and F. Vairel (eds), *Social Movements*, pp. 83–124.
Tamimi, A.S. (2001), *Rachid Ghannouchi: A Democrat Within Islamism*, Oxford: Oxford University Press.
Tarrow, S. (1998), *Power in Movement: Social Movements and Contentious Politics*, Cambridge, UK: Cambridge University Press.
Thompson, E.F. (2000), *Colonial Citizens: Republican Rights, Paternal Privilege and Gender in French Colonial Syria and Lebanon*, New York: Columbia University Press.

Thompson, E.F. (2013), *Justice Interrupted: The Struggle for Constitutional Government in the Middle East*, Cambridge, UK: Cambridge University Press.
Tilly, C. (2006), *Regimes and Repertoires*, Chicago, IL: University of Chicago Press.
Tilly, C. (2007), *Democracy*, Cambridge, UK: Cambridge University Press.
Tilly, C. and L.J. Wood (2009), *Social Movements, 1768–2008*, Boulder, CO: Paradigm Publishers.
Torelli, S., F. Merone and F. Cavatorta (2012), 'Salafism in Tunisia: challenges and opportunities for democratization', *Middle East Policy*, **19**(4), 140–54.
Tripp, C. (2007), *A History of Iraq*, Cambridge, UK: Cambridge University Press.
Tripp, C. (2013a), *The Power and the People: Paths of Resistance in the Middle East*, Cambridge, UK: Cambridge University Press.
Tripp, C. (2013b), 'Acting in and acting out: conceptions of political participation', in M. Freeden and A. Vincent (eds), *Comparative Political Thought*, London: Routledge, pp. 88–109.
Tuğal, C. (2009), 'Transforming everyday life: Islamism and social movement theory', *Theory and Society*, **38**(5), 423–58.
Turner, B.S. (1978), *Weber and Islam*, London: Routledge.
Turner, B.S. (1989), 'Outline of a theory of citizenship', *Sociology*, **24**, 189–217.
Turner, B.S. (2000), 'Islam, civil society, and citizenship: reflections on the sociology of citizenship and Islamic studies', in N.A. Butenschøn, U. Davis and M. Hassassian (eds), *Citizenship and the State in the Middle East: Approaches and Applications*, New York: Syracuse University Press, pp. 28–48.
Van Bruinessen, M. (1991), *Agha, Sheikh and Khan: Social and Political Structures of Kurdistan*, London: Zed Books.
Varisco, D.M. (2005), *Islam Obscured: The Rhetoric of Anthropological Representation*, New York: Palgrave Macmillan.
Vermeren, P. (2009), *Le Maroc de Mohammed VI: La Transition Inachevée* [The Morocco of Muhammad VI: The Interrupted Transition], Paris: La Découverte.
Vermeren, P. (2011), *Maghreb: Les Origines de la Révolution Démocratique* [Maghreb: Origins of the Democratic Revolution], Paris: Pluriel.
Vikør, K.S. (2005), *Between God and the Sultan: A History of Islamic Law*, London: Hurst & Co.
Volpi, F. (2011), 'Framing civility in the Middle East: alternative perspectives on the state and civil society', *Third World Quarterly*, **32**(5), 827.
Wedeen, L. (1999), *Ambiguities of Domination: Politics, Rhetoric, and Symbols in Contemporary Syria*, Chicago, IL: University of Chicago Press.
Wegner, E. (2011), *Islamist Opposition in Authoritarian Regimes: The Party of Justice and Development in Morocco*, New York: Syracuse University Press.
White, B. (2011), *The Emergence of Minorities in the Middle East: The Politics of Community in French Mandate Syria*, Edinburgh: University of Edinburgh Press.
Wickham, C.R. (2002), *Mobilizing Islam: Religion, Activism, and Political Change in Egypt*, New York: Columbia University Press.
Wickham, C.R. (2004), 'Strategy and learning in the formation of Egypt's Wasat Party', *Comparative Politics*, **36**(2), 205–28.
Wickham, C.R. (2011), 'The Muslim Brotherhood and democratic transition in Egypt', *Middle East Law and Governance Journal*, **3**(1–2), 204–23.
Wickham, C.R. (2013), *The Muslim Brotherhood: Evolution of an Islamist Movement*, Princeton, NJ: Princeton University Press.
Wiktorowicz, Q. (ed.) (2004), *Islamic Activism: A Social Movement Theory Approach*, Bloomington, IN: Indiana University Press.
Willis, M.J. (2012), *Politics and Power in the Maghreb: Algeria, Tunisia and Morocco from Independence to the Arab Spring*, London: Hurst & Co.
Zeghal, M. (2008), *Islamism in Morocco: Religion, Authoritarianism and Electoral Politics*, Princeton, NJ: Markus Wiener.
Zemni, S. (2013a), 'The extraordinary politics of the Tunisian Revolution: the process of constitution making' (unpublished paper).

Zemni, S. (2013b), 'From socio-economic protest to national revolt: mapping the workers origins of the Tunisian revolution', in N. Gana (ed.), *The Tunisian Revolution: Contexts, Architects, Prospects*, Edinburgh: Edinburgh University Press.

Zollner, B. (2009), *The Muslim Brotherhood: Hasan al-Hudaybi and Ideology*, London: Routledge.

Zubaida, S. (1999), 'Cosmopolitanism in the Middle East', in R. Meijer (ed.), *Cosmopolitanism, Identity and Authenticity in the Middle East*, Richmond: Curzon Press, pp. 15–33.

Zubaida, S. (2003), *Law and Power in the Islamic World*, London: IB Tauris.

Index

Abed-Kotob, S. 630
abeyance structures
   emotions and social movements 326, 327
   political opportunities and social movements 268
   women's movements 423–4
activism patterns and methods
   African protest movement *see* Africa, social movements and political citizenship, protest movement and social activism
   animal rights movement 533–4, 535
   'flash activism' 369
   gender and sexuality 76
   international human rights movement 443–52, 454
   internet activism 362–3, 369, 375–6
   political opportunities and social movements 262–3
   transnationalization of social movements, Global North activists' domination 351
   urban citizenship 139, 146
   urban governance, involvement of activists in 476
   see also collective action
Adam, B. 70, 248, 341
Adamishin, A. 457
Adams, J. 311
Aday, S. 375, 376
Africa
   anti-apartheid and post-apartheid movements, South Africa 347, 350, 449–50
   authoritarian rule 339–40, 352
   Green Belt Movement 407
   'nego-feminism' and inclusion of men 429
   neoliberal economic policies, South Africa 350
   sexual citizenship, South Africa 66, 71–2

Africa, social movements and political citizenship 604–27
   GDP and 'adjusted net savings' 607–8
   global capitalist crisis effects and 'Africa Rising' argument 605–8, 623–4
   overseas aid 606–7
Africa, social movements and political citizenship, Climate Justice movement 613–18
   Climate Action Network (CAN) 614
   climate damage 613
   Durban Group 614–15
   ecological debt and payment distribution problem 618–19
   Environmental Rights Action 615, 616–17
   fracking, opposition to 615–16
   global climate negotiations, inadequacy of 613
   Green Economy, criticism of 617–18
   market-based strategies and carbon trading, opposition to 613, 614–15
   'Million Climate Jobs' campaign 617
   Shell oil extraction involvement 615–17
   technological fixes and geo-engineering, opposition to 613
Africa, social movements and political citizenship, protest movement and social activism
   Botswana, public sector strikes 621
   Eastern Africa and neoliberalism 621
   Egypt protests 619–20
   far left movement risk 622–3
   labour militancy 610–11
   Nairobi, cost of living protests 621
   natural resources, protection of 610–11, 615–17
   and neoliberalism 621–3

religious-based insurgencies 611–12
rising food prices, effects of 610, 621
traditional class struggle, effects of 610
violent protests 609
West Africa, energy crisis 621–2
Agnew, R. 519, 523
Agnihotri, I. 590, 591
Agrawal, A. 581
Agulhon, M. 337
Agyeman, J. 124, 125
Ahmed, L. 631, 633
AIDS crisis 70, 320–23
Aizura, A. 79
Akhavi, S. 645
Akhtar, A. 530, 534, 538–9
Al-Awadi, H. 645, 646
Alavi, H. 584–5
Alexander, R. 590
Alimi, E. 269, 270
Allal, A. 643
Almeida, P. 269
Almond, G. 26, 27, 33, 37
Alvord, S. 346, 349
Amenta, E. 206, 227, 268, 269, 270, 272, 274
Amin, S. 620
Amnesty International (AI) 442, 444–5, 446, 448, 453
  see also international human rights movement
Anderson, B. 194
Andharia, J. 582
Andrée, P. 406, 407
Andrew, C. 483
Andrews, K. 208, 209, 210, 211, 272, 273
animal rights movement 518–43
  animal experimentation 522, 523, 533, 536, 538, 539
  animal liberation strand and utilitarianism 525, 527–9, 530
  animal protection strategies 524, 536
  animal rights strand 525, 529–31, 532
  animal welfare strand 525–7, 530
  Animals Australia 528–9
  animals as property 521
  Animals and Public Health 538–9
  anthropology 523, 524, 539
  capitalism, effects of 522
  counter-movements 536–7
  criminology 523
  criticism of 519–20
  cultural barriers 526–7
  ecological citizenship 118
  environmental movement links 519, 534, 538–9
  extremists (Radical Animal Liberation Movement (RALM)) 521, 524, 525, 530, 531–2
  factory farming 523, 527, 538
  future developments and research 537–9
  global awareness 525–6, 528–9
  history of 518–19, 535–6
  injustice, agency and identity 534–5
  media exposure 521, 524, 528–9, 530, 534
  moral shocks, use of 522, 526, 531
  movement strands 521, 524–5
  as new social movement 519, 520–21
  political opportunity structure (POS) 535–6
  political science 520, 531, 537–8, 539
  research overview 519–23
  research overview, assessment of middle-range theories 532–7
  research overview, most important results 524–32
  Royal Society for the Prevention of Cruelty to Animals (RSPCA) 525, 535–6
  social movement framing 533–4, 537
  social movement framing, role of animal rights activists 533–4, 535
  social psychology 523
  social sciences 519
  sociology 520–22, 534, 539
  speciesism 521–2, 528, 529
  Vegan Outreach 529–30
  and vegetarianism 522, 529–30, 534, 538
  women's movement 523
  World Society for the Protection of Animals (WSPA) 525–7
  Zoopolis 537–8

anthropology
  animal rights movement 523, 524, 539
  Arab world, political citizenship 629–30
Antony, W. 139
Appadurai, A. 145, 348, 349
Appiah, K. 351
Arab Spring 274, 319, 362, 368, 374, 375–6, 635
Arab world, political citizenship and social movements 628–60
  anthropology 629–30
  Arab uprisings, effects of 635
  authoritarian regimes and corporatism 629, 630, 631, 639–42, 648
  authoritarian regimes, social rights and 'authoritarian bargain' 641–2
  authoritarian rule, Middle East 339–40, 352
  citizenship history 634, 636–9
  citizenship studies 629–31
  citizenship studies, social history 630
  citizenship studies, social movement theory 630–36
  citizenship studies, social movement theory, comparative model 632
  civil society 630, 639–50
  cultural pluralism and end of cosmopolitan cities 639
  feminist studies 631, 633
  identity and loyalty issues 633
  'inclusion–exclusion' dichotomy 633
  individual and community, dichotomy between 633
  Islamic movements 630, 634
  leadership and personality cults 640
  marginalized citizens 635
  media and press liberalism 639, 649
  nationalism, rise of 638–41
  one-party systems 640–42
  patronage systems 630
  political economy 629, 635–6
  political 'participation' 632
  social movement theory 630–36
  state subsidies and control 641–2
  state violence, use of 641
  trade unionism, rise of 638–9, 641
  West, ideological differences from 635, 636
Arab world, political citizenship and social movements, politicization and demanding citizenship rights 642–52
  accountability and transparency demands 646
  austerity measures and 'bread riots' 643
  autonomy and resistance against state intervention and patronage 649
  civic responsibilities and civic/religious virtue 650
  civil rights 644
  constitutions 647
  cultural rights 644
  equal rights 651
  ethnic and religious minorities (or oppressed majorities) 651
  freedom of speech and media 649
  human rights 645–52
  ideological changes 648–9
  informal networks and 'non-movements' 651–2
  and Muslim Brotherhood 638, 645, 646, 648–9
  pluralism 647–8
  political rights 644
  political rights and parties 647
  professional organizations and civil society 649–50
  regional autonomy movements 651
  rule of law 646
  social rights 644
  youth movements 650–51
Aradau, C. 161
Arato, A. 465, 469
Archibugi, D. 39, 188, 193
Arendt, H. 57, 635
Arias-Maldonado, M. 109, 112, 120
Arluke, A. 518, 536–7
Armstrong, C. 185, 188
Armstrong, E. 99, 206, 228, 470
Aron, R. 155, 156, 158, 159, 162, 168, 169
Arquilla, J. 372
Arts, B. 406, 407
Ash, R. 214

Ashbee, Edward 493–517
Atluri, T. 62, 67, 71
Ault, A. 69
Australia
　AIDS policies 321, 322–3
　animal protection 520, 524, 528–9
　'boat people' 326
authoritarian regimes
　Arab world 629, 630, 631, 639–42, 648
　ICT revolution and social movements 374
　political opportunities and social movements 269–70
　transnationalization of social movements 339–40
authoritarianism
　environmental movement, Russia 404–5
　see also democracy; neoliberalism; republican citizenship
Ayeb, H. 635, 641, 643, 651
Ayres, J. 344, 361, 364, 373
Ayubi, N. 629, 641

Badie, B. 634
Bagguley, P. 245
Bailey, C. 424
Bair, J. 454
Bakardjieva, M. 367
Balibar, E. 26
Ball, P. 347, 456
Ballard, R. 340, 349
Balogun, J. 623–4
Banaszak, L. 268, 272, 273
Bandopadhyaya, J. 582
Bandy, J. 346
Banerjee, S. 575, 585
Barber, B. 7, 34, 135, 136
Barker, C. 318
Barker-Plummer, B. 209
Barnes, B. 519
Barney, D. 137
Barr, S. 125
Barrera, M. 498
Barry, B. 90, 91
Barry, J. 108, 110, 113–14, 116
Bash, H. 465
Bassey, N. 613, 616
Basu, A. 426

Basu, D. 587
Bauböck, R. 133, 135, 165–6, 173
Bauman, Z. 179–80, 185, 483
Baviskar, A. 572, 577, 580, 581, 582, 587, 594
Baxi, U. 592
Bayat, A. 631
Beaumont, J. 481
Becher, D. 475
Beck, U. 179, 192
Beiner, R. 156
Beinin, J. 337, 339–40, 350, 630, 631, 634–5, 639, 643, 648
Beirne, P. 519, 523
Beitz, C. 188, 454
Bell, D. 72, 73, 75, 109, 110, 111, 116, 117, 121, 496
Bellamy, R. 3, 6, 7, 53, 156, 163, 171, 178, 632
Benford, R. 14, 95, 338, 444, 502, 533, 534
Benhabib, S. 86–7, 181, 183–4, 188, 190
Bennani-Chraïbi, M. 631, 635, 643
Bennett, D. 369
Bennett, L. 344, 347, 353
Bennett, L. and S. 29, 36, 38
Bennett, W. 361, 362, 368, 369, 370, 373, 374
Benski, T. 314, 319–20, 327
Benton, T. 519, 521
Berglund, C. 120
Berlet, C. 499, 504, 507–8
Bernstein, M. 92, 93, 95, 98, 99, 206, 228, 470
Bernstein, T. 312, 550
Berry, J. 100–101
Betsill, M. 407
Bevington, D. 594
Beyer, J. 369, 375
Bhasin, T. 458
Bhattacharjee, D. 589, 590
Bhowmik, S. 589
Bian, Y. 563
Biano, L. 550
Bill, J. 630
Bimber, B. 365, 367, 369, 370
Biney, A. 624
Binnie, J. 72, 73, 75
Blee, K. 210
Bloemraad, I. 101

Blom, A. 325
Blumer, H. 264
Bob, C. 449, 457, 594
Boekkooi, M. 366, 367
Bogaert, K. 643, 652
Boggs, C. 280
Bohman, James 45–59
Boittin, J. 141, 144
Boltanski, L. 326–7, 526, 528
Bolzendahl, C. 38
Bomberg, E. 402
Bond, Patrick 249, 604–27
Bonds, E. 314
Bookchin, M. 110, 126
Borch, C. 328
Borchert, S. 495
Bosniak, L. 6, 180
Bosso, C. 396
Botman, S. 630
Boudet, H. 270
Boudreau, V. 269
Boulianne, S. 366
Bourdieu, P. 212, 215, 578
Bowden, B. 185
Boyce, J. 607, 608
Braine, N. 96, 97, 99
Brass, T. 576, 585
Brazil, homelessness and urban social movements 485–6
Brenner, N. 140, 466, 475
Britt, L. 312
Broad, D. 139
Brooks, D. 493, 504
Brower, M. 648
Brown, D. 343
Brown, M. 68, 69
Brown, N. 647, 648
Brulle, R. 211, 388, 389, 390, 391, 396, 399, 409
Brunsting, S. 367
Brysk, A. 347, 459
Buchanan, T. 453
Buechler, S. 235, 238, 336, 339, 371, 419, 470, 483, 527, 532–3, 536, 537, 539
Bullard, N. 252
Bullard, R. 408–9
Burack, C. 507
Burgess, E. 264
Burns, A. 362

Burns, N. 38
Bussemaker, J. 64, 65
Butenschøn, N. 633
Byres, T. 575
Byrne, P. 290

Cadeno-Roa, J. 314
Cadogan, P. 244
Cai, Y. 548, 551, 553, 560
Cain, B. 27
Calhoun, C. 95, 246
Canada
  animal welfare reforms 530
  environmental citizenship 109, 121
  multicultural policies 101
Caney, S. 192
capitalism *see* neoliberalism
carbon trading, opposition to, Africa 613, 614–15
  see also Africa, social movements and political citizenship, Climate Justice movement; environmental movement
Cardenas, S. 450
Caren, N. 209
Carpenter, R. 449
Carter, N. 109
Carty, V. 361
Carver, T. 61, 72
Castells, M. 144, 236, 284, 304, 345, 353, 371, 464, 467, 468, 472, 473–4, 475, 482, 486, 487
Castles, S. 87, 88, 180
Catney, P. 127, 128
Caute, D. 280
Cavatorta, F. 631, 647, 648
Cederlof, G. 581
Cefaï, D. 465
Cerny, P. 48, 181
Chadwick, A. 370, 374
Chafe, W. 425
Chafetz, J. 426
Chakrabarti, D. 587, 592, 593
Chakravarty, A. 573
Chapman, A. 456
Charvet, J. 188
Chasek, P. 406, 407
Chatterjee, P. 576, 577, 585, 588
Chatterji, A. 573
Chen, F. 551, 552

Chen, H. 372, 373
Chen, Y. 558, 560
Cheng, P. 564
Cherry, E. 519, 522
Chibber, V. 589, 590
child abuse and incest 322
  see also emotions and social movements
Childs, S. 65
China
  animal welfare, WSPA Libearty campaign 526
  'land grabbing' in Africa 605, 606, 607
  Tiananmen Square protest 318–19
  urban protests 484–5
China, social movements and political citizenship 547–71
  citizenship as civility 562–3
  citizenship as membership 563–5
  citizenship as membership, thin and thick 563–4
  citizenship as membership, village elections 564
  coercion use 560
  Confucianism 561
  cultural heritage influence 563
  ethical responsibility toward the collective good 561–2
  future research 565–6
  grievance studies and collective action 555–7
  grievance studies and collective action, and emotions 556
  institutional structure 558, 559
  international NGOs in China 563
  Labour Contract Law 552
  Liulitun waste incineration plants, campaign against 547–8
  mass media involvement 557
  outcome measurement, problems with 548
  political process and political opportunity structure 558–60
  political system and scale of actions 548
  resource mobilization 557–8
  rights consciousness and citizenship notions 560–62
  social movement scholarship 554–60
  strategy choices 548
  volunteers in community activities 562–3
China, social movements and political citizenship, in contemporary China 549–54
  environmental movements 553–4, 557, 559–60
  government organized 549–50
  hunger strikes 550
  internet networks 553
  labour movements 551–2, 557
  migrant workers' associations 552, 564
  peasants' movements 550–51, 555, 557, 559, 564
  Student Social Movement and political protest 550
  urban (homeowners) movements 552–3, 555, 556, 557, 562
  women's movements and gender equality 554
Chiodelli, F. 145
Cho, Y. 558
Chong, D. 290, 302
Choudry, A. 587, 594
Chow, J. 563
Christoff, P. 108, 118
citizenship
  concept 6, 7
  definition 178, 196
civic involvement
  duty to vote, democratic citizenship 32, 33, 36, 37, 41
  ecological citizenship 113–14
  friendship, republican citizenship 52–3
  see also urban citizenship
civil disobedience 262, 264–5
  see also political opportunities and social movements
Clark, Ann Marie 440–63
Clark, J. 351, 630
Clarke, K. 635, 648
Clarke, S. 124, 125
class struggle
  Africa, protest movement and social activism 610
  and global cities 144
  urban social movements 470, 485–6

Clemens, E. 273
climate change 113, 121, 128
   see also ecological citizenship; environmental movement
Cloward, R. 262, 361, 535
Coffé, H. 38
Cohen, C. 367
Cohen, J. 239, 246, 247, 465, 469
Cole, L. 408
Coleman, J. 212, 214, 215
collective action
   and free riders 289
   globalization of 478–9
   grievance studies, China 555–7
   identities, multicultural citizenship *see* multicultural citizenship, collective identity approach
   identities and subjectivities, post-structuralism 285
   international human rights movement 442
   local economic development 477–8
   national identity effects 98–9, 100–101
   new social movement (NSM) approach 239–41, 242–3, 246–7, 252
   and organizational layers, urban social movements 477
   policy change opportunities, and mobilization 271–3
   resistance to neoliberal forces 475–6
   South Asia, collective mobilization and violence 325
   Tea Party movement 496, 502–3
   transnationalization, large groups and small social networks 337–8
   urban social movements 468–72, 483, 485–6
   women's movements, identity construction and intersectionality 430–31
   see also activism patterns and methods
communitarian approach
   Arab world, individual and community, dichotomy between 633

ecological citizenship 128–9
   gender and sexuality 64–5
consumer demand effects, ecological citizenship 118–19, 126
consumer-as-activist, urban citizenship 139
Cooper, D. 71, 72, 77
Corell, E. 407
corporate power, demonstrations against 344–5
   see also neoliberalism
Corte, U. 216, 218
cosmopolitan citizenship
   cultural pluralism and end of cosmopolitan cities, Arab world 639
   democratic citizenship 39
   emerging, Europe 163
   global *see* global and cosmopolitan citizenship
   republican citizenship 47–8, 49
   see also transnationalization of social movements; urban citizenship
Costain, A. 268, 269, 272
Cousin, O. 237
Cox, L. 8, 235
Cress, D. 217, 226
Crick, B. 7, 134, 135
criminology, animal rights movement 523
Crook, S. 519
cultural issues
   citizenship rights, Arab world 639, 644
   cultural barriers, animal rights movement 526–7
   cultural connectedness, transnationalization of social movements 346–7
   democratic society and cultural minorities 86
   'framing', and transnationalization of social movements 337–8
   gender and sexuality 75–6
   heritage influence, China 563
   integration, need to move towards, Europe 159, 160
   multicultural citizenship *see* multicultural citizenship

new social movement (NSM)
    approach 236, 237–8, 245, 246
resources, uneven distribution and
    accessibility 215–17, 219, 220,
    222
Curtin, D. 108, 128–9, 159, 160

Dagger, R. 45–6, 47, 53, 54
Dahl, R. 27, 28
Dahrendorf, R. 561
Dallmayr, F. 184, 190–91, 192, 193
Dalton, Russell J. 2, 7, 25–44, 134, 336, 388, 390, 391, 412
Danyi, Paul 440–63
Darier, E. 109, 126
Das, A. 573, 577, 585
Das, D. 587
Davidson, A. 87, 88, 180
Davis, D. 448, 458
Dawes, R. 337
Dawisha, A. 634, 639
Day, R. 250, 251
De la Luz Inclan, M. 269
De Souza, M. 475, 485–6
Dean, H. 110, 114, 123
Deibert, R. 374
Deitelhoff, N. 447, 451
Delanty, G. 6, 60, 173
Della Porta, D. 1, 5, 234, 284, 285, 288, 311–12, 324, 337, 342, 353, 363, 368, 471, 478, 481, 634
Della Sala, V. 169
Dell'olio, F. 39
democracy
    challenges, post-structuralism 302–3
    and cultural minorities 86
    democratic component of
        citizenship, concerns over 181–2
    democratization of public policies 476
    and globalization 135
    ICT repression in democratic
        contexts and surveillance
        concerns 374–5
    involvement of citizens' movements 458–9
    principles of deliberative 481
    significance and ability to overcome
        limitations, urban social
        movements 469–70

    see also authoritarianism;
        neoliberalism; republican
        citizenship
democratic citizenship 25–44
    autonomy of citizen 30, 32, 33
    behavior and citizenship norms,
        interaction between 26
    citizenship norms 26–9
    citizenship norms, distribution of 31–2
    citizenship norms framework 32–5
    citizenship norms, social distribution 36–9
    civic duty to vote 32, 33, 36, 37, 41
    cosmopolitan citizenship 39
    definition 26–7
    educational patterns 37–8
    engaged citizenship 33, 34–5, 40–41
    engaged citizenship, new norms 36–7, 38
    equality and distributive justice 28, 30–32
    ethical and moral responsibility to
        others 28, 30–32, 33, 34, 37, 38, 39
    future research 40
    gender patterns 38–9
    generational patterns 36–7
    global responsibilities 28, 39–40
    importance of citizenship 40–41
    liberal and republican perceptions,
        differences between 27
    national patterns among established
        democracies 34–5
    native and immigrant populations,
        interaction between 39–40
    philosophical literature 28, 29–30
    post-material or self-expressive
        values 32, 34, 37
    public opinion surveys on citizenship
        norms 29–32
    public participation in politics 27,
        29–30, 34, 37–8, 40–41
    state authority, acceptance of, and
        social order 27–8, 30, 31–2, 33,
        34, 36–7, 38, 40
    transnational citizenship 39–40
    transnational citizenship, dual
        identities 39

demonstrations and civil disobedience 262, 264–5
  see also political opportunities and social movements
DeNardis, L. 375
Denoeux, G. 631
Denters, B. 30, 31, 32, 36
Derrida, J. 282, 283
Desai, A. 362, 369, 575, 583–4, 593
Desai, N. 591
Desrues, T. 651
Dhanagare, D. 575, 584, 585, 586
Diamond, J. 476
Diani, M. 1, 5, 215, 226, 284, 285, 288, 337, 353, 364, 391, 549, 634
digital technology effects
  digital rights movement 362, 369
  transnationalization of social movements 343–6
  see also ICT revolution and social movements
DiMaggio, A. 368, 495, 498–9
DiMaggio, P. 217
Dinan, D. 156, 168
Ding, D. 552
Disch, L. 500, 501
Dixon, C. 594
Dixon, M. 207
Dobson, A. 109, 110, 115–26*passim*, 191–2, 193, 388, 561
Doheny-Farina, S. 372
Doherty, B. 295, 388, 391, 392, 398, 399, 402, 406, 412, 413
Donald, R. 525
Donaldson, S. 537–8
Donnelly, J. 456, 458
Dorsey, J. 635, 651
Douay, N. 476, 484
Dowding, K. 289
Dower, N. 193, 195
Dowie, M. 391, 396, 397, 412
Downey, G. 393, 394
Doyle, T. 127, 128, 391, 406
Dryzek, J. 304, 396, 397
Dubet, F. 237, 468, 477
Dunlap, R. 389, 391, 393, 396, 397, 412
Dunleavy, P. 290, 304
Dunn, J. 314
Dupuy, C. 466

Duyvendak, J. 393, 395, 481
Dworkin, A. 426

Eagleton-Pierce, M. 361
Earl, Jennifer 353, 359–83
Eastern Europe
  environmental movement *see* environmental movement, Eastern Europe
  see also individual countries
Eckersley, R. 11, 108, 111, 116, 127, 388, 389, 409, 411, 519
ecological citizenship 107–32
  as activity rather than status 117–18, 127
  animal rights 118
  citizenship, justification for 110–11, 119
  civic participation 113–14
  climate champions 121
  climate change and anti-liberalism 113, 128
  communitarian approach 128–9
  consumer demand effects 118–19, 126
  critical environmental sociology and social practice approach 125–6
  ecological democracy, creation of 127–8
  empirical research 119–22
  and environmental citizenship, distinction between 110
  environmental regulation and environmental justice 116, 123, 124–5, 126–7
  equity and justice considerations 124–5
  feminist theories 122–3, 124
  future of 127–8
  future research 122
  global ecological citizenship and responsibilities (green cosmopolitanism) 114–19, 122
  history of concept 108–11
  institutional environmental agenda 107, 109, 110
  key virtues 116–17, 120–21
  liberal environmental citizenship 111–13, 117–18, 121, 126, 128
  minority ethnic communities 125

(post-)cosmopolitan ecological citizenship and responsibilities (green cosmopolitanism) 114–19, 122
private sphere, importance of 117, 123–4
pro-environmental behaviour 120–21
promotional methods 118, 120
public/private practice debate 118–19, 123–4, 126–7
republican ecological citizenship, individual green virtues 113–14
sustainable practices, encouragement of 114, 116, 118, 123
see also environmental movement
economic crisis effects
 anti-austerity movements 252–3
 European citizenship 172
 Occupy Movement 216, 252–3, 270, 478, 480
 Tea Party movement 498–9
 see also 'financial' headings
economic inequalities, and transnationalization of social movements 339
economic levers and sanctions, international human rights movement 449–50
Edelman, M. 336, 338, 339, 341, 344
Eder, K. 167, 243
education
 learning transfer, emergence of 300–301
 patterns, democratic citizenship 37–8
 pedagogical program, call for, cosmopolitan citizenship 191
Edwards, Bob 205–32, 499
Edwards, P. 344, 368
Einwohner, R. 272
Eisinger, P. 266
Ekine, S. 620–21
El Hachmi, H. 646
El-Ghobashy, M. 630, 646, 649
Elgar, R. 25
Elkins, D. 372
Eltham, B. 362
emotions and social movements 308–33
 anger model 309, 316, 320, 321
 'cementing' emotions 314
 emotional movement families 328
 'emotional resonance' 315
 emotions directed towards state or its institutions 324–5
 emotions and mobilization 308–9
 future research 327–8
 grievance studies and collective action, China 556
 humanitarian movement and human rights movement, contrast between 326–7
 institutionalization of public welfare programs 311
 intra-group conflicts 315
 intra-group mutual support 327
 member loyalty effects 310–11
 migrants and refugees 326
 'moral shocks' and mobilization 312–13, 327
 movements kept in abeyance 326, 327
 'nagging' protest events 319–21
 'nagging' protest events, grieving mothers' organizations 320
 'nagging' protest events, NAMES Project AIDS Memorial Quilt 320–21
 pioneer studies 311–13
 political control, regaining 310
 and political science theory 328
 research history and development 313–16
 secret ballot introduction 324
 self-division about self and society 316
 self-help groups 311–12, 315
 self-image improvement 312
 South Asia, collective mobilization and violence 325
 Soviet bloc, party-state relationships 324–5
 transnational mobilizing emotions 326–7
 victimization-related and self-assertive oppositional emotions, mixture of 313–14
emotions and social movements, challenging and shaping policies 321–4
 AIDS in Australia 322–3
 child abuse and incest 322

Disabled People's Movement (DPM) and Feminist Movement (FM)
  conflict 321–2
  gender codes and medical treatment 321
  NGOs and the Third Sector 323
  rape cases and feminist movement 324
emotions and social movements, transformative protest events 316–19
  Arab Uprisings 319
  China, Tiananmen Square protest 318–19
  France, storming of the Bastille 317
  Polish stockyard strike 318
  Serbian mass protests 317–18
Ems, L. 362
engaged citizenship 33, 34–7, 38, 40–41
  see also democratic citizenship
Enloe, C. 425
environmental issues
  Africa *see* Africa, social movements and political citizenship, Climate Justice movement
  environmental and ecological citizenship, distinction between 110
  groups, new social movement (NSM) approach 250, 252
  international human rights movement 451, 456
  sustainability and personal responsibility 192
  women's mobilization around 477–8, 483–4
environmental movement 387–417
  animal rights movement 519, 534, 538–9
  China 553–4, 557, 559–60
  differing strands 389–90
  future challenges and research 410–11
  green parties 401–2
  history of 388–90
  India 581–2
  nuclear energy conflict 393–5
  see also ecological citizenship
environmental movement, Eastern Europe 402–5
  anti-nuclear movements 403
  East European EMOs and green networks 404
  global EMOs 405
  Russian authoritarian rule 404–5
  Russian greenbelt protests 405
  Socio-Ecological Union umbrella organization 403–4, 405
  state-licensed environmental movement 403
environmental movement, EU and transformation of European environmentalism 399–401
  environmental Directives 400
  environmental movement organizations (EMOs) 387–8, 389–90, 396, 399–401
  Group of Ten lobby group 400
  organizational form, changes in 400–401
  umbrella organizations 399–400
environmental movement, institutionalization effects 395–9
  direct (e-)mail 396–7
  ecological modernization 397
  external institutionalization and political opportunity structure 397–8
  grassroots environmentalism 398
  homogenization concerns 397
  organizational growth 396–7
  radical environmentalism 398–9
environmental movement, new environmental movement 390–93
  Friends of the Earth 392–3, 395, 396, 406, 407, 411
  Greenpeace 392, 395, 396, 405, 406
  national-level environmental organizations 391–2
  scientific publications, influence of 390–91
  World Wide Fund for Nature 392, 396, 405, 406–7
environmental movement, transnationalization 406–8
  anti-dam movement 407
  environmental justice movement 408–10

environmental racism and environmental justice movement 408
global civil society 407–8
Global South 407, 410–11
and ICT use 407
and Third World poor 409–10
and toxic waste 408–9
Epstein, B. 234, 394
Epstein, S. 69, 70
equality issues
Arab world 651
and distributive justice, democratic citizenship 28, 30–32
ecological citizenship 124–5
see also multicultural citizenship; women's movements
Erskine, T. 189, 190
Eschenfelder, K. 362, 369
Escobar, A. 471
Etling, B. 374
Etzioni, A. 25
Europe
Aarhus Convention and environmental rights 112
environmentalism *see* environmental movement, EU and transformation of European environmentalism
EU Charter of Fundamental Rights (2000) 70
European Court of Human Rights, and cosmopolitan rights 184
national and transnational identities 39, 40, 53–4
as political community 53
protest movement, 1960s 1
see also individual countries
European citizenship 154–76
capitalist market citizenship, exclusionary nature of 160–61
citizenship enactment in trans-border relations and practices 161
'constructive' theory of citizenship 167
cosmopolitan citizenship, emerging 163

cultural integration and political integration, need to move towards 159, 160
as developing regulation 168–9
disagreement over term 155–9
economic crisis effects 172
essentialist vs constructivist ideas on viability of 156–61
exclusive membership decision of each member state, concerns over 159–60
future research 171–3
historical and institutionalist research, 166–71
institutional considerations 170–71
language considerations 162, 164
liberal democracies, dealing with nation-state framework 165–6
Maastricht Treaty, Union citizenship 154, 163
nation-state concept, dominance of 156–9, 161, 162, 164, 168, 172
normative research, desirability, problems and possibilities of citizenship 161–6
and political identity 167–8
post-national literature 159
process of citizenship building 169–70
republican citizenship construction 163–4
social rights 168–9
as special status of individual rights 171–2
supranationalism and concept of nationality 165–6, 170–73
third-country nationals, exclusion of 160
Evans, B. 124, 125
Evans, D. 72, 73, 79, 125, 126
Evans, Erin 259–78
Evans, P. 342
Evans, S. 243, 419, 420
Everett, J. 590, 592
Everson, M. 157
Eyerman, R. 5, 14, 242, 314

Fainstein, S. 466, 478
Falk, R. 173, 180, 186, 341
Fassin, D. 469

Index 673

Faulks, K. 633
female involvement, Tea Party movement 508–9
feminism and feminist studies
  Arab world 631, 633
  Disabled People's Movement (DPM) and Feminist Movement (FM) conflict 321–2
  ecological citizenship 122–3, 124
  liberal feminism and multicultural citizenship 90–91
  new social movement (NSM) approach 243, 245
  rape cases and feminist movement 324
  thinking blindspots, gender citizenship 74–5
  and urban activism 146
  urban citizenship 143–4
  women's movements and feminist movements, distinctions between 426–7
  see also gender and sexuality; women's movements
Ferree, M. 418, 421, 422, 425, 426, 432
Fetner, T. 208, 209, 210
Fielding, P. 369
Fillieule, O. 631, 635
financial circulation and uneven development, urban citizenship 143, 144, 147–8
financial donations, Tea Party movement 495, 500, 502, 513
financial resources 208–9, 211
  see also 'economic' headings; resource mobilization
Finger, M. 406, 408
Fireman, B. 309
Fisher, D. 364, 366, 367
Flam, Helena 308–33, 393, 394
Flank, L. 478
Flesher Fominaya, C. 8, 235, 250, 312
Fligstein, N. 321
Florini, A. 343
Fluekiger, J.-M. 521, 531
Flynn, C. 518
Foley, M. 209, 210, 214, 215
Formisano, R. 494, 500
Foster, G. 408
Foucault, M. 138–9, 282, 293

Foweraker, J. 284, 339
Fox, J. 343
fracking, opposition to, Africa 615–16
  see also Africa, social movements and political citizenship, Climate Justice movement; environmental movement
France
  animal activists 522
  Notre-Dame-des-Landes project 294, 295–6, 297, 298, 300–301
  Paris 'May events' 280
  storming of the Bastille 317
Franchescet, S. 65, 74
Francione, G. 520, 532, 533–4
Frank, J. 530
Franklin, A. 530
Franzén, M. 479
Fraser, N. 94
Freeman, J. 205, 223, 243
Freeman, P. 529–30
Frenzel, F. 244
Frickel, S. 207–8
Fricker, M. 50–51
Friedman, E. 406, 407, 443, 451, 454, 456, 457, 459, 548, 552, 554
Friedmann, J. 475
Friends of the Earth 392–3, 395, 396, 406, 407, 411
  see also environmental movement
Froissart, C. 552
Fuller, S. 62, 65
future research
  animal rights movement 537–9
  China, social movements and political citizenship 565–6
  democratic citizenship 40
  ecological citizenship 122
  emotions and social movements 327–8
  environmental movement 410–11
  European citizenship 171–3
  gender and sexuality 64, 71, 80–81
  global and cosmopolitan citizenship 198
  ICT revolution and social movements 367, 376, 377
  India, social movements 593–4
  new social movement (NSM) approach 253–4

post-structuralism, social movements and citizen politics 303
resource mobilization and social and political movements 228–9
Tea Party movement 512–13
transnationalization of social movements 352–3
urban social movements 482–6
women's movements 432–5

Gadgil, M. 578, 580, 581–2
Gallagher, M. 559
Gamson, W. 14–15, 95, 205, 261, 269, 271, 273, 309, 337, 503, 533, 534–5
Gandhi, N. 592
Ganesh, S. 368
Gao, B. 562
Gao, W. 551
Garcez, R. 315
Garcia, S. 481–2
Garner, R. 519, 520, 526, 529, 532, 533–4
Garrett, R. Kelly 344, 359–83
Garrido, M. 360, 364, 374
Garside, N. 109, 110
Gause, G. 631
Gaventa, J. 3
gender codes and medical treatment 321
gender patterns, democratic citizenship 38–9
gender and sexuality 60–85
  bisexual citizenship case 79
  common scholarly themes 75
  and communitarianism 64–5
  cultural concerns and injustices 75–6
  'fashionable' use of citizenship, concerns over 76
  feminist thinking blindspots 74–5
  future research 64, 71, 80–81
  gender and citizenship 62–7
  gender and citizenship, concept of 62–4
  gender diversity effects 63–4
  heterosexuality as basis for full citizenship 72
  human rights issues 75–6, 80
  international context 66–7
  intimate (sexual) citizenship 72–3
  masculinist nature of traditional approaches to citizenship 60, 62–3
  and neoliberalism 64, 77
  normalization moves 77
  policy and practice 63
  political activism, place for 76
  political science and gendered citizenship 65–6
  public–private inequalities 63
  and republicanism 64
  sexual citizenship, perceived uneven benefits 76–7
  sexual citizenship, universalist or particularist forms, debate over 78–81
  sexual and transgender citizenship 68–73
  terminology 61–2
  and traditional models of citizenship 64–5
  universalist approach, call for 80
  utility of concept of citizenship 74–5, 77
  Western-centric form of citizenship, moving beyond 66–7, 75
  women's agency in reshaping state institutions 67
  see also feminism and feminist studies
gender and sexuality, LGBT groups as social movements 68–71
  history of 68–9
  HIV/AIDS crisis 70
  lesbian and gay liberation movement 69–70
  political citizenship and participation 71–3
  queer perspective and anti-identity politics 70
  reformist strategies 70–71
  transnational networks and international organizations 70, 71–2
generational issues
  democratic citizenship 36–7
  Tea Party movement 506
gentrification and neoliberal urbanism 143, 144
  see also neoliberalism; urban citizenship

Germany
  airport protests 296
  green parties, and influence on national politics 402
Gerstenberg, O. 159, 160, 163
Giddens, A. 126, 388
Giesen, B. 167
Gillham, P. 209, 215, 217, 224, 226
Gillingham, J. 156, 157, 168
Gladwell, M. 362, 375, 376
Gledhill, J. 478
Glidden, B. 480
global and cosmopolitan citizenship 177–201
  citizen loyalty concerns 182
  citizenship definition 178, 196
  democratic component of citizenship, concerns over 181–2
  development of 183–6
  emergence of 179–86
  future research 198
  global civil society, emergence of 184–5
  global civil society, shortcomings 185
  global identities and goals 185–6
  global rights regime, development of 183–4
  globalization definition 179
  immigration issues 180–81
  liquidity metaphor 179
  nation-state, continued relevance 183, 194–5, 197–8
  political identity, shared 180, 196
  post-national citizenship 180–81
  prospects for 194–8
  and social divisions 180
  social solidarity, possible reinforcement of 183
  social and welfare rights 181, 182–4, 188–90
  supranational institutions, power of 181–2
  territorial citizenship decline 180–83
  territorial state, position of 179–80
  see also cosmopolitan citizenship
global and cosmopolitan citizenship, cosmopolitan citizenship
  communitarian criticism of 188–9, 190
  cultural and political orientations, dealing with diversity in 189–90, 197
  and democratic participation 193, 194, 197–8
  environmental sustainability and personal responsibility 192
  internationalism comparison 190
  as moral attitude 190–91, 192–3
  need for 187–94
  need for, humans as part of a common humanity 187–8, 191
  need for, justice as fairness (Rawls) theory 188
  pedagogical program, call for 191
  post-modern criticism of 189
  transnational political institutions, strengthening of 192–3, 194
  world parliament suggestion 193–4
globalization
  animal rights movement 525–6, 528–9
  capitalist crisis effects and 'Africa Rising' argument 605–8, 623–4
  climate negotiations, inadequacy of, Africa Climate Justice movement 613
  collective action and alter-globalization 478–9
  conflicts, involvement in 251–2
  counter-globalization movement 251, 252–3
  democracy and globalization 135
  Eastern Europe environmental movement 405
  ecological citizenship and responsibilities 114–19, 122
  effects, India social movements 582–3
  environmental movement 407–8
  gender and sexuality, LGBT groups as social movements 70, 71–2
  Global North and South, differences between 475, 476
  governance and civil society 345–7
  ICT and anti-globalization movement 361
  international NGOs in China 563
  internationalism comparison 190
  new social movement (NSM) approach 249–53

parliament of cities, suggestion of 135–6
responsibilities, and democratic citizenship 28, 39–40
and transnationalism, distinctions between 348–9
women's movements 421–5, 432
see also transnationalization of social movements
Glynos, J. 287, 293
Goheen, P. 141
Gökalp, D. 62, 67
Gold, T. 553
Goldman, M. 564
Goodwin, J. 99, 313, 314–15, 338, 537
Goonewardena, K. 143
Gordon, J. 639
Gottlieb, R. 388, 391, 412
Gough, K. 575, 583, 584, 585
Gould, D. 311, 312, 315–16
government involvement *see* state structures
Grabham, E. 79
Greenberg, C. 141
Greenpeace 392, 395, 396, 405, 406
see also environmental movement
Greenwood, J. 400
Gregory, T. 101
Greve, H. 209
Griggs, Steven 279–307
Grimm, D. 162, 164
Grossman, L. 362
Groves, J. 536–7
Guardino, M. 510
Guarnizo, L. 137, 138, 139
Gudavarthy, A. 592, 593
Guha, R. 388, 409–10, 572, 576, 577, 578, 580, 581–2, 583
Guidry, J. 342, 349
Gulia, M. 372
Gunning, J. 631
Guo, S. 552, 553
Guo, X. 556
Gupta, D. 272, 575, 578
Gurak, L. 361, 369
Guru, G. 573

Habermas, J. 51, 53–4, 55, 159, 160, 181–2, 188, 236, 243–4, 248, 285, 471, 519

Hacking, I. 279
Hackworth, J. 139, 479
Hafez, M. 631
Hafner-Burton, E. 458
Hagendoorn, L. 40
Hager, S. 160
Hailwood, S. 112
Hajer, M. 287, 397
Halavais, A. 360, 364, 374
Halfmann, D. 272
Halpern, C. 466
Halsaa, B. 62, 74
Hamel, Pierre 145, 464–92
Hannan, M. 346
Hannigan, J. 533, 534
Hansen, P. 160
Hansen, R. 184
Hards, S. 126
Hardt, M. 8
Harnisch, C. 649
Harris, D. 28, 142
Harvey, D. 3, 139, 140, 141, 143, 146, 344, 466, 471, 472, 478, 479, 577, 606
Hassin, S. 483
Hasson, S. 481
Haugbølle, R. 648
Hawkesworth, M. 422, 429
Haythornthwaite, C. 372
Hayward, T. 112, 116, 117, 119, 121
He, B. 564
health provision concerns, Tea Party movement 506, 511
Hearn, J. 61, 62, 63, 66, 68, 78, 79–80
Heater, D. 25, 41, 173
Heath, A. 101
Heberer, T. 553
Hedges, C. 149
Heimer, M. 564
Heise, D. 312
Held, D. 28, 39, 135, 179, 185, 188, 189, 193–4
Hertel, S. 454, 459
Herz, N. 8
Herzog, H. 67
Hess, B. 419, 421, 426
Hewitt, L. 207
Heydemann, S. 630, 635, 643
Hilderbrandt, T. 554
Hines, S. 79

Hirschman, A. 290, 310
Hirst, C. 466, 478
Hix, S. 156
Ho, P. 548, 553, 557
Hobson, B. 62, 94
Hoffmann, A. 635, 643
Hofstadter, R. 496, 503, 512
Holden, M. 481
Holloway, J. 251
Holmes, M. 327
Holston, J. 141, 145
Hooghe, M. 367
hooks, b. 431
Hopgood, S. 454
Hopkins, D. 314, 321–2
Howard, P. 369, 374
Howarth, David 279–307
Howell, J. 554
Howland, D. 562
Htun, M. 457
Huber, J. 426
human capital, and resource mobilization 209, 211, 213, 220, 221
human rights issues
  gender and sexuality 75–6, 80
  transnationalization of social movements 347
human rights movement
  Arab world 645–52
  and humanitarian movement, contrast between 326–7
  India 592–3
  international *see* international human rights movement
Humphrey, M. 531
hunger strikes, China 550
Hunt, Jayson 359–83
Hunt, S. 95
Hussain, M. 369, 374, 575

ICT revolution and social movements 3, 359–83
  anti-globalization movement 361
  and Arab Spring 374, 375–6
  digital rights movement 362, 369
  environmental movement 396–7, 407
  future research 367, 376, 377
  'hacktivism' 363
  internet activism consequences 375–6
  internet activism typologies 362–3
  internet networks, China 553
  micro-mobilization and participation 366–8
  micro-mobilization and participation, demographic characteristics and internet savvy, effects of 367–8
  micro-mobilization and participation, political participation and money donation 367
  online collective identity and community 371–3
  online collective identity and community, changes in understanding of 373
  repression in authoritarian contexts 374
  repression in democratic contexts and surveillance concerns 374–5
  strategic voting movement 361–2
  transnational social movements and ICT usage 373–4
  Zapatista movement, Mexico 360–61
ICT revolution and social movements, organizing ability and organizations 368–71
  cost and efficiency factors 368
  'flash activism' 369
  MoveOn liberal advocacy group 370
  and new social movement (NSM) theory 371
  organizational change as result of ICT usage 370
  organizing without organizations 369, 371
ICT revolution and social movements, theoretical debates 363–6
  alteration of underlying dynamics or processes 365–6, 368–70
  magnification of existing expectations 364–5
  offline organizing impact 364
  and resource mobilization (RM) and free-riding 364, 365, 369
  theoretical status quo as explanation 364

immigration *see* migration
India
  gender and sexuality 67, 71
  neoliberalism 485
  WSPA Pet Respect campaign 526–7
India, social movements 572–603
  Chipko movement 580–81, 582
  corruption watchdog body 583
  development-displacement-related movements 586–7
  future developments and research 593–4
  globalization effects 582–3
  human rights movements 592–3
  Indian Civil Liberties Union (ICLU) 592–3
  informal economy and industrial working class movements 587–90
  institutional decline 582–3
  Maoist movement and Operation Green Hunt 586–7
  new farmers' movements 584–7
  peasant movements 583–5, 586
  peasant and new farmer movements, hierarchical class structure 584–5
  People's Union for Civil Liberties (PUCL) 593
  Self-employed Women's Association of India (SEWA) 587–8
  strikes 588–9
  trade unions 587–90
  women's movements 587–8, 590–92
India, social movements, theoretical approaches 573–83
  colonial experiences, effects of 577–8
  Dalit movement (caste) politics 574, 576, 577, 579–80, 586
  dialectical-Marxist and related critical-structural approaches 575–8
  environmental movements 581–2
  new social movement approaches 578–80
  political ecology, cultural politics and popular democracy (micro-movements) 580–83
  political economy issues 578
  social policy for social welfare 575
  structural-functionalist approaches 574–5
  subaltern studies and political society 576–8, 580–81
Inglehart, R. 25, 27, 34, 37, 247, 371
Inglis, D. 518
injustice and dispossession perceptions, Tea Party movement 503–8
institutions
  anti-institutionalism, new social movement (NSM) approach 243, 245–6
  decline of, India 582–3
  emotions directed towards 324–5
  environmental agenda, ecological citizenship 107, 109, 110
  environmental movement *see* environmental movement, institutionalization effects
  institutional considerations, European citizenship 170–71
  institutionalization effects, and political opportunities 262, 263, 267–9
  international, and international human rights movement 447–9
  minority claims-making opportunities, multicultural citizenship 98–9
  post-institutionalization, new social movement (NSM) approach 250–51
  public welfare programs, institutionalization of 311
  standard setting and institution building, international human rights movement 445–7
  structure, China 558, 559
  supranational, republican citizenship 49–50, 53, 56–7
International Criminal Court, and cosmopolitan rights 184
international human rights movement 440–63
  activism patterns and methods 443–52
  agenda decentralization 442
  Amnesty International (AI) 442, 444–5, 446, 448, 453

bilateral human rights policies and foreign aid 445
environmental issues 451, 456
funding 443
growth and development 441–3, 459–60
human rights abuses, information and advocacy 443–5, 451, 455
human rights abuses, information and advocacy, local activists' role 444–5, 454
Human Rights Watch (HRW) 442–3, 446, 454
indigenous rights 451, 457
mobilization and collective organization 442
modern movement history 440–41
political involvement 442, 443, 444, 445–6, 447, 449–52
standard setting and institution building 445–7
standard setting and institution building, articulating new standards 445–6
and universal human rights 441–2
women's issues 451, 456, 457
international human rights movement, critical debates over 452–9
democracy and involvement of citizens' movements 458–9
impact of movement 457–9
legal coverage 456–7
maturation of movement 454–7
power-holders, influence of 454–5
state resistance, dealing with 454
technical aspects of documentation, assistance with, and information sharing 455–6
treaty ratification and international agreements 458
truth commissions 455–6
unique power of the human rights idea 453–4
international human rights movement, state accountability 447–52
accountability politics and discourse 450–51
domestic accountability 451–2, 457
economic levers and sanctions 449–50

leverage politics 448
powerful allies and international institutions, reaching out to 447–9
and transnational issue adoption considerations 449
and UN's human rights treaty review bodies 448–9
internet *see* ICT revolution and social movements
Isin, E. 2, 6, 9, 119, 133, 134, 136, 137, 138, 144, 149, 161, 632, 633–4
Islamic movements 630, 634
Muslim minorities and War on Terror 99–100, 102
see also Arab world, political citizenship and social movements
Ismael, T. 630
Ismail, S. 635, 652

Jacka, T. 554
Jacobs, D. 274
Jacobs, J. 142, 479–80
Jagers, S. 120–21, 122
Jamison, A. 3, 5, 14, 242, 391, 393
Jaoul, N. 325
Japan
Fukushima catastrophe 395
peace movement 326
Jasper, J. 95, 99, 240, 312–13, 314–15, 327, 338, 477, 519, 521, 522, 536, 540
Jeghllaly, M. 643
Jelin, E. 114
Jenkins, J. 205, 265, 274
Jin, J. 548
Joachim, J. 451
John, J. 575
Johnson, E. 207–8, 209, 210
Johnson, H. 346
Johnston, H. 95, 234, 240, 430
Jones, C. 193
Jones, K. 136–7
Jordan, G. 396, 412
Jordan, J. 250
Jordan, T. 362
Joseph, S. 633
Joshi, R. 590

Kabeer, N. 587
Kahn, R. 373
Kandil, H. 640, 643
Kane, Melinda 205–32
Kannan, K. 588, 591
Kant, I. 49, 54–5, 56, 177, 187–8
Kapoor, Dip 572–603
Karpf, D. 370, 375
Katsiaficas, G. 234, 243, 244
Katzarska-Miller, I. 185
Katzenstein, M. 421, 422, 426, 427, 428, 574, 578
Katzenstein, P. 348, 349
Katznelson, I. 466, 478
Kauffman, L. 91, 248
Kaufman, J. 554
Kavanaugh, A. 372
Keane, M. 561, 562
Keck, M. 270, 341, 342, 343, 346, 347, 406, 407–8, 444, 448, 450
Keddie, N. 633
Kelkar, G. 590
Kellner, D. 373
Kendall, L. 372
Keniston, K. 265
Kenney, S. 314
Khagram, S. 346, 349, 407, 578
Khalaf, A. 647
Killian, L. 93
Kim, H. 455
Kimport, K. 353, 364, 365–6, 367, 369, 370, 373
King, B. 208, 209, 210, 273
King, D. 314, 431
Kitschelt, H. 268, 393, 394, 402
Klandermans, B. 5, 6, 93, 206, 211, 338, 467
Klein, E. 426
Klein, N. 8, 248
Kleres, J. 311, 314, 323, 328
Klotz, A. 449, 450
Knox, P. 484
Köhler, B. 475, 480
Kolb, F. 393, 395, 524
Kollman, K. 70, 80
Kong, W. 548, 549, 552
König, C. 635, 643
Koopmans, R. 98, 99, 269, 338, 393, 395, 423
Kornhauser, W. 264

Kostakopoulou, T. 160, 167
Kothari, R. 572, 578, 582
Kratochwil, F. 349
Kreimer, S. 361
Kreiss, D. 370
Kriesi, H. 5, 98, 185, 234, 244, 245–6, 249, 250, 267, 268, 269
Krinsky, J. 480
Kristof, N. 426
Krueger, B. 367, 375
Kruks, S. 469
Kuechler, M. 336
Kumar, R. 485
Kurzman, C. 340
Kush, K. 208, 209, 210
Kymlicka, W. 6, 10, 25, 101, 156, 183, 537–8

labour militancy, Africa 610–11
labour movements
    China 551–2, 557
    working class and informal economy, India 587–90
Lacan, J. 282
Laclau, E. 280, 281, 282, 283, 286, 287, 291, 292, 304
Lacroix, S. 647, 650
Landman, T. 458
language considerations, European citizenship 162, 164
Lapid, Y. 349
Laraña, E. 95
Larson, J. 208
Latta, A. 109, 110, 124, 125, 128
Lauren, P. 440, 453
Le Sueur, J. 640, 641
leadership and personality cults, Arab world, political citizenship and social movements 640
learning transfer, emergence of 300–301
    see also education
Lee, C. 548, 551, 552
Leebaw, B. 326–7
Leenders, R. 635, 643
Lees, L. 143, 144
Lefebvre, H. 136, 140, 141, 142, 145, 147, 148, 478, 486
Leibfried, S. 169, 183
Leitz, L. 311, 312

Leonard, S. 64
Levi, M. 346
Levine, C. 243
Lewis, M. 633
Leydet, D. 6, 9, 10, 178, 194
LGBT groups *see* gender and sexuality, LGBT groups as social movements
Li, L. 548, 549, 551, 553, 559, 560, 561, 564
liberalism *see* neoliberalism
Liddle, J. 590
Lieberthal, K. 558
Lievrouw, L. 363
Lin, N. 212, 215
Linklater, A. 163, 164, 178, 183, 190, 193, 195
Lipset, S. 496
Lipsky, M. 265
Lister, R. 38, 60, 62, 63, 64, 65–6, 73, 78, 80, 199
Littig, B. 124
Liu, D. 554, 555, 556
Liu, L. 552
Liu, N. 550
Lo, C. 499, 500, 511
local issues
  campaigns against large infrastructure projects *see* post-structuralism, social movements and citizen politics, local campaigns against large infrastructure projects
  group support, Tea Party movement 500–501
  urban citizenship and local-scale arrangements, concerns over 136–7
  women's mobilization around 477–8, 483–4
Lockard, J. 372
Lockman, Z. 630, 639
Lockyer, A. 7
Logie, J. 361, 369
Lojkine, J. 464
Lombard, M. 475, 476, 481
Lombardo, E. 62
Long, J. 475
Lou, D. 563
Lu, C. 193

Lü, X. 550
Luciani, G. 629, 647
Ludden, D. 576
Luders, J. 265
Lundqvist, L. 120, 121
Lust-Okar, E. 647
Lustiger-Thaler, H. 77, 148, 477
Lynch, M. 374, 649

Maas, W. 154, 170
McAdam, D. 1, 5, 93, 98, 205, 206, 223, 225, 226, 238, 246, 260, 268, 269, 270, 310, 311, 314, 321, 336, 337, 338, 342, 348, 353, 533, 537, 634
McCall, L. 63, 78
McCammon, H. 207, 208, 209, 210, 224, 269, 433
McCarthy, J. 4, 12–13, 93, 205–17*passim*, 220, 223, 224, 228–9, 265, 308, 336, 422, 497, 499
McDonald, K. 241, 244, 252, 477
Macdonald, L. 65, 74
McEwan, C. 66
MacGregor, Sherilyn 107–32
McGrew, A. 185
McGurty, E. 209, 215, 223
Mackenzie, S. 144
McMichael, P. 342, 577, 586, 587, 588
Madrigal, A. 362
Maeckelbergh, M. 244, 251, 253, 480
Maghraoui, A. 641
Maghraoui, D. 647
Magnusson, W. 136, 145, 149
Maheu, L. 468, 469
Mair, P. 182
Maktabi, R. 633
Maloney, M. 396, 412
Maloutas, M. 66
Mann, M. 632, 642
Marcus, G. 328
Marcuse, H. 242
Marcuse, P. 140, 148
Margadant, T. 337
market-based strategies and carbon trading, opposition to, Africa 613, 614–15
  see also neoliberalism
Markham, W. 390, 391
Markkola, P. 66

Marks, G. 270
Marshall, T. 2, 6, 28, 30–31, 38, 60, 88–9, 112, 137, 168, 181, 259, 261, 482, 561, 631–2
Marston, S. 136
Martens, S. 553
Martin, A. 207
Martin, G. 245
Martin, P. 321, 324
Martinez-Alier, J. 388, 409–10, 581
Martinsson, J. 120, 121
Martuccelli, D. 468
Massoumi, Narzanin 86–106
material and financial resources 212–13, 219, 221, 224, 226–7
see also resource mobilization
Matheny, G. 528
Matsuzawa, S. 373, 374
Matti, S. 120
May, S. 89
Mayer, A. 646
Mayer, M. 402, 474, 487
Mazey, S. 399, 400
Mazumdar, V. 590, 591
Mecham, Q. 649
media involvement
 animal rights movement 521, 524, 528–9, 530, 534
 China 557
 press liberalism, Arab world 639, 649
 Tea Party movement 500
Meehan, E. 158, 168–9
Meer, Nasar 86–106
Mehta, L. 572, 577
Meier, P. 62
Meijer, Roel 628–60
Melo-Escrihuela, C. 109, 114, 118, 127, 128
Melucci, A. 92, 93, 205, 233–47*passim*, 250, 285, 304, 336, 430, 465, 468, 477
Membretti, A. 251
Merry, S. 456
Mertig, A. 389, 391, 393, 396, 397, 412
Mexico
 animal protection 526
 urban social marginalization 476, 481
 women's movements 65
 Zapatista movement 360–61

Meyer, David S. 2, 206, 259–78, 337, 433, 495, 536
Meyer, J. 217, 343, 346
Michelson, E. 556, 557, 559
Middle East *see* Arab world
Middlemiss, L. 126
migration
 democratic citizenship, native and immigrant populations, interaction between 39–40
 migrant workers' associations, China 552, 564
 migrants and refugees, emotions and social movements 326
 urban social movements 482
Mill, J.S. 46, 55–6
Miller, B. 466
Miller, D. 46, 47–8, 53–4, 162, 164, 177, 188–9, 195
Miller, W. 501, 502, 511, 513
Millett, K. 91
Milner, H. 37
Min, X. 562
Minkoff, D. 206, 210, 215, 269, 271, 273, 422
minority communities
 ecological citizenship 125
 institutionalised opportunities for claims-making 98–9
 see also multicultural citizenship
Mitchell, D. 143, 144
Mitchell, T. 630, 641
mobilization *see* activism patterns and methods; collective action
Modood, T. 86, 90, 91, 102
Moghadam, V. 425, 432, 631, 633
Mohanty, C. 429, 431, 434, 435
Mol, A. 126
Monro, Surya 60–85
Mooers, C. 336
Moore, B. 308–9, 584
moral attitude
 cosmopolitan citizenship 190–91, 192–3
 'moral shocks' and mobilization 312–13, 327
 'moral shocks', use of, animal rights movement 522, 526, 531
 Tea Party movement 507–8

moral resources 217–18, 219–20, 222, 224
  see also resource mobilization
Morgan, R. 451
Morgenthau, H. 447
Morozov, E. 362, 374, 375–6
Morris, A. 96, 97, 99, 205, 338
Mosca, L. 363, 368
Mottier, V. 61, 72
Mouffe, C. 148, 149, 280, 281, 282, 291, 304, 635
Mourtada, R. 374
Moustafa, T. 646
Moyn, S. 440, 453–4
Mthethwa, N. 605, 609
Mudu, P. 251
Mueller, C. 97, 338, 418, 421, 425, 426
Mueller, T. 252
Mueller-Rommel, F. 401–2
Muetzelfeldt, M. 185
Mukherji, P. 574, 584
multicultural citizenship 86–106
  citizenship challenge 86–8
  citizenship, Greek origins 87–8
  collective action, national identity effects 98–9, 100–101
  democratic society and cultural minorities 86
  equality and culture 88–9
  future directions 102
  inclusion and exclusion, tensions between 87
  institutionalised opportunities for minority claims-making 98–9
  liberal conception of universal citizenship, problems with 89
  liberal feminism comparison 90–91
  liberalism, recognition and multiculturalism 90–92
  multiculturalism, understanding of concept 91–2
  Muslim minorities and War on Terror 99–100, 102
  new social movements and recognition struggles 92–4, 98
  new social movements theory and multicultural political theory 94–9
  political identity framework 99–100

public policies, measurement problems 100–101
resource mobilization theory (RMT) 93
and secularism 102
  see also racial issues
multicultural citizenship, collective identity approach 94–5
  domination and subordination issues 96–7
  equality-based special issue movements 97
  liberation movements 97
  mobilization, cultures of subordination 96
  mobilization, solidarity and continuity of struggle over time 96
  and recognition struggles 95–7
  social responsibility movements 97, 99–100
Münkler, H. 29
Munro, Lyle 518–43
Murdie, A. 448, 458
Murphy, G. 346
Muslim minorities and War on Terror 99–100, 102
  see also Islamic movements
Myers, D. 364

Nadasen, P. 420, 424
Naples, N. 425, 426
Nash, J. 353, 519
Nash, K. 64, 236
Nathan, A. 561
nation-state concept
  dominance of, European citizenship 156–9, 161, 162, 164, 168, 172
  national government limitations 135, 137–8
  national patterns among established democracies 34–5
  national-level environmental organizations 391–2
  regional autonomy movements, Arab world 651
  see also sovereignty; state structures
national identity effects

multicultural citizenship 98–9, 100–101
and republican citizenship 53–4
nationalism, rise of, Arab world 638–41
Ndikumana, L. 607, 608
Nedelmann, B. 310
Negri, A. 8
Neier, A. 440, 444, 454
Nelkin, D. 519, 521, 536, 540
neoliberalism
  and Africa, social movements and political citizenship, protest movement and social activism 621–3
  capitalism effects, animal rights movement 522
  collective resistance to neoliberal forces, urban social movements, empirical research, learning from 475–6
  corporate power and neoliberal policies, demonstrations against, transnationalization of social movements 344–5
  democracies and nation-state framework, Europe 165–6
  ecological citizenship 111–13, 117–18, 121, 126, 128
  effects of 2, 8
  European market citizenship, exclusionary nature of 160–61
  and gender and sexuality 64, 77
  gentrification and neoliberal urbanism, urban citizenship 143, 144
  Global South, and neoliberal economic policies, in transnationalization of social movements 350–51
  market-based strategies and carbon trading, opposition to, Africa 613, 614–15
  and multicultural citizenship 89, 90–92, 97
  and republicanism, differences between 27
  and urban citizenship 139, 149
  see also authoritarianism; democracy; republican citizenship

Netherlands
  animal protection 520, 540
  human rights 448
  minorities in 101
Nettelfield, L. 447
Neumayer, E. 458
Nevitte, N. 32
new environmental movement *see* environmental movement, new environmental movement
new farmers' movements, India 584–7
new social movement (NSM)
  animal rights movement 519, 520–21
  criticism of, and transnationalization of social movements 336–7
  ICT revolution 371
  India 578–80
  multicultural political theory 94–9
  political opportunities and social movements 267–8
  recognition struggles, multicultural citizenship 92–4, 98
  transnationalization of social movements 336
  women's movements 422–5, 430–31
new social movement (NSM) approach 4, 233–58
  action, subjectivity and experience 241–2
  anti-austerity movements 252–3
  anti-institutionalism 243, 245–6
  autonomy versus representation 242–4
  collective identity 239–41, 242–3, 246–7, 252
  collective identity, and individual identity, interaction between 240, 242
  collective identity, tensions in 240
  counter-globalization movement 251, 252–3
  criticisms and debates 244–9
  criticisms and debates, new aspect, consideration of 245–7
  cultural focus 236
  culture and meaning 236, 237–8, 245, 246
  difference, appeal to 236
  direct action and civil disobedience 244

environmental groups 250, 252
and feminism 243, 245
future research 253–4
global conflicts, involvement in 251–2
globalization and newest social movements 249–53
historicity and social order 242
information societies' contribution 233–4
lifestylism and identity politics 248–9
local food movements 252
and the middle-classes 245
New Left and student movements 234–5
overview 233–5
politicization of daily life 243–4, 252
post-institutionalization 250–51
professionalized NGOs 250
resource mobilization and political process approaches 235–6, 237, 238, 240–41
shared approach, lack of 235–7
signs and symbols, interpretation of 238
sociological intervention method 237
strategy versus identity 247–8
submerged networks 241–2, 250–51
Nibert, D. 519, 521–2, 523
Nicholls, W. 475, 480, 481, 486
Nie, N. 37, 38
Niranjana, S. 590
Nnaemeka, O. 429
Nordhaus, T. 127
Norman, W. 25, 156
Norris, P. 367
Norton, A. 630
Noske, B. 518, 519, 523
nuclear energy conflict 393–5, 403
Nyers, P. 182, 635

Oberschall, A. 279, 289
O'Brien, K. 548, 549, 551, 558, 559, 561, 564
O'Brien, R. 342, 345, 457
Occupy Movement 216, 252–3, 270, 478, 480
see also economic crisis effects; urban citizenship; urban social movements
O'Donnell, G. 563
Offe, C. 243, 336, 481
Oleksy, E. 63, 72, 73, 78
Oliver-Smith, A. 572, 577, 587
Olives, J. 479
Olsen, Espen D.H. 154–76
Olson, M. 93, 266, 267, 289, 290, 304, 310
Olzak, S. 208, 209, 210, 211
Omvedt, G. 572, 573, 574, 575, 578–9, 580, 584, 585, 586, 590, 591, 592
one-party systems, Arab world 640–42
see also authoritarian regimes
Ong, A. 65, 135, 136, 139, 149
Oommen, T. 572, 573, 574, 575, 577, 578, 584, 587
organizations
  collective action and organizational layers 477
  development, Tea Party movement 500
  and ICT *see* ICT revolution and social movements, organizing ability and organizations
  organizational foundations, effects of strong 272–3
  social-organizational resources, uneven access 213–15, 219, 220–23
  urban social movements 473–4

Pace, M. 631
Padel, F. 573, 577
Pakulski, J. 519
Palacuer, F. 454
Pall, Z. 634
Palriwala, R. 591
Palumbo, A. 632
Pan, Y. 556
Pangsapa, P. 116
Panizza, F. 280
Papadopoulos, Y. 27
Pardo, M. 425, 426
Parekh, B. 86, 190
Pargeter, A. 642, 651
Park, R. 264
Parkin, F. 265

Parolin, G. 633
Parsa, M. 340
Patel, S. 588, 589, 591
Patel, V. 591
Pateman, C. 27, 60
Patil, C. 575
Patil, V. 431, 432, 433, 434
Patnaik, U. 575, 587
Peake, L. 143
Pearlman, W. 319
peasant movements
    China 550–51, 555, 557, 559, 564
    India 583–5, 586
Peckham, M. 364, 375
Peggs, K. 521–2
Pei, M. 556, 559, 561
Peksen, D. 450
Pellow, D. 408, 409
Pennel, C. 638, 639, 641
Perrow, C. 265
Perry, E. 553, 561, 564
Petersson, O. 29–30, 32, 36
Petronijewic[.], E. 317–18
Pettit, P. 45, 48, 50, 51, 52, 53
Phillips, A. 80
philosophical literature, democratic citizenship 28, 29–30
Pichardo, N. 95, 245, 371
Pickerill, J. 480
Pickvance, C. 464, 465, 467, 473, 474, 486, 487
Picolotti, R. 451
Pierson, P. 169
Pilny, A. 218
Piven, F. 262, 361, 535
Pizzorno, A. 239, 247, 310
Pleyers, G. 248, 251, 252
Plotke, D. 245, 336
Plummer, K. 72, 73, 75–6
Pogge, T. 187, 188, 194
Poland
    emotional anxiety 324–5
    stockyard strike 318
Polanyi, K. 137, 344, 608, 622, 623
policy change opportunities, and mobilization 271–3
    see also collective action
political community bonds, extent and scope 47–8
political ecology, India 580–83

political economy issues
    Arab world 629, 635–6
    India 578
political identity
    European citizenship 167–8
    multicultural citizenship 99–100
political involvement
    activism see activism patterns and methods
    animal rights movement 535–6
    Arab world 632
    class struggles and collective consumption 472–3
    gender and sexuality 71–3
    international human rights movement 442, 443, 444, 445–6, 447, 449–52
    new social movement (NSM) approach 243–4, 252
    political opportunities and social movements 266–7, 269–70
    'political opportunity' model 337–8, 339
    resource mobilization see resource mobilization and social and political movements
    Tea Party movement 493–4, 510–12
political opportunities and social movements 259–78
    abeyance structures 268
    authoritarian regimes 269–70
    demonstrations and civil disobedience 262, 264–5
    forms of change linked to movement activity 272
    'free-rider' tendency, overcoming 266
    institutionalization effects 262, 263, 267–9
    longitudinal analysis, need for 274–5
    mobilization and policy change opportunities 271–3
    movement politics and mainstream politics, ongoing connections 268–9
    and 'new social movements' 267–8
    organizational foundations, effects of strong 272–3
    political process approach, development of 266–71

political structures, effects of 266–7, 269–70
resource mobilization theories 265–6
scholarship before political process approach 264–6
shared knowledge of tactics and civic engagement 263–4
social capital and political activism 262–3
social movement definition 260–61
social movements and citizenship 260–64
transnational activism 270
political process model
cities and theory of social movements 470–71
political opportunities and social movements 266–71
political opportunity structure, China 558–60
resource mobilization 206, 227, 235–6, 237, 238, 240–41
political science theory
animal rights movement 520, 531, 537–8, 539
emotions and social movements 328
gendered citizenship 65–6
Polletta, F. 95, 240, 313, 314
post-structuralism, social movements and citizen politics 279–307
collective action and free riders 289
collective identities and subjectivities 285
democratic governance, challenges for 302–3
discourse analysis 281–3
discourse analysis, critical function 283, 286, 298
future research 303
group formation and collective mobilization 288–91
group formation and collective mobilization, classical model shortcomings and rational choice theory 289–91
group formation and collective mobilization, selective incentives 290–91
'group theory' and 'movement theory' 283–93

groups, movements and demands 286–8
groups, movements and demands, and dislocatory events 286–7
groups, movements and demands, and hegemony theory 287–8, 292–3, 298–300
interests and identities, identification and agency 291–3
leadership challenges 301–2
Paris 'May events' 280
post-structuralism definition 279–80
social movements and political parties, differences between 288
'sociology of action' approach 284–6
post-structuralism, social movements and citizen politics, dynamics of social movements and citizenship 296–301
chains of equivalences 298–300, 302
contingency and dislocation 297–8
learning transfer, emergence of 300–301
post-structuralism, social movements and citizen politics, local campaigns against large infrastructure projects 293–7
France, Notre-Dame-des-Landes 294, 295–6, 297, 298, 300–301
Germany, airport protests 296
new protests of bodily risk 295–6
UK, Heathrow Airport 294–5, 297–300
Postigo, H. 362, 369, 375
Postmes, T. 367
Poulsen, J. 312, 519, 522, 536
Powell, W. 217
Power, J. 320–21, 322–3
Predelli, L. 62, 78
Preuss, U. 159, 160, 162
Princen, P. 406, 408
private sphere, importance of, ecological citizenship 117, 123–4
protest movement
Africa see Africa, social movements and political citizenship, protest movement and social activism
see also activism
Pruijt, H. 480, 482

public participation in politics, democratic citizenship 27, 29–30, 34, 37–8, 40–41
public policies, measurement problems, multicultural citizenship 100–101
public space, use and control of, urban citizenship 141, 143, 145–6, 147, 149
public welfare, institutionalization of 311
public/private practice
  ecological citizenship 118–19, 123–4, 126–7
  gender and sexuality 63
Puig-i-Abril, E. 367
Purcell, M. 136
Putnam, R. 25, 27, 29, 36
Pye, L. 549, 561

Quataert, J. 440, 445, 446, 456, 457
Quintelier, E. 367

racial issues
  black communities finding freedom in public space of cities 146–7
  racialized populations and urban renewal 144
  Tea Party movement 505–6
  see also multicultural citizenship
Rainie, L. 373
Rao, A. 573, 580
Rao, M. 572, 574, 584
rape cases and feminist movement 324
Raschke, J. 243, 248
Rawls, J. 55, 156, 188
Ray, R. 422, 425, 574, 578, 591, 594
Read, B. 552, 553, 556, 562
Reddy, Movindri 334–58
Regan, T. 519, 521, 529
Reger, Jo 418–39
regional autonomy movements, Arab world 651
  see also Arab world, political citizenship and social movements; nation-state concept
Reid, E. 372, 373
Renteln, A. 453
republican citizenship 45–59
  civic friendship 52–3

commitment to community and common good 46–7, 54
commonalities, accepting variety of 48
communicative freedom 51, 52
construction, European citizenship 163–4
cosmopolitan forms 47–8, 49
distributive sovereignty and self-determination 56
domination concerns and epistemic justice 50–51
domination and use of normative powers 51–2
ecological citizenship, individual green virtues 113–14
Enlightenment critique 49–52, 55–6
freedom as non-domination 48–9, 50–51, 52, 56–7
freedom and self-determination 46
and gender and sexuality 64
humanity, inclusive of all 49–50
liberal and republican perceptions, differences between, democratic citizenship 27
modern republicanism, emergence of 52–5
and national identity 53–4
non-citizens, legal and civil status 54–5
participation in public life 55–6
political community bonds, extent and scope 47–8
supranational institutions 49–50, 53, 56–7
transformation of 45–7
see also authoritarianism; democracy; neoliberalism
resource mobilization
  China 557–8
  ICT revolution and free-riding 364, 365, 369
  multicultural citizenship 93
  new social movement (NSM) approach 235–6, 237, 238, 240–41
  political opportunities and social movements 265–6
  Tea Party movement 499

Index   689

resource mobilization and social and political movements 4, 205–32
   analytical utility, relevance of 206–7
   current utilization 207–12
   exchange relationships and source constraints 224–7
   financial resources 208–9, 211
   formation, maintenance, and closure of social movement organizations 210–11
   future research 228–9
   human capital 209, 211
   and indigenous political processes 206
   movement development, strategies, and outcomes 208–10
   political process model 206, 227
   resource attributes 218–20
   resource attributes, context-dependent 218–19
   resource attributes, proprietary resources 219–20
   social entrepreneurial approach 206
   social movement organization (SMO) 209–10
   under-utilization 211–12
resource mobilization and social and political movements, resource access mechanisms 220–24
   co-optation/appropriation 223
   patronage 224
   resource aggregation 223
   self-production 220–23
resource mobilization and social and political movements, resource types 212–18
   cultural resources, People's Mic 216
   cultural resources, uneven distribution and accessibility 215–17, 219, 220, 222
   human resources 213, 220, 221
   material and financial resources 212–13, 219, 221, 224, 226–7
   moral resources and legitimacy 217–18, 219–20, 222, 224
   social-organizational resources, uneven access 213–15, 219, 220–23
Reysen, S. 185
Rheingold, H. 344, 372

Richardson, Diane 60–85
Richardson, H. 51
Richardson, J. 399, 400, 401–2
Rieger, E. 183
Rifkin, J. 11
Riggle, E. 71
Risse, T. 450–51, 455, 456, 457, 459
Risse-Kappen, T. 341, 343, 347
Ritchie, M. 344
Roberts, J. 101
Robinson, W. 348, 498
Robnett, B. 315
Rochon, T. 237
Roggeband, C. 5, 6, 206
Rohlinger, D. 210, 269, 272–3
Rojas, H. 367
Ron, J. 449
Ronfeldt, D. 372
Roose, J. 391, 399
Rootes, C. 388, 389, 391, 395, 397, 401–2, 404, 412
Ropp, S. 456
Rosanvallon, P. 470, 635
Roseneil, S. 61, 66, 74, 78
Rossteutscher, S. 36, 37, 42
Roth, B. 420, 424, 468
Rousiley, M. 315
Rowan, B. 217
Roy, A. 486, 583
Roy, B. 583
Ru, X. 556
Rucht, D. 234, 336, 391, 465
Ruddick, S. 523
Rudig, W. 393, 394, 412
Ruedy, J. 634, 638
Ruggie, J. 349
Ruiz-Junco, N. 313
Rupp, L. 311, 326, 419, 421, 423, 432
Russia
   authoritarian rule 404–5
   Chernobyl catastrophe 394–5
   Soviet bloc, party-state relationships 324–5
Rutherford, B. 642, 646, 647, 648, 653
Ryan, M. 143, 146
Ryo, E. 208, 209, 210, 211

Saeidi, S. 62, 67
Salem, F. 374
Salima, Z. 643, 651

Sandercock, L. 482
Sanders, C. 518
Sangari, K. 590
Sanyal, K. 577, 588
Sarkar, T. 591
Sassen, S. 135, 144, 149, 180–81, 186, 348, 464, 470, 479, 482
Sassi, S. 372
Saunders, P. 464, 467–8
Saurin, J. 388
Saward, M. 160, 161
Scarce, R. 18, 398
Schifter, R. 457
Schlosberg, D. 408, 412–13
Schlumberger, O. 643
Scholl, Christian 233–58
Schrock, D. 315
Schudson, M. 25, 134, 137
Schulz, M. 360, 374
Schussman, A. 361, 369, 370, 375
Scott, A. 245, 285–6, 518
Scott, J. 141, 309, 339
Scott, R. 633, 648
Sears, A. 336
secret ballot introduction 324
    see also voting
Seidman, G. 341, 346, 347
Seidman, S. 69, 76
Selden, M. 564
self-help groups 311–12, 315
    see also emotions and social movements
Sen, I. 590, 591
Sengupta, C. 582
Serbia, mass protests 317–18
Sethi, H. 578, 582
sexuality
    and citizenship see gender and sexuality
    women and queer communities finding freedom in public space of cities 141, 146–7
    see also feminism and feminist studies; women's movements
Seyfang, G. 118, 121, 125
Shah, A. 577, 581, 587
Shah, G. 572, 573, 574, 584, 592, 593
Shah, K. 574, 590
Shah, N. 506, 592
Sharabi, H. 640

Sharife, K. 608, 618
Sharma, H. 584
Sharma, J. 575
Shaw, J. 159, 170
Shellenberger, M. 127
Shen, Y. 552, 553
Sheth, D. 572, 578, 582, 583
Shi, T. 559, 563, 564
Shils, E. 563
Shiva, V. 582
Shklar, J. 25, 28
Shore, C. 157–8, 159, 162
Shove, E. 125, 126
Sieverts, T. 147
Siim, B. 38
Sikkink, K. 270, 341, 342, 343, 346, 347, 406, 407–8, 444, 445, 447, 448, 450, 455, 456, 459
Silver, H. 475, 481
Simmons, B. 452, 458
Singer, P. 196, 521, 524, 527–8, 531, 532
Singerman, D. 633, 635, 652, 653
Singh, R. 572, 574, 575, 578, 579, 583, 584
SinghaRoy, D. 584
Sitrin, M. 251
Sivaramakrishnan, K. 581
Skocpol, T. 223, 500, 501, 503, 504, 505, 506, 508
Slater, T. 143
Smelser, N. 93, 284
Smith, C. 269
Smith, D. 144
Smith, G. 185
Smith, J. 8, 341, 342, 346, 373, 374, 446, 457, 459, 478, 480
Smith, K. 91
Smith, M. 108, 113, 114, 116, 137, 138
Smith, N. 143, 144
Sniderman, P. 40
Snow, D. 5, 14, 217, 226, 260, 338, 339, 444, 470, 477, 497, 502, 533, 534
Snyder, D. 510
Snyder, S. 442, 457
social activism, Africa see Africa, social movements and political citizenship, protest movement and social activism

social capital and political activism 262–3
social entrepreneurial approach, resource mobilization 206
social equity, and urban citizenship 135, 137–8
social media and transnational networking 338–9
social movements
  animal rights movement 533–4, 537
  Arab world *see* Arab world, political citizenship and social movements
  China *see* China, social movements and political citizenship
  multicultural citizenship 97, 99–100
  and political opportunities *see* political opportunities and social movements
  post-structuralism *see* post-structuralism, social movements and citizen politics
  and resource mobilization *see* resource mobilization and social and political movements
  and social sciences 4–8
  urban *see* urban social movements
social psychology, animal rights movement 523
social rights
  Arab world 644
  European citizenship 168–9
social welfare, India 575
sociological intervention method, new social movement (NSM) approach 237
sociology, animal rights movement 520–22, 534, 539
'sociology of action' approach, post-structuralism 284–6
Sodhi, J. 589
Somers, M. 143, 144, 149
Soule, S. 208, 209, 210, 272, 273, 470, 477, 480
South Africa *see under* Africa
South Asia, collective mobilization and violence 325
  see also individual countries
sovereignty
  'big government' and loss of sovereignty fears, Tea Party movement 503–4
  distributive, and self-determination, republican citizenship 56
  see also nation-state concept
Soysal, Y. 180, 181
Spaargaren, G. 126
Spitze, G. 426
Spragens, T. 52
Springborg, R. 630
Squires, J. 89, 102
Staggenborg, S. 210, 211, 262, 268, 272, 421, 422, 423, 424–6, 427, 428, 495, 536
Stammers, N. 19
standard setting and institution building, international human rights movement 445–7
Stansell, C. 141, 146
state accountability, international human rights movement *see* international human rights movement, state accountability
state authority, acceptance of, democratic citizenship 27–8, 30, 31–2, 33, 34, 36–7, 38, 40
state resistance, dealing with, international human rights movement 454
state structures
  effects of, transnationalization of social movements 343, 347
  emotions directed towards state or its institutions 324–5
  globalization challenges, transnationalization of social movements 348–9
  government and governed, relationship between 139, 142, 145, 149
  subsidies and control, Arab world 641–2
  see also nation-state concept
state violence, use of, Arab world 641
Statham, P. 98, 102, 269
Stears, M. 531
Stein, L. 363, 368
Stepan-Norris, J. 273
Steward, F. 108

Stohl, C. 368
Stoker, G. 25, 29, 180, 182, 196
Stokes, E. 584
Strange, C. 141, 146
subaltern studies and political society, India 576–8, 580–81
  see also India, social movements
submerged networks, new social movement (NSM) approach 241–2, 250–51
Subramanian, A. 581
Suchman, M. 217
Sulkunen, I. 65, 66
Sunstein, C. 519
supranationalism and concept of nationality, European citizenship 165–6, 170–73
Surana, P. 574
Susser, I. 474
sustainability issues
  sustainable practices, encouragement of 114, 116, 118, 123
  transnationalization of social movements 345–6
Sutherland, A. 519
Swaffield, J. 121
Swidler, A. 337
Swyngedouw, E. 127
Szasz, A. 408

Tadlock, B. 71
Taibbi, M. 496, 503
Taillant, J. 451
Tamimi, A. 630, 646, 648
Tamiotti, L. 408
Tao, Q. 562
Tapscott, C. 19
Tarkunde, V. 583
Tarrow, S. 1, 2, 5, 98, 246, 259, 262, 267, 269, 273, 279, 337, 341–2, 348, 351, 361, 364, 375, 423, 427, 449, 467, 468, 470, 527, 531–2, 535, 558, 634
Taylor, M. 290–91
Taylor, P. 362
Taylor, V. 95, 268, 273, 311, 312, 313, 315, 321, 326, 327, 339, 419–34*passim*
Tea Party movement 493–517
  agency 509–10
  'big government' and loss of sovereignty fears 503–4
  collective action frames 502–3
  female involvement 508–9
  future research 512–13
  generational discourses 506
  health provision concerns 506, 511
  identity definitions 508–9
  injustice and dispossession perceptions 503–8
  morality and faith 507–8
  origins 493, 498
  political impact of 493–4, 510–12
  producerism threat 504, 508
  racial discourses 505–6
Tea Party movement, as social movement 494–502
  'astroturf' character claims 494–5, 501
  collective behaviour and structural strain theories 496
  definition 497
  economic and labour market changes, effects of 498–9
  established conservative networks, influence of 499–500, 501–2
  financial donations 495, 500, 502, 513
  journalistic descriptions of 496
  local group support 500–501
  media involvement 500
  organizational development 500
  rejection of 494–5
  and resource mobilization theory 499
  rightist counter-movement perception 495–6
  and structural maladjustment and dispossession 496–8, 499
technology
  fixes and geo-engineering, opposition to, Africa Climate Justice movement 613
  ICT see ICT revolution and social movements
  technical aspects of documentation, international human rights movement 455–6
Thailand, WSPA Liberaty campaign 526

Thogersen, S. 564
Thompson, B. 420, 424
Thompson, D. 27
Thompson, E. 631, 633, 634
Thompson, L. 19
Thorburn, E. 149
Thornton, S. 248
Tijsterman, Sebastiaan 177–201
Tilly, C. 4, 98, 205, 206, 214, 261, 267, 279, 308, 314, 316, 335–6, 337, 344, 364, 422, 427, 443, 468, 470, 481, 563–4, 634
Tolley, H. 446, 448
Tomba, L. 553
Torgerson, D. 108, 127
Torres, B. 519, 522
Touraine, A. 92, 93, 233, 234, 236, 237, 240, 241–2, 251, 252, 284–5, 286, 336, 468
trade unions
  India 587–90
  rise of, Arab world 638–9, 641
transnationalization
  activism and political opportunities 270
  citizenship enactment in trans-border relations and practices, Europe 161
  cosmopolitan citizenship 192–3, 194
  democratic citizenship 39–40
  environmental movement *see* environmental movement, transnationalization
  gender and sexuality, LGBT groups as social movements 70, 71–2
  ICT revolution and social movements 373–4
  international human rights movement 449
  mobilizing emotions 326–7
  women's movements, Western women's movements as 'guide' 431–2
transnationalization of social movements 334–58
  agency analysis 342–3
  analysis problems 341–3
  authoritarian rule 339–40
  corporate power and neoliberal policies, demonstrations against 344–5
  cultural connectedness 346–7
  cultural 'framing' 337–8
  developing world 339
  digital technology effects 343–6
  economic inequalities, impact of 339
  future research 352–3
  global governance and civil society 345–7
  in Global South 338–9, 340, 349–51
  in Global South, and Global North activists' domination 351
  in Global South, and neoliberal economic policies 350–51
  globalization and transnationalism, distinctions between 348–9
  human rights and norms, influence on 347
  and new social movements (NSMs) 336
  and new social movements (NSMs), criticism of 336–7
  'political opportunity' model 337–8, 339
  'political opportunity' model, structural biases and undermining of subjective constructs, social constructionist approach 338
  small social networks and large collective action groups 337–8
  social media and transnational networking 338–9
  state structures, effects of 343, 347
  state systems and globalization challenges 348–9
  structural analysis 341–2
  sustainability issues 345–6
  theorizing social movements 335–51
  see also cosmopolitan citizenship; globalization; urban citizenship
Traugott, M. 337
Travaglino, G. 206
Tremblay, M. 71
Tripp, A. 432
Tripp, C. 631, 634, 639, 640
Tronto, J. 64

truth commissions, international
 human rights movement 455–6
Tsutsui, K. 346, 458
Tucker, K. 246
Tufekci, Z. 362, 375
Turner, B. 2, 6, 9, 72, 156, 632, 633
Turner, J. 525, 535
Turner, R. 93
Tyler, T. 27

Uberoi, V. 86
Uitermark, J. 142, 480, 481
UK
 Citizenship Survey 101
 Heathrow Airport project 294–5, 297–300
 McLibel trial 534
 Royal Society for the Prevention of Cruelty to Animals (RSPCA) 525, 535–6
universal human rights, and international human rights movement 441–2
universalist approach, call for, gender and sexuality 80
UN's human rights treaty review bodies 448–9
Upadhyaya, A. 575
urban citizenship 133–53
 actor involvement 142, 144–5
 Chicago School approach 143
 citizenship, democracy and class privilege 137–8
 citizenship as form of official membership 134
 city economy, nature of 142
 city as refuge and place of empowerment 140–41
 class struggle and global cities 144
 consumer-as-activist 139
 'critical urban theory 140
 definitions of concept 133–4
 democracy and globalization 135
 depoliticizing effects of technological innovation 137, 141–2
 engaged citizenship 134–5
 feminist approach 143–4
 feminist approach and creation of separate space for women 143–4
 feminists and urban activism 146
 financial circulation and uneven development 143, 144, 147–8
 gentrification and neoliberal urbanism 143, 144
 global parliament of cities, suggestion of 135–6
 government biopower and citizen surveillance 138–9
 government and governed, relationship between 139, 142, 145, 149
 in-between city and uneven infrastructure distribution 147–8
 local-scale arrangements, concerns over 136–7
 national government limitations 135, 137–8
 and neoliberal governance 139, 149
 Occupy Movement 216, 252–3, 270, 478, 480
 order and rhythm, active disruption of 145
 public sites, use and control of 143
 public space, disappearance through commercialization 147
 public space and political mobilization and protest 141, 145–6, 149
 racialized populations and urban renewal 144
 scholarship related to 133–4
 and social equity 135, 137–8
 uniqueness of individual cities 144–5
 urban crises, responses to 142–3
 urban nature 140–48
 women, blacks and queer communities finding freedom in public space of cities 141, 146–7
 see also civic involvement; cosmopolitan citizenship; transnationalization of social movements
urban social movements 464–92
 China (homeowners) 552–3, 555, 556, 557, 562
 definition problems 465–6, 473–4
 future research 482–6
 history of, and study isolation 464–5, 467–8

urban social movements, cities and theory of social movements 466–72, 483
  class conflicts 470, 485–6
  collective action 468–72, 483, 485–6
  collective action and action renewal 471–2
  collective action, recognition of the inherent ambivalence 469
  democratic significance and ability to overcome limitations 469–70
  historical contexts and conjunctures, influence of 466–7
  political process model 470–71
  sector-based and social transformation approaches, differences between 468–9
urban social movements, complementary approaches to primary research directions 479–82
  citizen participation 480–81
  citizenship and national identity 481–2
  immigration 482
  principles of deliberative democracy 481
  squatters' movements 480
  transformation of built environments 479–80, 484–5
urban social movements, empirical research, learning from 472–9
  actors and urban systems, transformation of relationships between 474–5
  collective action around local economic development 477–8
  collective action and organizational layers 477
  collective resistance to neoliberal forces 475–6
  context, relevance and importance of 475–6
  democratization of public policies 476
  Global North and South, differences between 475, 476
  globalization of collective action and alter-globalization 478–9
  organizational factors 473–4
  political class struggles and collective consumption 472–3
  sociology and theory of social movements 477
  urban governance, involvement of activists in 476
  urban struggles, case study approach 473
  urban struggles 'in' and 'of' the city, distinction between 474
  women's mobilization around environmental and local issues 477–8, 483–4
US
  citizenship norms 34–5, 36
  Global Justice Week protests 226–7
  Immigration and Naturalization Service 28
  Operation Rescue 216–17
  sit-in demonstrations, 1960s 1
  Tea Party movement see Tea Party movement
  Vegan Outreach 529–30
  women's movements 419–21, 423, 424, 427, 430

Vaid, S. 590
Vairel, F. 337, 339–40, 350, 631, 635
Valencia Sáiz, A. 111, 119
Van Aelst, P. 362, 373
Van de Donk, W. 364
Van der Heijden, Hein-Anton 1–22, 118, 127, 270, 387–417, 535, 559
Van Dyke, N. 209, 210, 224, 273
Van Koppen, C. 390
Van Laer, J. 362, 366, 367, 373
Van Rooij, B. 551, 560
Van Stekelenburg, J. 5
Van Willigen, M. 311, 321
Vasiljevic, S. 62
vegetarianism, and animal rights movement 522, 529–30, 534, 538
Verba, S. 26, 27, 33, 37
Vermeren, P. 638, 652
Vietnam, WSPA Libearty campaign 526
Vinz, D. 124
violent protests
  Africa 609
  South Asia 325

Vissers, S. 367
Voet, R. 64, 65
voting
　civic duty to vote, democratic citizenship 32, 33, 36, 37, 41
　secret ballot introduction, emotions and social movements 324
　strategic voting movement, ICT revolution and social movements 361–2

Wacquant, L. 475
Wagemakers, J. 645, 651
Waites, M. 70, 80
Walby, S. 60
Walgrave, S. 373
Walker, E. 210
Walker, J. 265
Walker, R. 348, 349
Walling, J. 501, 502, 513
Walsh, C. 252
Walzer, M. 28, 156, 190
Warleigh, A. 166
Warren, L. 79
Waterman, P. 341
Webster, R. 399, 400
Wedeen, L. 635, 640, 642
Weeks, J. 69, 72, 77
Wegner, E. 646, 648
Wei, F. 548, 562, 564
Weiler, J. 164–5
Weldon, S. 457
Wellman, B. 372, 373
Welzel, C. 27, 34, 37, 134, 371
Werkele, G. 478, 483
Western world
　gender and sexuality, Western-centric form of citizenship, moving beyond 66–7, 75
　ideological differences from Arab world 635, 636
　Women's movements *see* women's movements, global movement, Western women's movements as 'guide'
White, G. 555
White, M. 139
Whittier, N. 95, 262, 269, 311, 313–14, 315, 321, 322, 339, 420, 424, 425, 430, 433

Wickham, C. 631, 642, 645, 648, 649, 650, 651, 653
Wiener, A. 169–70
Wieviorka, M. 237
Wiktorowicz, Q. 630–31, 635
Wilkie, R. 518
Williams, R. 157, 211, 215
Williamson, V. 223, 500, 501, 503, 504, 505, 506, 508, 515
Wilson, A. 71, 76, 425, 431, 507
Wilson, C. 362, 375
Wilson, J. 265, 533
Wind-Cowie, M. 101
Wissen, M. 475, 480
Wolch, J. 481
Wolfe, A. 471, 519, 536
women
　animal rights movement 523
　finding freedom in public space of cities 141, 146–7
　gender and sexuality, agency in reshaping state institutions 67
　international human rights movement 451, 456, 457
　mobilization around environmental and local issues 477–8, 483–4
　Self-employed Women's Association of India (SEWA), India, social movements 587–8
women's movements 418–39
　abeyance period 423–4
　African 'nego-feminism' and inclusion of men 429
　community action research approach 434
　continuity studies and new social movement theory 422–5, 430–31
　future developments and research 432–5
　and gender equality, China 554
　global history 421–5, 432
　hostility towards 422
　India, social movements 587–8, 590–92
　issues other than feminism 425–8
　issues other than feminism, movement mobilization and outcomes 427–8
　issues other than feminism, social upheaval periods 425–6

mobilization rates and 'waves' 423–5, 433–4
mobilization rates and 'waves', white and 'mainstream' movement, predominance of 424
US movement history 419–21, 423, 424, 427, 430
US movement, women's studies programs 420–21
women of color 420
women's movements and feminist movements, distinctions between 426–7
see also feminism and feminist studies
women's movements, global movement, Western women's movements as 'guide' 428–32
collective identity construction and intersectionality 430–31
core female identity of motherhood 430
identity matrix 431
transnational mobilization and global connections 431–2
Wong, L. 552
Wong, W. 442, 449
Wood, E. 336, 339
Wood, L. 344, 634
Wood, Patricia Burke 119, 133–53
Woodman, S. 551
working class, and informal economy, India 587–90
World Society for the Protection of Animals (WSPA) 525–7
see also animal rights movement
World Trade Organization protests 270
World Wide Fund for Nature 392, 396, 405, 406–7
see also environmental movement
Wray, S. 361, 363

Wright, E. 336
WuDunn, S. 426

Xia, J. 562
Xiao, T. 548, 549, 552
Xiao, Y. 562
Xie, Lie 547–71
Xie, Y. 555, 556, 557, 560
Xiong, Y. 551
Xu, Q. 563

Yang, G. 314, 318–19, 550, 553, 554, 557
Yang, L. 556
Yang, Z. 555
Yanitsky, O. 403, 405, 412
Yearley, S. 533
Ying, X. 548, 551, 558, 559
Young, I. 90, 94, 95, 188, 234, 248, 471
Young, M. 272
youth movements, Arab world 650–51
Yu, J. 551, 564
Yu, Z. 552

Zald, M. 4, 13, 93, 205, 206, 208, 212, 214, 228–9, 238, 265, 308, 321, 336, 422, 497
Zarrow, P. 561
Zeghal, M. 646, 648
Zeitlin, M. 273
Zemni, S. 643
Zerhouni, S. 647
Zernike, K. 496
Zeskind, L. 505, 506
Zhang, J. 562
Zhang, L. 552, 557, 558, 560
Zhang, Z. 548
Zhao, D. 550, 552, 559
Zheng, Y. 555, 556
Zhu, J. 553, 557
Zhuo, X. 362, 368, 373, 374, 375
Zukin, C. 27, 470